# ETHICS AND CANADIAN CRIMINAL LAW

Other books in *Essentials of Canadian Law* Series

# ESSENTIALS OF
## CANADIAN LAW

# ETHICS AND CANADIAN CRIMINAL LAW

## HON. MICHEL PROULX

Quebec Court of Appeal

## DAVID LAYTON

of the Ontario Bar

IRWIN LAW

A Quicklaw Company

ETHICS AND CANADIAN CRIMINAL LAW
© Irwin Law Inc., 2001

Published in 2001 by
Irwin Law
Suite 930, Box 235
One First Canadian Place
Toronto, Ontario
M5X 1X8

ISBN: 1-55221-044-8


National Library of Canada Cataloguing in Publication Data

Proulx, Michel
    Ethics and Canadian criminal law

(Essentials of Canadian Law)
Includes bibliographical references and index.
ISBN 1-55221-044-8

    1. Criminal procedure–Moral and ethical aspects–Canada.
I. Layton, David II. Title. III. Series.

KE339.P76 2001          174'.3          C2001-901531-3


Printed and bound in Canada

1   2   3   4   5          05   04   03   02   01

# SUMMARY
# TABLE OF CONTENTS

# DETAILED
# TABLE OF CONTENTS

# ACKNOWLEDGMENTS

I should underline, at the outset, that the offer from the publishers to write this book came as a result of a suggestion to them by my colleague Louise Otis, following a panel on ethics in criminal law which was held in Montreal a few years ago and had a great success among the practitioners.

The realization of a lifetime project of this magnitude could not have been achieved without the contribution and support of so many great scholars and friends.

I am particularly indebted to my co-author who made this book possible. His passion for the subject and his dedication to quality in research were truly remarkable.

I would also like to thank the following, throughout Canada, for their comments on the text and their valuable time. My colleagues Melvin Rothman, Morris Fish and Joseph Nuss, the Honourable Michael Moldaver, J.A., The Honourable Fred Kaufman, Bruno Pateras, Q.C., Richard Shadley, Q.C., François Daviault, Raphaël Schachter, Q.C., Richard Masson, Lori Weitzman, Guy Cournoyer, Marc David, Suzanne Costom; Clayton Ruby, Q.C.; Alan D. Gold; Richard C.C. Peck, Q.C.; Joel E. Pink, Q.C.; Fred Ferguson, Q.C.; Daniel A. Bellemare, Q.C.

Special thanks are expressed to Daniel A. Bellemare, Q.C., Assistant Deputy Attorney General of Canada, who was intrumental in obtaining financial assistance extended by the Department of Justice for the publication of this book.

I appreciated, throughout the life of this project, the moral support of a great friend and colleague, Pierre A. Michaud, Chief Justice of the Quebec Court of Appeal.

I am also grateful to many other prominent jurists, too numerous to mention, who were a source of inspiration and guidance in my professional life as a defence attorney and a judge of the Quebec Court of Appeal. I would be happy if somehow, I were able to reflect their collective wisdom in this treatise.

I also wish to express my sincere gratitude to Micheline Mongeau, my administrative assistant, and my law clerk Marie-Lise Dufort. Their daily assistance was invaluable.

Finally, a special word for Brenda, my formidable partner in life. She has shown unconditional support as well as extraordinary patience and encouragement for this project. Along with our six daughters, and often our sons-in-law, she reminded me that no challenge can be met without special commitment and perseverance.

Michel Proulx, J.A.

Much love and thanks to my parents, Norman and Mary, and my partner Zoë Druick, for their exceptional encouragement and support during the writing of this book. I am also grateful to everyone at Shiller Layton Arbuck for their steadfast friendship, and for creating a working environment so conducive to outside projects. Finally, my appreciation goes out to my co-author, whose energy and enthusiasm for the subject of legal ethics is boundless, and who has taught me much over the past two years.

David Layton

# ABBREVIATIONS

**Canada**

| | |
|---|---|
| CBA Code | Canadian Bar Association, *Code of Professional Conduct* (Ottawa: Canadian Bar Association, 1998) (Chair: R.P. Fraser) |
| Alta. | Law Society of Alberta, *Code of Professional Conduct* |
| B.C. | Law Society of British Columbia, *Professional Conduct Handbook* |
| Man. | Law Society of Manitoba, *Handbook of Professional Conduct* |
| N.B. | Law Society of New Brunswick, *Professional Conduct Handbook* |
| Nfld. | Law Society of Newfoundland, *Code of Professional Conduct* |
| N.S. | Nova Scotia Barrister's Society, *Legal Ethics and Professional Conduct Handbook* |
| Ont. | Law Society of Upper Canada, *Rules of Professional Conduct* |

| | |
|---|---|
| P.E.I. | Law Society of Prince Edward Island, *CBA Code of Conduct* |
| Que. | Barreau du Québec, *Code of Ethics of Advocates/Code déontologie des avocats* |
| Sask. | Law Society of Saskatchewan, *Code of Professional Conduct* |
| N.W.T. | Law Society of the Northwest Territories, *Code of Professional Conduct* |
| Yukon | Law Society of Yukon, *Code of Professional Conduct* |

**United States**

| | |
|---|---|
| ABA Model Code | American Bar Association, *Mode Code of Professional Responsibility* (Chicago: American Bar Association, 1969) |
| ABA Model Rules | American Bar Association, *Model Rules of Professional Conduct* (Chicago: American Bar Association, 1983) |
| ABA Annotated Model Rules | American Bar Association, Center for Professional Responsibility, *Annotated Model Rules of Professional Conduct*, 4th ed. (Chicago: American Bar Association, 1999) |
| Third Restatement | American Law Institute, *Restatement of the Law, the Law Governing Lawyers*, rev. ed. (St. Paul, Minn.: American Law Institute, 2000) |
| ABA Prosecution Standards | American Bar Association, Criminal Justice Section, *ABA Standards for Criminal Justice: Prosecution Function and Defense Function*, 3d ed. (Chicago: American Bar Association, 1993), online: http://www.abanet.org/-crimjust/standards/pfunc_toc.html |
| ABA Defense Standards | American Bar Association, Criminal Justice Section, *ABA Standards for* |

# INTRODUCTION

## A. CRIMINAL LAWYERS' CONDUCT UNDER PUBLIC SCRUTINY

Last year, in the controversial case of *R. v. Murray*, the Ontario Superior Court of Justice acquitted a defence lawyer who had been charged with obstructing justice in connection with his handling of incriminating physical evidence.[1] Also in 2000, politician Stockwell Day settled a defamation suit arising from his criticism of a criminal counsel's role in challenging child pornography laws on behalf of a client.[2] Moving back slightly in time, in 1999 the Supreme Court of Canada rendered the judgment in *Smith v. Jones*, condoning the release of client confidences by lawyers for the purpose of protecting ascertainable members of the public from imminent and serious bodily harm.[3] In 1998 a prosecutor in Saskatchewan was charged, but not convicted, of obstructing justice by virtue of not disclosing his knowledge of police contact with prospective jurors in a high-profile murder case.[4] The year before, one of Canada's leading criminal defence counsel was held by a court to have breached his fiduciary duty to a client

---

1   *R. v. Murray* (2000), 144 C.C.C. (3d) 289 (Ont. S.C.J.).
2   See J. Mahoney, "Is it the End of Day?" *The Globe and Mail* (13 January 2001).
3   *Smith v. Jones* (1999), 132 C.C.C. (3d) 225 (S.C.C.) [*Smith*].
4   *R. v. Kirkham* (1998), 126 C.C.C. (3d) 397 (Sask. Q.B.).

by participating in a television program that focused on the client's conviction for criminal negligence causing death.[5]

The extensive press coverage of these cases shows that the public has a keen interest in ethics and criminal law and is often all too willing to denigrate lawyers (justifiably or not) for perceived improprieties. These examples also offer a smattering of the broad range of ethical issues that lawyers face in the practice of criminal law. In particular, they illustrate the complex range of duties, sometimes seemingly inconsonant, that a lawyer owes to a client and to the administration of justice. Such duties are closely connected to the lawyer's special role in the criminal justice system, a role that is reflected in ethical standards adopted by the legal profession. At the same time, lawyers often bring to bear a personal morality that helps to shape, and in difficult cases may conflict with, this singular role as advocate. To make matters more complicated still, lawyers are commonly called upon to make hard decisions in difficult circumstances, often with limited time for careful consideration. Frequently, there is no "right" answer to a particular ethical problem, although there may be many obviously bad ones.

The primary goal of this book is to help lawyers who practise criminal law identify and follow standards of conduct most acceptable to the profession, the public (including clients), and the individual practitioner. We also believe that the book will be of use to civil lawyers, judges, educators, students, and anyone else with an interest in law and ethics. The remainder of this Introduction sets out a road map outlining how we have approached our task.

# B. THE STUDY OF ETHICS AND CRIMINAL LAW

One can argue over the exact meaning of "legal ethics." At the risk of oversimplification, we prefer to avoid this debate. In this book, legal ethics is taken to encompass the study of lawyers' professional duties and thus the principles and standards that should guide lawyers in conducting a morally sound practice of law. Using this brief definition, we can move on to examine the factors influencing an ethics of law, the way in which ethical issues have been perceived over the past fifty

---

5    See *Stewart* v. *Canadian Broadcasting Corp.* (1997), 150 D.L.R. (4th) 24 (Ont. Gen. Div.).

years, and the hallmarks of our own perspective on what it means to be an ethical lawyer.

## 1) The Components of an Ethics of Law

The components that contribute to an ethics of professional conduct are diverse and fluid. A number of sources, taken together, serve to develop and reflect the general principles that shape lawyers' actions and ideals, including formal codes of professional responsibility, the views and writings of lawyers, events actually occurring in the courtroom, the demands and needs of clients, disciplinary decisions by governing bodies, judicial pronouncements, the expectations of the public, and the teachings and reflections that occur in law schools. These and other sources come together to constitute the legal culture that frames and influences ethical debate, and are discussed throughout this Introduction.

Our legal culture undergoes constant and inevitable change, and so too, then, do expectations and standards pertaining to lawyers' behaviour. What was contentious fifty years ago may seem totally unproblematic today, and vice versa. Or the preferred method of approaching an issue may change dramatically over time. Ideas about legal ethics by no means mutate daily, yet there is an undeniable malleability of emphasis regarding principles, concepts, and concerns. This topic, and hence its study, is definitely not static. Moreover, while certain ethical issues yield to reasonably clear answers, on many occasions identifying or applying the proper standards can be a maddeningly challenging exercise. Reasonable people can differ as to the proper ethical approach to apply in a given situation. Legal ethics is not an exact science, with every problem amenable to a set and indisputable resolution. What can be most frustrating about the study of lawyers' ethics is the elusiveness of a widespread consensus on many important issues.

## 2) Some Trends in Legal Ethics

The mutable and normative nature of legal ethics should not be news to anyone. We can see these attributes at work in reviewing trends that have occurred in legal ethics over the last half-century. In the years immediately following the Second World War, lawyers still saw themselves as members of a noble calling steeped in the honourable tradition of service to the community. In Canada, this view included a particularly strong commitment to uphold the tenets of the justice system; loyalty to the client, though extremely important, was arguably not a lawyer's pre-eminent duty. Personal morality, and thus a keen sense of right and wrong, pervaded this conception of the lawyer's role in society. In retrospect, one might question the particular values that the profession and individual lawyers chose to embrace, or criticize aspects of their approach as paternalistic or elitist. Nonetheless, the idea that the profession and its members should accept and promote a general responsibility to the community was ubiquitous.

In the 1960s and 1970s, American writers, led by Monroe Freedman and Charles Fried, articulated a theory of legal ethics under which lawyers are bound by a particularly potent allegiance to the client.[6] The lawyer's necessary and legitimate role as champion of the client within a rights-based adversarial system is the defining principle for adherents of this approach. The advancement of a client's rights within the system is the greater good that supports the lawyer's function as so-called "neutral partisan" or "client's friend." This especially strong "role morality" begins to crowd out the notion that a lawyer can legitimately pursue a personal morality or a larger duty to the public interest (beyond ensuring full access to the legal system for clients). That is to say, the lawyer's special role in the legal system usually provides a broad directive to undertake action on behalf of the client's cause that could conceivably viewed as immoral in other settings (or if not immoral, as raising a conflict between systemic duty and personal morality). We sense that this strongly client-centred approach has not enjoyed the same degree of acceptance in Canada as in the United States. Yet the idea that the vitality of the profession lies, above all else, in fidelity to the client is probably more widespread in Canada today than it was fifty years ago.[7]

In the last decade or so, the incipient study of legal ethics in Canada has felt and reflected the influence of a challenge to the conception of lawyer as neutral partisan for the client's cause, as a role player whose own morals are almost entirely subverted to those of the client. This influence is also evident in England and Wales and Australia.[8] Once again, the impetus for rethinking has largely come

---

6   See, for example, M. Freedman, *Lawyers' Ethics in an Adversary System* (New York: Bobbs-Merrill, 1975); and C. Fried, "The Lawyer as Friend: The Moral Foundation of the Lawyer-Client Relationship" (1976) 85 Yale L.J. 1060.

7   See, for example, D. Layton, "The Public Safety Exception: Confusing Confidentiality, Privilege and Ethics" (2001) 6 Can. Crim. L. Rev. 209 at 217, discussing the Criminal Lawyers' Association position regarding the new future-harm exception adopted by the Law Society of Upper Canada.

8   See, for example, A. Boon & J. Levin, *The Ethics and Conduct of Lawyers in England and Wales* (Oxford: Hart, 1999); and S. Ross, *Ethics in Law: Lawyers'*

from the United States, and in particular the so-called "New Ethics" school of thought promoted by academics such as David Luban, William Simon, and Deborah Rhode.[9] In Canada, advocates of this kind of re-examination of legal ethics include Allan Hutchinson, Donald Buckingham, Richard Devlin, Randal Graham, and especially Harry Arthurs (who for so long toiled as a voice in the wilderness in writing critically about Canadian legal ethics).[10] While these academics do not agree on all things, their approach is marked by a belief that good lawyering involves the active exercise of personal morality and a more acute sense of responsibility to society at large.

In some ways, the New Ethics approach reflects a return to the more traditional notion of tempered zealousness in lawyering.[11] It certainly rejects a role morality according to which the lawyer almost unquestioningly adopts and promotes the values of the client. Yet the New Ethics project is in part the progeny of critical legal studies, meaning that ideals traditionally espoused by the profession, and often encapsulated in the tired phrase, "the best traditions of the bar," are fair game for examination, criticism, and modification. For instance, the adversarial system and its precepts are often dissected with a somewhat jaundiced eye. While academics such as David Luban are willing to accept the adversarial system in the criminal law context, and so are we, the notion that justice must always equate with a vigorous adversarial system is no longer sacred.[12] This approach to legal ethics is challenging and interesting, and long overdue.[13]

---

*Responsibility and Accountability in Australia*, 2d ed. (Sydney: Butterworths, 1998).

9    See, for example, W. Simon, "Ethical Discretion in Lawyering" (1988) 101 Harv. L. Rev. 1083; D. Luban, *Lawyers and Justice: An Ethical Study* (Princeton, N.J.: Princeton University Press, 1988); and D. Rhode, "Ethical Perspectives on Legal Practice" (1985) 37 Stan. L. Rev.

10   See, for example, A. Hutchinson, *Legal Ethics and Professional Responsibility* (Toronto: Irwin Law, 1999); R. Devlin, "Normative, and Somewhere to Go? Reflections on Professional Responsibility" (1995) 33 Alta. L. Rev. 924; D. Buckingham, "Rules and Roles: Casting Off Legal Education's Moral Blinders for an Approach that Encourages Moral Development" (1996) 9 Can. J. L. & Jur. 111; R. Graham, "Moral Contexts" (2001) 50 U.N.B.L.J. 77; and H. Arthurs, "Counsel, Client and Community" (1973) 11 Osgoode Hall L.J. 437.

11   See J. Bickenbach, "The Redemption of the Moral Mandate of the Profession of Law" (1996) 9 Can. J. L. & Jur. 51.

12   See, for example, D. Cayley, *The Expanding Prison: The Crisis in Crime and Punishment and the Search for Alternatives* (Toronto: Anansi Press, 1998).

13   As a final point, the trends discussed above should not be mistaken for completely discrete approaches that bear no common ground, nor can writers or

## 3) Our Approach

Our book is aimed at practitioners who require immediate guidance applicable to the legal system as it currently operates. The lawyer today whose client is about to commit perjury is working within a rights-based adversarial process and a particular ethical framework provided by, among other sources, the governing body's rules of professional conduct and the *Criminal Code*. Lawyers undoubtedly take on a role morality that demands and justifies actions that might seem wrong or unpalatable in another context. In this respect, our approach to resolving ethical problems is not terribly daring and leans only tentatively towards the prescriptive. Nonetheless, within a traditional framework we have tried to re-emphasize attributes of lawyering that sometimes get lost in the adversarial, rights-focused world of criminal trial practice.

In particular, lawyers must constantly reflect on what they are doing, and why, and appreciate how their actions affect the client, the legal system, and the public at large. Ethical lawyering requires assessment and reassessment at many stages, not an unthinking acceptance of neutral partisanship or the rote application of a written rule of professional conduct. Lawyers should also recognize that harm to the public is not automatically justified by dint of the function that they perform as criminal counsel. Whether harm might occur, and whether it can be tolerated, is part of the individual lawyer's assessment. Furthermore, and accordingly, lawyers *do* exercise personal morality in approaching ethical issues, and so they must be prepared to accept responsibility for the decisions made. Accepting the legitimacy of a systemic role morality does not erase the fact that lawyers are moral agents whose actions have real repercussions.

As a last point, one often encounters lists of ethical duties owed by lawyers to clients, the courts, the profession, and the public. In this respect, zeal, candour, diligence, competency, integrity, confidentiality, independence, fairness, honesty, dignity, avoidance of conflict, and other concepts are often mentioned, and rightly so. But making lists of ethical duties can be a bit numbing and, without more, of questionable utility. At the risk of unduly simplifying matters, we group a lawyer's duties to the client under a single overarching principle, that of loyalty owed by a fiduciary. Similarly, duties owed to everyone else can be

---

lawyers invariably be slotted into one or another of the trends. There is a substantial expanse of common ground shared by each school of thought.

traced to a fundamental obligation to uphold the integrity of the legal system employed to determine criminal matters.

Expressed at such a level of generality, these two guiding principles are extremely malleable and provide little more than a beginning in discussing ethical issues. For instance, proponents of any of the schools of thought referred to above would accept these principles as central to the practice of law. However, we must start somewhere, and concomitant fidelity to the client and the legal system is the almost universally accepted point that we have chosen. In fact, many of the chapters in this book illustrate a common theme in most contemporary discussions of ethics and criminal law: the challenge to accommodate the duty of loyalty to the client with the obligation to maintain the integrity of our justice system. As if arriving at an acceptable balance between these responsibilities were not difficult enough, there is also the constant need to incorporate the lawyer's personal morality into the mix.[14]

# C. CANADIAN WRITINGS

Not so long ago, scant attention was paid to ethical matters in Canadian texts and law journals.[15] The paucity of writing in the area was positively embarrassing, especially when compared to the reams of information available in the United States. Lawyers in Canada seemed largely content to leave the discussion of ethics to the occasional article in a trade newspaper, the after-dinner speech, and war stories told in the robing room or pub. Fortunately, however, times are changing. While there is still a gap to be filled,[16] during the last decade or so a sorry state of affairs has begun to change. Several Canadian texts devoted to the subject of law and ethics have joined Orkin's previously

---

14  Even on the extremely robust view of zealousness endorsed by Monroe Freedman, lawyers possess discretion in making and implementing ethical choices. Few would deny that within Freedman's paradigm the lawyer's personal morality plays a role in exercising such discretion.

15  A number of the available Canadian writings, current to 2000, are included in a helpful bibliography appended to the Law Society of Upper Canada's new Rules of Professional Conduct: see online, http://www.lsuc.on.ca/services/contents/bibliography.shtml.

16  See the excellent analysis in A. Dodek, "Canadian Legal Ethics: A Subject in Search of Scholarship" (2000) 50 U.T.L.J. 115.

solitary 1957 work, *Legal Ethics*.[17] Proceedings have been published from two projects on legal ethics, representing a substantial contribution to the subject area.[18] The Supreme Court of Canada's 1990 ruling in *MacDonald Estate* v. *Martin* has spawned articles on conflict of interest.[19] Increasingly, the Canadian Bar Association and various professional governing associations are publishing consultation documents or advisory papers that consider particular ethical problems.[20]

Yet, despite the modest beginnings of a developed literature on legal ethics in this country, the number of publications devoted to matters of ethics and *criminal law* lags considerably behind. In Canada, the leading global discussion of ethics for the criminal law practitioner probably remains a 1969 panel discussion involving several prominent Ontario lawyers and judges, and an article of roughly the same vintage written by the esteemed G. Arthur Martin.[21] Canadian texts on legal

---

17  Main texts presently available in Canada include Hutchinson, above note 10; G. MacKenzie, *Lawyers and Ethics: Professional Responsibility and Discipline* (Toronto: Carswell, 1993); B. Smith, *Professional Conduct for Lawyers and Judges* (Fredericton, N.B.: Maritime Law Book, 1998); D. Lundy, G. MacKenzie, & M. Newbury, *Barristers and Solicitors in Practice* (Toronto: Butterworths, 1998); D. Buckingham, J. Bickenbach, R. Bronaugh, & B. Wilson, *Legal Ethics in Canada: Theory and Practice* (Toronto: Harcourt Brace, 1996) [*Legal Ethics in Canada*]; and M. Orkin, *Legal Ethics: A Study of Professional Conduct* (Toronto: Cartwright, 1957).

18  See the published proceedings from a 1994 conference held in Calgary, entitled "A New Look: A National Conference on the Legal Profession and Ethics" (1995) 33 Alta. L. Rev. 719ff; and the publication of papers prepared as part of a project conducted by the Westminster Institute, in (1996) 9 Can. J. L. & Jur. 3ff.

19  *MacDonald Estate* v. *Martin*, [1990] 3 S.C.R. 1235 [*MacDonald Estate*] (see, for example, P. Glenn, "*MacDonald Estate* v. *Martin*" Case Comment (1991) 70 Can. Bar Rev. 351; and P. Perell, "Defences to the Motion to Disqualify for Conflict of Interest" (1998) 20 Advocates' Q. 469.

20  See, for example, Law Society of British Columbia, Proceeds of Crime Subcommittee, *The Impact of Proceeds of Crime Legislation on the Practice of Law* (August 1990) 7 Benchers' Bulletin (Supp.); and the extensive work of the Law Society of Upper Canada's Task Force on Review of the Rules of Professional Conduct over a lengthy period prior to last year's adoption of new rules of professional conduct in Ontario.

21  "Panel Discussion: Problems in Advocacy and Ethics" in Law Society of Upper Canada, *Defending a Criminal Case* (Toronto: R. De Boo, 1969) 279; and G. Arthur Martin, "The Role and Responsibility of the Defence Advocate" (1970) 12 Crim. L.Q. 376. See also C. Savage, "The Duties and Conduct of Crown and Defence Counsel in a Criminal Trial" (1958-59) 1 Crim. L.Q. 164; and F. Schroeder, "Some Ethical Problems in Criminal Law" in Law Society of Upper Canada, *Representing an Arrested Client and Police Interrogation* (Toronto: R. DeBoo, 1963) 87.

ethics all address criminal law issues, but their attention is quite legitimately focused on the profession more broadly and so tends to lack comprehensiveness. Ethics is partly situational, and discussion of ethical dilemmas is most useful when directly addressing situations in which criminal lawyers find themselves.

Reassuringly, signs of change have begun to appear on the horizon in the criminal law context. The Canadian Supreme Court's recent decision in *Smith* v. *Jones* has, just like *MacDonald Estate*, spawned several articles.[22] The Court's 2001 ruling in *R.* v. *McClure*, which recognizes an exception to legal-professional privilege where innocence is at stake, promises to do the same.[23] The University of New Brunswick's law journal has just published a written forum inspired in part by the controversy arising over the *Murray* case.[24] The Criminal Lawyers' Association, Canada's largest organization of criminal defence lawyers, devoted its 2000 annual conference to the examination of ethical issues, and the proceedings produced a number of written works on the subject. The National Criminal Law Program, held every summer and bringing together criminal law experts from across the country, often yields excellent papers on ethical issues.[25] But, despite these positive developments, there is still a long way to go before Canadians can boast of a healthy literature on ethics and criminal law.

By contrast, in the United States there are entire texts, of high quality, devoted solely to matters of professional responsibility and the criminal lawyer.[26] More especially, articles on ethics and criminal law

---

22  *Smith*, above note 3 (see, for example, A. Kapoor, "Public Safety and Private Communications: Keeping Up With the Jones'" Kapoor's Criminal Appeals Review 1 (7 May 1999), online: QL (KCAR 1999/003); W. Renke, "Secrets and Lives — The Public Safety Exception to Solicitor-Client Privilege: *Smith* v. *Jones*" Case Comment (1999) 37 Alta. L. Rev. 1045; and A. Dodek, "The Public Safety Exception to Solicitor-Client Privilege: *Smith* v. *Jones*" (2001) 34 U.B.C. L. Rev. 293).

23  See, for example, D. Layton, "*R.* v. *McClure*: The Privilege on the Pea" (2001) 40 C.R. (5th) 19.

24  (2001) 50 U.N.B.L.J. 1679ff ("Forum: Legal Ethics"). The same volume also contains several other articles on the subject of legal ethics.

25  The Program is run by the Federation of Law Societies of Canada. Unfortunately, materials presented at the National Criminal Law Program and Criminal Lawyers' Association meetings are not readily available to non-participants.

26  See, for example, J. Burkoff, *Criminal Defense Ethics: Law and Liability*, rev. ed. (St. Paul: West, 2000); J. Hall, *Professional Responsibility of the Criminal Lawyer*, 2d ed. (New York: Clark Boardman Callaghan, 1996); and R. Uphoff, ed., *Ethical Problems Facing the Criminal Defense Lawyer: Practical Answers to Tough Questions* (Chicago: American Bar Association, 1995).

in various American law journals are legion. Of course, quantity of writing is not necessarily indicative of the quality of ethical behaviour exhibited by practising lawyers in any given jurisdiction. Yet surely the more that practitioners and academics write about ethics in the criminal law context, the better developed will be the profession's thinking and actions regarding ethical issues.

## D. CANADIAN GOVERNING BODIES AND RULES OF PROFESSIONAL CONDUCT

Lawyers in Canada are substantially self-regulated,[27] and governing bodies for the profession in Canada exist in each provincial jurisdiction. These bodies enjoy significant control over many aspects of the profession, including admission, training, continuing education, discipline, and competency standards. Also deserving mention is the Canadian Bar Association (CBA), a national organization of lawyers. In contrast to the provincial law societies, membership in the CBA is voluntary and the group does not formally regulate the profession. However, the *de facto* influence of the CBA in many areas, including professional standards, is considerable. The CBA has membership in excess of 35,000, including approximately two-thirds of all lawyers practising in Canada, and boasts resources that rival those of the larger provincial law societies. It is active in many issues affecting lawyers and the public and provides important links for Canadian lawyers that cross provincial boundaries.[28]

Codes of professional conduct are primarily a phenomenon of the twentieth century, and the first prominent effort to produce a code in Canada was the CBA's 1920 Canons of Legal Ethics.[29] The current CBA Code of Professional Conduct (CBA Code) was initially approved by the organization's National Council in 1974 and then revised in 1987.

---

27   For the worse, some would argue: see H. Arthurs, "The Dead Parrot: Does Professional Self-Regulation Exhibit Vital Signs?" (1995) 33 Alta. L. Rev. 800. In Quebec, the government plays a more prominent regulatory role, since the *Professional Code*, R.S.Q. 1977, c. C-26, governs a large number of professions, including law. The Office des Professions administers the *Code*, monitoring the bar's activity in training, admitting new lawyers, setting standards of competency, and so on.

28   Much of the information on the CBA is taken from the organization's website: see online http://www.cba.org.

29   In referring to these documents, we will use the terms "standards," "codes," and "rules" interchangeably.

A number of provincial law societies have adopted the CBA Code holus-bolus, while others have used the Code as a basic template and made modest alterations or additions.[30] The trend among Canadian law societies, however, is to create codes of conduct that are more detailed, comprehensive, and contemporary. This trend translates into rules that bear diminishing resemblance to the CBA Code, the prime example being the ethical code employed by the Law Society of Alberta. The governing bodies in Ontario, Nova Scotia, and British Columbia also use codes that show, to varying degrees, decreasing reliance upon the text of the CBA Code. In New Brunswick, the Law Society is currently considering adoption of a new code of ethics, based on a draft prepared by Professor Beverley Smith.

In Canada, written codes promulgated by the law societies offer a formal expression of standards of conduct expected of lawyers. They say a lot about the role that lawyers play in the legal system and about the profession's collective beliefs and expectations as to appropriate behaviour.[31] There is a constant tension between the desire to articulate lofty ideals in a hortatory code while at the same time providing specific and practical guidance to lawyers who encounter ethical problems. All Canadian codes on some level try to accomplish both tasks. In every jurisdiction, violation of a governing body's ethical code can lead to disciplinary proceedings and attendant punitive consequences. Realistically, however, the behaviour most likely to be targeted by a governing body for investigation and disciplinary proceedings is fraud perpetrated on a client or failure to respond to requests for information.

While important in the context of self-regulation by the profession, the codes do not carry the force of law in civil or criminal litigation. In other words, courts are by no means bound by the provisions of the rules of professional responsibility adopted by a particular law society. Nevertheless, a court often considers the CBA Code and/or a govern-

---

30   See, for example, the rules of professional conduct in Prince Edward Island, Newfoundland, Manitoba, Saskatchewan, the Northwest Territories, and Nunavut. Some governing bodies have adopted the CBA Code in addition to another set of written ethical guidelines: see, for example, New Brunswick, the Northwest Territories, and Yukon Territory).

31   There are, however, arguments against using formal codes of ethics, some of which are canvassed by M. Wilkinson, C. Walker, & P. Mercer in "Do Codes of Ethics Actually Shape Legal Practice?" (2000) 45 McGill L.J. 645. More supportive of the role of codes, though advocating change, is G. MacKenzie, "The Valentine's Card in the Operating Room: Codes of Ethics and the Failing Ideals of the Legal Profession" (1995) 33 Alta. L. Rev. 859.

ing body's code of conduct where relevant to an issue at hand. The Supreme Court of Canada has held as much in the conflict-of-interest case of *MacDonald Estate*, observing that:

> A code of professional conduct is designed to serve as a guide to lawyers and typically it is enforced in disciplinary proceedings. See, for example, *Law Society of Manitoba v. Giesbrecht* (1983), 24 Man. R. (2d) 228 (C.A.). The courts, which have inherent jurisdiction to remove from the record solicitors who have a conflict of interest, are not bound to apply a code of ethics. Their jurisdiction stems from the fact that lawyers are officers of the court and their conduct in legal proceedings which may affect the administration of justice is subject to this supervisory jurisdiction. Nonetheless, an expression of a professional standard in a code of ethics relating to a matter before the court should be considered an important statement of public policy.[32]

The rules of professional conduct promulgated by a law society and the CBA Code can therefore influence decision making in the courts.

## E.  COMMON LAW AND STATUTORY AND CONSTITUTIONAL PRINCIPLES

Questions of legal ethics frequently (though not always, or even usually) involve pronouncements from the courts. A dissatisfied client may sue a lawyer for negligence, violation of fiduciary duty, breach of contract and so on, requiring an assessment of the propriety of the lawyer's actions. In the criminal sphere, convicted clients are increasingly likely to ground an appeal on an allegation that trial counsel was ineffective. There may also be numerous occasions during a trial where the presiding judge is required to make a ruling that includes an assessment of counsel's conduct, a common example being a decision whether to remove a lawyer from the record because of an alleged conflict of interest. Finally, lawyers who push the envelope regarding acceptable ethical behaviour may be subject, rightly or wrongly, to criminal charges that fall to be determined in a court of law.

These sorts of judicial rulings involve diverse areas of substantive law, spanning the gambit from torts to equity to constitutional principles. Additionally, such rulings contribute to the development of an ethics of professional conduct for lawyers. What a judge has to say

---

32   *MacDonald Estate*, above note 19 at 1244–46.

about counsel's actions, while not necessarily tantamount to a binding standard, will frequently spark and influence debate in the area. In the realm of ethics and criminal law, constitutional principles as interpreted by the courts are especially important. The client-lawyer relationship is closely entwined with a multitude of constitutional guarantees, including legal-professional confidentiality and privilege, the right to the effective assistance of counsel, the ability to choose one's lawyer, control of the conduct of the defence, and many others. Thus, while we have not endeavoured to write a text on constitutional law or criminal procedure, these subjects are important to understanding ethics in the criminal law context.

## F.  A COMPARATIVE APPROACH

The lack of an extensive body of Canadian writing in the field of ethics and criminal law means that reference to other jurisdictions can provide helpful guidance. So, too, can professional codes and case law from other countries that employ a broadly similar system of criminal justice. As mentioned, writings in the United States offer a rich discussion of many ethical problems that can confront the criminal lawyer, and we have accordingly looked to the American experience for guidance. After all, we share with the United States a common law legal system based on adversary principles, a constitutionally entrenched bill of rights, and a unified profession. On the other hand, the American context is not perfectly replicated in Canada.[33] To pick one example, professional organizations in the United States often do not regulate attorneys, the courts frequently bearing responsibility for adopting and enforcing standards of professional conduct. Solutions to ethical issues that may be perfectly acceptable in the United States are thus not necessarily appropriate for use here, depending upon the context. Nonetheless, our admittedly *ad hoc* review of what is happening in the United States is hopefully useful in providing a taste of different perspectives from a similar legal system.

We have also considered the Commonwealth approach to various ethical problems, the main sources of comparison being England and Wales and Australia. Both of these jurisdictions have a long history of dividing lawyers into two categories: barristers, who appear in court to

---

33    See, for example, A. Woolley, "Integrity in Zealousness: Comparing the Standard Conceptions of the Canadian and American Lawyer" (1996) 9 Can. J. L. & Jur. 61.

litigate matters, and solicitors, who perform legal work outside the courtroom and instruct barristers where litigation is necessary. In most of Canada, all lawyers are notionally both barristers and solicitors.[34] Granted, some lawyers attend at court frequently while others virtually never set foot in a courtroom, yet the division between barristers and solicitors traditionally observed in England and Wales and Australia has never really been reflected in this country.[35] Rules of professional conduct adopted by Canadian governing bodies thus apply to all lawyers, while in England and Wales solicitors follow standards set out in their Law Society's Guide to the Professional Conduct of Solicitors and barristers adhere to their General Council's Code of Conduct of the Bar of England and Wales.[36] Once again, we must be careful to recognize that differences in legal cultures may account for different perspectives regarding ethical issues, and sometimes these differences militate against importing a solution from another country in an attempt to solve a Canadian problem.

# G. AMERICAN PUBLISHED STANDARDS OF PROFESSIONAL CONDUCT

American codes of professional conduct are more numerous and comprehensive than those used in England and Wales or Australia and have probably had a greater influence upon analogous Canadian codes. It is thus worth reviewing the main standards of professional responsibility used by lawyers in our neighbour to the south, especially since we refer to these standards quite often in the text.

In the United States, the leading professional organization for lawyers is the American Bar Association (ABA), more or less the counterpart of the CBA. The ABA promulgated a set of ethical canons in 1908, representing one of the earliest Anglo-American attempts at providing lawyers with a broad set of guidelines. These Canons of

---

34 In Quebec, the barrister/solicitor distinction was never employed, not even as a fiction. More important was the distinction between advocate and notary.

35 See *Legal Ethics in Canada*, above note 17 at 1–4. Moreover, the distinction is eroding in the land of its origin, given the increased ability of English and Welsh solicitors to appear as courtroom advocates.

36 See, respectively, Law Society, *The Guide to the Professional Conduct of Solicitors*, 8th ed. (London: Law Society, 1999); and General Council, *Code of Conduct of the Bar of England and Wales* (London: The Council, 1990), especially Annex "H" (Written Standards for the Conduct of Professional Work, Standards Applicable to Criminal Cases).

Professional Ethics were based on a similar document produced by the Alabama Bar Association in 1887, which in turn was substantially influenced by the lectures of Judge George Sharswood. The Canons subsequently influenced the form and content of the CBA's 1920 Canons of Legal Ethics.

However, the ABA's Canons were criticized by some as being unduly vague and hence of not much use to practitioners.[37] Others have argued that the Canons were irredeemably tainted because they aimed to exclude people from the legal profession on the basis of gender, class, and race.[38] In any event, the ABA has subsequently produced three major documents of interest to the criminal lawyer, namely, the Model Code of Responsibility, the Model Rules of Professional Conduct, and the Standards for Criminal Justice. Also of prime importance, though not produced by the ABA, is the American Law Institute's (ALI) Restatement of the Law Governing Lawyers. We will briefly discuss each of these four documents in a little more detail.

## 1) ABA Model Code of Professional Responsibility

In 1969 the Model Code of Professional Responsibility was introduced by the ABA, replacing the Canons. Most state and federal jurisdictions in the United States adopted the Model Code, albeit sometimes in revised form. An interesting component of the Model Code is the distinction drawn between "disciplinary rules" and "ethical considerations." Disciplinary rules set out minimum standards of behaviour, the violation of which can warrant formal investigation and censure. In contrast, ethical considerations are of an aspirational nature, providing ideals for which lawyers are encouraged (but not required) to strive. The ABA Model Code also includes "canons," which are axiomatic norms intended to express in general terms the standards applicable to lawyers' behaviour.

As noted immediately below, the Model Code has been superseded by the ABA's Model Rules. However, the Code remains relevant as an important commentary on ethical standards, and also because almost one-third of American jurisdictions currently retain formal, enforceable standards based upon the Code. We thus make occasional mention of the Code's approach to ethical issues in this text. Disciplinary

---

37    See C.W. Wolfram, *Modern Legal Ethics* (St. Paul: West, 1986) 53–56.
38    See M. Freedman, *Understanding Lawyers' Ethics* (New York: Matthew Bender, 1990) at 3–4.

rules are prefaced by the letters "DR," while ethical considerations are indicated by a reference to "EC."

## 2)  ABA Model Rules of Professional Conduct

In 1983 the ABA's House of Delegates approved the Model Rules of Professional Conduct. These written standards jettisoned the distinction between disciplinary rules and ethical considerations used in the Model Code, instead utilizing the "rules and commentary" approach familiar to Canadian lawyers. Since their initial inception, the Model Rules have been amended roughly thirty times, and the ABA is currently considering a major revision based on November 2000 proposals made by the Ethics 2000 Commission on the Evaluation of the Rules of Professional Conduct.[39] Approximately two-thirds of American jurisdictions have adopted ethical codes based on the Model Rules. The application and interpretation of the Model Rules is subject to consideration by formal and informal opinions issued by the ABA Committee on Ethics and Professional Responsibility.[40] We make frequent reference to the Model Rules in this book and have also incorporated certain opinions of the ABA Committee on Ethics and Professional Responsibility.

## 3)  ABA Criminal Justice Section's Standards for Criminal Justice

In 1968 the ABA Criminal Justice Section published standards for the practice of law by criminal lawyers, which were approved by the House of Delegates in 1971. Chief Justice Warren Burger called the Standards "the single most comprehensive and probably the most monumental undertaking in the field of criminal justice ever attempted by the American legal profession in our national history."[41] Today, the Standards are in their third edition, and cover a wide range of topics including the Defense Function and Prosecution Function. The organ-

---

39   For an update on the work of the Ethics 2000 Commission, see the ABA Center for Professional Responsibility website, online at http://www.abanet.org/cpr.

40   Also, the ABA Center for Professional Responsibility has published an excellent annotated version of the Model Rules: see American Bar Association, *Annotated Model Rules of Professional Conduct*, 4th ed. (Chicago: American Bar Association, Center for Professional Responsibility, 1999).

41   Quoted from the ABA Criminal Justice website, online at http://www.abanet.org/crimjust/standards.

ization of the Standards is somewhat similar to the Model Rules, with black letter standards followed by commentaries.[42]

The Standards are not enforceable codes, rather being intended as a guide to professional conduct and performance. Unlike the ABA's Model Code and Rules, they have not been taken up for use in regulating attorneys at the state and federal level. Nonetheless, the Standards represent a concerted effort, produced by and for criminal lawyers, to provide guidance in ethical matters. Certainly, American courts have often looked to the Standards in assessing the propriety of impugned lawyer conduct. We make frequent reference to the Standards, given that they provide a valuable assessment of many ethical issues pertaining to the practice of criminal law.

## 4)  The ALI's Restatement of the Law Governing Lawyers

The American Law Institute drafts and publishes restatements of law, model codes, and other proposals for legal reform. In 2000 the ALI released its eagerly anticipated Restatement of Law Governing Lawyers, often called the "Third Restatement."[43] This massive two-volume effort comprises an exhaustive review of the law pertaining to the work of lawyers and includes extensive material pertaining to lawyers' ethics. The work is organized in the form of black letter standards, followed by commentaries and examples that tend to be more discursive than those provided in the ABA Model Rules. In addition, the Third Restatement includes "Reporter's Notes" with reference to each rule, focusing on case law and other references pertinent to the topic at hand.[44] The Third Restatement thus offers a new perspective on many ethics issues, compiled by leading experts, and also a handy overview of the statutory landscape, case law, and academic commentary in the United States.

---

42   The Standards' reporter is Professor John Burkoff, the author of a leading American text on ethics and criminal law: see *Criminal Defense Ethics: Law and Liability*, above note 26.

43   American Law Institute, *Restatement of the Law, the Law Governing Lawyers*, rev. ed. (St. Paul: American Law Institute, 2000) ["*Third Restatement*"]. Somewhat confusingly, there were no previous restatements covering the law governing lawyers.

44   The Reporter for the Third Restatement is Professor Charles Wolfram of Cornell Law School, a highly respected writer on legal ethics: see *Modern Legal Ethics*, above note 37.

# H. TOPICS COVERED

In this book, we have directed our attention to subject areas that reflect many of the most common and/or demanding ethical issues confronting criminal lawyers. A brief synopsis of these subject areas, organized on a chapter-by-chapter basis, is as follows:

**Chapter 1, Defending the Guilty:** The defence of an accused individual often involves working towards the acquittal of the guilty. Sometimes a defence lawyer has irresistible knowledge that the client is in fact guilty. This chapter examines the restrictions upon the conduct of the case where a lawyer possesses such knowledge. Also, we introduce the notion that a defence lawyer plays a special role in the system, a role based largely upon a duty of loyalty owed to the client. As presaged by the above discussion of New Ethics, the question becomes the extent to which this role is necessarily tempered by fidelity to the truth-finding function of the criminal justice system.

**Chapter 2, Choosing and Refusing Clients:** The discussion of role morality for lawyers continues in this chapter, where we try to determine when, if ever, a lawyer can refuse the case of a prospective client. Social opprobrium and personal distaste for a client or cause can work against accepting a retainer, yet refusal to take on a matter can restrict an individual's access to justice.

**Chapter 3, Decision Making:** Who controls the conduct of a case? The traditional view in Canada is that criminal lawyers reign supreme in deciding how to carry out the litigation. On this view, the client holds ultimate authority with respect to only a few (albeit important) matters, such as the decision on how to plead or whether to testify. However, a more sophisticated approach, which gives credence to the client's right to control the conduct of the case, is gaining support in Canada. We adopt this newer model and examine how it might apply in especially difficult circumstances, including where the client is disabled or a young person or has disappeared or demands a frivolous litigation manoeuvre.

**Chapter 4, Confidentiality:** One of the central aspects of a lawyer's duty of loyalty to the client is the concomitant obligation to keep confidential all information obtained as a result of the retainer. The duty of confidentiality infuses pretty much every single aspect of a lawyer's work. In this chapter, we examine its justification, breadth and operation. We also discuss the important distinction between the ethical duty of confidentiality and the rule of evidence known as legal-professional privilege.

**Chapter 5, Possible Confidentiality Exceptions:** While confidentiality is a mainstay of the client-lawyer relationship, competing societal values often push for the disclosure of confidences. Public safety may be in jeopardy, or the court may have been misled. The exact nature of permissible derogations from the duty of confidentiality is often contentious and unclear, which is why we refer to "possible" confidentiality exceptions. We review the instances where confidential information can perhaps be revealed absent the client's consent, and we also argue against excessively wide exceptions to the basic rule of non-disclosure.

**Chapter 6, Conflict of Interest:** A conflict of interest occurs whenever a lawyer's duty of loyalty to a client is compromised by a competing interest. A threat to the client's confidences is often, though not always, implicated. Perhaps more than with any other ethical issue, principles concerning conflict of interest are frequently the subject of judicial application. This chapter therefore contains an extensive discussion of relevant case law. Principal topics include the pitfalls and benefits of multiple representation, the problems that can arise in relation to former clients, and the efficacy of client waivers.

**Chapter 7, Client Perjury:** The lawyer faced with anticipated or completed client perjury is called upon to wend his or her way through an ethical minefield. There is no shortage of opinion on offer from commentators as to the proper course of action, yet consensus is elusive on many points. The discussion in this chapter provides, in a fashion that will by now be familiar to the reader, an example of the tension between a lawyer's duty of loyalty to the client and adherence to the integrity of the truth-finding function of the criminal justice process.

**Chapter 8, Plea Discussions:** A substantial majority of criminal cases end in a guilty plea. It is thus crucial for criminal lawyers to pursue an ethical course of action even where the issue of guilt may ultimately not be disputed. Many of the elements of the client-lawyer relationship discussed in chapter 3 are elaborated upon at this juncture, including the need for full consultation with the client and respect for the client's goals and desires. A particularly thorny problem concerns the client who maintains innocence yet insists on pleading guilty.

**Chapter 9, Incriminating Physical Evidence:** Client perjury is likely the paradigm topic of discussion regarding lawyers' ethics in the United States. In Canada, the story of convicted murderer Paul

Bernardo, his lawyer Ken Murray and the famously concealed video-tapes has currently made the proper handling of incriminating physical evidence the hot ethical issue for Canadian lawyers and the public. Nonetheless, the often feeble efforts of the profession to address ethical problems particular to criminal lawyers come to the forefront with the *Murray* case. We attempt to provide guidance as to how this admittedly vexing problem can be approached.

**Chapter 10, Fees and Disbursements:** It is probably fair to say that criminal lawyers trail behind their civil counterparts in ascribing sufficient attention to ethical issues involving fees and disbursements. The idea that barristers belong to a noble calling with minimal interest in financial gain may be a harmless fiction, but not where the result is non-itemized, fixed-fee accounts provided to the client absent any explanation as to how the fee was arrived upon. Fee issues do not hold the drama of, for instance, the problem of handling incriminating physical evidence. Nonetheless, many important ethical issues are thrown up with regards to the exchange of money for services between client and lawyer.

**Chapter 11, Termination:** Client-lawyer relationships usually start with fond hopes for a happy partnership that achieves the best possible result. For a variety of reasons, not always within the control of the parties, the relationship may end sooner than expected. This chapter reviews some of the circumstances where a lawyer can or must end the representation, the manner by which this step should be taken, and the duties attendant upon termination.

**Chapter 12, The Prosecutor:** Many of the principles discussed above are relevant to lawyers who prosecute criminal offences. But the special role of the prosecutor demands the refinement of these principles, often in a substantial manner. Most notably, Crown counsel acts as a "minister of justice," in the public interest, and accordingly must temper or control zealous advocacy in a way not required of defence counsel. This chapter examines the nature of the prosecutor's function, as well as the way in which this function operates in the particular circumstances of a criminal case.

# I.  SCOPE OF THE BOOK AND RECOMMENDATIONS MADE

This book does not attempt to cover every ethical dilemma that a criminal lawyer may encounter.[45] Instead, we have aimed to draw out general principles from the problems that are canvassed, and to provide concrete suggestions for a great many instances where the proper course of action for the criminal lawyer is not immediately clear. In doing so, we have made use of examples in the text, in many instances employing scenarios borrowed from actual cases, as a means of illustrating relevant principles and warning of dangerous ethical snares. Additionally, special emphasis is given to certain points through the use of bold type and headings such as "caveat," "caution," "recommendation," and so on. There is no magic in these particular terms, other than to make sure that the point in question does not escape the reader's attention. The reader will also notice that selected bibliographies have been provided after each chapter. These bibliographies, though not comprehensive, include many of the sources that we have reviewed and found useful.

At the end of each chapter we summarize our views and frequently offer opinions pertaining to the particular problem or subject area at hand. In doing so, we are not proposing a black letter code for criminal lawyers, and we have not weighed each word with the exactitude required in drafting such a document. Rather, we offer these views in the hope that lawyers are aided in arriving at their own decisions regarding ethical matters, and to help stimulate debate in an area of study that is still in its infancy in Canada. Indeed, we note with some pride, if not an equal amount of modesty, that the Law Society of Upper Canada has drawn upon our recommendations in proposing a draft rule and commentary on the handling of incriminating physical evidence.[46] Of course, this process of interplay between the many sources that contribute to a criminal lawyers' ethics is exactly what this book is about.

---

45   Examples of areas to which we devote minimal attention are statements to the media, the conduct of an appeal, and contacts with judges, witnesses, and jurors.

46   See Law Society of Upper Canada, *Report to Convocation: Special Committee on Lawyer's Duties with Respect to Physical Evidence Relevant to a Crime* (22 March 2001) at para. 7.

It is our hope that this work represents a modest beginning to what will become a better-developed area of discussion and debate in publications, firms, courtrooms, and law schools, indeed in any forum used by people interested in criminal law to discuss matters of ethics. No doubt some of our proposals will be rejected, modified, or ignored. New Ethicists may view our positions as too tentative or naively retrograde, while practising defence lawyers may complain that we have too readily undermined the sacrosanct principle of loyalty to the client. The point, however, is not to glean favourable reviews but rather to spark discussion and thought. We thus optimistically look forward to a second edition of this book in which the Introduction can point to a burgeoning body of work on ethics and criminal law.

## FURTHER READINGS

ARTHURS, H., "The Dead Parrot: Does Professional Self-Regulation Exhibit Vital Signs?" (1995) 33 Alta. L. Rev. 800

ARTHURS, H., "Counsel, Client and Community" (1973) 11 Osgoode Hall L.J. 437

BICKENBACH, J., "The Redemption of the Moral Mandate of the Profession of Law" (1996) 9 Can. J. L. & Jur. 51

BOON, A., & LEVIN, J. *The Ethics and Conduct of Lawyers in England and Wales* (Oxford: Hart Publishing, 1999)

BUCKINGHAM, D., J. BICKENBACH, R. BRONAUGH, & B. WILSON, *Legal Ethics in Canada: Theory and Practice* (Toronto: Harcourt Brace, 1996)

BUCKINGHAM, D., "Rules and Roles: Casting Off Legal Education's Moral Blinders for an Approach that Encourages Moral Development" (1996) 9 Can. J. L. & Jur. 111

BURKOFF, J., *Criminal Defense Ethics: Law and Liability*, rev. ed. (St. Paul: West Group, 2000)

CAYLEY, D., *The Expanding Prison: The Crisis in Crime and Punishment and the Search for Alternatives* (Toronto: Anansi Press, 1998)

DEVLIN, R., "Normative, and Somewhere to Go? Reflections on Professional Responsibility" (1995) 33 Alta. L. Rev. 924

DODEK, A., "Canadian Legal Ethics: A Subject in Search of Scholarship" (2000) 50 U.T.L.J. 115

DODEK, A., "The Public Safety Exception to Solictor-Client Privilege: *Smith* v. *Jones*" (2001) 34 U.B.C. L. Rev. 293

DOWNIE, J., "A Case for Compulsory Legal Ethics Education in Canadian Law Schools" (1997) Dal. L.J. 224

FREEDMAN, M., *Lawyers' Ethics in an Adversary System* (New York: Bobbs-Merrill, 1975)

FREEDMAN, M., *Understanding Lawyers' Ethics* (New York: Matthew Bender, 1990)

FRIED, C., "The Lawyer as Friend: The Moral Foundations of the Lawyer-Client Relation" (1976) 85 Yale L.J. 1060

GLENN, P., "*MacDonald Estate* v. *Martin*" Case Comment (1991) 70 Can. Bar Rev. 351

GRAHAM, R., "Moral Contexts" (2001) 50 U.N.B.L.J. 77

HALL, J., *Professional Responsibility of the Criminal Lawyer*, 2d ed. (New York: Clark Boardman Callaghan, 1996)

HAMILTON, J., "Metaphors of Lawyers' Professionalism" (1995) 33 Alta. L. Rev. 833

HUBERMAN, M., "Integrity Testing for Lawyers: Is It Time?" (1997) 76 Can. Bar Rev. 47

HUTCHINSON, A., "Calgary and Everything After: A Postmodern Re-Vision of Lawyering" (1995) 33 Alta. L. Rev. 768

HUTCHINSON, A., *Legal Ethics and Professional Responsibility* (Toronto: Irwin Law, 1999)

JACKSON, J., "Truth and Compromise in Criminal Justice: A Critique of Trial Practice and Lawyers' Ethics" (1997) 48 N. Ir. L.Q. 321

KAPOOR, A., "Public Safety and Private Communications: Keeping Up with the Jones'", Kapoor's Criminal Appeals Review 1 (7 May 1999), online: QL (KCAR 1999/003)

KONIAK, S., "Law and Ethics in a World of Rights and Unsuitable Wrongs" (1996) 9 Can. J. L. & Jur. 11

LAYTON, D., "*R.* v. *McClure*: The Privilege on the Pea" (2001) 40 C.R. (5th) 19

LAYTON, D., "The Public Safety Exception: Confusing Confidentiality, Privilege and Ethics" (2001) 6 Can. Crim. L. Rev. 209

LUBAN, D., "Introduction: A New Canadian Legal Ethics?" (1996) 9 Can. J. L. & Jur. 3

LUBAN, D., *Lawyers and Justice: An Ethical Study* (Princeton, N.J.: Princeton University Press, 1988)

LUNDY, D., G. MACKENZIE, & M. NEWBURY, *Barristers and Solicitors in Practice* (Toronto: Butterworths, 1998)

MACKENZIE, G., "Breaking the Dichotomy Habit: The Adversary System and the Ethics of Professionalism" (1996) 9 Can. J. L. & Jur. 33

MACKENZIE, G., *Lawyers and Ethics: Professional Responsibility and Discipline* (Toronto: Carswell, 1993)

MACKENZIE, G., "The Valentine's Card in the Operating Room: Codes of Ethics and the Failing Ideals of the Legal Profession" (1995) 33 Alta. L. Rev. 859

MARTIN, G., "The Role and Responsibility of the Defence Advocate" (1970) 12 Crim. L.Q. 376

ORKIN, M., *Legal Ethics: A Study of Professional Conduct* (Toronto: Cartwright, 1957)

"Panel Discussion: Problems in Advocacy and Ethics" in Law Society of Upper Canada, *Defending a Criminal Case* (Toronto: R. De Boo, 1969) 279

PERELL, P., "Defences to the Motion to Disqualify for Conflict of Interest" (1998) 20 Advocates' Q. 469

PUE, W., "In Pursuit of Better Myth: Lawyers' Histories and Histories of Lawyers" (1995) 33 Alta. L. Rev. 730

PUE, W., "Becoming 'Ethical': Lawyers' Professional Ethics in Early Twentieth Century Canada" (1990) 20 Man. L.J. 227

RENKE, W., "Secrets and Lives — The Public Safety Exception to Solicitor-Client Privilege: *Smith* v. *Jones*" Case Comment (1999) 37 Alta. L. Rev. 1045

RHODE, D., "Ethical Perspectives on Legal Practice" (1985) 37 Stan. L. Rev. 589

ROSS, S., *Ethics in Law: Lawyers' Responsibility and Accountability in Australia*, 2d ed. (Sydney: Butterworths, 1998)

SAVAGE, C., "The Duties and Conduct of Crown and Defence Counsel in a Criminal Trial" (1958-59) 1 Crim. L.R. 164

SCHROEDER, F., "Some Ethical Problems in Criminal Law" in Law Society of Upper Canada, *Representing an Arested Client and Police Interrogation* (Toronto: Law Society of Upper Canada, 1963) 87

SIMON, W., "Ethical Discretion in Lawyering" (1988) 101 Harv. L. Rev. 1083

SKURKA, S., & J. STRIBOPOULOS, "Professional Responsibility in Criminal Practice" in Law Society of Upper Canada, *42nd Bar Admission Course, 2000, Criminal Procedure Reference Materials* (Toronto: Law Society of Upper Canada, 2000) c. 1

SMITH, B., *Professional Conduct for Lawyers and Judges* (Fredericton: Maritime Law Book, 1998)

WILKINSON, M., C. WALKER, & P. MERCER, "Do Codes of Ethics Actually Shape Legal Practice?" (2000) 45 McGill L.J. 645

WOLFRAM C.W., *Modern Legal Ethics* (St. Paul: West, 1986)

WOOLLEY, A., "Integrity in Zealousness: Comparing the Standard Conceptions of the Canadian and American Lawyer" (1996) 9 Can. J. L. & Jur. 61

# CHAPTER 1

# DEFENDING
# THE GUILTY

## A. INTRODUCTION

Almost every defence lawyer has been asked, whether by family, friends, or strangers, "How can you defend a guilty person?"[1] The layperson probably has no problem with counsel representing such an accused on a guilty plea. What raises his or her ire is the defence lawyer who helps the guilty client try to avoid conviction. In response to this challenge, the lawyer can often deflect the enquiry by posing other questions in reply, such as "How can you say that a person is guilty before the verdict?" "But guilty of what?" or "How do you know the person is guilty?" But the persistent interlocutor, not satisfied with these partial answers, may push on further and say: "What I mean is, how can you defend an accused person that *you know* is guilty?" It is this issue — how can counsel fight against the conviction of a client who is known to be guilty — that is discussed in this chapter.

Defending an accused who has confessed his or her guilt to counsel, or whom counsel otherwise knows to be guilty, has been described as "the supreme test problem in the ethics of advocacy."[2] It encapsu-

---

1   See B. Babcock, "Commentary: Defending the Guilty" (1983–84) 32 Clev. S. L. Rev. 175 at 175: "I have answered that question hundreds of times, never to my inquirer's satisfaction, and therefore never to my own."

2   H. Macmillan, "The Ethics of Advocacy" in J. Ames, *Jurisprudence in Action: A Pleader's Anthology* (New York: Baker, Voorhis, 1953) at 307 (originally pub-

lates an existential question that goes to the very core of a defence lawyer's mission. Academics who study the adversarial, rights-based nature of our criminal justice system have long grappled with issues surrounding the defence of the guilty client, and if anything the debate has grown more intense of late. As we will see, controversy prevails among many commentators regarding how best to handle the difficult problems related to this issue. Of course, it is practising lawyers and their clients who are most immediately affected by the issue, which engages diverse ethical duties (to the client, the administration of justice, and the profession) and implicates counsel's own conscience and sense of morality. Yet, on a broader scale still, this issue foments public debate (and, in many cases, misunderstanding) as to the fundamental rights of the accused and the various aims of the criminal justice system. There are few things more galling to the public than defence counsel's zealous and aggressive representation of a client who is "obviously" guilty.

## B. RELATED RULES OF PROFESSIONAL CONDUCT

The CBA Code of Professional Conduct serves as the main point of reference in setting the standards applicable to the defence of an accused who is known to be guilty, with most Canadian governing bodies adopting the same or very similar text.[3] The CBA Code seeks to promote the need for zealous representation of the client, but without countenancing the improper subversion of the truth. Chapter IX of the Code, pertaining to "The Lawyer as Advocate," begins with the following general rule: "[W]hen acting as an advocate, the lawyer must treat the tribunal with courtesy and respect and must represent the client resolutely, honourably and within the limits of the law." The so-called

---

lished in Rt. Hon. Lord Macmillan, *Law and Other Things* (Cambridge, U.K.: University Press, 1937).

3   See, for example, Ont. r. 4.01(1); N.S. ch. 10, comm. 10.3–10.7; Alta. ch. 10, comm. 1 & 14.2; and Yukon Part 3, r. 6. In contrast, the Quebec and British Columbia ethical codes do not mimic the CBA Code rule. Both codes recognize the general need to balance zealous representation with honest dealing, but without offering much more in the way of guidance. The result in both jurisdictions is a less useful directive for defence lawyers, essentially going no further than making the point, reflected in Commentary 10 to the CBA Code's rule, that a lawyer's private opinion as to a client's guilt does not justify a mediocre defence: see Que. s. 2.04; and B.C. c.h I, r. 3(5) & (6).

"guiding principles" for this rule are found in Commentary 1 and continue the theme as follows:

Commentary 1

Guiding Principles

1. The advocate's duty to the client "fearlessly to raise every issue, advance every argument, and ask every question, however distasteful, which he thinks will help his client's case" and to endeavour "to obtain for his client the benefit of any and every remedy and defence which is authorized by law" must always be discharged by fair and honourable means, without illegality and in a manner consistent with the lawyer's duty to treat the court with candour, fairness, courtesy and respect.

The Code goes on to isolate certain conduct that is prohibited, including:

Commentary 2

2.   The lawyer must not, for example:

(b) knowingly assist or permit the client to do anything that the lawyer considers to be dishonest or dishonourable;

. . .

(e) knowingly attempt to deceive or participate in the deception of a tribunal or influence the course of justice by offering false evidence, misstating facts or law, presenting or relying upon a false or deceptive affidavit, suppressing what ought to be disclosed or otherwise assisting in any fraud, crime or illegal conduct; . . . .

These principles are useful in ascertaining the ethical limits imposed on counsel who represents a client known to be guilty. In addition, the commentaries in Chapter IX of the CBA Code offer still greater specificity with respect to the role of defence counsel. Commentary 10 states:

Commentary 10

Duties of Defence Counsel

10. When defending an accused person, the lawyer's duty is to protect the client as far as possible from being convicted except by a court of competent jurisdiction and upon legal evidence sufficient to support a conviction for the offence charged. Accordingly, and notwithstanding the lawyer's private opinion as to credibility or

merits, the lawyer may properly rely upon all available evidence or defences including so-called technicalities not known to be false or fraudulent.

Most relevant of all is Commentary 11, which deals directly with our topic and reads as follows:

> 11. Admissions made by the accused to the lawyer may impose strict limitations on the conduct of the defence and the accused should be made aware of this. For example, if the accused clearly admits to the lawyer the factual and mental elements necessary to constitute the offence, the lawyer, if convinced that the admissions are true and voluntary, may properly take objection to the jurisdiction of the court, or to the form of the indictment, or to the admissibility or sufficiency of the evidence, but must not suggest that some other person committed the offence, or call any evidence that, by reason of the admissions, the lawyer believes to be false. Nor may the lawyer set up an affirmative case inconsistent with such admissions, for example, by calling evidence in support of an alibi intended to show that the accused could not have done, or in fact had not done, the act. Such admissions will also impose a limit upon the extent to which the lawyer may attack the evidence for the prosecution. The lawyer is entitled to test the evidence given by each individual witness for the prosecution and argue that the evidence taken as a whole is insufficient to amount to proof that the accused is guilty of the offence charged, but the lawyer should go no further than that.

Also of interest is the approach taken in New Brunswick. There, the Professional Conduct Handbook states that

> [t]he lawyer is an advocate and not an agent. The function of counsel is to plead his client's case on the record before the court. Therefore, unless the counsel is sworn and testifies, it is improper for counsel to state his personal belief about his client's cause. See *Boucher v. The Queen* (1955) S.C.R. 16 at page 26 (Supreme Court of Canada). *In a criminal matter, the opinion of counsel as to his client's guilt or innocence is not only totally irrelevant to the issue, but it must not be expressed to the court at all.*[4]

The articulation of this principle does not permit a lawyer to mislead the court in presenting a client's case.[5] But this ethical guideline does

---

4    N.B. Part C, r. 11 (emphasis added).
5    See N.B. Part B, r. 2.

serve to emphasize that defence counsel is fully justified in defending a client known to be guilty.

Some other jurisdictions employ guidelines similar to those found in Commentaries 10 and 11 of the CBA Code, including England and Wales and Australia.[6] In the United States, the approach is more varied and arguably less comprehensive. The ABA Model Code makes the point that counsel should not seek to be excused from taking a brief because he or she believes that the defendant is guilty, but it addresses only the situation where counsel is appointed by the court or asked by a bar association to undertake the representation.[7] Moreover, neither the ABA Model Code nor the newer ABA Model Rules offer much direct insight into the limits placed upon counsel who knows that a client is guilty. Rather, the Model Code and Model Rules contain a general prohibition against counsel knowingly making a false statement of material law or fact to a tribunal, or offering evidence that the lawyer knows to be false.[8] The Third Restatement and the ABA Defense Standards contain a similar prohibition.[9] Yet the Standards for Criminal Justice flesh out one aspect of the problem in more detail, regarding the cross-examination of a truthful witness. According to Defense Standard 4-7.6(b), "defense counsel's belief or knowledge that the witness is telling the truth does not preclude cross-examination."[10]

# C. GENESIS OF THE PRESENT RULES

Nineteenth-century philosopher Jeremy Bentham famously went so far as to argue that a lawyer who receives a confession of guilt becomes an

---

6    See, for example, General Council, *Code of Conduct of the Bar of England and Wales* (London: The Council, 1990) [*Bar Code of Conduct*] Annex "H" (Written Standards for the Conduct of Professional Work, Standards Applicable to Criminal Cases) §13 (Confessions of Guilt); Law Society, *The Guide to the Professional Conduct of Solicitors*, 8th ed. (London: Law Society, 1999), §21.20; New South Wales Barristers' Rules, r. 33; and Bar Association of Queensland Rules, r. 33. Overall, there are some differences among these ethical standards, though usually of a minor nature.

7    See ABA Model Code EC 2-29, as well as the discussion in C.W. Wolfram, *Modern Legal Ethics* (St. Paul: West, 1986) at 587, note 21 and accompanying text. The ABA Model Rules do not have an exact counterpart, but compare ABA Model Rule 6.2.

8    See ABA Model Rule 3.3; and ABA Model Code DR 7-102(A).

9    See Third Restatement §120; and ABA Defense Standard 4-7.5(a).

10   The implication of this provision is discussed further in section K(1), "Cross-Examining the Truthful Witness," in this chapter.

accessory after the fact if he undertakes a defence at trial.[11] Yet Bentham's view was by no means common currency among his contemporaries who practised criminal law. As early as 1840, the profession in England was forced to grapple with the issue of defending the client who is known to be guilty in the celebrated *Courvoisier* case.[12] Courvoisier was charged with the murder of his aristocratic employer, Lord Russell, and was defended by Charles Phillips, a leading counsel of the day. After the trial, which ended with the conviction and eventually the hanging of the accused, it was publicly revealed that on the second day of the proceedings Courvoisier had confessed his guilt to Phillips. Phillips then consulted with Baron Parke, who, according to the English practice at the time, was assisting Lord Chief Justice Tindal in the case. Though reportedly "much annoyed" with Phillips's initiative,[13] Baron Parke enquired as to whether the accused still wished to be defended by Phillips. On receiving an affirmative answer, Baron Parke told Phillips that he "was bound to do so, and to use all fair arguments arising on the evidence."[14]

The *Courvoisier* case not only generated much controversy at the time but ultimately influenced the "ethical canons of lawyers in England, America, and wherever the Anglo-American system of legal representation has taken hold."[15] By the early twentieth century, the idea that a lawyer has a duty to defend vigorously a client known to be guilty was fairly well established. In England, this duty was affirmed in an extremely influential report released by the General Council of the

---

11    See J. Bentham, *Rationale of Judicial Evidence: Specially Applied to English Practice*, Vol. VII, Book IX in J. Bowring, ed., *The Works of Jeremy Bentham* (Edinburgh: W. Tait, 1838-43) 474.

12    See *R. v. Courvoisier* (1840), 9 C. & P. 362, 173 E.R. 869 (N.P.) [*Courvoisier*]. The ethical issues thrown up by *Courvoisier* are not discussed in the reported case, but they were well publicized at the time and have been canvassed by a great many commentators. A thorough and entertaining discussion of *Courvoisier* is provided by D. Mellinkoff, *The Conscience of a Lawyer* (St. Paul: West, 1973).

13    See Mellinkoff, above note 12 at 138.

14    Phillips's recounting of the story was eventually published in *The Times*, 20 November 1849, in the form of his correspondence with Samuel Warren. The letters exchanged between Phillips and Warren are reprinted by G. Sharswood, *An Essay on Professional Ethics*, 4th ed. (Philadelphia: T. & J.W. Johnson, 1876) App. 1 at 183ff.

15    Mellinkoff, above note 12 at 131. See also F. Schroeder, "Some Ethical Problems in Criminal Law" in Law Society of Upper Canada, *Representing an Arrested Client and Police Interrogation* (Toronto: R. De Boo, 1963) 87 at 94; and R. Lawry, "Cross-Examining the Truthful Witness: The Ideal Within the Central Moral Tradition of Lawyering" (1996) 100 Dick. L. Rev. 563 at 569 & 572.

English Bar in 1915.[16] The Council had been asked by the Bar Committee of Shanghai "to advise on the propriety of Counsel defending on a plea of 'Not guilty' a prisoner charged with an offence, capital or otherwise, when the latter has confessed to Counsel himself the fact that he did commit the offence charged."[17] In its report, the Council answered by confirming that in such circumstances a lawyer often has a duty to continue with the defence,[18] but at the same time it set out certain limitations aimed at preventing counsel from misleading the court. The influence of the Council's report in Canada can hardly be overemphasized: the text of the report was reproduced almost verbatim in the 1974 CBA Code and today forms the vast bulk of the CBA Code's Commentary 11 (and by extension, the comparable ethical rules adopted by most Canadian governing bodies).[19]

By the 1930s, the notion that a lawyer could represent a client known to be guilty was sufficiently well established, at least among practitioners, that the High Court of Australia could state, in response to the assertion by counsel that receiving a client's confession represented "the worst predicament that he had encountered in all his legal career":

> Why he should have conceived himself to have been in so great a predicament, it is not easy for those experienced in advocacy to understand.[20]

This chiding comment was made in one of the leading Commonwealth cases on the subject, *Tuckiar* v. *R.*[21] During the trial, the accused admit-

---

16   The 1915 report is reproduced in its entirety in U.K., Supreme Court of Judicature, *The Annual Practice* (London: Sweet & Maxwell, 1917) at 2433–2434 [*The Annual Practice*].

17   *The Annual Practice*, *ibid.*, at 2433. It is Macmillan, in "The Ethics of Advocacy," above note 2 at 321–22, who reports that the request for advice came from the Bar Committee of Shanghai.

18   However, in the Council's view the duty usually did *not* apply where the confession came prior to trial, as is discussed below in section G, "Accepting or Continuing With the Retainer of a Client Known to Be Guilty," in this chapter.

19   The 1920 CBA Canons of Legal Ethics do not borrow the language of the 1915 report (although the defence of the client known to be guilty is dealt with at §2(5) & (6)). Commentary 11 of the current CBA Code is reproduced above in section B, "Related Rules of Professional Conduct," in this chapter. Footnote 23 to Commentary 11 makes reference to the report, though without clearly revealing the substantial extent to which this portion of the CBA Code relies upon the Council's work.

20   *Tuckiar* v. *R.* (1934), 52 C.L.R. 335 at 346 (H.C. Austl.) [*Tuckiar*].

21   *Ibid.*

ted to his lawyer that he had committed the crime. Counsel responded by passing on this information to the judge and opposing counsel during a meeting in chambers, and he went so far as to recount the substance of his client's confession in open court following the jury's verdict of guilt.[22] The High Court strongly disagreed with counsel's actions and, in a statement that has become a classic description of a criminal defence lawyer's duty, noted that

> [w]hether he be in fact guilty or not, a prisoner is, in point of law, entitled to acquittal from any charge which the evidence fails to establish that he committed, and it is not incumbent on his counsel by abandoning his defence to deprive him of the benefit of such rational arguments as fairly arise on the proofs submitted.[23]

These sentiments remain valid in Canada, not to mention much of the Commonwealth and the United States. The hard question, about which there is no strong consensus, concerns how far defence counsel can go in defending the guilty client.

## D. RATIONALE FOR DEFENDING ONE KNOWN TO BE GUILTY

The rationale that permits a lawyer to defend a client known to be guilty is inextricably linked to the nature of our criminal justice system, including the role that the system assigns to defence counsel. Crucially, the criminal justice process is adversarial. The opposing sides are responsible for presenting their own cases by bringing forward evidence, cross-examination, argument, and other forensic methods, and partisanship is an integral part of this process. The decision as to guilt is made not by the parties themselves but by a neutral trier of fact. The adversarial system is commonly thought to be an excellent means of arriving at a reliable determination as to "what happened."[24]

The criminal justice system may be adversarial in nature, but the accused and prosecution are not always subject to the same rules.

---

22    *Ibid.* at 343–44.

23    *Ibid.* at 346.

24    This claim has been subject to much criticism, especially by American academics of the New Ethics school. For a taste of the New Ethics approach, see the Review Essay Symposium devoted to William Simon's *The Practice of Justice: A Theory of Lawyers' Ethics*, found at (1999) 51 Stan. L. Rev. 867–1006. In Canada, see the authors cited in the Introduction at note 10.

Rather, the system incorporates certain fairness or due process concerns.[25] These concerns, which can be organized within the broad notion of the principle against self-incrimination,[26] serve to provide an accused with special protections vis-à-vis the powerful and sometimes overweening state. In this regard, specific guarantees are provided by the common law, the *Criminal Code*, and in Canada the *Charter of Rights and Freedoms*. The latter's provisions include:

1. the right to be presumed innocent until proven guilty according to law after a fair and public hearing by an independent and impartial tribunal,[27] which, most crucially for our discussion, means that the Crown bears the onus of making out its case on proof beyond a reasonable doubt;[28]

2. the right to silence[29] and the privilege against self-incrimination[30];

3. the right to a full answer and defence;[31] and

---

25   See J. Jackson, "Truth and Compromise in Criminal Justice: A Critique of Trial Practice and Lawyers' Ethics" (1997) N. Ir. L.Q. 321 at 325–327; D. Paciocco, "Evidence About Guilt: Balancing the Rights of the Individual and Society in Matters of Truth and Proof" (2001) 80 Can. Bar Rev. 433; and R. Peck, "The Adversarial System: A Qualified Search for Truth" (2001) 80 Can. Bar Rev. 456.

26   In *R. v. Jones* (1994), 89 C.C.C. (3d) 353 at 369 (S.C.C.) [*Jones*], Lamer C.J.C. suggests that the principle against self-incrimination is the unifying principle of our criminal justice system. Note that Chief Justice Lamer's review of the principle, though set out in a dissent, is subsequently adopted by a majority of the Court in *R. v. S.(R.J.)* (1995), 96 C.C.C. (3d) 1 at 25 (S.C.C.) [*S.(R.J.)*].

27   See *Canadian Charter of Rights and Freedoms*, Part I of the *Constitution Act, 1982*, being Schedule B to the *Canada Act 1982* (U.K.), 1982, c. 11, s. 11(d) [*Charter*]; *R. v. Oakes* (1986), 24 C.C.C. (3d) 321 (S.C.C.); and *R. v. Vaillancourt* (1987), 39 C.C.C. (3d) 118 (S.C.C.).

28   See *R. v. Dubois* (1985), 22 C.C.C. (3d) 513 (S.C.C.) [*Dubois*]; *R. v. Lifchus* (1997), 118 C.C.C. (3d) 1 at 6, 10–11 & 13 (S.C.C.), amended (1998), 120 C.C.C. (3d) vi (S.C.C.); *R. v. Starr* (2000), 147 C.C.C. (3d) 449 at 540–543 (S.C.C.); and *R. v. Avetysan* (2000), 149 C.C.C. (3d) 77 at 82–83 (S.C.C.).

29   See *R. v. Hebert* (1989), 57 C.C.C. (3d) 1 (S.C.C.); and *R. v. Chambers* (1990), 59 C.C.C. (3d) 321 (S.C.C.).

30   The privilege against self-incrimination can be seen to encompass both the privilege of a witness not to answer incriminating questions *and* the non-compellability of an accused person: see, for example, *S.(R.J.)*, above note 26 at 27–35. The latter aspect of the privilege, which is enshrined in s. 11(c) of the *Charter*, above note 27, is especially relevant to our discussion: see *Dubois*, above note 28 at 531–32; *Canada v. Amway of Canada Ltd.* (1989), 68 C.R. (3d) 97 at 104–05 and 111–12 (S.C.C.).

31   See, *Criminal Code*, R.S.C. 1985, c. C-46, s. 650(3); and *R. v. Stinchcombe*, [1991] 3 S.C.R. 326.

4.  the right to counsel of choice[32] and to the effective assistance of
    counsel.[33]

Taken together, these guarantees give any accused — whether
innocent or guilty — the ability, indeed the right, to resist any effort to
cause his or her defeat or otherwise to assist in the prosecution.
Conversely, the Crown must use its own resources to marshal the evidence and cannot force the accused's cooperation in doing so.[34] The
lawyer who vigorously defends the accused who is known to be guilty
sends a message to police and prosecution alike that fair and complete
evidence will be needed if they hope to secure a conviction, with an
attendant benefit for all accused. Such a defence also recognizes an
inherent dignity and autonomy in even the culpable accused, who is
deserving of fair procedures as he or she goes through the criminal justice process. The result may be the acquittal of persons who have
committed criminal offences — in a sense, the overprotection of the
guilty — but society has deemed this to be an acceptable price to pay
in exchange for the adequate protection of individual rights.

It can scarcely be gainsaid that defence counsel plays a particularly
crucial role in ensuring that the accused receives a fair trial and is able
to exercise any applicable common law and constitutional rights.
Because the workings of the criminal justice system seem complex,
unfamiliar, and often intimidating to laypeople, the system relies upon
defence counsel to represent accused persons. The skilled advocate
who performs competently helps to ensure that the verdict is reliable
and hence maintains public confidence in the administration of justice.
But more than this, defence counsel plays a central role in ensuring
that the accused is able to assert his or her common law and constitutional rights within the adversarial system. Additionally, the lawyer
who represents an accused without judging his or her guilt arguably

---

32  The right to counsel of choice is discussed in *R. v. McCallen* (1999), 131 C.C.C.
    (3d) 518 (Ont. C.A.). The more general right to representation by counsel at
    trial has been recognized by a number of Canadian appeal courts: see, for exam-
    ple, *McCallen, ibid.; Howard* v. *Stony Mountain Institution Disciplinary Court*
    (1984), 19 C.C.C. (3d) 195 (Fed. C.A.), quashed (*sub nom. R. v. Howard* (1987),
    41 C.C.C. (3d) 287 (S.C.C.); *R. v. Howell* (1995), 103 C.C.C. (3d) 302
    (N.S.C.A.), aff'd (1996), 110 C.C.C. (3d) 192 (S.C.C.); and *R. v. Sechon* (1995),
    104 C.C.C. (3d) 554 (Que. C.A.).
33  See, for example, *R. v. B.(G.D.)* (2000), 143 C.C.C. (3d) 289 (S.C.C.); *R. v.
    Joanisse* (1995), 102 C.C.C. (3d) 35 (Ont. C.A.), leave to appeal to S.C.C.
    refused (1997), 111 C.C.C. (3d) vi (S.C.C.); and *R. v. Delisle* (1999), 133
    C.C.C. (3d) 541 (Que. C.A.) [*Delisle*].
34  See *Dubois*, above note 28 at 531–32; and *Jones*, above note 26 at 366–74.

furthers the important values of individual freedom and autonomy, as well as equality of access to the law. For these reasons, defence counsel assumes a partisan duty to represent zealously the client's interests and should feel no compunction in putting forward a defence for a guilty client. The principle that a guilty person must be defended preserves the integrity of the criminal justice system and, more generally, society itself. Ultimately, the lawyer's actions in defending the guilty client are justified by the particular role that counsel plays in an adversarial, rights-based legal system.[35]

## E. RATIONALE FOR RESTRICTING COUNSEL IN THE CONDUCT OF THE CASE

While strong advocacy in the cause of a client is seen to be an ethically desirable professional attitude, regardless of whether the client is known to be guilty, a lawyer's loyalty to the client is subject to constraints. The law permits an accused to insist that the Crown prove its case according to the justice system's applicable standards and rules, and to challenge and test the Crown case within an adversarial setting. But the law does not allow an accused, nor counsel acting on his or her behalf, to act dishonestly or fraudulently in conducting the defence. We therefore see a balance between the legitimate pursuit and exercise of an accused's rights in conducting a defence, and the need to ensure that lawyers do not knowingly mislead the court and hence unacceptably subvert the truth-finding function of the criminal justice process. Lord Reid aptly articulated the need for a balance in his oft-quoted judgment in *Rondel v. Worsley*:

> Every counsel has a duty to his client fearlessly to raise every issue, advance every argument, and ask every question, however distasteful, which he thinks will help his client's case. But, as an officer of the court concerned in the administration of justice, he has an overriding duty to the court, to the standards of his profession, and to the public, which may and often does lead to a conflict with his client's wishes or with what the client thinks are his personal interests. Counsel must not mislead the court, he must not lend himself to casting aspersions on the other party or witnesses for which there is no sufficient basis in the information in his possession, he must not withhold authorities or documents which may tell against his clients

---

35   The concept of a lawyer's "role morality" is also examined in chapter 2.

but which the law or the standards of his profession require him to produce.[36]

Along these same lines, our ethical codes place restrictions on counsel's partisanship.in order to prevent him or her from knowingly misleading the court.[37] Counsel who exceeds the proper bounds of partisanship risks attracting not only disciplinary action but criminal prosecution.[38] Such restrictions obviously bear upon the lawyer who represents a client known to be guilty. Counsel who has unassailable knowledge of a client's guilt is limited in conducting the defence, for this knowledge means that evidence or assertions to the contrary will mislead the court. To take an easy example, counsel who has received a clear, unequivocal, and reliable confession from the accused cannot knowingly mislead the court by calling a false alibi.[39] As we shall see, however, the line between conduct that merely forces the Crown to prove its case and that which serves to mislead the court is not always easy to discern.

# F. ACQUIRING KNOWLEDGE THAT THE CLIENT IS GUILTY

Given that counsel faces possible restrictions in acting for a client who is known to be guilty, the preliminary issue arises as to when counsel can be said to have obtained such knowledge.[40]

---

36  *Rondel* v. *Worsley*, [1969] 1 A.C. 191 at 227–28. See also the judgment of Holroyd Pearce L.J. in *Meek* v. *Fleming*, [1961] 2 Q.B. 366 at 379–80 (C.A.). *Rondel* v. *Worsley* has recently been overruled in *Arthur JS Hall & Co.* v. *Simons*, [2000] 3 All E.R. 673 at 680 (H.L.), but not in any way that undermines Lord Reid's comments.

37  See, for example, CBA Code ch. IX comms. 2(b) & (e), reproduced above in section B, "Related Rules of Professional Conduct," in this chapter.

38  Actions that serve to mislead the court may constitute crimes under the *Criminal Code*, above note 31, such as party to perjury (ss. 21 & 131); counselling perjury (ss. 22, 131, & 464); fabricating evidence (s. 137); and obstructing justice (s. 139). See, for example, *R.* v. *Sweezey* (1987), 39 C.C.C. (3d) 182 at 188 (Nfld. C.A.).

39  See, for example, CBA Code ch. IX, comm. 10 & 11.

40  See also section F(1), "Acquiring Knowledge that the Client Intends to Commit Perjury," in chapter 7.

## 1)  The Basic Presumption Against Judging the Client's Culpability

Counsel's role in the criminal justice system is neither to judge the client nor to arrive at a personal determination as to the client's guilt. The expressions of this sentiment by distinguished lawyers and commentators are legion and frequently hackneyed. "A client is entitled to say to his counsel, I want your advocacy, not your judgment; I prefer that of the Court," stated Baron Bramwell in a much repeated quotation from *Johnson* v. *Emerson and Sparrow*.[41] Just as famous are the comments of defence lawyer Thomas Erskine in *R.* v. *Paine*:

> If the advocate refuses to defend, from what he may think of the charge or the defence, he assumes the character of the judge; nay, he assumes it before the hour of judgment; and in proportion to his rank and reputation, puts the heavy influence of perhaps a mistaken opinion into the scale against the accused, in whose favour the benevolent principle of the English law makes all presumptions, and which commands the very judge to be his counsel.[42]

Daniel Soulez-Larivière, a Parisian lawyer who has written a masterful book on the ethics of advocacy, says: "À . . . chacun son métier. Aux juges de juger, aux avocats de défendre. Un avocat qui veut se faire juge de son client se trompe de métier, mélange les fonctions, affaiblit la sienne pour le plus grand mal de toute l'institution judiciaire."[43] To the same effect, David Mellinkoff has advised that a lawyer should never let his or her "own conscientious scruples stand in the way of a proper defence for his client."[44]

That a lawyer reasonably believes the client to be guilty is thus largely irrelevant to the conduct of the defence at trial. Certainly, such a belief does not, without more, preclude counsel from calling evidence that suggests the client's innocence or from making submissions to the same effect before a jury. Moreover, counsel who limits a defence based on no more than a personal suspicion that the client is

---

41   (1871), L.R. 6 Ex. 329 at 367.

42   *R.* v. *Paine* (1792), 22 St. Tr. 358 at 412.

43   D. Soulez-Larivière, *L'Avocature* (Paris: Éditions du Seuil, 1995) at 245. His words can be translated as: "To each their role. To judges to judge, to lawyers to defend. A lawyer who wants to judge his own client is mistaken as to his profession, mixes up respective functions and weakens his own function to the detriment of the entire judicial system."

44   Mellinkoff, above note 12 at 191.

guilty may be denying the client access to constitutional rights.[45] In instances where the lawyer's suspicions are wrong, implementing such limitations may cause (or contribute to) an unreliable verdict. As G. Arthur Martin said, "I have heard many unlikely stories in my time from defendants; some surprisingly, turned out to be true. Some cases look impossible; intensive preparation indicates that they are not really so."[46]

R. v. Delisle,[47] a fairly recent case of the Quebec Court of Appeal, illustrates the substantial damage that a lawyer can cause by too quickly judging the client. There, the victim of a serious assault identified the accused as one of several assailants. The accused insisted to counsel that this identification was erroneous, and that a man named Kevin Carl was the person who, in the others' company, participated in the assault. The lawyer disregarded the accused's story, based on his own evaluation of the case, and did not investigate the possibility that Carl was the real culprit. Counsel did not call his client at trial, thinking that he could win the case by attacking the sufficiency of the identification evidence. The accused was convicted.

Following the conviction but prior to sentencing, Carl contacted the lawyer, confiding that he was the person responsible for the acts attributed to the accused. Counsel attempted in vain to have the case reopened based on this new information. On appeal, however, the information from Carl was introduced as fresh evidence. Writing for the Court, Mr. Justice Proulx held that

> [i]n the case at bar, counsel for the appellant totally misunderstood the role which was his, by setting himself up as the judge of his client instead of respecting his client's instructions and truly defending his client's interests. Taking into account what we know now as a result of fresh evidence, this demonstrates even more the danger for counsel of relying upon his impressions.[48]

The conviction was consequently quashed based on a breach of the right to competent counsel, which in turn violated the appellant's right to make full answer and defence.[49]

On the other hand, it cannot be denied that counsel's opinion regarding the nature and strength of the case against the client will

---

45   See, for example, *Johns v. Smyth*, 176 F. Supp. 949 at 952 (E.D. Va. 1959).
46   G. Arthur Martin, "The Role and Responsibility of the Defence Advocate" (1970) 12 Crim. L.Q. 376 at 387.
47   Above note 33.
48   *Ibid.* at 558.
49   *Ibid.*

almost certainly influence the advice given to the client. After objectively assessing the strength of the Crown's case, a lawyer should advise the client regarding the prospect of success at trial.[50] It may also be that counsel's considered view of the Crown evidence will lead him or her (with the client's informed consent) to adopt a defence or tactic that is most consistent with the evidence, the idea being to avoid undermining the integrity of the defence position by fruitlessly attacking unassailable evidence. Obviously, there is a distinction between providing the client with informed, candid, and reasonable advice, which is ethically permissible, and rushing to judgment against the client so as to limit the defence unduly, which is not.

## 2) The Exception: Irresistible Knowledge of Guilt

We can begin by concluding that, in the great majority of cases, a lawyer is not justified in restricting the conduct of the defence based merely upon his or her personal view of a client's guilt. However, occasionally, after careful investigation and thorough assessment, a lawyer may reach such a level of certainty with respect to the client's culpability that he or she "will have as much reason to feel confidence in concluding that a client is guilty as charged as to feel confidence about anything else."[51] Indeed, we sometimes forget that the lawyer's special position as recipient of confidential information that must not be shared with third parties may actually make him or her *better* able to determine what is true or false than is the prosecutor, judge, or jury.[52] In these unusual cases, the lawyer is surely restricted in the conduct of the defence by the ethical codes' prohibition against *knowingly* assist-

---

50   See, for example, *R. v. Hall* (1968), 52 Cr. App. R. 528 at 534–35, as well as the discussion in A. Gold, "Abuse of Power by the Defence Bar" in Law Society of Upper Canada, *The Abuse of Power and the Role of an Independent Judicial System in its Regulation and Control* (Toronto: R. De Boo, 1979) 617 at 632; and Martin, above note 46 at 396. The impact that counsel's opinion can have upon the course of the case can hardly be overstated, and is also discussed below in section I, "The Need For Full Consultation With the Client," in this chapter, and in detail in section K, "Duty to Advise the Client," in chapter 8.

51   Wolfram, above note 7 at 586.

52   See D. Rhode, "Ethical Perspectives on Legal Practice" (1985) 37 Stan. L. Rev. 589 at 618–20. *Contra* J. Silver, "Truth, Justice, and the American Way: The Case *Against* the Client Perjury Rules" (1994) 47 Vand. L. Rev. 339 at 383, arguing that defence counsel are often biased against their clients and have access to unreliable evidence.

ing in dishonest action, presenting false evidence, or otherwise misleading the court.[53]

Little has been written in Canada regarding the factual basis necessary to justify the conclusion that a lawyer is knowingly misleading the court.[54] Canadian ethical codes typically place express restrictions on counsel who has received a "clear" confession from his or her client.[55] These rules also state that the lawyer must be "convinced" that the admissions are true, and they prohibit the lawyer from calling any evidence that he or she "believes to be false."[56] In British Columbia, the rules of professional conduct speak of a lawyer being "certain that the client or witness intends to offer false testimony,"[57] while Alberta's rules refer to the lawyer being "satisfied that the client committed a crime."[58] Based on these standards, an unequivocal and reasonable subjective belief in the client's guilt seems sufficient to activate ethical restrictions pertaining to the conduct of the defence. But a question remains as to whether a lawyer can look to any source of information in arriving at the determination that a client is guilty. Canadian ethical rules usually do not directly address the possibility that knowledge of guilt can come from sources other than the client. Alberta is an exception in this regard, insofar as knowledge of falsity can be based upon the lawyer's "personal knowledge *or* the client's admission."[59]

In the United States, the matter of knowledge has received more attention, usually in the closely related context of client perjury, and several fairly stringent tests have been adopted or suggested.[60] A "firm factual basis" is one such test, interpreted by some courts to require "clearly established" or "actual knowledge" based upon an admission

---

53    See, for example, CBA Code ch. IX, comm. 2(b), 2(e), & 10.
54    See, however, A. Hutchinson, *Legal Ethics and Professional Responsibility* (Toronto: Irwin Law, 1999) at 157 (arguing that the lawyer must have no doubt that a client intends to mislead the court).
55    See, for example CBA Code ch. IX, comm. 11.
56    *Ibid.*
57    B.C. ch. 8, r. 6.
58    Alta. ch. 10, r. 14 comm. 14.2.
59    *Ibid.* (emphasis added).
60    For a review of some of the relevant case law and academic commentary, see M. Freedman "But Only If You Know," in R. Uphoff, ed., *Ethical Problems Facing the Criminal Lawyer: Practical Answers to Tough Questions* (Chicago: American Bar Association, 1995) at 138–39; and E. Wilkinson, "'That's A Damn Lie!': Ethical Obligations of Counsel When a Witness Offers False Testimony in a Criminal Trial" (2000) 31 St. Mary's L.J. 407 at 411–15.

by the client.[61] Other standards have been suggested that appear to be more demanding, such as "beyond a reasonable doubt,"[62] "clear and convincing evidence,"[63] "an undeniable conclusion,"[64] and "absolutely no doubt."[65] The efficacy of these types of standard has been questioned in the Third Restatement, on the ground that the prime focus should be upon the state of mind of the lawyer.[66] We agree, with the qualification that, while the subjective belief of the lawyer is important, in many instances the lawyer's personal assessment depends upon the quantity and quality of factual information pointing to guilt.

Despite the fact that Canadian ethical codes tend to focus on instances where there has been a confession from the client (at least in specifically addressing the limitations placed upon a criminal defence lawyer), we believe that the rationale against misleading the court should apply where counsel reasonably draws an irresistible conclusion of guilt from available information.[67] Some defence lawyers may see this position as a heresy.[68] Yet in our view it is unacceptable for counsel to put up a defence that he or she believes is false, or to suggest that someone else may have committed the crime, regardless of

---

61   See, for example, *United States ex rel. Wilcox v. Johnson*, 555 F.2d 115 at 122 (3d Cir. 1977); and *United States v. Long*, 857 F.2d 436 at 444 (8th Cir. 1988), cert. denied 502 U.S. 828 (1991). Compare *State v. Berrysmith*, 944 P.2d 397 at 401 (Wash. App. 1997) (a "firm factual basis" need not necessarily include the client's admission).

62   *United States v. Del Carpio-Cotrina*, 733 F. Supp. 95 (S.D. Fla. 1990); *Shockley v. State*, 565 A. 2d 1373 at 1379–80 (Del. Sup. Ct. 1989); and *Commonwealth v. Alderman*, 437 A.2d 36 at 39 (Pa. Super. 1981).

63   Third Restatement §120, comm. "c" (Reporter's Note).

64   W. Brazil, "Unanticipated Client Perjury and the Collision of Rules of Ethics, Evidence, and Constitutional Law" (1979) 44 Mo. L. Rev. 601 at 608–09.

65   N. Lefstein, "Client Perjury in Criminal Cases: Still in Search of an Answer" (1988) 1 Geo. J. Legal Ethics 521 at 528.

66   Third Restatement §120, comm. "c" & Reporter's Note. See also ABA Model Rule 3.3, Legal Background ("When Does a Lawyer 'Know' that a Client Intends Perjury"); and the definition of "knowingly" provided in the "terminology" section of the Model Rules (the word "knowingly" "denotes actual knowledge of the fact in question. A person's knowledge may be inferred from circumstances").

67   See Lefstein, above note 65 at 529; and E. Kimball, "When Does a Lawyer 'Know' Her Client Will Commit Perjury?" (1988) 2 Geo. J. Legal Ethics 579 at 583–84.

68   See J. Mitchell, "The Ethics of the Criminal Defense Attorney — New Answers to Old Questions" (1980) 32 Stan. L. Rev. 293 at 296–98, note 12: "I am never convinced beyond a reasonable doubt of someone's factual guilt unless they admit their crime to me under reliable circumstances"; and Silver, above note 52 at 358–92.

exactly how he or she comes to the knowledge that the client is undoubtedly the culprit. The justification for prohibiting a lawyer from knowingly misleading the court should thus apply whether the knowledge of falsity comes from the client's confession or from other reliable sources of information. Consequently, although a lawyer must resist passing judgment on his or her client except in rare cases, there are some situations where he or she cannot escape the obvious conclusion and the attendant ethical constraints. Counsel is precluded from reaching such a conclusion, however, absent a careful investigation of all relevant aspects of the case.[69]

**Example:** Trial counsel successfully challenges the admissibility of completely and unassailably incriminating DNA evidence that connects her client to the crime. Such evidence is excluded, not on the basis of reliability concerns but rather owing to a serious *Charter* infringement. Even without the DNA evidence, the case against the client is remarkably strong. The client refuses to discuss the facts of the case with counsel but makes it clear that she wishes to plead "not guilty." In such a case, counsel is justified in concluding that she knows the accused to be guilty, even though there has been no admission of guilt. This knowledge will result in limitations regarding the conduct of the defence at trial.

**Variation:** Let us alter the facts of the above example, so that the client insists to counsel that he is innocent. He believes that the DNA evidence is incorrect, but has no thoughts as to how or why the error exists. Nor can he explain the other evidence against him, and persists in telling counsel wildly and demonstrably inconsistent and unbelievable accounts of the events in issue. Counsel undertakes an exhaustive investigation of all facets of the DNA and other evidence, including retaining scientific experts and a private investigator, but turns up no evidence to support the client's view. This example is much more contentious, given the client's express position, but we believe that on these facts counsel can conclude that she has irresistible knowledge of guilt, and accordingly accept some restrictions in handling the case.

---

69   See ABA Defense Standard 4-4.1 (Duty to Investigate.) See also R. v. *Elliott* (1975), 28 C.C.C. (2d) 546 at 549 (Ont. C.A.), as well as the discussion below in section F(3), "A Common Example of Irresistible Knowledge of Guilt: The Confession," in this chapter (in the context of confessions).

## 3) A Common Example of Irresistible Knowledge of Guilt: The Confession

The most likely manner by which a lawyer learns of a client's guilt is by means of a reliable, unequivocal, and unrecanted confession. Sometimes the confession is made publicly, in a non-confidential setting, so that the prosecutor and presiding judge know of its existence. For instance, the client may admit guilt in a statement made to police, or during testimony on a *voir dire*, or in a prior proceeding in which he or she is a witness (not an accused). Other times, the confession is made only to counsel, in strict confidence, as happened in the *Courvoisier* and *Tuckiar* cases.[70] In theory, there is no qualitative difference between a public confession and one that is made only to counsel. Counsel is subject to the same limitations in either instance. But in practice, differences may arise. The primary distinction stems from the fact that the Crown, and sometimes the judge, is usually aware of the public confession. As a result, the Crown or judge may intervene in the trial process if of the view that the defence lawyer is acting unethically in the conduct of the case.

**Example I:** An accused is charged with first-degree murder. He has confessed to police and seeks to exclude the confession during a pretrial *voir dire*. In the course of the *voir dire*, the accused clearly admits his guilt by conceding the truth of his incriminating statement (though not its voluntariness). The confession is ruled inadmissible, following which the accused pleads not guilty. Assuming that counsel is satisfied that the client told the truth on the *voir dire*, the confession will restrict the conduct of the defence. Moreover, because the Crown and judge were privy to the confession, either might decide to object if counsel appears to act unethically during the trial.[71]

**Example II:** At a trial for the murder of V, the accused calls M as a surprise witness for the defence. After claiming protection under section 5 of the *Canada Evidence Act*, M testifies that he was the murderer, and that the accused had nothing to do with the crime. The accused is acquitted. Despite the fact that M has claimed statutory protection against the use of his testimony, the Crown subsequently charges him with murder on the basis that the claim was made improperly. Once again, as long as counsel for M in the subsequent trial is satisfied that

---

70    Above notes 12 and 20, respectively. Both cases are discussed above in section C, "Genesis of the Present Rules," in this chapter.

71    This example is taken from *R. v. Leblanc* (1996), Montreal (Sup. Ct.).

the confession is true, the options available in running the defence will be constricted. As an aside, however, a legitimate course of action would be to argue against admission of M's testimony at the second trial. In fact, M's counsel would have a paramount duty, on behalf of the client, to fight for the exclusion of the admission.[72]

Whether a confession is made publicly or in confidence, counsel must always ensure, to borrow the terminology of the CBA Code, that the accused has clearly admitted the factual and mental elements necessary to constitute the offence charged.[73] It is essential that the lawyer be thoroughly familiar with the legal delineation of the offence in question and clarify exactly the facts to which the client admits. Sometimes the law is not clear as to the ambit of a criminal offence, in which case any non-frivolous legal issue should be resolved in favour of the client.[74] An admission may be made as a means of expressing moral guilt, despite the absence of legal liability. Some clients may wrongly assume that they are guilty, being unfamiliar with available defences such as self-defence, intoxication, or lack of criminal responsibility. Many clients are not aware of common law or constitutional rights that may permit the exclusion of inculpatory evidence. Additionally, a client may make an admission, whether or not during a confidential conversation with counsel, which is inconsistent or vague to the extent that no certainty as to guilt can be established. It is also possible that the client confesses to the crime on one occasion, only to recant at a later date. Most typically, a client may be alleged to have made an inculpatory statement to police but informs counsel that the statement was never made or was untrue.

In all of these examples, counsel must do whatever he or she can to reduce the uncertainty. As the ABA Defense Standards recognize, a lawyer has a duty to investigate the facts and law relevant to a case, a duty that persists even where the client has admitted his or her guilt.[75] The irony in this approach may be that counsel secures information

---

72  This example is based on the cases of *R. v. Duhamel* (1971), Montreal (Sup. Ct.) (Nichols J.) (the initial trial in which M testified), and *R. v. Morin* (1972), Montreal (Sup. Ct.) (Bisson J.) (the subsequent trial of M). Counsel in *Morin* was eventually successful in having his client's testimony excluded. We will come back to this case later, in section K(2), "Cross-Examining the Perjurious or Mistaken Witness," in this chapter.

73  See CBA Code ch. IX, comm. 11.

74  See, for example, *McCoy v. Court of Appeals of Wisconsin, District 1*, 486 U.S. 429 at 444 (1988) [*McCoy*].

75  See ABA Defense Standard 4-4.1. See also *Sankar v. State of Trinidad and Tobago*, [1995] 1 All E.R. 236 at 241 (P.C.) [*Sankar*].

that serves to limit the conduct of the defence.[76] However, this price is worth paying in order to ensure that counsel is thoroughly prepared to conduct the case, and the approach has the added benefit of lessening the possibility that he or she will be accused of wilful blindness.

**Example I:** X is charged with bigamy. He firmly believes that he is guilty, admitting to counsel that he married his current wife without obtaining a divorce from his first wife. Counsel reviews the statutory definition of bigamy and learns that a defence exists where the first spouse has been continually absent for seven years immediately preceding the second marriage, provided that the accused did not know that the spouse was alive.[77] Upon ascertaining further facts from the client, counsel concludes that X can avail himself of this defence.[78]

**Example II:** C is charged with the murder of her husband, who was stabbed to death in his bed. She tells the police that she committed the murder and gives a detailed confession of her involvement in the crime. A day later, she reiterates her confession under oath at a coroner's inquest. C is accordingly charged with murder and remanded for psychiatric assessment. A psychiatrist treating C subsequently receives a visit from M, who says that he had been C's lover for some time before the murder and is the real killer. M also admits to a friend that he had some unspecified involvement in the murder. However, when confronted by the police, M repudiates his story, and the police do not pursue the matter. Prior to trial, C recants her confession during an interview with a psychiatrist and blames M for the crime. Faced with a number of inconsistent statements, counsel is fully justified in proceeding on the basis that the client is not admitting to any liability, and in running a defence that seeks to paint M as the true killer.[79]

**Example III:** Continuing with the last scenario, assume that C is acquitted, and the Crown charges M with the murder. C is to be the main Crown witness at trial. Counsel for M must ascertain his client's position regarding the prior statements. If M repudiates the inculpatory statements, and sticks by his statement to the police, counsel cannot come to the irresistible conclusion that M is guilty. Alternatively,

---

76   See Silver, above note 52 at 388.

77   See *Criminal Code*, above note 31, s. 290(2)(b).

78   This problem is taken from an example given by J. Sedgwick in "Panel Discussion: Problems in Ethics and Advocacy" in Law Society of Upper Canada, *Defending a Criminal Case* (Toronto: R. De Boo, 1969) 279 at 287–88.

79   This problem is roughly based on the facts in *R. v. Maleau* (1987), 12 Q.A.C. 104 (C.A.) [Maleau].

if M refuses to discuss the matter with counsel, the inconsistent statements will likely serve to preclude any conclusion that the client is guilty. However, if M confesses to counsel in a clear and convincing manner, and counsel is satisfied as to the confession's truth, the conduct of the defence faces certain limits.[80]

These examples emphasize that, before imposing any restrictions on the conduct of the defence, the lawyer must believe that the client's admission is true.[81] The most sincere sounding confession of guilt can, on further examination, turn out to be false. People occasionally confess to crimes that they have not committed.[82] The admission may be made in an attempt to protect the true culprit.[83] Or the client may be suffering under a mental affliction that causes delusions. Some clients falsely confess in the belief that the admission will put an early end to the unpleasant stress and strain of the criminal process. To guard against these false confessions, counsel must ask probing questions of the client, review the Crown's case, and, where warranted, undertake independent investigation.[84]

## 4)  Avoidance Techniques: Restricting Client-Lawyer Communications, Wilful Blindness, "Woodshedding," and Viewing Guilt as Completely Irrelevant

Some lawyers may be tempted to skirt the ethical limitations imposed where there is irresistible knowledge of a client's guilt by strenuously

---

80   In *Maleau, ibid.*, we do not know what the accused told his counsel. It is interesting, however, that the accused did not testify at his trial and did not take the stand on a retrial ordered after a successful appeal. At both trials, the defence lawyer vigorously cross-examined C on her prior inconsistent statements, with the aim of painting her as the real killer. We address the propriety of cross-examining the truthful witness in section K(1), "Cross-Examining the Truthful Witness," in this chapter.

81   See, for example, CBA Code ch. IX, comm. 11.

82   See D. Pannick, *Advocates* (Oxford: Oxford University Press, 1992) 158; Mellinkoff, above note 12 at 149–50; and Pool, "Defending the 'Guilty' Client" (1979) 64 Mass. L. Rev. 11 at 15.

83   A historical example of a client who may have falsely confessed to counsel prior to trial, in the hope of saving family members from conviction, is related by C. Allen, "R. v. *Dean*" (1941) 57 L.Q. Rev. 85 at 105–06. However, Allen appears to conclude that the client's confession was true, for he intimates that prudent counsel would not have taken the case after hearing the confession.

84   See ABA Defense Standard 4-4.1.

avoiding any such knowledge. One strategy is rarely to discuss the facts of the case with the client, and in particular never to ask the deadly question, "Did you do it?" A related tack is to avoid acquiring any knowledge from outside sources that might threaten counsel's carefully cultivated ignorance. Another approach is to encourage the client to develop an exculpatory version of events, without much regard for the version's validity. This method is commonly known by the colloquial terms "woodshedding" or "horseshedding," and is sometimes also referred to as "the lesson." Still other lawyers may choose to view a clear and unequivocal confession as absolutely irrelevant, on the putative ground that legal guilt is always unknowable prior to the final verdict, and guilt thus plays no part in the role of the advocate.[85]

**Example I (Restricting Communications):** D faces a charge of theft and retains a lawyer. The lawyer forms the view that D is probably guilty, but he instructs D that he does not want to hear anything about the facts of the case. The reason for this restriction is that the lawyer does not wish to receive a confession from the client that might serve to limit the conduct of the defence. Counsel represents the client at trial and, in challenging the Crown case and making final submissions, strongly suggests that another individual committed the theft.

**Example II (Woodshedding):** A lawyer acts for a client who is charged with fraud. The client informs counsel that he did not commit the *actus reus* of the offence. After reviewing the disclosure, counsel determines that the client's assertion will not succeed at trial, but that a colour of right defence might offer the prospect of an acquittal. Counsel therefore tells the client that he should reconsider his original story and provides him with a written summary of the facts that would establish colour of right. She also gives him a copy of the Crown disclosure for his perusal and tells him to make sure that any new story is consistent with the disclosure.[86]

---

85  See S. Ross, *Ethics in Law: Lawyers' Responsibility and Accountability in Australia,* 2d ed. (Sydney: Butterworths, 1998) at 442 (quoting a lawyer).

86  In Otto Preminger's film *Anatomy of a Murder,* adapted from J. Voelker's 1958 novel of the same name (written under the pseudonym "Robert Traver"), the lawyer tells his client: "If the facts are as you have stated them so far, you have no defence, and you will probably be electrocuted. On the other hand, if you acted in a blind rage, there is a possibility of saving your life. Think it over, and we will talk about it tomorrow." This example is cited, and presumably seen to demonstrate improper behaviour, in the commentary to ABA Defense Standard 4-3.2. Contrast the approving view of the fictional lawyer's conduct offered by M. Freedman, "Professional Responsibility of the Criminal Defense Lawyer: The Three Hardest Questions" (1966) 64 Mich. L. Rev. 1469 at 1478–82.

The above methods of avoiding or ignoring knowledge of the client's guilt are problematic. Let us start with the lawyer who refuses to discuss the facts of the case with his or her client. A lawyer requires full information in order to provide competent and useful legal advice.[87] To restrict artificially the flow of information between client and lawyer thus clashes with the proper role of counsel and may serve to harm the client. For instance, the client may be prevented from revealing exculpatory information that *helps* his or her cause. Being deprived of inculpatory information may also lead to counsel being surprised or unprepared at trial, with resultant damage to the defence cause. As the commentary to ABA Standard 4-3.2 states:

> The client is usually the lawyer's primary source of information for an effective defense. An adequate defense cannot be framed if the lawyer does not know what is likely to develop at trial. The lawyer needs to know essential facts, including the events surrounding the act charged, information concerning the defendant's background, and the defendant's record of prior convictions, if any. In criminal litigation, as in other matters, information is the key guide to decisions and action. The lawyer who is ignorant of the facts of the case cannot serve the client effectively.[88]

Complete candour and honesty between client and lawyer can serve only to improve the strength of any legitimate defence. Deliberate ignorance fostered by restricting the normal flow of communication is not recommended.[89]

Granted, it may be that the client decides of his or her own accord not to discuss the facts of the case with counsel. In such an event, counsel should carefully explain the advantages of making full disclosure in a confidential setting. If the client persists in refusing to provide any information, counsel has not received an inculpatory admission and will probably have greater latitude in mounting a defence. At the same time, counsel has made a valid effort to inform

---

87    See ABA Defense Standard 4-3.2(a): "As soon as practicable, defense counsel should seek to determine all relevant facts known to the accused. In so doing, defense counsel should probe for all legally relevant information without seeking to influence the direction of the client's responses."

88    ABA Defense Standard 4-3.2, commentary (footnote omitted).

89    See ABA Defense Standard 4-3.2(b): "Defense counsel should not instruct the client or intimate to the client in any way that the client should not be candid in revealing facts so as to afford defence counsel free rein to take action which would be precluded by counsel's knowing of such facts."

himself or herself for the purpose of providing complete and competent legal advice, and cannot be faulted if the defence suffers because of the client's recalcitrance.

The problems presented by other avoidance techniques are generally even more glaring. Counsel who woodsheds a client with the aim of encouraging a particular version of events runs the risk of complicity in manufacturing false evidence. It is one thing to make sure that the client understands his or her position based on the law, but quite another to encourage and then rely upon a fabricated version of events. As for the lawyer who ignores a clear and truthful confession based on the view that knowledge of guilt is irrelevant, he or she is placing excessive emphasis on the need for zealous advocacy and concomitantly risks acting unethically or illegally by misleading the court. The argument that the truth is never known until a legal determination of guilt is made suffers from a confusion of concepts. Legal guilt is not the equivalent of factual truth, but we can surely say that counsel knows something to be true prior to the trier of fact's final determination. Finally, a lawyer whose subjective suspicions are aroused should never intentionally avoid acquiring information concerning a case for the purpose of remaining ignorant of facts that, if known, would limit his or her conduct of the defence. The deliberate ignorance of such facts can be equated with actual knowledge, according to the doctrine of wilful blindness.[90]

As a last point, counsel who is tempted to employ some or all of the above techniques to avoid acquiring knowledge of a client's guilt risks public exposure, which in turn may lead to disciplinary action or criminal charges. A dispute between the client and his or her counsel may lead to an ineffective counsel claim, bringing the fact of an ignored confession to light on appeal. In R. v. Li, for example, the client argued on appeal that his trial counsel had been labouring under a conflict of interest.[91] The fresh evidence introduced on appeal revealed that counsel had received a confidential confession from the client. This information led the appeal court to consider whether trial counsel had acted

---

90   For discussions of wilful blindness, though not in the context of a lawyer's state of knowledge, see, for example, R. v. Duong (1998), 124 C.C.C. (3d) 392 at 401–02 (Ont. C.A.); and R. v. Hajian (1998), 124 C.C.C. (3d) 440 at 447–48 (Que. C.A.). Note that wilful blindness is a subjective state of mind and does not exist simply because counsel has been careless or negligent.

91   R. v. Li, [1993] B.C.J. No. 2312 (C.A.) (QL), leave to appeal to S.C.C. refused (1994), 178 N.R. 395 (S.C.C.) [Li], discussed in section K(3), "Presenting Truthful Evidence as Part of the Defence, Knowing that the Trier of Fact May Use the Evidence to Arrive at a False Conclusion," in this chapter.

inappropriately in cross-examining Crown witnesses on the issue of identity and calling a defence. Another possibility is that the client may discharge counsel and retain a new lawyer, who on learning of shameless woodshedding reports former counsel to the appropriate governing body. Or perhaps the client decides to cooperate with the police and, in the course of providing a sworn, videotaped statement or testifying in court for the prosecution, reveals counsel's impropriety. The lesson is simple. Counsel can never safely assume that unethical behaviour will be shielded by lawyer-client privilege.

# G. ACCEPTING OR CONTINUING WITH THE RETAINER OF A CLIENT KNOWN TO BE GUILTY

In its 1915 report, the General Council of the English Bar addressed the issue of whether or not counsel should accept or continue with a retainer upon receiving a confession from the client. The proper course of action, according to the Council, depended upon the timing of the confession in relation to the commencement of the trial:

> Different considerations apply to cases in which the confession has been made before the advocate has undertaken the defence and to those in which the confession is made subsequently during the course of the proceedings.
>
> If the confession has been made before the proceedings have been commenced, it is most undesirable that an advocate to whom the confession has been made should undertake the defence, as he would most certainly be seriously embarrassed in the conduct of the case, and no harm can be done to the accused by requesting him to retain another advocate.
>
> Other considerations apply in cases in which the confession has been made during the proceedings, or in such circumstances that the advocate retained for the defence cannot retire from the case without seriously compromising the position of the accused.[92]

The Council thus determined that a lawyer receiving a confession prior to trial was not only justified in rejecting or ending the retainer but, absent serious compromise to the defence case, was obligated to do so.

---

92  *The Annual Practice*, above note 17 at 2433.

While some commentators have shared the Council's view,[93] the idea that a lawyer must reject a retainer upon receiving a confession of guilt from a client or prospective client seems strange from a contemporary Anglo-American perspective. The theoretical underpinnings that justify counsel acting for the client who is known to be guilty apply equally at *all* stages of the process, whether before, during, or after the trial.[94] Once one accepts the rationale behind the defence of the guilty, there is no reason why counsel must refuse to undertake the case simply because the confession is made prior to trial. It has been suggested that the client will suffer harm where counsel stays on the case, for "having been apprised of his client's guilt or the untruthfulness of certain vital testimony, it is highly doubtful if he could plead the case effectively and affect 'warmth for his client' without his being plagued by conscience that he was acting as a false dissembler."[95] Yet this reasoning similarly fails to appreciate the nature of the criminal justice system and the role of defence counsel. Moreover, a lawyer who receives a client's confession during the trial is surely no better (or worse) placed to plead the case effectively.

There are also practical problems associated with the notion that counsel cannot accept a retainer upon receiving a confession prior to the start of trial. Where a lawyer follows the General Council's dictate, and refuses to take on a case because he or she has received a confession from the prospective client, the problem will likely be transferred to another counsel. If the client persists in being completely candid, and repeats the confession to other lawyers, he or she may never be able to acquire counsel.[96] On the other hand, if the client decides to withhold the confession from subsequent counsel, the system has worked to discourage the very openness and free flow of information that is necessary for a successful client-lawyer relationship.[97]

---

93   See Schroeder, above note 15 at 92; D. Ipp, "Lawyers' Duties to the Court" (1998) 114 L.Q. Rev. 63 at 87; and Allen, above note 83 at 103–04 & 106–07.

94   Regarding the rationale that supports counsel acting in defence of a client known to be guilty, see section D, "The Rationale For Defending One Known to be Guilty," in this chapter. As for the application of this rationale during various stages of the criminal justice process, see section K, "Limitations on the Conduct of the Defence," and L, "Limitations Existing at the Pre-Trial and Sentencing Stages," in this chapter.

95   Schroeder, above note 15 at 92.

96   See "Panel Discussion: Problems in Advocacy and Ethics," above note 78 at 292–94.

97   This argument is expanded upon in section F(4), "Avoidance Techniques: Restricting Client-Lawyer Communications, Wilful Blindness, Woodshedding,

Today, the ethical rules guiding English barristers and solicitors contain no prohibition against taking on or keeping a case where counsel has received a confession prior to trial.[98] The position espoused by the General Council in 1915 is no longer followed. We have seen that Canadian ethical codes typically espouse the general view that defence counsel is justified in undertaking the defence of the client who is known to be guilty.[99] Given that the rules of professional conduct in Canada do not contain a prohibition against accepting or continuing with a retainer where knowledge of guilt is acquired prior to the start of trial, it seems safe to say that the General Council's position carries no credence in this country. There may be a debate as to whether a lawyer who receives a confession prior to trial has a *discretion* to reject or end the retainer,[100] but there is no doubt whatsoever that he or she is not obligated to do so.[101]

# H. THE NEED TO MAINTAIN CONFIDENTIALITY

Frequently, counsel's knowledge concerning the guilt of the client comes from confidential information, most often in the form of a client confession. In such a case, counsel is bound by the duty of confidentiality owed to the client and is prohibited from sharing the information with anyone else.[102] Sadly, this duty has not always been followed.

---

and Viewing Guilt as Completely Irrelevant," in this chapter, regarding the avoidance technique of restricting client-lawyer communications.

98   See *Bar Code of Conduct*, above note 6, Annex "H" (Written Standards for the Conduct of Professional Work, Standards Applicable to Criminal Cases) §13 (Confessions of Guilt); and *The Guide to the Professional Conduct of Solicitors*, above note 6 at §21.20.

99   See, for example, CBA Code ch. IX comm. 10 & 11.

100  See Hutchinson, above note 54 at 155 (advocating a discretion). We prefer the view, expressly adopted by the ethical rules in New Brunswick that a lawyer has a duty to provide a vigorous defence even where a confession has been received from the client, and cannot unilaterally end the retainer simply because he or she has received the confession: see N.B. Part C, r. 6.

101  See *McCoy*, above note 74 at 435: "At trial level, defense counsel's view of the merits of his or her client's case never gives rise to a duty to withdraw." This view is shared by the panel members in "Panel Discussion: Problems in Advocacy and Ethics," above note 15 at 292–94 (see especially the succinct and persuasive position taken by G. Arthur Martin at 294).

102  See *Tuckiar*, above note 20 at 346–47. Also see generally chapter 4. The issue of maintaining confidentiality becomes more contentious and complex in the case

The lawyers in the *Courvoisier* and *Tuckiar* cases acted improperly by sharing information of their clients' guilt with the presiding judge and others.[103] Taking such action not only violates the client's confidence but may compromise the judge's ability to try the case fairly.[104]

It is equally unacceptable to reveal a client's incriminating confidences by way of cryptic comment, or to make statements that imply impropriety on the part of the client.[105] The resulting harm to the client can be seen in *R. v. Colpitts*,[106] where the accused had made inculpatory statements to the police in relation to a charge of murdering a prison guard. At trial, he testified that these statements to police were untrue and explained the earlier lies by alleging that he wanted to protect the real killer, who was a friend at the time. The accused's testimony was likely sabotaged in advance, however, by defence counsel's damning pronouncement to the judge and jury, made just prior to calling his client to the stand:

> My Lord, yes, I am going to call one witness for the defence, and that will be Reginald Colpitts, the accused. And, Sir, I must — as a matter of professional ethics — do assert that this is going to happen against my better judgment and counsel. But Mr. Colpitts has decided to take the stand and I — of course — will act as examiner.[107]

This pronouncement was ill-advised, intimating the real possibility that the client had admitted guilt to counsel but was nonetheless insistent on taking the stand and committing perjury.[108] At the very least, defence counsel implicitly revealed that there had been a very serious disagreement between client and lawyer.

---

of perjury by the client: see sections F(4)(f), "Disclosure of the Intended Perjury," and G(3)(b), "Disclosure," in this chapter.

103 The facts of these cases, and the nature of defence counsels' respective breaches of confidentiality, are set out in section C, "Genesis of the Present Rules," in this chapter.

104 See Mellinkoff, above note 12 at 136.

105 The issue is not without complication, however: see the discussion below in section K(4), "Submissions that Rely upon Truthful Evidence to Suggest a False Conclusion," in this chapter.

106 (1965), [1966] 1 C.C.C. 146 (S.C.C.).

107 *Ibid.* at 156.

108 Mr. Justice Spence, who penned the majority reasons in *Colpitts*, stated that these remarks, in conjunction with the trial judge's charge, "could only suggest, and strongly suggest, to the jury that they could place no reliance upon the evidence given by the appellant in his defence": *ibid* at 157. Also telling was defence counsel's address to the jury, in which he made exceedingly little reference to his client's testimony: *ibid.* at 155.

# I. THE NEED FOR FULL CONSULTATION WITH THE CLIENT

Regardless of when counsel obtains irresistible knowledge that the client is guilty, it is imperative that the client be kept fully informed as to the impact that such knowledge may have upon the retainer, especially including any related restrictions on the conduct of the defence.[109] As Commentary 11 of the CBA Code directs, in the context of client confessions to counsel, "admissions made by the accused to the lawyer may impose strict limitations on the conduct of the defence *and the accused should be made aware of this.*"[110] Having received a confession of guilt, it is unacceptable for counsel thereupon to change the defence strategy unilaterally without consultation with the client.[111]

# J. PRELIMINARY ADVICE FOR COUNSEL WHO LEARNS OF A CLIENT'S GUILT ONLY AT TRIAL

A lawyer who receives a confidential confession from the accused (or who otherwise comes to an irresistible conclusion that the accused is guilty) during the course of a trial is placed in a particularly difficult predicament. Time constraints and the pressures of the trial make it hard to engage in careful consideration of the available options. Yet, to the fullest extent possible, such consideration is demanded of counsel.

There are several steps that a lawyer must take or consider in reacting to the mid-trial confession. First, the impact of counsel's knowledge on the trial process must be determined in the context of the case at hand and then discussed with the client.[112] Second, if the client refuses to accept any applicable restrictions, he or she may decide to discharge counsel.[113] Where the client does not discharge the lawyer, but nonetheless persists in refusing to accept any necessary limitations on the defence, counsel is usually justified in seeking the court's permission to withdraw from the case. Third, counsel remains bound by

---

109 See *Li*, above note 91 at para. 64.
110 CBA Code ch. IX, comm. 11 (emphasis added).
111 See *Sankar*, above note 75.
112 See the discussion above in section I, "The Need For Full Consultation With the Client," in this chapter.
113 See *Li*, above note 91 at para. 64.

duties of confidence and loyalty to the client and should not divulge any lawyer-client communications.[114] These duties apply even where counsel is discharged or attempts to get off the record. Fourth, it may be appropriate, if not obligatory, for counsel to consult independent counsel in an attempt to resolve the problem (and concomitantly to minimize the possibility of later complaints by the client). Naturally, the client must be kept fully informed of all interactions with independent counsel. Fifth, and finally, some of these steps may require a short break in the trial proceedings. To this end, counsel should request an adjournment, though in doing so no confidential information can be released.

**Example:** X is charged with murder. He gives a statement to police that, while largely incriminating, opens up the possibility of several defences, including provocation, mistake, and self-defence. X tells counsel that the statement made to police is true, and counsel accordingly cross-examines several Crown identification witnesses with the aim of raising one of these defences. Counsel intends to call X as a witness to provide further evidence in support of the defence. However, just as counsel is poised to start the defence case, X confidentially confesses that the exculpatory portions of the statement to police are untrue and that the killing was intentional and unprovoked. Counsel immediately decides to abandon any defence based on these portions of the statement, and unilaterally chooses not to call the accused to the stand. He delivers a curt jury address, in which he states only that the jury is justified in convicting the accused if satisfied that the Crown has met its burden of proof. This response is inadequate and represents a breach of counsel's duty to keep the client informed. The better approach would have been to follow the steps recommended above, starting with an adjournment request in order to provide some time for consultation with the client and independent counsel.[115]

---

114 See the discussion in Section H, "The Need to Maintain Confidentiality," in this chapter.

115 This example is adapted from the facts in *Sankar*, above note 75. In that case, it was not absolutely clear that the accused made a confession to counsel, though the inference that he had done so was strong. The Privy Council ruled that counsel failed to investigate the issue fully with the client and explain any available options, and added that, if necessary, an adjournment should have been sought for this purpose: *ibid.* at 241.

# K. LIMITATIONS ON THE CONDUCT OF THE DEFENCE

We have discussed the rationale behind limiting counsel's conduct of a defence where he or she knows that the client is guilty.[116] The question becomes, once defence counsel obtains such knowledge, what is permissible and what is precluded? The general limitation is simply stated: the lawyer may not conduct the defence so as to mislead the court knowingly. Narrowing our focus, the propriety (or impropriety) of certain specific defence tactics is made fairly clear in Chapter IX, Commentary 11 of the CBA Code.[117] To recap Commentary 11's substance, using the exact language of the provision, counsel who has received a clear and unequivocal confession from the accused

> may properly take objection to the jurisdiction of the court, or to the form of the indictment, or to the admissibility or sufficiency of the evidence;

> must not suggest that some other person committed the offence;

> must not . . . call any evidence that, by reason of the client's admissions, the lawyer believes to be false;

> [must not] set up an affirmative case inconsistent with the client's admission of guilt, for example by calling evidence in support of an alibi intended to show that the accused could not have done, or in fact had not done, the act;

> may test the evidence given by each individual witness for the prosecution and argue that the evidence taken as a whole is insufficient to amount to proof that the accused is guilty of the offence charged, but the lawyer should go no further than that.[118]

Most codes of professional responsibility in Canada, England and Wales and Australia track the wording in Commentary 11 and hence adopt the same ethical guidelines.[119] The leading American standards

---

116 See section E, "Rationale for Restricting Counsel in the Conduct of the Case," in this chapter.

117 Set out in full in section B, "Related Rules of Professional Conduct," in this chapter.

118 CBA Code ch. IX, comm. 11.

119 See the discussion in section B, "Related Rules of Professional Conduct," in this chapter.

for ethics are less likely to specify what is acceptable, and what is not, in conducting a defence for the client known to be guilty.[120]

Let us look more closely at the examples provided by Commentary 11. The Commentary's determination that certain behaviour is (or is not) permissible is consistent with the basic notion that a lawyer who has received a confession from the client can utilize defences that are not reliant upon information or submissions known to be false.[121] Because of the case-to-meet theory of our criminal justice system, and as Commentary 11 makes clear, counsel can therefore raise a jurisdictional issue, challenge the validity of the indictment, oppose the admissibility of evidence, or argue that the Crown has failed to prove its case beyond a reasonable doubt. As long as the particular defence does not mislead the court, counsel's conduct is legitimate. By the same token, counsel is prohibited from running any defence that involves knowingly misleading the court. As Commentary 11 states, it is improper to call evidence that counsel knows to be false, such as a bogus alibi, or to cross-examine a witness in an effort to suggest that another party committed the offence.

In many instances, Commentary 11 provides lawyers with relatively straightforward and uncontentious guidance. There are few who would contend, for example, that defence counsel is ethically justified in calling alibi witnesses that he or she knows to be part of a criminal conspiracy to exonerate the guilty client. But the propriety of other courses of conduct is not so obvious and is not commented upon by Commentary 11. The truly difficult scenarios create controversy because they seem to fall within a grey area, where testing the Crown's case (permissible) seems to risk misleading the court (impermissible). Three provocative and interrelated scenarios that are often raised in ethical debates are:

1.  How far can counsel go in testing the reliability of a truthful witness, including his or her general character? For instance, is it proper to cross-examine the witness in order to show that her vision is poor and that she did not have her glasses on, or that she has prior convictions that suggest dishonesty?

2.  Can defence counsel call truthful evidence as part of the defence case, where the evidence is then used to suggest that the client did not commit the crime? What if such evidence is employed only to support the argument that the prosecution has failed to meet its

---

120  *Ibid.*
121  CBA Code ch. IX, comm. 10.

onus? To continue with the example of identification, assume that a Crown witness accurately testifies that she saw the accused commit the crime. Yet her testimony is inaccurate to the limited extent that she indicates that the culprit was 1.80 metres tall and 75 kilograms in weight. Can the defence call truthful evidence from a witness who testifies that the accused is 1.70 metres in height and weighs only 65 kilograms?

3. Can counsel make final submissions that suggest a possible defence, based on evidence led by the Crown, even though the defence is inconsistent with counsel's knowledge of the client's guilt?

Examining these three scenarios allows us to delve into some of the most controversial debates concerning the ethical limits applicable where defence counsel knows that the client is guilty.

## 1)   Cross-Examining the Truthful Witness

The possibility that defence counsel may be ethically limited in cross-examining the truthful witness has been the subject of much discussion by commentators. There are several arguments presented against permitting a lawyer to attack the reliability of the truthful witness. First, such action is akin to calling false evidence, for the cross-examination may serve to convince the judge and jury that certain facts, known to be false by counsel, are true.[122] Indeed, it has been noted that defence counsel who uses cross-examination to attack the truthful witness's reliability has arguably has gone further than counsel who knowingly calls a false alibi. The latter counsel merely brings out the alibi by means of non-leading questions, while the usual cross-examination technique is more aggressive and most likely involves counsel expressly suggesting falsehoods. Second, the importance that our justice system ascribes to cross-examination as a forensic technique does not justify permitting counsel to mislead the judicial process. Third, cross-examining the truthful witness to suggest unreliability may well cause the witness harm, an unfair result given that he or she has testified truthfully. The harm visited upon the truthful witness seems especially egregious where the attack is made upon his or her sincerity, the aim of defence counsel being to suggest that the witness is a liar. Fourth, given that counsel will really know that a witness is truthful

---

122 See M. Freedman, *Understanding Lawyers' Ethics* (New York: Matthew Bender, 1990) at 164; and M. Freedman, *Lawyers' Ethics in an Adversary System* (New York: Bobbs-Merrill, 1975) at 45.

only in rare cases, the impact of curtailing cross-examination will be limited. Finally, the need to protect individual autonomy and dignity against the power of the state does not justify the use of any means to secure acquittal where the accused is factually guilty, to the lawyer's knowledge. Truth as a systemic goal should not be completely ignored in pursuit of rights-based concerns.

The arguments for the other side, that is to say, in support of permitting defence counsel to attack the reliability of the truthful witness, are familiar to the reader by this point. The central tenet in favour of allowing such conduct is the nature of the defence advocate's role in our criminal justice system. A central function of the system, and the lawyer's function within it, is to ensure that the Crown proves its case on a standard of proof beyond a reasonable doubt. It is therefore legitimate for counsel to test the strength of the prosecution case, including by cross-examination that questions the reliability of the truthful witness.[123] Perhaps the most-quoted expression of this position is offered by Justice White of the Supreme Court of United States, who in the 1967 decision of *United States* v. *Wade* stated that

> [a]bsent a voluntary plea of guilty, we . . . insist that [defence counsel] defend his client whether he is innocent or guilty. The State has the obligation to present the evidence. Defense counsel need present nothing, even if he knows what the truth is. He need not furnish any witnesses to the police, or reveal any confidences of his client, or fur-

---

123  See, for example, K. Pye, "The Role of Counsel in the Suppression of Truth" [1978] Duke L.J. 921 at 945. This rationale is also accepted by D. Luban, "Partisanship, Betrayal and Autonomy in the Lawyer-Client Relationship: A Reply to Stephen Ellmann" (1990) 90 Colum. L. Rev. 1004 at 1031, especially note 98. However, at 1026–35, *ibid.*, Luban argues (modifying his earlier position in *Lawyers and Justice: An Ethical Study* (Princeton, N.J.: Princeton University Press, 1988) at 150–52) that there is one situation where the need to hold the state to its burden and standard of proof in a criminal case is insufficient reason to permit the aggressive cross-examination of a truthful witness, namely, where the witness is the female victim of a sexual assault. Luban argues that the male patriarchy is a powerful institution posing a chronic threat to the well-being of women, and that protecting women from this threat necessitates limiting the cross-examination of the truthful female witness. This position is rejected by Freedman, *Understanding Lawyers' Ethics*, above note 122 at 167–68, but he nonetheless manifests discomfort at the criminal justice system's treatment of female sexual assault victims by stating that he does not accept rape cases in the first place. Luban's view is also criticized by W. Simon, "The Ethics of Criminal Defense" (1993) 91 Mich. L. Rev. 1703 at 1710; and S. Ellmann, "Lawyering for Justice in a Flawed Democracy" Book Review of *Lawyers and Justice: An Ethical Study* by D. Luban (1990) 90 Colum. L. Rev. 116 at 155–56.

nish other information to help the prosecution's case. If he can confuse a witness, even a truthful one, or make him appear at a disadvantage, unsure or indecisive, that will be his normal course. Our interest in not convicting the innocent permits counsel to put the State to its proof, to put the State's case in the worst possible light, regardless of what he thinks or knows to be the truth. Undoubtedly, there are some limits which defense counsel must observe but more often than not, defense counsel will cross-examine a prosecution witness, and impeach him if he can, even if he thinks the witness is telling the truth, just as he will attempt to destroy a witness whom he thinks is lying. In this respect, as part of our modified adversary system and as part of the duty imposed on the most honourable defense counsel, we countenance or require conduct which in many instances has little, if any, relation to the search for truth.[124]

Obviously, this position restricts the truth-finding goal in the rare individual case, in furtherance of systemic ends that seek to protect individual rights against the overreaching power of the state.

There are other arguments in favour of giving defence counsel significant latitude in cross-examining the truthful witness. Professor Monroe Freedman, one of the more provocative and controversial writers on the subject of criminal law and ethics, stresses the harm that a limited cross-examination would cause to the client-lawyer relationship.[125] If the candid client informs the lawyer of his or her guilt, but the lawyer responds by restricting the conduct of the defence to the client's detriment, the duty of confidentiality has been compromised and the promotion of unrestricted communication between lawyer and client dealt a serious blow. Moreover, as clients eventually learn to keep certain information secret from lawyers, in order to avoid a restricted defence, the result will be that counsel engages in the same vigorous and attacking cross-examination of the truthful witness. A rule that forbids counsel from knowingly undertaking such a cross-examination thus carries the seeds for its own undermining. It has also been suggested, in a related vein, that failure to cross-examine the truthful witness, or the insistence on placing substantial restrictions on the cross-examination, will fatally violate confidentiality by signalling to judge and jury that the lawyer believes the witness to be reliable.[126] Finally, a much more novel justification relies on a sort of nullification

---

124 *United States* v. *Wade*, 388 U.S. 218 at 257–58 (1967).
125 See *Understanding Lawyers' Ethics*, above note 122 at 167.
126 See A. Kaufman, *Problems in Professional Responsibility*, 3d ed. (Boston: Little, Brown, 1990) at 775.

doctrine, where cross-examination of the truthful witness is permitted because the normal working of the justice system is perceived to operate in an unjustly harsh and discriminatory way.[127]

Most commentators ultimately take the position that defence counsel can legitimately subject the truthful witness to a vigorous and aggressive cross-examination. The CBA Code does not clearly prohibit such conduct, expressly permitting counsel to "test the evidence given by each individual witness for the prosecution" despite possessing clear and unequivocal knowledge of the client's guilt.[128] As Gavin MacKenzie argues that, given this wording, and in light of the principle expressed in Commentary 10, "one is impelled to conclude that clearer language would be required to alter the traditional view that it is entirely proper for criminal counsel to discredit or impeach the evidence of witnesses whom they know are testifying truthfully and accurately."[129] In the United States, the influential ABA Defense Standards state that the defence lawyer's knowledge that a witness is telling the truth does not prelude cross-examination.[130] We believe that the arguments in favour of permitting a lawyer to challenge even the truthful witness are more convincing, and given the position of the Canadian codes of professional responsibility, counsel who takes such action is not acting unethically. Indeed, there is arguably a duty to undertake this sort of cross-examination,[131] assuming that the exercise is properly conducted and legitimately serves to advance the accused's case.

How would this position work in practice? A frequently used example posits that an elderly and frail woman is called by the Crown to identify the accused. The accused has confessed to his counsel, who accordingly knows that the identification evidence is accurate. Counsel is nonetheless justified in cross-examining the witness so as to test the

---

127 See Simon, above note 123 at 1722–28; and D. Luban, "Are Criminal Defenders Different?" (1993), 91 Mich. L. Rev. 1729 at 1755–59, 1764–65. Simon favours more of an *ad hoc* approach, determined by the lawyer on the facts of each individual case, while Luban seems more inclined to use this rationale to support a blanket license for aggressive defence tactics.

128 CBA Code ch. IX, comm. 11.

129 See G. MacKenzie, *Lawyers and Ethics: Professional Responsibility and Discipline* (Toronto: Carswell, 1993) at §7.4.

130 See ABA Defense Standard 4-7.6(b). Interestingly, the first edition of the ABA Defense Standards, released in 1971, took the opposite view: "[A lawyer] should not misuse the power of cross-examination or impeachment by employing it to discredit or undermine a witness if he knows the witness is testifying truthfully." The shift from the first edition's position to that taken in the third edition is trenchantly criticized by Lawry, above note 15 at 577–80.

131 See Li, above note 91 at para. 66.

strength of her evidence. In this respect, counsel can delve into the poor lighting in the area, any obstructions or distractions in the vicinity of the witness's sightline, the lack of prior familiarity with the accused, the briefness of the opportunity to see the culprit, and so on, all with the aim of suggesting that the prosecution has not proved its case beyond a reasonable doubt.

The above example is used most famously by Freedman.[132] In Freedman's treatment, however, the facts are decidedly different in that the accused is innocent. The elderly witness testifies truthfully that the accused was in the vicinity of the crime scene just five minutes before the crime, a robbery, occurred. The accused admits to counsel that he was at the location but insists that he was walking *away* from the scene of the crime, and is innocent. Unfortunately, another prosecution witness has testified inaccurately, but convincingly, to having seen the accused commit the robbery. The testimony of the elderly witness, if believed by the trier of fact, will be used by the prosecution to corroborate the inaccurate witness and probably result in the accused's wrongful conviction. On this scenario, permitting counsel to attack the reliability of the elderly witness is arguably less problematic, for the ultimate aim is to exonerate an innocent accused and thus prevent a wrongful conviction. However, Professor Harry Subin, who in an influential article expressed a general scepticism as to the propriety of counsel attacking the reliability of the truthful witness, is tentatively unwilling to concede that such conduct may be justified in order to exonerate an innocent accused.[133] Most writers, including Freedman and Subin, choose not to draw a distinction based on whether or not the client is known to be guilty.

Some commentators, though prepared to accept that defence counsel can ethically attack the general reliability of a truthful witness, draw the line at an attack on character.[134] Others, while perhaps less troubled by the "attack on character" scenario, nonetheless find the issue particularly difficult and are unable to offer a firm opinion as to

---

132 See *Understanding Lawyers' Ethics*, above note 122, cc. 6 & 8.

133 See H. Subin, "The Criminal Lawyer's 'Different Mission': Reflections on the 'Right' to Present a False Case" (1987) 1 Geo. J. Legal Ethics 125 at 150–51, note 113.

134 See, for example, Macmillan, above note 2 at 325; Sedgwick, above note 78 at 319 (though he retreats somewhat after hearing a comment made by G. Arthur Martin); and M. Blake & A. Ashworth, "Some Ethical Issues in Prosecuting and Defending Criminal Cases" [1998] Crim. L. Rev. at 20 & 30, especially at the text accompanying note 21.

whether such conduct is permissible.[135] There is no doubt that the prospect of undermining the credibility of a truthful witness by attacking character is particularly unnerving. Permitting counsel to do so, in effect to label the witness as a liar, arguably goes too far because of the resultant harm to the witness's reputation.

Consider the example provided by the *Courvoisier* case. After Courvoisier had confessed to Phillips, his lawyer, the prosecution called Charlotte Piolaine as a witness. Piolaine testified that the accused, whom she knew by reason of his having worked for her in the past, left a quantity of plate with her for safekeeping shortly after the killing. It was irrefutably clear that the plate had belonged to the victim, and hence this evidence was terribly incriminating to Courvoisier. In cross-examining Piolaine, Phillips attacked her character, the purpose being to discredit her testimony. Mellinkoff describes the effect on the witness as follows:

> She enters the courtroom an unknown innkeeper of London, and she leaves — after performing a public service — accused of keeping a disreputable house, her sex life made public, and her integrity suspect, her whole narrative held up to public ridicule.[136]

If we assume that Courvoisier expressly told his lawyer that Piolaine's testimony was accurate,[137] the attack on her character is potentially troubling. Suggesting that a witness might be inaccurate or mistaken is one thing, but insisting that he or she is committing perjury is quite another.

Yet the rationale for permitting counsel to test the Crown case seems to apply equally where counsel is faced with a truthful witness whose character is open to attack. Hiving off challenges to character from the category of ethically permissible cross-examination is especially hard to justify if one is prepared to accept the propriety of an attack on credibility based upon a truthful witness's *animus* against the accused or any other motive to lie.[138] Is it any worse to expose a wit-

---

135 See, for example, G. Arthur Martin, "Panel Discussion: Problems in Advocacy and Ethics," above note 78 at 320; and A. Boon & J. Levin, *The Ethics and Conduct of Lawyers in England and Wales* (Oxford: Hart, 1999) at 364–65.

136 Mellinkoff, above note 12 at 186–87.

137 As Mellinkoff tells the story, *ibid.* at 206, it is not obvious that Phillips knew the witness' testimony to be truthful *in all respects*. Given that she came forward to the authorities only after the trial had commenced, it is possible that she was complicit in the crime, and through fear of discovery decided to save herself and betray her confederate by means of partially false testimony.

138 This "hiving off" approach is taken by Blake & Ashworth, above note 134 at 20.

ness's prior conviction for perjury, than to bring out his or her bad feelings towards the accused? In either case, defence counsel is asking the jury to consider the possibility that the witness is knowingly telling untruths. We therefore prefer the view that counsel can use cross-examination to attack the character of the witness who is known to be truthful, by for instance, exposing priors acts of dishonesty. This is *not* to say, however, that defence counsel should in fact launch an attack on a truthful witness's character just because such conduct is not ethically improper. In many cases, there are tactical disadvantages in undertaking such cross-examination.[139] For example, raising the issue of bad character with a sympathetic witness may turn the trier of fact against the accused and so harm the defence case. Or counsel may reasonably decide that, although it is open to argue that the witness's testimony should be questioned by reason of his or her bad character, there is a better chance of acquittal if the cross-examination focuses solely upon the possibility that the witness is mistaken.

It must be stressed, however, that defence counsel does not have absolutely free rein to challenge the character of a witness who is known to be truthful. The rules of professional conduct prohibit the *needless* abuse, hectoring, harassment, or inconveniencing of a witness.[140] That is to say, such treatment is not justified absent some legitimate benefit to the client's case. It is proper to expose any frailties in the witness's testimony on points that are relevant to the issue of guilt, including concerns relating to the witness's character. But the client who insists that the witness be degraded or demeaned purely out of spite must be told in no uncertain terms that such conduct is impermissible.[141] Respect for the privacy and dignity of the witness, as well as the administration of justice, are pre-eminent where there can be no countervailing forensic benefit for the client.

## 2) Cross-Examining the Perjurious or Mistaken Witness

Addressing a slightly different point, it seems to be well accepted that perjury must be rejected, including a perjury directed at convicting the

---

139 This point is made in the commentary to ABA Defense Standard 4-7.6(b), and for that matter it applies to any attack upon the reliability of the witness who is known to be truthful.

140 See, for example, CBA Code ch. IX, comm. 2(k) & (l).

141 Lawyers have an "ethical responsibility, however, to refrain from attacking witnesses' character or morality in cases in which their credibility is not really in issue": MacKenzie, above note 129 at §4.14.

obviously guilty client.[142] The same applies where counsel is confronted with testimony that, while not perjurious, is otherwise inaccurate. Counsel is therefore completely justified in using cross-examination to challenge testimony that is known to be perjurious, mistaken, or exaggerated, this even though the client has confessed his or her guilt.[143] Counsel should also be able to attack a witness where there is uncertainty as to whether or not the witness is telling the truth, once again regardless of the fact that counsel has received a confession from the accused. On this scenario, the known information (that the client is guilty) is not inconsistent with the possibility that the witness is lying or mistaken.

**Example:** The accused is charged with murder and in confidence confesses his guilt to counsel. Just prior to trial, the Crown discloses a witness who claims to have received a jailhouse confession from the accused. The accused vehemently denies having discussed the case with the witness. Counsel is perfectly justified in vigorously attacking the credibility of the witness and alleging he is liar, all the while knowing that his client is guilty.[144]

## 3) Presenting Truthful Evidence as Part of the Defence, Knowing that the Trier of Fact May Use the Evidence to Arrive at a False Conclusion

We have seen that the rules of professional responsibility preclude counsel who has received a confession from setting up "an affirmative case" inconsistent with the client's admission.[145] In this regard, the rules specify that counsel cannot call any evidence that he or she knows to be false, such as an alibi intended to show that the accused

---

142 Even commentators who strongly insist that counsel can never impeach a truthful witness are willing to accept that false portions of the testimony are properly subject to challenge: see, for example, Subin, above note 133 at 150.

143 This scenario arose in *Li*, above note 91, where two witnesses correctly identified the accused, but were mistaken in describing his hairstyle and fluency in English. Defence counsel had received a confession of guilt from his client, but was not held to be precluded from attacking the faulty aspects of the identification evidence through cross-examination: *ibid.* at para. 68. *Li* is discussed further below in section K(3), "Presenting Truthful Evidence as Part of the Defence, Knowing that the Trier of Fact May Use the Evidence to Arrive at a False Conclusion," in this chapter.

144 This example is adapted from the facts in *Morin*, above note 72, discussed above in the text accompanying note 72.

145 CBA Code ch. IX, comm. 11.

did not commit the offence.[146] But what about calling witnesses who testify to facts that counsel believes to be truthful, or at least does not believe to be false, in an effort to raise a reasonable doubt? Suppose that counsel has received a confession, and the Crown calls an eyewitness who truthfully identifies the accused but inaccurately describes some material aspect of the accused's physical characteristics, say height or weight. Can defence counsel call a witness to challenge this inaccuracy, despite being saddled with the knowledge that the client is indeed guilty?

This very scenario has been considered by the British Columbia Court of Appeal in the case of *R. v. Li.*[147] There, the accused was charged with robbing a jewellery store. On the day of the robbery, two store clerks identified the accused from a photograph as one of the perpetrators. But neither clerk was absolutely certain of the identification, and their descriptive statements to police contained some discrepancies when measured against the accused's true physical characteristics. In particular, it appears that the witnesses provided police with a description of the accused that included inaccurate information respecting his fluency in the English language and his hairstyle. Sometime prior to trial, the accused told his counsel that he participated in the robbery. At the trial itself, the accused did not testify. However, defence counsel called two witnesses who testified as to the accused's hairstyle at the time in question, as well as to his capacity to speak and understand English.[148] The aim of this evidence was to undermine the clerks' identification testimony, although this defence failed and the accused was convicted.

The accused appealed on the ground that trial counsel had been acting while under a conflict of interest.[149] The Court of Appeal agreed that a conflict existed and, among other things, went on to consider whether the failure to call the accused as a witness at trial constituted an adverse consequence of the conflict.[150] After concluding that defence counsel was precluded from calling the accused as a witness, given his knowledge that the accused was guilty, the court examined the propriety of defence counsel calling witnesses to provide evidence

---

146 *Ibid.*

147 Above note 91.

148 *Ibid.* at para. 66.

149 The conflicting interest was said to arise from defence counsel's current representation of several individuals who were associated with the accused and the robbery but had been charged separately.

150 *Li,* above note 91 at paras. 56–68.

of fluency in English and hairstyle. Writing for the court, McEachern C.J. stated:

> Having received an admission from the accused that he robbed the store, [trial counsel] was required to refrain from setting up any inconsistent defence. He was entitled, however, indeed under a duty, to test the proof of the case in every proper way. Thus, in my view, it was not improper for [trial counsel] to call two independent witnesses who gave uncontroversial evidence about the hairstyle of the accused and about his fluency in English. Those matters might have raised a reasonable doubt about the reliability of the identification evidence given by the jewellery store clerks.
>
> On this point, I agree with [appellant counsel's] argument that if the evidence of the Crown was that an assailant was about 6 feet in height, a counsel defending an accused who has privately admitted guilt, could properly call evidence to prove the real height of the accused was less or more than that.
>
> Thus, it does not appear that [trial counsel] breached any ethical rule by continuing to act after the accused admitted he participated in the Burnaby robbery. He cross-examined the witnesses and sought to raise a doubt about identification (which was the only hope the accused had). He did not call the accused or put up any defence inconsistent with the facts believed by him to be true.[151]

The English scholars Meredith Blake and Andrew Ashworth have argued that the conduct of the defence in *Li* "may come close to setting up an affirmative defence" that counsel knows to be false[152] and hence extend beyond a mere testing of the prosecution case. A less equivocal condemnation of the practice seen in *Li* is made by Professor Harry Subin.[153] But does the *Li* example constitute "going too far," in that counsel is putting forward an affirmative defence that involves misleading the court? Is it misleading for counsel who has challenged, through cross-examination, inaccurate aspects of otherwise truthful eyewitness testimony to take the further step of bringing forward truthful defence witnesses to attack the same inaccuracies?

Drawing a bright line between cross-examination ("legitimate") and calling evidence as part of the defence case ("illegitimate") is not especially attractive. After all, in many instances cross-examination can be used to bring out the same type of truthful evidence. Suppose, for

---

151  *Ibid.* at paras. 66-68.
152  Blake & Ashworth, above note 134 at 20.
153  See, for example, Subin, above note 133 at 126.

example, that instead of calling defence witnesses, counsel in *Li* brought out identical information regarding hairstyle and proficiency in English by cross-examining the arresting police officers.[154] Or perhaps this evidence comes out during examination-in-chief, without any active involvement by defence counsel.[155] The ethical propriety of eliciting evidence in the cause of obtaining an acquittal should depend not on distinguishing between forensic techniques but rather on the potential truthfulness of the evidence and the purpose to which it is put.

To forbid counsel absolutely from calling truthful evidence as a means of attacking the prosecution case, where counsel knows of the client's guilt, may lead to unpalatable results. Let us assume for the moment that a lawyer, confronted with the fact pattern from the *Li* case, decides not to call defence evidence that would successfully challenge the inaccurate part of the identification testimony. Despite cross-examination on the point, the witnesses hold convincingly firm in their inaccuracies. The result might be that the trier of fact accepts the identification evidence and convicts the accused, based in part on evidence known by defence counsel to be inaccurate. In a system where the prosecution bears the onus of proving guilt beyond a reasonable doubt, this result is unacceptable. As we have argued above, counsel should be entitled to attack inaccurate evidence,[156] and this license should extend to calling truthful evidence as part of the defence case.

Perhaps the best answer to this difficult issue is that defence counsel can follow the approach condoned in *Li* and argue that the witness is partly wrong in his description of the culprit. Moreover, on the broader issue of whether or not the identification is correct, counsel can legitimately suggest that the witness *might* be mistaken, and refer to the inaccuracies in support of this argument, including the evidence of any truthful defence witness. Yet counsel cannot contend that the witness is *in fact* mistaken, for to do so would amount to the assertion of a position that is inconsistent with the admission of guilt. In essence, counsel can legitimately utilize the evidence brought out in cross-examination, and the truthful evidence of the defence witnesses, to

---

154 Along these lines, also see the example offered by J. Mitchell, "Reasonable Doubts Are Where You Find Them: A Response to Professor Subin's Position on the Criminal Lawyer's 'Different Mission'" (1987) 1 Geo. J. Legal Ethics 339 at 343–44 ["Reasonable Doubts"], where truthful evidence is brought out in cross-examination.

155 *Ibid.* at 353–54.

156 See section K(2), "Cross-Examining the Perjurious or Mistaken Witness," in this chapter.

argue that the Crown has not proven its case, and can aggressively assert that aspects of the identification are erroneous. But this same evidentiary ammunition cannot be used in support of a contention that counsel knows to be false, namely, that the accused did not commit the crime.

A variation on the issue that we have been discussing arises where the prosecution unintentionally leads evidence that is known by defence counsel to be false. But instead of challenging the false evidence, counsel determines that the error, if uncorrected, can be used to his or her client's advantage. Counsel may thus decide to call truthful defence evidence that, taken in conjunction with the erroneous prosecution evidence, suggests that the accused did not commit the crime.

**Example:** The defendant is charged with robbery. The victim identifies the defendant as the robber but mistakenly tells the police that the robbery occurred at 10:30PM, when it actually occurred at 10:00PM. The police put the mistaken time in their report. There is no way for either the victim or the police to know that they have the time wrong. Meanwhile, the defendant, seeing the wrong time in the police report, admits to his lawyer that he committed the robbery, but at 10:00PM, not 10:30PM. The defendant went directly from the robbery to a bar that he habitually frequents. Several of his friends and the bartender can provide him with an alibi for any time after 10:15PM, thus covering the period during which the victim believes the robbery took place. When the victim testifies to the wrong time at trial, what should the lawyer do about presenting the alibi?[157]

As we have discussed in connection with the *Li* case, it is permissible for counsel to call truthful evidence in response to the prosecution case, given the case-to-meet principle that underlies the criminal justice system. The lawyer can then use this evidence to argue that the prosecution has not proven its case, although it would be improper to assert that the client is innocent.

---

157  This example comes from a 1987 Michigan State Bar Committee ethics opinion (reported in (1987) 3 Laws. Man. on Prof. Conduct (ABA/BNA) 44). The Bar Committee concluded that "it is perfectly proper to call to the witness stand those witnesses on behalf of the client who will present truthful testimony."

# 4) Submissions that Rely upon Truthful Evidence to Suggest a False Conclusion

It has always been accepted that, to quote the words of Baron Parke in the *Courvoisier* case, counsel can "use all fair arguments arising from the evidence."[158] Is it "fair," however, to make submissions based on truthful evidence where the practical result may be to mislead the trier of fact? In the alibi problem discussed immediately above, for instance, we have already intimated that the defence lawyer breaches no ethical rules by suggesting that the prosecution has not proven its case and by relying on truthful witnesses in support of the claim. Yet it has been argued, not unreasonably, that counsel's submission may be viewed by the trier of fact as an assertion that a factual possibility, known by counsel to be false, is actually true.[159] The risk of deception is greatest where the submissions are made to a jury, which is less likely than a judge to twig to the qualified, "case not proven" language used by defence counsel.

This problem is most likely to arise where the prosecution has no trouble proving the *actus reus* of an offence but proof of the *mens rea* component is open for debate. Take the case of an accused charged with receiving stolen property. Irrefutable police evidence shows that he was observed loading stolen electronic equipment into the back seat of a car. The accused's mental state becomes crucial — did he know that the property was stolen? An argument in support of the defence is that the actions of the accused, in placing the property in the back seat of the car, instead of using the trunk, are consistent with the belief that the property was not stolen. But suppose that the accused tells counsel that he knew the property to be stolen and that he used the back seat only because the trunk was stuck shut. Can counsel nonetheless argue to the jury, based on the evidence presented by the Crown, that "the accused obviously had no idea that the property was stolen, otherwise he would have concealed the equipment in the trunk, not the exposed back seat"?[160]

---

158 See above note 14 and accompanying text.
159 Simon, above note 123 at 1718.
160 This scenario is based on a case described by James Kunen, and discussed in Simon, above note 123 at 1704, 1717–19. The same scenario is also taken up by D. Luban, "Are Criminal Defenders Different?" (1998) 91 Mich. L. Rev. 1729 at 1760–60. An analogous problem is examined by Mitchell in "Reasonable Doubts," above note 154 at 343–44.

This problem demonstrates that putting the prosecution to its proof can simultaneously work to deceive the trier of fact. Certainly, the language used by defence counsel in the above example seems calculated to suggest forcefully that the accused is factually innocent. But if counsel chooses not to raise the weakness in the Crown case, the mistaken inference may nonetheless be made by the trial judge in the charge or by some of the jurors during the deliberations. Once again, the best compromise answer to this troubling dilemma may be that counsel can put the possibility to the jury, despite knowing it to be false, but in doing so cannot assert that the possibility is in fact true.

This approach, though it permits a certain amount of zealousness, undoubtedly limits counsel's options in presenting the defence during submissions to the trier of fact. In this respect, counsel's ethical restrictions create a type of "frozen defence" where certain techniques are prohibited.[161] It may also be that counsel's careful balancing of the sometimes conflicting ethical dictates — allegiance to the client and honesty in dealing with the court — twigs the judge and prosecutor to the probability that the client has confessed. Nevertheless, this compromise provides the maximum protection that our adversarial criminal justice system can offer to one who, despite his confession to counsel, wishes to contest guilt.

# L. LIMITATIONS EXISTING AT THE PRE-TRIAL AND SENTENCING STAGES

So far, the discussion has mainly focused on the ethical difficulties that arise during the conduct of the trial, in the pre-conviction stage. However, counsel who represents one known to be guilty must take equal care respecting steps taken prior to trial and during sentencing.

Beginning with the pre-trial stage, we have already seen that irresistible knowledge of a client's guilt does not require counsel to refuse or end a retainer.[162] Nor does a pre-trial confession of guilt received from the client require counsel to focus all energies on reaching a plea resolution. Counsel must review the case to ensure that the confession is clear, unequivocal, and true, and even then he or she has a duty to consider any available defences and to discuss these defences with the

---

161  The term "frozen defence" is used by Ross, above note 85 at 439.

162  See section G, "Accepting or Continuing with the Retainer of a Client Known to Be Guilty," in this chapter.

client. There will certainly be instances where the client decides to plead guilty and instructs counsel to seek a plea agreement, but any such decision should be fully informed and based on the considered advice of counsel. Finally, the limits that knowledge of a client's guilt imposes on the conduct of the defence extend to pre-trial proceedings, such as a preliminary inquiry or a *Charter* application to exclude evidence. As in any other context, counsel operates under a general prohibition not to mislead the court.

As for the sentencing stage, in the event that the client pleads or is found guilty, counsel remains bound by the prohibition against misleading the court. The CBA Code's general precepts thus apply to cross-examination, defence evidence, and oral or written submissions that take place during sentencing proceedings. For instance, a client may admit to counsel that an aggravating fact alleged by the Crown during sentencing is true but instruct counsel not to concede the fact. Counsel has a duty to advocate the client's desired position but is governed by those same limitations generally applicable at the pre-conviction stage of a proceeding.[163]

There is an argument that the principle against self-incrimination has less force once an accused has been convicted.[164] If this point is accepted, the constitutional imperatives that provide part of the rationale for defending the client who is known to be guilty are weakened at the sentencing stage. It might follow that the ethical limits placed on defence counsel during sentencing are more restrictive. On the other hand, the "case-to-meet" nature of the criminal justice process retains some force at sentencing, at least with respect to disputed facts; that is, the Crown has the onus to prove such facts on a standard of proof beyond a reasonable doubt.[165] Moreover, the adversarial process, though admittedly relaxed with respect to non-contentious issues, continues to apply in the sentencing process.[166] Thus, while the issue has attracted little attention, and the application of constitutional rights in the sentencing context remains to be fully fleshed out by the courts,[167] we prefer the view that the ethical guidelines operating prior

---

163 See the limitations outlined in section K, "Limitations on the Conduct of the Defence," in this chapter.

164 See, for example, *Jones,* above note 26 at 394.

165 See *R. v. Gardiner,* [1982] 2 S.C.R. 368 [*Gardiner*].

166 See *ibid.*

167 Compare the majority position in *Jones,* above note 26, with *R. v. MacDougall* (1998), 128 C.C.C. (3d) 483 (S.C.C.). See also the interpretation of *Gardiner,* above note 165, as a principle against self-incrimination case, offered by Chief Justice Lamer in *R. v. Pearson* (1992), 77 C.C.C. (3d) 124 at 137 (S.C.C.). This

to conviction apply in more or less the same fashion during the sentencing process.

# M. SUMMARY AND RECOMMENDATIONS

The legitimacy of defending the guilty client is second nature to any criminal lawyer, the justification lying in an adversarial criminal justice system that affords the accused the right to resist any effort to cause his or her defeat or otherwise assist in the prosecution (section D). But counsel is not permitted to deceive the court in the course of defending a client. The difficulty in remaining loyal to the client without misleading the court is most pronounced where the line between resisting the prosecution and putting forward an affirmative case begins to blur (section E). The following guidelines set out our recommended view of the limitations that defence lawyers face in conducting the case of a client who is known to be guilty.

1.  Counsel's role in the criminal justice system is neither to judge the client nor to arrive at a personal determination as to the client's guilt. A lawyer is generally not precluded from calling evidence that suggests the client's innocence or making submissions to the same effect (section F(1)).
2.  However, where a lawyer reasonably draws an irresistible knowledge of a client's guilt, based on careful investigation and a thorough assessment of the case, he or she will be restricted in the conduct of the case by the ethical prohibition against knowingly assisting in deceiving the court (section F(2)).
3.  Irresistible knowledge of a client's guilt can come from a client's confession, which is the more usual form, or from other information available to the lawyer (sections F(2) & (3)).
4.  It is improper for a lawyer to avoid knowledge of a client's guilt by restricting client-lawyer communications, remaining wilfully blind, woodshedding the client, or viewing guilt as completely irrelevant to the function of a defence lawyer (section F(4)).
5.  There is no ethical principle that prevents a lawyer from accepting or continuing with the retainer where he or she has irresistible knowledge that the client is guilty (section G).

---

interpretation is accepted by the majority in R. v. *Noble* (1997), 114 C.C.C. (3d) 385 at 430 (S.C.C.).

6.  It will usually be the case that counsel's irresistible knowledge as to the client's guilt comes from confidential information. Accordingly, counsel is prohibited from sharing the knowledge with anyone else (section H).

7.  It is imperative that the client be fully informed as to any limitations that counsel's knowledge of guilt may have upon the conduct of the defence (section I).

8.  Where a lawyer acquires irresistible knowledge of a client's guilt only at trial, time constraints and litigation pressures cannot impede a prudent assessment of the problem. Appropriate measures include discussion with the client, maintaining client confidentiality, consultation with independent counsel, and a request for an adjournment (section J).

9.  Because of the case-to-meet theory of our criminal justice system, it is entirely appropriate for counsel who acts for the guilty client to raise a jurisdictional issue, challenge the validity of the indictment, oppose the admissibility of evidence, or argue that the Crown has failed to prove its case beyond a reasonable doubt (section K).

10. Limitations on the conduct of the defence where counsel has irresistible knowledge that the client is guilty all stem from the prohibition against misleading the court. Some fairly straightforward restrictions include the prohibitions not to suggest that another person committed the offence, not to call evidence that the lawyer knows to be false and not to call evidence in support of a fabricated alibi (section K).

11. The truly difficult scenarios create controversy because they seem to fall within a grey area, where testing the Crown's case (permissible) seems to risk misleading the court (impermissible). Three especially provocative and interrelated hypothetical problems, and our recommended responses, are set out below:

    a.  cross-examining the truthful witness: Counsel can permissibly challenge the truthful witness in cross-examination, and may even have a duty to do so, assuming that the exercise is properly conducted and legitimately serves to advance the accused's case. Such cross-examination can include an examination of the witness's motives or an attack on character, although it may be tactically unwise to adopt this latter strategy (section K(1)).

    b.  cross-examining the perjurious or mistaken witness: A defence lawyer is always justified in attacking the evidence of a perjurious or mistaken witness, regardless of irresistible knowledge of the client's guilt (section K(2)).

c. truthful evidence that supports a false conclusion: Counsel can legitimately utilize truthful evidence brought out in cross-examination, and the accurate evidence of defence witnesses, to argue that the Crown has not proved its case. However, the same evidence cannot be used to suggest that a conclusion known to be false is in fact true (section K(3)).

d. submissions based on truthful evidence that may mislead the court: It is not improper for counsel to argue a possibility to the trier of fact, despite knowing that the possibility is not true. However, counsel cannot go so far as to assert that the false possibility is actually true (section K(4)).

12. The limitations that counsel faces when conducting the defence of a client who is known to be guilty are not restricted to the trial proper. Rather, counsel's actions are equally constrained in relation to any aspect of the case, including pre-trial applications and sentencing hearings (section L).

## FURTHER READINGS

ALLEN, C., "R. v. Dean" (1941) 57 L.Q. Rev. 85

BABCOCK, B., "Commentary: Defending the Guilty" (1983–84), 32 Clev. St. L. Rev. 175

BENTHAM, J., Rationale of Judicial Evidence: Specially Applied to English Practice, Vol. VII, Book IX in J. Bowring, ed., The Works of Jeremy Bentham (Edinburgh: W. Tait, 1838-43)

BLAKE, M., & A. ASHWORTH, "Some Ethical Issues in Prosecuting and Defending Criminal Cases" [1998] Crim. L.R. 16

BOON, A., & J. LEVIN, The Ethics and Conduct of Lawyers in England and Wales (Oxford: Hart, 1999)

BOWMAN, A,. "Standards of Conduct for Prosecution and Defense Personnel: An Attorney's Viewpoint" (1966) 5 Am. Crim. L. Rev. 23

BRAZIL, W., "Unanticipated Client Perjury and the Collision of Rules of Ethics, Evidence, and Constitutional Law" (1979) 44 Mo. L. Rev. 601

BURGER, W., "Standards of Conduct for Prosecution and Defense Personnel: A Judge's Viewpoint" (1966) 5 Am. Crim. L. Rev. 11

BURKOFF, J., *Criminal Defense Ethics: Law and Liability*, rev. ed. (St. Paul: West, 2000)

DAL PONT, G., *Lawyers' Professional Responsibility in Australia and New Zealand* (North Ryde, N.S.W.: LBC Information Services, 1996)

ELLMANN, S., "Lawyering for Justice in a Flawed Democracy" Book Review of *Lawyers and Justice: An Ethical Study* by D. Luban (1990) 90 Colum. L. Rev. 116

FORTUNE, W., R. UNDERWOOD, & E. IMWINKELRIED, *Modern Litigation and Professional Responsibility Handbook: The Limits of Zealous Advocacy* (New York: Little, Brown & Co., 1996)

FREEDMAN, M., "But Only If You Know" in R. Uphoff, ed., *Ethical Problems Facing the Criminal Lawyer* (Chicago: American Bar Association, 1995) c. 10

FREEDMAN, M., *Lawyers' Ethics in an Adversary System* (New York: Bobbs-Merrill, 1975)

FREEDMAN, M., "Professional Responsibility of the Criminal Defense Lawyer: The Three Hardest Questions" (1966) 64 Mich. L. Rev. 1469

FREEDMAN, M., *Understanding Lawyers' Ethics* (New York: Matthew Bender, 1990)

FULLER, L., "The Adversary System" in H. Berman, ed., *Talks on American Law*, rev. ed. (Washington: Voice of America Forum Lectures, 1972)

GILLERS, S., "Can a Good Lawyer Be A Bad Person?" (1986) 84 Mich. L. Rev. 1011

GOLD, A., "Abuse of Power by the Defence Bar" in Law Society of Upper Canada, *The Abuse of Power and the Role of an Independent Judicial System in its Regulation and Control* (Toronto: R. De Boo, 1979) 617

HALL, J., *Professional Responsibility of the Criminal Lawyer*, 2d ed. (New York: Clark Boardman Callaghan, 1996)

HAZARD, G., & W. HODES, *The Law of Lawyering: A Handbook on the Model Rules of Professional Conduct*, 2d ed. (Englewood, N.J.: Prentice Hall, 1993)

HUTCHINSON, A., *Legal Ethics and Professional Responsibility* (Toronto: Irwin Law, 1999)

IPP, D., "Lawyers' Duties to the Court" (1998) 114 L.Q. Rev. 63

JACKSON, J., "Truth and Compromise in Criminal Justice: A Critique of Trial Practice and Lawyers' Ethics" (1997) 48 N. Ir. L.Q. 321

KAUFMAN, A., *Problems in Professional Responsibility*, 3d ed. (Boston: Little, Brown, 1990)

LAWRY, R., "Cross-Examining the Truthful Witness: The Ideal Within the Central Moral Tradition of Lawyering" (1996) 100 Dick. L. Rev. 563

LEFSTEIN, N., "Client Perjury in Criminal Cases: Still in Search of an Answer" (1988) 1 Geo. J. Legal Ethics 521

LEVY, E., *Examination of Witnesses in Criminal Cases*, 4th ed. (Toronto: Carswell, 1999)

LUBAN, D., "Are Criminal Defenders Different?" (1993) 91 Mich. L. Rev. 1729

LUBAN, D., *Lawyers and Justice: An Ethical Study* (Princeton, N.J.: Princeton University Press, 1988)

LUBAN, D., "Partisanship, Betrayal and Autonomy in the Lawyer-Client Relationship: A Reply to Stephen Ellmann" (1990) 90 Colum. L. Rev. 1004

MACKENZIE, G., *Lawyers and Ethics: Professional Responsibility and Discipline* (Toronto: Carswell, 1993)

MACMILLAN, H., "The Ethics of Advocacy" in J. Ames, *Jurisprudence in Action: A Pleader's Anthology* (New York: Baker, Voorhis, 1953) 307 (originally published in Rt. Hon. Lord Macmillan, *Law and Other Things* (Cambridge, U.K.: University Press, 1937)

MARTIN, G. ARTHUR, "The Role and Responsibility of the Defence Advocate" (1970) 12 Crim. L.Q. 376

MATHEW, L., "Counsel's Duties to the Court and to the Client — Is There a Conflict?" (August 1984), 3 Advocates' Soc. J. 3

MELLINKOFF, P., *The Conscience of a Lawyer* (St. Paul: West, 1973)

MITCHELL, J., "The Ethics of the Criminal Defense Attorney — New Answers to Old Questions" (1980) 32 Stan. L. Rev. 293

MITCHELL, J., "Reasonable Doubts Are Where You Find Them: A Response to Professor Subin's Position on the Criminal Lawyer's 'Different Mission'" (1987) 1 Geo. J. Legal Ethics 339

NOONAN, J., "The Purposes of Advocacy and the Limits of Confidentiality" (1966) 64 Mich. L. Rev. 1485

ORKIN, M., *Legal Ethics: A Study of Professional Conduct* (Toronto: Cartwright, 1957) at 107 (reprinted in (1959) 1 Crim. L.Q. 170)

PACIOCCO, D., "Evidence About Guilt: Balancing the Rights of the Individual and Society in Matters of Truth and Proof" (2001) 80 Can. Bar Rev. 433

"Panel Discussion: Problems in Advocacy and Ethics" in Law Society of Upper Canada, *Defending a Criminal Case* (Toronto: R. De Boo, 1969) 279

PANNICK, D., *Advocates* (Oxford: Oxford University Press, 1992)

PECK, R., "The Adversarial System: A Qualified Search for Truth" (2001) 80 Can. Bar Rev. 456.

PEPPER, S., "The Lawyer's Amoral Ethical Role: A Defense, a Problem and Some Possibilities" [1986] Am. B. Found. Res. J. 611

PEPPER, S., "Lawyers' Ethics in the Gap Between Law and Justice" (1999) S. Tex. L. Rev. 181

POOL, J., "Defending the 'Guilty' Client" (1979) 64 Mass. L. Rev. 11

PYE, K., "The Role of Counsel in the Suppression of Truth" [1978] Duke L.J. 921

REVIEW ESSAY SYMPOSIUM on W. Simon, *The Practice of Justice: A Theory of Lawyers' Ethics*, found at (1999) 51 Stan. L. Rev. 867–1006

RHODE, D., "Ethical Perspectives on Legal Practice" (1985) 37 Stan. L. Rev. 589

RHODE, D., "Symposium Introduction: In Pursuit of Justice" (1999) 51 Stan. L. Rev. 867

ROSS, S., *Ethics in Law: Lawyers' Responsibility and Accountability in Australia*, 2d ed. (Sydney: Butterworths, 1998)

SCHROEDER, F., "Some Ethical Problems in Criminal Law" in Law Society of Upper Canada, *Representing an Arrested Client and Police Interrogation* (Toronto: R. De Boo, 1963) 87

SHARSWOOD, G., *An Essay on Professional Ethics*, 4th ed. (Philadelphia: T. & J.W. Johnson & Co., 1876)

SIMON, W., "The Ethics of Criminal Defense" (1993) 91 Mich. L. Rev. 1703

SIMON, W., "Reply: Further Reflections on Libertarian Criminal Defense" (1993) 91 Mich. L. Rev. 1767

SKURKA S., & J. STRIBOPOULOS, "Proessional Responsibility in Criminal Practice" in Law Society of Upper Canada, *42nd Bar Admission Course, 2000, Criminal Procedure Reference Materials* (Toronto: Law Society of Upper Canada, 2000) c. 1

SMITH, B., *Professional Conduct for Lawyers and Judges* (Fredericton: Maritime Law Book, 1998) c. 8

SOULEZ-LARIVIÈRE, D., *L'Avocature* (Paris: êditions du Seuil, 1995)

STARRS, J., "Professional Responsibility: Three Basic Propositions" (1966) Am. Crim. L. Rev. 17

SUBIN, H., "The Criminal Lawyer's 'Different Mission': Reflections on the 'Right' to Present a False Case" (1987) 1 Geo. J. Legal Ethics 125

SUBIN, H., "Is This Lie Necessary? Further Reflections on the Right to Present a False Defense" (1988) 1 Geo. J. Legal Ethics 689

U.K., SUPREME COURT OF JUDICATURE, *The Annual Practice* (London: Sweet & Maxwell, 1917)

WOLFRAM, C.W., *Modern Legal Ethics* (St. Paul: West, 1986)

# CHAPTER 2

# CHOOSING AND REFUSING CLIENTS

## A. INTRODUCTION

There are several distinct aspects to the question of lawyers choosing and refusing clients. First, there are those facets of client selection that should normally raise no substantial ethical dilemmas. For example, it may be that refusing a prospective client is completely uncontroversial, because the suggested retainer would manifestly involve a breach of the rules of professional conduct. Similarly, it is beyond dispute that a lawyer cannot refuse a potential client based on a ground prohibited by human rights statutes. Second, and more contentious and difficult, is the issue as to whether a lawyer enjoys a general discretion to reject a potential client. The classic presentation of the problem lies in the case of the unpopular or repugnant client. As we will see, Canadian rules of professional conduct do not preclude a lawyer from exercising some discretion in deciding whether to accept a case. However, it remains to determine exactly how this discretion should be exercised. Third, assuming that a lawyer properly decides not to accept a retainer, certain duties are nevertheless owed to the individual whose matter has not been taken on. Prime among these duties are to assist in finding counsel and to maintain the prospective client's confidentiality.

# B. INSTANCES WHERE COUNSEL CANNOT ACT

On occasion, a lawyer must reject an available retainer, usually because the representation would effectively undermine the proper basis of a client-lawyer relationship or otherwise require the lawyer to engage in unethical conduct. Accordingly, a lawyer is required to refuse a case in the following circumstances:

1. **Conflict of interest:** A lawyer cannot act if the brief would involve labouring under an irresolvable conflict of interest.[1]
2. **Potential to be a witness:** Since most jurisdictions prevent counsel from appearing as a witness in a case in which he or she represents a litigant, a proposed retainer that raises a very real spectre of the lawyer testifying should be rejected.[2]
3. **Lack of competence:** It is unacceptable for a lawyer to act in a case where he or she is unable to provide competent representation.[3]
4. **Continuing retainer with another lawyer:** A client may approach counsel asking for representation while already represented by another lawyer in the same matter. The new client cannot be accepted unless the pre-existing retainer has been terminated.[4]
5. **Illegal purpose:** The rules of professional conduct prohibit a lawyer from taking on any case that would require a breach of the law.[5]

In short, a retainer that necessitates the violation of ethical rules cannot be accepted.

# C. ACCEPTING A COURT-ORDERED RETAINER

Most Canadian rules of professional conduct expressly state that a lawyer must accept a court-ordered retainer.[6] These rules provide no

---

1   See generally chapter 6.
2   See section L(1), "Counsel's Alleged Involvement in Facts Relevant to the Retainer," in chapter 6.
3   See section I(1), "Competence and the Rules of Professional Conduct," in chapter 3.
4   See section O, "Duties of a Potential Successor Lawyer and a Sucessor Lawyer," in chapter 11.
5   See, for example, CBA Code ch. III,, comm. 7; ch. IX, Rule; ch. XIII,, comm. 3.

general discretion to refuse a potential client where counsel is mandated to take the case by judicial order. However, and despite the silence of most Canadian rules on the point, we believe that counsel has a duty to decline a court-ordered representation where there exists a "substantial ethical justification" for doing so.[7] Lack of competence or an irresolvable conflict of interest are examples of a substantial ethical justification.[8] To hold otherwise would be to countenance a flawed client-lawyer relationship in circumstances where the client and/or the administration of justice would suffer attendant harm. Naturally, the existence of a substantial ethical justification should be reviewed with the court, subject to any restrictions imposed by a duty of confidentiality, and the court's permission to decline the retainer should ordinarily be obtained.

Less clear, in terms of a valid ground to refuse a court-ordered retainer, is the case in which the court requires counsel to undertake an extremely lengthy matter for meagre compensation. In the United States, where court-appointments are common, the ABA Model Rules expressly permit a lawyer to refuse an appointment where "representing the client is likely to result in an unreasonable financial burden on the lawyer."[9] Canadian ethical rules do not follow suit and arguably preclude counsel from refusing to act in the face of such an order, even though the result might be to destroy a legal practice and drive the lawyer into bankruptcy. However, in most provinces, given the existence of legal aid programs, court-ordered representation is fairly rare. If anything, intervention by the court is most likely to be requested by defence counsel, in cases where legal aid plans are seen not to provide adequate compensation.[10]

# D. PROHIBITING DISCRIMINATION

As we will shortly discuss, Canadian lawyers are not obligated to accept all prospective clients (assuming counsel's competency and the client's ability to pay the required fee). However, there is one area

---

6    See, for example, CBA Code ch. XIV,, comm. 6.
7    The phrase "substantial ethical justification" is borrowed from the Alberta Code of Professional Conduct: see Alta. ch. 1, comm. 4; and ch. 5, comm. 1.
8    As are any of the factors set out in section B, "Instances Where Counsel Cannot Act," in this chapter.
9    ABA Model Rule 6.2(b).
10   See, for example, *R. v. Chan* (2000), 276 A.R. 1 (Q.B.).

where lawyers are prohibited from declining employment: most rules of professional conduct, including the CBA Code, forbid discrimination on the same grounds generally prohibited by human rights legislation.[11] These rules are drafted broadly enough to encompass the decision whether or not to provide legal services.[12] The result is that a lawyer cannot refuse a case on grounds that typically include race, language, national or ethnic origin, colour, religion, age, sex, sexual orientation, marital status, family status, or disability.[13] It is also improper for a lawyer to provide an inferior quality of service based on discriminatory grounds.[14]

Breaching the rules of professional conduct pertaining to improper discrimination risks a human rights complaint and constitutes unethical conduct that could lead to disciplinary action by the governing body. In several American jurisdictions that employ comparable anti-discrimination provisions, a finding of professional misconduct cannot be made without a prior judicial determination of discrimination.[15] This precondition does not apply in Canada, meaning that a governing body can initiate a disciplinary proceeding without the need for a pre-existing adverse finding from a court or human rights tribunal.

One might ask, however, whether a lawyer's distaste for a client based on a prohibited ground might be so severe as to undermine the quality of representation should he or she be forced to continue with the case. Obviously, permitting the lawyer to refuse the case in these circumstances holds the potential to render the anti-discrimination rule patently ineffective. Yet the alternative may leave the client with poor-quality representation, meaning that the lawyer is violating the

---

11   See, for example, CBA Code ch. XX, Rule; Alta. ch. 1, r. 8; Ont. r. 5.04(1); B.C. ch. 2, r. 3; N.S. ch. 24; Man. ch. 21; and Nfld. ch. XX. For a review of the profession's response in Ontario, see C. Curtis, "Alternative Visions of the Legal Profession in Society: A Perspective On Ontario" (1995) 33 Alta. L. Rev. 787 at 788–89.

12   See, for example, CBA Code ch. XX, comm. 1(a); Ont. r. 5.04(2); Quebec *Professional Code*, R.S.Q. 1977, ch. C-26, s. 57; and Alta ch. 1, r. 8 & comm.

13   This list of prohibited grounds of discrimination is taken from Chapter XX of the CBA Code. The grounds forbidden by various governing bodies are similar, but differences do exist from jurisdiction to jurisdiction. For instance, the Law Society of Manitoba has adopted a very broad range of prohibited grounds: see Man. ch. 21. In Nova Scotia, the Barristers' Society lists many grounds of prohibited discrimination, yet does not purport to enumerate all such grounds: see N.S. ch. 24.

14   See, for example, Ont. r. 5.04(2).

15   See, for example, N.Y. Code of Professional Responsibility DR 1-102(A)(6) & EC 1-7; and Cal Rules of Professional Conduct 2-400(C).

ethical rule that demands competent service.[16] Nonetheless, attenuating the lawyer's choice seems justified because the alternative may unfairly limit access to the legal system, cause substantial emotional and psychological damage to the rejected client, and result in attendant harm to the image of the profession. Ultimately, the message that governing bodies send by virtue of anti-discrimination rules may therefore be that lawyers who are unable to set aside repugnance for the client on certain specific grounds should not be practising law.

## E. THE UNPOPULAR OR REPUGNANT CLIENT: SETTING UP THE PROBLEM

Perhaps the most difficult problem associated with the decision to accept or reject a case arises from the example of the unpopular or repugnant client.[17] Taking on a notoriously abhorrent case can cause the lawyer considerable personal risk and discomfort. He or she may be subject to intense criticism in the media and from family and friends. Other clients, both potential and existing, may decide that they are not comfortable with the lawyer's decision to act, with the result that business suffers. Colleagues may shun the lawyer, not wanting to court societal displeasure by any sort of association. Caution may lead the lawyer to perpetual inaction, as the following comment, written in the mid-1960s, laments:

> The average lawyer hesitates to participate in the controversial issues of his time. He wonders what his other clients might think. He wonders about the social consequences to himself, his wife, and his family. And he listens to the enemy within. This enemy speaks in a

---

16    See section I(3), "Competence and the Rules of Professional Conduct," in chapter 3.

17    Some indication of the dilemma facing the profession in this regard is reflected in the changing position of Monroe Freedman, who is usually not one to equivocate with respect to ethical issues. In his first book, *Lawyers' Ethics in an Adversary System* (New York: Bobs-Merrill, 1975) at 11, Freedman argued that lawyers must accept any prospective client. Shortly thereafter, however, Freedman performed a volte-face, arguing that lawyers should be morally accountable for the clients that they choose to represent: see *Understanding Lawyers' Ethics* (New York: Matthew Bender, 1990) at 66–70. See an interesting footnote to Freedman's change of heart, in R. Zitrin & C. Langford, *Legal Ethics and the Practice of Law* (Charlottesville, Va.: Michie, 1995) at 49–50, reporting his role in a debate concerning the propriety of a lawyer defending accused death-camp guard John Demjanjuk.

thousand voices, now whispering caution and then whining fear, now pleading in reasonable accents for practicality and self-interests, and then shouting direful predictions of disaster. But above all the voice says wait: wait until your prestige is secure, your voice more powerful; wait for the right time, for the right case. But the right case at the right time seldom comes. And while the lawyer waits, the voice of the demagogue is unanswered and the unpopular client's right to counsel goes by default.[18]

The lawyer may also encounter very real difficulties in undertaking the representation in a competent manner, struggling to overcome strongly held personal views in an effort to provide the client with zealous advocacy. The lawyer's individual autonomy and dignity, as reflected in his or her personal morality, is thus not always easily sublimated to the role of advancing a client's case.[19]

Of course, by virtue of their daily work, criminal lawyers have made basic choices about the propriety of representing accused persons, and they are presumably comfortable with such representation based upon the special role that a defence lawyer plays in the justice system. We have examined this role and its justifications in the chapter on defending the guilty.[20] If one can accept that the justice system is a necessary and good institution, and that the lawyer must undertake special duties to ensure that the system operates properly, then such duties, to the extent that they may superficially clash with common or non-legal morality, are arguably justified.[21] In a sense, the lawyer acts pursuant to a role morality that requires actions and attitudes not demanded of (and perhaps even shunned by) other members of society. Indeed, it is not going too far to suggest that a community consensus exists to the effect that defence lawyers play an important function that justifies representing individuals who may well be

---

18   D. Pollitt, "Counsel for the Unpopular Cause: The 'Hazard' of Being Undone" (1964–65) 43 N.C. L. Rev. 9 at 17–18.

19   It has been observed that "[t]he decision to act for a particular client is always a moral choice, implicating the lawyer's personal views of whether or not a 'moral lawyer' can assist a particular client in pursuit of a given goal": see R. Graham, "Moral Contexts" (2001) 50 U.N.B.L.J. 77 at 104.

20   See chapter 1, especially section D, "The Rationale for Defending One Known to Be Guilty," in chapter 1.

21   For a discussion of role morality and the lawyer, see L. Griffin, "The Lawyer's Dirty Hands" (1993) 8 Geo. J. Legal Ethics 219. See also the illuminating discussion in D. Luban, *Lawyers and Justice: An Ethical Study* (Princeton, N.J.: Princeton University Press, 1988) at 6 & 7.

guilty.[22] Consequently, in the great majority of cases, representing an accused is completely unproblematic for the lawyer whose practice is devoted to criminal law.

On the other hand, the problem of whether or not a criminal lawyer should accept a repellent client is not merely hypothetical. In recent times we have seen substantial controversy caused by criminal lawyers who decide to accept, or reject, the case of an unpopular client. In the leading child-pornography case of *R. v. Sharpe*,[23] the accused was for a time unable to obtain representation, at least in part because of the unpalatable nature of the charges.[24] Or consider the decision made by Phil Rankin, a Jewish lawyer involved in human rights issues, who was approached to take the case of an accused charged with a murder having significant racist overtones. Mr. Rankin decided not to accept the retainer, on the basis that he was unable to guarantee that his legal work would not be adversely affected by his personal views.[25] More recently, politician Stockwell Day ignited a firestorm of controversy, and attracted a defamation suit, by accusing a criminal lawyer of promoting the possession of child pornography by launching a constitutional challenge on behalf of an individual accused of such a crime.[26]

Some lawyers occasionally balk at representing a particular individual who is accused with an especially heinous crime. But other advocates go farther and adopt broad policies that shun representation for certain categories of client. Somewhat similarly, a lawyer may make a principled decision to restrict the representation so that a position that the lawyer finds distasteful is not advanced. Common examples of these approaches include refusing to defend an accused charged with any sex-related offence,[27] declining to represent anyone facing charges in a racist crime,[28] or rejecting the case of a potential client who wishes

---

22  See *Goddard* v. *Day*, [2000] A.J. 1375 at paras. 22–24 (Q.B.) (QL) [*Day*].

23  (2001), 150 C.C.C. (3d) 321 (S.C.C.).

24  He ultimately retained one of British Columbia's leading criminal counsel to handle the appeals. Shortly after the Supreme Court of Canada rendered its decision, Mr. Sharpe reported his counsel to the Law Society.

25  See R. Matas, "Murder Case Tests Lawyer's Beliefs: *The Globe and Mail* (25 April 1998) A5; and "Lawyer Declines Murder Case" *The Globe and Mail* (27 April 1998) A3.

26  See J. Mahoney, "Is it the End of Day?" *The Globe and Mail* (13 January 2001). The lawsuit was eventually settled, with Mr. Day paying $60,000 in damages and very substantial legal costs to Mr. Goddard.

27  See, for example, A. Hall, "We Say No and We Mean No!" (1990) 140 New L.J. 284; and R. Raymond, "The Profession's Duty to Provide; A Solicitor's Right to Choose" (1990) 140 New L.J. 285.

28  See, for example, "Lawyer Declines Murder Case," above note 25.

to inform against a co-accused in return for a more lenient sentence.[29] Other defence lawyers choose never to represent a police officer charged with a crime, or may avoid acting for higher-level drug traffickers or alleged members of biker gangs.

Lawyers who restrict their practice in this manner are allowing strongly held personal views about morality to guide their work, something that we usually do not begrudge members of society. The problem is that, if enough criminal lawyers restrict their practice in these ways, some accused persons may have considerable trouble in finding a competent lawyer. The issue thus becomes whether or not to accommodate a lawyer's morality, which may reflect views held by the populace at large, at the risk of limiting access to the legal system for certain accused persons. One approach to this problem, called the cab-rank rule, absolutely precludes a lawyer from bringing to bear personal moral views in deciding whether to accept a proffered retainer. We now turn to look at the cab-rank rule and some of the arguments made by its proponents and detractors.

# F. THE CAB-RANK RULE

In England and Australia, barristers have long adopted the cab-rank rule of accepting clients.[30] This rule is held up as an exemplar of the profession's unremitting dedication to ensure access to justice for all members of society. Reviewing the content of the cab-rank rule, as well as its justifications, will help us to determine whether the rule delivers on this lofty promise.

## 1) The Cab-rank Rule and Its Justification

The cab-rank rule, as its name implies, requires barristers to accept any client who requests legal representation, provided that a proper fee is paid and the lawyer is available and competent to take on the work.

---

29   See, for example, B. Tarlow, "The Moral Conundrum of Representing the Rat" (August 1995) 29 The Champion 15.

30   In England and Wales, see General Council, *Code of Conduct of the Bar of England and Wales* (London: The Council, 1990), r. 501; and Law Society, *The Guide to the Professional Conduct of Solicitors*, 8th ed. (London: Law Society, 1999) Annex 21A (Law Society's Code for Advocacy) §2.4.2 (implementing a version of the rule for solicitors who engage in litigation). In Australia, see, for example, The New South Wales Barristers' Rules, r. 85; and Bar Association of Queensland Rules, r. 85.

The central feature of the rule is that barristers do not choose clients based upon the nature of the case or the individual. Consequently, an invidious cause or an odious individual will not be denied access to legal representation. To put the matter another way, which criticizes any system that permits lawyers a substantial choice in deciding whether to accept clients: "To the extent that the advocate picks and chooses between potential clients on the basis of whether their conduct and opinions are acceptable to him, he is, implicitly, associating himself with his clients and their causes and giving a personal endorsement to the submissions he makes on their behalf."[31] Such freedom of choice may mean that lawyers refuse to take on unpopular cases or clients, not wishing to attract opprobrium for the choices made.[32] Conversely, taking away all freedom of choice arguably insulates lawyers from public criticism for accepting an unpopular client: the lawyer elides personal responsibility by pointing to the noble mandate of the cab-rank rule. The cab-rank rule thus helps to promote justice, for no one is forced to go without counsel or to settle for a second-rate lawyer because leading counsel is unwilling to risk social opprobrium by taking on the case. One of the classic expressions of the cab-rank rule's importance in this respect comes from Lord Erskine, who took on the case of the unpopular revolutionary Tom Paine. He stated: "From the moment that any advocate can be permitted to say that he will or will not stand between the Crown and the subject arraigned in the court where he daily sits to practise, from that moment the liberties of England are at an end."[33]

A secondary justification for the cab-rank rule is that a lawyer who assesses the viability or propriety of a potential client's case as a precursor to accepting or declining the retainer may be in error.[34] A valid cause, and the assertion of a legitimate legal right, could be rashly spurned in the result. On this view, lawyers who choose their clients are usurping the role of a judge or jury. It is better to leave the final decision-making function to the court and to accept that zealous argument by a non-judgmental advocate is the best means of achieving justice.

We can see that the cab-rank rule is the apotheosis of role morality at work, actually requiring lawyers to set aside personal convictions

---

31  D. Pannick, *Advocates* (Oxford: Oxford University Press, 1992) at 135.
32  *Ibid.* at 141.
33  Quoted in *Rondel* v. *Worsley*, [1967] 3 All E.R. 993 at 1029 (H.L.) [*Rondel*].
34  See R. Wasserstrom, "Lawyers as Professionals: Some Moral Issues" (1975) 5 Hum. R.Q. 1 at 9–10 (though not endorsing a cab-rank rule).

by accepting all clients. Lord Reid has articulated the importance of the lawyer's function within the justice system in this regard, in the well-known case of *Rondel v. Worsley*:

> It has long been recognised that no counsel is entitled to refuse to act in a sphere in which he practices, and on being tendered a proper fee, for any person however unpopular or even offensive he or his opinions may be, and it is essential that that duty must continue: justice cannot be done and certainly cannot be seen to be done otherwise. If counsel is bound to act for such a person, no reasonable man could think the less of any counsel because of his association with such a client, but, if counsel could pick and choose, his reputation might suffer if he chose to act for such a client, and the client might have great difficulty in obtaining proper legal assistance.[35]

The legal system promotes a moral good, and a function of the advocate is to ensure access to justice by taking on all clients. The morality of the lawyer's role thus demands that he or she set aside personal views as to the propriety of a client's actions, and perhaps also depart from standards of morality generally espoused by the community at large.

In Canada, it could also be observed that a cab-rank rule, if utilized, would promote the constitutional rights to legal representation[36] and counsel of choice[37] and the autonomy and dignity of the individual in controlling decisions of fundamental importance to his or her criminal defence.[38] Granted, lawyers are not state actors who are bound by the constitution in their daily activities. Yet the notion that lawyers should have some obligation to advance these constitutional rights can be seen as emblematic of their crucial role in the justice system and a fair exchange for the valuable monopoly granted to the profession by the state.[39]

---

35   *Rondel*, above note 33 at 998. The same sentiments are expressed by Lord Pearce at 1029–1030, *ibid.* and by Lord Upjohn, *ibid.* at 1033. See also the Australian case of *Giannarelli v. Wraith* (1988), 165 C.L.R. 543 at 580 (H.C. Austl.) (per Brennan J., but contrast the tepid support for the rule offered by Dawson J. at 594) [*Giannarelli*].

36   See, for example, *R. v. Howell* (1995), 103 C.C.C. (3d) 302 (N.S.C.A.), aff'd (1996), 110 C.C.C. (3d) 192 (S.C.C.); and *R. v. Sechon* (1995), 104 C.C.C. (3d) 554 (Que. C.A.).

37   See, for example, *R. v. McCallen* (1999), 131 C.C.C. (3d) 518 (Ont. C.A.).

38   See, for example, *R. v. Swain* (1991), 63 C.C.C. (3d) 481 at 505–507 (S.C.C.).

39   A. Thornton, "The Professional Responsibility and Ethics of the English Bar," in *Legal Ethics and Professional Responsibility* (Oxford: Clarendon Press, 1995) 53 at 68.

## 2) An Example: The Case of *Goddard* v. *Day*

The purported utility of the cab-rank rule can be illustrated by looking at the facts in the case of *Goddard* v. *Day*,[40] already referred to above. Mr. Day, at that time a member of Alberta's Legislative Assembly, wrote a letter to a Red Deer newspaper criticizing criminal lawyer and school trustee Lorne Goddard for his role in defending a man charged with possessing child pornography. The letter appeared to use the mere act of representation, which included a constitutional challenge to provisions of the *Criminal Code*,[41] as a basis for suggesting that Mr. Goddard personally supported the possession, and even the production, of child pornography.[42] Mr. Goddard responded by launching a defamation suit against Mr. Day.

One of the defences attempted by Mr. Day in the defamation litigation asserted that Mr. Goddard, by virtue of the role played by lawyers in advancing their clients' causes, must have personally endorsed his client's legal arguments. For example, an amended Statement of Defence filed by Mr. Day stated that Mr. Goddard:

> . . . as a member of the Law Society of Alberta, made certain legal representations as to the rights of individuals in Canada to possess child pornography and as to the unconstitutionality of s. 163.1(4) of the Criminal Code of Canada, which representations were made on March 26, 1999 in the Court of Queen's Bench of Alberta in the case of R. v. *Valley*. As such, the Plaintiff must, in accordance with the obligations of a Barrister being a member of the Law Society of Alberta, have actually believed or alternatively did in fact believe that those said representations as to the rights of individuals and as to the unconstitutionality of s. 163.1(4) of the Criminal Code of Canada fairly and accurately represented the law in Canada at the time the Plaintiff made the representations on behalf of his client, Kevin Valley.[43]

Mr. Day then argued that the public so despises child pornography that a lawyer who makes constitutional arguments in support of an accused charged with possession of such material would as a matter of course be hated and despised, be the subject of ridicule, be shunned or avoided, and be adversely affected in the estimation of others.[44]

---

40   Above note 22.
41   See R. v. *V.(K.L.)*, [1999] A.J. No. 350 (Q.B.) (QL).
42   The text of the letter is reprinted in "Is it the End of Day?," above note 26.
43   *Day*, above note 22 at para. 4 (emphasis added).
44   *Ibid.* at para. 21.

This brazen association of a defence lawyer's personal beliefs with the actions of a client, and the conduct of the defence, represents exactly the sort of problem that supporters of the cab-rank rule seek to avert. If Mr. Goddard had absolutely no choice but to accept the accused as a client, it would be less likely that the public would conclude that he endorsed the actions of his client and subject him to ridicule and hatred. On the other hand, we will revisit the *Goddard* v. *Day* decision below, in order to show how an interlocutory ruling in the case is not especially supportive of the cab-rank rule.[45]

## 3)  Room for a Lawyer's Personal Viewpoint

Does the cab-rank rule provide absolutely no room for a lawyer to employ his or her personal views in conducting a case? It has been suggested that, while the cab-rank rule is of the utmost importance to the proper functioning of the legal system, the lawyer who adheres to the rule is not precluded from exercising moral persuasion upon the client.[46] On this view, it is perfectly legitimate not only to advise the client as to the legal pitfalls and weaknesses in a case but also to discuss the morality of achieving the client's desired goal. By the same token, through dialogue with the client, a lawyer may come to accept that the retainer's objectives are not repugnant after all.

We should query, however, whether a lawyer has an affirmative obligation to put his or her moral concerns squarely to the client prior to accepting the retainer.[47] If this step is taken, the lawyer may effectively avoid the entire controversy surrounding whether lawyers should decline cases based on personal beliefs or opinions. Counsel who finds a potential client's cause to be highly unpalatable, and who candidly mentions such concerns to the prospective client, will often not be hired in the first place. Of course, there are clients who not unreasonably prefer to be represented by a lawyer who is publicly associated with condemnation of the alleged crime. Clearly, these clients believe that the trier of fact and/or society at large will infer that the lawyer is acting only because the defence position has obvious merit.

---

45   See the discussion in section G(2), "Justification for the American Position," in this chapter.

46   See Pannick, above note 31 at 153.

47   As is suggested by G. Dal Pont, *Lawyers' Professional Responsibility in Australia and New Zealand* (North Ryde, N.S.W.: LBC Information Services, 1996) at 48. If the potential client is not put off by the lawyer's disclosure, and wishes to proceed with the retainer, Dal Pont argues that the retainer must be accepted.

# 4)  Criticism of the Cab-rank Rule

The cab-rank rule asserts an impressive vision of the legal profession's role in ensuring that all accused persons have access to justice. There is a substantial question, however, as to whether the rule truly operates in accord with its Pollyanna supporting theory. Consider, for instance, that a great many exceptions are permitted under the cab-rank rule. A lawyer can legitimately reject a case for many reasons, including incompetence to act, conflict of interest, inability of the client to pay the required fees, and a busy schedule that does not permit counsel to take on the case.[48] These and other exceptions to the cab-rank rule effectively provide lawyers with considerable discretion in deciding whether or not to accept a client. It has thus been persuasively argued that the cab-rank rule is largely a myth or fiction, and that lawyers who purport to follow the rule in fact are able to pick and choose clients with relative freedom, rejecting cases that they find distasteful by imposing especially stringent fee requirements or claiming an excessively busy schedule.[49]

While there is still considerable support for the cab-rank rule in England and Wales, the panegyric testimonials traditionally surrounding the rule have been tempered of late, no doubt in part because of the honest recognition that the rule is open to easy avoidance. Contrast the staunch defence of the cab-rank rule by Lord Reid in *Rondel* v. *Worsley*, quoted above,[50] with the equivocal and tepid support offered by Lord Steyn in the recent House of Lords decision in *Arthur JS Hall & Co.* v. *Simons.*[51] In deciding that the cab rank rule cannot be relied upon to help justify granting barristers an immunity from liability for negligence,[52] Lord Steyn stated:

> First, there is the ethical 'cab rank' principle. It provides that barristers may not pick and choose their clients. It binds barristers but not

---

48  See, for example, the many exceptions countenanced by *Bar Code of Conduct*, above note 30, r. 501. In Australia, some rules of professional conduct attempt to restrict the discretion by expressly forbidding lawyers from setting an inordinately high fee for the purpose of avoiding a case: see, for example, The New South Wales Barristers' Rules, r. 86; and Bar Association of Queensland Rules, r. 86.

49  See, for example, S. Ross, *Ethics in Law: Lawyers' Responsibility and Accountability in Australia*, 2d ed. (Sydney: Butterworths, 1998) at 174–175.

50  See the text accompanying note 35.

51  [2000] 3 All E.R. 673 (H.L.) [*Arthur JS Hall*].

52  The opposite position was taken in *Rondel*, above note 33, which was overruled. Both cases are discussed in more detail in section C(3), "A Different Line of Canadian Judicial Authority," in chapter 3.

solicitor advocates. It cannot therefore account for the immunity of solicitor advocates. It is a matter of judgment what weight should be placed on the 'cab rank' rule as justification for the immunity. It is a valuable professional rule. But its impact on the administration of justice in England is not great. In real life a barrister has a clerk whose enthusiasm for the unwanted brief may not be great, and he is free to raise the fee within limits. It is not likely that the rule often obliges barristers to undertake work which they would not otherwise accept.[53]

It has also been argued that, despite the existence of the cab-rank rule, the public persists in associating lawyers with actions or legal positions taken by their clients.[54] In other words, the principle of independence that underlies the rule, and aims to promote access to the justice system by shielding lawyers from public criticism, simply does not achieve its professed goal.

# G. THE AMERICAN POSITION: A GREATER FREEDOM OF CHOICE FOR THE LAWYER

In the United States, the major professional governing bodies have never mandated the cab-rank rule, although some lawyers have chosen to follow its precepts. Instead, the American approach to client selection overtly affords the lawyer significant choice on the matter of client selection, in stark contrast to the theory behind the cab-rank rule.

## 1) Rules of Professional Conduct in the United States

Most jurisdictions in the United States do not employ a cab-rank rule, rather permitting a lawyer substantial freedom in deciding whether to take on a case. The Third Restatement goes the farthest of the major ethical codes in this regard, stating quite succinctly that: "[l]awyers are generally as free as other persons to decide with whom to deal, subject to generally applicable statutes such as those prohibiting certain kinds of discrimination. A lawyer, for example, may decline to undertake a

---

53   *Arthur JS Hall*, above note 51 at 680. To similar effect, see also the comments of Lord Hope at 714 *ibid.* More solicitous of the cab-rank rule's continuing role in the administration of justice is Lord Hobhouse, at 738 *ibid.*

54   See Ross, above note 49 at 182.

representation that the lawyer finds inconvenient or repugnant."[55] The ABA's Model Code and Model Rules, as well as the ABA Defense Function Standards, if slightly less strident, are generally to the same effect.[56] But contrast this with the position adopted by statute in California, where the Business and Professions Code states that an attorney has a duty "never to reject, for any consideration personal to him or herself, the cause of the defenseless or the oppressed."[57] Yet this dictate is not especially unique, merely replicating the oath taken by many attorneys in the United States upon their call to the profession. One suspects that California attorneys are therefore no more likely than other American lawyers to embrace the cab-rank rule.

The American position is not without certain significant exceptions, however, and also must be viewed in light of aspirational precepts contained in most rules of professional conduct. For instance, counsel must take on a case, absent "good cause" to refuse, where representation of a client is mandated by court order.[58] "Good cause" is not exhaustively defined in the rules, but among other things it is said to include circumstances where "the client or the cause is so repugnant to the lawyer as to be likely to impair the client-lawyer relationship or the lawyer's ability to represent the client."[59] Unless this standard is met, mere distaste for the client, or a desire to avoid public opprobrium by taking on a case, does not excuse counsel from the court appointment. It is also worth mentioning that, despite the general freedom given to American lawyers to accept or reject a proffered retainer, the rules of professional conduct urge lawyers not to shun a prospective client. The ABA Model Code is among the clearest in this regard, stating that "[r]egardless of his personal feelings, a lawyer should not decline representation because a client or a cause is unpopular or community reaction is adverse."[60] In this respect, the Code notes,

---

55   Third Restatement §14. comm. "b." To similar effect, see §16, comm. "b"; and §32, comm. "j."

56   See ABA Model Rules 1.2(b) & 6.2, comm. 1; ABA Model Code EC 2-29 and EC 2-30; and ABA Defense Standard 4-1.6.

57   Cal. *Business and Professions Code* §6068(h).

58   See ABA Model Rule 6.2. ABA Model Code EC 2-29 speaks of "compelling reasons" that might allow counsel to refuse a court-ordered retainer.

59   See ABA Model Rule 6.2(c), as well as the comparable ABA Defense Standard 4-1.6(d). See also ABA Model Code EC 2-29 & EC 2-30.

60   ABA Model Code EC 2-27. EC 2-28 further provides that a lawyer should not reject a proffered retainer simply because he or she wishes to avoid "adversary alignment against judges, other lawyers, public officials, or influential members of the community." See also ABA Defense Standard 4-1.6(b); and ABA Model Rule 1.2, comm. 3.

somewhat in the manner of arguments supporting the cab-rank rule, that legal services must be available to all litigants.[61]

## 2) Justification for the American Position

Several arguments are frequently forwarded to support the American position that a lawyer should have a general discretion to refuse a prospective client. First, the duties associated with a retainer, once assumed, are admittedly onerous. Counsel is restricted in his or her ability to withdraw from the case. The legal system should therefore not lightly impose upon lawyers the fiduciary obligations associated with legal representation. Second, the quality of legal representation may actually suffer if counsel is forced to accept cases in which he or she does not wish to act. The cab-rank rule, on this view, can actually harm the client, who is not assured of counsel who can zealously act in the cause at hand. Third, the client-lawyer relationship is by its very nature a contractual arrangement based on the consent of both parties. Forcing a lawyer to accept a client impinges on the freedom to contract. Fourth, it does not necessarily follow that providing a lawyer with discretion in selecting clients invariably results in the lawyer being associated with the views and positions of those individuals whose cases are accepted. A legal system can endeavour to divorce a lawyer's personal views from those of the client even where some choice in accepting a case is permitted. Indeed, ABA Model Rule 1.2(b) directly addresses this point, providing that "[a] lawyer's representation of a client, including representation by appointment, does not constitute an endorsement of the client's political, economic, social or moral views or activities."[62]

The notion that a lawyer's perceived independence (and personal reputation) can survive acceptance of a retainer for an unpopular client, despite the absence of the cab-rank rule, was accepted in an interlocutory ruling rendered in *Goddard* v. *Day*. Though a Canadian case, the court's ruling nicely articulates a justification for the American approach, along the lines espoused by ABA Model Rule 1.2(b). Remember that Mr. Day contended that a criminal lawyer is personally associated with the cause or behaviour of any client that he or she chooses to represent. However, this contention was rejected as part of a successful motion to strike a portion of the statement of defence. Rather, the Court accepted that criminal lawyers carry out an

---

61   See ABA Model Code EC 2-26. See also ABA Model Rule 1.2, comm. 3.
62   ABA Model Rule 1.2(b).

important function in the legal system, one that permits advocacy on behalf of an accused without leading to a personal association with the client's impugned actions. In this regard, the court stated:

> I do not doubt that there are some people who would follow the path suggested by the Defence in terms of their estimation of the Plaintiff. However, that is not the test. The test is whether or not it is plain and obvious that the Defence discloses no reasonable defence. I am satisfied that the allegation that someone is a criminal lawyer, or a politician would tend to adversely affect that person in the estimation of some other people. The same might be said of practically every appellation which describes a position or occupation taken by a person. Those other people would not be reasonable people.
>
> I am satisfied that reasonable people would not hate, or despise, or subject a person to ridicule, shun or avoid that person, or consider that person to be a lesser person in their estimation because that person has made a Constitutional argument in a criminal court.
>
> Reasonable people are concerned about the constitutional liberties of fellow citizens. Reasonable people support the Constitution of Canada or at the very least, support the right of other citizens to rely upon the protection afforded by that Constitution.[63]

The court thus accepted that the public understands the role of an advocate in an adversarial, rights-based legal system and does not think less highly of a criminal lawyer based on the clients that he or she chooses to represent.

On the other hand, supporters of the cab-rank rule have little use for the notion that a provision in the nature of Model Rule 1.2(b), or platitudes of the sort offered in *Goddard* v. *Day*, can shield lawyers from public criticism for choosing particular clients and thus promote access to the justice system.[64] The fact of the matter, according to these commentators, is that affording lawyers any discretion in choosing clients invariably means that counsel's neutrality within the legal system is lost. If a lawyer has decided to represent a client, when he or she is free to decline the retainer, then it is fair game to attack the lawyer for manifesting an allegiance to the client's cause. In this context, the bald statement that a lawyer does not endorse a client's position, so the argument goes, is ineffective and unconvincing. Certainly, some of the justifications for the traditional American position are open to question, at least if the aim is to provide a rationale for a totally unfettered

---

63  *Day*, above note 22 at paras. 22–24.
64  See Pannick, above note 31 at 140.

discretion to refuse a client.[65] Moreover, there have been periods in the history of American lawyering where the reluctance of the profession to provide representation for unpopular clients or causes has made access to justice truly difficult.[66]

However, in response to this attack from cab-rank supporters, surely a lawyer can derive some support from the principled notion that he or she is helping to provide access to the justice system, and does not personally endorse a client's views or activities, without the need for a cab-rank rule. Indeed, a similar criticism can be levelled at the cab-rank rule as it apparently operates in practice. That is to say, the cab-rank rule has so many exceptions, and provides such leeway to lawyers to avoid unwanted cases, that the associated bedrock principle of counsel's absolute independence is arguably divorced from reality. David Pannick, who presents a strong case in favour of the cab-rank rule, recognizes that there are legitimate exceptions to the rule. He also concedes that some advocates in England and Wales avoid unwanted clients by manipulating these exceptions to their advantage. But rather than recognize that the cab-rank rule might not be so very different, in practice, from the freedom of choice afforded American lawyers, he denigrates the critics who refuse to adhere to the cab-rank rule.[67] Nevertheless, one can legitimately question a tenacious adherence to a principle that has never really played out according to plan in the real world. At the end of the day, it thus appears that the cab-rank rule is not so very different, in effect, from ABA Model Rule 1.2(b).

## 3)  "The Last Lawyer in Town"

One way to reduce the possibility that legal services will be denied a deserving individual under the American approach is to encourage lawyers to act for the repugnant client where to refuse representation would leave the client without a lawyer. Thus, the lawyer should take

---

65   An excellent critique of the traditional justifications, from the perspective of one who supports an anti-discrimination ethical rule, is provided in R. Begg, "Revoking the Lawyers' License to Discriminate in New York: The Demise of a Traditional Professional Prerogative" (1993) 7 Geo. J. Legal Ethics 275 at 287–303.

66   See Pollitt, above note 18 (focusing on the refusal of many lawyers to act in civil rights cases and matters involving communism); and D. Goldberger, "The 'Right to Counsel' in Political Cases: The Bar's Failure" (1979), 43 Law & Contemp. Probs. 321 (discussing the famous *Skokie* case).

67   See Pannick, above note 31 at 137 & 144–145. See also *Giannarelli* above note 35 at 580 (per Brennan J.).

on a case where he or she is notionally "the last lawyer in town." The ABA Model Rules evince an attraction to this approach, albeit without imposing an affirmative ethical duty on the lawyer.[68] Limiting the lawyer's choice to refuse a client in "the last lawyer in town" scenario therefore helps somewhat to address the legitimate concern that freedom of choice in selecting clients might serve to leave some individuals without any legal representation.

A valid criticism of a "last lawyer in town" exception to freedom of choice for the lawyer in selecting clients is that the lawyer still exercises choice respecting the vast majority of clients who do not fall within the exception. One is thus arguably left with a general undermining of the objectivity so essential to the lawyer's role within the legal system. Moreover, this approach tends to place the burden of representation on the few lawyers who do not hesitate before taking on unpopular cases. Indeed, if all lawyers exercised the discretion not to accept an unpopular client or cause, relying on professional colleagues to act in troublesome cases, clients might frequently be left without any lawyer.[69] It can also be persuasively argued that the client is left with a restricted choice of counsel and may be forced to accept representation by a lawyer who, though competent, is not particularly well suited to conduct the case.

# H. CANADIAN RULES OF PROFESSIONAL CONDUCT

With a general understanding of two distinct ethical models regarding client selection, we can turn to look at the position in Canada.

## 1) The Text of the Rules

Most Canadian rules of professional conduct emphasize the importance of access to legal services and explicitly urge lawyers to "make

---

68    See ABA Model Rule 1.2, comm. 3; and Model Rule 6.2, comm. 1.

69    For this reason, G. Hazard & W. Hodes, *The Law of Lawyering: A Handbook on the Model Rules of Professional Conduct*, 2d ed. (Englewood, N.J.: Prentice Hall, 1993) at §6.2(101) suggest that in deciding whether to take on a case, a lawyer should approach the problem as though he or she were in fact the last lawyer in town. This fictional device thus becomes a potent means of restricting the ability to refuse a potential client, as opposed to a narrow exception to the expansive freedom usually enjoyed by lawyers in deciding whether to accept a case.

legal services available to the public in an efficient and convenient manner that will command respect and competence."[70] "It is essential," say these rules, "that a person requiring legal services be able to find a qualified lawyer with a minimum of difficulty or delay."[71] These ambitious statements of principle might lead one to conclude that a lawyer must take on any case, regardless of the unpopularity of the cause. However, the rules are decidedly ambivalent in this regard, the position set out in the CBA Code being representative:

> The lawyer has a general right to decline particular employment (except when assigned as counsel by a court) but it is a right the lawyer should be slow to exercise if the probable result would be to make it very difficult for a person to obtain legal advice or representation. Generally speaking, the lawyer should not exercise the right merely because the person seeking legal services or that person's cause is unpopular or notorious, or because powerful interests or allegations of misconduct or malfeasance are involved, or because of the lawyer's private opinion about the guilt of the accused. As stated in commentary 4, the lawyer who declines employment should assist the person to obtain the services of another lawyer competent in the particular field and able to act.[72]

While most Canadian governing bodies closely follow the CBA Code's lead, others have adopted different approaches to the issue of declining employment. The British Columbia Professional Conduct Handbook takes the novel position of making no express reference to the issue. It might therefore be thought that lawyers in this province have relatively free rein to accept or reject prospective clients. However, the Handbook urges lawyers to accept any representation assigned by the court.[73] More generally, if somewhat obscurely, the Handbook states that the oaths taken by lawyers upon admission to the bar are "solemn undertakings to be strictly observed."[74] The oath currently taken by British Columbia lawyers does not include an obligation to accept all cases. Contrast the oath in Ontario, which states: "You shall neglect no one's interest . . . you shall not refuse cases of

---

70  See, for example, CBA Code ch. XIV, Rule; N.S. ch. 15, Rule; Ont. r. 3.01; and Alta. ch. 1, rule 4.

71  See, for example, CBA Code ch. XIV, comm. 1; N.S. ch. 15, Guiding Principles; and Ont. r. 3.01 (commentary).

72  See, for example, CBA Code ch. XIV, comm. 6; N.B. Part C, r. 4; N.S. ch. 15, comm. 15.4; and Ont. r. 3.01 (commentary).

73  See B.C. ch. 1, r. 1(3).

74  B.C. ch. 1, r. 5(5).

complaint reasonably founded . . . ."[75] The Ontario wording on its face mandates that a lawyer accept any non-frivolous case, and it can be seen to equate with the cab-rank rule favoured by barristers in England and Wales. Similar wording is used elsewhere in Canada, and in the attorney's oath commonly employed in the United States, despite the fact that the cab-rank rule is clearly not adopted.[76]

Equally unique is the Quebec Code of Ethics of Advocates, which states: "[t]he advocate may accept or refuse a mandate."[77] Apparently, the message is that lawyers in Quebec are under no duty to accept a particular client. Yet the Code also implores that lawyers "must in no way interfere with the right of a client to choose his advocate." This latter provision could be interpreted to prevent a lawyer from rejecting a client who wishes to engage his or her services. After all, declining a proffered retainer surely operates to interfere with the client's right of choice regarding legal counsel. Lawyers in Quebec thus face ambiguity in trying to determine the Code's position on client selection.

In Alberta, the Code of Professional Conduct is more transparent and to the point. It provides that "a lawyer must not decline to act in a meritorious matter unless the lawyer makes reasonable efforts to assist the client in obtaining competent representation."[78] The Alberta Code then fleshes out this rule in a commentary that states:

> Rule #1: "Client" in the context of Rule #1 includes a potential or prospective client. A lawyer is generally entitled to decline to act in any matter provided that reasonable efforts are made to ensure that a meritorious cause does not go unrepresented. Such efforts would normally consist of referring the client to a firm member, directing the client to a lawyer referral service or legal aid program, or identifying for the client two or three lawyers believed to be competent in the area in question.
>
> A lawyer should be slow to exercise the right to decline a representation when the client is disadvantaged in some respect, particularly if the court has requested that the lawyer act for the

---

75 See, for example, the oath administered in Ontario, set out in Bylaw 11, passed pursuant to the *Law Society Act*, R.S.O. 1990, ch. L.8.

76 See ABA Defense Standard 4-1.6, commentary on "Unpopular Clients" (the lawyer promises never to reject "from any consideration personal to myself, the cause of the defenseless or oppressed").

77 Que. s. 3.05.01. See also s. 2.04, which provides that "the advocate may undertake the defence of a client no matter what his personal opinion may be on the latter's guilt or liability."

78 Alta. ch. 5, r. 1.

disadvantaged client. See Commentary 4 of Chapter 1, *Relationship of the Lawyer to Society and the Justice System*, for a discussion of the considerations that apply. If a lawyer is permitted or obliged by this Code to decline a representation requested by the court, that lawyer must then cooperate with the court, if so requested, in reasonable efforts to obtain other counsel for the client.

It is improper to decline a representation solely because it involves allegations of misconduct on the part of a colleague. The client with a meritorious claim against a lawyer should not encounter undue difficulty in obtaining competent representation. A willingness to act in such a situation as well as to report ethical violations to the Law Society is consistent with a lawyer's duties to the profession and the public. See also Rule #4 and accompanying commentary of Chapter 3, *Relationship of the Lawyer to the Profession.*

Elsewhere, the Alberta Code stipulates that a lawyer must refuse representation where personal distaste regarding the client or cause is so great that "an impairment of professional judgment" would result if the retainer were accepted.[79]

In the commentary to a different rule, the Alberta Code also mentions the potential problem raised by the unpopular client. This commentary implicitly asks that lawyers take on unpopular clients, but at the same time makes clear that there is no ethical requirement to do so:

With respect to objectives or beliefs of a client that a lawyer finds objectionable although they are neither illegal nor involve the lawyer in unethical conduct, one should generally overcome the inclination to pass moral judgment. While the lawyer is entitled to decline to act in a meritorious matter provided that reasonable steps are taken to assist the client in finding competent representation (see Rule #1 of Chapter 5, *Accessibility and Advertisement of Legal Services*), it is usually the unpopular client who will encounter the most difficulty in obtaining legal assistance. Representing a client does not constitute approval of the client's views or activities, and representation by a lawyer with personal reservations may be preferable to no representation at all.[80]

---

79   Alta. ch. 2, comm. 2.
80   Alta. ch. 9, comm. 11.

Interestingly, the last sentence of this commentary ascribes to the "representation does not equate with a personal endorsement" position taken by ABA Model Rule 1.2(b).[81]

The Alberta rules and commentary show a modest degree of similarity to the CBA Code's position. However, the license to refuse cases is stated less equivocally and thus appears broader. Under the Alberta rules, declining employment because an individual's cause is unpopular is not problematic, provided that the lawyer takes reasonable steps to assist in obtaining representation for the individual. Moreover, a lawyer is not required to take on a case simply because the request is made by a court. On the other hand, there is a recognition that lawyers should not shy away from representing unpopular clients. Overall, the Alberta approach is thus very similar to the position taken by the ABA Model Rules and Code.

## 2) Divining the Meaning of the Canadian Rules

We have examined the cab-rank rule used in England and Wales and Australia, and have compared this approach to the greater degree of choice provided American lawyers in deciding whether to accept an individual's case. What is the import of the Canadian rules? Gavin MacKenzie argues that the rules of professional conduct in Canada come very close to endorsing the cab-rank principle, given that lawyers are asked not to reject a client because of unpopularity, and urged to be especially slow to refuse a case where the individual will have difficulty in obtaining legal representation.[82] He also draws substantial support from the terms of the barrister's oath used in some provinces which we have already seen is suggestive of a cab-rank rule. Yet Professor Allan Hutchinson takes the opposite view, arguing that the Canadian rules afford lawyers the general freedom openly to assert personal morality in deciding whether to accept a retainer. As for Canadian case law on point, there is nothing in the way of binding authority and little more in the realm of principled dicta. One of the few judicial pronouncements in this area, offered by Mr. Justice Krever in *Demarco* v. *Ungaro*, expresses doubt as to whether Ontario lawyers have ever had an obligation to accept any client and rejects the exis-

---

81   ABA Model Rule 1.2(b) is discussed in section G(2), "Justification for the American Position," in this chapter.

82   G. MacKenzie, *Lawyers and Ethics: Professional Responsibility and Discipline* (Toronto: Carswell, 1993) at §4.2.

tence of such a duty in civil litigation.[83] Beyond Mr. Justice Krever's observation, the case law offers no real guidance.

That MacKenzie and Hutchinson can hold such diametrically opposed views regarding the same rules suggests that Canadian ethical codes could stand clarification. Granted, the rules employed in Alberta are unambiguous in stating that a lawyer has no obligation to accept employment. We have also seen that Canadian governing bodies adopt a type of cab-rank rule regarding certain prohibited grounds of discrimination.[84] Otherwise, however, the provisions modelled on the CBA Code, as well as the British Columbia and Quebec approaches, defy a straightforward interpretation. The CBA Code, in particular, simultaneously expresses potentially conflicting views. A general right to decline employment is granted, but at the same time lawyers are urged (though not required) to ensure that all individuals have access to legal services. The desire not to leave a prospective client without legal services comes through more strongly than is the case in most American ethical codes. Yet, ultimately, we are driven to the view that Canadian rules afford lawyers a general right to decline representation, and that lawyers thus have discretion in deciding whether to take on a client.

Moreover, we accept the justification behind affording the lawyer some discretion in choosing or refusing clients. There are commentators, including professors Hutchinson, David Luban, and Monroe Freedman, who unabashedly promote the idea that lawyers have a moral obligation to choose clients carefully, with an eye to the larger social good.[85] This approach involves jettisoning much of the rhetoric that surrounds the cab-rank rule, while at the same time refusing to embrace uncritically all justifications for the traditional American position. It also admits that barriers to access to justice relate much more to a client's economic position than to a lawyer's freedom of choice in accepting or declining a client's case.[86] There is also a recognition that, apart from the somewhat rare "last lawyer in town" scenario, one lawyer's decision not to take a case will often not preclude an individual from finding another competent lawyer willing to accept the representation. But, most important, the argument endorsing a degree of

---

83 *Demarco* v. *Ungaro* (1978), 21 O.R. (2d) 673 at 694–695 (H.C.J.).

84 See section D, "Prohibiting Discrimination," in this chapter.

85 See A. Hutchinson, *Legal Ethics and Professional Responsibility* (Toronto: Irwin Law, 1999) at 74–76; *Lawyers and Justice*, above note 21 at c. 8; and *Understanding Lawyers' Ethics*, above note 17 at 68.

86 See *Understanding Lawyers' Ethics*, above note 17 at 69–70; and J. Major, "Lawyers' Obligation to Provide Legal Sergices" (1995) 33 Alta. L. Rev. 719.

freedom of choice rejects, or at least tempers, the Diceyan notion that lawyers are morally neutral providers of access to justice. Decisions regarding what type of law to practise, fees to be charged, and the arguments to be placed before the court all have an impact on the greater administration of justice. In these and many other respects, lawyers shape the structure and process of the system within which they work. Accordingly, permitting lawyers a limited ability to reject certain clients, and thereby to shape the larger legal system, is not especially startling or out of character with their actual role.

There is much to commend this notion that lawyers should be permitted to employ their personal morality, and concomitantly be open to public evaluation on this basis, in deciding which clients to represent. True, there is a very real concern in criminal matters, where the accused faces a loss of liberty and serious social stigma, that competent lawyers must generally be willing to take on cases for unpopular clients. There certainly can be no legal obligation to *refuse* a retainer on such grounds.[87] Yet allowing lawyers a narrow discretion to decline a case based on heartfelt moral grounds, as the ethical rules in Canada and the United States do, is a tenable proposition. The question becomes, what guidelines should a lawyer follow in exercising the discretion to refuse a case?

## I.  SUGGESTIONS FOR EXERCISING THE DISCRETION TO ACCEPT OR REJECT A CLIENT

In our view, and consistent with the Canadian rules of professional conduct, there are different ways in which a lawyer's personal views can legitimately influence the decision whether to accept a client or cause.

### 1)  Refusal Where the Quality of Representation Would Suffer

A lawyer must reject a retainer where personal distaste concerning the potential client or cause is so severe that the lawyer can reasonably conclude that the quality of legal representation would suffer as a

---

87  See sections B, "Related Rules of Professional Conduct," and D, "The Rationale for Defending One Known to Be Guilty," in chapter 1.

result.[88] This sort of situation is really tantamount to the problem of incompetence.[89] If the lawyer cannot provide competent representation because of his or her personal beliefs, the brief should not be accepted. The same conclusion follows where the potential client's personality is so abrasive or vile to the lawyer as to impede fatally the duties demanded of any competent advocate. In either case, acceptance of the retainer, followed by compromised representation, would constitute a breach of the lawyer's duties of loyalty and competence to the client.[90] To be blunt, there is no room for the exercise of discretion in such an event, and the lawyer must reject the proffered employment.[91]

## 2) Responsible Exercise of the Discretion to Accept or Refuse a Case

Where a discretion clearly exists, the question becomes, what factors can be taken into account in choosing or refusing a particular client or cause? The aim is to strike an appropriate balance between a lawyer's legitimate exercise of personal morality and the potential client's right to access the justice system. In this regard, primary considerations include:

1. The lawyer should hold a sincere belief in the immorality of the representation. Fatuously or disingenuously claiming that a prospective client's case is objectionable does not meet the grade.
2. The repugnance should relate to concerns intimately connected to the representation at hand and not merely to the personality of the client. Provided that a personality clash does not irreparably cripple the client-lawyer relationship, the difficult client should not be rejected merely because he or she rubs the lawyer the wrong way.
3. A desire to avoid public opprobrium and to skirt the substantial economic harm to a lawyer's practice that can flow as a result are

88   See Alta. ch. 2, comm. 2.
89   See C.W. Wolfram, "A Lawyer's Duty to Represent Clients Repugnant and Otherwise" in D. Luban, ed., *The Good Lawyer: Lawyers' Roles and Lawyers' Ethics* (Totowa, N.J.: Rowman & Allanheld, 1984) 214 at 224.
90   See Tenn. Sup. Ct. Bd. of Professional Responsibility, Ethics Comm., Op. 96-F-140 (1996), where a lawyer sought to be removed from a case on the ground that his religious and moral beliefs would impair the quality of representation provided to a client. The client wanted legal representation in seeking waiver of the parental approval requirement for an abortion.
91   The one exception to this basic proposition may come when a lawyer's distaste arises out of a prohibited ground of discrimination. See section D, "Prohibiting Discrimination," in this chapter.

also legitimate factors to take into account. On the other hand, counsel should be slow to allow public opinion to shape his or her decision.

4.  Against the lawyer's moral discomfort in taking on the case must be weighed the importance of representation for the client. In most criminal law matters, the client will be facing possible stigma from a conviction, and perhaps also a serious impingement upon liberty. Access to the protections offered by the legal system through the help of counsel will thus constitute a valuable, perhaps even essential, interest. The strength of this interest must not be ignored or unreasonably discounted.

5.  The lawyer should also take into account the likelihood that the prospective client can obtain competent representation from other counsel (the "last lawyer in town" factor). This consideration is expressly mentioned by the CBA Code, which states that a lawyer should be slow to exercise the general right to decline employment if the probable result would be to make it difficult for a person to obtain legal advice or representation.[92]

6.  The CBA Code also states that a lawyer's private opinion about the guilt of an accused person should not constitute the basis to decline employment.[93] Utilizing this rationale for refusing a client would be at odds with a central tenet of the criminal defence lawyer's role. Once a lawyer decides to practice criminal law, choosing a client based upon the likelihood that he or she is guilty or not guilty is unacceptable.

7.  A client cannot be turned away based upon an ethically prohibited ground of discrimination.[94]

8.  As a final point, we have already mentioned that some criminal defence lawyers habitually refuse to take on entire categories of representation, for example, all individuals facing sex-related charges or all individuals who wish to cooperate with the prosecutor.[95] While uncomfortable with uncompromising refusals to represent clients who fall within a particular category of case, we

---

92  See CBA Code ch. XIV, comm. 6.

93  *ibid.*

94  See section D, "Prohibiting Discrimination," in this chapter.

95  This issue recently proved divisive and contentious among members of the Criminal Lawyers' Association (CLA). Some CLA members supported the decision of the Community and Legal Aid Services Programme (CLASP) at Osgoode Hall Law School not to represent men accused of domestic violence. Other CLA members strongly criticized the CLASP policy: see R. Martin, "Embodying Courage, Integrity, and Ability" *Law Times* (11 June 2001) at 6.

accept that a dedicated and highly competent criminal lawyer can have a profound moral objection to taking on certain types of representation. There must be a limit, however, on the scope of a lawyer's crisis of conscience regarding representation in criminal matters.[96] To take an extreme, defending only innocent clients so undermines the philosophical basis of defence work that the proper response should be not to practise criminal law in the first place.

## J.  DUTIES ARISING ONCE A RETAINER IS REFUSED

Where a lawyer decides not to accept a retainer, for whatever legitimate reason, it is advisable to take certain measures designed to protect the interests of both the lawyer and the individual whose case has been declined. A primary duty owed to the rejected individual is to help in finding a suitable lawyer.[97] Subject to the rules pertaining to referrals,[98] the lawyer should generally not charge for providing assistance in this regard. As for the extent to which the declining lawyer must provide assistance, we agree with the Alberta Code of Professional Conduct, which states that "such efforts would normally consist of referring the client to a firm member, directing the client to a lawyer referral service or legal aid program, or identifying for the client two or three lawyers believed to be competent in the area in question."[99] Of course, where the individual is seeking a lawyer to implement an illegal scheme, no duty arises in the first place. To assist under such circumstances would be to flirt with becoming a party to the illegality.[100]

There are other steps that can or must be taken by a lawyer in conjunction with a decision not to accept the case of a prospective client.

---

96  See A. Smith, "When Ideology and Duty Conflict" in R. Uphoff, ed., *Ethical Problems Facing the Criminal Lawyer: Practical Answers to Tough Questions* (Chicago: American Bar Association, 1995) c. 2 at 18.

97  See, for example, CBA Code ch. XIV, comm. 4; N.S. ch. 15, comm. 15.1 & 15.2; and Ont. r. 3.01 (commentary).

98  See section N, "Referrals," in chapter 10.

99  Alta. ch. 5, comm. 1.

100 This subject is addressed in an analogous context in Section N, "Other Duties Upon Termination," in chapter 11. Also see Alta. ch. 5, comm. 1, stating that a potential client whose position "is clearly without merit" is owed no duty of assistance in finding a lawyer.

First, the lawyer should be very clear with the individual that the case is not being accepted, to prevent any misunderstandings. The safest course is to set out in writing a quick review of the meetings or contacts leading up to the final decision to reject the retainer. Second, where the case demands that the individual take prompt legal action, for instance, where a trial is quickly approaching, the lawyer should stress the importance of retaining counsel immediately. Third, any documents or other property that have come into the lawyer's possession should be returned to the individual, although the lawyer may wish to make a copy for his or her own records. Fourth, counsel owes the individual whose case is not accepted a duty of confidentiality that precludes release of secrets to third parties unless authorized by the client.[101]

# K.  SUMMARY AND RECOMMENDATIONS

Our preferred approach to the question of choosing and refusing clients is as follows:

1.  Counsel must not accept a retainer in cases where to do so would require a violation of the law or any ethical obligations. For instance, a lawyer must not take on a case in circumstances that amount to an irresolvable conflict of interest, or if the lawyer is not competent to handle the matter (section B).
2.  A court-ordered retainer usually must be accepted, although a substantial ethical justification likely excuses the lawyer from acting (section C).
3.  Most Canadian rules of professional conduct expressly forbid discrimination in choosing clients on the same grounds prohibited by human rights legislation (section D).
4.  One of the most difficult problems associated with the decision whether to accept a proffered retainer arises in the case of the repugnant or unpopular client. Different jurisdictions have approached this problem in different ways, always with an eye to ensuring all accused persons wide access to the justice system. In England and Wales, the cab-rank rule ostensibly prevents lawyers from rejecting a client on the basis of moral distaste. In the United States, ethical codes give the lawyer freedom of choice in deciding

---

101  See section H, "Some Applications of the Ethical Duty of Confidentiality," in chapter 4.

whether to take on a case, yet urge him or her to accept unpopular clients where possible (sections D, F, & G).

5. Canadian ethical codes are not entirely clear regarding a lawyer's obligations in choosing or refusing a prospective client. However, the applicable rules can be reasonably read to afford lawyers the discretion to reject a case even though the client can pay the required fee and there is no ethical impediment to acting (section H).

6. We believe that a lawyer should enjoy some discretion in deciding whether or not to take on the case of an unpopular client. The question becomes how should the discretion should be exercised (sections H(2) & I).

7. An overriding ethical imperative is that a lawyer must reject a retainer where personal distaste concerning the potential client or cause is so severe that the lawyer can reasonably conclude that the quality of legal representation would suffer as a result (section I(1)).

8. In other instances, where the client or cause is unpopular, yet the lawyer reasonably believes that the quality of representation will not suffer if the case is accepted, the following guidelines are suggested:

   a. The lawyer should hold a sincere belief in the immorality of the representation.

   b. The repugnance should relate to concerns intimately connected to the representation at hand and not merely to the personality of the client.

   c. Counsel should be very slow to allow public opinion to shape his or her decision.

   d. The lawyer must take into account the importance of representation for the client.

   e. A further factor is the likelihood that the prospective client can obtain competent representation from other counsel.

   f. The lawyer's private opinion about the guilt of an accused person should not constitute the basis to decline employment. Once a lawyer decides to practice criminal law, choosing a client based upon the likelihood that he or she is guilty or not guilty is unacceptable.

   g. A client cannot be turned away based upon an ethically prohibited ground of discrimination.

   h. While uncomfortable with uncompromising refusals to represent clients who fall within a particular category of case, for instance all persons charged with a sex-related offence, we accept that a dedicated and highly competent criminal lawyer can have a profound moral objection to taking on certain types of representation (section I(2)).

9. Where the lawyer rejects the potential client, reasonable assistance should be provided, free of charge, in finding another competent advocate (section G).

## FURTHER READINGS

BEGG, R., "Revoking the Lawyers' License to Discriminate in New York: The Demise of a Traditional Professional Prerogative" (1993) 7 Geo. J. Legal Ethics 275

BOON, A., & J. LEVIN, *The Ethics and Conduct of Lawyers in England and Wales* (Oxford: Hart, 1999)

BURKOFF, J., *Criminal Defense Ethics: Law and Liability*, rev. ed. (St. Paul: West, 2000)

COOPER, H., "Representation of the Unpopular: What Can the Profession Do About this Ethical Problem?" (1974) 22 Chitty's L.J. 333

CURTIS, C., "Alternative Visions of the Legal Profession in Society: A Perspective On Ontario" (1995) 33 Alta. L. Rev. 787

DAL PONT, G., *Lawyers' Professional Responsibility in Australia and New Zealand* (North Ryde, N.S.W.: LBC Information Services, 1996)

FREEDMAN, M., *Lawyers' Ethics in an Adversary System* (New York: Bobs-Merrill, 1975)

FREEDMAN, M., *Understanding Lawyers' Ethics* (New York: Matthew Bender, 1990)

FRIED, C., "The Lawyer as Friend: The Moral Foundation of the Lawyer-Client Relationship" (1976) 85 Yale L.J. 1060 at 1078–1079

GRAHAM, R., "Moral Contexts" (2001) 50 U.N.B.L.J. 77

GRIFFIN, L., "The Lawyer's Dirty Hands" (1993) 8 Geo. J. Legal Ethics 219

HALL, A., "We Say No and We Mean No!" (1990) 140 New L.J. 284

HALL, J., *Professional Responsibility of the Criminal Lawyer*, 2d ed. (New York: Clark Boardman Callaghan, 1996)

HAZARD, G., & W. HODES, *The Law of Lawyering: A Handbook on the Model Rules of Professional Conduct*, 2d ed. (Englewood, N.J.: Prentice Hall, 1993)

HUTCHINSON, A., *Legal Ethics and Professional Responsibility* (Toronto: Irwin Law, 1999)

LUBAN, D., *Lawyers and Justice: An Ethical Study* (Princeton, N.J.: Princeton University Press, 1988)

MACKENZIE, G., *Lawyers and Ethics: Professional Responsibility and Discipline* (Toronto: Carswell, 1993)

MAJOR, J., "Lawyers' Obligation to Provide Legal Services" (1995) 33 Alta. L. Rev. 719

MILLER, J., "Free Exercise v. Legal Ethics: Can a Religious Lawyer Discriminate in Choosing Clients?" (1999) 13 Geo. J. Legal Ethics 161

OLENDER, J., "Let Us Admit Impediments" (1959) 20 U. Pitt. L. Rev. 749

PANNICK, D., *Advocates* (Oxford: Oxford University Press, 1992)

POLLITT, D., "Counsel for the Unpopular Cause: The 'Hazard' of Being Undone" (1964–65) 43 N.C. L. Rev. 9

PROULX, M., "The Defence of the Unpopular or Repugnant Client: Some of the Hardest Questions" (2000) 5 Can. Crim. L. Rev. 221

QUICK, B., "Ethical Rules Prohibiting Discrimination by Lawyers: The Legal Profession's Response to Discrimination on the Rise" (1993) 7 Notre Dame J.L. Ethics & Pub. Pol. 5

RAYMOND, R., "The Profession's Duty to Provide; A Solicitor's Right to Choose" (1990) 140 New L.J. 285

ROSS, S., *Ethics in Law: Lawyers' Responsibility and Accountability in Australia*, 2d ed. (Sydney: Butterworths, 1998)

SMITH, A., "When Ideology and Duty Conflict" in R. Uphoff ed., *Ethical Problems Facing the Criminal Lawyer: Practical Answers to Tough Questions* (Chicago: American Bar Association, 1995) c. 2

TARLOW, B., "The Moral Conundrum of Representing the Rat" (August 1995) 29 The Champion 15

THORNTON, A., "The Professional Responsibility and Ethics of the English Bar" in R. Cranston, ed., *Legal Ethics and Professional Responsibility* (Oxford: Clarendon Press, 1995) 53

WASSERSTROM, R., "Lawyers as Professionals: Some Moral Issues" (1975) 5 Hum. Rts. Q. 1

WOLFRAM, C.W., *Modern Legal Ethics* (St. Paul: West, 1986)

WOLFRAM, C.W., "A Lawyer's Duty to Represent Clients, Repugnant and Otherwise" in D. Luban, ed., *The Good Lawyer: Lawyers' Roles and Lawyers' Ethics* (Totowa, N.J.: Rowman & Allanheld, 1984) 214

ZITRIN, R., & C. LANGFORD, *Legal Ethics in the Practice of Law* (Charlottesville, Va.: Michie, 1995)

# CHAPTER 3

# DECISION MAKING

## A. INTRODUCTION

A principal function of the client-lawyer relationship is to arrive at decisions regarding the conduct of the case. In this regard, the client and lawyer have distinct roles and bring different strengths and interests to the process. The client, charged with a criminal offence, faces social stigma and serious restrictions upon liberty if convicted. He or she may have a number of objectives that relate to the legal representation, going beyond the obvious goal of escaping conviction if possible. The client will also often possess information that can be instrumental in identifying and carrying out these objectives. As for the lawyer, he or she possesses experience and knowledge with respect to the legal system, to a degree that the client simply cannot hope to match. The lawyer also has professional obligations, not to mention personal principles and preferences, which shape the way that the defence is conducted.

These and other attributes of the client and the lawyer have the potential to influence the decision making process of the professional relationship. The question becomes, how is the decision to be made? As we shall see, criminal defence practitioners in Canada have traditionally favoured granting the lawyer near absolute control over the conduct of the defence, what is often called the lawyer-control model. However, contemporary thought in the area is more and more inclined to reject this traditional approach as overly paternalistic. Moreover, the development of constitutional standards of competence in conducting a defence has placed definite strictures on a lawyer's ability to direct an accused client's litigation. We may thus be witnessing a sea change in Canadian perspectives concerning the allocation of decision making authority in a criminal case. A "cooperative" model, which encourages mutual decision making involving the client and lawyer, is starting to gain pre-eminence as the preferable template for structuring the professional relationship.

# B. DECISION MAKING AND THE RULES OF PROFESSIONAL CONDUCT

Many Canadian rules of professional conduct contain no direct reference to the general locus of decision making authority in the client-lawyer relationship. Specifically, the CBA Code makes no mention of this subject,[1] and hence those governing bodies that follow the CBA's ethical guidelines show a similar lacuna. Yet there are some governing bodies that address this important topic. The British Columbia rules seem to suggest, though without great clarity, that a lawyer is generally required to carry out the client's instructions.[2] In New Brunswick, the situation is substantially clearer, for a lawyer has an express duty to follow the instructions of the client, the Professional Conduct Handbook stating that: "[i]t is a lawyer's duty to advise and give his client the best judgement and the lawyer must seek and follow the client's instructions — unless the instructions are illegal or improper. For example, the lawyer must obtain instructions from his client before rejecting an offer of settlement."[3] It might be argued, however, that the reference to "improper" instructions is sufficiently vague that the New Brunswick standard is rendered ambiguous. Do "improper" instructions encompass only those directions that would involve breaching the rules of ethical conduct? Or does this term include any instruction to conduct the case in a manner that the lawyer reasonably deems to be tactically or strategically inadvisable?

---

1    An exception is the CBA Code's recognition that the decision whether to plead guilty is solely within the power of the client and is not to be made by the lawyer: see section F, "Related Rules of Professional Conduct," in chapter 8.

2    See B.C. ch. 1, r. 3(6).

3    N.B. Part C, r. 7. See also rule 3, which provides that "the lawyer is not the judge of his client's case, and if there is a reasonable prospect of success, the lawyer is justified in proceeding to trial".

In Alberta, the Code of Professional Conduct contains significantly more detail and commentary pertaining to decision making. Lawyers in Alberta are directed to "obtain instructions from the client on all matters not falling within the express or implied authority of the lawyer."[4] The underlying principle, states the commentary to the applicable rules, is that the lawyer must follow the client's instructions.[5] There are, however, exceptions. The lawyer "must not implement instructions of a client that are contrary to professional ethics and must withdraw if the client persists in such instructions."[6] The Alberta rules also stress that the lawyer must competently advise the client, based upon all known facts and law, prior to obtaining the client's instructions.[7]

In the United States, the major ethical codes devote more attention to the issue of decision making authority and offer several different approaches to the division of powers and responsibilities. The ABA Model Code tends to leave the main decision making powers with the client, subject to the lawyer having a certain amount of autonomy in areas "not affecting the merits of the cause or substantially prejudicing the rights of the client."[8] The ABA Model Rules flesh out the issue a little more fully. The Rules state that a normal client-lawyer relationship is based upon the assumption that the client, when properly advised and assisted, is capable of making decisions about important matters.[9] In this vein, the Model Rules give the client pre-eminence in making decisions concerning the objectives of the representation, provided that the lawyer is not required to commit an illegal or unethical act.[10] The Model Rules also specifically state that, in a criminal case, the lawyer shall abide by the client's decision, after consultation with the lawyer, as to the plea to be entered, whether to waive a jury trial, and whether the client will testify.[11] Yet, crucially, the Rules do not necessarily require that the lawyer abide by the client's wishes when it comes to the *means* taken to achieve the desired objectives of the representa-

---

4    Alta. ch. 9, r. 5.
5    See Alta. ch. 9, comm. G.1.
6    Alta. ch. 9, r. 10.
7    See Alta. ch. 9, r. 2, 4, 12 & 14.
8    ABA Model Code EC 7-7 & 7-8. See also ABA Model Code DR 7-101, which provides that a lawyer is to "seek the lawful objectives of his client."
9    See ABA Model Rule 1.14, comm. 1.
10   See ABA Model Rule 1.2.
11   See ABA Model Rule 1.2(a).

tion.[12] In short, the ABA Model Rules adopt a loose distinction between objectives and means, according to which decision making power is allocated, respectively, to the client and the lawyer.

The ABA Defense Standards for Criminal Justice illustrate yet another approach to the question, one that is especially robust in allocating decision making power to the lawyer:

Standard 4-5.2 Control and Direction of the Case

(a) Certain decisions relating to the conduct of the case are ultimately for the accused and others are ultimately for defense counsel. The decisions which are to be made by the accused after full consultation with counsel include:
  i)   what pleas to enter;
  ii)  whether to accept a plea agreement;
  iii) whether to waive a jury trial;
  iv)  whether to testify in his or her own behalf; and
  v)   whether to appeal.

(b) Strategic and tactical decisions should be made by defense counsel after consultation with the client where feasible and appropriate. Such decisions include what witnesses to call, whether and how to conduct cross-examination, what jurors to accept or strike, what trial motions should be made, and what evidence should be introduced.

(c) If a disagreement on significant matters of tactics or strategy arises between defense counsel and the client, defence counsel should make a record of the circumstances, counsel's advice and reasons, and the conclusion reached. The record should be made in a manner which protects the confidentiality of the lawyer-client relationship.[13]

The ABA Defense Standards thus provide the lawyer with considerable power to make decisions concerning the conduct of the defence, and probably go farther than any major North American ethical code towards embracing a lawyer-control model of decision making.

---

12   See ABA Model Rule 1.2, comm. 1. On the other hand, two areas where the client is given the final say over "means" pertain to the expense to be incurred and concern for third parties who may be affected aversely by a proposed action: *ibid*. Even with these two exceptions, the ABA Model Rules are arguably more inclined than is the predecessor Code to provide a lawyer with the power to override the client's wishes in conducting a case.

13   ABA Defense Standard 4–5.2.

Much closer to the opposite end of the spectrum, though with an emphasis on consultation reminiscent of the cooperative model, is the position taken by the Third Restatement. Once one works through the meaning of several interlocking provisions, there remains no doubt that, in the case of disagreement, the client has the final say on almost all matters concerning the representation, and the lawyer must follow the client's instructions.[14] Only where the client's instructions require conduct that counsel reasonably believes to be illegal or unethical, or would intrude upon counsel's ability to make immediate decisions during the course of a trial where there is no time for consultation, can a lawyer refuse to comply with a client's wishes.[15] Additionally, the Third Restatement promotes the idea that a client and lawyer can mutually agree upon the division of decision making responsibility best suited to the circumstances of the case.[16]

Turning to England and Wales, the two branches of the profession take different approaches to the issue of decision making. Barristers operate under ethical guidelines somewhat approximating the CBA Code, in that not much is said regarding the authority to determine how the defence is to be conducted. However, some clues are provided in the bar's Code of Conduct. While certain sections of the Code ascribe decision making authority to the client (for example, decisions regarding the plea and whether to give evidence),[17] others suggest that the lawyer retains control over the conduct of the defence. Most notably, the Code states: "[A] barrister when conducting proceedings at Court is personally responsible for the conduct and presentation of his case and must exercise personal judgment upon the substance and purpose of statements made and questions asked."[18] This lawyer-control approach is supported by leading judicial decisions from England and Wales.[19]

More direct and daring, at least from a United Kingdom perspective, is the Law Society's directive to solicitors who perform defence advocacy:

---

14   See Third Restatement §20–24.
15   See Third Restatement §23.
16   See Third Restatement §21.
17   See General Council, *Code of Conduct of the Bar of England and Wales* (London: The Council, 1990) [*Bar Code of Conduct*], Annex "H" (Written Standards for the Conduct of Professional Work, Standards Applicable to Criminal Cases) §12.3 & §12.4.
18   *Ibid.* at §5.10(a).
19   See the discussion in section C(1), "Martin's Lawyer-Control Model," in this chapter.

It is an implied term of the retainer that the advocate is free to present the client's case at the trial or hearing in such a way as he or she considers appropriate. If the client's express instructions do not permit the solicitor to present the case in a manner which the solicitor considers to be the most appropriate, then unless the instructions are varied, the solicitor may withdraw from the case after seeking the approval of the court to that course, but without disclosing matters which are protected by the client's privilege.[20]

This approach breaks from the traditional view endorsed by the bar. Rather than allowing the advocate a broad discretion to simply ignore the client's views, the Law Society effectively provides that a solicitor must either accept instructions or withdraw from the representation.

## C. CANADIAN CASE LAW AND COMMENTARY ON DECISION MAKING AUTHORITY

Just as the various ethical codes reveal diverse approaches to the decision making process in the conduct of a case, so have Canadian commentators and judges endorsed a wide range of options. However, the dominant response to the issue, at least where the representation of criminal accused are concerned, flows primarily from the opinions of the late G. Arthur Martin. Just over thirty years ago, this distinguished criminal practitioner, and soon to be court of appeal judge, endorsed a staunch lawyer-control model, essentially giving the lawyer a very substantial license to guide the conduct of a criminal defence as he or she sees fit.[21] Martin's handling of the issue has had a profound influence on subsequent commentators and the case law, especially in Ontario.[22] It is thus apposite to look at his position more closely.

---

20  The Law Society, *The Guide to the Professional Conduct of Solicitors*, 8th ed. (London: The Law Society, 1999) at §21.20(2).

21  G. Arthur Martin, "The Role and Responsibility of the Defence Advocate" (1969) 12 Crim. L.Q. 376. Martin expressed similar views in "Panel Discussion: Problems in Advocacy and Ethics" in Law Society of Upper Canada, *Defending a Criminal Case* (Toronto: R. De Boo, 1969) 279 at 282–286.

22  For instance, Martin's general approach is urged upon students taking the bar admissions course in Ontario: see S. Skurka & J. Stribopoulos, "Professional Responsibility in Criminal Practice" in Law Society of Upper Canada, *42nd Bar Admission Course, 2000, Criminal Procedure Reference Materials* (Toronto: Law Society of Upper Canada, 2000) c. 1 at 20–22.

## 1) Martin's Lawyer-Control Model

To begin with, Martin set out the sensible proposition that a lawyer's function extends far beyond the simplistic role of unquestionably carrying out all of the client's wishes. Rather, he stated, in a much quoted passage, that "[t]he defence counsel is not the *alter ego* of the client. The function of defence counsel is to provide professional assistance and advice. He must, accordingly, exercise his professional skill and judgment in the conduct of the case and not allow himself to be a mere mouthpiece for the client."[23] Among other things, rejecting the "mere mouthpiece" role requires that a lawyer become fully familiar with the law and facts pertaining to the case and advise the client accordingly as to the best course of action. It also supports the corollary notion that a lawyer cannot justify illegal or otherwise unethical conduct on the fallacious reasoning that he or she is acting pursuant to the client's instructions.

Yet Martin went considerably beyond a simple rejection of the "mere mouthpiece" role for defence counsel. He additionally stipulated that a lawyer must have absolute control over the conduct of the case, with quite limited exceptions, and believed that the lawyer should be permitted to override the client's express instructions on almost any matter. For support, he drew upon the analogy of the surgeon and patient: the surgeon cannot possibly take instructions from a patient as to how an operation should be performed, and so the lawyer must similarly be able to reject the client's directions in conducting a criminal defence.[24] This analogy holds an easy charm, but its potency evaporates once one considers several counter arguments. First, in this hypothetical case, the doctor surely has no right to proceed with an operation against the patient's wishes, even if entirely correct as to the best course of action. Current ethical rules for doctors preclude imposing treatment against a patient's wishes.[25] Second, the client may desire treatment options that, while reasonable, are not favoured by the sur-

---

23   Martin, above note 21 at 382.

24   *Ibid.* at 383, borrowing in part from American Bar Association, Advisory Committee on the Prosecution and Defense Functions, *Tentative Draft Standards Relating to the Prosecution Function and the Defense Function* (Washington, D.C.: American Bar Association, 1970) [*Tentative Draft Standards*].

25   See, for example, Canadian Medical Association, *Code of Ethics of the Canadian Medical Association* (Ottawa: Canadian Medical Association, 1996), para. 15: "Respect the right of a competent patient to accept or reject any medical care recommended"; and Canadian Medical Association, *Joint Statement on Preventing and Resolving Ethical Conflicts Involving Health Care Providers and Persons Receiving Care* (Ottawa: Canadian Medical Association, 1998).

geon. Should the patient's wishes be ignored? Once again, the medical profession has adopted guidelines that generally defer to the client's wishes.[26] It may be correct to say that a surgeon cannot conduct an operation in an incompetent manner because the patient has so instructed, but the surgeon-patient analogy falls short of generally advancing Martin's lawyer-control model.

Martin also relied upon legal precedent for his position, in particular the decision of the House of Lords in *Rondel* v. *Worsley*.[27] In that famous case, the plaintiff sued his criminal counsel for negligence arising out of the conduct of the defence to a charge of grievous bodily harm. The impugned actions included a failure to re-examine a defence witness, to cross-examine two prosecution witnesses regarding the nature of the injury, and to call certain defence witnesses. The House of Lords ruled that a barrister has absolute immunity from an action for negligence arising out of the conduct of a case at trial.[28] In coming to this conclusion, several of the judges endorsed the view that a barrister must be accorded total control in the conduct of the defence. To a certain extent, this endorsement represented the uncontroversial recognition that counsel cannot violate the rules of professional conduct at the client's behest.[29] However, at other points in the judgment, the law lords left no doubt that the barrister who acts in the good-faith belief that the client's best interests require certain actions is under no duty to follow his or her client's instructions to the contrary.[30] The only exceptions to this general rule appeared to be that the client had the final say in deciding whether or not to plead guilty,[31] and whether to testify in his or her defence.[32]

Martin seized upon the sentiments expressed in *Rondel* v. *Worsley*, concluding that "a Canadian lawyer has the same right and duty to exercise his or her own judgment and discretion as the English barris-

---

26  *Ibid.*

27  [1967] 3 All E.R. 993 (H.L.) [*Rondel*].

28  In any event, the House of Lords was of the view that the plaintiff had no reasonable defence available to him at trial and would have been convicted no matter whether counsel followed his instructions: see, for example, *Rondel, ibid.* at 997 ("F" & "I") (per Lord Reid); 1015 ("H"); and 1016 ("C") (per Lord Pearce).

29  *Ibid.* at 998 ("G" & "H" (per Lord Reid); 1011 ("E") (per Lord Morris); 1027 ("I") (per Lord Pearce); and 1034-1035 (per Lord Upjohn).

30  *Ibid.* at 999 ("C" & "D") (per Lord Reid ); 1011 ("F" & "G"); 1013 ("H") (per Lord Morris); 1016, 1027–1028 (per Lord Pearce); 1034 (per Lord Upjohn); and 1039-1041 (per Lord Pearson).

31  *Ibid.* at 1033 ("F") (per Lord Upjohn).

32  *Ibid.* at 1013 ("D") (per Lord Morris).

ter with respect to his conduct of a case in court."[33] Indeed, Martin went so far as to approve the following sentiments of Lord President Inglis in the Scottish case of *Batchelor v. Pattison and Mackersy* (referred to by several judges in *Rondel v. Worsley*):

> . . . the nature of the advocate's office makes it clear that in the performance of his duty he must be entirely independent, and act according to his own discretion and judgment in the conduct of the cause for his client. *His legal right is to conduct the cause without any regard to the wishes of the client, so long as his mandate is unrecalled,* and what he does bona fide according to his own judgment will bind his client, and will not expose him to any action for what he has done, even if the client's interests are thereby prejudiced.[34]

The emphasis in the above quote comes from Martin. This perspective leads, not surprisingly, to the conclusion that the lawyer, not the client, makes virtually all decisions concerning the case, including what witnesses to call, whether a witness should be cross-examined, and if so how.[35] Martin would have left the client only with the final say regarding the decisions on how to plead, the mode of trial, and whether to testify, ostensibly because these areas involve fundamental rights.[36] (Indeed, on an earlier occasion Martin went even farther, recognizing the pre-eminence of counsel in decision making on all matters excepting the choice as to how to plead to the charge.)[37] Moreover, he allowed that the client could at any time fire a lawyer who refused to accept instructions, and that the lawyer could withdraw from the case where disagreement led to a complete breakdown in the client-lawyer relationship.[38]

## 2) Subsequent Canadian Commentary and Case Law

Martin's views were by no means novel at the time that he expressed them.[39] The same points were to be found in the proposed first edition

---

33   Martin, above note 21 at 385.

34   *Batchelor* v. *Pattison and Mackersy* (1876), 3 R. 914 at 918 (Sess.), quoted by Lords Morris, Pearce and Pearson in *Rondel*, above note 27 at 1007, 1019 & 1040, and spoken of approvingly by Lord Upjohn at 1034.

35   Martin, above note 21 at 386.

36   *Ibid.* at 386–388.

37   See "Panel Discussion: Problems in Advocacy and Ethics," above note 21 at 283.

38   See Martin, above note 21 at 384, 387.

39   For earlier cases ascribing to the view, see *R.* v. *MacTemple* (1935), 64 C.C.C. 11 (Ont. C.A.); *Judson* v. *McQuain* (1923), 53 D.L.R. 348 (C.A.); and *Wilson* v. *Huron & Bruce (United Counties)* (1862), 11 U.C.C.P. 548. Yet Martin's views

of the ABA Defense Standards.[40] But, moving ahead three decades, Martin's lawyer-control approach remains very much in fashion in Canada. Subsequent Canadian authors have generally adhered to Martin's position, or at least have reiterated the position without any adverse comment.[41] Moreover, Ontario courts have on occasion embraced the idea that defence lawyers can ignore a client's instructions on most matters without violating any ethical principles. The main exceptions to this general rule would essentially be those areas identified by Martin as fundamental to the client's defence, including the decisions whether to plead guilty and whether to testify.[42]

In *R. v. Samra*,[43] for example, the appellant sought to overturn his murder conviction on the ground, among others, that a lawyer acting as *amicus curiae* had improperly made submissions contrary to the appellant's clearly expressed position. In addressing this argument, Rosenberg J.A. commented upon the proper role of defence counsel. First, he noted that two lawyers retained by the appellant to assist at trial had simply taken action at the appellant's bidding, failing to exercise any independent judgment. This role was not expressly said to be improper, but, as Mr. Justice Rosenberg readily observed, "such is not the role of properly retained defence counsel."[44] Second, Rosenberg J.A. pointedly referred to, and adopted, Martin's broad view of defence

---

were not universally accepted in Canada. Compare the largely contrary position of M. Orkin, *Legal Ethics: A Study of Professional Conduct* (Toronto: Cartwright, 1957) at 95.

40  See *Tentative Draft Standards*, above note 24 at 174, referred to by Martin, above note 21 at 382–383.

41  See, for example, J. Hoolihan, "Ethical Standards for Defence Counsel" in Canadian Bar Association, *Studies in Criminal Law and Procedure* (Agincourt, Ont.: Canada Law Book, 1972) at 124; A. Maloney, "The Role of the Independent Bar" in Law Society of Upper Canada, *The Abuse of Power and the Role of an Independent Judicial System in its Regulation and Control* (Toronto: R. De Boo, 1979) 49 at 61ff; F. Hoskins, "The Players of a Criminal Trial" in J. Pink & D. Perrier, eds., *From Crime to Punishment: An Introduction to the Criminal Justice System*, 4th ed. (Toronto: Carswell, 1999) at 177–178; A. Hutchinson, *Legal Ethics and Professional Responsibility* (Toronto: Irwin Law, 1999) at 94; and G. MacKenzie, *Lawyers and Ethics: Professional Responsibility and Discipline* (Toronto: Carswell, 1993) at §4.11 (4-21–23).

42  See, for example, *R. v. Lamoureux* (1984), 13 C.C.C. (3d) 101 at 105 (Que. C.A.); *R. v. Prosser*, [1980] 3 W.W.R. 499 (Sask. Dist. Ct.) (how to plead); and *R. v. Smith* (1997), 120 C.C.C. (3d) 500 at 506–08, 510–11 (Ont. C.A.) (whether to testify).

43  (1998), 129 C.C.C. (3d) 144 (Ont. C.A.) [*Samra*], leave to appeal to S.C.C. refused (1997), 46 C.R.R. (2d) 276n (S.C.C.).

44  *Ibid.* at 158.

counsel's decision making powers. Accordingly, he concluded that, assuming for the sake of argument that the *amicus curiae* had made the impugned submissions while acting as defence counsel, to do so even over the express disapproval of the client was unproblematic.[45]

## 3) A Different Line of Canadian Judicial Authority

The adoption of Martin's views in *Samra* is by no means unique in our criminal law jurisprudence.[46] Yet one can detect a different line of Canadian legal authority that is less comfortable with allowing a lawyer to ignore a client's instructions in conducting a defence. For one thing, some Canadian courts have commented that the right of counsel to control the conduct of a criminal defence must conform to reasonable professional standards, including the exercise of reasonable skill and judgment in the best interests of the client.[47] But more than this, in *R. v. Swain* the Supreme Court of Canada has provided substantial ammunition for an approach that gives the client greater control. While not directly addressing the issue of a lawyer overriding a client's instructions, the Court emphasized the fundamental importance of allowing an accused control over his or her own defence.[48] The reasoning in *Swain*, based on respect for the autonomy and dignity of human beings, seems potentially at odds with Martin's lawyer-control approach. Moreover, *Swain* specifies that the accused's right to control the conduct of the defence includes not only the decision whether to have counsel and whether to testify but also the determination as to what witnesses to call.[49] This latter component of the right, pertaining to witnesses called as part of the defence, undoubtedly goes farther

---

45  *Ibid.* at 158–59.

46  See, for example, *Sherman* v. *Manley* (1978), 19 O.R. (2d) 531 at 534 (Ont. C.A.) [*Sherman*], leave to appeal to S.C.C. refused (1978), 19 O.R. (2d) 531n (S.C.C.); *R.* v. *White* (1997), 114 C.C.C. (3d) 225 at 253 (Ont. C.A.) [*White*], leave to appeal to S.C.C. refused (1997), 46 C.R.R. (2d) 276n (S.C.C.); *Stewart* v. *Canadian Broadcasting Corp.* (1997), 150 D.L.R. (4th) 24 at 83–88 (Ont. Gen. Div.) [*Stewart*]; and *Wenn* v. *Goyer*, [1986] B.C.J. No. 822 at para. 20 (S.C.) (QL) [*Wenn*].

47  See, for example, *Stewart*, above note 46 at 83, 87–88; *White*, above note 46 at 247 & 253. *R.* v. *Joanisse* (1995), 102 C.C.C. (3d) 35 at 72–74 (Ont. C.A.) [*Joanisse*], leave to appeal to S.C.C. refused (1997), 111 C.C.C. (3d) vi (S.C.C.).

48  *R.* v. *Swain* (1991), 63 C.C.C. (3d) 481 at 505–06 (S.C.C.) [*Swain*]. On the facts, the Court was dealing with a prosecution attempt to influence the type of defence put before the trier of fact (namely, to raise the insanity defence against the accused's wishes).

49  *Ibid.* at 505–06.

than the traditional lawyer-control approach. A similar departure from the Martin view is evidenced in the *Swain* Court's ruling that an accused must have control over the decision whether a particular defence should be relied upon, in particular the defence of not criminally responsible.[50]

**Example:** Counsel is retained to represent a client charged with a serious sexual assault. The client insists that he was not present at the scene of the crime and wants to put forward an alibi defence. While by no means certain that the client's defence is false, counsel is convinced that a defence of consent stands a much better chance of success. Against the client's express instructions, counsel cross-examines the complainant on the issue of consent, and in doing so effectively concedes that the client participated in sexual activities with the complainant. Two alibi witnesses identified by the client are not called to the stand, nor does the client testify on his own behalf. On this scenario, the reasoning of G. Arthur Martin largely supports counsel's decisions. The one possible exception would be the failure to call the client as a witness, and yet counsel's earlier decisions probably forced the client to "agree" not to testify. In contrast, the principles set out in *Swain* suggest that overriding the client's express instructions on this important aspect of the defence is unethical, even though defence counsel has the best interests of the client at heart.[51]

**Example:** Defence counsel undertakes to have his client visit a psychiatrist and to provide the resulting report to the Crown. He makes the undertaking in exchange for the Crown's consent to bail, and because he believes the psychiatric assessment will aid in preparing the defence. Absent the client's informed consent, however, this course of action clashes with the *Swain* principles.[52]

The leading Canadian case that elucidates principles articulated in *Swain* to support a less paternalistic model of decision making author-

---

50    *Ibid.*
51    The facts for this scenario are taken largely from the case of *R. v. McLoughlin*, [1985] 1 N.Z.L.R. 106 (C.A.) [*McLoughlin*]. The court in that case held that "counsel most certainly had no right to disregard [the client's] instructions. Following any advice he thought proper to give to his client, his duty was either to act on the instructions he then received or to withdraw from the case." *McLoughlin* is discussed farther below at notes 102 and 129 and accompanying text.
52    See *R. v. L.(C.K.)* (1987), 39 C.C.C. (3d) 476 (Ont. Dist. Ct.), where defence counsel gave the undertaking without first obtaining instructions. The court subsequently held that privilege was not waived, and the psychiatric report need not be disclosed.

ity is *R. v. Delisle*,[53] the facts of which are set out in more detail else-where.[54] Suffice it here to say that defence counsel refused to investigate or call as a witness an individual that the accused regarded as the true culprit in a serious assault, and also declined to call the accused in his own defence. Simply put, the lawyer did not believe his client, and conducted the case accordingly, albeit contrary to the client's instructions. The accused was convicted.

On appeal, information from the individual allegedly responsible for the assault was introduced as fresh evidence. Writing for a unanimous court, Mr. Justice Proulx agreed with the sentiments of Martin that a lawyer is not the mere mouthpiece of the client.[55] On the other hand, Proulx J.A. was unprepared to grant the lawyer absolute control over the conduct of the defence regardless of the client's instructions. To the contrary, he held that a lawyer, while under a duty to provide competent advice, including a duty to attempt to dissuade a client from making a rash decision, must not disregard the client's final instructions.[56] Where the disagreement is particularly fundamental, the proper response is for the lawyer to withdraw from the case, not to ignore the client's wishes and proceed as the lawyer thinks best.[57] Accordingly, the appeal was allowed on the grounds that trial counsel failed to provide effective legal assistance, to the appellant's prejudice, by neglecting to investigate the potential witness and refusing to call the client to the stand.[58]

A distinct yet related area of the case law that deserves mention concerns the ability of a client to sue a lawyer for negligence in the conduct of a criminal defence. In Canada, our courts have never endorsed the rule of absolute immunity set out in *Rondel v. Worsley*.[59]

---

53   (1999), 133 C.C.C. (3d) 541 (Que. C.A.) [*Delisle*]. See also R. v. *Taylor* (1992), 77 C.C.C. (3d) 551 at 567 (Ont. C.A.).

54   See section F(1), "The Basic Presumption Against Judging the Client's Culpability," in chapter 1.

55   *Delisle*, above note 53 at 555.

56   *Ibid*. Further support for the notion that a client's instructions should be followed, in lieu of which withdrawal is the only option, is found in R. v. *Brigham* (1992), 79 C.C.C. (3d) 365 at 380–381 (Que. C.A.) [*Brigham*], although that case dealt with the decision of the accused whether to testify.

57   *Delisle*, above note 53 at 555.

58   *Ibid*. at 557.

59   Above note 27. Leading decisions include *Demarco v. Ungaro* (1979), 21 O.R. (2d) 673 (H.C.J.) [*Demarco*]; and *Wernikowski v. Kirkland, Murphy & Ain* (1999), 141 C.C.C. (3d) 403 (Ont. C.A.), leave to appeal to S.C.C refused (2000), 264 N.R. 196n (S.C.C.). Other cases of interest, involving attacks on the conduct of counsel in criminal or quasi-criminal proceedings, include *Wenn*,

As well, in *Arthur JS Hall & Co.* v. *Simons*,[60] the House of Lords recently reconsidered the rule granting barristers immunity from negligence suits, and it concluded that the *ratio* in *Rondel* v. *Worsley* is no longer supportable on policy grounds and must be overturned. A dissenting minority would have retained the rule of immunity in cases involving the conduct of a criminal trial, on the ground that such an attack on the barrister's performance should properly come in the criminal appeal process. But the notion that barristers are not bound to follow the instructions of their clients in conducting a trial, in deference to their higher duty to the court and the administration of justice, so prevalent in *Rondel* v. *Worsley*, was not emphasized in any of the law lords' reasons in *Arthur JS Hall*. This change in the law in England and Wales certainly undercuts the broad rationale for the lawyer-control model that Martin extracted from *Rondel* v. *Worsley*.

Of course, even before the decision in *Arthur JS Hall*, criminal counsel in Canada could be, and occasionally were, sued for negligence. There is also no reason why a lawsuit could not be brought for breach of contract or fiduciary duty in relation to the conduct of a defence at trial. Granted, there are significant potential obstacles on the plaintiff's road to success, including a reluctance of the courts to find a lawyer liable for "a mere error in judgment."[61] Nonetheless, the existence of a standard of negligence against which the conduct of a trial lawyer can be measured is good support for the argument that ethical rules should not accord a lawyer absolute power over most decisions made in the course of conducting the defence.

## 4)   The Decision in *R.* v. *B.(G.D.)*

The latest judicial contribution to the debate over counsel's decision making authority comes from the Supreme Court of Canada, in the intriguing case of *R.* v. *B.(G.D.)*.[62] The appellant had been charged with committing sexual and indecent assaults upon his adopted daughter, and prior to the trial he provided his lawyer with a taped recording of

---

above note 46; *Blackburn* v. *Lapkin* (1996), 28 O.R. (3d) 292 (Gen. Div.) [*Blackburn*]; *Boudreau* v. *Benaiah* (1998), 37 O.R. (3d) 686 (Gen. Div.), appeal allowed in part (2000), 46 O.R. (3d) 737 (C.A.); *Bartolovic* v. *Bennet*, [1996] O.J. No. 961 (Gen. Div.) (QL); and *Anastasakos* v. *Allen* (1996), 16 O.T.C. 413 (Ont. Gen. Div.).

60   [2000] 3 All E.R. 673 (H.L.).

61   See for example, *Demarco*, above note 29 at 693; *Blackburn*, above note 58 at 309; and *Bartolovic*, above note 59 at para. 11.

62   (2000), 143 C.C.C. (3d) 289 (S.C.C.) [*B.(G.D.)*].

the complainant in which she denied the allegations during a conversation with her mother (the appellant's wife). However, for tactical reasons counsel decided not to play the tape in cross-examining the complainant. The appellant was convicted on two of three counts, and on appeal he alleged that the failure to utilize the tape was made contrary to his express instructions and represented a denial of the effective assistance of counsel and a miscarriage of justice.

In dismissing the appeal, Mr. Justice Major made several points that relate to our discussion. First, he noted that the constitutional standard for effective assistance from counsel is not the exact equivalent of a lawyer's ethical obligations. Rather, "the question of the competence of counsel is usually a matter of professional ethics and is not a question for the appellate courts to consider."[63] In particular, if the client suffers no prejudice, the performance of counsel becomes irrelevant on appeal, and any concerns are left to the profession's self-governing body.[64] Second, Mr. Justice Major felt that the lawyer's decision not to use the tape was reasonably made. In fact, he accepted that counsel had probably taken the best course of action in all the circumstances, because aspects of the tape potentially undermined the credibility of the appellant's wife, who was the key defence witness, and the complainant's denial of abuse was arguably coerced.[65]

Third, the appellant posited that, even if the decision of trial counsel was entirely reasonable, there was nonetheless an obligation to inform the appellant of the decision not to use the tape and accord the appellant an opportunity to take part in the decision. However, Mr. Justice Major expressly refused to determine whether defence counsel had such a duty.[66] Instead, the finding that the lawyer's decision was tactically sound meant that the effective assistance of counsel was not denied. If any issue regarding the need to obtain the client's consent arose, it properly fell within the realm of professional conduct governed by the Law Society of Alberta based on prevailing ethical standards.[67] In this respect, and as an interesting aside, Alberta is one of the few jurisdictions where the governing body has expressly adopted an ethical standard contrary to Martin's lawyer-control model.[68] Yet the Supreme Court made no reference to the particular Alberta rule on

---

63    *Ibid.* at 292 & 298.

64    Ibid. at 298.

65    *Ibid.* at 298–99. The basis for this decision is elaborated upon at 300–01, *ibid.*

66    *Ibid.* at 299.

67    *Ibid.* at 299.

68    See Alta. ch. 9, comm. G.1.

point, nor did the Court make any comment regarding Martin's philosophy on the subject. These silences perhaps make sense, given that the applicable Alberta ethical rules are very different from Martin's model, and that the issue of the appropriate ethical standard is said by the Court to be distinct from the constitutional question as to whether trial counsel acted effectively.

While the decision in *R. v. B.(G.D.)* professes that ethical issues are often distinct from effective assistance from counsel claims, Mr. Justice Major went on to observe that

> [w]here, in the course of a trial, counsel makes a decision in good faith and in the best interests of his client, a court should not look behind it save only to prevent a miscarriage of justice. *While it is not the case that defence lawyers must always obtain express approval for each and every decision made by them in relation to the conduct of the defence, there are decisions such as whether or not to plead guilty, or whether or not to testify that defence counsel are ethically bound to discuss with the client and regarding which they must obtain instructions.* The failure to do so may in some circumstances raise questions of procedural fairness and the reliability of the result leading to a miscarriage of justice.
>
> On the facts of this case, I conclude that counsel had the carriage of the defence and the implied authority to make tactical decisions, as the ones made here, in the best interests of the client. In any event, the failure to obtain specific instructions did not affect the outcome of the trial. There was no miscarriage of justice.[69]

Major J. thus directly comments upon the substance of a lawyer's ethical obligations. At the same time, however, he deftly skirts the issue as to whether or not, on the facts, the trial lawyer knowingly overrode the client's wishes regarding the conduct of the defence. He did note, however, that in the proceedings below a specially appointed commission of inquiry concluded that "counsel was evasive in communicating his decision to the appellant."[70] In particular, the Alberta Court of Appeal had noted, based on the commissioner's report, that "[a]s to whether trial counsel clearly advised his client before trial that he would not use the tape, trial counsel testified that each time the matter came up he expressed no great enthusiasm for the evidence, but that it may well be that he had, at the opening of the trial, never quite said explicitly that

---

69   *B.(G.D.)*, above note 62 at 299 (emphasis added).
70   *Ibid.* at 299.

he would not introduce it."[71] It also appears that, based on the penultimate sentence set out in the lengthy quotation above, the Supreme Court accepted that counsel did not have "specific instructions" from the client that the tape not be used.[72]

# D. RE-EVALUATING THE TRADITIONAL LAWYER-CONTROL APPROACH

Given that the conventional lawyer-control model, as described by G. Arthur Martin, holds considerable sway within the culture of Canadian criminal lawyers, it is worth examining the underlying justifications for this approach. In doing so, one can identify ways in which Martin's views can be substantially modified in order to fashion a contemporary model of Canadian criminal lawyering.

## 1) Justifications for the Traditional Lawyer-control Approach

Numerous arguments have been put forth to justify allocating an untrammelled decision making power to the lawyer on most strategic and tactical matters involving the conduct of the defence. First, it is sometimes said that the lawyer's experience and learning in the complexities of the law and the procedures of a criminal trial are all but incomprehensible to the average accused person, at least absent an impractical amount of study and learning.[73] Allowing a lawyer the freedom to conduct the case as he or she thinks fit results in a better defence and promotes a fair and just result.[74] Second, the point is made that decisions must frequently be made on the spur of the moment during a trial, without time for the niceties of consultation with the client.[75] Counsel is well equipped to make such snap decisions, yet his or her performance will be hampered if the client is constantly engaged in second-guessing. Third, some contend that the lawyer is more objec-

---

71   *R. v. B.(G.D.)* (1999), 133 C.C.C. (3d) 309 at 319 (Alta. C.A.).

72   To the same effect, see also the discussion in *B.(G.D.)*, above note 62 at 301–02.

73   See, for example, ABA Annotated Model Rule 1.2, Legal Background (Relationship to Agency Principles); and ABA Defense Standard 4-5.2, Commentary.

74   See for example, *Rondel*, above note 27 at 1028 (per Lord Pearce); and *Stewart*, above note 46 at 83.

75   See, for example, *Stewart*, above note 46 at 87.

tive and less emotionally involved than the client regarding the outcome of the matter, and hence is better able to arrive at the best decision respecting the means of conducting the case. Fourth, it is said that carrying out an unsound tactical or strategic course of action at the client's insistence may leave the lawyer open to a later claim in negligence[76] or provide the basis for an allegation of ineffective assistance from counsel on appeal.[77] Fifth, acceding to the client's wishes might be thought to prolong the trial process unnecessarily, and hence prove costly and time-consuming, to the detriment of the administration of justice.[78] Sixth, the lawyer owes duties to the administration of justice that prohibit the application of certain means in the conduct of the case, despite the instructions of the client to the contrary. For instance, the lawyer cannot accept a client's direction to mislead the court.

Finally, under the lawyer-control model, the lawyer is still obligated to provide the client with thorough advice, provided that circumstances reasonably permit the time to do so.[79] Accordingly, although the lawyer holds the ultimate decision making authority, it would be wrong to suggest that the client's views are totally ignored or that the client is being kept in the dark regarding developments. It is also important to remember that timely and clear communication with the client, and a real respect for the client's opinion, can minimize the possibility of substantial disagreement concerning the conduct of the defence.[80] Consider, for instance, the circumstances in *R. v. B.(G.D.)*. The Supreme Court of Canada determined that trial counsel's conduct was strategically sound. Remarkably, however, these ostensibly sound reasons were not communicated to the client. In fact, it appears that the client was never actually told that the tape would not be used in the conduct of the defence. If one accepts that trial counsel's preferred course of action regarding the tape was justified, a candid discussion

---

76  See, for example, *Rondel*, above note 27 at 1013 (per Lord Morris); and Hutchinson, above note 41 at 94.

77  A slightly similar way of making the same argument is to say that the lawyer must never act below the accepted standard of competence in conducting a defence, regardless of whether he or she is instructed to do so by the client: see MacKenzie, above note 41 at §4.11 (4–23), and the discussion below in section I, "A Client's Insistence that the Lawyer Act 'Incompetently,'" in this chapter.

78  See, for example, *Rondel*, above note 27 at 1028 (per Lord Pearce).

79  See, for example, "Panel Discussion: Problems in Advocacy and Ethics," above note 21 at 284 (G. Martin).

80  See, for example, *Brigham*, above note 56 at 380; and G. Bisharat, "Pursuing a Questionable Suppression Motion" in R. Uphoff, ed., *Ethical Problems Facing the Criminal Defense Lawyer: Practical Answers to Tough Questions* (Chicago: American Bar Association, 1995) c. 5 at 63.

with the client on the point presumably stood an excellent chance of yielding firm instructions not to use the recording. Hypothetically, it was also possible that by fully discussing this important aspect of the case with the client, and hearing the client's opinion, trial counsel would have amended his opinion, concluding that the client's instructions to use the tape were best suited to a favourable resolution of the case.

## 2)  Questioning the Justifications

Many of the various concerns used to justify a lawyer-control model are far from specious, in particular the need for competent and ethical conduct by the lawyer. However, by and large these concerns can be accommodated without ascribing final decision making power to the lawyer in the realm of strategy and tactics. Moreover, some of the justifications for a lawyer-control model are simply unconvincing. In particular, the notion that a client can never hope to understand the basic process of a criminal matter is extremely suspect. It is more likely that some lawyers do not take the proper time to explain the workings of the system, or care little for the client's views in any event. Most important, if we take seriously the principles of individual autonomy and dignity articulated in *R. v. Swain*, affording the client considerable decision making power is paramount.[81] After all, it is the client who risks stigma and punishment if he or she is convicted following the trial. To withhold decision making authority from the client thus represents misguided paternalism, and for all the proffered justifications may, more than anything else, primarily reflect the relative powerlessness of most criminal accused.

There are other reasons to look askance at the traditional lawyer-control model. Consider, for instance, that where the lawyer takes positive action in conducting a defence contrary to the client's instructions, the result may be to disclose confidential information. Calling a witness against the client's wishes, where the existence of the witness comes to the lawyer's attention only because of the professional relationship, arguably breaches the duty of confidentiality. Cross-examination of a Crown witness on a sensitive matter, contrary to the client's wishes, will often have the same effect. There is no recognized exception to the rule of confidentiality that applies merely because the lawyer in good faith believes that disclosure is in the best

---

81    This position is strongly argued by M. Freedman, *Understanding Lawyers' Ethics* (New York: Matthew Bender, 1990) in chapter 3.

interests of the client.[82] Accordingly, the duty of confidentiality militates against a bold lawyer-control model of representation.

Additionally, it must be recalled that a client may have broad and diverse objectives that go beyond simply avoiding a conviction or minimizing a court-imposed punishment. Maybe the client has political aims that would benefit from a full-blown trial and is not interested in bringing a pre-trial motion that might circumvent the entire process. Or perhaps the client desires to bring a non-frivolous pre-trial motion to exclude evidence, partly as a means of exposing police misconduct, even though the chances of success are marginal. Consider also the client who refuses to call a helpful witness because he or she wishes to spare that individual's privacy, or declines to attack a third party as a possible culprit out of a sense of loyalty to that person. From the lawyer's perspective, implementing these objectives may be misguided or harm the prospects of an acquittal. Yet are such goals improper or totally irrelevant to the representation? Not, we believe, if one takes the autonomy and dignity of the client seriously.

## 3) Updating the Traditional Approach: Increasing Client Involvement

We believe that the traditional lawyer-control model should be substantially updated to reflect the fiduciary nature of the professional relationship and to give greater credence to the client's free will and decision making abilities. A more sophisticated and finely nuanced approach is required, what could be called a cooperative model.[83] A central feature of this model demands the unimpeded exchange of information between client and lawyer, and a mutual trust and a joint responsibility for a great deal of the decision making. The lawyer, having arrived at a complete understanding of the facts and law, must provide the client with competent advice. Counsel can recommend that the client make a particular decision, provided that he or she does not overwhelm the client's freedom of choice. Approaching decision making in this manner empowers the autonomy and dignity of both client

---

82   See chapter 5.
83   See, for example, C.W. Wolfram, *Modern Legal Ethics* (St. Paul: West, 1986) at 156; and S. Ross, *Ethics in Law: Lawyers' Responsibility and Accountability in Australia*, 2d ed. (Sydney: Butterworths, 1998) at 197.

and lawyer, and promotes a full and free exchange of information and dialogue that leads to decisions most favourable to the client's goals.[84]

Of course, no amount of good-faith communication and comprehensive preparation by the lawyer can avoid the occasional dispute with a client as to the proper conduct of a defence. Where the disagreement is intractable, the following broad guidelines may be helpful:

1. The lawyer can never accept instructions that require illegal or unethical action.[85]

2. The client has the ability to terminate the retainer at any time, and if this step is taken the lawyer has no choice but to get off the record.[86]

3. Conversely, where the relationship has suffered a complete breakdown by reason of the disagreement, the lawyer may be permitted or forced to withdraw from the representation.[87] Yet withdrawal should not be utilized as an easy method of avoiding compliance with the client's instructions, especially where the trial is imminent or ongoing.[88] Using the threat of withdrawal to browbeat the client into submission, thus effecting a desired change in the instructions, is also improper.

4. If the relationship is not irreparably ruptured by reason of the dispute, the client should make the final determination regarding the course of action to be taken. That is to say, in the ordinary course the lawyer should carry out any non-frivolous and otherwise ethical course of action that is desired by the client.

Adopting a cooperative model is not always easy. Lawyers may have difficulty communicating technical information to clients in simple, easily understood language. The lawyer's patience may be severely tested on occasion. Lawyers must also resist succumbing to the temptation to frame issues and disclose information in a way that unfairly presents their preferred option in the best light. Problems can also arise where a client feels overwhelmed by the predicament of criminal

---

84   See D. Rosenthal, *Lawyer and Client: Who's in Charge?* (New York: Russell Sage Foundation, 1974) c. 2, reporting on a study that suggests a cooperative model is more likely to lead to a good outcome in personal-injury cases.

85   This restriction is discussed further in section H, "Instructions that Require Unethical Conduct from the Lawyer," in this chapter.

86   See also section C, "Rules of the Court," in chapter 11.

87   See, for example, *Sherman*, above note 46 at 536. See also the discussion in section G, "Discretionary Withdrawal by the Lawyer," in chapter 11.

88   See also the discussion in section I(3), "Decision Making That Accommodates Ethical and Constitutional Concerns," in this chapter.

charges and seeks comfort by abdicating responsibility for making important decisions. Similarly, a client may view the lawyer as expert and experienced and downplay his or her own opinions as a result. Furthermore, it has been pointed out that the cooperative model is more costly and time-consuming than other approaches to decision making, especially compared to a lawyer-control model that arguably requires less communication between client and lawyer.[89] Finally, the cooperative model provides less of a check against clients carrying out immoral, albeit legal, actions that a lawyer might justifiably refuse to pursue under a lawyer-control approach.

These potential difficulties cannot be ignored. Yet we believe that a cooperative model that assigns final decision making authority to the client in most instances offers the best allocation of responsibility in the professional relationship. The remainder of this chapter focuses in more detail upon particular problems associated with the traditional lawyer-control model, and fleshes out how the cooperative approach might operate in particular instances.

## E.  INFORMING AND ADVISING THE CLIENT

A cooperative model of lawyering demands a high level of trust and communication between client and counsel. Such an approach dovetails neatly into the lawyer's general duty to keep the client informed and advised as to all matters relevant to the representation, and to do so promptly.[90] This duty encompasses not merely the provision of information necessary to make particular decisions but also alerting the client to the basic fact that a decision must be made. Moreover, as part of the duty to inform and advise, a lawyer should respond in a timely and complete manner to any request from the client for information concerning the case. Naturally, a key rationale for the obligation to keep the client informed and advised is that the client can thereby effectively make decisions concerning the conduct of the defence. Absent proper information and advice from the lawyer, the client's ability to make decisions will be seriously hampered. As a com-

---

89   See Ross, above note 83 at 202.

90   See, for example, CBA Code ch. III. An egregious example of counsel failing to keep the client informed occurred in *R. v. Watkins* (2000), 149 C.C.C. (3d) 279 (Ont. C.A.), where the client was not told that the counsel's associate would appear at the sentencing hearing (by reason of the original counsel's scheduling problems).

ment to ABA Model Rule 1.4 states: "The client should have sufficient information to participate intelligently in decisions concerning the objectives of the representation and the means by which they are to be pursued, to the extent the client is willing and able to do so."[91]

The lawyer's advice will usually include the exercise of persuasion based on competent strategic/tactical judgment. But more than this, we believe that a lawyer is permitted to bring his or her personal morality to bear in offering advice to the client. By doing so, the lawyer may alert the client to factors that had not previously been considered. Providing the lawyer with such latitude, albeit short of allowing veto power over the client's final decision, recognizes that lawyers are human beings with individual conceptions of good. In this respect, the lawyer's role in the decision making process is not amoral or concerned solely with the best interests of the client.

The provision of advice necessary to meet a lawyer's ethical obligations varies with a number of factors. In some instances, the sophistication and experience of a client may permit fairly brief contact for the purpose of providing advice. Conversely, a client who is entirely new to the legal system, suffers from a mental impairment or has difficulty speaking the lawyer's language may require much more attention and effort from the lawyer in order to meet this ethical imperative. The time available for consultation is also a factor to consider, although the lawyer should not place the client in a pressure situation by neglecting to discuss an important issue until the eleventh hour. Other factors that bear on the manner in which advice is given include the importance of the decision to the outcome of the case and the client's express or implied objectives in the litigation.

## 1) A Possible Exception: Keeping Information from a Client

An issue sometimes arises concerning the propriety of intentionally keeping relevant information from the client. As a general principle, withholding relevant information breaches the duty to keep the client informed and is thus improper.[92] However, in rare instances such action is acceptable, for instance, where the court orders counsel not to make disclosure to the client. It may also be that the lawyer harbours a legitimate and reasonable fear that disclosure to the client will lead to

---

91   ABA Model Rule 1.4, comm. 1.

92   See for example, CBA Code ch. II, comm. 7(a), stating that the failure to keep the client reasonably informed falls short of a competent quality of service.

the serious bodily harm of a third party or cause substantial harm to the client.[93] In these latter circumstances, the lawyer may be justified in at least delaying release of the information to the client.[94] Furthermore, where a lawyer has gained confidential information from one client, and that information is relevant to a legal matter involving another client, disclosure to the latter client is prohibited (and the lawyer is faced with a conflict-of-interest problem).[95]

# F.  DECISIONS FUNDAMENTAL TO THE CONDUCT OF THE DEFENCE

Many commentators and some ethical codes reserve for the client the ultimate say regarding decisions on matters seen to be particularly fundamental to the conduct of the defence, most notably the decisions how to plead and whether to testify. A representative list of such fundamental matters is set out in ABA Defense Standard 4-5.2(a).[96] In Canada, those rules of professional conduct that follow the lead of the CBA Code stipulate that a lawyer must leave the final decision whether to plead guilty to the client[97] yet do not mention any other decisions as falling within the sole authority of the client. In England and Wales, the Code of Conduct of the Bar provides that the decisions regarding the plea and whether to testify belong to the client.[98] For those who would afford the client final decision making authority on most aspects of the representation, leaving so-called fundamental decisions to the client is simply an application of the general principle. But for writers, judges, and practitioners who believe that the lawyer should have free rein in conducting many aspects of the defence, these select fundamental decisions are, by their very nature, so important that an excep-

---

93 This justification is analogous to the future-harm exception to the duty of confidentiality, discussed in section G, "Future Harm or Public Safety," in chapter 5.

94 See ABA Model Rule 1.4, comm. 4; Third Restatement §20, comm. "b"; §24, comm. "c"; and §46, comm. "c."

95 Regarding confidential information and conflict of interest, see chapters 4 & 6.

96 In the United States, see also the Third Restatement §22(1); and ABA Model Rule 1.2(a).

97 See, for example, CBA Code ch. IX, comm. 12, including the footnote reference.

98 See *Bar Code of Conduct*, above note 17, Annex "H" (Written Standards for the Conduct of Professional Work, Standards Applicable to Criminal Cases) at §12.3 (plea) & §12.5 (testifying).

tion to the usual principle of lawyer-control must be made.[99] On this latter view, justification for giving the client decision making authority is sometimes said to flow from the fact that an accused has a constitutional right to choose how to conduct these particular aspects of the defence. Moreover, the law may require that a decision be made by the client in order to have effect, the best example being the decision whether to plead guilty.[100] It has also been pointed out that society has an interest in ensuring a degree of personal confrontation between the accused and the state at certain key junctures in the criminal trial process, an interest that is bolstered by reserving decision making power to the client.[101]

Given that decisions regarding the plea and whether to testify usually play a central role in the conduct and resolution of a criminal case, we wholeheartedly agree that the client is best suited to make the final call. Yet, consistent with our general cooperative view of decision making, we do not restrict the client's power to decide to these limited areas. Nor do we agree that these specific decisions will always be more "fundamental" than any others in a criminal case. In fact, isolating those decisions that are fundamental to the representation is notoriously difficult. Consider, for instance, that proponents of the lawyer-control model have not traditionally viewed the calling of defence witnesses (other than the accused) and the scope of cross-examination as falling within the client's sole power to decide. Yet calling a particular witness or pursuing a line of inquiry in cross-examination can be absolutely crucial to the prospects of success for a particular defence. It is certainly easy to envision circumstances where impeding the defence in either respect would constitute a constitutional violation.[102]

It may also transpire that the refusal to follow a client's instructions respecting an area not traditionally seen as "fundamental" will substantially affect a decision that falls within the realm of the client's

---

99   See, for example, ABA Defense Standard 4-5.2 (commentary on "Allocation of Decision-making Power"); Hutchinson, above note 41 at 94; and R. Fry, "Calling Defense Witnesses: Whose Case is This Anyway?" in Uphoff, above note 80, c. 6 at 77.

100  See section C, "Constitutional and Other Legal Facets of a Guilty Plea," in chapter 8.

101  This point is made in the Third Restatement §22, comm. "b."

102  See, for example, R. v. Osolin (1993), 86 C.C.C. (3d) 481 at 516–18 (S.C.C.) (importance of cross-examination as a forensic tool); R. v. Michelin (1999), 62 C.R.R. (2d) 349 (Ont. Gen. Div.) (failure to call witnesses undermines the defence).

absolute decision making power. For instance, a refusal to bring a pre-trial motion might necessarily involve preventing the client from testifying on such a motion. Or assume that the client wishes to advance an alibi defence but does not want to testify. If the lawyer refuses to call the witness, one could argue that the client has been forced into the stand, having no other means of advancing the defence. Still with the alibi example, suppose that the client wants to testify. The lawyer could effectively preclude the client from doing so by cross-examining Crown witnesses in a manner that concedes the client's presence during the incident in question.[103] In sum, many decisions made concerning the conduct of a trial are interrelated. It is not always easy to isolate the client's decision regarding how to plead or whether to testify from the lawyer's decisions pertaining to other aspects of the litigation.

Given the difficulty in justifying the very narrow ambit of fundamental decisions that the traditional lawyer-control model affords the client, it is perhaps advisable to widen the scope of the client's powers and to place any decision that has a substantial impact on the outcome of the case within his or her control.[104] In determining whether a decision will have a substantial impact, one might look to the potential influence upon the outcome regarding guilt or sentencing given the broad context of the case, the importance ascribed by the client to the decision, whether the lawyer's interests conflict with those of the client, whether reasonable persons would disagree as to how the decision should be made, and whether the trial process can feasibly be halted to permit the client to participate in making the decision.[105] Better yet, however, an endorsement of the cooperative model would alleviate the problem altogether, giving the client the final say on most matters connected with the case.

---

103 This tactic was employed in *McLoughlin*, above note 51, with just such an impact on the client's ability to testify.

104 The Third Restatement §22(1) takes a related approach, in so far as authority is ordinarily irrevocably reserved to the client regarding enumerated fundamental *and comparable* decisions (*i.e.*, there is no closed set of fundamental matters, in contrast to ABA Defense Standard 4-5.2(a)).

105 These factors are borrowed almost verbatim from the Third Restatement §22, comm. "e."

# G. DECISIONS THAT MUST BE MADE QUICKLY DURING THE COURSE OF A TRIAL

Once a trial proceeding is under way, lawyers are required to make a bevy of decisions in conducting the defence. Some decisions are undeniably crucial to the outcome of the case, while others may be less significant. The need to make certain decisions can be predicted far in advance, yet many issues arise on the spur of the moment, without warning, and require an immediate response. The criminal justice system insists upon a degree of consistent momentum during the trial process. If the proceedings could be adjourned every time an action had to be taken, for the purpose of making a decision with the client's considered input, the process would bog down and the quality of justice would suffer. Accordingly, it makes good sense for the lawyer to possess an implied authority to render those decisions that must be made immediately in response to sudden developments, and without time for consultation.[106] A perfect example is an objection to a question posed by Crown counsel.

This approach to decision making does not mean that a lawyer must keep the client in the dark regarding events occurring at trial. The trial process, and the role to be played by client and lawyer, should be explained to the client well in advance. Moreover, while a lawyer will likely not be able to predict every instance where an immediate decision is required, he or she can generally explain the types of decision that may be made during the trial. It is certainly possible and appropriate to obtain advance instructions or input from the client with respect to some such matters. It is also worth emphasizing that a decision on an absolutely crucial matter is sometimes suddenly required in a manner that could not be predicted in advance. Courts will generally recognize that the defence could not have anticipated the issue arising, and will readily permit an adjournment for the purpose of consultation between client and counsel. A lawyer should therefore request an adjournment for this purpose whenever a decision legitimately needs the client's informed input.[107]

---

106  It has been suggested that such decisions are within the sole power of the lawyer to make, at least to the extent that the trial process does not permit interruption for the purpose of consultation between client and lawyer, and thus these decisions can never be left to the client: (see Third Restatement §23, comm. "d".

107  See, for example, *Joanisse*, above note 47 at 73–74 (per Doherty J.A. in dissent).

# H. INSTRUCTIONS THAT REQUIRE UNETHICAL CONDUCT FROM THE LAWYER

A lawyer cannot take on a retainer where its terms involve undertaking unethical conduct, which includes any action that facilitates an illegality.[108] In the same fashion, a lawyer who has properly accepted a retainer, having no inkling that improper conduct will be requested, cannot carry out subsequently revealed instructions that require a breach of the rules of professional conduct.[109] Thus, a lawyer cannot accede to a client's insistence that a witness be called for the purpose of giving false exculpatory testimony.[110] There is also a strong argument that the lawyer must reject instructions that involve taking frivolous action, as discussed below.[111] It may also be necessary to undertake investigation or review information provided by the client prior to deciding whether to implement questionable instructions. This sort of investigation or review is definitely advisable where the lawyer strongly suspects that the information is inaccurate and knowledge of the inaccuracy would render the requested conduct unethical.[112]

If a client refuses to alter or revoke instructions that demand unethical conduct on the part of the lawyer, the lawyer faces a dilemma. On the one hand, he or she is normally obligated to abide by the client's wishes and owes the client a general duty of loyalty. On the other hand, there exists a duty to the profession and the administration of justice, in essence a duty to society at large, not to act unethically. What can the lawyer do? Disclosing the improper instructions to the court or Crown counsel is usually not an option, because the duty of confidentiality will be breached.[113] Continuing on with the retainer, and conducting the defence in a manner that rejects the problematic instructions, is no better as a solution. Such a course of action has the advantage of avoiding the unethical conduct yet works to undermine

---

108 See the discussion in section B, "Instances Where Counsel Cannot Act," in chapter 2.

109 See, for example, N.B. Part C, r. 7; Alta. ch. 9, r. 10; and Third Restatement §23.

110 The question as to how a lawyer should react where the *client* insists on testifying falsely is more difficult, and forms the subject matter of chapter 7.

111 See section J, "Frivolous Tactics," in this chapter.

112 See, for example, Alta. ch. 9 comm. 2.

113 Accommodating the duty of confidentiality with the need not to mislead the court is discussed in section K, "Duty Not to Mislead the Court," in chapter 5; section F(4)(f), "Disclosure of the Intended Perjury," in chapter 7; and section M, "Confidentiality," in chapter 11.

the client's decision making authority and will often cause a total breakdown in the client-lawyer relationship. Therefore, the only realistic option is probably to withdraw from the representation, although this response to the problem is not always ideal. The various difficulties facing counsel whose client steadfastly insists that unethical conduct be carried out are discussed in detail in the chapter on client perjury.[114]

# I.   A CLIENT'S INSISTENCE THAT THE LAWYER ACT "INCOMPETENTLY"

It may be that the client insists on mounting a defence in a manner that an objective and adequately informed person would view as rash or unreasonable. In extreme cases, were the lawyer to pursue such a course of action of his or her own accord, an appeal court might conclude that the client was denied the assistance of effective counsel. Is the lawyer obligated to follow ill-advised instructions that hold the potential to bring disaster for the defence (and perhaps additionally to support a successful appeal ground of ineffective assistance of counsel)?

## 1)   Competence and the Rules of Professional Conduct

Canadian rules of professional conduct invariably include reference to a lawyer's duty to provide competent service to the client.[115] For the purposes of our discussion regarding decision making, there are two primary facets to this duty. First, the lawyer must strive to maintain, on an ongoing basis, an acceptable degree of knowledge in his or her area of practice. Second, the lawyer must exercise sound judgment and skill, including adequate preparation and communication with the client, in providing representation in a particular case. The duty of competency also has other components, though slightly less important to the matter at hand. For example, a lawyer must not take on or continue with a case if he or she is not competent to provide representa-

---

114  See section F(4)(a), "Withdrawal," in chapter 7.

115  See, for example, CBA Code ch. II; Alta. ch. 2; B.C. ch. 1, r. 3(1) & 3; N.S. ch. 2 and ch. 3; N.B. Part C, r. 5 & 7; Ont. r. 2.01; Que. ss. 3.01.01, 3.02.03 & 3.03.01; and Yukon Part 1, r. 1 & 2.

tion, and should aid the client in finding alternative counsel who is competent.[116]

The rationale behind an ethical rule mandating competency is that a high quality of service best promotes the legal rights and interests of the client and, by extension, bolsters society's interest in a reliable and fair criminal justice system.[117] A competent lawyer will also find that his or her reputation benefits from providing a high quality of service, with a consequent favourable impact on the public's perception of the administration of justice.[118] Based on these justifications for a duty of competence, there is no doubt that a lawyer is ordinarily obligated, and also has a personal incentive, to conduct a defence in a manner best calculated to yield a favourable result for the client. The dilemma arises when a client desires representation of a sort that runs counter to the lawyer's competent judgment. Canadian rules of professional conduct do not provide the lawyer with guidance on this point.

## 2) The Constitutional Right to Effective Assistance of Counsel

It is well established that an accused person enjoys a constitutional right to effective assistance from counsel.[119] Accordingly, the usual assumption that an accused is bound by the acts of counsel in conducting the case (at least vis-à-vis third parties and the court) can be circumvented in some instances. The logic behind the right to effective assistance from counsel is essentially the same as the primary justification for an ethical duty of competence: the client's systemic rights, and the reliability and justness of the outcome, are best promoted by effective advocacy.[120]

The right to effective assistance from counsel is most often raised on appeal, after the accused has been convicted. The approach favoured by Canadian courts in assessing whether the right has been

---

116 See sections B, "Instances Where Counsel Cannot Act," and "Duties Arising Once a Retainer is Refused," in chapter 2.

117 See, for example, Alta. ch. 2, comm. G.1.

118 See, for example, Ont. r. 2.01(1) (commentary).

119 Leading cases establishing this right include B.(G.D.), above note 62; R. v. Toussaint (1984), 16 C.C.C. (3d) 544 (Que. C.A.); R. v. Garofoli (1988), 41 C.C.C. (3d) 97 (Ont. C.A.); Brigham, above note 56; Joanisse, above note 47; R. v. W.(W.) (1995), 100 C.C.C. (3d) 225 (Ont. C.A.); Delisle, above note 53; and R. v. Rideout (1999), 182 Nfld. & P.E.I.R. 227 (Nfld. C.A.), aff'd [2001] S.C.J. No.28 (QL).

120 See Joanisse, above note 47 at 57.

infringed is derived from the leading American case of *Strickland* v. *Washington*.[121] The *Strickland* standard will be met where the appellant establishes two things; first, that counsel's acts or omissions constituted incompetence; and second, that a miscarriage of justice resulted.[122] The Supreme Court of Canada has recently pronounced upon the nature of this two-prong test in *R. v. B.(G.D.)*, stating

> Incompetence is determined by a reasonableness standard. The analysis proceeds upon a strong presumption that counsel's conduct fell within the wide range of reasonable professional assistance. The onus is on the appellant to establish the acts or omissions of counsel that are alleged not to have been the result of reasonable professional judgment. The wisdom of hindsight has no place in this assessment.
>
> Miscarriages of justice may take many forms in this context. In some instances, counsel's performance may have resulted in procedural unfairness. In others, the reliability of the trial's result may have been compromised.
>
> In those cases where it is apparent that no prejudice has occurred, it will usually be undesirable for appellate courts to consider the performance component of the analysis. The object of an ineffectiveness claim is not to grade counsel's performance or professional conduct. The latter is left to the profession's self-governing body. If it is appropriate to dispose of an ineffectiveness claim on the ground of no prejudice having occurred, that is the course to follow (*Strickland, supra*, at p. 697).[123]

This quotation underlines the fact that, as we have already seen, ethical standards of competence do not equate exactly with the constitutional guarantee of effective assistance from counsel.[124]

---

121 466 U.S. 668 (1984). *Strickland* has been adopted by the Supreme Court of Canada in *B.(G.D.)*, above note 62 at 298. A different approach, focusing more firmly upon the impact of counsel's actions or omissions, has been used elsewhere in the Commonwealth, as described and endorsed in *Delisle*, above note 53 at 549–54.

122 *B.(G.D.)*, above note 62 at 298.

123 *B.(G.D.)*, above note 62 at 298.

124 See the discussion in section C(4), "The Decision in *R. v. B.(G.D.)*," in this chapter.

## 3) Decision-Making That Accommodates Ethical and Constitutional Concerns

Under Martin's conception of the lawyer-control model, the lawyer has total freedom (and probably an affirmative duty) to reject the client's imprudent instructions, unless of course the matter involves one of the few areas where the client is accorded the final say. In this regard, Martin said: "Counsel, however, is not bound to follow instructions which are *unreasonable* and in proper cases is entitled to refuse to act for a client who rejects his advice."[125] The cooperative approach is less susceptible to a black-and-white answer where the client's instructions are patently unreasonable. However, provided that the client has been fully and competently advised as to the pitfalls of the desired action,[126] there is a good argument that a lawyer ascribing to the cooperative method should not override the client's final decision. For one thing, it does not follow that an appeal court would find that counsel was ineffective on this scenario, at least not within the meaning of the constitutional law on this point. Rather, the client has made an informed decision, against counsel's advice, regarding the conduct of the case, and cannot be heard to complain that his or her lawyer refused to override the strenuously desired course of action.[127] On this view, the lawyer who carries out the instructions is not constitutionally ineffective. It is also worth stressing that the constitutional standard for competency, as articulated in the first prong of the *Strickland* test, is very forgiving of the lawyer's decisions. If the client's preferred course of action is not entirely unreasonable, the incompetence standard may not be met, regardless of whether the client or lawyer made the final decision.

Moreover, in the majority of instances where the client pushes the lawyer to take a course of action that may well damage the defence, the

---

125 Martin, above note 21 at 387 (speaking in the context of the decision how to plead).

126 In effect, there must have been a valid waiver of the benefits that would normally be expected to accrue under the rejected course of conduct, pursuant to the test outlined in *Korponey v. Canada (A.G.)* (1982), 65 C.C.C. (2d) 65 (S.C.C.). There may also be a positive duty to attempt to dissuade the client from embarking on a terribly unwise course of action: see *Joanisse*, above note 47, at 72.

127 See, for example, *Joanisse*, above note 47 at 77. In our view, however, there may be instances where the conviction is so suspect that a new trial is warranted, despite the fact that the client's rash conduct was responsible for the miscarriage of justice.

appeal court is not required to assess the propriety of counsel's conduct. Crucially, courts of appeal often profess to prefer resolving the issue on the basis of a lack of prejudice, where possible and appropriate to do so. The quotation set out above from *B.(G.D.)* goes so far as to require this approach.[128] In other words, if the client was destined to lose the case regardless of the impugned action, there is a good possibility that the lawyer's conduct will not lead to a finding of ineffective assistance. For instance, suppose that the client insists on a pre-trial motion that stands little chance of success. If the lawyer proceeds with the motion, the end result may be a waste of time and money but without any adverse impact on the final determination of guilt or innocence.

In some cases, however, the client's instructions may be resolutely and undeniably unreasonable *and* hold the strong potential for a conviction that could perhaps be otherwise avoided. Counsel has some leeway to withdraw from the case owing to the client's terribly ill-advised directions.[129] Naturally, withdrawal is a more realistic option when attempted well before the commencement of trial, and accordingly it is best to bring the disagreement to a head, where possible, before the retainer progresses too far. Additionally, counsel does not have the right or obligation to withdraw in every instance where a client rejects good advice.[130] Yet where the client's rejection of counsel's advice manifests or creates a total and irrevocable breakdown of the relationship, there is no choice but to withdraw (with the court's permission if required). This level of dysfunction in the professional relationship will surely be reached where the client insists on action that the lawyer reasonably believes is destined to result in a serious miscarriage of justice.

## J.  FRIVOLOUS TACTICS

Most Canadian rules of professional conduct preclude counsel from mounting a frivolous argument. The CBA Code states:

> In civil matters it is desirable that the lawyer should avoid and discourage the client from resorting to frivolous or vexatious objections

---

128  *B.(G.D.)*, above note 62 at 298.
129  See, for example, *Delisle*, above note 53 at 555.
130  Note that passages in *McLoughlin*, above note 51 at 107, and *Delisle*, above note 53 at 555, can be read to suggest the contrary.

or attempts to gain advantage from slips or oversights not going to the real merits, or tactics that will merely delay or harass the other side. Such practices can readily bring the administration of justice and the legal profession into disrepute.[131]

The Alberta Rules are more succinct, simply providing that "the lawyer must not take any step in the representation of the client that is clearly without merit."[132] Yet both the CBA and Alberta codes leave criminal counsel without much guidance. The CBA rule is expressly said to pertain to civil matters, which might appear to suggest that criminal counsel can make frivolous arguments with impunity.[133] As for the Alberta rule, one can be forgiven for asking whether criminal counsel is precluded from defending an accused person simply because the prosecution has an overwhelmingly strong case.

There are sound reasons for prohibiting frivolous claims and arguments, even in criminal matters. Such activity wastes valuable time and resources and delays the system in reaching a just and final outcome. It may also be that the client is actually harmed by the mounting of a frivolous argument. The judge and/or jury may become frustrated with defence counsel, and by association with the accused, and begin to look askance at other, entirely valid, aspects of the defence case. Putting forth a completely groundless argument may also alienate Crown counsel, with the result that he or she is less likely to exercise discretion in favour of the accused regarding other, more important, aspects of the case. Additionally, counsel who employs frivolous measures in litigation has a legitimate reason to fear a serious loss of reputation and respect from colleagues and other clients.[134]

At the same time, an accused person is presumed innocent until proven guilty and has a constitutional right to require the Crown to prove the charge beyond a reasonable doubt. In light of these fundamental constitutional rights, it is crucial that the ethical rule against frivolous arguments contain an exception permitting defence counsel to require that the Crown prove all essential elements of the offence.[135]

---

131 CBA Code ch. IX, comm. 7 (footnotes omitted). See also Man. ch. 9, comm. 7; Sask. ch. 9, comm. 7; Alta. ch. 10, r. 1 and 2; and N.S. ch. 10, comm. 10.10.

132 Alta. ch. 10, r. 1.

133 Also causing confusion is the fact that the footnote to the CBA Code rule cites fairly diverse provisions from other jurisdictions, yet for some reason does not cite the key American Rules that are directly on point, namely, ABA Model Rule 3.1 and ABA Model Code DR 7-102 (a)(1) & (2).

134 Bisharat, above note 80 at 67.

135 See *Abraham* v. *Jutsun,* [1963] 2 All E.R. 402 at 404 (C.A.), holding that defence counsel has a positive duty to make any point that he or she believes to be

To this end, in the United States the major ethical codes contain an express exception that permits the defence of the proceedings so as to require that the prosecutor establish every necessary element of the offence.[136] This sort of exception should be employed in Canada as well, and in its absence should be viewed as implied.

The exception allowing counsel for an accused to require that the prosecution prove every element of the case does not give a defence lawyer carte blanche to mount hopeless arguments. For instance, a motion to exclude evidence that is totally without merit, where the accused bears the onus of proving a *Charter* breach, goes beyond simply requiring the Crown to prove all elements of the case. The question becomes to determine whether or not an argument is frivolous. One could adopt a means test, an ends test, or a combination of the two. A means test would focus upon whether the purpose of making the argument is primarily to harass the opposing party.[137] An ends test would ask whether the argument is so lacking in merit that there is no legitimate possibility of acceptance by the court.[138] We believe that both the means and ends of the proposed action can be taken into account in determining whether an argument is frivolous. However, there may be fine line between an argument that is truly frivolous and one that has only a faint hope of succeeding, or between an argument intended primarily to harass an opponent and one that simply happens to have such an impact. On this score, the benefit of the doubt should be given to defence counsel who in good faith determines that an argument is not frivolous. After all, if counsel fails to bring an argument that turns out to have real merit, the result may be a claim of ineffective assistance of counsel.

There is some Canadian case law regarding defence counsel's professional obligations and the mounting of frivolous defences or tactics. In *R. v. Samra*, the Ontario Court of Appeal raised the hypothetical case of a lawyer who is asked by the client to make submissions that are "foolish or ill-advised or contrary to established legal principle and doctrine."[139] The court offered the view that defence counsel, not being

---

"fairly arguable" on behalf of an accused (per Lord Denning). More generally, see chapter 1, in particular section D, "The Rationale for Defending One Known to Be Guilty," in chapter 1.

136  See ABA Model Rule 3.1; and Third Restatement §110(b).

137  See the definition in ABA Model Rule 3.1, comm. 2.

138  See the discussion at Third Restatement §110, comm. "d"; and ABA Model Rule 3.1, comm. 2.

139  *Samra*, above note 43 at 158.

the alter ego of the client, is not required to make such submissions.[140] No opinion was provided as to whether counsel owes a duty to the court *not* to make such submissions, although the tenor of the judgment is inclined in this direction.

A different example is provided in *R. v. White*, where the appellant argued that trial counsel was ineffective on a diverse number of grounds and suggested that such ineffectiveness was in part illustrated by the decision to launch a hopeless interlocutory proceeding in the appeal court. In addressing this contention, the Ontario Court of Appeal stated that the application in question "had virtually no chance of succeeding" and yet was not prepared to say that counsel was unquestionably wrong to launch the proceeding. The court's primary response to the appellant's position was that, assuming for the sake of argument that counsel should not have taken the action, no prejudice to the accused occurred. But in any event, held the court:

> Branding as incompetent the bringing of an application that admittedly had previously met with judicial disapproval and had almost no chance of succeeding but that could not harm the interests of the client, flies in the face of the advocate's professional duty "fearlessly to raise every issue, advance every argument, and ask every question, however distasteful, which he thinks will help his client's case": see The Code of Professional Conduct of the Canadian Bar Association (1988), ch. IX.[141]

The decision in *White* thus suggests that counsel can properly bring an application that verges on the frivolous, and somewhat startlingly hints that he or she has a positive duty to so do.

## K. THE LAWYER IS UNABLE TO OBTAIN INSTRUCTIONS

Occasionally, a lawyer is unable to obtain instructions from the client. A prime example is the case of the client who disappears and cannot be located. A different instance of a lawyer being unable to obtain instructions occurs where the client simply refuses to provide any direction on a key aspect of the conduct of the defence. In either instance, and indeed in any case where the lawyer, despite reasonable efforts, cannot

---

140 *Ibid.*
141 *White*, above note 46 at 259.

obtain instructions, the usual response is to withdraw.[142] Certainly, continuing with the representation is not a viable option, given that the lawyer cannot properly conduct a defence absent the client's direction and input.

It may be, however, that certain uncontroversial steps can be taken without express instructions. Thus, where a client disappears, counsel may decide to order disclosure and review the materials, in the hope that the client will reappear before any substantial action is required with respect to the case. Such steps are proper only if reasonably viewed as falling within the express or implied authority provided to the lawyer by the client. It may also be that the client has a routine court appearance yet does not appear as required. Counsel may not have had sufficient time to attempt to locate the client and may be unsure as to the cause of the absence. In this situation, there is nothing wrong with informing the court of the dilemma, and asking for a short adjournment for the purpose of making inquiries.[143] If the client is located prior to recommencement of court proceedings, the lawyer's request for an adjournment has avoided a possible arrest and charge for failure to appear at court.[144]

Finally, a question arises as to what steps a lawyer should take in attempting to locate the missing client. The Alberta Code of Professional Conduct offers sage advice on this point, stating:

> Circumstances dictating the extent of a lawyer's efforts to locate a missing client include the facts giving rise to the inability to contact the client and importance of the issue on which instructions are sought. A wilful disappearance may mandate a less strenuous attempt at location, while the potential loss of a significant right or remedy will require greater efforts. In the latter case, the lawyer should take such steps as are reasonably necessary and in accordance with the lawyer's implied authority to preserve the right or remedy in the meantime. Once a matter moves beyond the implied authority of the lawyer and all attempts to locate the client have been unsuccessful,

---

142  See Alta. ch. 9, comm. 5 & 6.

143  An appearance as agent may be possible in a summary matter, or counsel may ask for the issuance of a "bench warrant with discretion" for a hybrid or straight indictable charge.

144  Contrast the suggestion made in *Lavallee* v. *Canada (A.G.)* (2000), 143 C.C.C. (3d) 187 at 198 (Alta. C.A.), to the effect that a lawyer requires express authority from the client to engage in litigation. However, the court is arguably referring to the initial *commencement* of litigation.

the lawyer may be compelled to withdraw since a representation may not be continued in the absence of proper instructions.[145]

# L.  CLIENT UNDER A DISABILITY

Representing a client whose ability to make decisions is impaired, whether by reason of age, physical disability, mental problems, substance abuse, or any other characteristic, presents unique and challenging problems. Our favoured model for decision making in the professional relationship, in which the client enjoys substantial control subject to a few carefully circumscribed limits, requires re-evaluation in circumstances where the client has difficulty participating meaningfully in the process. As a general rule, the lawyer's primary aim should be, as far as reasonably possible, to maintain a normal relationship with the client.[146] Conversely, a lawyer should not take advantage of a client's disability in order to provide a less than adequate level of service.[147] Establishing normality and ensuring competency in the professional relationship may require taking extraordinary and innovative steps that would be unnecessary, and perhaps even inappropriate, with other clients.

## 1)  Canadian Rules of Professional Conduct

The Law Societies in Ontario and Alberta are alone among Canadian governing bodies in specifically addressing the role of counsel who represents a client under a disability. Both bodies encourage lawyers to take steps reasonably calculated to foster informed decision making by the client. For instance, the Ontario Rules of Professional Conduct address the issue as follows:

> When a client's ability to make decisions is impaired because of minority, mental disability, or for some other reason, the lawyer shall, as far as reasonably possible, maintain a normal lawyer and client relationship.

*Commentary*

---

145 Alta. ch. 9, comm. 6.

146 See, for example, Ont. r. 2.02(6). This standard is set out in ABA Model Rule 1.14(a) and is elaborated upon in ABA Comm. on Ethics and Professional    .
Responsibility Formal Op. 404 (1996).

147 See, for example, *State ex rel. Nebraska State Bar Ass'n* v. *Walsh*, 294 N.W.2d 873 (Neb. 1980); and *Florida Bar* v. *Betts*, 530 So. 2d 928 (Fla. 1988).

A lawyer and client relationship presupposes that the client has the requisite mental ability to make decisions about his or her legal affairs and to give the lawyer instructions. A client's ability to make decisions, however, depends on such factors as his or her age, intelligence, experience, and mental and physical health, and on the advice, guidance, and support of others. Further, a client's ability to make decisions may change, for better or worse, over time. When a client is or comes to be under a disability that impairs his or her ability to make decisions, the impairment may be minor or it might prevent the client from having the legal capacity to give instructions or to enter into binding legal relationships. Recognizing these factors, the purpose of this rule is to direct a lawyer with a client under a disability to maintain, as far as reasonably possible, a normal lawyer and client relationship.

A lawyer with a client under a disability should appreciate that if the disability of the client is such that the client no longer has the legal capacity to manage his or her legal affairs, then the lawyer may need to take steps to have a lawfully authorized representative appointed, for example, a litigation guardian, or to obtain the assistance of the Office of the Public Guardian and Trustee or the Office of the Children's Lawyer to protect the interests of the client. In any event, the lawyer has an ethical obligation to ensure that the client's interests are not abandoned.[148]

The Alberta approach takes a slightly different tack, dividing the problem into two components.[149] First, what should the lawyer do if he or she feels that a client is not able to provide instructions because of a disability? Second, where the legal representative of an incompetent client retains a lawyer, how should instructions be obtained? Starting with the first issue, the Alberta Code of Professional Conduct properly recognizes that, once a lawyer determines that the client is unable to provide instructions owing to incapacity, the proper response is to make reasonable efforts to cause the appointment of a legal representative for the client.[150] In the meantime, prior to the appointment being made, the lawyer is directed to continue to act in the best interests of the client to the extent that instructions are implied or as otherwise permitted by law.[151] Of course, the greatest difficulty may well be in deciding whether the client lacks the capacity to instruct counsel on

---

148  Ont. r. 2.02(6) & commentary.
149  See Alta. ch. 9, r. 7 & 8.
150  See Alta. ch. 9, r. 7(a).
151  See Alta. ch. 9, r. 7(b).

the matter at hand.[152] The Code states that this determination is ultimately a legal, not an ethical, determination.[153]

Under the Alberta Code, once a legal representative has been appointed, and retains counsel in respect of a matter, there are client-lawyer duties owed to both the representative and the disabled individual.[154] The difficulties begin where the best interests of the disabled person and the representative's instructions appear to diverge. The Code provides that the lawyer must obey good-faith instructions from the representative, even if he or she feels that the instructions are not in the best interests of the disabled person.[155] However, the lawyer facing this predicament is sometimes afforded the option of withdrawing from the case.[156] Moreover, if the instructions are not provided in good faith or fall outside the representative's proper authority, and appear contrary to the best interests of the disabled person, the lawyer "must take such steps as are reasonably necessary to protect the interests" of the disabled individual.[157]

## 2) General Guidelines

A lawyer should not close his or her eyes to the possibility that a client suffers from some level of disability. Equally, however, legal counsel must not rashly conclude that a client harbours a serious inability to understand the trial process and make decisions pertaining to the case. We believe that a lawyer should generally assume that the client is competent and yet remain finely attuned to factors such as age, education, life experience, culture and psychiatric history that may point to potential problems. Guidelines in dealing with the client who exhibits a level of disability include:

1.  Undertake all reasonable efforts to ascertain the client's wishes, and otherwise carry on a functional client-lawyer relationship,

---

152 The client may have substantial competency problems in certain regards yet be reasonably able to provide instructions on the points central to the retainer: see Alta. ch. 9, comm. 7.

153 See Alta. ch. 9, comm. 7.

154 See Alta. ch. 9, r. 8 & commentary.

155 See Alta. ch. 9, r. 8(a).

156 *Ibid.*

157 Alta. ch. 9, r. 8(b). Compare the Third Restatement §24(3), which permits the lawyer to disobey the legal representative's instructions where the lawyer knows that the instructions represent or will cause a violation of the representative's legal duties to the client.

which will probably require specially tailoring communications to best overcome obstacles created by the disability.[158]

2.  Where the disability is likely temporary, as is usually the case where a client is under the influence of alcohol or other drugs, if feasible postpone taking any important steps in the representation until the problem has dissipated.

3.  If the client simply cannot provide the lawyer with any instructions on important aspects of the case, seek the appointment of a legal representative.[159] It has been suggested that withdrawal is a valid option,[160] but we are disinclined to agree, at least absent extraordinary circumstances.

4.  Where the lawyer is absolutely forced to take action, but is unable to obtain clear instructions, make the decision that counsel reasonably perceives the client would make if competent.[161]

5.  Approach the client's family and friends, as well as appropriate health-care or other professionals, in an effort to determine the preferable manner of communicating with the client and interpreting his or her wishes.

At the end of the day, there is no doubt that the lawyer may play a more active role in the relationship, and in the decision making process, in direct proportion to the client's degree of disability. Always, however, the goal is to respect the client's autonomy and dignity in making decisions, to the extent reasonably possible given the nature of the impairment.

## 3)  Fitness to Stand Trial

One of the most difficult problems in providing representation for a client who suffers from a disability arises when counsel suspects that a fitness hearing should be held, and yet the client strongly objects. Is counsel able to disclose his or her concerns to the court? Can he or she

---

158  See Third Restatement §24(1).

159  See Third Restatement §24(4).

160  See *Green* v. *Livermore* (1940), 74 C.C.C. 240 at 242 (Ont. H.C.J.).

161  Fairly recent amendments to the ABA Model Rules outline counsel's ability to act for a incompetent client, absent the appointment of a legal representative, where the health, safety, or financial interest of the client is threatened with imminent and irreparable harm: see ABA Model Rule 1.14, comm. 6. See also Third Restatement §24(2).

initiate a fitness hearing against the wishes of the client? These are provocative questions that do not yield easy answers.[162]

We can start by noting the possibility that counsel may wish to obtain the advice of a mental-health expert regarding the client's predicament, and the possibility of questioning the client's fitness to stand trial, despite the absence of instructions to do so.[163] The objection can be made that, absent the client's consent, such action violates the lawyer's duty of confidentiality. Provided that counsel has a real concern on the issue of fitness, and no more confidential information is revealed than is necessary, consultation with an expert is justified. In this regard, it is worth remembering that the expert will ordinarily be bound by the same duty of confidentiality that applies to the lawyer.[164]

It may be that, after obtaining expert advice, the lawyer feels it necessary to launch a fitness hearing and to present evidence. We believe that this drastic step may be justified in limited circumstances.[165] After all, by undertaking the conduct of the case in court, the lawyer is arguably implicitly representing that the accused is fit to stand trial. Certainly, the lawyer is proceeding on the assumption that the client is exercising some level of decision making authority within the bounds of a workable professional relationship. If the relationship is fractured by reason of real fitness issues, nonetheless proceeding to conduct the trial undermines the client's autonomy and the proper role of counsel.[166]

---

162 For an impressive discussion of the issues, see R. Uphoff, "The Decision to Challenge the Competency of a Marginally Competent Client: Defense Counsel's Unavoidably Difficult Position" in Uphoff, above note 80, c. 3.

163 See ABA Comm. on Ethics and Professional Responsibility, Informal Op. 1530 (1989).

164 Both the lawyer and expert are, however, subject to the potential application of the future harm exception, discussed in section G, "Future Harm or Public Safety," in chapter 5.

165 We have found little Canadian case law on point, but several American cases support this position, including *State* v. *Johnson*, 395 N.W.2d 176 (Wis. 1986); *United States* v. *Boigegrain*, 155 F.3d 1181 (10th Cir. 1998), cert denied 525 U.S. 1083 (1999). See also ABA Mental Health Standard 7-4.2(c), providing that the lawyer should move for an evaluation of the accused's competency to stand trial when in possession of a "good faith doubt" as to competence. If the client objects, defence counsel may ask for a fitness assessment, and in any event should disclose his or her concerns to the court and prosecution. The Third Restatement §24, comm. "d" also condones counsel taking such action, where to do so is reasonably calculated to advance the client's legitimate objective or interests as the client would define them if able to do so.

166 In *Joanisse*, above note 47 at 52–53, the comments of Mr. Justice Doherty suggest that counsel may have a professional obligation to bring a client's lack of fitness to the attention of the court. See also *Brigham*, above note 56 at 379–80.

Prior to raising the issue of fitness with the court, counsel must do his or her best to discuss the matter fully with the client. Also, counsel must recognize that there may be valid reasons why an accused does not want to pursue the fitness inquiry. There may be a legitimate wish to avoid the stigma of the assessment or an adverse finding, the hospitalization and treatment that can attend on such a process, or the delay associated with an assessment. On the other hand, however, an assessment will sometimes work to the client's immediate benefit. The process may occur quickly, and involve treatment that results in drastic improvement in the client's mental state, allowing for the instruction of counsel without any impediment.

If, after such discussions as the client's condition allows, counsel and client agree that the best course of action is to raise the competency issue, then the choice to proceed accordingly is relatively simple. If the lawyer has misgivings, but the client is adamant that he or she wishes to pursue a fitness hearing, counsel should usually abide by these instructions. In other cases, the client may be unable to express any cogent opinion. Counsel may therefore want to consider appointing a legal representative. But apart from this option, if the inability to instruct makes it impossible to conduct a defence, we feel that the lawyer has no option but to alert the court of the problem. The only other alternative might be to seek the Crown's agreement to divert the matter because of the client's condition, something that may be appropriate where the charges are minor.

**Example:** Client X is in pre-trial detention. He is likely not fit to stand trial, and counsel cannot obtain any sensible instructions. However, the charge is not serious. The Crown refuses to entertain a mental health diversion but is willing to have the client plead guilty in exchange for time served. The client is clearly in distress at the prospect of continued incarceration. Counsel doubts that the client is competent to enter a plea, and yet having thoroughly investigated the case, is convinced that the Crown will be able to obtain a conviction if the matter goes to trial. It has been argued that on these facts, counsel can represent the client on a guilty plea and not raise the competency

---

In R. v. *Gero* (2000), 147 C.C.C. (3d) 562 (Alta. C.A.) [*Gero*], defence counsel raised concerns regarding fitness despite his client's strong assertion that he wished to proceed with the trial. See also M. Martin, "Defending the Mentally Ill Client in Criminal Matters: Ethics, Advocacy, and Responsibility" (1993) 52 U.T. Fac. L. Rev. 73 at 127 ["Defending the Mentally Ill Client"].

issue in court.[167] However, if the court raises the issue of its own accord, there is little that counsel can do to prevent an inquiry.[168]

## 4)  Raising the NCR Defence

The question of overriding a competent client's decision not to raise an NCR (not criminally responsible) defence is distinct from the fitness issue, and in our view it is less problematic. The major point of differentiation derives from the fact that the client who refuses to advance an NCR defence is, in the lawyer's view, generally competent to make decisions regarding the conduct of the defence.[169] As we have seen, Canadian constitutional law accords the client total freedom in deciding whether to plead guilty.[170] The reasoning behind this conclusion seems to apply equally to the decision to put forward, or not, an NCR defence. Indeed, the Supreme Court of Canada's decision in R. v. *Swain* asserts that an accused person has a constitutional right to control the conduct of the defence in various respects, including the decision whether or not to rely upon the insanity defence.[171] It therefore seems that defence counsel must accept the client's instructions not to pursue an NCR defence, as long as the client's ability to make the decision is not impaired.[172] This conclusion does not absolve the lawyer of the duty to  inform the client fully as to the advantages and disadvantages of arguing for an NCR verdict, and of providing his or her opinion on the point.[173]

Note, however, that *Swain* also recognizes that society has an interest in preventing the conviction of people who are not truly guilty of a criminal offence by reason of incompetence.[174] The Court went so far

---

167 See Uphoff, above note 162 at 35.

168 See *Criminal Code*, R.S.C. 1985, c. C-46, s. 672.23, permitting the Crown or court to raise the fitness issue. In R. v. *Peitrangelo* (2001), 152 C.C.C. (3d) 475 (Ont. C.A.), the court held that the trial judge erred in ignoring ample evidence that the accused was unfit and refusing to hold a fitness hearing. See also *Gero*, above note 166.

169 It has been held that "an accused who has not been found unfit to stand trial must be considered capable of conducting his or her own defence": *Swain*, above note 48 at 505.

170 See the discussion in section F, "Decisions Fundamental to the Conduct of the Defence," in this chapter.

171 *Swain*, above note 48 at 505–06.

172 See "Defending the Mentally Ill Client," above note 166 at 129.

173 See *Alvord* v. *Wainwright*, 469 U.S. 956 at 961 (1984), per Justice Marshall in dissent.

174 *Swain*, above note 48 at 508–09.

in this regard as to permit the Crown to raise the NCR issue of its own accord, and against the wishes of the accused, following a guilty verdict.[175] The Court stated that "[t]he accused is not the only person who has an interest in the outcome of the trial; society itself has an interest in ensuring that the system does not incorrectly label insane people as criminals."[176] The NCR issue, on this view, can reasonably be brought to the court's attention in the post-guilt phase of a case. Can defence counsel therefore take similar action, against the client's wishes? In considering this possibility, we must remember that the prosecutor does not owe an accused the obligations of loyalty inherent in a client-lawyer relationship, and to a substantial extent is able (and expected) to conduct the state's case in a manner that harms the best interests of the accused. We thus draw a distinction between the Crown's ability to raise the NCR issue and the propriety of a defence lawyer doing so.[177] Simply put, defence counsel should not impose his or her views on the client in this regard.

Counsel should recognize that a client may have many legitimate reasons for viewing an NCR defence with distaste. He or she may want to obtain total vindication from the judicial process by means of an acquittal, and may reject any notion that the alleged offence involved incompetent behaviour. The client may also prefer a set and limited jail term to the more indeterminate confinement that can result from an NCR finding. Furthermore, the stigma of an NCR finding and the psychiatric treatment to which he or she might be subjected as a result may be anathema to some clients. There can also be tactical reasons to avoid an NCR defence, including the hope that withholding the defence from the trier of fact will improve the chances of acquittal or focus more attention on a diminished responsibility defence. Finally, raising NCR may hurt the client on sentencing, if the defence is rejected, or render the Crown less amenable to an acceptable plea resolution prior to trial. These are points worth discussing with the client in arriving at a final decision on the matter.

---

175  *Ibid.* at 512–18.
176  *Ibid.* at 512.
177  However, defence counsel can always raise the NCR issue in the post-guilt phase pursuant to the client's informed instructions: see *Swain, ibid.* at 516.

# M. THE REPRESENTATION OF YOUNG PEOPLE

How do the basic ground rules for cooperative decision making affect counsel who represents a young person in a criminal proceeding? To varying degrees, our society views children and adolescents as unable to make many fundamental decisions affecting their welfare, and regards young people as dependent upon the care and guidance of parents or legal guardians. The legal system has thus deemed that young people have limited capacity in numerous respects. A prime example is the inability of a minor to commence a civil action without a litigation guardian. In the realm of criminal law, no person can be convicted of an offence committed while under the age of twelve.[178]

Yet young people between the ages of twelve and seventeen who commit offences proscribed by the *Criminal Code* are subject to prosecution under the *Young Offenders Act*.[179] Moreover, the developmental issues or legal incapacities that typically relate to young people do not necessarily preclude a normal client-lawyer relationship in the context of criminal proceedings under the *Act*. Rather, the provisions of the *Act* make it clear that a youth charged with a criminal offence has the right to "retain and instruct counsel without delay *and to exercise that right personally, at any stage of the proceedings*."[180] The *Young Offenders Act* also stipulates that

> [y]oung persons have rights and freedoms in their own right, including those stated in the *Canadian Charter of Rights and Freedoms* or in the *Canadian Bill of Rights*, and in particular a right to be heard in the course of, and to participate in, the processes that lead to decisions

---

178  See *Criminal Code*, above note 168, s. 13.

179  See *Young Offenders Act*, R.S.C. 1985, c. Y-1, ss. 2(1) (definition of "young person"), & 5(1).

180  *Ibid.*, s. 11(1) (emphasis added). The original version of s. 11(1) made no reference to this right being exercised personally, and in *R. v. W.(W.)* (1985), 20 C.C.C. (3d) 214 (Man. C.A.) was interpreted as having no impact upon the common law rule. At common law, held the court, a youth charged with a criminal office could not retain counsel directly, but rather a lawyer could be retained only by a guardian, next friend, or guardian *ad litem*. For this reason, the court concluded that a lawyer must take instructions from the adult responsible for the retainer, as opposed to the youth. Following the decision in *W.(W.)*, Parliament amended s. 11(1) of the *Young Offenders Act* to insert the phrase "and to exercise that right personally": see R.S.C. 1985, c. 24 (2nd Supp.), s. 9.

that affect them, and young persons should have special guarantees of their rights and freedoms.[181]

These provisions of the Act strongly suggest that the relationship between a young person charged with a criminal offence and his or her lawyer is similar to any other client-lawyer relationship. Moreover, since codes of professional conduct in Canada typically do not articulate any special role for counsel who represents a young person charged with an offence, presumably the basic approach applicable to an adult accused applies.

Furthermore, committees struck by both the Law Society of Upper Canada and the Quebec bar have expressed the opinion that a youth who is able to comprehend the circumstances relevant to the charge and instruct counsel has the same decision making authority vis-à-vis counsel as would an adult accused.[182] This position is generally accepted in United States[183] and is advocated by leading commentators in Canada.[184] In other words, as is the case with an adult client, counsel must act as an advocate, zealously seeking to achieve the client's goals. Moreover, counsel must keep the young person informed and follow his or her instructions, even if given against the advice of counsel and arguably not in the client's best interests. An amicus curiae model, where counsel attempts to aid the court in achieving a result that is fair for all participants and society as a whole, is thus rejected, as is the "champion" or "guardianship model," whereby counsel's view of the client's best interests can sometimes override instructions to the contrary.

---

181  See Young Offenders Act, above note 179, s. 3(1)(e).

182  See Quebec Bar Committee on the Legal Representation of Children, The Legal Representation of Children: A Consultation Paper (1996) 13 Can. J. Fam. L. 49; and Law Society of Upper Canada, Report on the Legal Representation of Children (Toronto: Law Society of Upper Canada, 1981).

183  See, for example, ABA Model Rule 1.2(a) & 1.14; Third Restatement §24; Institute of Judicial Administration and the American Bar Association Joint Commission on Juvenile Justice Standards, Standards Relating to Counsel for Private Parties (Cambridge, Mass.: Ballinger, 1976); and National Advisory Committee for Juvenile Justice and Delinquency Prevention, Standards for the Administration of Juvenile Justice (Washington, D.C.: Department of Justice, 1980).

184  See, for example, N. Bala, Young Offenders Law (Concord: Irwin Law, 1997) at 174–75; P. Platt, Young Offenders Law in Canada, 2d ed. (Markham, Ont.: Butterworths, 1995) at 308–09; and J. Wilson, Wilson on Children and the Law (Markham, Ont.: Butterworths, 1994) at §6.18 & §7.20.

# 1)  Making Sure That the Client-Lawyer Relationship Works

The cooperative approach to the client-lawyer relationship applies whether or not the client is a young person. Yet defence counsel who represents a young person must take special care to ensure that the relationship operates properly. By dint of less extensive life experience and education, as well as developmental factors, young people are not as likely as adults to understand the workings of the criminal justice system. Studies suggest that young people often hold significant misconceptions about principles and facts fundamental to the system's operation.[185] In many instances, the role of counsel therefore includes educating the young person as to the operation of the system, in language suitable to his or her stage of development. This educational function ensures that the young person is fully informed, and thus able to make competent decisions pertaining to his or her legal representation.

# 2)  The Role of the Parent

Parental support and involvement during the course of a proceeding can be of great value to a young person charged with a criminal offence. It is thus often appropriate for counsel to meet with a young person's parents and to keep them informed as to the progress of the case. Parents may also be able to aid directly in the preparation of the case, for instance, by helping to put in place rehabilitative programs for their offspring in anticipation of a sentence hearing. As noted above, however, counsel defending a young person does not take instructions from the parents, unless the young person is incapable of making decisions and the parent is appointed as a guardian ad litem.

A parent's view as to the proper resolution of the case may be very different from that of the young person. The parent may prefer a delay prior to seeking bail in order to teach the young person a lesson, or insist on a guilty plea, or view a custody disposition as preferable for the young person's future development. Conversely, where the parent risks liability arising out of the young person's acts, he or she may press for an acquittal at all costs even though such an approach is contrary

---

185 See, for example, M. Peterson-Dadala, R. Abramovitch, & J. Duda, "Young Children's Legal Knowledge and Reasoning Ability" (1997) 39 Can. J. Crim. 145; and M. Peterson-Dadala & R. Abramovitch, "Children's Knowledge of the Legal System: Are They Competent to Instruct Legal Counsel?" (1992) 34 Can. J. Crim. 139.

to the young person's wishes. Regardless of the parent's wishes, counsel must leave the decision making authority with the client.

The duties attendant upon a client-lawyer relationship are thus not typically owed to the parents. In addition, these duties often restrict the degree and nature of counsel's interaction with parents. Obligations of loyalty, competence, confidentiality, and disclosure are owed to the young person, not the parents, and dealings with the parents are permitted only where counsel holds a reasonable expectation that these obligations to the client will be bolstered as a result. The limited nature of the relationship between counsel and the young person's parents should be made clear to the young person at the beginning of the retainer. As well, interaction with parents should take place only with the consent of the young person. Some young people may not want any parental involvement or may wish for only limited communication between lawyer and parents, in which case counsel must abide by these directions.

## N. USING THE RETAINER TO DEFINE THE DECISION-MAKING AUTHORITY

The client and lawyer may for perfectly good reasons wish to adopt a specific allocation of decision making authority, and accordingly provide for their preferred version in the retainer agreement.[186] Consequently, the terms of a retainer may relegate certain decisions to the lawyer, to be made in the ordinary course without the need for consultation with the client.[187] In effect, the client is giving the lawyer the express authority to act within a defined realm. The Third Restatement has taken this concept the furthest of the major Anglo-American ethical codes. Subject to certain restrictions, the Restatement allows the client and lawyer to agree which of them will make specified decisions, and also stipulates that the allocation of decision making authority can be amended by mutual agreement as the representation progresses.[188]

---

186 See, for example, *Stewart*, above note 46 at 46–52 & 83, where the retainer agreement expanded the degree of control normally provided to a criminal lawyer at common law. This case expressly leaves aside the question as to whether a retainer can *narrow* counsel's common law ability to control the case, apparently out of a potential concern that unethical behaviour may be demanded of the lawyer: *ibid.* at 88.

187 See for example, Alta. ch. 9, comm. 5.

188 See Third Restatement §21(1).

Are there nonetheless certain decisions that should not in the ordinary course be left to the lawyer, regardless of the client's desire to do so? It is fair to say that crucial steps to be taken as part of the conduct of the defence always require specific consultation with the client and clear instructions at the time that the decision is being made. At the least, such crucial steps include the decisions as to how to plead to the charge, the advisability of having a jury trial (where such an option is available), whether the client should testify, and the launching of an appeal following conviction.[189] It is beyond dispute that these and comparable decisions must be left to the client in the absence of an agreement otherwise. Most ethical codes and commentators would go yet farther and prohibit a client and lawyer from agreeing to leave these decisions to the lawyer's sole discretion. However, the Third Restatement precludes a client-lawyer agreement that would leave sole decision making authority to the lawyer on these particular matters only in two instances, namely, where the client is required by law to participate personally in or approve of the decision, and where the client wishes to revoke an agreement to leave such matters to the lawyer (*viz.*, the initial agreement is never irrevocable).[190]

## O. KEEPING A WRITTEN RECORD OF DISAGREEMENTS AND RESOLUTIONS

Regardless of the lawyer's preferred approach to decision making, the prudent course is to keep a written record of any substantial disagreement that occurs between counsel and client during the course of the retainer.[191] Matters that should be memorialized include the issue in dispute, the advice given, the client's reaction and instructions, and the course actually taken. This record can help resolve factual disputes as to what happened and what was said if the lawyer's conduct is later attacked on appeal or in disciplinary proceedings. Such a record can also on occasion aid the client, lending support to a version of events that is disputed by the Crown on appeal. Additionally, the process of recording circumstances surrounding the dispute will serve to remind

---

189 See Alta. ch. 9, comm. 5.
190 See Third Restatement §21(1) & §22.
191 See ABA Defense Standard 4-5.2(c).

the lawyer of the importance of communicating fully with the client. To this extent, the result may be a satisfactory resolution of the disagreement.

# P. SUMMARY AND RECOMMENDATIONS

Our preferred approach to the issue of decision making authority in the client-lawyer relationship is as follows:

1.  Most Canadian rules of professional conduct devote little or no attention to the question of decision making authority in the client-lawyer relationship. The main exception is found in Alberta, where the Code of Professional Conduct discusses the issue in considerable detail (section B).
2.  The best-known and most influential Canadian opinion on decision making authority in the criminal law context comes from the late G. Arthur Martin. Martin endorsed a traditional lawyer-control model, under which most decisions pertaining to the conduct of the defence are left to the absolute discretion of the lawyer. Martin accorded the final say to the client only in very limited circumstances, most notably regarding the decisions how to plead and whether to testify as part of the defence case (section C(1)).
3.  Martin's views have been endorsed in some Canadian cases (section C(2)).
4.  A different approach is to provide the client with final decision making authority in recognition of a broad constitutional right to determine the conduct of the defence, a right derived from the autonomy and dignity of the individual. This approach has been endorsed in other Canadian cases (section C(3_).
5.  The Supreme Court of Canada has obliquely addressed the issue of decision making in the case of *R. v. B.(G.D.)* but without offering any firm opinion on the point (section C(4)).
6.  We prefer the model of allocating decision making authority that seeks to empower the client in recognition of his or her individual autonomy and dignity. This approach is sometimes called the cooperative model (section D).
7.  In employing a cooperative model to make decisions regarding the conduct of the defence, it is imperative that the lawyer keep the client informed and provide thorough advice. Absent proper information and advice, the client's ability to make decisions will be seriously hampered (section E).

8. On the lawyer-control approach, a limited number of fundamental decisions are nonetheless left to the client, for example, the plea decision, waiver of a jury trial, the determination whether to testify and the decision whether to appeal. While we agree that such decisions should be left to the client, our endorsement of the cooperative model means that we favour granting the client much wider decision making authority (section F).

9. Even under a cooperative approach, there are instances where the trial process demands an immediate decision without providing the opportunity for prior consultation with the client. In such cases, the lawyer effectively holds final decision making authority. However, where a decision is important to the defence, and obtaining an adjournment is feasible, the lawyer should attempt to stop proceedings in order to acquire the client's considered input (section G).

10. A lawyer must never accept instructions from a client that require unethical conduct (for example, to call a witness to the stand for the purpose of offering perjured testimony) (section H).

11. The cooperative model requires a lawyer to follow a client's instructions even where to do so may, in the lawyer's reasonable opinion, have a negative impact on the defence. Naturally, the client must first be advised as to the pitfalls of the desired action. In extreme cases, however, the client's refusal to follow the lawyer's advice may manifest or create a total and irrevocable breakdown of the relationship. In such instances, the lawyer has no choice but to withdraw from the representation (section I).

12. A lawyer cannot carry out instructions that involve frivolous action or argument. At the same time, however, the lawyer can legitimately require the prosecution to establish every necessary element of the offence charged (section J).

13. Where the lawyer is unable to obtain instructions from the client, reasonable steps should be taken to alleviate the problem. Where such steps are unsuccessful, withdrawal is usually the only option, given that the lawyer cannot properly conduct a defence absent the client's direction and input (section K).

14. Where a client suffers from some disability or impairment that impedes the ordinary decision making process, the lawyer must nonetheless strive to maintain a normal professional relationship. Doing so is not always easy or possible (sections L & L(1)).

15. General guidelines for dealing with the client who suffers from some level of disability or impairment include:

a. Undertake all reasonable efforts to ascertain the client's wishes, and otherwise carry on a functional client-lawyer relationship, which will probably require specially tailoring communications to overcome obstacles created by the disability.

b. Where the disability is likely temporary, as is usually the case where a client is under the influence of alcohol or other drugs, if feasible postpone taking any important steps in the representation until the problem has dissipated.

c. If the client simply cannot provide the lawyer with any instructions on important aspects of the case, seek the appointment of a legal representative.

d. Where the lawyer is absolutely forced to take action, but is unable to obtain clear instructions, make the decision that counsel reasonably perceives the client would make if competent.

e. Approach the client's family and friends, as well as appropriate health-care or other professionals, in an effort to determine the preferable approach in communicating with the client and interpreting his or her wishes (section L(2)).

Particular examples of the issue arising can be seen where a client is possibly unfit to stand trial yet opposes raising the issue (section L(3)).

16. Where a client is fit to stand trial, yet wishes to forego a viable NCR defence, counsel should generally abide by such instructions (section L(4)).

17. In representing a young person in a criminal matter, the lawyer should utilize the cooperative model, all the while taking any special measures required to ensure that the client understands the criminal justice process and is able to make informed decisions (section M).

18. The allocation of decision making authority can be expressly addressed in the retainer agreement. However, we believe that some decisions, such as the decision how to plead, should never be left to the lawyer's sole discretion, not even where ostensibly permitted by written agreement between client and lawyer (section N).

19. It is prudent to keep a written record of any substantial disagreement that occurs between client and lawyer during the course of representation (section O)

# FURTHER READINGS

BALA, N., *Young Offenders Law* (Concord, Ont.: Irwin Law, 1997)

BISHARAT, G., "Pursuing a Questionable Suppression Motion" in R. Uphoff, ed., *Ethical Problems Facing the Criminal Defense Lawyer: Practical Answers to Tough Questions* (Chicago: Criminal Justice Section of American Bar Association, 1995) c. 5

BLAKE, M., & A. ASHWORTH, "Some Ethical Issues in Prosecuting and Defending Criminal Cases" (1998) Crim. L. Rev. 16

BOON, A.& J. LEVIN, *The Ethics and Conduct of Lawyers in England and Wales* (Oxford: Hart, 1999)

BURKOFF, J., *Criminal Defense Ethics: Law and Liability*, rev. ed. (St. Paul: West, 2000)

BURGER, W., "Standards of Conduct for Prosecution and Defense Personnel" (1966) 5 Am. Crim. L. Rev. 11

CALARCO, P., "The Ontario Court of Appeal Gives a Green Light to Relitigate Convictions by Suing Your Lawyers" (2000) 31 C.R. (5th) 129

FINK, J., "Who Decides: The Role of Parent or Guardian in Juvenile Delinquency Representation in R. Uphoff, ed., *Ethical Problems Facing the Criminal Defense Lawyer: Practical Answers to Tough Questions* (Chicago: American Bar Association, 1995) c. 9

FREEDMAN, M., *Understanding Lawyers' Ethics* (New York: Matthew Bender, 1990)

FRY, R., "Calling Defense Witnesses: Whose Case is This Anyway?" in R. Uphoff, ed., *Ethical Problems Facing the Criminal Defense Lawyer: Practical Answers to Tough Questions* (Chicago: Criminal Justice Section of American Bar Association, 1995) c. 6

HOOLIHAN, J., "Ethical Standards for Defence Counsel" in Canadian Bar Association, *Studies in Criminal Law and Procedure* (Agincourt, Ont.: Canada Law Book, 1972) 124

HOSKINS, F., "The Players of a Criminal Trial" in J. Pink & D. Perrier, eds., *From Crime to Punishment: An Introduction to the Criminal Justice System*, 4th ed. (Toronto: Carswell, 1999)

HUTCHINSON, A., *Legal Ethics and Professional Responsibility* (Toronto: Irwin Law, 1999)

Law Society of Upper Canada, *Report on the Legal Representation of Children* (Toronto, Law Society of Upper Canada, 1981)

MACKENZIE, G., *Lawyers and Ethics: Professional Responsibility and Discipline* (Toronto: Carswell, 1993)

MALONEY, A., "The Role of the Independent Bar" in Law Society of Upper Canada, *The Abuse of Power and the Role of an Independent Judicial System in its Regulation and Control* (Toronto: R. De Boo, 1979) 49

MARRUS, E., "Please Keep My Secret: Child Abuse Reporting Statutes, Confidentiality, and Juvenile Delinquency" (1998) 11 Geo. J. Legal Ethics 509

MARTIN, G. ARTHUR, "The Role and Responsibility of the Defence Advocate" (1969) 12 Crim. L.Q. 376

MARTIN, M., "Defending the Mentally Ill Client in Criminal Matters: Ethics, Advocacy, and Responsibility" (1993) 52 U.T. Fac. L. Rev. 73

MLYNIEC, W., "Who Decides: Decision Making in Juvenile Delinquency Proceedings" in R. Uphoff, ed., *Ethical Problems Facing the Criminal Defense Lawyer: Practical Answers to Tough Questions* (Chicago: American Bar Association, Criminal Justice Section, 1995)

ORKIN, M., *Legal Ethics* (Toronto: Cartwright, 1957)

"Panel Discussion: Problems in Advocacy and Ethics" in Law Society of Upper Canada, *Defending a Criminal Case* (Toronto: R De Boo, 1969) 279

PETERSON-DADALA, M.R ABRAMOVITCH, & J. DUDA, "Young Children's Legal Knowledge and Reasoning Ability" (1997) 39 Can. J. Crim. 145

PETERSON-DADALA, M., & R. ABRAMOVITCH, "Children's Knowledge of the Legal System: Are They Competent to Instruct Legal Counsel?" (1992) 34 Can. J. Crim. 139

PLATT, P., *Young Offenders Law in Canada*, 2d ed. (Markham, Ont.: Butterworths, 1995)

QUEBEC BAR COMMITTEE ON THE LEGAL REPRESENTATION OF CHILDREN, "The Legal Representation of Children: A Consultation Paper" (1996) 13 Can. J. Fam. L. 49

ROSENTHAL, D., *Lawyer and Client: Who's in Charge?* (New York: Russell Sage Foundation, 1974)

ROSS, S., *Ethics in Law: Lawyers' Responsibility and Accountability in Australia*, 2d ed. (Sydney: Butterworths, 1998)

SKURKA, S., & J. STRIBOPOULOS, "Professional Responsibility in Criminal Practice" in Law Society of Upper Canada, *42nd Bar Admission Course, 2000, Criminal Procedure Reference Materials* (Toronto: Law Society of Upper Canada, 2000) c. 1

SYMPOSIUM, "Solicitor/Client Privilege and the Mentally Incapable Older Client" (2000) 19 Est. & Tr. J. 171

UPHOFF, R., "The Decision to Challenge the Competency of a Marginally Competent Client: Defense Counsel's Unavoidably Difficult Position" in R. Uphoff, ed., *Ethical Problems Facing the Criminal Defense Lawyer: Practical Answers to Tough Questions* (Chicago: Criminal Justice Section of American Bar Association, 1995) c. 3

WASSERSTROM, R., "Lawyers as Professionals: Some Moral Issues" (1975) 5 Hum. Rts. Q. 105

WILSON, J., *Wilson on Children and the Law* (Markham, Ont.: Butterworths, 1994)

WOLFRAM, C.W., *Modern Legal Ethics* (St. Paul: West, 1986)

# CHAPTER 4

# CONFIDENTIALITY

## A. INTRODUCTION

The lawyer's duty to keep confidential all information received as a result of representing a client is a linchpin of the professional relationship. The scope of this duty is exceptionally broad, demanding that counsel take great care in handling all information pertaining to or affecting a client. At the same time, there are exceptions to the duty of confidentiality that permit, and sometimes even demand, disclosure of such information by the lawyer. Determining the instances where exceptions should apply raises some of the most controversial and daunting ethical problems facing the criminal bar today.

This chapter examines the lawyer's duty of confidentiality with an eye to some of the problems and concerns that can arise in a criminal practice. Possible justifications for breaching confidentiality are discussed in other chapters, including chapter 5 (Possible Confidentiality Exceptions), chapter 7 (Client Perjury), and chapter 9 (Incriminating Physical Evidence).

## B. RATIONALE

The standard justification for imposing a duty of confidentiality upon lawyers is that the client who is assured of complete secrecy is more likely to reveal to his or her counsel all information pertaining to the case.[1] The lawyer who is in possession of all relevant information is better able to advise the client and hence provide competent service.[2] The client's legal rights are furthered, as is the truth-finding function of the adversarial system.[3] Additionally, the obligation to maintain confidentiality fosters the autonomy and dignity of the client by protecting his or her privacy.[4] Finally, the duty of confidentiality is closely connected to the overarching duty of loyalty owed by a lawyer to the client. The obligation to be loyal would be compromised if a lawyer could use information so as to cause adverse impact to the client. A complete bar on the unauthorized use of confidential information by counsel, even where no adverse impact is possible, accordingly serves a prophylactic function that helps to ensure undivided loyalty.

In promoting effective legal advice, the duty of confidentiality not only benefits the individual client but also serves a broader societal interest. As already noted, a client who is able to rely upon the assurance of confidentiality is more likely to receive sound legal counsel. As a result, he or she is more likely to obey the law and, if charged with a crime, is better able to mount a defence. It is in the public interest that both ends be encouraged, and the duty of confidentiality thus advances fundamental systemic goals.

## C. THE RULES OF PROFESSIONAL CONDUCT

All Canadian rules of professional conduct strongly assert the lawyer's duty of confidentiality. The CBA Code's applicable rule states:

---

1    See, for example, *R. v. McClure* (2001), 151 C.C.C. (3d) 321 at 331–32 (S.C.C.) [*McClure*]; and *Wilder* v. *Ontario (Securities Commission)* (2001), 197 D.L.R. (4th) 193 at 208–09 (Ont. C.A.).

2    CBA Code ch. IV, comm. 1.

3    See, for example, *R. v. Joanisse* (1995), 102 C.C.C. (3d) 35 at 57 (Ont. C.A.) [*Joanisse*], leave to appeal to S.C.C. refused (1997), 111 C.C.C. (3d) vi (S.C.C.).

4    The importance of autonomy and dignity in the context of the right to counsel of choice has been recognized in *R. v. McCallen* (1999), 131 C.C.C. (3d) 518 (Ont. C.A.). More generally, see also the discussion in *R. v. Swain* (1991), 63 C.C.C. (3d) 481 at 505–06 (S.C.C.). Privacy arguments have been given constitutional import in the context of confidential communications between client and counsellor/psychiatrist in *R. v. O'Connor* (1995), 103 C.C.C. (3d) 1 (S.C.C.); and *R. v. Mills* (1999), 139 C.C.C. (3d) 321 (S.C.C.). See also *M.(A.)* v. *Ryan* (1997), 143 D.L.R. (4th) 1 (S.C.C.). The same reasoning likely pertains to client-lawyer communications. See *R. v. Robillard* (2000), 151 C.C.C. (3d) 296 at 307 & 309 (Que. C.A.) [*Robillard*].

> The lawyer has a duty to hold in strict confidence all information concerning the business and affairs of the client acquired in the course of the professional relationship, and should not divulge such information unless disclosure is expressly or impliedly authorized by the client, required by law or otherwise permitted or required by this Code.[5]

The breadth of the duty of confidentiality imposed by the ethical rules will be discussed in detail below. It is worth stressing at this point, however, that the Canadian rules do not merely import a definition of confidentiality that has independently been delineated elsewhere, for instance, by the common law or equity. Rather, the rules typically purport to provide lawyers with a free-standing, self-contained definition of confidentiality.

# D. COMPARISON WITH LEGAL-PROFESSIONAL PRIVILEGE

The similarities and differences between the ethical rule of confidentiality and legal-professional privilege are important, and are at least ostensibly recognized in our rules of professional conduct.[6] Legal-professional privilege is a class privilege that attaches to certain confidential communications that either pass between lawyer and client as part of the professional relationship or pass between the lawyer or client and third parties for the dominant purpose of litigation.[7] The concept of confidentiality is accordingly central to the privilege.

---

5   CBA Code ch. IV, Rule. See also B.C. ch. 5, r. 1; Alta. ch. 7, Statement of Principle; Sask. ch. IV, Rule; N.S. ch. 5, Rule; Ont. r. 2.03(1); Man. ch. 4, Rule; N.B. Part C, r. 5; Que. s. 3.06; and Yukon Part 1, r. 3.

6   See, for example, CBA Code ch. IV, comm. 2; Alta. ch. 8, comm. G.3; N.S. ch. 5, comm. 5.1; Ont. r. 2.03(1) (commentary); Man. ch. IV, comm. 2; Sask. ch. IV, comm. 2. At common law, the leading case establishing the distinction is *Descôteaux* v. *Mierzwinski* (1982), 70 C.C.C. (2d) 385 (S.C.C.) [*Descôteaux*]. See also the earlier case of *Slavutych* v. *Baker* (1975), 55 D.L.R. (3d) 224 (S.C.C.) [*Slavutych*], where the court draws the same sort of distinction between confidentiality and privilege. More recently, similar sentiments are found in *Stevens* v. *Canada (Prime Minister)* (1998), 161 D.L.R. (4th) 85 at 94–95 (F.C.A.) [*Stevens*]; and *Lavallee* v. *Canada (A.G.)* (1998), 126 C.C.C. (3d) 129 at 147-148 (Alta. Q.B.), aff'd (2000), 143 C.C.C. (3d) 187 (Alta. C.A.) [*Lavallee (C.A.)*].

7   The term "legal-professional privilege" is used here to encompass both client-lawyer privilege and litigation privilege, as is done in C. Tapper, *Cross and Tapper on Evidence*, 9th ed. (London: Butterworths, 1999) at 438 (where a more detailed and precise definition of the term is provided). For a comprehensive

Despite this important similarity, crucial distinctions exist between a lawyer's ethical duty of confidentiality and legal-professional privilege.[8] First, the privilege applies only in proceedings where the lawyer may be a witness or otherwise compelled to produce evidence relating to the client. The ethical rule of confidentiality is not so restricted, operating even where there is no question of any attempt to compel disclosure by legal process. Second, legal-professional privilege encompasses only matters communicated in confidence by the client, or by a third party for the dominant purpose of litigation. Once again, the rule of confidentiality is broader, covering all information acquired by counsel whatever its source. Third, the privilege applies to the communication itself, does not bar the adduction of evidence pertaining to the facts communicated if gleaned from another source, and is often lost where other parties are present during the communication. In contrast, the rule of confidentiality usually persists despite the fact that third parties know the information in question or the communication was made in the presence of others.

The subtle and complicated interplay between confidentiality and privilege is relevant to many ethical questions that confront a criminal lawyer.[9] Unfortunately, discussion of these concepts in the case law is sometimes muddled or, if taken out of context, confusing. To provide but one example, courts will sometimes hold that a communication is not privileged because it was not intended to be "confidential," yet this same communication may well be considered confidential within the meaning of the ethical rules.[10] In other words, the term "confidential" can be used in different ways at different times. We will return to the distinction between the evidentiary rule of privilege and the ethical duty of confidentiality at various points in this chapter, as well as the chapter on possible exceptions to the duty. For the moment, it may be helpful to provide a few preliminary examples:

**Example:** Penitentiary officials seek to open and review letters sent between inmates and their legal counsel, on the ground that such a

---

review of legal-professional privilege in Canadian law, see J. Sopinka, S. Lederman, & A. Bryant, *The Law of Evidence in Canada*, 2d ed. (Toronto: Butterworths, 1999) at 14.42ff. The "dominant purpose" test for litigation privilege was recently endorsed in *General Accident Assurance Co.* v. *Chrusz* (1999), 45 O.R. (3d) 321 (C.A.).

8    See *Robillard*, above note 4 at 305–08.

9    See, for example, D. Layton, "The Public Safety Exception: Confusing Confidentiality, Privilege and Ethics" (2001) 6 Can. Crim. L. Rev. 209.

10   For a concrete instance where a court so held, see the discussion at note 97, below.

review is required in the interests of institutional security. If the inmates seek to stop this practice, they cannot rely upon legal-professional privilege, given that the institution has no plan to use the communications as evidence in court. Nonetheless, the common law rule of confidentiality may well provide inmates with some remedy. Moreover, the ethical duty of confidentiality imposed by the rules of professional conduct will prevent counsel who writes or receives such letters from disclosing any of the information to a third party. This ethical duty will persist despite the inapplicability of the privilege, and it continues to apply even where the common law permits penitentiary officials some limited license to review the letters.[11]

**Example:** An accused is charged with robbery. Counsel has received disclosure detailing the results of police surveillance of her client during the day of the offence. The facts outlined in the disclosure are not privileged, and it is clear that the surveillance officers can testify at trial as to their observations. Nevertheless, the ethical rule of confidentiality prohibits the lawyer from revealing the facts set out in the disclosure to third parties.[12]

**Example:** A client consults counsel with respect to the law concerning electronic surveillance. Counsel eventually forms the opinion that the client is seeking information that will help him to avoid detection by police in connection with a narcotics deal. She sternly tells him not to break the law, and promptly ends the interview. Counsel wisely decides to make detailed notes of the meeting in case the propriety of her advice is ever challenged by the client or police. Subsequently, the police visit the lawyer, asking her to reveal voluntarily the contents of the interview and provide them with any notes. The communications between counsel and client come within the crime-fraud exception to legal-professional privilege, and will probably not be protected if the lawyer is subpoenaed to testify or subjected to a search warrant. However, the lawyer's ethical duty of confidentiality arguably prevents her from otherwise disclosing the communications or notes to police.[13]

---

11    This example is based on the facts in *Canada* v. *Solosky* (1979), 50 C.C.C. (2d) 495 (S.C.C.) [*Solosky*], a case that must really be read in light of the discussion in *Descôteaux*, above note 6 at 399.

12    The possibility that the lawyer is free to reveal such information once the facts come out in open court is discussed in section C, "Public Knowledge," in chapter 5.

13    The issues raised by this example are discussed in detail in section I, "Possible Crime-Fraud Exception," in chapter 5. The proper handling of this problem is also affected by the possible application of the future-harm exception to the eth-

# E. COMPARISON WITH CONFIDENTIALITY AT COMMON LAW AND EQUITY

Bodies of law external to the ethical rules of professional conduct work to protect and enforce client-lawyer confidences. As we have seen, the law of evidence implicitly gives effect to client-lawyer confidentiality by affording legal-professional communications a class privilege.[14] The law of agency also enforces client-lawyer confidences, the lawyer taking on numerous duties as agent, including the duty of confidentiality.[15] One can also find robust protection of a client's right to confidentiality in the law of fiduciaries more generally[16] and in the willingness of equity to enjoin a breach of confidence.[17]

These legal and equitable manifestations of confidentiality bear close resemblance to the ethical obligations imposed by rules of professional conduct. However, as the example of legal-professional privilege shows, a lawyer's ethical obligations can differ from legal rules concerning confidences. The same can be said, though perhaps to a lesser degree, for the substantive duties of confidentiality imposed by the common law and equity. Though significant similarities exist, these legal and ethical duties are neither exactly coterminous with nor necessarily determined by the ethical duties defined by a lawyer's professional governing body.[18]

---

ical duty of confidentiality: see section G, "Future Harm or Public Safety," in chapter 5. Yet on the facts here, we are assuming that the preconditions necessary to set up the future-crime exception have not been satisfied.

14  It has been said that the substantive right to confidentiality first took the form of this rule of evidence: see *Descôteaux*, above note 6 at 398.

15  See, for example, G. Fridman, *The Law of Agency* (Toronto: Butterworths, 1996) at 46–48.

16  See, for example, M. Ellis, *Fiduciary Duties in Canada* (Toronto: Carswell, 1993) c. 9.

17  See *Slavutych*, above note 6 at 229–30.

18  See, for example, *MacDonald Estate* v. *Martin*, [1990] 3 S.C.R. 1235 at 1245–46 [*MacDonald Estate*]; *Stewart* v. *Canadian Broadcasting Corp.* (1997), 150 D.L.R. (4th) 24 at 101–08 (Ont. Gen. Div.) [*Stewart*]; *R.* v. *Murray* (2000), 144 C.C.C. (3d) 289 at 309 (Ont. S.C.J.); and *R.* v. *Jenkins* (2001), 152 C.C.C. (3d) 426 at 436 (Ont. S.C.J.). See also the discussion at note 97, below, and the issues canvassed in section I, "Possible Crime-Fraud Exception," in chapter 5.

# F.  CONSTITUTIONAL PRINCIPLES

As we have already noted,[19] the ability of an accused to make full answer and defence is often dependent upon obtaining the help of a lawyer. For this reason, the right to counsel has been recognized by many courts, and in many contexts.[20] Yet the right to counsel requires more than simply a guarantee that counsel can act for an accused. Among other things, an accused must enjoy the benefit of confidentiality if the relationship with counsel is to operate effectively.[21] For this reason, courts have afforded clients a fundamental legal and civil right to maintain legal-professional confidences, a right applicable to both the evidentiary and substantive aspects of legal-professional confidentiality.[22] Constitutional protections such as the right to full answer and defence, the right to counsel, and the right to be secure from unreasonable search and seizure thus come into play. It has also been suggested that the *Charter of Rights and Freedoms*' principle against self-incrimination can work to protect client-lawyer confidences,[23] although the interface between this protean principle and the

---

19   See section D, "The Rationale for Defending One Known to Be Guilty," in chapter 1.

20   Most obviously, s. 10(b) of the *Canadian Charter of Rights and Freedoms*, Part I, of the *Constitution Act, 1982*, being Schedule B to the *Canada Act 1982* (U.K.), 1982, c. 11 [*Charter*] guarantees the right to counsel on arrest or detention. While the Supreme Court of Canada has not definitively established that the *Charter* provides for a right to counsel at trial (see, for example, *New Brunswick (Minister of Health and Community Services)* v. *G.(J.)* (1999), 177 D.L.R. (4th) 124 at 156 (S.C.C.); *R.* v. *Prosper* (1994), 92 C.C.C (3d) 353 at 373 (S.C.C.)), several provincial appeal courts have come to this conclusion: see, for example, *Joanisse*, above note 3 at 58; *R.* v. *Romanowicz* (1999), 138 C.C.C. (3d) 225 at 237 (Ont. C.A.); *R.* v. *Sechon* (1995), 104 C.C.C. (3d) 554 (Que. C.A.); and *R.* v. *Howell* (1995), 103 C.C.C. (3d) 302 (N.S.C.A.), aff'd (1996), 110 C.C.C. (3d) 192 (S.C.C.).

21   See, for example, *Smith* v. *Jones* (1999), 132 C.C.C. (3d) 225 at 230–31 (S.C.C.) [*Smith*], per Major J. (dissenting); and *McClure*, above note 1 at 331–32.

22   See, for example, *Solosky*, above note 11 at 510; *Descôteaux*, above note 6 at 409–13; *Geffen* v. *Goodman Estate* (1991), 81 D.L.R. (4th) 211 at 231–32 (S.C.C.) [*Geffen*]; and *A.(L.L.)* v. *Beharriell* (1995), 103 C.C.C. (3d) 92 at 120–21 (S.C.C.); *Smith*, above note 21 at 239–41; and *McClure*, above note 1 at 329.

23   See *Smith*, above note 21 at 231 & 235–36, per Major J. (dissenting); and *R.* v. *Chan* (2000), 146 C.C.C. (3d) 494 at 499–501 (Alta. C.A.).

client-lawyer relationship is perhaps best viewed as a subsidiary aspect of the right to counsel.[24]

# G. REMEDIES

The lawyer who breaches the ethical duty of confidence is exposed to a panoply of possible legal proceedings brought at the client's behest. The client may launch disciplinary proceedings for violation of the rules of professional conduct.[25] He or she can also sue for breach of fiduciary duty, contract, or duty of care arising out of counsel's actions, seeking remedies as diverse as damages, an injunction enjoining misuse of the information, an accounting and disgorgement of profits, and/or delivery up or destruction of documents containing the confidential information.[26] Breach or threatened breach of a confidence may also lead to a claim of privilege in extant legal proceedings,[27] ground an application to have counsel removed from the record for conflict of interest,[28] or fuel an appeal based on an allegation of ineffective counsel.[29] Finally, a serious breach of confidentiality may also contravene the *Criminal Code*.[30]

---

24 For instance, a document is *not* protected by the principle against self-incrimination simply because it passes from client to lawyer. The client-lawyer relationship cannot be used as a "principle against self-incrimination clearing house" to protect material that is otherwise legitimately subject to seizure by search warrant or production by subpoena *duces tecum*: see, for example, *Fisher* v. *United States*, 425 U.S. 391 (1976); *R.* v. *King*, [1983] 1 All E.R. 929 (C.A.); and *British Columbia (Securities Commission)* v. *Branch* (1995), 97 C.C.C. (3d) 505 at 524 (S.C.C.). See also the sentiments expressed in *Susan Hosiery Ltd.* v. *M.N.R.*, [1969] 2 Ex. C.R. 27 at 34 (Ex. Ct.); and *Stevens*, above note 6 at 94 & 97–98).

25 See, for example, *Law Society of Upper Canada* v. *Vujic*, [1995] L.S.D.D. No. 7 [*Vujic*].

26 See generally F. Bennett, *Confidentiality in a Solicitor and Client Relationship* (1989) 23 L. Soc. Gaz. 251; M. Ellis, above note 16, c. 20; Fridman, above note 15, at 177–79; and *Wernikowski* v. *Kirkland, Murphy & Ain* (2000), 141 C.C.C. (3d) 403 at 410 (Ont. C.A.).

27 See, for example, above note 21.

28 See, for example, *MacDonald Estate,* above note 18.

29 See the analogous situation in *R.* v. *Samra* (1998), 129 C.C.C. (3d) 144 (Ont. C.A.), where an alleged breach of confidence by *amicus curiae* who formerly represented the appellant at trial formed one ground of appeal.

30 See, for example, *United States* v. *ReBrook*, 837 F. Supp. 162 (S.D. W. Va. 1993), where the lawyer for a state lottery was charged with insider trading based on an alleged misuse of confidential information.

# H. SOME APPLICATIONS OF THE ETHICAL DUTY OF CONFIDENTIALITY

The duty of confidentiality owed a client by counsel has an expansive scope and comes to bear in countless situations. Some of the most important attributes of the duty, which serve to emphasize its great breadth, are set out below.

## 1) Information from All Sources Included

A key aspect of the duty of confidentiality, which is largely responsible for its tremendous reach, is that information from any and all sources is covered.[31] It matters not, for example, that the information comes from a third party rather than the client. Nor does it necessarily matter that legal-professional privilege does not apply.[32] Confidentiality will even arise where information relating to the client comes unexpectedly or through unusual channels, for instance, where counsel happens to learn of the information from another client, through casual reading or by overhearing gossip.[33]

## 2) All Forms of Information Are Covered

The duty of confidentiality applies to all forms of information relating to a client, including oral, documentary, electronic, photographic, and digital.[34]

## 3) Information Received by Employees and Agents

The ambit of confidentiality extends to information provided to agents for the lawyer. Thus, information obtained by a law clerk, secretary, or private investigator will be impressed with a confidential nature and attract the same ethical obligations as would information coming directly to the lawyer.[35]

---

31   See, for example, CBA Code ch. IV, comm. 2, which states: "The ethical rule ... applies without regard to the nature or source of the information or to the fact that others may share the knowledge."

32   See section D, "Comparison with Legal-Professional Privilege," in this chapter.

33   See CBA Code ch. IV, comm. 7; and Third Restatement §59, comm. "b."

34   See Third Restatement §59, comm. "b."

35   See, for example, *Commonwealth* v. *Mrozek*, 657 A.2d 997 (Pa. Super. 1995), where an individual's inculpatory statement to a lawyer's secretary was held to be confidential and privileged; *Robillard*, above note 4 at 300, treating a *bona*

## 4)  Risk of Harm to Client and Altruistic Purpose of Disclosure Are Irrelevant

The prohibition against disclosing a client confidence does not dissipate simply because the client is not exposed to any risk of harm. Canadian rules of professional conduct thus make no distinction between cases where disclosure or use will likely harm a client and those instances where the risk of adverse impact is non-existent.[36]

**Comparison:** The Third Restatement allows a lawyer to use or disclose confidential information where there is no reasonable prospect that doing so will adversely affect a material interest of the client, provided that the information is not used for the lawyer's gain and that the client has not instructed the lawyer to the contrary.[37] We prefer the more cautious approach adopted by Canadian ethical codes, which serves to prevent unexpected harm or an erroneous assessment of risk by counsel.

Similarly, the lawyer's duty to maintain confidentiality applies regardless of the use to which the information may be put.[38] The application of confidential information for the benefit of a third party, be it another client of the lawyer or otherwise, is clearly prohibited. So is the use of such information for the lawyer's own benefit or for a purpose that has a philanthropic, neutral, or undetermined effect.

## 5)  Both Disclosure and Use Prohibited

It is possible to make use of confidential information without expressly disclosing the information to a third party.[39] As an example, counsel

---

*fide* communication between the client and the lawyer's secretary as confidential; and *R. v. Peruta* (1992), 78 C.C.C. (3d) 350 (Que. C.A.), in which the same approach was taken respecting the applicability of legal-professional privilege to witness statements taken by a private investigator working for the defence.

36   See, for example, CBA Code ch. IV, comm. 5; and Alta. ch. 7, r. 1.

37   Third Restatement §60(1), comm. "c(i)" & "c(ii)." The Third Restatement views the risk of adverse impact as irrelevant where the lawyer stands to gain personally, on the ground that there is a special need for prophylactic measures in cases of self-interest: see §60(2), & comm. "j".

38   See, for example, CBA Code ch. IV, comm. 5; Ont. r. 2.03(6) (commentary; and N.S. ch. 5, comm. 5.4.

39   See, for example, Third Restatement §60, the wording of which takes care to prohibit both disclosure *and* use. C.W. Wolfram, *Modern Legal Ethics* (St. Paul: West, 1986) at 304–05, also discusses how information can be used in breach of the duty of confidentiality without necessarily involving overt disclosure.

might learn from a client that a certain business opportunity exists, and simply act on the information to take advantage of the opportunity without necessarily revealing any information to a third party. While Canadian rules of professional conduct can be criticized for failing to recognize a possible distinction between the disclosure and use of confidential information, their general tenor undoubtedly embraces both concepts.[40]

**Example:** During the course of the representation, counsel learns that his client's marriage is in desperate straits, and that the couple is experiencing sexual problems. Without discussing this matter with anyone else, counsel uses the information to embark on a sexual relationship with the client's wife. He has thereby breached the duty of confidentiality.[41]

## 6) Information Can be Confidential Even in the Absence of a Retainer

Some Canadian rules of professional conduct are worded so as to provide that information acquired "in the course of [the] professional relationship" is subject to the duty of confidentiality.[42] In *Descôteaux* v. *Mierzwinski*, the Supreme Court of Canada made clear that the professional relationship arises as soon as a potential client has his or her first dealing with the lawyer's office in order to obtain legal advice.[43] The wording used in the ethical rules is thus broad enough to cover pre-retainer discussions, and all information acquired at this point is confidential, even if the lawyer is retained only later or not at all.

**Caution:** A lawyer who quite legitimately does not wish to be bound by a duty of confidentiality *vis-à-vis* a non-client, for instance because of a potential for conflict of interest, should exercise care in communi-

---

40  To be fair, Canadian rules do contain language that seems intended to cover the use of confidential information despite the absence of overt disclosure: see, for example, CBA Code ch. IV, comm. 5.

41  See *Szarfer* v. *Chodos* (1986), 54 O.R. (2d) 663 (H.C.J.), aff'd (1988) 66 O.R. (2d) 350 (C.A.).

42  See, for example, CBA Code ch. IV, Rule.

43  *Descôteaux*, above note 6 at 401.

cating with that person.[44] Simply refusing to accept a retainer may be inadequate to prevent a duty from arising.[45]

## 7) Duty Survives End of Retainer

It is clear that the duty of confidentiality owed to a client continues after the retainer has come to an end.[46] The tenacious persistence of the duty is said to be justified given the basic rationale behind the obligation of confidentiality: if confidential information can be revealed once the retainer ends, the client is less likely to be completely candid with his or her lawyer while the retainer continues.[47]

**Advice:** Counsel must guard against the improper disclosure of confidential information at that point where the retainer comes to an end. Sometimes the client-lawyer relationship has broken down in a way that fosters acrimony. Even so, and barring the application of a self-defence or any other recognized exception to the duty, counsel cannot use confidential information to harm the client.[48] Moreover, where counsel withdraws from the record, care should be taken not to reveal client confidences to any third parties, including the court.[49]

## 8) Duty Survives Death of Client

The duty of confidentiality is in a sense perpetual, encompassing confidential information held by counsel even after the death of a client or former client.[50] It has nonetheless been argued that a less robust duty of confidentiality should apply where a client or former client has died.

---

44 This caution is made express in the Alberta rule: see Alta. ch. 7, comm. G.1.
45 Some of the steps that can be taken to minimize risk in this regard are discussed in section O(7), "Meeting a Potential Client: Avoiding Conflict Problems in Advance," in chapter 6.
46 See, for example, CBA Code ch. IV, comm. 4; N.S. ch. 5, comm. 5.3; Ont. r. 2.03(1); Man. ch. 4, comm. 4; Sask. ch. IV, comm. 4; Alta. ch. 7, r. 5 & comm. 5; and B.C. ch. 5, r. 4.
47 The other justifications for the duty of confidentiality also arguably support continuation of the duty after the retainer ends: see section B, "Rationale," in this chapter.
48 See *Vujic*, above note 25.
49 This topic is discussed in section C, "Rules of the Court," in chapter 11.
50 Alberta is alone among Canadian jurisdictions in expressly providing that the duty of confidentiality continues after death (see Alta. c.7, r. 5 and commentary), but other jurisdictions impliedly come to the same result by placing no end-point on the obligation of confidentiality to former clients: see the rules cited at note 46, above.

The paradigmatic case that is often raised postulates that disclosure will potentially exculpate an accused or convicted person whom counsel for a deceased client has good reason to believe is innocent. A standard application of professional conduct rules arguably prohibits disclosure in such a case,[51] and case law has traditionally endorsed a strict application of legal-professional privilege even where a client is deceased.[52] For instance, a number of American courts have held that the privilege prevents reception into evidence of communications between lawyer and a deceased client for the purpose of helping to demonstrate an accused's innocence.[53] It is interesting to compare the reluctance to breach the privilege exhibited in these decisions with other cases where courts have allowed a lawyer to testify for the *prosecution* at the trial of an accused charged with killing the deceased client.[54]

Yet permitting limited disclosure after death surely has minimal adverse impact on client-lawyer relations, and seems justified where an accused or convicted person's innocence is at stake. If one accepts that a deceased client has a substantially reduced interest in confidentiality, it is not much of a stretch to conclude that the possibility that confidences will in certain limited circumstances be disclosed after death will not place a significant chill on the free flow of information between lawyer and client. We recognize that a client can legitimately wish for confidentiality after death, for instance, to protect his or her reputation or to avoid adverse impact on loved ones.[55] However, a care-

---

51   No Canadian rule expressly allows disclosure on this scenario, apart from the possible application of the future-harm exception discussed in section G(3), "Type of Harm: Focus on Crimes," in chapter 5.

52   The general rule of evidence that client-lawyer communications are privileged although the client has died is discussed in *Geffen*, above note 22 at 232; and *Swidler & Berlin* v. *United States*, 524 U.S. 399 (1998) [*Swidler & Berlin*]. As *Geffen* notes, the rule is relaxed to permit a lawyer to give evidence in wills cases.

53   See, for example, *State* v. *Macumber*, 544 P.2d 1084 (Ariz., 1976); *People* v. *Modzelewski*, 611 N.Y.S. 2d 22 (N.Y.A.D. 1994); and *People* v. *Pena*, 198 Cal. Rptr. 819 at 828 (Ct. App. 1994). Also of interest is *Herrara* v. *Collins*, 506 U.S. 390 (1993), where a lawyer breached a confidence to come forward with such information, yet the issue of privilege was not raised.

54   See, for example, *State* v. *Gause*, 489 P.2d 830 (Ariz. 1971), vacated on other grounds, 409 U.S. 815 (1972); *State* v. *Kump*, 301 P.2d 808 (Wyo. 1956). A Canadian case where the privilege was set aside for just such a purpose, ostensibly on the basis of the client's best interests and the administration of justice, is *R.* v. *Jack* (1992), 70 C.C.C. (3d) 67 (Man. C.A.).

55   See *Swidler & Berlin*, above note 52 at 407.

fully circumscribed exception, for example, one applicable only where innocence is a stake, need not ignore such interests.[56] Moreover, some support for easing the duty of confidentiality where a wrongful conviction looms large can be taken from the emergence of an "innocence-at-stake" exception to legal-professional privilege.[57] However, it should not be assumed that this development regarding the privilege can solve the dilemma single-handed. Yet again, we must stress that an exception to legal-professional privilege does not necessarily permit a lawyer to breach confidentiality absent compulsion by court process. Often the lawyer will alone be aware of the exculpatory information, meaning that no other interested party has any reason or basis to invoke the court process in order to defeat the privilege. In such a case, the ethical rule of confidentiality must permit disclosure independent of any exception to the privilege if the information is ever to see the light of day.

On the other hand, it is possible to permit disclosure in this scenario without creating a special exception relating to deceased clients. A general innocence-at-stake exception to the duty of confidentiality could be recognized. Or consider the application of the future-harm exception presently found in most Canadian rules of professional conduct. The typical future harm exception would permit or even mandate disclosure where the exculpatory information would serve to prevent a prospective crime.[58] A potential or continuing miscarriage of justice will not fall within this definition where no prospective or ongoing *crime* is threatened, meaning that the future-harm exception has no application.[59] However, a cautious expansion of the future harm exception, let us say to encompass non-criminal future harm involving death or serious bodily injury, offers an attractive solution to our problem.

---

56   See generally B. Hood, "The Attorney-Client Privilege and a Revised Rule 1.6: Permitting Limited Disclosure after the Death of the Client" (1997) 7 Geo. J. Legal Ethics 741; *Swidler & Berlin*, above note 52, per O'Connor J. (dissenting); *contra* S. Frankel, "The Attorney-Client Privilege After the Death of the Client" (1992) 6 Geo. J. Legal Ethics 45.

57   See, for example, *Smith*, above note 21 at 242–43; *R. v. Campbell* (1999), 133 C.C.C. (3d) 257 at 295–96 (S.C.C.) [*Campbell*]; and most recently *McClure*, above note 1, which formally establishes an innocence-at-stake exception to legal-professional privilege.

58   See, for example, CBA Code ch. IV, comm. 11; Sask. ch. IV, comm. 11; Ont. r. 2.03(3); N.S. ch. 5, r. 5.12; and Alta. ch. 7, r. 8(c). The future harm exception is discussed in detail in section G, "Future Harm or Public Safety," in chapter 5.

59   See section G(3), "Type of Harm: Focus on Crimes," in chapter 5. Unique in this regard is Ont. r. 2.03(3), which permits disclosure where necessary to prevent serious bodily harm, whether criminal or not.

This approach, which is examined further in chapter 5, could take the death of the client into account to the extent that counsel is provided with a discretion regarding disclosure.[60] That is to say, where the future-harm exception has potential application, a client's death can reasonably be seen to reduce the interest in maintaining confidentiality, so that a lawyer may be more inclined to exercise the discretion to reveal the information in question.

## 9) Information Received after the Retainer Has Ended

The CBA Code does not purport to impose confidentiality with respect to information obtained by the lawyer *after* the professional relationship has ended, and most of the provincial governing bodies take the same stance.[61] However, the text of the Nova Scotia rule departs from this approach by imposing the duty of confidentiality where information is acquired by the lawyer "as a result of" the professional relationship with the client. The ambit of the Nova Scotia rule thus appears to cover information received *after* the professional relationship has ended, provided that the lawyer comes by the information as a result of having formerly represented the client.

**Example:** Counsel A practises in Nova Scotia. She has been discharged by her client, who retains Counsel B. Shortly thereafter, Crown counsel calls Counsel A to discuss ongoing settlement negotiations and, despite learning that the retainer has ended, updates Counsel A as to the status of the case. Several months later, Counsel B phones Counsel A to obtain information regarding the early stages of the case and, in doing so, necessarily reveals recent non-public developments pertaining to the client's matter. The information acquired by Counsel A, whether from the Crown or Counsel B, should be kept confidential even though obtained after the professional relationship has ended.

This limited extension of the obligation of confidentiality beyond the strict timeline of the professional relationship is warranted. If former counsel is free to publicize or exploit information acquired subsequent to, but as a result of, a prior professional relationship with the client, the client may delay discharging a lawyer in whom he or she no longer has confidence. It is also possible that the client is less willing to provide complete disclosure to a new lawyer, at least initially, on the fear that the information will be passed on to former counsel in the

---

60   See section G(8), "The Lawyer's Discretion," in chapter 5.

61   CBA Code ch. IV, Rule. See also Ont. r. 2.03(1); Sask. ch. IV, Rule; B.C. ch. 5, comm. 1; and Alta. ch. 7, Statement of Principle.

course of discussions necessary for the transfer of the file. We therefore agree with the approach to this issue taken in Nova Scotia. The wording could follow the text used in Nova Scotia, or it could refer to information "relating to the representation of the client."[62]

## 10) Literary Works

All Canadian rules of professional conduct refer, with some trepidation, to a lawyer's participation in literary works. The CBA Code's treatment of this subject has been followed in several Canadian jurisdictions. It states:

> The fiduciary relationship between lawyer and client forbids the lawyer to use any confidential information covered by the ethical rule for the benefit of the lawyer or a third person, or to the disadvantage of the client. *The lawyer who engages in literary works, such as an autobiography, memoirs and the like, should avoid disclosure of confidential information.*[63]

This wording has been seen simply to confirm that the usual duty of confidentiality applies where literary works are concerned, as opposed to imposing a less onerous or optional duty by virtue of the qualifier "should."[64] Ascribing this meaning to the language used in the Code essentially replicates the stricter wording used in British Columbia, Nova Scotia, and Alberta.[65] Consequently, Canadian lawyers have no special license or discretion to reveal confidential information in literary works, and remain bound by the obligation to keep client confidences secret.

## 11) Gossip and Shoptalk

A lawyer should never engage in idle gossip that serves to reveal confidential information, not even with the closest of family or friends. This obvious proscription is set out in most Canadian rules of professional conduct.[66] By the same token, these rules provide that the lawyer

---

62    This latter phrase is employed by Third Restatement §59; and ABA Rule 1.6(a).
63    CBA ch. IV, comm. 5 (emphasis added); see also Ont. r. 2.03(6).
64    See *Stewart*, above note 18 at 112.
65    See B.C. ch. 5, r. 5; and N.S. ch. 5, r. 5.5. In Alberta, no specific mention is made of literary works, meaning that the general prohibition applies: see Alta. ch. 7, Statement of Principle.
66    See, for example, CBA Code ch. IV, comm. 7; Ont. r. 2.03 (commentary); B.C. ch. 5, r. 8; N.S. ch. 5, r. 5.7; Sask. ch. IV, comm. 7; and Alta. ch. 7, comm. 1.

who hears gossip concerning the client's affairs should keep such information confidential and not recount the information to third parties.[67] The fact that information may come to the lawyer for reasons totally unconnected with the relationship, as would be the case with gossip overheard in a restaurant, is irrelevant.

"Shoptalk," used here to mean the discussion of legal matters between or among lawyers, ranging from an informal discussion at lunch to a question-and-answer session at a professional conference, raises more complicated issues. Lawyers routinely engage in shoptalk to aid in the conduct of a client's case, and shoptalk also serves the important function of continuing legal education. Starting with a non-contentious case, it makes sense to permit a lawyer to engage in such discussions with members of the same firm. Indeed, Canadian ethical rules provide that, absent instructions to the contrary, the authority to do so can be implied.[68] The other lawyers in the firm, as well as staff and agents, owe the client a duty of confidentiality wide enough to encompass such shoptalk.

More complicated is the case involving shoptalk with lawyers outside the firm, for these lawyers do not ordinarily owe the client a duty of confidentiality. A number of respected commentators nonetheless view "extra-firm" shoptalk as an acceptable phenomenon.[69] This position is acceptable only where the discussion presents no realistic risk of harm to the client. Moreover, the client's identity should not be revealed, even implicitly, unless necessary, and the conversation should always be discreet. If these guidelines are followed, one could view such talk as impliedly authorized by the client.[70] Most clients would want counsel to canvas ideas and strategies as a means of improving the quality of representation. It may also be that communication with a fellow lawyer is purged of identifying characteristics to the point that no confidential information is disclosed. Ultimately, revealing confidential information to non-firm colleagues, for purposes other than education, professional development, or the benefit of the

---

67   *Ibid.*

68   See, for example, CBA Code ch. IV, comm. 9.

69   See, for example, G. Hazard & W. Hodes, *The Law of Lawyering: A Handbook on the Model Rules of Professional Conduct*, 2d ed. (Englewood, N.J.: Prentice Hall, 1993) at §1.6 (202); J. Hall, *Professional Responsibility of the Criminal Lawyer*, 2d ed. (New York: Clark Boardman Callaghan, 1996) at §28:30; and Third Restatement §60, comm. "h."

70   This view is taken by Hall, above note 69. Naturally, the client could foreclose this implied consent by instructing counsel not to engage in shoptalk: see section B(2), "Implied Authority," in chapter 5.

client in question, is impossible to countenance and must be prohibited.

The Canadian rules of professional conduct are less than completely clear regarding the propriety of shoptalk.[71] Words such as "gossip," "indiscreet," and "shoptalk" are not used in any precise way, and conversations with lawyers and non-lawyers are discussed separately without indicating what differences, if any, might exist. Certainly, however, the Canadian rules are reasonably open to the interpretation that discussion of a client's case with another lawyer is acceptable if carried out discreetly and for a proper purpose. More clarity is provided by the Australian Bar Association's Advocacy Rules, which provide that no breach of the duty of confidence is committed by the barrister who simply seeks professional assistance or advice from another barrister or who shows a brief to a student.[72] This approach raises a correlative question as to the duty, if any, of the lawyer who *receives* information in this capacity. In our view, shoptalk that discloses confidential information is permissible in the narrow circumstances defined above, but accommodation should be made for a concomitant requirement that the recipient lawyer treat the information as confidential. Such an extension of the ethical duty of confidentiality is justified where it is reasonable in all the circumstances for the recipient lawyer to expect that the information is intended to be kept secret.[73] The Australian Advocacy Rules impose such a duty on the recipient,[74] and in our view this position should also apply in Canada.

**Recommendation:** Counsel who seeks the advice of a lawyer outside the firm should make sure that the recipient lawyer understands the need maintain confidentiality. Sometimes the circumstances of the consultation in themselves make clear this need, but other cases may require counsel to obtain the recipient lawyer's express agreement not to disclose or use information before proceeding with the discussion. Counsel should also exercise care to avoid seeking advice from a

---

71 See, for example, CBA Code ch. IV, comm. 7, adopted by most Canadian governing bodies. Much clearer is the Alberta commentary, though query the scope of implied authorization: Alta. ch. 7, comm. 1.

72 Australian Bar Association Advocacy Rules (1995), r. 105. See also *McKaskell* v. *Benseman*, [1989] 3 N.Z.L.R. 75 at 88 (H.C.) [*McKaskell*].

73 The notion of a duty of confidentiality owed by a lawyer to another lawyer's client is not entirely novel; see the discussion of joint defence arrangements in section I, "Joint Defences," in chapter 6.

74 Australian Bar Association Advocacy Rules (1995), r. 106. It does not follow, however, that the recipient lawyer is placed in a fiduciary relationship with the client: see *McKaskell*, above note 72 at 89.

lawyer who is in a conflict position *vis-à-vis* the matter or who is known to be a gossip.

# I. POSITIVE DUTY TO SAFEGUARD CONFIDENTIAL INFORMATION

The duty of confidentiality requires more of a lawyer than merely keeping quiet about client secrets. The ethical obligation also imposes an important positive duty to safeguard client confidences by taking reasonable steps to secure all such information.[75] Consequently, the acquisition, storage, retrieval, and communication of confidential information must be subject to controls reasonably designed and managed to prevent unauthorized disclosure. Whether the steps taken are reasonable will depend upon a number of factors, including the degree of risk that disclosure will occur, the foreseeability and seriousness of any resulting damage, the burden of taking steps to avoid the damage, and any relevant instructions provided by the client.

## 1) Safeguarding Confidential Information and Shared Office Space

The security of physical items, such as hard-copy documents, can be easily maintained by using locks, alarm systems, and adequate storage facilities. However, special care must be taken where two or more lawyers share office space but are not members of the same firm. A lawyer who shares space in this way must ensure that confidential information cannot be accessed by non-associated lawyers. Each lawyer's office should have a lock, as should filing cabinets located in common areas, and shared support staff should ideally have little or no access to confidential materials. If these steps are impractical, for instance, where non-associated lawyers wish to share a secretary, the

---

75  Closely related to this duty is the ethical rule that specifically imposes an obligation on a lawyer to observe all relevant rules and laws regarding the preservation and safeguarding of a client's property. Where no such rules or laws exist, or their interpretation is in doubt, the lawyer must care for the property in the manner of a careful and prudent owner. See, for example, CBA Code ch. VIII; Sask. ch. VIII; B.C. ch. 7.1; Ont. r. 2.07. See also Alta. ch. 7, r. 3, which encompasses "confidential" property. These rules expressly recognize the close relation between the preservation of a client's property and the duty of confidentiality: see for example, CBA Code ch. VIII, comm. 5.

only alternative may be to treat the group as a true firm for the purposes of the ethical rule regarding confidentiality.[76]

**Comparison:** In Alberta, lawyers who practise independently but share office space are treated as members of the same firm for the purpose of the confidentiality rule.[77] This approach is not expressly taken by other Canadian ethical rules on confidentiality.[78]

## 2) Phones and E-mail

Security concerns may be more difficult to address with respect to newer technologies. Cordless and non-digital cellphones present a real risk of eavesdropping, whether intentional or not, and should not be used for any matter of import without first warning the client of this distinct possibility.[79] More generally, the nature of a defence lawyer's practice makes electronic surveillance a possibility in certain instances. Despite the protection afforded lawyers by the applicable *Criminal Code* provisions,[80] in such cases it is prudent to avoid communicating on issues of substance by telephone, fax, or pager unless urgent circumstances offer no reasonable alternative.

As for communication via computer products, the burgeoning use of e-mail raises some unique concerns. Even absent secure encryption, there is arguably a reasonable expectation of privacy in e-mail that permits its general use without the need for the express consent of the client. Yet where information is sensitive, it is safest to obtain consent,

---

76 This approach would also have a substantial impact on conflict of interest issues. See the discussion in section M, "Affiliated Lawyers: Imputation of Conflict of Interest," in chapter 6.

77 See Alta. ch. 7, comm. G.2 & interp. 4(j).

78 However, most Canadian governing bodies treat lawyers who share office space as though they were partners or associates in the same firm for at least some conflict-of-interest purposes, an approach that implicitly engages notions of confidentiality: see the discussion in section M(1), "Office-Sharing Arrangements," in chapter 6.

79 See the review in J. Hall, *Search and Seizure,* 2d ed. (New York: Clark Boardman Callaghan, 1993) at §33.16–21. See also *R. v. Solomon* (1993), 85 C.C.C. (3d) 496 (Que. Mun. Ct.), aff'd (1996), 139 D.L.R. (4th) 625 (Que. C.A.), aff'd (1997), 118 C.C.C. (3d) 351 (S.C.C.); and *R. v. Larson* (1996), 192 A.R. 58 (Prov. Ct.).

80 See ss. 186(2) & (3) of the wiretap provisions in the *Criminal Code,* R.S.C. 1985, c. C-46, the aim of which is to exclude *bona fide* communications between lawyer and client. For a case in which the police brazenly breached client-lawyer communications, much to the court's chagrin, see *Robillard,* above note 4 at 307–10.

utilize encryption, or perhaps even forego the use of e-mail all together. There may also be merit in attaching a standard warning to all e-mail communications along the lines of that typically found on fax transmissions.

## 3) Handling Confidential Information in a Public Place

A lawyer must also exercise caution when handling confidential material in a public space.[81] Leaving a confidential document in an office reception area or courtroom may result in the disclosure of information to a third party. Similarly, working or talking at close quarters, such as in a court-house corridor or on an aeroplane, can expose a client's confidences to third parties who overhear or view confidential information.

## 4) Supervising Employees and Agents

The lawyer's positive duty to guard against breaches of confidentiality extends to require adequate and proper training of lawyers and non-lawyers who are working at the firm, and to ensure that confidences are protected by agents who come into contact with confidential material (such as bank employees, private investigators, couriers, photocopy services, and experts). Most Canadian rules can be read so as to recognize this aspect of the positive duty only where the lawyer has disclosed confidential information to such people.[82] The better view is that the lawyer has an obligation to ensure that all others who work at a firm or are contracted to provide services act in such a way so as to preserve confidentiality, even if they themselves are not privy to confidential information. This approach is taken in Alberta, where the applicable rule simply states that "[a] lawyer must take reasonable steps to ensure the maintenance of confidentiality by all persons engaged or employed by the lawyer."[83]

---

81   See Alta ch. 7, r. 3, comm. 3.
82   See, for example, CBA Code ch. IV, comm. 9; Ont. r. 2.03(1). See also Ont. r. 5.01.
83   Alta. ch. 7, r. 4. See also B.C. ch. 5, r. 2. See also Wolfram, above note 39 at 892–95; and ABA Rule 5.3.

## 5)  Keeping Confidential Information Secure after the Retainer has Ended

The duty to ensure the safekeeping of a client's information continues after the retainer has ended, given that the predicate duty of confidentiality survives the termination of the client-lawyer relationship. The lawyer must therefore handle the former client's file with care.[84] The file should be returned to the client or stored in a secure location. In our view, as a general rule the file cannot be destroyed unless the client consents, in which case the destruction must be carried out so as to prevent any breach of confidentiality. In sensitive cases, shredding will be required.

Absent client consent, there may be certain occasions where a file can be destroyed, but the need to avoid possible harm to the client must always remain paramount. Given that appeals and retrials can extend the life of a case, and that details regarding a closed file can be relevant to a subsequent civil or criminal proceeding, we believe that counsel should wait at least six years before destroying a file absent consent of a client. Even then, to be safe, counsel is advised to take reasonable steps to contact the client and determine his or her wishes. Finally, a lawyer must never destroy a client's file, no matter how much time has elapsed, where there are legitimate grounds to believe that the client's interests may be harmed as a result.[85]

# J.  DUTY TO ASSERT CONFIDENTIALITY

Related to the positive duty to safeguard information is the obligation of counsel to assert confidentiality when information is sought by a third party. This duty has been recognized at common law,[86] and in particular it applies where counsel is served with a subpoena to testify or produce documents relating to a client or is subject to a search war-

---

84  In this regard, also see the ethical rules regarding the preservation of a client's property set out in note 75, above.

85  In *Professional Responsibility of the Criminal Lawyer* above note 69 at §28:32, Hall goes so far as to argue that files can never be destroyed absent a client's consent.

86  *Bell v. Smith* (1968), 68 D.L.R. (2d) 751 (S.C.C.). See also *Lavallee*, above note 6 at 200–01.

rant pertaining to a client's file.[87] Counsel who is subject to the compulsion of court process must raise any non-frivolous claim of privilege, and should be generally aware of the relevant common law, statutory provisions, and constitutional principles.[88]

## K. DUTY TO WARN CLIENT

Lawyers have a duty to inform a client of the scope of the confidentiality obligation, including possible exceptions. Failure to do so could leave the client with a false sense of security and result in counsel's liability where information not covered by the confidentiality rule is used or released. On the other hand, a lawyer need not review with the client every last aspect of the duty of confidentiality. Rather, a warning is required only where reasonably necessary in the circumstances (including the risk of disclosure and the foreseeability and extent of attendant harm to the client). The case of two or more co-accused represented by the same lawyer provides a good example: the special application of the duty of confidentiality must always be fully discussed with all co-accused.[89] Other examples include a client who is about to be assessed by a defence psychiatrist (future-harm exception),[90] a sexual-assault complainant who retains a lawyer to bring a civil suit against the perpetrator (innocence-at-stake exception to legal-professional privilege),[91] and the appellant who contemplates raising ineffective assistance of counsel as a ground of appeal (self-defence exception and/or waiver).[92]

---

87   Recommended responses to a subpoena or search warrant are discussed in section P, "Subpoenas and Search Warrants," in this chapter.

88   See especially B.C. ch. 5, r. 14, which stresses that this duty arises where a lawyer is required under any federal or provincial legislation to produce a document or provide information that is or may be privileged. A need to assert privilege over a client's file is emphasized by many Canadian codes of professional conduct as part of the duty to preserve the client's property; see, for example, CBA Code ch. VIII, comm. 6; Sask. ch. VIII, comm. 6; N.S. ch. 9, r. 9.7; Ont. r. 2.07(6).

89   See, for example, Ont. r. 2.04(6)(b).

90   See *Smith*, above note 21.

91   See *McClure*, above note 1.

92   See *R. v. B.(G.D.)* (2000), 143 C.C.C. (3d) 289 (S.C.C.).

Caveat: The duty to warn must not be misused as a veiled threat to dissuade a client from making a complaint against counsel. For instance, a trial lawyer should not cow a client with horror stories of widespread loss of confidentiality and privilege in order to head-off a claim of ineffective assistance. If the circumstances present a possible conflict between counsel's desire to avoid a complaint or civil liability and the client's best interests, independent legal advice will probably be necessary.

## 1) An Example: Representing the Young Person

An area of special concern is avoiding the release of confidential information when representing a young person, and making sure that the young person understands the ambit of the ethical duty. A young person should be clearly told that the duty of confidentiality applies to prevent the disclosure of confidences to all third parties, including parents. Confidential information should be revealed only with the young person's informed consent. Moreover, counsel must take special care to advise the young person as to the inapplicability of legal-professional privilege with respect to information provided to parents, and to avoid scrupulously the release of information that could later be used against the young person in court. The best course is usually to exercise great caution with respect to information made available to parents and to make the young person aware of the potential problems when information is shared with parents. Counsel should make a habit of not discussing the actual details of the case with the young person when his or her parents are present.

Example: Counsel represents a young person on a charge of assault bodily harm arising out of a schoolyard brawl. At his first meeting with the client, counsel includes the parents in all the discussions, including the client's inculpatory review of the events in issue. The Crown's case is quite weak on the issue of identification, and after discussions with counsel the client ultimately decides to plead not guilty, leaving the prosecution to prove the allegation. Serious difficulties with this strategy can arise, however, because of the initial meeting with the parents. The parents may decide to go to the police or Crown with their information, believing that their son should not attempt to avoid responsibility for the offence. Equally, the Crown may independently decide to subpoena the parents to testify at trial on a material point and illicit damming statements as part of its case.

## L. CONFIDENTIALITY AND INFORMATION REVEALING THE IDENTITY OF A CLIENT

Information indicating the identity of a client, as well as the related fact that a retainer exists, is typically not the subject of legal-professional privilege.[93] An exception to this general rule appears to exist where the fact of identity is closely connected to the nature of the retainer, where disclosure by the lawyer would represent the last link in connecting the client to a crime or perhaps where identity is inextricably intertwined with other clearly privileged information.[94] Where legal-professional privilege does apply, there is no doubt that a client's identity will be confidential within the meaning of the rules of professional conduct. The ethical rules in Canada go much further, however, placing a general obligation on counsel not to reveal the identity of a client or the fact of being consulted unless required by the nature of the retainer.[95] Whether or not privilege covers the information is irrelevant. Imposing this duty of confidentiality on counsel is warranted, for revelation of a client's name by criminal counsel may fuel gossip and cause embarrassment, ridicule, or financial harm.

**Two Examples:** Our first example sees a lawyer approached by a prospective client. The client tells the lawyer that he has been involved in a fatal car accident and wishes to determine whether he can come forward without risking a criminal charge. The lawyer accepts the retainer, the purpose of which is to attempt negotiations with the authorities so as to achieve the client's objective. Our second example sees the lawyer retained to act for a prominent businesswoman who has been charged with shoplifting. In only the first scenario will privilege operate to shield the lawyer from the operation of legal process that attempts to expose the client's identity.[96] However, leaving the

---

93   See, for example, *Ontario (Securities Commission)* v. *Greymac Credit Corp.* (1983), 41 O.R. (2d) 328 at 338 (Div. Ct.) [*Ontario (Securities Commission)*]; and *Lukas* v. *Lawson* (1993), 13 O.R. (3d) 447 (Gen. Div., Master Donkin).

94   See, for example, *R.* v. *Fink* (2001), 149 C.C.C. (3d) 321 at 334 (Ont. C.A.) [*Fink*]; *Lavallee (C.A.)*, above note 6 at 204–07; and *R.* v. *Sauvé*, [1965] C.S. 129.

95   See CBA Code, ch. IV, comm. 3; Alta. ch. 7, r. 2; Ont. r. 2.01(1); B.C. c. 5, comm. 3; and N.S. ch. 5, comm. 5.2.

96   As already noted, legal-professional privilege can operate with respect to the identity of a client. Privilege was found to exist on facts resembling this example in *Thorson* v. *Jones* (1973), 38 D.L.R. (3d) 312 (B.C.S.C.). See also the high-profile American case of *Baltes* v. *Doe*, 4 Laws. Man. on Prof. Conduct (ABA/BNA) 356 (Fla. Cir. Ct. 1988), (discussed in Hazard & Hodes, above note 69 at §1.6

possibility of legal compulsion aside, in *both* examples counsel is forbidden from revealing the client's identity to any third party by operation of the ethical duty of confidentiality.[97]

**Caution:** Counsel who accepts a retainer involving secrecy as to the client's identity must carefully investigate whether legal-professional privilege will apply in the event that adverse parties attempt to compel disclosure of this information. As noted, if the privilege does not apply, counsel could be forced to disclose the information in response to a subpoena, despite the ethical rule of confidentiality. Naturally, the client must be informed of any such risk. In addition, great care should be taken to ensure that the client's identity is not inadvertently revealed. In extreme cases, where the press and/or police are eager to obtain the client's identity, counsel may want to consider retaining another lawyer to provide extra insulation against unintended revelation.

In spite of the general ethical prohibition against revealing a client's identity, it would be wrong to say that the fact of retainer and the identity of one's client can never be disclosed. Much to the contrary, disclosure of this confidential information will be permitted in accordance with the client's implied or express authorization.[98] In particular, counsel has the implied authority to reveal information pertaining to a client's identity where to do so is a necessary part of the retainer.[99] In the vast majority of cases, a defence lawyer cannot effectively represent a client without informing the court, Crown counsel, and others of this fact. On the other hand, this implied authority obviously does not permit disclosure for purposes unrelated to the proper representation of the client.

---

(105); and J. Przypyszny, "Public Assault on the Attorney-Client Privilege, Ramification of *Baltes* v. *Doe*" (1990) 3 Geo. J. Legal Ethics 351).

97  It has been suggested that legal-professional privilege usually does not cover the client's identity because such information is not confidential: see, for example, *Ontario (Securities Commission)*, above note 97 at 338. This approach does not take account of the difference between the evidentiary rule of privilege and the duty imposed by the ethical rules, and it should not be taken to mean that lawyers are unconstrained in disclosing a client's identity.

98  See the discussion of express and implied authority in section B, "Authorized Disclosure," in chapter 5.

99  Revelation of a client's identity is expressly permitted by many rules of professional conduct where, "the nature of the retainer requires such disclosure": see, for example, CBA Code ch. IV, comm. 3.

# M. WHEREABOUTS OF THE UNLOCATED OR FUGITIVE CLIENT

Somewhat related to the tricky question of whether counsel can reveal a client's identity is the more common case of the unlocated or fugitive client. A client may seek advice from a lawyer regarding police attempts to conduct a suspect interview or execute an arrest warrant. A client may also contact counsel after absconding while on bail or escaping from prison. Yet another possibility is that a subpoenaed witness contacts counsel after failing to appear in court as required. In any of these circumstances, counsel may learn of the client's whereabouts or obtain information that could help to reveal the client's location. It is also possible that friends or relatives of the client provide counsel with similar information. How does the duty of confidentiality operate in these sorts of situations?

As was the case regarding the issue of a client's identity, it is helpful to start by considering both legal-professional privilege and the duty of confidentiality. Looking to the privilege, there is scant Canadian authority on point, but the law regarding identity appears to be applicable.[100] That is to say, the location of one's client is usually not protected by privilege, but the privilege will apply where the client's location is closely connected to the subject matter of the retainer. Of course, if the client seeks advice regarding how to evade capture, the crime-fraud exception to the privilege may apply.[101]

Turning to the related question of confidentiality, it is clear that where counsel is compelled by judicial process to reveal such information, and a court determines that the privilege is inoperative, the rules of professional conduct mandate disclosure.[102] None the less, prior to the application of court process, the better view is that counsel's broad obligation to keep information confidential precludes the revelation of

---

100   See, for example, Sopinka, Lederman & Bryant, above note 7 at §14.47, where a client's identity and whereabouts are impliedly treated in a similar way. In the United States, authority is divided as to the applicability of privilege where a client's location is in issue. The leading case finding that legal-professional privilege has at least some application is *In re Nackson*, 555 A.2d 1101 (N.J. 1989), while a position somewhat less accommodating to the privilege is taken in *Commonwealth v. Maguigan*, 511 A.2d 1327 (Pa. 1986). We are attracted to the interpretation of these cases offered by Hazard & Hodes, above note 69 at §1.6 (113).

101   See, for example, *Descôteaux*, above note 6 at 404–05, 413; and *Campbell*, above note 57 at 291–95.

102   See section D, "Disclosure Required by Law," in chapter 5.

an unlocated or fugitive client's whereabouts.[103] Certainly, no Canadian code of professional conduct contains an exception that unambiguously mandates disclosure of this sort of information. Yet, if in the circumstances it can be said that the client's continued status as a fugitive constitutes on ongoing criminal offence, some Canadian future-harm exceptions permit disclosure.[104] Future-harm exceptions may also apply if, altogether apart from the client's status as a fugitive, there are reasonable grounds to believe that the client is likely to commit other crimes. However, leaving aside the possible application of the future-harm exception, a prohibition against disclosure should apply even where a fugitive client expressly seeks counsel's help in avoiding capture. In such a case, counsel can do no more than advise the client against breaking the law and seek to convince him or her to surrender. As long as Canadian law does not criminalize mere non-disclosure by counsel,[105] and absent the applicability of the future-harm exception, counsel cannot violate the confidence by revealing the client's location to the authorities.

**Warning:** Counsel must never aid or abet a fugitive client's efforts to evade capture. Any action that helps the client in this regard is unethical and also exposes counsel to criminal censure.[106]

---

103 ABA Comm. on Ethics and Professional Responsibility, in Formal Op. 349 (1984) effectively adopts this position by withdrawing previous opinions that held to the contrary. However, the American position is subject to some debate, in part because of the legacy wrought by these various opinions.

104 See section G(5), "The Need for *Future* Harm," in chapter 5.

105 If Canadian law criminalized the mere failure to disclose a fugitive's whereabouts, counsel would be forced to reveal the information pursuant to the both the required by law and self-defence exceptions: see sections D, "Disclosure Required by Law," and E, "Lawyer Self-Defence," in chapter 5. However, our law does not operate to this effect: see, for example, *Criminal Code*, above note 80, s. 139 (obstructing justice), "the gist of which is *doing an act* which has a tendency to pervert or obstruct the course of justice and which is done for that purpose": *R. v. May* (1984), 13 C.C.C. (3d) 257 at 260 (Ont. C.A.) (emphasis added).

106 See *Criminal Code*, above note 80, s. 22 (counselling), ss. 23 & 463 (accessory after the fact); and s. 139 (obstructing justice), as well as Canadian ethical rules that restrict counsel from acting illegally in aid of a client's cause: see, for example, CBA Code ch. IX.

# N. INADVERTENT DISCLOSURE

At one time, legal-professional privilege was considered lost by virtue of accidental interception or even theft of the underlying confidential information.[107] More recently, Canadian courts have shown a willingness to depart from this unforgiving stance.[108] Accordingly, the privilege will likely be maintained despite inadvertent disclosure to a third party if in the circumstances it can be said that waiver has not occurred. Factors applicable in determining whether waiver has occurred include how the documents were released, whether prompt attempts were made to recover the documents once disclosure was discovered, the timing of the application to retrieve the documents, the number and nature of the third parties who received the documents, whether or not unfairness would result if other parties were not allowed to use the documents, and the impact on the court process.[109] We can thus say that, in cases where counsel takes reasonable precautions to protect a confidence, there is a strong argument that waiver does not occur (and hence privilege is not lost) merely because information has been unintentionally disclosed.

A lawyer's ethical duty of confidentiality is implicated in several ways by the accidental disclosure scenario. First, the positive duty to protect confidences from disclosure means that counsel must take steps to prevent this scenario from occurring.[110] Second, if unintentional disclosure does occur, counsel has an obligation, pursuant to the same duty, to take promptly all reasonable steps to retrieve the information and prevent further dissemination. This obligation exists even if the information is irrelevant to matters at issue in a court proceed-

---

107 The classic statement of this position is found in *Calcraft* v. *Guest*, [1898] 1 Q.B. 759 (C.A.). Support for the same view is also found in *Descôteaux*, above note 6 at 396 (note 3) & 400; and *R.* v. *Dunbar* (1982), 68 C.C.C. (2d) 13 at 42 (Ont. C.A.) [*Dunbar*]. Limited respite from this strict rule was traditionally offered by equity, which would enjoin use of confidential documents that had been unlawfully or improperly obtained: see *Ashburton (Lord)* v. *Pape*, [1913] 2 Ch. 469 (C.A.) [*Ashburton*].

108 See, for example, *Airst* v. *Airst* (1998), 37 O.R. (3d) 654 at 657–60 (Gen. Div.) [*Airst*]; *Supercom of California Ltd.* v. *Sovereign General Insurance Co.* (1998), 37 O.R. (3d) 597 at 606 (Gen. Div.); P. Perell, "*Royal Bank* v. *Lee*" Case Comment (1993) 72 Can. Bar Rev. 72; P. McWilliams, *Canadian Criminal Evidence*, 3d ed. (Aurora: Canada Law Book, 1999) at §35:10760. See also the possible discretion referred to in *Dunbar*, above note 107 at 42–43.

109 See, for example, *Airst*, above note 108 at 659–60.

110 The positive aspect of the duty is discussed in section I, "Positive Duty to Safeguard Confidential Information," in this chapter.

ing. Third, counsel's ethical duty of confidentiality will usually persist altogether apart from any question of privilege. Thus, counsel remains under a duty to refrain from using or disclosing the information even where the privilege has been lost.

The last two points regarding the duty of confidentiality apply with equal, if not greater, vigour where information is disclosed because of the illegal or improper actions of a third party, for instance, where the document has been stolen. It is worth adding that, where information is obtained by such nefarious means, it is almost certain that legal-professional privilege will continue to operate. Moreover, where the illegal or improper acts are carried out by government actors such as the police, a breach of sections 7, 8, and/or 10(b) of the *Charter* has likely occurred, implicating the remedial possibilities envisaged by section 24.[111]

What happens where the tables are turned, so that a lawyer finds himself or herself in receipt of confidential information that has been obtained by improper means or inadvertently disclosed? Consider the example where Lawyer A receives documents from Lawyer B, who acts for a co-accused. The documents are being provided pursuant to a joint defence arrangement whereby research on several legal points is being exchanged. To her surprise, Lawyer A discovers among the documents a written statement provided to Lawyer B by his client, and can only assume that the statement has been disclosed in error. The British Columbia rules of professional conduct expressly address this kind of situation, providing that:

15. A lawyer who has access to or comes into possession of a document which the lawyer has reasonable grounds to believe belongs to or is intended for an opposing party and was not intended for the lawyer to see, shall:
(a) return the document, unread and uncopied, to the party to whom it belongs; or
(b) if the lawyer reads part or all of the document before realizing that it was not intended for him or her, cease reading the document and promptly return it, uncopied, to the party to whom it belongs, advising that party:

---

111 See, for example, *Weatherford* v. *Bursey*, 429 U.S. 545 at 550–52 (1977); as well as Canadian cases that stress the importance of privacy in exercising the right under s. 10(b) of the *Charter*, above note 20, including *R.* v. *Jackson* (1993), 86 C.C.C. (3d) 233 (Ont. C.A.); *R.* v. *Butler* (1995), 104 C.C.C. (3d) 198 (B.C.C.A.); and *R.* v. *Kennedy* (1995), 103 C.C.C. (3d) 161 (Nfld. C.A.).

(i)  of the extent to which the lawyer is aware of the contents, and

(ii)  what use the lawyer intents to make of the contents of the document.[112]

The rules of professional conduct in Alberta take a similar approach.[113]

A variation is taken by the Third Restatement, which provides that counsel is under an obligation to return the documents only where the circumstances of disclosure do not destroy the privilege.[114] That is to say, if the privilege is gone, the document can be kept and used. The British Columbia and Alberta rules are arguably stricter, in that counsel must refrain from reviewing the document if he or she is aware that disclosure was not intended. In Alberta, however, where counsel inadvertently reviews the document, the possible loss of privilege may become immediately relevant. In such a case, the Alberta rule provides that the issue as to use of the document must be resolved by agreement or by the court, and that until such resolution is achieved it is improper to use the document or disclose the document's contents.[115]

To act otherwise than as required by the British Columbia or Alberta rules may be more advantageous to one's client. However, a lawyer's duty to act zealously in the client's best interests is not without its limits. The ethical rules provide that a lawyer must not take advantage of a mistake on the part of another lawyer if to do so would obtain for the lawyer's client a benefit to which the client has no *bona fide* claim or entitlement.[116] At the least, in circumstances where privilege is unlikely to be lost, the approach taken in British Columbia and Alberta is to be preferred. Returning the document also bolsters the credibility and integrity of the individual lawyer, not to mention the profession as a whole. Counsel should also consider the possibility that on another occasion he or she will make the same sort of mistake, in which case his or her client will benefit from the recipient lawyer's adherence to the British Columbia/Alberta approach. Moreover, from a practical point of view, a decision to examine the inadvertently dis-

---

112 B.C. ch. 5, r. 15. The interests implicated by this scenario are fully discussed in ABA Comm. on Ethics and Professional Responsibility, Formal Op. 368 (1992) (Inadvertent Disclosure of Confidential Materials). This Opinion takes a position similar to the B.C. rule.

113 See Alta. ch. 4, r. 8 & commentary.

114 See Third Restatement §60, comm. "m," and related Reporter's Note.

115 See Alta. ch. 4, comm. 8.

116 See especially Alta. ch. 4, r. 3. A somewhat convoluted version of this rule is found in other jurisdictions: see, for example, CBA Code ch. XVI, comm. 4; Ont. r. 6.03(3).

closed document may hurt one's client by creating a conflict-of-interest that mandates withdrawal from the case. The conflict-of-interest problem can occur if, despite inadvertent disclosure of the document, legal-professional privilege is found by a court to apply. In such a case, the counsel receiving the document may not be allowed to use it as part of his or her case and could conceivably be forced from the record.[117] Finally, there may be circumstances where counsel can successfully argue that inadvertent disclosure constitutes waiver or comes within an independent exception to legal-professional privilege (such as the innocence-at-stake or crime-fraud exceptions). In such cases, counsel may be able to compel production of the information.

Where the information reaches counsel as a result of deceit or illegal means, such as theft or fraud, there is less dispute as to the proper course of action.[118] Counsel who is aware of the impropriety may be liable for any damage caused by using such information, and in any event must take steps to return the information and cannot pass it on to his or her client.[119] This result is especially apposite where the information in question comes into the possession of Crown counsel under circumstances where privilege is not lost, given the constitutional implications of both legal-professional privilege and the underlying principle of confidentiality.[120] Also, such information arguably falls within the Crown's obligation to disclose, and at a minimum any accused affected by the contents should be informed that the information has come into the Crown's possession.[121]

---

117  Compare *Re Markovina* (1991), 57 B.C.L.R. (2d) 73 (S.C.), as well as the discussion of conflict-of-interest problems sometimes confronting lawyers who participate in joint defence arrangements in section I, "Joint Defences," in chapter 6.

118  The Alberta ethical rules touch on the subject of counsel's obligation where documents are acquired by improper means: see Alta. ch. 4, r. 8 & commentary. See also the Canadian ethical rules dealing with the limits placed on the lawyer's actions as an advocate (for example, CBA Code ch. IX).

119  See Third Restatement §60, comm. "m." See also *Re Markovina*, above note 117; and *Ashburton*, above note 107.

120  See, for example, *People* v. *Knippenberg*, 362 N.E.2d 681 (Ill. 1977).

121  However, if such an accused is not the party whose legal-professional privilege is in issue, disclosure should be limited to notice that the Crown is in possession of a document over which privilege may well exist. If necessary, the issue of privilege would subsequently be determined by the court.

## O. CO-CLIENTS

Where not prevented from doing so by conflict-of-interest problems, counsel may represent two or more co-accused. In such an instance, counsel is not bound by any duty of confidence to one client vis-à-vis the other(s).[122] He or she actually has a positive obligation to inform each client as to all relevant information received from the other(s).[123] Remember that counsel will have fully explained the workings of the duty of confidentiality to all affected clients before taking on such a retainer.[124]

It may be possible in some circumstances to erect a limited duty of confidentiality between co-clients. This arrangement can be instituted only where the clients concerned provide informed consent. Yet, in criminal cases involving co-accused, this approach is fraught with danger, even given the necessary precondition that conflict-of-interest concerns not be fatal. Certainly, if information relevant to the defence of one client cannot be disclosed by reason of an agreement to limit confidentiality, counsel will likely have a conflict-of-interest. Only the most innocuous information could validly be the subject of such an agreement.

Another wrinkle regarding the application of the duty of confidentiality to co-clients occurs where one client tries to renege on the usual sharing arrangement. Suppose that, despite having given informed consent to multiple representation, Client A provides information to counsel with the express instruction that it not be shared with the co-accused, Client B. This scenario places counsel in a position of divided loyalty: failure to disclose will betray the duty to keep Client B informed, while disclosure will violate Client A's instructions. In such a case, counsel must withdraw unless Client A can be persuaded to share the information. Where counsel is forced to withdraw for this reason, the question still arises as to whether he or she can disclose the information to Client B. It has been suggested that there is a discretion to disclose if the adverse impact on Client B of non-disclosure exceeds the adverse impact that disclosure will have on Client A.[125] There may

---

122 See especially Alta. ch. 7, r. 8(d) & commentary. Other Canadian ethical rules discuss confidentiality and co-clients in the context of conflict-of-interest: see, for example, CBA Code ch. V, comm. 5.

123 *Ibid.*

124 See the discussion in section J, "Duty to Assert Confidentiality," in this chapter; and section O(1), "Consultation with the Client," in chapter 6.

125 See Third Restatement §60, comm. "l."

also be a discretion, whether in the alternative or not, to at least inform Client B that a matter seriously affecting his or her interests has arisen.[126]

# P. SUBPOENAS AND SEARCH WARRANTS[127]

As already noted, counsel has a positive duty to prevent disclosure of a client's confidences.[128] When the threatened breach arises by reason of an attempt to compel the release of information by court process, carrying out this duty will invariably involve asserting legal-professional privilege. The following discussion examines some of the difficulties that arise, as well as recommended responses, where counsel is served with a subpoena or subjected to a search warrant.

## 1) Subpoenas

Counsel who is served with a subpoena usually has adequate time to consider carefully his or her response. It is wise to begin by contacting another lawyer for the purpose of providing legal assistance. Another lawyer should also represent the client in any attempt to quash or otherwise challenge the subpoena. Depending on the circumstances, the subpoenaed counsel may want or require separate counsel (for instance, where a conflict-of-interest arises and counsel's unique concerns warrant representation).

Counsel acting on behalf of the client and/or subpoenaed lawyer in an attempt to quash or resist a subpoena should determine the availability of an immediate appeal in case of an adverse ruling.[129] If such an appeal route has any realistic potential, and the client so instructs counsel, preparations should be made in advance of the ruling so that the necessary procedural steps, including an application for a stay pending appeal, can be undertaken immediately if the subpoena is upheld.

---

126 See Third Restatement §60, comm. "l."
127 See also section D, "Disclosure Required by Law," in chapter 5.
128 See section J, "Duty to Assert Confidentiality," in this chapter.
129 For instance, where the client whose lawyer has been subpoenaed is a witness in the proceeding, it may be that an interlocutory appeal can be brought, with leave, directly to the Supreme Court of Canada: see the discussion in section D, "Disclosure Required by Law," in chapter 5. Of late, however, the Supreme Court has urged Parliament to foreclose this direct appeal route: see *McClure*, above note 1 at 339.

## 2)  Search Warrants

Being the subject of a search warrant often places counsel in a difficult position, with little time to carefully consider all options prior to reacting. Counsel who is faced with a search warrant may want to take some or all of the steps set out below. Crucially, all members and employees of the firm should know in advance how to react to a search warrant, just as the inhabitants of an office are generally aware of the required procedure for a fire drill. Each lawyer and staff member will ideally be provided with a written checklist of steps to take when confronted with a search warrant.

Possible steps to take in responding to a search warrant include:

1.  If notified in advance of the search warrant, separate the documents sought by the parties executing the warrant and place these documents in a secure place. Take careful notes of this procedure so that continuity of the documents can be established if need be. Under no circumstance should any document be destroyed or hidden.

2.  Make copies of the documents for the client to aid him or her in making informed decisions regarding the search.[130] If time permits, counsel may want to compile an inventory of the documents.

3.  Immediately notify the client. It may be appropriate to suggest that he or she retain independent legal counsel, for instance, where the propriety of lawyer's conduct is potentially in issue. Any instructions of import should be provided in writing if time and logistics permit.

4.  Counsel should review the statute under which the search warrant has been issued and the state of case law on point. Note that section 488.1 of the *Criminal Code* will apply to most searches carried out under federal legislation, a notable exception being a search pursuant to the *Income Tax Act*.[131] Most provinces have a similar provision governing the search and seizure of potentially privi-

---

130  This step avoids the need to bring an application to obtain copies, for instance under s. 488.1(9) of the *Criminal Code*, above note 80.

131  See s. 488.1(2) & (11) of the *Criminal Code*, *ibid.*, as well as s. 232 of the *Income Tax Act*, R.S.C. 1985, c. 1 (5th Supp.). The procedure under the latter statute is similar to the *Criminal Code* provisions. Note that s. 232(3.1) of the *Income Tax Act* provides for the same procedure where an officer is about to inspect or examine documents or where the minister has required a lawyer to produce a document.

leged materials.[132] Currently, several provincial appeal courts have ruled that section 488.1 is unconstitutional.[133]

5. Counsel should consider obtaining legal advice from another lawyer and also calling his or her governing association for input.[134] If the authorities executing the warrant have not already done so,[135] counsel may wish to request that a representative from the governing association attend during the execution of the warrant.

6. Call a meeting of all lawyers and staff to review the procedure to be followed upon the arrival of the parties executing the warrant.

7. On the arrival of any parties seeking to seize confidential documents, ask to see the search warrant and supporting materials, and also ask the parties for identification. If no search warrant is provided, counsel must refuse to provide any files.[136] However, once a search warrant is proffered by the proper authorities, counsel must cooperate to the extent required by the warrant. Refusal to do so raises the risk of being charged with obstructing justice.

8. If copies of the search warrant and supporting materials are not provided, ask to make copies of the originals.

9. Carefully read the search warrant and supporting materials. Ensure that the warrant has not expired. If the warrant is valid, keep the parties executing the warrant to its terms.

10. If no warning has been given prior to the arrival of the parties executing the search warrant, ask for an opportunity to carry out as many of steps 1-6 above as possible.[137] It may be worthwhile asking for a substantial period of time to carry out these steps, perhaps

---

132 See for example, s. 160 of the Ontario *Provincial Offences Act*, R.S.O. 1990, ch. P.33.

133 See, for example, *Fink*, above note 94; *Lavallee (C.A.)*, above note 6; *White, Ottenheimer & Baker* v. *Canada (Attorney General)* (2000), 146 C.C.C. (3d) 28 (Nfld. C.A.); *Canada (A.G.)* v. *Several Clients*, [2000] N.S.J. No. 384 (C.A.) (QL). See also *Festing* v. *Canada (A.G.)* (2000), 31 C.R. (5th) 203 (B.C.S.C.). If the Supreme Court of Canada upholds these decisions, Parliament will almost certainly amend the impugned *Criminal Code* provision.

134 Many governing bodies have written guidelines that are useful in assessing what steps should be taken.

135 In some jurisdictions the police are advised or required to take this step: see *Lavallee (Q.B.)*, above note 6 at 524 & 536 (Appendix "B," para. 1).

136 See the discussion in *Agnes Securities Ltd.* v. *British Columbia* (1976), 31 C.C.C. (2d) 154 (B.C.S.C.).

137 The client and counsel do not necessarily have a right to take these steps prior to the execution of the search warrant.

several days. It is quite likely, however, that this request will be refused, especially given the limited lifespan of most search warrants.[138] If the authorities are not prepared to provide any time to carry out some or all of these steps, counsel should nonetheless attempt to do so as the search and seizure is progressing.

11. Absent a clear, express and fully informed waiver by the client, inform the parties executing the search warrant that the materials sought are confidential and claim legal-professional privilege on behalf of the client.[139] It is crucial that the privilege be claimed prior to providing the documents to the police, given that the terms of the applicable legislation may require such in order to preserve the privilege.[140]

12. A search warrant does not determine the application of legal-professional privilege, and therefore the parties executing the warrant should not be reviewing the contents of any confidential items.[141] Also, remember that a search warrant does not provide the bearer with any right to conduct interviews with lawyers or staff members. Lawyers must keep this point in mind, and staff should be informed not to talk to the parties executing the warrant. To pro-

---

138 See *Joseph* v. *M.N.R.* (1985), 20 D.L.R. (4th) 577 (Ont. H.C.); and *1013808 Ontario Inc.* v. *Revenue Canada* (1994), 94 D.T.C. 6532 (Ont. Gen. Div.) accept the possibility that counsel may be permitted a reasonable time to produce requested documents, but these cases do not involve search warrants that pertain to an alleged criminal offence. Note that s. 488.1(8) of the *Criminal Code*, above note 80, provides that no officer shall seize any documents without affording a reasonable opportunity for a claim of solicitor-client privilege to be made.

139 Note that s. 488.1(2) of the *Criminal Code, ibid.*, and subsections 232(3) & (3.1) of the *Income Tax Act*, above note 131, require that privilege be claimed on behalf of a "named client."

140 For instance, s. 488.1(2) of the *Criminal Code*, above note 80, and subsections 232(3) & (3.1) of the *Income Tax Act*, above note 131, are drafted in terms that suggest that the protective procedure made available by the provisions is activated only where privilege is claimed prior to the police taking possession of the materials in question. Note that s. 488.1(8) of the *Code* requires that counsel be afforded a "reasonable opportunity" to claim privilege. This heavy reliance upon counsel's prompt claiming of the privilege has been a major basis for some courts to hold the legislation unconstitutional: see the cases cited at note 133, above.

141 See *Robillard*, above note 4 at 308.

tect against inadvertent slips and ensure a consistent approach, it is advisable to nominate one or two lawyers to handle all interaction with the parties executing the warrant.

13. Counsel should ask to be allowed to collect the sought-after documents and provide these to the police, rather than having the police conduct a full-scale search of the law office. Taking this initiative serves to minimize disruption in the office and reduce the possible breach of confidentiality with respect to materials not properly the subject of the search warrant. The authorities may welcome such assistance, unless of course counsel is himself or herself suspected of involvement in illegal activities.

14. A search warrant can operate to permit the seizure of computer data, and the parties executing the warrant are permitted to use computer equipment in the office for this purpose.[142] If possible counsel should provide the requested information himself or herself (or have a technician or other staff member do so), in order to minimize the possibility that confidential information pertaining to other clients will be revealed. If the parties executing the warrant insist on carrying out the search themselves, counsel should monitor their actions with this same aim in mind.

15. Unless privilege is waived, counsel should affix a seal on the materials or insist on being present when the seal is affixed.

16. Sometimes the applicable legislation requires that the materials be deposited with a specific custodian but permits alternative arrangements to be made by agreement.[143] Consider whether alternative arrangements might be desirable. In any event, ascertain from the parties executing the warrant exactly where the materials are being taken, so that any appropriate objection or alternative arrangements can be made and reduced to writing.[144]

17. Make thorough notes regarding the entire process, and have all staff do the same — if a dispute arises as to how the search was

---

142 See for example, subsections 487(2.1) & (2.2) of the *Criminal Code*, above note 80. Also note that s. 488.1(1) of the *Code* defines "document" so as to include any material on which is recorded or marked anything that is capable of being read or understood by a computer system or other device.

143 In particular, see s. 488.1(2)(b) of the *Criminal Code, ibid.*, and note that this provision requires that any such agreement be reduced to writing.

144 *Ibid.*

conducted or other aspects of the events, such notes may be invaluable. It may also be wise to have at least two lawyers present at all times so that corroboration will be available if a factual dispute arises, or, if the technology is available, to videotape the events.

18. Once the search has been completed, discuss the events with the client, or independent counsel acting on behalf of the client, and seek further instructions from the client if necessary. If independent counsel has not been retained, consider whether a conflict-of-interest might arise so as to necessitate new counsel for the client.

19. If instructed to continue acting for the client, take any steps required or advisable under the applicable legislation. Most notably, consider bringing an application to a court for the purpose of determining whether legal-professional privilege applies.[145] Such an application usually must be brought within a strict time period. For instance, section 488.1(3) of the *Criminal Code* requires that the client apply within fourteen days for an order setting a date for a hearing to determine the privilege issue.[146] In bringing this or any other application where privilege is asserted, counsel will likely be a witness and is thus almost certainly precluded from representing the client.[147]

---

145 Another option is to challenge the validity of the warrant under s. 8 of the *Charter*, above note 20, altogether apart from the procedure set out in s. 488.1 of the *Criminal Code*, above note 80. This sort of application could be brought prior to charges being laid, seeking the return of the documents under s. 24(1) of the *Charter*. If charges have been laid, the application can seek not only the return of the documents but also their exclusion from evidence pursuant to s. 24(2). The grounds for such an application would not be restricted to issues of legal-professional privilege. Yet another option is to bring an application for an order denying access to the information used to obtain the search warrant: see for example, s. 487.3 of the *Criminal Code*, as well as *R. v. Flahiff* (1998), 123 C.C.C. (3d) 79 (Que. C.A.).

146 The *Income Tax Act*, above note 131, adopts the same timeline. Provincial timelines may vary: see, for example, s. 160(5) of Ontario's *Provincial Offences Act*, above note 132, which requires that a motion for an order sustaining the privilege be made on notice no later than thirty days after the seizure. If for some reason counsel is unable to contact the client, and a relevant time deadline is close to expiring, an application should be brought asking the court for directions.

147 In some jurisdictions, another lawyer from the same office may be able to argue the application. A cautionary tale regarding counsel's role on the application is presented by *R. v. Morra* (1991), 68 C.C.C. (3d) 273 (Ont. Gen. Div.), where one of the lawyers arguing the application attempted to rely upon his own affidavit. Ultimately, the judge ruled that there was no proper affidavit material before the court, and went on to find that there was no evidence upon which to base a proper claim of legal-professional privilege.

# Q. SUMMARY AND RECOMMENDATIONS

Our summary and recommendations regarding the ethical duty of confidentiality are as follows:

1. The major justification for protecting confidences that pass between client and lawyer lies in a desire to promote candid communications within the professional relationship, the better to further the client's legal rights within an adversarial system (section B).
2. All Canadian rules of professional conduct strongly assert the lawyer's duty of confidentiality, in extremely broad terms (section C).
3. The ethical duty of confidentiality is not exactly commensurate with legal-professional privilege, though the two concepts are closely related (section D).
4. The ethical duty of confidentiality is also analogous to legal principles at common law and equity that serve to protect confidences (section E).
5. Constitutional principles further many of the same aims that the ethical duty of confidentiality seeks to promote. In particular, our courts have recognized that clients have a fundamental legal and civil right to maintain legal-professional confidences (section F).
6. The lawyer who improperly breaches a client's confidence may be subject to a panoply of possible legal proceedings, including a disciplinary hearing, civil litigation, and/or an ineffective-assistance-of-counsel claim made by a convicted client on appeal (section G).
7. Specific applications of the ethical duty of confidentiality include:
   a. Information from all sources is included in the duty (section H(1)).
   b. All forms of information are covered by the duty (section H(2)).
   c. The duty is wide enough to embrace information received by employees and agents of the lawyer (section H(3)).
   d. The fact that violation of the confidence risks no harm to the client, or serves an altruistic purpose, is irrelevant (section H(4)).
   e. It is improper for a lawyer to violate a client's confidences by using the information, even where such use does not involve disclosure to a third party (section H(5)).
   f. Information can be confidential even in the absence of a formal retainer (section H(6)).
   g. The duty of confidentiality survives the end of the retainer (section H(7)).
   h. The duty of confidentiality persists although the client or former client has died (section H(8)).

     i.    Information received after a retainer has ended may fall within the duty of confidentiality, if it is provided to former counsel as a result of the erstwhile professional relationship (section H(9)).

     j.    Literary works produced by a lawyer are subject to the ordinary duty of confidentiality (section H(10)).

     k.    Gossip and shoptalk occurring outside of a law firm must not reveal or use confidential information. However, a lawyer may be impliedly authorized to seek input from lawyers outside the firm in order to handle better the client's matter (section H(11)).

8.    Lawyers are under a positive duty to safeguard confidential information, which includes implementing adequate security measures where office space is shared and guarding against too casual a use of cell phones and e-mail. Also, after a retainer has ended, the file should not be destroyed if there is any legitimate ground to believe that the client's interests may be harmed as a result (section I).

9.    There is a duty to assert confidentiality where the client's secrets are threatened, for instance, by a subpoena or search warrant directed at the lawyer (section J).

10. Lawyers have a duty to inform the client as to the scope and nature of the confidentiality obligation. This duty includes informing the client of exceptions to the duty that might reasonably hold the potential to apply in the circumstances (section K).

11. Special care regarding the duty of confidentiality must be taken when counsel represents a young person. The young person must be advised as to the broad ambit of the duty, and counsel also must take care not to release confidential information to the client's parents absent informed consent from the client (section K(1)).

12. While the identity of a client is not always covered by legal-professional privilege, the ethical duty of confidentiality is usually applicable to prohibit a lawyer from disclosing the name of a client (other than as required to further the client's representation) (section L).

13. A lawyer has no duty to reveal the location of a fugitive client. However, in communicating with such a client, counsel must never aid or abet the client's efforts to evade capture (section M).

14. Inadvertent disclosure does not necessarily operate to destroy a client's confidentiality interest or legal-professional privilege. Moreover, counsel who receives inadvertently disclosed confidential information may have an ethical duty not to make use of the material (section N).

15. Counsel who represents two or more clients in the same matter cannot ordinarily maintain confidentiality as between the clients.

Rather, the general rule is that any information relevant to the retainer must be shared with all of the clients (section O).

16. Counsel should strive to protect a client's confidences whenever faced with a subpoena or search warrant. A search warrant can present special problems, owing to the usual lack of advance warning and immediate pressure for counsel to comply. The prudent lawyer will therefore establish in advance a procedure for responding to any search warrant aimed at confidential information. A detailed list of points to consider in this regard is set out in the text above (section P).

## FURTHER READINGS

Burkoff, J., *Criminal Defense Ethics: Law and Liability*, rev. ed. (St. Paul: West, 2000)

Ellis, M., *Fiduciary Duties in Canada* (Toronto: Carswell, 1993) c. 9

Bennett, F., "Confidentiality in a Solicitor and Client Relationship" (1989) 23 L. Soc. Gaz. 251

Frankel, S., "The Attorney-Client Privilege After the Death of the Client" (1992) 6 Geo. J. Legal Ethics 45

Freedman, M., *Lawyers' Ethics in an Adversary System* (New York: Bobbs-Merrill, 1975)

Freedman, M., "Professional Responsibility of the Criminal Defense Lawyer: The Three Hardest Questions" (1966) 64 Mich. L. Rev. 1469

Freedman, M., *Understanding Lawyers' Ethics* (New York: Matthew Bender, 1990)

Fridman, G., *The Law of Agency* (Toronto: Butterworths, 1996)

Guth, D., "Retention and Disposition of Client Files: Guidelines for Lawyers" (1988) 46 Advocate 229

Hall, J., *Professional Responsibility of the Criminal Lawyer*, 2d ed. (New York: Clark Boardman Callaghan, 1996)

Hall, J., *Search and Seizure*, 2d ed. (New York: Clark Boardman Callaghan, 1993)

Hazard, G. & W. Hodes, *The Law of Lawyering: A Handbook on the Model Rules of Professional Conduct*, 2d ed. (Englewood, N.J.: Prentice Hall, 1993)

Hillyer, S., "The Attorney-Client Privilege, Ethical Rules of Confidentiality, and Other Arguments Bearing on Disclosure of the Fugitive Client's Whereabouts" (1995) 68 Temp. L. Rev. 307

HOOD, B., "The Attorney-Client Privilege and a Revised Rule 1.6: Permitting Limited Disclosure After the Death of the Client" (1997) 7 Geo. J. Legal Ethics 741

HRICIK, D., "E-mail and Client Confidentiality: Lawyers Worry Too Much about Transmitting Client Confidences by Internet E-mail" (1999) 11 Geo. J. Legal Ethics 459

HUTCHINSON, A., *Legal Ethics and Professional Responsibility* (Toronto: Irwin Law, 1999)

JONES, R., "Client Confidentiality: A Lawyer's Duties with Regard to Internet E-mail" online, www.kuesterlaw.com/netethics/bjones.htm

LAYTON, D., "The Public Safety Exception: Confusing Confidentiality, Privilege and Ethics" (2001) 6 Can. Crim. L. Rev. 209

LEFSTEIN, N., "Legal Ethics: Confidentiality and the Fugitive Client" (1986) 1:3 Criminal Justice 16

MACKENZIE, G., *Lawyers and Ethics: Professional Responsibility and Discipline* (Toronto: Carswell, 1993)

MCWILLIAMS, P., *Canadian Criminal Evidence*, 3d ed. (Aurora, Ont.: Canada Law Book, 1999)

PACIOCCO, D. & L. STUESSER, *The Law of Evidence*, 2d ed. (Concord, Ont.: Irwin Law, 1999)

PERELL, P., "*Royal Bank v. Lee*" Case Comment (1993) 72 Can. Bar Rev. 72

PIZZIMENTI, L., "The Lawyer's Duty to Warn Clients About Limits on Confidentiality" (1990) 39 Cath. U.L. Rev. 441

PRZYPYSZNY, J., "Public Assault on the Attorney-Client Privilege, Ramification of *Baltes v. Doe*" (1990) 3 Geo. J. Legal Ethics 351

ROGERS, J., "Ethics, Malpractice Concerns Cloud E-mail, Online Advice" (1996) 12 Laws. Man. omn Prof. Conduct 59

SOPINKA, J., S. LEDERMAN & A. BRYANT, *The Law of Evidence in Canada*, 2d ed. (Toronto: Butterworths, 1999)

TAPPER, C., *Cross and Tapper on Evidence*, 9th ed. (London: Butterworths, 1999)

WOLFRAM, C.W., *Modern Legal Ethics* (St. Paul: West, 1986)

# CHAPTER 5

# POSSIBLE CONFIDENTIALITY EXCEPTIONS

## A. INTRODUCTION

The duty of confidentiality is central to the integrity of client-lawyer relationships, and the profession and administration of justice more generally. However, there are other societal values that in some cases trump the duty, permitting or even mandating disclosure of confidential information. For this reason, the rules of professional conduct contain various possible exceptions to the obligation of confidentiality, often grappling with the question of exactly when confidentiality can give way by reason of inconsistency with important countervailing values. Other exceptions are based on the client's authority to release information or on the recognition that widespread public awareness of information may render the lawyer's obligation otiose. While the possible exceptions most commonly suggested by Canadian ethical rules are dealt with in this chapter, their application in certain special circumstances are canvassed separately elsewhere in this book.[1]

As we shall see, the possible exceptions to the duty of confidentiality are frequently controversial, and perhaps as a result they are often framed differently in different jurisdictions. It is therefore important that counsel consult the ethical rules applicable in his or her jurisdiction and not blithely assume any sort of consistency from province

---

1   See, for example, chapters 7 & 9.

to province. Even then, in some instances an exception is only vaguely described or hinted at by the rules, which as a result may offer only minimal guidance for practising lawyers. In yet other cases, exceptions provide a discretion as to whether disclosure should be made, leaving counsel with a difficult moral decision as to the proper course to take. With these forewarnings, we can now look at some of the instances where Canadian ethical rules may operate to relieve counsel from the obligation to keep client information confidential.

# B. AUTHORIZED DISCLOSURE

The disclosure of otherwise confidential information is permitted where authorized by the client.[2] After all, the lawyer's duty of confidentiality is for the benefit of the client, and the rationale for maintaining confidentiality dissipates where the client can be said to permit disclosure. Authorized disclosure can be viewed either as an exception to the duty of confidentiality or instead as not coming within the scope of the duty to begin with. At least some of the Canadian rules of professional conduct support this latter view.[3] However, the commentaries to these rules also appear to perceive of authorization as an exception, and we prefer this view, if only as a means of emphasizing the importance of protecting confidentiality in the ordinary course. Authorization comes in two forms, express or implied, each of which will be considered in turn.

## 1) Express Authority

Disclosure can be expressly authorized by the client.[4] If waiver of confidentiality is clear and unambiguous, consent can even permit use or disclosure that risks harm to the client.[5] In any case of express consent, however, counsel must make sure that the client fully understands the ramifications of disclosure, including the possibility that legal-professional privilege will be lost. Counsel must competently advise the client in this respect, and where the action being considered raises a possible conflict-of-interest, independent legal advice may be neces-

---

2   See, for example, CBA Code ch. IV, Rule &, comm. 9; Alta. ch. 7, r. 8(e) & comm.; B.C. ch. 5, r. 11(a); Ont. 2.03(1); and N.B. Part B, r. 5.
3   See the various rules cited at note 2, above.
4   *Ibid.*
5   See Third Restatement §61, comm. "b."

sary.[6] It is possible that, although fully informed consent is obtained, conflict-of-interest concerns cannot be alleviated.[7] It may be, for example, that a potential conflict-of-interest involving two clients is waived only by one, or that, despite a knowing waiver by both clients, the court is not prepared to treat the conflict problem as resolved.

In the United States, ABA Model Rule 1.6(a) and the Third Restatement §61 require counsel to consult with the client prior to obtaining express consent. A similar approach is taken in Alberta, where the commentary to the rules stipulates in part:

> A client's express authorization of disclosure or use of confidential information must be genuine and informed. A lawyer must take reasonable steps to ensure that the client understands how such disclosure or use will affect the client's interests, particularly if the lawyer stands to incur personal benefit from the client's waiver of confidentiality.[8]

In contrast, most other Canadian rules of professional conduct dealing with confidentiality do not make clear that express consent must be fully informed. However, this requirement is usually set out in the related area of conflict-of-interest, and in any event it is surely mandated as part of a lawyer's duties to serve the client in a conscientious, diligent, and efficient manner and to be honest and candid when advising a client.[9]

The importance of providing complete and competent advice on the issue of waiving confidentiality is brought home when one considers that disclosure to a third party may result in the loss of legal-professional privilege. Any real risk that privilege will be lost, as well as the possible resulting harm, must be included in counsel's discussion with the client.

**Example**: A client is in custody on serious charges and has prepared and provided to counsel a summary of his whereabouts on the day of the offence. The client is concerned that his parents have a complete

---

6    The disclosure and independent legal advice requirements pertaining to conflict-of-interest are discussed in section O, "Duty of Counsel to Address the Conflict Problem As Soon As Possible," in chapter 6.

7    See, for example, *R. v. Robillard* (1986), 28 C.C.C. (3d) 22 (Ont. C.A.), and the discussion of waiver and conflict-of-interest at in section N, "Waiver," in chapter 6.

8    Alta. ch. 7, comm. 8(e).

9    See, for example, the discussion in section O, "Duty of Counsel to Address the Conflict Problem As Soon As Possible," in chapter 6, as well as CBA Code ch. II, Rule &, comm. 7(a); and ch. III, Rule &, comm. 1-4.

understanding of the case, and to this end he asks counsel to send them a copy of the summary. Counsel should not take this step without first making the client aware of the possible loss of privilege and the attendant harm.[10]

## 2) Implied Authority

A lawyer is also permitted to reveal or use confidential information based on a client's implied authority.[11] Authority can ordinarily be implied where disclosure or use is necessary in order to advance the client's interests regarding the subject matter of the retainer. Often included in the scope of implied authority will be disclosure to other lawyers, secretaries, and clerks who work with or for the firm, as well as outside contractors such as lawyers, private investigators, and prospective expert witnesses. These sorts of people are frequently employed by counsel to aid a client's cause, and disclosure or use of confidential information is required for this purpose.[12]

Implied authority will also permit counsel to disclose or use confidential information as required in the ordinary course of running a law practice. Bookkeepers, accountants, bankers, governing body auditors, computer technicians, and others may thus come into contact with client information without breaching the duty of confidentiality.[13] Only the Alberta rules specifically refer to this aspect of implied authority, but the wording of the more general provisions found in other Canadian jurisdictions easily accommodates such disclosure.[14]

Authority may also be implied to permit counsel to disclose or use confidential information when dealing with people who are not employed to work on behalf of the client or lawyer. For instance, in certain circumstances counsel may divulge confidential information to the police or Crown. Examples include information provided to the

---

10   See *R. v. Kotapski* (1981), 66 C.C.C. (2d) 78 (Que. S.C.), aff'd (1984), 13 C.C.C. (3d) 185 (Que. C.A.), where counsel sent such a document to a former client's wife and privilege was lost. It may be that counsel has a duty to discuss possible loss of privilege with even a former client (read together, the commentaries to Alta. ch. 7, r. 5 & 8(e) arguably suggest as much).

11   See the rules cited at note 2, above.

12   These people will owe a duty of confidentiality to the client, and the lawyer will be responsible for taking reasonable steps to ensure that they do not improperly use or disclose confidences: see the discussion in sections H(3), "Information Received by Employees and Agents," and I(4), "Supervising Employees and Agents," in chapter 4.

13   The point made in note 12, above, applies equally here.

14   See Alta. ch. 7, r. 8(c) &, comm. See also the rules cited at note 2, above.

authorities as part of an effort to avoid charges being laid, to negotiate a plea resolution, or to press any other point on behalf of the client. In disclosing confidential information to third parties who are adverse in interest, counsel must naturally exercise caution. While a lawyer has some discretion in this regard, authority should not be implied to permit disclosure that presents a real risk of harm to the client. Where the lawyer has any doubt on this score, the issue of disclosure should be fully canvassed with the client and express instructions obtained.[15]

Implied authority works to legitimize a myriad of disclosures and uses of client information that would otherwise be considered confidential. It must always be remembered, however, that implied authority is subject to countermand by the client. That is to say, where a client forbids a particular disclosure or use of confidential information, authority to do so can never be implied. The client's will is sovereign in this respect, and he or she can restrict dissemination of information to any number of people, including even a lawyer's own associates.[16] While on the subject of sharing information with other members and employees of the firm, it is worth making the tangential point that screening measures taken to avoid a conflict-of-interest problem may also present a bar to the dissemination of information.[17]

# C. PUBLIC KNOWLEDGE

As already mentioned, the ethical duty of confidentiality applies to much information that would not attract legal-professional privilege because it has been shared with third parties. For example, let us assume that a lawyer acts for a client charged with fraud. During the trial, the lawyer has lunch with the client and several of the client's friends who are unconnected with the matters in dispute in the case. Discussion among the friends turns to the client's business affairs, and

---

15   In *R. v. L(C.K.)* (1987), 39 C.C.C. (3d) 476 (Ont. Dist. Ct.), defence counsel improperly put the client's confidences at risk by undertaking to disclose a defence psychiatric assessment to the Crown. The client was not informed of the planned disclosure prior to the undertaking being made. The court ruled that, despite the undertaking, privilege was not waived.

16   See, for example, CBA Code ch. IV, comm. 9; Sask. ch. IV, comm. 9; Ont. r. 2.03(1); B.C. ch. 5, r. 11(b); and N.S. ch. 5, Rule &, comm. 5.10. Alberta's rule is the most detailed and lucid on this point: see Alta. ch. 7, r. 8(e) & commentary.

17   The purpose and effect of screening measures are discussed in section M(2), "Screening," in chapter 6.

the lawyer acquires information on this point. While such communications are not privileged, they are nonetheless confidential under the rules of professional conduct.[18] This type of "public" conversation (and we use the term loosely) falls within the ambit of the duty of confidentiality.

The question arises, however, as to whether the duty persists even where the information is widely known in the public sphere.[19] Many Canadian rules of professional conduct suggest that information may be so well known or readily available as to release counsel from any obligation of confidentiality. Typical is the CBA Code, which states with respect to the rule of confidentiality: "Although the Rule may not apply to facts that are public knowledge, the lawyer should guard against participating in or commenting upon speculation concerning the client's affairs or business."[20] Other provincial governing bodies do not recognize a "public-knowledge" exception. The British Columbia rules contain no reference to the possibility that information within the public's knowledge is not confidential.[21] The Alberta standards go further still, expressly stating that a lawyer must not disclose any confidential information, "regardless of its source and whether or not it is a matter of public record."[22]

While a lawyer must be guided by the particular rules applicable in his or her jurisdiction, the public-knowledge exception implied by the CBA Code and many provincial rules must be approached with caution. In our view, the knowledge must beyond all doubt be a matter of public record, to such an extent that it can be said to be "generally known." In this regard, it has been suggested that even information accessible to members of the public will remain confidential where acquisition requires special knowledge, unusual effort, or substantial expenditure.[23] The difficulty in determining when a sufficient level of

---

18   See, for example, Ont. r. 2.03(1); and *Stewart* v. *Canadian Broadcasting Corp.* (1997), 150 D.L.R. (4th) 24 at 111 (Ont. Gen. Div.) [*Stewart*], to the effect that "widely known information may still be confidential information within this rule."

19   One of the clearest articulations of such an exception is found in the Third Restatement §59, which defines confidential information so as *not* to encompass "information that is generally known."

20   CBA Code ch. IV, comm. 8. To similar effect are Ont. r. 2.03(1); N.S. ch. 5, r. 5.9. See also *Ott* v. *Fleishman* (1983), 46 B.C.L.R. 321 at 322–323 (S.C.), providing that information which is "already notorious" when received by a lawyer is not confidential.

21   See B.C. ch. 5.

22   Alta. ch. 7, r. 1 & commentary.

23   See Third Restatement §59, comm. "d."

public dissemination has been reached is plain. Moreover, other ethical obligations come to bear where counsel is considering the use or disclosure of information that is potentially within the public's knowledge. Notably, the duty of loyalty prevents counsel from taking any action that can reasonably be said to cause harm to a client or former client, at least where the harm is caused in relation to the subject matter of the retainer or a related matter.[24] This prohibition applies regardless of whether the duty of confidentiality is engaged, and hence the public-knowledge exception becomes irrelevant where the broader duty of loyalty prohibits disclosure or use of information to the disadvantage of a client or former client.[25]

To date, the most detailed discussion of confidentiality, loyalty, and public knowledge in Canadian case law can be found in *Stewart* v. *Canadian Broadcasting Corp.*[26] In *Stewart*, defence counsel participated in a television broadcast that examined a former client's case. The information revealed by the broadcast was readily available in trial transcripts and had been the subject of widespread media coverage roughly twelve years previous.[27] An important holding in *Stewart* is that defence counsel did not run afoul of Ontario's ethical rule of confidentiality by participating in the program. In the court's view, the only information disclosed by the broadcast was "public" within the meaning of Ontario's counterpart to the CBA Code commentary quoted above: the information was therefore not confidential.[28] A crucial caveat to this holding, however, may be that information pertaining to most criminal trials, though available to members of the public who attend court or order transcripts, is not sufficiently notorious to fall outside the duty of confidentiality.[29] We are inclined to this position. The client whose case is not widely reported in the media should not automatically lose the protection offered by the duty of confidentiality with respect to matters that take place in open court. Public

---

24  CBA Code ch. V, comm. 8; Ont. r. 2.04(4); B.C. ch. 6, r. 7; Sask. ch. V, comm. 8. See *Stewart*, above note 18 at 127–63; as well as *R. v. Speid* (1983), 8 C.C.C. (3d) 18 at 22 (Ont. C.A.).

25  Contrast the approach taken in Alberta, where the rule concerning conflict-of-interest and former clients addresses only the issue of confidential information: see Alta. ch. 6, r. 3. As noted already, however, Alberta expressly rejects the notion that public information is excluded from the duty of confidentiality.

26  Above note 18.

27  *Ibid.* at 112–13 & 127–28.

28  *Ibid.* at 110–13. See also Ont. r. 2.03(1).

29  *Ibid.* at 162.

knowledge arguably means more than simply knowledge revealed in a form accessible to the public.

While *Stewart* exonerated counsel with respect to an alleged breach of the duty of confidentiality, the court was keenly aware that the duty of loyalty owed a former client can operate to prevent a lawyer from employing widely known information (or indeed taking any steps) to the client's disadvantage. Specifically, the court held that "careful, competent and responsible criminal defence counsel should and do take into account the risk of harm to a former client in deciding whether to discuss publicly a former client or the former client's case, [even] when all relevant information is in the public domain."[30] Counsel in *Stewart* was ultimately found to have acted inappropriately by participating in a broadcast that was harmful to the former client's interests.

**Opinion:** Counsel contemplating the use or disclosure of information that might be "public" within the meaning of applicable ethical rules must consider both the duty of confidentiality and the wider duty of loyalty. Overall, the safest course is to err liberally on the side of non-disclosure. Where possible, counsel should check with the client or former client to obtain express authorization rather than relying on this rather foggy limitation to the duty of confidentiality.[31] If the client objects to the requested use or disclosure, then, absent exceptional circumstances, counsel should comply.[32] Refusal to abide by a current client's instruction in this regard will likely require withdrawal from the case. Ultimately, counsel must never proceed against the wishes of a client or former client where to do so would violate the duty of loyalty.

---

30   *Ibid.* at 97. Note that the court reached this result based on legal and equitable principles, and not the rules of professional conduct. We prefer, however, to interpret Commentary 13 to former Ontario Rule 5 (now r. 2.04(4)) as imposing a duty of loyalty that would apply on the facts of *Stewart*, in particular by reading the phrase "acting against a former client" to encompass non-litigation activities undertaken in pursuit of the lawyer's personal interests (contrast the more restrictive language found in B.C. ch. 6, r. 7). Moreover, we believe that a broad ethical duty of loyalty can be derived from a lawyer's general duties of integrity and competence, in which case the ethical rules mirror the principles articulated in *Stewart*.

31   As noted, in Alberta, and perhaps also British Columbia, there is no public knowledge exception, and thus consultation with the client is counsel's only option: see notes 20–21, above.

32   Compare the contrary approach taken by counsel in *Stewart*, above note 18 at 98–100.

# D. DISCLOSURE REQUIRED BY LAW[33]

Canadian rules of professional conduct all provide that a lawyer must disclose confidential information where required to do so by law or order of the court. This exception is somewhat awkwardly put by the CBA Code and several provincial governing bodies, which recognize the exception only inferentially, as part of the following direction to counsel:[34] "When disclosure is required by law or by order of a court of competent jurisdiction, the lawyer should always be careful not to divulge more information than is required."[35] Preferable is the straightforward language used in Alberta, where the rules simply provide that "a lawyer must disclose confidential information when required to do so by law."[36]

The Alberta Rule obviously mandates disclosure, providing counsel with no discretion on the point. The other Canadian jurisdictions are not so clear in this regard, by reason of their indirect wording. The distinction can be important. Some counsel might choose to risk contempt of court rather than disclose a confidence if given the choice under the rules of ethics. The CBA Code's language could conceivably accommodate this interpretation. However, the exception's wording seems to assume that the lawyer must disclose where required by law or court order. The better view, in light of a lawyer's duty to abide by the dictates of the law,[37] is that counsel must disclose information where compelled by statute or court order.

---

33  See also section P, "Subpoenas and Search Warrants," in chapter 4, discussing counsel's obligations where served with a subpoena or subjected to a search warrant.

34  ABA Model Rule 1.6 is far worse; no exception is even implicitly recognized in the text of the rule, and lawyers are thus left to adopt a "forced exception": G. Hazard & W. Hodes, *The Law of Lawyering: A Handbook on the Model Rules of Professional Conduct*, 2d ed. (Englewood, N.J.: Prentice Hall, 1993) at §1.9(402).

35  CBA Code IV, comm. 13. See also Sask. ch. IV, comm. 13; Ont. r. 2.03(2); and N.S. ch. 5, comm. 5.13. Compare the British Columbia provision, which uses the phrase "shall not" to more clearly emphasize that disclosure is forbidden unless required by process of law: see B.C. ch. 5, r. 13.

36  Alta. ch. 7, r. 8(c), which is elaborated upon by, comm. 8(c).

37  See generally CBA Code ch. IX (The Lawyer as Advocate); and ch. XIII (The Lawyer and the Administration of Justice). Also keep in mind that contempt of court can constitute a criminal offence: see s. 9 of the *Criminal Code*, R.S.C. 1985, c. C-46, as well as A. Mewett & P. Sankoff, *Witnesses* (Toronto: Carswell, 1999) at §8.1. A lawyer's duty to reveal non-privileged confidential information, where compelled by court process, is also affirmed in *Lavallee* v. *Canada (A.G.)* (2000), 143 C.C.C. (3d) 187 at 207 (Alta. C.A.) [*Lavallee*].

Often the legal imperative to disclose will come by way of a court ruling that legal-professional privilege does not apply. For instance, the court may decide that the information in question was never afforded the privilege, that the privilege was waived, or that an exception is applicable.[38] It is also possible that legislation forces disclosure. The *Income Tax Act* and *Criminal Code* provisions regarding the search and seizure of a lawyer's file certainly require counsel to surrender up documents, subject, of course, to a judicial determination of the privilege issue.[39] In the United States and the United Kingdom, legislation imposes reporting requirements on lawyers who receive large amounts of money from or in relation to clients, and the federal government is about to impose somewhat similar statutory duties on lawyers in Canada.[40]

When faced with an attempt to use statutory or other legal process to obtain confidential information, counsel has a duty to raise any non-frivolous argument that might reasonably serve to thwart disclosure. Most obviously, legal-professional privilege can often be asserted, but other legal arguments may also be apposite. For instance, another exclusionary rule may apply, such as the prohibition against hearsay or bad character evidence. Similarly, rules of statutory interpretation can be brought to bear[41] and/or constitutional arguments invoked.[42] While any reasonably tenable objection to disclose must be raised, indis-

---

38   For instance, the privilege might not apply to begin with because of the presence of a third party, or the actions of the client may be taken as implied waiver. Exceptions to the privilege include the crime-fraud exception, discussed in *R. v. Campbell* (1999), 133 C.C.C. (3d) 257 at 291–95 (S.C.C.) [*Campbell*]; the public-safety exception created by *Smith v. Jones* (1999), 132 C.C.C. (3d) 225 (S.C.C.) [*Smith*]; and the innocence-at-stake exception recognized most recently in *R. v. McClure* (2001), 151 C.C.C. (3d) 321 (S.C.C.) [*McClure*].

39   See ss. 231.3 & 232(3) of the *Income Tax Act*, R.S.C. 1985, c. 1 (5th Supp.); and s. 488.1 of the *Criminal Code*, above note 37. Section 488.1 imports the procedure previously suggested by *Descôteaux v. Mierzwinski* (1982), 70 C.C.C. (2d) 385 (S.C.C.) [*Descôteaux*]. If this provision is eventually held to be unconstitutional, following the lead of *Lavallee*, above note 37, and other provincial courts of appeal, *Descôteaux* could presumably continue to apply in the absence of new legislation.

40   This topic is reviewed in section R, "Reporting Requirements, Confidentiality, and Privilege," in chapter 10.

41   Important in this respect are the rules of interpretation articulated in *Descôteaux*, above note 39 at 400.

42   See, for example, *Lavalle*, above note 37.

putably frivolous attempts to mount legal arguments against disclosure are improper.[43]

The possibility of appealing an adverse ruling that compels disclosure raises a further issue. The Alberta rules of professional conduct go so far as to require, at least in some circumstances, temporary non-compliance with a court order pending appeal. Specifically, counsel is obliged *not* to submit to a court order if he or she believes in good-faith, based on reasonable grounds, that the order is in error and the law does not require disclosure.[44] In such a case, the Alberta rule requires that counsel withhold disclosure pending final adjudication of the matter.[45] Only at the point where appeal routes have been exhausted does the duty subside.

There are good reasons for providing counsel with a limited discretion to withhold disclosure in the face of a plainly erroneous court order that is appealable. To a certain extent, a client's right to confidentiality will have been irrevocably damaged once the information is disclosed, regardless of whether he or she is successful on appeal. Third parties will have been privy to the information against the client's wishes, and in some cases media reports may result in widespread dissemination.[46] Of course, as the Alberta position indicates, counsel cannot remain uncooperative unless he or she holds a good-faith belief that the law as properly interpreted does not require disclosure. Moreover, the client's informed position must be taken into account; refusal is not an option if the client does not wish to appeal.

While a discretion to refuse compliance in certain circumstances makes some sense, it is less easy to support a rule (such as Alberta's) that makes non-disclosure mandatory. This point can be explored by looking at the potential impact on counsel of refusal depending upon the availability of appeal routes. In some instances, an interlocutory appeal will be possible, such as where the client is a Crown witness or other third party, and counsel can apply for an interim stay while wait-

---

43  This position is taken by the Third Restatement, §63, comm. "b." The impropriety of frivolous methods is discussed in section J, "Frivolous Tactics," in chapter 3.

44  See Alta. ch. 7, r. 8(b), as interpreted by the accompanying commentary.

45  *Ibid.*

46  These points are made in *Maness* v. *Meyers*, 419 U.S. 449 (1975), though on slightly different facts. *State* v. *Schmidt*, 474 So.2d 899 (Fla. App. 1985), which follows the approach in *Maness* v. *Meyers*, provides an example of a court upholding counsel's decision not to comply with a disclosure order prior to appellate review.

ing for the appeal to be determined.[47] In other cases, especially where counsel's client or former client is an accused, only a post-conviction appeal may be possible.[48] Refusing to reveal confidential information where an interlocutory appeal is prohibited exposes counsel to a much greater risk of contempt, given that a contempt hearing will likely be heard prior to any post-conviction appeal.

Granted, perhaps a contempt hearing can be postponed until the appeal is heard, especially if the issue arises in Alberta and on the facts counsel is arguably obligated under the rules to refuse compliance pending appeal. But apart from this possibility, an ethical rule that mandates refusal under these circumstances is somewhat harsh, for the lawyer could conceivably be sent to jail. It is therefore our view that a discretionary approach is preferable, leaving the final choice regarding non-compliance pending appeal to the individual lawyer.[49] In coming to this conclusion, we take comfort from the fact that a successful post-conviction appeal can at least lessen the adverse impact of disclosure at trial. Where the error is such that the proviso does not apply, a new trial will be held during which the information cannot be used. If the proviso applies, the erroneous ruling of the trial judge is presumably no longer effective. One may legitimately ask, however, whether the client must bring civil proceedings if he or she wishes the return of any disclosed documents or to prevent a further use or dissemination of the information in question.

## E.  LAWYER SELF-DEFENCE

Virtually all jurisdictions recognize that a lawyer has the right to use or disclose confidential information to the extent necessary to defend

---

47  See, for example, *A.(L.L.)* v. *Beharriell* (1995), 103 C.C.C. (3d) 92 (S.C.C.); and *Dagenais* v. *Canadian Broadcasting Corp.* (1994), 94 C.C.C. (3d) 289 (S.C.C.). The appeal in such an instance is heard by the Supreme Court of Canada (with leave), although the Court has recently urged Parliament to provide for provincial appellate review: see *McClure, above note 38* at 339. *Beharriell* is a case where a stay was granted pending the interlocutory appeal.

48  See, for example, *R.* v. *King* (1992), 74 C.C.C. (3d) 191 (P.E.I.S.C.(A.D.)); and *R* v. *Wilder* (1996), 110 C.C.C. (3d) 186 (B.C.C.A.). More generally, see *R.* v. *Mills* (1986), 26 C.C.C. (3d) 481 (S.C.C.); *R.* v. *Meltzer* (1989), 49 C.C.C. (3d) 453 (S.C.C.); and D. Layton, "The Pre-trial Removal of Counsel for Conflict of Interest: Appealability and Remedies on Appeal" (1999) 4 Can. Crim. L. Rev. 25.

49  This position is taken by the Third Restatement §63, comm. "b."

against an allegation of wrongdoing.[50] The best rationale for this exception is that lawyers would otherwise be defenceless against groundless charges of impropriety, and that where it is a client who makes the allegation the usual duty of confidentiality has been waived.

## 1) Basic Scope of the Self-Defence Exception

Instances where the exception might apply include the case where a client charges counsel with participating in a criminal act, brings a civil suit or disciplinary complaint against counsel, or alleges on appeal that trial counsel rendered ineffective legal assistance. As the ineffective-legal-assistance example makes clear, it does not matter that the allegation has been made in a proceeding to which the lawyer is not a party.[51]

It is also worth noting that the self-defence exception permits disclosure or use of confidential information not only to defend a lawyer from attack by a client but also to protect associated lawyers and non-lawyers who are subject to allegations of impropriety. The text of most of the Canadian rules expressly covers a lawyer's associates or employees.[52] Those rules that do not on their face extend so far, such as the Alberta rule, should be interpreted in this manner. An allegation that a secretary counselled an obstruction of justice or misappropriated a client's money would thus fall within the exception. As well, the logic behind protecting "associates or employees," to use the words of the CBA Code, justifies extending the exception to any agent who is subject to attack.[53]

---

50   See, for example, CBA Code IV, comm. 10; Ont. r. 2.03(4); B.C. r. notes 1 & 2; Alta. ch. 7, r. 8(f); N.S. c.5, r. 5.11. Surprisingly, New Brunswick has no comparable exception, though presumably this sort of disclosure is permissible by forced implication.

51   See, for example, *R. v. Dunbar* (1982), 68 C.C.C. (2d) 13 at 39 (Ont. C.A.). Though dealing with legal-professional privilege, *Dunbar* demonstrates that counsel can reveal confidences in self-defence even though he or she is not a party to the legal proceeding (former counsel was called as a witness by a co-accused to rebut the erstwhile client's allegations of impropriety). See also *R. v. Li*, [1993] B.C.J. No. 2312 (C.A.) (QL) [*Li*]; and *R. v. Delisle* (1999), 133 C.C.C. (3d) 541 at 548 (Que. C.A.).

52   See the rules cited at note 50, above.

53   See the Third Restatement §64, comm. "d."

## 2) Use of Confidential Information Only to the Extent Necessary

As with all exceptions to the duty of confidentiality, use or disclosure of the information is permitted only to the extent necessary in order to achieve the countervailing purpose, in this case to mount a defence.[54] The lawyer must therefore assess the seriousness of the allegation and determine the minimum amount of confidential information required to counter effectively the charge of misconduct. Some allegations may be so far-fetched or ludicrous as to call for no response or perhaps simply a blanket refutation. Others may on their face appear to be valid and justify an extensive revelation of lawyer-client communications.

The need to keep the disclosure or use of confidential information to a minimum also applies with respect to the people to whom confidences are revealed. For instance, dissemination to the media might be warranted if the client's allegations are made or reported in that forum, but otherwise in most cases would not be permitted. Similarly, an allegation of misconduct made solely to a governing body would probably not justify the revelation of confidences to any person or entity other than that body.

**Warning**: A lawyer must never threaten to use the self-defence exception as a means of dissuading a client from making or proceeding with a complaint. In some instances, the potential divergence of the client's interests from those of the lawyer will make necessary independent legal advice for the client.

## 3) Allegations by a Third Party

A particularly difficult scenario sees the lawyer subject to allegations of wrongdoing made not by the client but by a third party such as the police or Crown. Most Canadian rules of professional conduct are framed broadly enough to encompass such third-party claims,[55] but Alberta's rule is phrased more narrowly, permitting relaxation of the duty of confidentiality for the purpose of "defending a claim or allega-

---

54   See Li, above note 51, where the court held that counsel had gone too far in disclosing confidential information that was not strictly speaking necessary to counter the allegation of misconduct. If counsel is unsure whether disclosure of particular information is justified, Li suggests that one option may be to file a sealed response with the court.

55   See the rules cited at note 50, above; and *Wilder* v. *Ontario (Securities Commission)* (2001), 197 D.L.R. (4th) 193 at 209 (Ont. C.A.) [*Wilder*]. See also Third Restatement §54 and ABA Model Rule 1.6(b)(2).

tion in a dispute with a client."[56] This distinction may hold great importance. Allegations made against a lawyer by the police or Crown often occur under circumstances where legal-professional privilege is lost owing to the crime-fraud exception. However, such is not always the case, an example being a complaint by a third party to the lawyer's governing body concerning non-criminal conduct. Moreover, a lawyer may legitimately wish to respond promptly to a third-party allegation in a non-judicial forum, in which case the potential loss of privilege does not serve to permit use or disclosure of confidences.[57] For these reasons, permitting a self-defence exception where a third party alleges impropriety is justified.

Nevertheless, before using or disclosing information in response to a third-party allegation, it is especially important that counsel make efforts to discuss the matter with his or her client. Unlike the more usual case, where it is the client who makes the allegation, the client may well be unaware of the dispute. In discussing the problem with the client, counsel should request that the client authorize use or revelation of confidential information only to the extent necessary to counter the allegation.[58] Where notifying the client would jeopardize counsel's ability to mount an effective defence, it may be appropriate to dispense with this requirement.

The interests of counsel and client can easily diverge where the police or Crown allege criminal conduct by counsel (whether or not the client is also said to be implicated). Rendering advice to the client under these circumstances will usually be impossible because of conflict-of-interest concerns, and in any event will require independent legal advice for the client. In this regard, consider the cautionary tale revealed in *R. v. Joubert*,[59] where counsel continued to provide advice to a client after police executed a search warrant at his office. On the facts of the case as reported, it seems clear that the police were not ruling out the possibility that counsel was implicated in money-launder-

---

56   Alta. ch. 7, r. 8(f).

57   This point is valid only if one agrees with the position taken below, in section I, "Possible Crime-Fraud Exception," that the crime-fraud exception to legal-professional privilege does not permit disclosure absent compulsion by court process.

58   See Third Restatement §64, comm. "e" (Reporter's Note); and ABA Rule 1.6, comment (Dispute Concerning Lawyer's Conduct).

59   (1992), 69 C.C.C. (3d) 553 (B.C.C.A.), reconsideration refsed (1992), 13 B.C.A.C. 116 (C.A.), leaveto appeal to S.C.C. refused (1992), 147 N.R. 396n (S.C.C.)

ing activities, and yet counsel continued to provide legal advice to the client.

**Prohibition**: Using or disclosing confidential information to defend oneself against allegations of misconduct by the police or Crown is permitted only where the allegation pertains to the client's retainer. Counsel is not allowed to breach confidentiality as a means of obtaining leniency from the police or Crown with respect to conduct unrelated to the representation. Conversely, Crown counsel should never threaten or bring unfounded charges against a defence lawyer in an effort to force the revelation of otherwise confidential information that can then be used against the client.[60] Defence counsel who encounters such a tactic is placed in a terrible bind. If at all possible, he or she should hold off making disclosure, all the while protesting vigourously, but there may be no choice except to reveal some information if charges are in fact laid.

## 4) Anticipated Allegation

To the extent that Canadian rules of professional conduct typically speak of the lawyer defending against "any allegation," they may be broad enough to cover the use or disclosure of confidential information where an allegation of misconduct, though made, has not yet led to a formal complaint or charge.[61] It is not clear, however, whether the rules permit counsel to mount a purely pre-emptive defence. The impetus for such action could occur where counsel discovers part way through a retainer that the client is using his or her services for a criminal purpose. Remaining silent may increase the risk of being charged, convicted or held civilly liable. Despite the increased erosion of confidentiality, permitting a pre-emptive breach has been advocated by at least one leading commentator.[62] Where no other option can reasonably be seen to protect counsel, disclosure may be justified. For instance, in *Finers* v. *Miro*,[63] a law firm managing assets for a client

---

60   See *Wilder*, above note 55 at 209.

61   Compare the position in Australia, where a formal complain or charge may be required: see S. Ross, *Ethics in Law: Lawyers' Responsibility and Accountability in Australia* (Sydney: Butterworths, 1998) at 271–72.

62   See Hazard and Hodes, above note 34 at §1.6(306). The Law Society of Upper Canada implicitly addresses the pre-emptive defence option in the commentary to Rule 2.03(3), and apparently condones whistle-blowing where justified by the self-defence exception found in Rule 2.03(4).

63   [1991] 1 All E.R. 182 (C.A.) [*Finers*].

learned that the assets were potentially subject to a constructive trust in favour of a third party who alleged fraud by the client, and that the firm also faced possible liability to the third party. In these circumstances, the court permitted the firm to make partial disclosure of otherwise confidential information.[64] However, prior to taking this extreme step, counsel should consider alternative actions that stop short of whistle-blowing, including immediate cessation of the retainer and action to preserve evidence that will aid in demonstrating innocence if an allegation of misconduct arises in the future.[65]

## F. FEE DISPUTES

Closely related to the self-defence exception is the widespread recognition that lawyers can use confidential information to the extent necessary to establish or collect fees.[66] Though currently well established, this exception has been criticized on the ground that lawyers are merely favouring their own financial interests, avoiding the much more stringent rules applicable when the interests of non-lawyers are put in jeopardy.[67] In any event, the restriction of this exception to circumstances where disclosure is necessary to protect the lawyer's interests demands special emphasis. The mere fact that a lawyer seeks to advance his or her position in a fee dispute does not justify widespread revelation of all confidences.[68]

A wrinkle arises where counsel has an agreement with a third party to pay the fee. It may conceivably be possible to infer the authority to reveal a confidence where a fee-related dispute occurs with the third

---

64  To the extent that *Finers*, *ibid.*, can be taken to hold that the crime-fraud exception to legal-professional privilege completely releases a lawyer from any obligation of confidentiality, one must take into account §16.02(1) of the ethical rules governing solicitors in England and Wales (set out in section T3, "Searching for Guidance in the Rules of Professional Conduct," in this chapter).

65  A general discussion of the "duped lawyer" problem can be found in section J, "The Problem of Unwitting Involvement by Counsel in Criminal Acts," in this chapter.

66  See, for example, CBA Code IV, comm. 10; Ont. r. 2.03(5); Sask. ch. IV, comm. 10; N.S. ch. 5, comm. 5.9; and Alta. ch. 7, r. 8(f). The B.C. rule engages this exception by implication, insofar as authority to use or disclose confidential information can be implied where a fee dispute arises: see B.C. ch. 5, notes 1 & 2.

67  See D. Layton, "*R. v. McClure*: The Privilege on the Pea" (2001), 40 C.R. (5th) 19 at 26–27.

68  See, for example, *Piercy v. Piercy* (1990), 48 B.C.L.R. (2d) 145 at 152 (C.A.).

party. However, relying upon implied authority is untenable where disclosure would harm the client, and, absent express consent, counsel may be foreclosed from even a necessary use of confidential information.[69] On the other hand, counsel can to some extent minimize the problem when arranging the terms of the retainer, for instance, by obtaining express authority from the client in advance or by carefully crafting the terms of the contract with the third party.[70] Most Canadian rules of professional conduct do not flag this issue and on their wording would seem to permit the same use of confidential information even where a fee dispute concerns a third party.[71]

## G. FUTURE HARM OR PUBLIC SAFETY

The exception to the duty of confidentiality covering the prevention of future-harm is especially contentious. This exception relaxes the lawyer's ordinary duty to the client in an attempt to strike a balance with the need to protect members of the public from preventable harmful acts. The ethical rules adopted by the CBA Code and each provincial governing body invariably contain a future-harm exception, and in *Smith* v. *Jones* the Supreme Court of Canada has recognized a comparable "public-safety" exception to both the common law duty of confidentiality and legal-professional privilege. As we shall see, ascertaining the scope of, and relationship between, the various professional conduct and judge-made exceptions is not always easy. We will begin by looking in turn at the ethical rules and the Supreme Court's approach, and then move on to examine some of the issues raised by these exceptions.

As a prelude, however, note that we use the term future-harm to refer to the general exception found in all Canadian rules of professional conduct. The term "public-safety" is used to refer to the Supreme Court of Canada's exception to both the duty of confidential-

---

69  See, for example, Third Restatement §65, comm. "e"; and C.W. Wolfram, *Modern Legal Ethics* (St. Paul, West, 1986) at 310–11.

70  Such steps may well raise conflict-of-interest concerns, but then again many third-party payment arrangements do so — and hence require independent legal advice — even absent this issue of possible fee disputes: see section J, "Third-Party Payment of Fees," in chapter 6.

71  See, for example, the rules cited at note 66, above. Contrast ABA Model Rule 1.6(b)(2), which encompasses only a claim "on behalf of the lawyer in a controversy between the lawyer and the client," thus approximating the Alberta rule cited at note 56, above.

ity and legal-professional privilege, as discussed below in section G(2). Another term sometimes used when the prevention of harm is being discussed is the "crime-fraud exception." As explained below, in section I, we use "crime-fraud" to refer to a particular exception to legal-professional privilege, and argue against the existence of a comparable exception to the ethical duty of confidentiality. There is no magic in the use of these various terms. For instance, in R. v. Campbell, the Supreme Court of Canada occasionally speaks of a future-harm exception in discussing what we choose to call the crime-fraud exception.[72] What is important, however, is to define one's terms carefully and to be consistent in their use.

## 1) The Rules of Professional Conduct

The rules of professional conduct reveal considerable disparity in delineating the future-harm exception. The most expansive approach is arguably employed in New Brunswick, where a lawyer has the discretion to reveal communications relating to a criminal or fraudulent transaction unless the client has been charged with a criminal offence, and is mandated to make disclosure where the information concerns a serious crime.[73] The CBA Code takes a different tack, stating: "Disclosure of information necessary to prevent a crime will be justified if the lawyer has reasonable grounds for believing that a crime is likely to be committed and will be mandatory when the anticipated crime is one involving violence."[74] The CBA Code makes an important distinction based upon the seriousness of the future crime, a distinction that determines whether disclosure is discretionary or mandatory. This approach is followed in many provinces, including Saskatchewan, Manitoba, Newfoundland, and Prince Edward Island.[75] A variation on the CBA Code's approach is employed in Alberta, where the mandatory aspect of the rule applies more narrowly, extending only to "prevent a crime likely to result in death or bodily harm."[76] Nova Scotia's version is perhaps stricter still, adopting only the mandatory portion of exception found in the CBA Code (that is, if a crime does not involve violence, disclosure is never permitted).[77] British Columbia has a narrow

---

72  *Campbell*, above note 38 at 291–95.
73  See N.B. Part C, r. 5.
74  CBA Code ch. IV, comm. 11.
75  See, for example, Sask. ch. IV, comm. 11; Man. ch. IV, comm. 11; Nfld. ch. IV, comm. 11; and P.E.I. ch. IV, comm. 11.
76  Alta. ch. 7, r. 8(c).
77  See N.S. ch. 5, r. 5.12.

future-harm exception: counsel is permitted (and never required) to disclose confidential information only where necessary to prevent a crime involving death or serious bodily harm.[78] Ontario recently adopted a new future-harm exception along these same lines.[79] Rule 2.03(3) of the Ontario Rules of Professional Conduct is much more detailed than most other Canadian future-harm exceptions, stating:

> Where a lawyer believes upon reasonable grounds that there is an imminent risk to an identifiable person or group of death or serious bodily harm, including serious psychological harm that substantially interferes with health or well-being, the lawyer may disclose, pursuant to judicial order where practicable, confidential information where it is necessary to do so in order to prevent the death or harm, but shall not disclose more information than is required.[80]

Finally, Quebec ostensibly has no future-harm exception at all. However, given the exceedingly sparse attention paid to matters of confidentiality in Quebec's ethical code, and the general absence of *any* exceptions to the duty of confidentiality, it is hard to fathom the exact state of affairs in the province.[81] Can it be that lawyers in Quebec are never allowed to reveal confidences to avoid future-harm? Perhaps, but the absence of any exceptions makes one wonder if the lack of a future-harm dispensation is an oversight.

The British Columbia and new Ontario future-harm exceptions somewhat resemble the ABA's Model Rule 1.6(b)(1), which states that "a lawyer may reveal [confidential] information to the extent that the lawyer reasonably believes necessary to prevent the client from committing a criminal act that the lawyer believes is likely to result in imminent death or substantial bodily harm."[82] The ABA Model Code, immediate predecessor to the Model Rules, at first glance appears to adopt a wider exception, for the lawyer may disclose where necessary to prevent any crime.[83] The potentially broad scope of the Model Code

---

78    B.C. ch. 5, r. 5.12.
79    See Ont. 2.03(3). The genesis of the new Ontario exception is discussed in D. Layton, "The Public Safety Exception: Confusing Confidentiality, Privilege and Ethics" (2001) 6 Can. Crim. L. Rev. 209 ["The Public Safety Exception"].
80    Ont. r. 2.03(3).
81    See Que. s. 3.06.03, setting out a lawyer's basic obligation to keep a client's secrets.
82    ABA Model Rule 1.6(b)(1). Note, however, that in early August, 2001, the ABA House of Delegates voted to remove the references to "criminal" and "imminent." The result is a somewhat wider exception.
83    See ABA Model Code DR 4-101(C)(3).

provision has been reined in, however, by an interpretation that requires belief beyond a reasonable doubt before disclosure is justified.[84] State governing bodies have by no means uniformly embraced the ABA's current Model Rule. Only a small minority has adopted Rule 1.6(b)(1) *in toto*, while a greater number have retained the Model Code version of the future-harm exception. Still other state governing associations have adopted future-harm exceptions that do not adhere exactly to either the Rules or the Code. In sum, depending upon the jurisdiction, disclosure may be mandatory, permissive, or a combination of both, and the targeted harm may focus upon death/substantial physical injury, certain serious crimes, any criminal act, or any criminal or fraudulent act.[85]

Turning to England, the bar's Code of Conduct provides that a barrister must preserve a client's confidences and cannot reveal such information to any third party absent prior consent or as permitted by law.[86] The Code of Conduct contains no future-harm exception, meaning that barristers are not permitted to disclose confidential matters for the purpose of preventing anticipated damage. However, England's Law Society takes a much different stance, more consistent with the approaches adopted in most North American jurisdictions. Though subject to a general duty of confidentiality, "a solicitor may reveal confidential information to the extent that he or she believes necessary to prevent the client or a third party committing a criminal act that the solicitor believes on reasonable grounds is likely to result in serious bodily harm."[87] In addition, the Law Society requires disclosure of confidential information in certain situations involving the prevention of harm to children.[88]

## 2) The Decision in *Smith* v. *Jones*

Until recently, Canadian courts had not commented on the future-harm exception to the duty of confidentiality. This lacuna has been filled by the Supreme Court of Canada's decision in the unusual case

---

84  See J. Hall, *Professional Responsibility of the Criminal Lawyer*, 2d ed. (New York: Clark Boardman Callaghan, 1996) at §28.6.

85  See the handy review of the state provisions in Hall, *ibid.* at §28.6, and especially §28.6A (cumulative supplement).

86  See General Council, *Code of Conduct of the Bar of England and Wales* (London: The Council, 1990), r. 603.

87  The Law Society, *The Guide to the Professional Conduct of Solicitors*, 8th ed. (London: Law Society, 1999) at §16.02(3).

88  *Ibid.* at §16.02(4).

of *Smith* v. *Jones*.[89] There, the Court endorsed a public-safety exception to legal-professional privilege, an exception that the majority of the Court found to apply where "the facts raise real concerns that an identifiable individual or group is in imminent danger of death or serious bodily harm."[90] Although the facts in *Smith* v. *Jones* concern disclosure by a defence psychiatrist, and hence more properly engage litigation privilege, the majority treated the case as one of client-lawyer privilege, reasoning that if the latter privilege yields in a given circumstance, *a fortiori* the litigation privilege covering a psychiatrist must do the same.[91] The entire Court was of the view that the clarity, seriousness, and imminence of the risk are the three most important factors in assessing whether the exception is engaged, and discussed each of these factors in some detail.[92]

One might legitimately ask whether *Smith* v. *Jones* deals only with an exception to legal-professional privilege and does not purport to comment on or affect in any way the future-harm exception to the common law duty of confidentiality. After all, throughout the discussion the Court speaks almost entirely in terms of privilege, and ostensibly has little to say with respect to the broader, non-evidentiary duty of confidentiality. Would such a limited reading of the case, if supported by the Court's reasons, matter? Perhaps. It is possible to conceive of an exception to legal-professional privilege that requires disclosure by counsel where compelled by court process, but at the same time to employ a narrower exception, or perhaps no exception at all, with respect to the duty of confidentiality. There could thus be instances where counsel would be forced to disclose information if compelled by subpoena or search warrant, yet otherwise would be precluded from disclosing the same information (or at least permitted a discretion to withhold disclosure). Conversely, the exception to the duty of confidentiality could be broader than an exception to the privilege. On this view, in certain circumstances, counsel would be permitted or even mandated to disclose otherwise confidential information in order to prevent future-harm, yet the information would not fall within the parameters of the exception to legal-professional privilege. Counsel could not be compelled to release such infor-

---

89   Above note 38.

90   This particular formulation of the test is found, *ibid.*, at 251. At 249, the majority also states that "as a general rule, if the privilege is to be set aside the court must find that there is an imminent risk of serious bodily harm or death to an identifiable person or group."

91   *Ibid*, at 239.

92   *Ibid.* at 234–35 & 249–51.

mation, and if he or she voluntarily decided to do so the information would arguably be excluded from use as evidence against the client in court.[93]

However, while the Court's terminology could perhaps be clearer, there can be little doubt that the majority decision in *Smith* v. *Jones* establishes a public-safety exception to the common law duty of confidentiality, and not merely an exception to legal-professional privilege. We reach this conclusion for a number of reasons. First, on the facts of the case, the party in possession of the confidential information was not actually compelled by court process to make disclosure, but rather himself applied to the court for permission to do so. Granted, the offender (for he had already pleaded guilty) invoked privilege to prevent disclosure of the information in court, which in a sense typifies the case where the rule of evidence applies. As well, the majority reasons apparently permit the use of the information as evidence on the offender's sentencing, another hallmark of a decision pertaining to privilege. Yet the crucial preliminary decision, whether articulated or not by the majority, must have been that the psychiatrist who held the information was permitted, even absent compulsion by court process, to disclose. This foundational holding surely must operate equally to allow disclosure outside the courtroom and whether or not the information is to be used as evidence.

A second indication that the Court's decision has an impact on the common law duty of confidentiality arises from the affirmation of the decision of the appeal court below, which permitted, rather than mandated, release of the information.[94] Arguably, the concept of a discretion to disclose points to the lawyer possessing an ability to override the normal duty to maintain client confidences. Third, the Court expressly stated that the exception could apply to justify disclosure of information directly to a victim, or the police or Crown, without the need for the type of involvement by the court system that usually indicates a privilege at work.[95] Fourth, the Court stated that the public-safety exception has its origins in *Canada* v. *Solosky*, an earlier decision that has been said not to involve the evidentiary rule of privilege but

---

93  This position is suggested in "The Public Safety Exception," above note 79.

94  See *Smith*, above note 38 at 256; but see the comments accompanying note 126, below.

95  See *Smith*, above note 38 at 254–55. See, however, section G(9), "Procedure," in this chapter, discussing instances where prior judicial authorization may be needed.

rather the common law duty of confidentiality.[96] Finally, the decision in *Smith v. Jones* makes the point that "by necessary implication, if a public-safety exception applies to solicitor-client privilege, it applies to all classifications of privileges *and duties of confidentiality*."[97]

If *Smith v. Jones* is best viewed as a case that bears upon both a lawyer's common law duty of confidentiality and the scope of legal-professional privilege, it still remains to explore the parameters of the public-safety exception and also to determine how the exception bears upon the analogous ethical duty set out in Canadian rules of professional conduct. In some ways the exception is easy to apply, but in other respects there remains much uncertainty.

## 3) Type of Harm: Focus on Crimes

One of the most striking features of the various future-harm exceptions utilized by the CBA Code and provincial governing bodies is that, apart from the new Ontario rule, all are restricted to future crimes.[98] As currently framed, only in Ontario does the exception condone disclosure of confidential information where serious preventable harm would flow from a *non-criminal* occurrence. At least in the context of our ethical rules, it would therefore not be out of place to refer to a "future-crime" (as opposed to a future-harm) exception.[99]

**Example I**: X gets into a car accident with another driver. Police investigate but correctly decide not to press charges; X is clearly not criminally at fault. The other driver is injured and sues X civilly. X's counsel retains a doctor to examine the plaintiff. The doctor's report reveals that the plaintiff has an aortic aneurysm which is life-threatening if left untreated. The plaintiff's own doctor has failed to detect the condition, but X is adamant that counsel not disclose the information to the other side. Under most Canadian ethical rules, counsel must comply with X's instructions.[100]

---

96   See *Smith*, above note 38 at 243; and *Descôteaux*, above note 39 at 396–97, and especially at 398–400.

97   *Smith*, above note 38 at 239 (emphasis added).

98   New Brunswick's exception applies to "criminal or fraudulent transactions," but the impact of including the reference to non-criminal frauds does not constitute a substantial expansion.

99   The "future-crime" terminology is used, for example, by G. MacKenzie, *Lawyers and Ethics: Professional Responsibility and Discipline* (Toronto: Carswell, 1993) at §3.4.

100  This example borrows heavily from the famous case of *Spaulding v. Zimmerman*, 116 N.W.2d 704 (Minn. 1962). It is not a far stretch to suppose that, faced with

**Example II**: Counsel acts for a client who is going through a severe depression as a result of outstanding criminal charges. The client tells counsel that he is going to commit suicide by taking an overdose of sleeping pills at his home that evening. Counsel has a heated discussion with the client in an attempt to dissuade him, following which it appears that the client's mind is unchanged. Early in the evening, counsel drives to the client's house. The lights and a stereo are on, and the client's car is in the driveway, but no one answers the door. Repeated phone calls go unanswered. Because suicide is not a crime in Canada,[101] in no province except Ontario will the future-harm exception allow counsel to call for help. Indeed, the prohibition will apply even if counsel, finding the front door open, enters the house to discover the client lying unconscious on the floor and clutching an empty bottle of sleeping pills.

The failure of our ethical rules to accommodate cases where future-harm does not arise from a criminal act is highly problematic. The fact that future-harm flows from a crime perhaps imposes a greater moral obligation on a lawyer to make disclosure, given the lawyer's position as an officer of the court. Nevertheless, providing not even a *discretion* to reveal information where necessary to prevent serious but non-criminal future-harm places confidentiality on too high a plane. For this reason, the Ontario rules aptly contain a future-harm exception that extends beyond criminal acts.[102]

*Smith* v. *Jones* appears to have substantially departed from the approach taken in Canadian ethical rules by abandoning criminality as a precondition necessary to invoke the public-safety exception. In rendering its decision, the Court was obviously aware of the ethical rules promulgated by various provincial governing bodies, making specific reference to the future-harm exception employed in British Columbia and the *previous* version used in Ontario.[103] Both of these ethical rules

---

this terrible scenario, counsel outside Ontario would ignore the apparent inapplicability of the future-harm exception and make disclosure.

101  See s. 241 of the *Criminal Code*, above note 37, which makes it a crime only to counsel, aid or abet a person to commit suicide.

102  See Ont. r. 2.03(3). See also the Third Restatement §66 (which covers non-criminal death or serious bodily harm); and §67 (which covers any non-criminal fraud that threatens a substantial financial loss and involves the use of counsel's services). As noted, in early August, 2001, the ABA House of Delegates voted to remove the reference to criminal acts, meaning that Model Rule 1.6 no longer requires that substantial bodily harm or death relate to a crime.

103  See *Smith*, above note 38 at 248. The old Ontario rule was set out in Rule 4, commentary 11 of the Professional Conduct Handbook.

focus on criminal acts. Yet in formulating and defining the public-safety exception, the Court at no time stated that the harm to be avoided must constitute a crime in order to justify disclosure, nor does anything in the Court's reasoning necessarily require such a restriction. It therefore appears that the common law duty of confidentiality is subject to a public-safety exception that is in this respect broader than the future-harm exceptions found in most Canadian rules of professional conduct. Admittedly, however, the Court does not directly address the issue as to whether the public-safety exception can apply to non-criminal future-harm, and no such determination was required on the facts of the case. It thus cannot be said with absolute certainty that the issue is settled.

The fact that the various Canadian professional governing bodies have adopted future-harm exceptions that are incongruent is often unproblematic. A lawyer is usually bound only by the ethical dictates of a single law society, rendering other jurisdictional approaches of primarily academic interest. But a real dilemma may arise where a lawyer's governing body has adopted a future-harm exception which is inconsistent with the Supreme Court of Canada's public-safety exception. Consider the possibilities that arise where future non-criminal harm can be averted only if counsel discloses confidential information against a client's wishes. If the public-safety exception articulated by *Smith* v. *Jones* is permissive (which for the moment appears to be the case), then the lawyer who chooses to disclose will necessarily be breaching the rules of his or her professional body.[104] Only if the court's exception is mandatory will the dilemma be solved, for as we have seen, the rules of professional conduct create an exception to the duty of confidentiality where disclosure is required by law.[105] Practically speaking, it may be that few governing bodies would discipline a lawyer for making disclosure where permitted (but not required) by rule of law, in circumstances where he or she acted reasonably to avoid non-criminal death or serious bodily harm. Nonetheless, the potential for inconsistency between *Smith* v. *Jones* and the ethical rules on the issue of future *crime* as a precondition of disclosure warrants attention. In particular, the CBA and Canadian gov-

---

104 Seeking a declaration from a court in order to activate the "required by law" exception does not necessarily avoid the problem. In *Smith*, *ibid.*, the Supreme Court affirmed the decision of the appeal court below to the effect that a mandatory order could not be made in response to a request for a declaration: see the discussion accompanying note 126, below.

105 See section D, "Disclosure Required by Law," in this chapter.

erning bodies should follow the lead of the Law Society of Upper Canada and abandon the "crime" precondition to the future-harm exception.

We can sum up by looking at the following example. Client X is terminally ill and tells counsel that he committed a murder for which Y was convicted and sentenced to life in prison. X refuses to permit counsel to reveal this information and dies shortly thereafter. Counsel thoroughly checks into the facts of the case and becomes convinced that X was telling the truth. Counsel also comes to the firm conclusion that Y was not convicted because of any untoward tampering with the trial process, and reasonably believes that the conviction could be set aside if X's admission was disclosed. Almost all Canadian rules of professional conduct do not permit disclosure on these facts.[106] There is no future-crime to be prevented, and the duty of confidentiality persists even after a client's death. Moreover, while an innocence-at-stake exception has been recognized regarding legal-professional privilege,[107] the duty of confidentiality arguably yields only via the "required by law" exception, where counsel is compelled by court process to reveal the information (*i.e.* there is no innocence-at-stake exception to the ethical duty of confidentiality).[108] However, if the public-safety exception in *Smith* v. *Jones* applies to preventable non-criminal harm, voluntary disclosure by counsel may be allowed at common law. Counsel outside of Ontario who relies on this reading of *Smith* v. *Jones* to justify disclosure has nonetheless probably breached the ethical dictates of his or her governing body.

---

106  The two exceptions may be Ontario and New Brunswick (in the latter province, if on the facts X's counsel was not "advising a client who has been charged with a criminal offence": see N.B. Part C, r. 5). A much harder situation arises where we alter the facts so that X has not died. In a well known Alabama case, Leo Frank was convicted of murder and then lynched by an angry mob. It was later learned that the real killer had confessed to his attorney, who remained silent prior to the lynching: see B. Williams, "Some Secrets Are Not Worth Keeping," [1998] Crim. L. Bull. 1 at note 104.

107  See *McClure*, above note 38.

108  See section H(7), "Duty Survives End of Retainer," in chapter 4. The argument against fashioning an exception to the duty of confidentiality simply because there exists an apparently analogous exception to legal-professional privilege is addressed in detail in section I, "Positive Duty to Safeguard Confidential Information," in chapter 4 (in the context of the crime-fraud exception).

## 4) Type of Harm: Death or Serious Bodily Harm

*Smith* v. *Jones* may take an expansive approach by jettisoning the requirement that the future-harm constitute a crime, yet in another sense the Supreme Court's decision seems to embrace a restrictive view of the type of harm sufficient to activate the public-safety exception. Again and again, the Court speaks of the exception as applying in order to prevent "serious bodily harm or death," apparently excluding all other types of harm. At one point, the Court goes so far as to say that

> the disclosure of planned future-crime without an element of violence would be insufficient reason to set aside solicitor-client privilege because of fears of public-safety. For the public-safety interest to be of sufficient importance to displace solicitor-client privilege, the threat must be to occasion serious bodily harm or death.[109]

To restrict the exception in this way is to leave practitioners in a serious bind. As mentioned, in every jurisdiction except British Columbia, Ontario, and perhaps Quebec, the ethical future-harm exception is wide enough to cover injury that does not involve death or serious bodily harm. If counsel chooses to disclose confidential information pertaining to lesser types of harm, and has acted properly in accordance with the rules imposed by his or her governing body, has the common law duty of confidentiality been unjustifiably violated? A client could certainly make this argument in civil proceedings for breach of confidentiality.[110]

In our view, the adverse impact sought to be avoided by future-harm exceptions should *not* be confined to physical harm constituting death or serious bodily harm. A multi-million dollar fraud may hold no risk of physical harm yet have an utterly devastating impact on many individuals. The importance of threatened death or serious bodily harm in defining and applying the exception must not be downplayed, but at the same time lawyers should at least have a discretion in deciding whether to make disclosure where other types of serious harm are threatened. Another option would be to permit disclosure to prevent substantial economic harm only where the client has used the lawyer's

---

109 *Smith*, above note 38 at 250.

110 In *Smith*, *ibid.* at 254, the majority states that an application to the court for a declaration may operate to protect a lawyer contemplating disclosure "from legal consequences." One possible implication of this comment is that an erroneous revelation of confidential information, made absent judicial permission, attracts civil liability (however, see the comment at note 136, below).

services to perpetrate a fraud.[111] It should be noted, however, that the Law Society of Upper Canada considered including non-physical harm in its new future-harm exception, and after a spirited debate the proposal was defeated.[112]

As a last point, the problem of an unduly narrow delineation of "type of harm" by *Smith* v. *Jones* may be tempered, or perhaps even entirely alleviated, by the Court's proffered definition of "serious bodily harm." In this respect, the majority notes that serious psychological harm may suffice, so long as the psychological harm "substantially interferes with the health or well-being of the complainant."[113] The exact scope of this phrase remains to be determined, but there is an argument that catastrophic economic loss may come within the definition.[114]

## 5) The Need for *Future* Harm

Most ethical rules, whether Canadian, American, or Commonwealth, make an exception for certain types of harm that occur in the future and are thus preventable.[115] The same can be said for the public-safety exception described by *Smith* v. *Jones*. Both the ethical rules and the Supreme Court's exception are arguably broad enough to encompass an ongoing crime. A kidnapping may extend for days or even weeks. An attempted murder crystallizes when a client places an explosive on an airplane, but a murder does not occur until the bomb goes off.[116] A fraudulent investment scheme may actually deprive the victims of

---

111 See Third Restatement §67, discussed in section J(5), "A Potential New Exception," in this chapter.

112 See "The Public Safety Exception," above note 79.

113 *Smith*, above note 38 at 250, quoting from *R.* v. *McCraw* (1991), 66 C.C.C. (3d) 517 at 524 (S.C.C.). A slightly broader definition of serious bodily harm is provided in the next paragraph in *McCraw*, encompassing "any hurt or injury, whether physical or psychological, that interferes in a substantial way with the physical or psychological integrity, health or well-being of the complainant."

114 Compare the apparently narrower definition employed by the Third Restatement §66, comm. "c": "Serious bodily harm . . . includes life-threatening illness and injuries and the consequences of events such as imprisonment for a substantial period and child sexual abuse. It also includes a client's threat of suicide."

115 In lonely contrast, however, is New Brunswick's exception, which appears to cover past crimes as long as the client is not charged. Indeed, this ill-conceived exception arguably applies even where the client is charged with the crime, if the information is communicated to a lawyer who is retained on an unrelated matter.

116 This particular example is given in Alta. ch. 7, comm. 8(c).

funds only after many months. In all of these cases, there is a prospective crime that surely comes within the meaning of most Canadian ethical rules, as well as the scope of the public-safety exception set out in *Smith* v. *Jones* (leaving aside the issue of serious bodily harm or death).

**Example I**: Client X has kidnapped and hidden a young child. Now under arrest, he refuses to cooperate with the police. However, X tells his counsel that the child is tied up in a locked storage shed on a deserted country lot, and was alive when he last saw her two days previous. X refuses to provide this information to the police or to allow the lawyer to do so because the girl can identify him. Under Canadian future-harm exceptions, as well as the public-safety exception articulated in *Smith* v. *Jones*, counsel is either permitted or mandated to release this information in order to save the child's life.[117]

In contrast, where a crime is definitely complete the exception does not apply, and counsel cannot reveal confidential information. Limiting the exception to instances where a crime is prospective can be explained by the obvious fact that completed harm can no longer be prevented. Yet hard cases can arise which test this restriction.

**Example II**: Vary the previous example so that X is arrested one month after the child's disappearance. He tells the lawyer that the child is dead and provides the location of the body. On hearing X's story, the lawyer forms the view that the body will yield damning DNA evidence which will shore up an otherwise vulnerable Crown case. Learning of the arrest, the child's family is frantic to recover the body. However, the future-crime exceptions set out in the Canadian rules of professional conduct do not apply. Revealing the information will not prevent a crime, and the importance of maintaining confidentiality is especially strong. The fact that X may go free for a heinous crime does not in itself justify disclosure.

A fact situation somewhat similar to this last example arose in the Lake Pleasant Bodies case, where two counsel not only refused to reveal the location of their client's victims, but attempted to use the information to plea bargain.[118] The facts and legal aftermath of the case

---

117 A more complicated version of this scenario occurred in *Henderson* v. *State*, 962 S.W.2d 544 (Tex. Crim. App. 1997) [*Henderson*], cert. denied (1998) 525 U.S. 978. It is unclear on the facts of *Henderson* whether the lawyer had reason to believe that the girl was alive, but police apparently entertained some slight hope in this regard.

118 A tactic also seen in *Henderson*, *ibid.*

can be founds in the reported case of *People* v. *Belge*.[119] One might ask whether the inability to recover the body could constitute serious bodily harm for the victims' families under the broad definition suggested in *Smith* v. *Jones*, discussed above at in section G(4). More extreme still is the argument that serious bodily harm as described in *Smith* v. *Jones* can encompass the severe psychological pain felt by a victim or a victim's family if a perpetrator is not caught, convicted and punished. These examples demonstrate the weakness that would attend an overly wide and elastic definition of harm, namely, that the public-safety exception would threaten to obliterate altogether the duty of confidentiality.

**Example III**: Let us alter the last example so that, based on information provided by X, counsel reasonably forms the opinion that X has killed several other children, and that if released he is likely to continue the killings. In this situation, under the rules of professional conduct counsel may be permitted or even mandated to disclose information to prevent future-harm to other children.[120] Query whether disclosure sufficient to protect this class of future victims could be made without exposing the client to harm in relation to past criminal acts.

## 6) Disclosure Must be Necessary

Most Canadian rules of professional conduct specify that disclosure can be made only where necessary to prevent the specified future-harm.[121] This precondition emphasizes the importance of maintaining confidentiality wherever possible. If the use or revelation of confidential information is not required, for example, where there are alternative ways of preventing the harm, breach of the duty is not justified. An implied corollary is that disclosure should be made only to the extent necessary to prevent harm.[122] Only information sufficient to avoid the harm should be released, and only to those persons who need be notified in order to achieve this purpose.

---

119 372 N.Y.S.2d 798 (Co. Ct. 1975), aff'd 376 N.Y.S.2d 771 (1975), aff'd 359 N.E.2d 377 (1976).

120 Disclosure will be mandated in all jurisdictions except British Columbia and Ontario: see section G(1), "The Rules of Professional Conduct," in this chapter.

121 New Brunswick alone fails to impose this restriction upon the future-harm exception. In our view, the absence of this restriction is unjustifiable. It is to be hoped that the governing body in New Brunswick is prepared to infer a "necessity" precondition.

122 See *Smith*, above note 38 at 252.

## 7) Duty to Confer with the Client

The requirement that disclosure be necessary to prevent a future-harm is closely connected with counsel's positive duty to confer with the client prior to making disclosure, assuming that circumstances permit. If counsel is to be satisfied, to use the guidelines set out by the Supreme Court in *Smith* v. *Jones*, that the harm is clear, serious, and imminent, discussion with the client where practicable is often essential.[123] Upon discussing the matter with the client, counsel may learn that his or her fears were unjustified. Or, where the client has the power to prevent the harm, counsel may be able to convince the client to do so. In other cases, counsel may secure the client's consent to use or reveal a certain amount of confidential information. Even if some information is eventually revealed over the objections of the client, a pre-revelation discussion may better equip counsel to make disclosure in the manner least damaging to the client. These examples illustrate why counsel should make all reasonable efforts to speak to the client prior to acting under the future-harm exception. Failure to do so may result in the disclosure of confidential information that was not necessary in order to prevent future-harm.

Granted, it may not always be possible or prudent to confer with one's client prior to disclosing information pursuant to the future-harm exception. In certain circumstances, time constraints or the unavailability of the client will reasonably justify foregoing this step in the process. In other instances, speaking with the client may jeopardize efforts to prevent the harm or create a new risk of serious harm (whether to the lawyer or a third party). It may also be, in the rarest of cases, that discussing the issue with the client is obviously futile and hence not worth pursuing. Counsel's "default mechanism," however, should be to consult with the client in advance of releasing any information, absent good reasons to forego this step in the process.

## 8) The Lawyer's Discretion

As we have seen, many professional governing bodies have chosen to provide counsel with a discretion in deciding whether to make disclo-

---

123 This duty is not expressly mentioned in *Smith* v. *Jones*, yet surely is mandated by counsel's ethical obligations. The general duty to inform and advise the client has already been discussed in section E, "Informing and Advising the Client," in chapter 8.

sure in order to prevent a future-harm.[124] Yet the decision in *Smith v. Jones* is not so clear on the matter. At certain points, the Court uses mandatory language, suggesting that the exception *must* be applied if the necessary preconditions are met.[125] On the other hand, the Court affirms the decision of the British Columbia Court of Appeal regarding the form of the order. The Court of Appeal expressly modified the mandatory order made by the judge at first instance, ruling that disclosure of the information in question was permitted.[126] In our view, however, it is important to recognize that the Court of Appeal did not reach its decision after a reasoned consideration of the nature of the public-safety exception, but rather seemed most concerned with the remedial limits imposed by the rules of the court concerning declarative relief. Despite the Supreme Court's affirmation of the appeal court's order, it is thus still open to argue that the public-safety exception mandates disclosure where the necessary preconditions are met.

If we assume that a discretion does indeed exist, at least in some instances, regarding the application of the future-harm exception, the question arises as to what factors a lawyer should consider in coming to a decision. The standards employed in many Canadian future-harm exceptions as a precondition to acquiring a discretion in the first place suggest several possible factors; so, too, does the test formulated in *Smith v. Jones*.[127] Nevertheless, counsel should take care not to act precipitously: the applicable standard must be met *before* moving on to consider the exercise of a discretion. Once the discretion is activated, factors that counsel may want to take into account include:

1. **Probability that harm will occur:** Under most ethical rules a lawyer's discretion will arise only once he or she believes that the defined harm is likely to occur, which means that a certain degree of probability has already been established by the time the question

---

124 See the discussion in section G(1), "The Rules of Professional Conduct," in this chapter.

125 See *Smith*, above note 38 at 248 ("In rare circumstances, these public interests may be so compelling that the privilege *must* be displaced"); 251 ("If after considering all appropriate factors it is determined that the threat to public-safety outweighs the need to preserve solicitor-client privilege, then the privilege *must* be set aside"); and 254 ("In light of these conclusions, the solicitor-client privilege attaching to Dr. Smith's report, to the extent provided by the order of Henderson J., *must* be set aside") (emphases added).

126 See *Smith v. Jones*, [1997] B.C.J. No. 3136 (S.C.) (QL) [*Smith (B.C.S.C.)*], varied (1998), 62 B.C.L.R. (3d) 198 (C.A.).

127 Factors concerning the probability of harm, as well as type and extent of harm, immediately come to mind in this regard.

of discretion arises. In *Smith* v. *Jones*, the Supreme Court of Canada speaks of probability in terms of the existence of a "clear risk to an identifiable group or person."[128] However, some "likely" harms are more probable than others. A lawyer may be more inclined to disclose a confidence where harm is absolutely certain, as opposed to some high yet lesser degree of likelihood.

2. **Type (including extent) of harm**: This factor is also implied by most ethical rules, as well as *Smith* v. *Jones*,[129] insofar as only certain types of harm can trigger the discretion. But even within the scope of the discretion, distinctions between type of harm may influence a lawyer's action. For instance, in jurisdictions where the discretion can arise with respect to any sort of crime whatsoever, physical harm may provide a greater pull for disclosure than will non-physical damage. At the other extreme, where harm is potentially reversible, such as with the eventual return of a stolen car, disclosure is less likely to occur.

3. **Immediacy of harm**: Another consideration is the immediacy of the possible harm.[130] A threat that is unlikely to be carried out for many months may militate towards leaving confidentiality intact, at least for the time being.[131] In sharp contrast, a harm that may occur within minutes of the lawyer receiving the information may legitimately lead him or her to err on the side of disclosure.

4. **Role of the client**: Counsel may be more inclined to reveal a confidence where the client has used him or her as an unwitting dupe to carry out the intended harmful act. For instance, a lawyer who learns that he or she has unknowingly been drawn into an impending fraud engineered by a client can take account of the client's role. Contrast the case where the impending harm in no way involves the client and instead is the sole responsibility of a third party.[132] As a caveat, however, counsel must always be wary of judging a client's moral culpability. For this reason, the fact that a

---

128 *Smith*, above note 38 at 249–50.

129 Ibid. at 250, where seriousness of harm is discussed by the majority.

130 See generally the discussion of "imminence" in *Smith*, *ibid.* at 251.

131 Compare *Smith*, *ibid.* at 251, where the court suggests (somewhat oddly) that a threat to commit murder in three years' time will be imminent if a reasonable bystander would be convinced that the killing would be carried out. Also note that the ABA House of Delegates has removed the "imminence" requirement from Model Rule 1.6 (as of August 2001).

132 In contrast to the Canadian rules of professional conduct, note that ABA Model Rule 1.6(b)(1) covers only the case where a *client* is likely to commit a future-crime.

client is implicated in the anticipated harm should not be overemphasized.

5. **Role of the lawyer**: As just mentioned, the lawyer may have unwittingly played a role in exposing a third party to future-harm, whether or not arising out of a client's improper manipulation of the professional relationship. The lawyer may harbour legitimate concerns regarding personal responsibility for causing the harm, and take these into account in exercising the discretion. A valid desire to circumvent subsequent attribution of blame by the party who is poised to suffer harm may also be a proper consideration for the lawyer.[133] However, given the potential for conflict-of-interest, the lawyer should be slow to give effect to these concerns absent reasoned advice from knowledgeable colleagues or the professional governing body.

6. **Impact on client**: If the harm can be averted without any adverse impact on the client, the discretion is more likely to be exercised in favour of disclosure. Conversely, serious repercussions for the client will make counsel less likely to disclose. Determining the impact on a client is not always easy. Consider an example where counsel receives a call from the client's brother. The brother says that the client has left the house with a gun, intent on killing a Crown witness. Calling the witness and/or the police might lead to a charge of attempted murder yet be to the client's advantage because timely intervention potentially avoids the more serious charge of first degree murder.[134] This example also demonstrates how the disclosure of information received from a third party who is not himself or herself bound by a duty of confidentiality (*viz.*, the brother) may present less risk of adverse impact to the client than if the information comes directly from the client himself. Where the third party's information is likely discoverable by the police, even if only after the crime has been committed, revelation by the lawyer may have little additional adverse impact for the client.

7. **Impact on the lawyer's practice**: Counsel may fear that his or her professional practice will suffer harm by reason of being labelled a

---

133 See the discussion of the self-defence exception to the duty of confidentiality, in section E, "Lawyer Self-defence," in this chapter.

134 It could be argued that privilege operates to protect the client from adverse use of the disclosed information in subsequent legal proceedings, yet this approach seems to be implicitly precluded by the majority judgment in *Smith*, above note 38: see "The Public Safety Exception," above note 79.

whistle-blower. Certainly, it is possible that existing or prospective clients will view disclosure as tantamount to working with the police or Crown and will refuse to be represented by counsel. Yet it is our view that counsel should be exceedingly slow to rely upon possible harm to his or her own business interests in approaching the question of discretion. Favouring financial gain over preventing serious bodily harm to a third party smacks of unseemly self-interest, and understandably tends to lower the public's level of respect for the legal profession and the administration of justice.

8.  **Reliance on the lawyer by the victim:** If the lawyer knows that the potential victim of the crime is placing some reliance on him or her with respect to the matter, for example, an elderly and unsophisticated mother who is acting as surety, this factor can be taken into account.

9.  **Impact on the legal system:** It is legitimate for counsel to take into account the impact that his or her decision will have upon the administration of justice. Counsel should not cower before the vagaries of public opinion but on the other hand may want to consider the position of the hypothetical reasonable person properly appraised of all the facts.[135]

10. **Lawyer's personal view:** Lawyers are human beings and can reasonably differ on the proper approach to certain ethical issues. Counsel's own moral compass will always play some role in the decision whether or not to disclose a confidence under a future-harm exception. Some counsel may feel so strongly that confidences must be preserved, even while recognizing that not everyone takes this view, as to almost always decide in favour of non-disclosure.

These factors are not intended to be all-inclusive. Moreover, all relevant factors must be considered together, the ultimate question being whether in counsel's view the need to keep client information confidential is outweighed by the importance of preventing likely future-harm. Finally, it is our view that counsel should be given significant leeway in exercising the discretion.[136]

---

135  It is, after all, this same hypothetical person who helps to ascertain whether a disqualifying conflict-of-interest exists: see *MacDonald Estate* v. *Martin*, [1990] 3 S.C.R. 1235.

136  The Third Restatement, in §66(3) and §67(4), goes so far as to grant counsel an absolute, unreviewable discretion in this regard. On a related point, *Smith*, above note 38 at 244, expressly leaves unanswered the question as to whether a doctor (and hence, presumably, a lawyer as well) can be held liable for deciding

## 9) Procedure

*Smith* v. *Jones* offers insight into the procedures available to the lawyer who contemplates using or disclosing confidential information pursuant to a future-harm exception. On the facts of the case, a defence psychiatric expert believed that the release of confidential information was necessary to prevent serious future-crimes by an offender who had pleaded guilty and was awaiting sentencing. The psychiatrist brought an action in the superior court for a declaration permitting him to release the information, and gave notice to the offender's counsel. The psychiatrist also sought, and was granted, leave to commence the action using pseudonyms for both parties and for an *in camera* hearing.[137] The court record was sealed and a publication ban was imposed, measures that the Court of Appeal and Supreme Court of Canada continued pending a final determination of the matter.[138] Once the Supreme Court released its decision, the record was unsealed and the publication ban removed to the extent that legal-professional privilege had been overridden.[139]

The decision of the majority in *Smith* v. *Jones* generally approves of the procedure undertaken by the psychiatrist.[140] Counsel may therefore wish to adopt this sort of approach, where time and other circumstances permit, in order to ensure that disclosure is not made precipitously. Indeed, in Ontario the new rules of professional conduct specifically state that disclosure under the future-harm exception be made "pursuant to judicial order where practicable."[141] A judicial determination that disclosure is permitted or mandated will presumably protect counsel from disciplinary or civil proceedings by the client, while an order forbidding disclosure may well have the same

---

not to make a discretionary disclosure. Case law bearing upon a doctor's civil liability for failing to disclose, or conversely for disclosing, confidential information where public-safety is at stake is cited in "The Public Safety Exception," above note 79 at note 113.

137 See *Smith* (B.C.S.C.), above note 126 at para. 38.

138 See *Smith*, above note 38 at 255. Note, however, that the Supreme Court of Canada refused to hear the appeal *in camera*: *ibid.* at 256.

139 *Ibid.* at 255–56. Many of the details concerning the confidential information, including matters not revealed in the Supreme Court of Canada's decision, have since been reported in the press: see "The Public Safety Exception," above note 79.

140 *Smith*, above note 38 at 254.

141 Ont. r. 2.03(3).

effect in relation to any third party who suffers harm as a result of non-disclosure.[142]

Relying on judicial guidance to resolve a problem involving the future-harm exception may be ideal, but sometimes circumstances may arise that do not permit the luxury of a court proceeding. The Supreme Court of Canada recognized as much in *Smith* v. *Jones*, the majority suggesting that "it might be appropriate to notify the potential victim or the police or a Crown prosecutor, depending on the specific circumstances."[143] The dissent also approved of disclosure absent prior judicial approval "in rare cases where an individual poses an instant risk such that even an *ex parte* application to the court is not possible."[144] The Ontario ethical rules speak of obtaining prior judicial approval "where practicable." Overall, the tenor of the decision in *Smith* v. *Jones*, taken in conjunction with the recently adopted position of the Law Society of Upper Canada, suggest that counsel should bring the matter to a court's attention prior to making disclosure where reasonably practicable.

# H. FUTURE-HARM ACCRETIONS: COURT AND NATIONAL SECURITY

Several Canadian governing bodies have adopted, or make vague reference to, exceptions to the duty of confidentiality that aim to prevent harm either in a specific location (a court facility) or of a particular dimension (national security or emergency). Such exceptions can be seen as accretions upon the future-harm exception, but it is open to debate whether they add anything of true value concerning the protection of important public-safety interests.

## 1) Court Security

A number of jurisdictions have included an exception expressly aimed at preventing harm at a court-house. For instance, the CBA Code provides that

> [t]he lawyer who has reasonable grounds for believing that a dangerous situation is likely to develop at a court facility shall inform the

---

142 A possible counter-argument is set out at note 104, above.

143 *Smith*, above note 38 at 255.

144 *Ibid.* at 236 (not dissenting on this point).

person having responsibility for security at the facility and give particulars. Where possible the lawyer should suggest solutions to the anticipated problem such as:

(a) the need for further security;

(b) that the judgment be reserved;

(c) such other measures as may seem advisable.[145]

Other jurisdictions do not have this provision, including Alberta, British Columbia, and Nova Scotia.

The "likely development of a dangerous situation" would seem to equate with the likelihood that a crime involving violence will be committed. On this reading, the court-security rule adds little to the future-harm exception as found in the CBA Code. However, it is not entirely clear that "a dangerous situation" embraces only physical violence. On this view, while the future-crime exception in the CBA Code provides a discretion where the crime does not involve violence, the court-security exception counsel allows for no discretion where a court facility is at risk. If the court-security exception is interpreted in this expansive way, perhaps the lawyer's special duties to the court and the administration of justice can be relied upon for justification. Yet the notion that a lesser degree of protection should be provided to third parties where danger arises outside a court facility seems callous and biased.

The court-security exception is further marred by the apparent failure to ensure that disclosure of confidential information is necessary to foreclose the possibility of danger. However, we are of the view that this limitation can be read into the exception. Accordingly, if counsel is confronted with a dangerous situation at a court facility, he or she should release confidential information only to the extent necessary to prevent the anticipated harm. Moreover, prior to releasing any information, counsel should discuss the matter with the client if circumstances permit. If the client is not responsible for the danger, he or she may well consent to the disclosure of information. Even if the client is complicit in the threat, counsel may be able to avert the danger by convincing the client to call off the anticipated action. In sum, the guidelines already discussed above regarding the future-harm exception are useful in approaching the problem of danger at a court facility.[146]

As a final point, it used to be that the Law Society of Upper Canada endorsed a court-security exception similar to that found in the CBA Code. Because Ontario had only a discretionary future-harm excep-

---

145 CBA Code ch. IV, comm. 12; and *former* Ont. r. 11, comm. 6.

146 See especially sections G(6), "Disclosure Must be Necessary," and G)(7), "Duty to Confer with the Client," in this chapter.

tion, and yet mandated disclosure where court-security was compromised, a sharp distinction was being drawn based on the location of an anticipated crime. This favouritism was, it is submitted, extraordinarily difficult to fathom or support. However, Ontario's new Rules of Professional Conduct, while still evincing a court-security provision, now stipulate that the provision is subject to the general duty of confidentiality.[147] Apparently, there is no longer an independent exception applicable to court-security, as opposed to other locations where future-harm might occur.

## 2)  National Security or Emergency

New Brunswick, alone among the Canadian provinces, expressly creates an exception to the duty of confidentiality, "when the national interest makes disclosure imperative."[148] A number of other governing bodies follow the CBA Code's lead in making a much more oblique reference to "national emergency." Specifically, these jurisdictions employ footnote 9, which purports to comment upon and relate to the self-defence exception, and states (somewhat mysteriously): "There is no duty or privilege where a client conspires with or deceives his lawyer: *The Queen* v. *Cox* (1885), L.R. 14 Q.B.D. 153 (C.C.R.). *Cf. Orkin at p. 86 as to the exceptions of crime, fraud and national emergency.*"[149] The reference, of course, is to Orkin's well known book on professional conduct, published in 1957.[150] Closer observation reveals that the passage in Orkin refers to an exception to legal-profession privilege.[151] But the question remains, what does this footnote mean? And more generally still, should there be an exception to the duty of confidentiality for matters of national interest?

We can start by looking at the common law with respect to confidentiality and privilege. While there may be an emerging national-security exception to legal-professional privilege,[152] the elliptical mention of "national emergency" in a footnote to the rules of professional conduct should not be seen to create any comparable exception

---

147  See Ont r. 4.06(3), as well as r. 2.03(1) (commentary).

148  N.B. Part C, r. 5.

149  See CBA Code ch. IV, comm. 10, footnote 9 [emphasis added]. Footnote 9 is discussed further in section I(3), "Searching for Guidance in the Rules of Professional Conduct," in this chapter.

150  See M. Orkin, *Legal Ethics: A Study of Professional Conduct* (Toronto: Cartwright, 1957).

151  *Ibid.*

152  See *Smith*, above note 38 at 242

to the duty of confidentiality. Once again, an exception to the privilege does not necessitate a loss of confidentiality in the absence of compulsion by court process. A mere footnote that recommends comparison or review of a 1957 comment about legal-professional privilege, without more, should not be taken to impinge on the lawyer's duty to keep client information confidential.

As for the New Brunswick approach, there is little to be said in favour of this rather stark national interest exception. For one thing, lawyers deserve some guidance as to its meaning and scope; figuring out where the national interest "mandates" disclosure, to use the terminology of the rule, is difficult in all but the most obvious cases. This observation leads us to a more general critique. Serious national threats involving physical harm will surely fall within future-harm exceptions; consider a client who is going to blow up the Parliament buildings while the House of Commons is in session. More subtle threats, for instance, criminal acts with national economic or diplomatic repercussions, will also fall within many Canadian future-harm exceptions. To the extent that existing future-harm exceptions are possibly inadequate where the national interest is concerned, the first step should be to consider wholesale reform to these or other pre-existing exceptions.[153] Providing special dispensation for a rather amorphous "national interest" appears difficult to justify.

# I. POSSIBLE CRIME-FRAUD EXCEPTION

We now turn our focus to a question that has garnered little attention in Canada: is there a crime-fraud exception to the ethical duty of confidentiality? By "crime-fraud exception," we mean an exception that would permit or mandate disclosure by counsel, *even in the absence of compulsion by court process*, whenever circumstances existed sufficient to engage the crime-fraud exception to legal-professional privilege. Answering this question requires that we begin by examining the nature and parameters of this exception to the privilege.

---

153 Aspects of the debate in this regard are discussed in sections E, "Lawyer Self-Defence," and J, "The Problem of Unwitting Involvement by Counsel in Criminal Acts," in this chapter.

## 1) The Crime-Fraud Exception to Legal-Professional Privilege

The crime-fraud exception to legal-professional privilege applies to communications with a lawyer that are in themselves criminal or are knowingly made for the purpose of obtaining legal advice to facilitate the commission of a crime.[154] The justification for this exception is inextricably linked with the grounds necessary to establish the privilege in the first place. Communications between lawyer and client are protected by privilege if made within the usual and ordinary scope of professional employment.[155] This requirement means that the communications need be made for the purpose of seeking legal advice, as opposed to some other purpose.[156] Where the client seeks advice for the purpose of assisting in a crime or fraud, there can be no privilege because such advice is not within the usual and ordinary scope of a lawyer's professional employment.[157] At bottom, a policy decision is being made to the effect that these communications constitute an abuse of the client-lawyer relationship, do nothing to advance the rationale underlying legal-professional privilege, and thus should not be fostered by means of the protection afforded by a privilege.

Still on the subject of privilege, it is worth noting that the crime-fraud exception is *not* commensurate with the public-safety exception to legal-professional privilege described in *Smith* v. *Jones*. Among other things, the crime-fraud exception applies only where the communications are in themselves criminal or the client seeks legal advice in furtherance of committing a crime or fraud. If a client merely informs counsel of an intention to commit a crime or somehow reveals an uncontrollable propensity to do so, and is not seeking legal advice in order to further an illegal purpose, the crime-fraud exception does not apply. Rather, only where the prospective crime involves death or serious bodily harm, and counsel reasonably believes that disclosure is necessary to prevent the crime, will the public-safety exception will be engaged. Another difference between the two exceptions lies in the fact that the crime-fraud exception does not require any degree of likelihood that a crime will be committed.

---

154  See *Campbell*, above note 38 at 291–95.
155  See *Canada* v. *Solosky* (1979), 50 C.C.C. (2d) 495 at 507 (S.C.C.)[ *Solosky*]; and *Descôteaux*, above note 38 at 398.
156  See *Solosky*, above note 155 at 507; *Descôteaux*, above note 39 at 398 & 413; and *Campbell*, above note 38 at 289.
157  See *Solosky*, above note 155 at 507; *Descôteaux* , above note 39 at 398 & 413; and *Campbell*, above note 38 at 291–93.

**Example**: Client X is arrested for conspiracy to traffic in narcotics and released on bail. X tells counsel that a substantial amount of cash proceeds from drug deals that occurred during the time period covered by the charge are being held in a safety deposit box. He proposes that counsel launder the cash through her trust account in exchange for a percentage of the proceeds. Counsel has a long talk with X, explaining the impropriety of such action and providing a number of reasons why he should forget about trying to launder the money. At the conclusion of the conversation, X agrees to abandon his proposal and counsel reasonably believes X's assurance. Counsel takes detailed notes of the entire conversation.

This example does not fall within the public-safety exception to legal professional privilege, most especially because counsel does not reasonably believe that disclosure is necessary to prevent a future-crime. Nevertheless, the crime-fraud exception *does* apply, and legal-professional privilege could not be invoked to ward off, for example, a search warrant with respect to counsel's notes.[158]

## 2) Envisioning a Similar Exception to the Duty of Confidentiality

Our discussion so far has focused on the possible displacement of legal-professional privilege by the crime-fraud exception. The next logical step is to revisit our initial query, namely, whether there exists a crime-fraud exception to *the ethical duty of confidentiality*. Crucially, such an exception would allow a lawyer to disclose information received from a client to a third party, such as the police or Crown counsel, completely apart from any question of compulsion by court process. If we return to the last example, concerning the money-laundering proposal put to counsel, the implications of extending the crime-fraud exception to the duty of confidentiality become concrete. Assume that no one else has any reason to suspect that the client was considering a plan to launder the money through counsel's trust

---

158 In order to displace the privilege, there must be a *prima facie* case to suppose that the exception applies; see J. Sopinka, S. Lederman, & A. Bryant, *The Law of Evidence in Canada*, 2d ed. (Toronto, Butterworths, 1999) at §14.59. It seems that the court can review the communications in issue in order to determine whether the privilege applies: see *Campbell*, above note 38 at 295; and *R. v. Bencardino* (1973), 15 C.C.C. (2d) 342 (Ont. C.A.). On the facts in this example, privilege may exist in relation to some of the communications between counsel and client.

account. In such a case, counsel will not be subpoenaed or served with a search warrant regarding the communications, and the crime-fraud exception to privilege will never come into play. But if the crime-fraud exception also works to release counsel from any ethical duty of confidentiality, counsel is nevertheless free to inform the police of the communications. The result would obviously be catastrophic for the client.

There are numerous less exotic instances where a crime-fraud exception to the duty of confidentiality might come to bear. Consider the client who asks counsel to provide a bogus excuse in order to obtain a bench warrant with discretion, suggests fabricating an alibi or offering perjured testimony, seeks advice regarding the best way to ensure that a Crown witness does not attend at trial, or provides counsel with an obviously forged employer's letter for use on sentencing. A crime-fraud exception to the duty of confidentiality would permit counsel to report the client to the authorities in these and many other cases, even where counsel has succeeded in dissuading the client from the proposed illegality. Such an incursion into the duty is potentially enormous, making it important to determine whether this sort of exception in fact exists.

## 3) Searching for Guidance in the Rules of Professional Conduct

National professional organizations in the United Kingdom and United States offer two different approaches to the issue of a crime-fraud exception. In the United Kingdom, solicitors are not bound by an ethical duty of confidence where communications occur in an attempt to further a crime or fraud:

> 16.02 The duty to keep a client's confidences can be overridden in certain exceptional circumstances.
>
> 1. The duty of confidentiality does not apply to information acquired by a solicitor where he or she is being used by the client to facilitate the commission of a crime or fraud, because that is not within the scope of a professional retainer. If the solicitor becomes suspicious about a client's activities the solicitor should normally assess the situation in light of the client's explanations and the solicitor's professional judgement.[159]

---

159 *The Guide to the Professional Conduct of Solicitors*, above note 87 at §16.02(1).

The opposite tack is taken in the ABA Model Rules, a position reached only after intense and sometimes acrimonious debate.[160] Simply put, ABA Rule 1.6 does not permit disclosure of communications, in the absence of court process, just because the crime-fraud exception to legal-professional privilege theoretically applies.[161]

In contrast to the stance taken in the United Kingdom or by the ABA Model Rules, many Canadian rules of professional conduct are frustratingly obscure on the question of whether crime-fraud communications must remain confidential. Almost no jurisdiction directly addresses the existence or non-existence of such an exception, and arguments can be marshalled either way. In support of a crime-fraud exception, one can point to numerous judicial pronouncements to the effect that crime-fraud communications are not confidential.[162] The non-confidential nature of such communications would by definition relieve counsel of any obligation to keep the information secret. There is also a statement in *Smith* v. *Jones* to the effect that, by necessary implication, an exception that applies to legal-professional privilege also applies to all duties of confidentiality.[163] On this reasoning, because there is indisputably a crime-fraud exception to the privilege, communications falling within the scope of the exception would not fall within the ambit of the duty of confidentiality. Furthermore, the CBA Code and several provincial rules of professional conduct contain two footnotes to the rule governing confidentiality that point towards a crime-fraud exception to the ethical obligation. Footnote 9 says that, "there is no duty or privilege where a client conspires with or deceives his lawyer,"[164] while footnote 10 opines that, "to oust privilege the communication must have been made to execute or further a crime or

---

160 See, for example, the discussion in the Third Restatement §67, comm. "c" & Reporter's Note "b"; and A. Kaufman, *Problems in Professional Responsibility*, 3d ed. (Boston: Little, Brown, 1989) at 210–13 (in the context of past fraud committed with the unwitting help of counsel, a situation where the issue of possible limits on the duty of confidentiality often arises).

161 See the text of Rule 1.6 and also the discussion in the Legal Background (Disclosure upon Discovery of Client Crime or Fraud). See also Hazard & Hodes, above note 34 at §1.6 (307–15). As these sources indicate, the ABA position has *not* led to a well-defined, easily applied, or universally accepted rule.

162 See, for example, *Descôteaux*, above note 39 at 398 & 413–14; and *Campbell*, above note 38 at 291.

163 *Smith*, above note 38 at 239. See also the discussion in section G(2), "The Decision in *Smith* v. *Jones*," in this chapter.

164 CBA Code ch. IV, footnote 9, citing the early but influential crime-fraud case of *R.* v. *Cox and Railton* (1884), 14 Q.B.D. 153 (C.R.); and N.S. ch. 5 footnote 9.

fraud — it must be prospective as distinguished from retrospective."[165] Finally, from a policy perspective it can be argued that the client who attempts to utilize counsel's services to commit a crime has perverted the proper purpose of the professional relationship. Communications that are criminal in themselves or knowingly seek an illegal end are in no way necessary to further a client's legal representation and fall outside the rationale that justifies the ethical duty of confidentiality.

These points in favour of a crime-fraud exception to the duty of confidentiality cannot be dismissed outright. But we believe that, on closer examination, the Canadian ethical rules as currently constituted do not permit such an exception. For one thing, the CBA Code and every provincial governing body arguably define the general duty of confidentiality broadly enough to cover communications knowingly made for the purpose of facilitating a crime or fraud. Remember that these ethical rules do not rely on common law or equitable definitions of confidentiality in delineating the scope of the duty,[166] a fact that weakens the relevance of judicial pronouncements regarding crime-fraud communications and confidentiality. In the same vein, the case law that at first glance appears to support an exception must be seen in context. Usually the courts are speaking of a loss of the confidentiality that is necessary to ground legal-professional privilege,[167] or the inability of a substantive rule of confidentiality to protect communications from use or interception by a third party.[168] Permitting voluntary disclosure by a fiduciary who has a duty of loyalty to the client, including a duty not to reveal information received regarding a client's affairs, is taking matters significantly further. That is to say, case law forcing compliance with court process or refusing to stop interference by a third party does not necessarily equate with an ethical rule that condones voluntary disclosure by counsel. Confidentiality as defined by the rules of professional conduct can be, and in many cases is, wider than confidentiality at common law.[169]

As for the two CBA Code footnotes that seem to imply a crime-fraud exception, in our view these should not be read so as to permit disclosure by counsel. It is important to note that neither footnote stands independently as an unclouded and discrete exception.

---

165  CBA Code ch. IV, footnote 10, citing *R. v. Bennett* (1964), 41 C.R. 227
     (B.C.S.C.). As an aside, this footnote appears to confuse the distinction between
     the evidentiary rule of privilege and the ethical duty of confidentiality.
166  See section C, "The Rules of Professional Conduct," in chapter 4.
167  See, for example, *Campbell*, above note 38.
168  See, for example, *Solosky*, above note 155.
169  See, for example, the discussion in sections C–E in chapter 4.

Footnote 9 purports to bear upon the self-defence exception, while footnote 10 ostensibly comments on the future-harm exception. Both can legitimately be viewed as glosses on these two well-established exceptions, exceptions that are not defined coterminously with the crime-fraud exception to legal-professional privilege. To elaborate, footnote 9 can be read to support the view that a lawyer who is deceived by the client may be in a position where disclosure is necessary for the purpose of self-defence. Also note that footnote 9 makes reference to a comment in Orkin's *Legal Ethics*.[170] Orkin seems to propose that crime-fraud circumstances allow counsel to disclose "where called upon to do so by due process of the court." This approach simply makes use of the "required by law" exception described above in section D. Orkin then appears to advocate a mandatory duty to disclose for serious crimes and a discretionary ability to do so for minor offences, a passage that comes close to mimicking the CBA Code's future-harm exception. As for footnote 10, this reference arguably does no more than suggest that circumstances falling within the crime-fraud exception to legal-professional privilege will on occasion serve to activate the future-harm exception to the ethical duty of confidentiality.

Establishing a crime-fraud exception based on two cryptic (and, it must be said, confusing) footnotes is difficult to countenance, and it is instructive that Alberta, British Columbia and Ontario do not include these footnotes in their rules. In fact, Alberta's rules, which are unique in Canada by virtue of their relative clarity on this point, quite firmly exclude the possibility of a crime-fraud exception to the duty of confidentiality.[171] As for Ontario, the Law Society of Upper Canada has included a commentary to its new rule on confidentiality that relates to the issue of crime-fraud and disclosure:

*Commentary*

A lawyer employed or retained to act for an organization, including a corporation, confronts a difficult problem about confidentiality when he or she becomes aware that the organization may commit a dishonest, fraudulent, criminal, or illegal act.

This problem is sometimes described as the problem of whether the lawyer should "blow the whistle" on his employer or client. Although the Rules of Professional Conduct make it clear that the lawyer shall not knowingly assist or encourage any dis-

---

170 Orkin, above note 150 at 86.
171 See Alta. ch. 7, r. 8, read in conjunction with Rule 7 and the cross-references provided in the commentary to r. 7.

honesty, fraud, crime, or illegal conduct (rule 2.02(6)), it does not follow that the lawyer should disclose to the appropriate authorities an employer's or client's proposed misconduct.

Rather, the general rule, as set out above, is that the lawyer shall hold the client's information in strict confidence, and this general rule is subject to only a few exceptions. Assuming the exceptions do not apply, there are, however, several steps that a lawyer should take when confronted with the difficult problem of proposed misconduct by an organization. The lawyer should recognize that his or her duties are owed to the organization and not to the officers, employees, or agents of the organization. The lawyer should therefore ask that the matter be reconsidered, and the lawyer should, if necessary, bring the proposed misconduct to the attention of a higher (and ultimately the highest) authority in the organization despite any directions from anyone in the organization to the contrary. If these measures fail, then it may be appropriate for the lawyer to resign in accordance with the rules for withdrawal from representation (rule 2.09).[172]

This commentary, dealing primarily with circumstances that most commonly crop up in the work of a solicitor or in-house counsel, seems to recognize that the crime-fraud exception to client-lawyer privilege is not exactly commensurate with any exception to the ethical duty of confidentiality. The lawyer who discovers that he or she has been a client's dupe in committing a planned or ongoing fraud does not have free rein to "blow the whistle." An Ontario lawyer confronted with the circumstances described in the commentary will thus usually be required to maintain the client's confidences.

In sum, there is a strong case that Canadian rules of professional conduct do not contain an exception to the duty of confidentiality that is strictly analogous to the crime-fraud exception to legal-professional privilege. Additionally, where *carefully crafted* future-harm or self-defence exceptions do not apply, there is little reason to permit voluntary disclosure by counsel in every case where a crime-fraud communication has occurred. Often prospective harm to the public will not be prevented, there is no past harm to mitigate, and the lawyer's own interests are not unfairly jeopardized. What is more, disclosure will frequently provide the police with evidence to be used in prosecuting the client. Consequently, even though crime-fraud communications would not be protected by privilege if a lawyer was sub-

---

172 Ont. r. 2.03(3) (commentary).

poenaed or a legal file seized pursuant to a search warrant, we believe that counsel is not permitted to disclose a crime-fraud communication absent legal compulsion or the application of another recognized exception to the duty of confidentiality.[173]

# J.  THE PROBLEM OF UNWITTING INVOLVEMENT BY COUNSEL IN CRIMINAL ACTS

Our discussions of the future-harm exception and the apparent absence of a crime-fraud exception to the ethical duty of confidentiality segue nicely to the examination of a potentially difficult problem: the case of the lawyer who learns that he or she has been unwittingly used by a dishonest client to further or commit a crime. Looking at this problem helps to illuminate the relationship among some of the exceptions to the lawyer's obligation to keep client confidences secret. But more than this, the exercise underlines possible weaknesses in Canadian ethical rules as they currently stand and points the way to potential amendments.

## 1)  The Crime-fraud Exception to Legal-Professional Privilege

We can start by observing that, by virtue of the crime-fraud exception to legal-professional privilege, the privilege will not cover client-lawyer communications where the client uses the lawyer's services to perpetrate a crime.[174] As we have just seen, however, the fact that legal-professional privilege will not apply where a lawyer is compelled by court process to reveal information does not necessarily mean that the lawyer can volunteer the same information absent legal compulsion.[175] It thus seems that the crime-fraud exception to legal-professional privilege may not help the lawyer who wishes to make voluntary disclosure, for instance, in order to remedy harm already caused by the client's illegal activities. (Of course, if our conclusions regarding the non-existence of

---

173  This is not to say, however, that the status quo is satisfactory, as elaborated upon in section J, "The Problem of Unwitting Involvement by Counsel in Criminal Acts," in this chapter, and especially in section J(4)–(5).

174  See section I(1), "The Crime-Fraud Exception to Legal Professional Privilege," in this chapter.

175  See section I(1)–(3).

a crime-fraud exception to the duty of confidentiality are wrong, the duped-lawyer scenario presents no real problem at all, and counsel will have a broad discretion to release information.)

## 2) The Future-Harm Exception

What about the future-harm exception? If the duped-lawyer scenario involves an entirely completed crime, the obligation of confidentiality is not abrogated by this exception, which applies only to prospective harms.[176] The case where the crime is still ongoing raises different possibilities. As already discussed, in most Canadian jurisdictions the ethical rules provide counsel with at least a discretion to reveal confidential information in order to prevent a future-crime, including an ongoing crime.[177] What is more, the fact that the client used counsel's services for an illegal purpose can be factored in when deciding how to exercise this discretion.[178] Yet in British Columbia and Ontario this approach will probably be foreclosed, given that the rules of professional conduct limit the scope of the future-harm exception to cases where a crime involves death or serious bodily harm.[179] Unless his or her services have been used in relation to a future-crime of this sort, British Columbia and Ontario counsel cannot rely on the exception to reveal confidential information in order to avoid preventable harm to potential victims.

## 3) The Self-Defence Exception

There is yet another analytical approach to the "duped lawyer" scenario that arguably permits disclosure where a lawyer has unwittingly participated in an entirely completed crime or, in the case of counsel from British Columbia or Ontario, has unknowingly helped in the

---

176 Once again, however, the New Brunswick exception, not being restricted to future-harm, seems to provide a different answer. Since by definition the communications between client and lawyer pertain to a crime with which the client has not been charged, the New Brunswick lawyer has at least the discretion to breach confidentiality.

177 See section G, "The Need for Future Harm," in this chapter.

178 See the discussion in section G(i), "The Lawyer's Discretion," in this chapter.

179 As already noted, the British Columbia rule follows the lead of the ABA Rule 1.6(b)(2); see the discussion section G(1), "The Rules of Professional Conduct," in this chapter. The same result may also flow from the public-safety exception of *Smith*, above note 38 (see section G(4), "Type of Harm: Death or Serious Bodily Harm," in this chapter), which was the template for Ontario's future-harm exception.

commission of a future-crime that does not involve death or serious bodily harm. Lawyers have a discretion to reveal confidential information in order to defend against allegations of misconduct.[180] Whether this self-defence exception should apply in our duped-lawyer scenario depends upon whether its scope extends to cover *anticipated* allegations. As discussed above, we are of the opinion that in some cases the exception can be read this broadly.[181]

**Warning:** If the self-defence exception is seen to permit disclosure in such circumstances, it should be used only where the lawyer reasonably and in good-faith believes that an allegation of misconduct is likely to arise in the future. In particular, the exception can never be employed disingenuously as a means of exacting revenge against the client.

## 4) The Possible Inapplicability of Any Exception

It may be that no recognized exception to the ethical duty of confidentiality applies in the case of a duped lawyer. It could be, for instance, that the crime is completed or abandoned part way through, and counsel is unlikely to be blamed if the client's dishonesty later comes to light. In British Columbia and Ontario, it could also be that the client refuses to abandon a future-crime that does not involve death or serious bodily harm. Probably the best way of dealing with the difficult duped-lawyer situation, in those cases where the future-harm and self-defence exceptions do not apply, is to take the following steps. To begin with, and if feasible in the circumstances, attempt to persuade the client to take any actions necessary to avoid future-harm or to remedy past damage. If consultation with the client is not practical or proves fruitless, immediately put an end to the retainer.[182] The delicate question of how counsel should withdraw, and whether he or she can disaffirm or retract any opinion, document, or statement connected with the illegal act, is dealt with elsewhere.[183] At this juncture, suffice it to say that the distinction between a "noisy" withdrawal and the overt and unequivocal use or release of confidential information is

---

180  See section E, "Lawyer Self-Defence," in this chapter.
181  See section E(4), "Anticipated Allegation," in this chapter.
182  This option is recommended in the Legal Commentary to ABA Model Rule 1.6(b)(2), "Disclosure Upon Discovery of Client Crime or Fraud."
183  See sections F, "Mandatory Withdrawal by the Lawyer, O, "Discretionary Withdrawal by the Lawyer," and M(2), "Withdrawal As Implied Disclosure of Confidential Information," in chapter 11.

sometimes difficult to discern. One should therefore guard against viewing the withdrawal option as a simple way to avoid the problem concerning confidentiality.

As a final point, note that these recommended steps may also be helpful where counsel determines that an exception to the duty of confidentiality is applicable but decides to exercise his or her discretion in favour of non-disclosure.

## 5) A Potential New Exception

The interstices of the crime-fraud exception to legal-professional privilege and the various existing exceptions to the ethical duty of confidentiality can be troubling when held up against the duped-lawyer scenario. Where the client has misused the client-lawyer relationship to plan or commit a crime, and refuses to abandon the project and/or, if applicable, rectify or mitigate any damage done, there is a good argument in favour of permitting disclosure. A liberal interpretation of the self-defence exception could conceivably cover most such cases, but justifying increased disclosure in the name of lawyer self-interest does little to improve the reputation of the profession in the eyes of the public. If there is to be a change in the ethical rules on this point, protecting society from serious harm and discouraging individuals from abusing the client-lawyer relationship should be the guiding principles.

While adopting a wholesale crime-fraud exception constitutes too great an impingement upon the duty of confidentiality, there is much to recommend an attenuated and more focused exception that takes account of the policy factors just mentioned. In fact, as we shall shortly see, Canadian ethical rules may already contain an exception to the duty where a lawyer's services have been used to mislead the court and disclosure will serve at least in part to rectify the problem. Also of interest is the approach embraced by the American Law Institute's Third Restatement. The Third Restatement includes an exception under which a lawyer may use or disclose confidential information to the extent reasonably necessary to rectify or mitigate a substantial financial loss arising from a completed crime or fraud, provided that the fraud was committed through the client's use of the lawyer's services.[184] Disclosure is permitted only where the lawyer fails to persuade the client to take action necessary to rectify or mitigate the loss, and, in these attempts at persuasion, counsel should advise of the ability to

---

184 See Third Restatement §67(2).

disclose absent consent as a last resort.[185] As the commentary to this exception recognizes, the discretion recognized in the exception "may to an unknowable extent lessen some clients' willingness to consult freely with their lawyers," but the social benefits of allowing a lawyer to mitigate or rectify substantial financial loss in the described circumstances warrant such a risk.[186]

# K.  DUTY NOT TO MISLEAD THE COURT

Canadian rules of professional conduct often define the basic obligation of confidentiality so as to allow a lawyer to divulge confidential information where permitted or required under the rules themselves.[187] One of the rules that potentially creates an exception to the duty of confidentiality is commonly found under the rubric "The Lawyer as Advocate."[188] This rule places limits upon the zealousness with which a lawyer can champion the client's case, and in large part it focuses upon the duty not to mislead the court. The basic rationale behind the rule is simple: the truth-finding function of the judicial process can never knowingly be subverted by counsel.

A classic and difficult instance where counsel's duty not to mislead the court clashes with the duty of confidentiality arises where a client intends to commit or already has committed perjury. We discuss the client-perjury problem in considerable detail in chapter 7, and in doing so we canvas many of the issues bearing upon the uneasy relationship between counsel's duty not to mislead the court and the obligation to keep client information confidential. It is sufficient at this stage to provide a more general review of the matter. The proper approach to the problem changes depending upon whether or not the court has already been misled and when counsel discovers the truth. As a discussion aid, we will comment from time to time upon the case of counsel who learns that his or her client has been charged under a false name.[189]

---

185  See Third Restatement §67(3).

186  Third Restatement §67, comm. "b."

187  See, for example, CBA Code ch. IV Rule; N.S. ch. 5, Rule; and Sask. ch. IV, Rule. Also take note of the similar approach taken by Alta. ch. 7, Statement of Principle, and r. 8. Contrast other jurisdictions where the basic obligation is not so defined: see, for example, B.C. ch. 5, r.; and Ont. r. 2.03(1).

188  See, for example CBA Code ch. IX; Alta. ch. 10; B.C. ch. 8; Ont. r. 4.01; and N.S. ch. 14.

189  On this topic, see E. Nilsen, "Disclose or Not: The Client with a False Identity," in R. Uphoff, *Ethical Problems Facing the Criminal Lawyer: Practical Answers to*

## 1) The Court Has Not Yet Been Misled

Where a client urges counsel to mislead the court through action or inaction, it is axiomatic that counsel must never accede to the request.[190] The CBA Code states that a lawyer must represent the client "by fair and honourable means, without illegality and in a manner consistent with the lawyer's duty to treat the court with candour, fairness, courtesy and respect."[191] In particular, according to Commentary 2 of the Code's "Lawyer as Advocate" rule, the lawyer must not:

> b) knowingly assist or permit the client to do anything that the lawyer considers to be dishonest or dishonourable;
> e) knowingly attempt to deceive or participate in the deception of a tribunal or influence the course of justice by offering false evidence, misstating the facts or law, presenting or relying upon a false or deceptive affidavit, suppressing what ought to be disclosed or otherwise assisting in any fraud, crime or illegal conduct; or
> j) knowingly permit a witness to be presented in a false or misleading way or to impersonate another.[192]

What the lawyer cannot do is clear, meaning that the first task facing counsel whose client advocates misleading the court is to attempt to dissuade the client from the intended plan. If despite counsel's best efforts the client is adamant, counsel must ordinarily withdraw from the case. As the CBA Code states: "If the client wishes to adopt a course that would involve a breach of this Rule, the lawyer must refuse and do everything reasonably possible to prevent it. If the client persists in such a course the lawyer should, subject to the Rule relating to withdrawal, withdraw or seek leave of the court to do so."[193] As we have seen, in counsel's ending the retainer, the duty of confidentiality applies to prevent disclosure of any confidential information.[194]

---

Tough Questions (Chicago: American Bar Association, 1995) c. 15; and The Guide to the Professional Conduct of Solicitors, above note 87, Annex 21F (Guidance – Citation of Criminal Convictions – Misleading the Court).

190  See, for example, CBA Code ch. IX, comm. 4; Ont. r. 4.01(5); N.S. ch. 14, r. 14.3; and Alta. ch. 10, comm. 14.2.

191  CBA Code ch. IX, Rule.

192  CBA Code ch. IX, comm. 2(b), (e) & (j) (footnotes omitted). See also Sask. ch. IX, comm. 2(a), (e) and (j); N.S. ch. 14 Guiding Principles (b), (e) & (f); B.C. ch. 8, r. 1(b) & (h); Ont. r. 4.01(2)(b), (e) & (j); and Alta. ch. 10, r. 13–14, 20 & 24.

193  CBA Code ch. IX, comm. 4 (footnotes omitted). See also N.S. ch. 14, r. 14.3; B.C. ch. 8, r. 2-3 & 7–8; Ont. r. 4.01(5); and Alta. ch. 10, comm. 14.2.

194  See section H(7), "Duty Survives End of Retainer," in chapter 4.

Let us consider how these general guidelines apply to the client who is charged under a false name and wants counsel to provide representation under the phony moniker. To flesh out the scenario a little bit, assume that the client has been charged and released on a promise to appear. She used the false name because a significant criminal record would have hurt her chances of obtaining bail and, if convicted, would count against her on sentencing. Counsel faced with this situation cannot reveal the client's true identity to third parties without breaching the duty of confidentiality in a way that causes the client substantial harm.[195] However, representing the client under a false name will necessarily mislead the court, breaching counsel's duty in this regard. For this reason, Alberta and British Columbia specifically prohibit counsel from misrepresenting to the court the identity of the lawyer's client.[196] Other Canadian rules typically speak of a narrower duty not to permit a *witness* to be presented in a false or misleading way or to impersonate another, a duty that would apply to the client upon taking the stand.[197] However, the more general duty set out in these rules, such as CBA Code, Chapter IX, Commentary 2(b) and (e), quoted above, surely forecloses counsel from appearing before the court on any occasion where the falsehood is perpetuated. It is also worth mentioning that acting on such a retainer as if nothing is remiss may also constitute a criminal offence.[198] One might also ask whether helping the client to find new counsel in the knowledge that the client intends to persist in using the false identity constitutes participation in an attempt to obstruct justice.

Extricating oneself from this dilemma in the early stages of a retainer is typically not difficult. Counsel must begin by advising the client that proceeding under a false name constitutes a criminal offence, and that counsel cannot represent the client under such circumstances. Attempts should be made to dissuade the client from per-

---

195 See *Attorney Grievance Commission of Maryland* v. *Rohrback*, 591 A.2d 488 at 494 (Md. 1991) [*Rohrback*].
196 See Alta. ch. 10, r.13; and B.C. ch. 10, r. 1(h).
197 See the citations provided at note 192, above.
198 Depending upon the nature of the case and the course of the proceeding, counsel may be open to charges under the *Criminal Code*, above note 36, such as perjury (s. 131); fabricating evidence (s. 137); obstructing justice (s. 139); counselling (s. 22); and accessory after the fact (ss. 23 & 463). This point is made in CBA Code ch. IX, footnote 8; N.S. ch. 14 footnote 6; and Sask. ch. IX, footnote 8; Ont. r. 10, note 8, and demonstrated by *R.* v. *Guttman* (1992), 73 C.C.C. (3d) 62 (Man.foot C.A.); and *R.* v. *Doz* (1984), 12 C.C.C. (3d) 200 (Alta. C.A.).

sisting in this course.[199] The client may well decide to reveal her true identity to the authorities upon realizing that the truth will probably come out at some point in the future, and that the longer she continues the charade the harsher the consequences upon her being found out. Moreover, if counsel forms the view that disclosure is permitted against the client's wishes, in order to prevent a prospective fraud on the court, the client must be warned in advance.[200] Where the client is persuaded to reveal her true identity, counsel's difficulty is solved. However, if the client refuses to abandon her assumed name, counsel cannot continue to act in any capacity.

**Warning**: Counsel who knows of a client's false identity should avoid taking any step, whether in or out of court, that could be construed as aiding in the deception. In our view, appearing on a set date is improper, as is negotiating a plea agreement with the Crown, this even if counsel fully intends to withdraw prior to a trial or plea unless the client abandons the ruse.[201]

Once counsel has withdrawn from the case, the obligation of confidentiality generally continues to work to prevent disclosure of the client's true identity. As for the duty to be candid with the court, this obligation operates only to prohibit a lawyer from knowingly participating in deception. The duty is no longer engaged once the representation has ended (assuming for the moment that counsel played no role, not even unknowingly, in misleading the court). Yet it may be that the future-crime exception applies to permit disclosure. Suppose that the client tells counsel that she intends to retain a new lawyer and, having learned about ethical and criminal law restrictions on professional conduct, will make sure to keep her true identity a secret. This

---

199 Matters to cover in remonstrating with the client are discussed in section F(2), "Admonishing the Client to Tell the Truth," in chapter 7.

200 As discussed below, the future-harm exception may apply to permit disclosure. If counsel takes the position that he or she can take this drastic step, and seriously contemplates doing so, the client must be informed in advance: see section G(7), "Duty to Confer with the Client," in this chapter).

201 See *Law Society of Upper Canada* v. *Brown*, [1997] L.S.D.D. No. 93 (QL), where counsel was convicted of obstructing justice and reprimanded by his governing body for knowingly defending a client who used a false name. See also *Office of Disciplinary Counsel* v. *Hazelkorn*, 480 N.E.2d 1116 (Ohio 1985); and *State* v. *Casby*, 348 N.W. 2d 736 (Minn., 1984) (both cases where counsel negotiated a plea agreement, and in doing so was seen to have misled the prosecutor). In *Rohrback*, above note 195, counsel was found to have violated the governing ethical rules by (among other things) speaking to a probation officer on behalf of a client who was using a false name.

scenario may leave counsel with the reasonable belief that the client will commit a criminal act by proceeding to trial under a false name. Under the rules of professional conduct in most Canadian jurisdictions, counsel's knowledge may be sufficient to permit disclosure under the future-harm exception.[202] Counsel has a discretion in determining whether to reveal the information, however, and in our view would be entirely justified in maintaining confidentiality.[203]

Where counsel decides to make disclosure, he or she can do so only to the extent necessary to prevent the crime,[204] a purpose that is arguably achieved by divulging the truth only to subsequent counsel. In most jurisdictions, it is a relatively simple matter for counsel to determine who is currently representing a former client. Once the second counsel has been provided with the information, he or she can no longer act. However, the second counsel may decide to maintain the confidence after the client retains a third lawyer. At this point, the original counsel may either make disclosure to the new lawyer, decide that disclosure to other parties is now warranted, or conversely choose to take no further action at all. If the client defends himself or herself, disclosure to the Crown or court may be the only way to prevent the fraud.

## 2) The Court Has Already Been Misled in a Continuing Matter

What about the case where counsel has unintentionally participated in events that serve to mislead the court and the matter is still ongoing? A lawyer may discover, for instance, that he or she unwittingly placed a deceitful affidavit before the court or called a witness who committed perjury. These cases obviously demand some sort of action by counsel, in light of the duty to rectify that is set out in all Canadian ethical rules. In this respect, most governing bodies follow the lead of Commentary 3 to the CBA Code's "The Lawyer as Advocate" rule, which reads as follows:

---

202 See section G(1), "The Rules of Professional Conduct," in this chapter.
203 See Nilsen, above note 189 at 222. The issue of discretion in approaching the future-harm exception is discussed in section G(8), "The Lawyer's Discretion," in this chapter.
204 See section G(6), "Disclosure Must be Necessary," in this chapter. Consider whether, pursuant to *Smith*, above note 38, counsel must make an application to the court prior to revealing the information: see section G(9), "Procedure," in this chapter).

The lawyer who has unknowingly done or failed to do something that, if done or omitted knowingly, would have been in breach of this Rule and discovers it, has a duty to the court, subject to the Rule relating to confidential information, to disclose the error or omission and do all that can reasonably be done in the circumstances to rectify it.[205]

An important point is that the emphasis in Commentary 3 is on remedying the deception where counsel has unwittingly played a role in misleading the court.

### a)   Determining Whether the Duty to Rectify is Engaged

A preliminary question may arise as to whether the duty to take remedial action is engaged. Several issues related to the scope of the duty of candour and the obligation to rectify can be dealt with by looking at the following examples:

#### i)   False Evidence Not Led Intentionally

Consider the case where counsel leads evidence from a mistaken witness who does not intend to mislead the court. There is no doubt that the duty of candour prohibits counsel from knowingly offering such evidence, for in doing so he or she would be intentionally deceiving the court. But the wording of most Canadian ethical rules is also broad enough to encompass circumstances where counsel unknowingly offers such evidence, and only later comes to realizes its falsity. To paraphrase the wording in Commentary 3, where counsel has unknowingly done something that, if done knowingly, would have been in breach of the duty of candour, the remedial duty applies.

**Example:** Suppose that a client informs counsel that she was at a concert at the time a crime was committed. She provides a ticket stub setting out the relevant date and time. But counsel investigates further and discovers that the concert ticket mistakenly lists the wrong date. Though the client's recollection, based on the erroneous ticket, may be honestly held, counsel cannot keep quiet and allow the client to testify to the falsehood. The same issue arises where the client testifies in good-faith, though falsely, and subsequently counsel learns of the true state of affairs.

---

205  CBA Code ch. IX, comm. 3 (footnote omitted). See also Sask. ch. IX, comm. 3; N.S. ch. 14, comm. 14.2; and Ont. r. 4.01(5);. See also B.C. ch. 8, r. 4 & 8.

## ii)  Deception by Opposing Party's Witness

Defence counsel cross-examines a Crown witness at a preliminary inquiry. In responding to counsel's questions, the witness commits perjury. Defence counsel is aware of the perjury but wishes to leave the deception uncorrected until trial, at which time the witness's lies will be exposed in front of the trier of fact. In our view, this approach does not violate the duty of candour towards the court, for counsel is not attempting to practice a deception on the administration of justice. Rather, the opposing party's witness has done so, and defence counsel will ultimately bring out the truth at trial.

## iii)  Mistake Regarding Client's Record

Client X is about to be sentenced. Counsel knows that X has a record, but the Crown tells the court that "there appear to be no prior convictions." On these facts, counsel has no duty to inform the court of the truth, not even if the court expressly relies on the lack of a record in determining the sentence.[206] In fact, the duty of confidentiality prevents him or her from doing so. On the other hand, counsel's duty of candour precludes making any comment or submission that suggests that X has no record or that relies upon the Crown's misstatement. If the court asks defence counsel whether the Crown's statement is correct, the proper response is either to tell the truth (if the client consents) or to inform the court that he or she cannot corroborate the Crown's position.[207]

## iv)  Deception during Cross-examination by Opponent

Defence counsel calls an alibi witness who testifies without incident during examination-in-chief. In cross-examination by Crown counsel, however, the witness tells a lie regarding a material fact. The language of some ethical rules is open to the interpretation that the duty to remedy the deception applies only where the fraud is perpetrated in the course of evidence brought out by counsel's questioning and is not engaged on cross-examination by an opponent.[208] Yet this view would allow counsel to restrict himself or herself to eliciting truthful testi-

---

206  See, for example, Alta. ch. 10, comm. 14.1. In *R. v. Brooks* (2001), 153 C.C.C. (3d) 533 at 544 (Ont. S.C.J.), Hill J. made the related point that an accused is not required to provide information regarding his or her criminal record at a bail hearing, nor should defence counsel do so absent the client's consent.

207  See Alta. ch. 10, r. 14 & 16, plus associated commentaries. See also the guidelines adopted by the Law Society for England and Wales, *The Guide to the Professional Conduct of Solicitors*, above note 87, Annex 21F at 405–06.

208  See, for example, CBA Code ch. IX, comm. 2(b), (e) & (j).

mony during a circumscribed examination-in-chief, knowing all the while that lies will inevitably be told during cross-examination and that these lies can go unchecked. The preferable approach, in light of the rationale underlying counsel's obligation of candour, is to extend the duty to remedy to any deceptive evidence proffered by counsel's witness. *A fortiori*, counsel cannot intentionally choose to avoid certain areas in examination-in-chief, on the assumption that the client will be asked about those areas in cross-examination and be able to lie in response.[209]

### v)   Material Issue

A defence witness informs counsel that he lied about his age while on the stand. The witness admits to having consistently told the same lie for years, in all situations, out of vanity. Counsel reasonably concludes that this lie is not material to any facet of the case because, among other things, the witness's credibility is not in issue. Nevertheless, Commentary 3 of the CBA Code appears to apply to all instances where the court is deceived, regardless of the extent to which the deception may or may not be relevant to matters in issue. Strictly speaking, any false statement is a fraud on the court.

Yet, if a false statement involves a truly immaterial or trivial matter, and there is no possibility that the court will be misled regarding relevant issues of fact, the impetus to take remedial action is less strong. ABA Model Rule 3.3 therefore impresses counsel with a remedial duty only where the deception concerns material evidence and hence requires no rectifying steps in response to our example.[210] However, materiality must be broadly defined. Counsel's personal opinion that a fact is unlikely to influence a decision does not constitute immateriality. Rather, it must be objectively clear that the fact cannot influence the trier of fact in any way at all.

### vi)   Waiting until the End of Trial

Client X informs counsel that an alibi witness has lied in favour of the defence position. The trial is near completion, and counsel is fairly certain that the powerful Crown case will lead to a conviction. The ques-

---

209  See for example, *Committee on Professional Ethics v. Crary*, 245 N.W.2d 298 (Iowa 1976); *In re A.*, 554 P.2d 479 (Or. 1976); and E. Wilkinson, "'That's a Damn Lie!': Ethical Obligations of Counsel When a Witness Offers False Testimony in a Criminal Trial" (2000) 31 St. Mary's L.J. 407 at 438 & 445–47.

210  See ABA Rule 3.3(a)(4). See also ABA Rule 3.3(a)(1), which refers to a "material fact," as does the Third Restatement §120(2).

tion has been raised, can counsel wait to see whether this reasonably expected conviction in fact materializes?[211] If the conviction occurs, the deception has arguably had no impact on the case, and there is no need to take any remedial steps. If, contrary to expectations, the accused is acquitted, counsel will be forced to rectify the deception. This "waiting game" does not seem to jibe with the wording of Commentary 3 of the CBA Code and is unlikely to be endorsed by governing bodies in Canada.

### b)    Initial Responses: Remonstration and Withdrawal

Once counsel has determined that the duty to rectify is engaged, the initial response must be to discuss the matter with the client and to advocate disclosure of the falsehood to the court. If the client refuses to do so, counsel is probably justified in applying to the court to get off the record.[212] Assuming that withdrawal is not a problem,[213] the more contentious issue, to which we next turn, is whether counsel has an obligation to inform the court of the true state of affairs.

### c)    The Disclosure Issue and the CBA Code

We have already reviewed Commentary 3 of the CBA Code's "The Lawyer as Advocate" rule.[214] This Commentary is central to any discussion of a possible duty to disclose, given that most Canadian governing bodies have adopted its language verbatim. A crucial initial observation can be made regarding Commentary 3: the obligation to correct a misimpression is expressly said to be subject to the rule relating to confidentiality, which, taken at face value, seems to represent a significant restriction. Unfortunately, when it comes to potential impact on the duty of confidentiality, the actual import of Commentary 3 is terribly obscure. Why? One genesis of confusion flows from the footnote to this Commentary. Footnote 13 asks the reader to compare the Commentary to portions of the New Brunswick Professional Conduct Handbook as well as provisions in the ABA Model Code.[215] The New Brunswick rules expressly state that counsel who learns of a client's participation in fraudulent testimony must

---

211 See Wolfram, above note 69 at 659–60.
212 See section G(3)(a), "Withdrawal," in chapter 7, and more generally chapter 11.
213 The case where withdrawal is a problem is dealt with in chapter 7. See also Nilsen, above note 189 at 222–23.
214 See the text accompanying note 205, above.
215 The rules cited in footnote 13 are N.B. Part B, r. 8, and ABA Model Code DRs 7–102(B) & 4–101(C)(2).

withdraw from the case *and* inform the court of the deception.[216] However, the rules cited from the ABA Model Code permit revelation of a fraud perpetrated by the client "except where the information is protected as a privileged communication," a caveat that the ABA Ethics Committee has interpreted in Formal Opinion 341 so as to prevent disclosure of confidential information.[217] Interestingly, the caveat was introduced by the ABA's House of Delegates in 1974 and was thereafter adopted by eighteen states, but in 1983 the ABA Model Rules came into force, Rule 3.3 of which contains no such caveat and clearly requires disclosure. Why the CBA Code, which was adopted in 1987, refers only to the Model Code, and does not mention Model Rule 3.3, is difficult to fathom. Perhaps the CBA Code is showing a preference for the ABA Code as interpreted by Formal Opinion 341. Or maybe the CBA Code is contrasting the two different approaches taken by New Brunswick and the ABA Code. Another possibility is that the Canadian drafters were not cognizant of either Formal Opinion 341 or Model Rule 3.3. Regardless of the true explanation, footnote 13 is a terrible muddle.

The indefatigable reader might also look for guidance in footnote 14 to Commentary 4, dealing with the duty to withdraw. Footnote 14 fails to shed further light on the issue, however, since it merely suggests a comparison with the New Brunswick rule just mentioned (although this time providing the text of the rule).[218]

Perhaps our dilemma can be solved by looking at Commentary 2(e) to the CBA Code, which, as noted above, sets out a broad prohibition against knowingly "suppressing what ought to be disclosed or otherwise assisting in any fraud, crime or illegal conduct."[219] The lengthy footnote 8 to Commentary 2(e) discusses a case in which counsel knowingly engaged in such conduct[220] and sets out a number of criminal offences which may be implicated. It then reproduces por-

---

216  N.B. Part B, r. 8.

217  See ABA Model Code DR 7-102(B)(1), as interpreted by ABA Comm. on Ethics and Professional Responsibility, Formal Op. 341 (1975) and discussed in ABA Comm. on Ethics and Professional Responsibility, Formal Op. 353 (1987).

218  Footnote 14 also cites ABA Model Code DR 2-110(B)(2), but this provision concerns the withdrawal of counsel and adds nothing to the debate regarding disclosure.

219  Commentary 2(e) is quoted in its entirety in section K(1), "The Court Has Not Yet Been Misled," in this chapter.

220  See *Banks* v. *Hall*, [1941] 2 W.W.R. 534 (Sask. C.A.).

tions of two judgments. *Myers v. Elman* is quoted to the effect that "[a] solicitor who has innocently put on file an affidavit by his client which he has subsequently discovered to be certainly false owes it to the Court to put the matter right at the earliest date if he continues to act."[221] Next, *Re Ontario (Crime Commission)* is quoted as follows: "[Counsel] had full knowledge of the impropriety of the paragraphs in the affidavit . . . [and] is bound to accept responsibility for [them]. . . . If he knows that his client is making false statements under oath and does nothing to correct it, his silence indicates, at the least, a gross neglect of duty."[222]

What can we glean from footnote 8? Gavin MacKenzie suggests that this footnote may place a gloss on the duty to rectify and thus operate to mandate the disclosure of confidential information in order to correct the court's misimpression.[223] This interpretation, though tenable, is open to legitimate question for a couple of reasons. First, as already noted, the express wording of Commentary 3 subjects the duty to correct a court's misimpression to a limitation where confidential information would be revealed. Reading a footnote to another commentary so as to mandate disclosure of confidential information seems to render the express limitation otiose — it is hard to imagine any rational drafter of rules and commentaries taking such a convoluted route to create an exception to the duty of confidentiality. Second, a careful reading of the quotations set out in footnote 8 by no means unequivocally mandates disclosure. The quote from *Myers v. Elman* appears only to require disclosure *if counsel continues to act after discovering the problem.*[224] Nothing is said about the case where counsel is able to withdraw from the record. As for *Re Ontario (Crime Commission)*, counsel there was personally aware of the matters

---

221 *Myers v. Elman* (1939), [1940] A.C. 282 at 293–94 (H.L.), per Viscount Maugham, quoted at CBA Code ch. IX, footnote 8. The CBA Code provides a more lengthy quote, but the section reproduced here is the most relevant.

222 *Re Ontario (Crime Commission)* (1962), 37 D.L.R. (2d) 382 at 391 (Ont. C.A.), quoted at CBA Code ch. IX note 8. Note that leave to appeal was refused by the Supreme Court of Canada.

223 See MacKenzie, above note 99 at §7.5, in the discussion accompanying notes 62–63 (MacKenzie's complete position is ascertained through cross-referencing §4.13, and in particular the discussion accompanying notes 133–36). In a charitable understatement, MacKenzie notes that Commentary 3 "is not a model of clarity."

224 This interpretation of Viscount Maugham's words gains strength when one reads the full text of pages 293 and 294 and not merely the quote reproduced in footnote 8.

described in his client's affidavit. The court's comments seem directed to counsel's impropriety in *knowingly* helping to produce an improper affidavit. The comment denigrating counsel who "does nothing to correct [the deception]" can thus be read consistently with a course of action by which, immediately upon learning of the deception, the lawyer takes steps to dissuade the client from committing the fraud and, if unsuccessful, does no more than successfully apply to withdraw from the case.

## d) Disclosure: Looking Beyond the CBA Code

The unsatisfactory state of Commentary 3 perhaps reflects a disagreement within the profession that has led to a deliberately vague (and hence unhelpful) position. Compare the approach in British Columbia, where the rules contain no footnotes hinting that counsel may be permitted to breach confidentiality in order to correct a misapprehension of the type being discussed.[225] Or consider the applicable rules in Alberta, which unequivocally state that confidentiality cannot be breached in such a case.[226] Equally direct, as we have seen, is the converse approach taken in New Brunswick, at least with respect to a fraud perpetrated by a client.[227] A broader "pro-disclosure" tack is also evident in ABA Model Rule 3.3, which states:

> (a) A lawyer shall not knowingly:
> > (2) fail to disclose a material fact to a tribunal when disclosure is necessary to avoid assisting a criminal or fraudulent act by the client;
> > (4) offer evidence that the lawyer knows to be false. If a lawyer has offered material evidence and comes to know of its falsity, the lawyer shall take reasonable remedial measures.

---

225 See B.C. ch. 8, r. 8 (among the cross-references in this rule, note especially that ch. 10, r. 9 prohibits counsel from disclosing confidential information when withdrawing from a case). Also note that the Law Society of Upper Canada has recently adopted new ethical rules which do not contain footnote 8: see Ont. r. 4.01(2).
226 See Alta. ch. 10, r. 15 (the reference made by this rule to ch. 7 and confidentiality, including r. 7 and the associated commentary, is crucial). However, the position in Alberta is not entirely clear, as elaborated upon in section G(3), "Remedial Measures Where the Client Refuses to Correct the Perjury," in chapter 7.
227 See N.B. Part B, r. 8.

(b) The duties stated in paragraph (a) continue to the conclusion of a proceeding, and apply even if compliance requires disclosure of information otherwise protected by Rule 1.6 [i.e. the rule setting out a lawyer's duty of confidentiality].[228]

At the end of the day, various jurisdictions provide different answers to the disclosure issue (or, in the case of the CBA Code, no real answer at all). We favour the position taken by the ABA, mandating disclosure of confidential information as a last resort where counsel has unknowingly helped to mislead the court. Although disclosure will in many cases deprive the client of an adversarial advantage, and may also lead to serious adverse consequences such as a charge of perjury or attempt to obstruct justice, the integrity of the truth-finding process cannot be compromised by the actions of counsel. It is true that numerous constitutional rights are implicated by the duty of confidentiality and hence risk violation whenever the duty is breached,[229] yet surely these guarantees are not so broad as to permit the client a right to utilize or otherwise rely upon the services of counsel in order to mislead the court.[230]

### e)    Revisiting the Case of the Client Who Employs a False Identity

Returning to our "false identity" scenario, let us vary the facts to assume that the client is held for a bail hearing and counsel successfully obtains her release. Counsel then negotiates a joint submission with the Crown and represents the client when the guilty plea is entered. The matter goes over for sentencing, and only at this point does the client inform counsel of the deception.

There is no doubt that counsel who knowingly represents a client under a false name is in breach of the duty to be candid with the court.

---

228 ABA Model Rule 3.3. See also ABA Model Rule 1.2, which prohibits a lawyer from knowingly assisting a client in criminal or fraudulent conduct. The same position is taken by the ABA Defense Standards; see ABA Defense Standard 4-7.5(a), and the accompanying commentary.

229 See section F, "Constitutional Principles," in chapter 4.

230 A recent case that discusses the competing interests without reaching a firm conclusion is *R. v. Samra* (1998), 129 C.C.C. (3d) 144 at 164–69 (Ont. C.A.). *Amicus curiae* released confidential information in order to correct a misleading submission made by counsel for the accused. The court expressly declined to rule on whether *amicus curiae* could have remained silent in the face of this untrue allegation: *ibid.* at 168–69. An even more recent case that appears to reject disclosure as an option is *R. v. Jenkins* (2001), 152 C.C.C. (3d) 426 (Ont. S.C.J.). *Jenkins* is discussed in more detail throughout chapter 7.

Accordingly, where counsel unwittingly does so, but discovers the deception before the proceedings have concluded, all Canadian rules of professional conduct require that counsel attempt to rectify the court's misapprehension. Doing so mandates making an effort to convince the client of the necessity to correct the falsehood.[231] Where the client refuses to reveal the truth, in Alberta (and probably British Columbia) counsel cannot disregard his or her instructions. The only remaining option is to withdraw from the case, and to do so without revealing any confidential information. In New Brunswick, the ethical rules stipulate that counsel must withdraw from the case and disclose the deception to the court. In the remaining Canadian jurisdictions, the proper approach is not immediately evident, and counsel should, if at all possible, contact his or her governing body for guidance. If it is determined that disclosure is required, counsel must warn the client of this duty prior to releasing the information. On learning that the fraud will inevitably be discovered, the client may agree to inform the court of the deception.

**Recommendation:** Counsel should always carefully document all communications and events relevant to a false identification issue, including advice sought from other counsel or an advisory service, in order to protect against any later allegation of complicity in deceiving the court.

## 3) The Court Has Been Misled in a Concluded Matter

A lawyer may find out that he or she has been the unwitting party to a fraud on the court following the conclusion of the retainer. For instance, a defence witness may have committed perjury by testifying in support of a fabricated alibi, but the lawyer discovers the fraud only after a conviction has been entered. ABA Model Rule 3.3 and the Third Restatement both provide that the duty to remedy the deception ends at the conclusion of the proceeding.[232] It has been suggested that such an endpoint is not reached until the time for launching an appeal has

---

231  See ABA Model Rule 3.3, comm. 5.
232  See ABA Rule 3.3; and Third Restatement §180, comm. "h." Not all American jurisdictions mirror this approach; for instance, in Oklahoma, counsel's duty persists even after the proceedings have concluded: see Oklahoma Model Rule, 3.3(b).

lapsed or, if an appeal is undertaken, the appellate process has concluded.[233]

It has been said that the need to ensure finality in proceedings, combined with an attenuated responsibility upon counsel once the matter has ended, justifies the American approach.[234] Yet if Commentary 3 of the CBA Code's "Lawyer as Advocate" rule is read so as to include a duty to disclose, the duty is apparently not restricted to the duration of proceedings. Many counsel in Canada, most obviously including New Brunswick counsel, may thus be under a perpetual duty to reveal a deception once discovered.

**Example I:** Client X is found guilty of a minor theft after a trial during which no defence is called. The Crown asks for a suspended sentence, but the court accedes to defence counsel's request for a conditional discharge, given X's lack of prior convictions. Three months later, defence counsel meets X on the street. X tells the lawyer that he was lucky to have escaped with a conditional discharge, and was glad that he used an assumed name to hide his many prior convictions. Given that the appeal period has expired, under ABA Rule 3.3 the proceedings can be said to have concluded and counsel has no obligation to make disclosure. Canadian rules, to the extent that they mandate disclosure, arguably contain no such restriction.[235]

**Example II:** Counsel calls an unsuccessful alibi defence at trial, including testimony by the accused. She appeals on behalf of the client, on the ground that the trial judge misdirected himself regarding the law on alibi and misappreciated the alibi evidence. Appeal counsel is retained for the client. In the week before the appeal is to be heard, the client informs trial counsel that he lied on the stand and that the alibi is false. Even though the trial has concluded, the CBA Code appears to require trial counsel to take remedial measures to correct the perjury,

---

233  See Hazard & Hodes, above note 34 at §3.3 (301), suggesting that counsel's duties may also persist where the rules of the court permit an application to reopen the case on grounds of fraud.

234  See Hazard & Hodes, *ibid.*; and Nilsen, above note 189 at 224.

235  See *Office of Disciplinary Counsel* v. *Heffernan*, 569 N.E.2d 1027 (Ohio 1991), cert. denied 502 U.S. 856 (1991), where counsel was disciplined for failing to make disclosure upon learning of his client's deception several months after the proceeding had ended. Note that the Ohio ethical rule mirrors the pre-1974 ABA Model Code provision DR 7-102(B)(1); *viz.*, the rule contains no caveat, and also does not limit the duty to disclose to the currency of the proceeding.

including disclosure if necessary.[236] Appeal counsel's duty may play out differently, for he did not participate in presenting and relying upon the false evidence.[237] Nevertheless, the appeal lawyer is bound by the ethical rules that prevent counsel from knowingly assisting the client in dishonest conduct or deceiving the court.[238] At the least, he cannot argue on the appeal that the trial judge misappreciated the alibi evidence.[239]

# L.  SUMMARY AND RECOMMENDATIONS

The duty of confidentiality is one of the pillars upon which the client-lawyer relationship is built. This duty is nonetheless subject to numerous potential exceptions. Our summary and recommendations regarding possible confidentiality exceptions are as follows:

1. Confidential information can be released or otherwise used by a lawyer with the client's express or implied consent (section B).
2. Information that is widely known in the public sphere may no longer be confidential, although not all Canadian rules of professional conduct recognize such an exception. Also, altogether apart from any public knowledge exception that might exist, a lawyer has a duty of loyalty that may restrict the adverse use of information relevant to a client's matter (section C).
3. A lawyer is obligated to reveal confidential information where required to do so by law or court order. However, before capitulating too quickly, counsel has an obligation to raise any non-frivolous argument that might reasonably serve to avoid disclosure. Also, there may be some room for counsel to delay compliance with an erroneous court order while launching and awaiting the result of an appeal (section D).

---

236 See CBA Code ch. IX, comm. 3.
237 Consider, however, whether the client's conduct constitutes a continuing crime until the appeal is concluded. If so, the future-crime exception to the duty of confidentiality may apply in some Canadian jurisdictions.
238 See CBA Code ch. IX comms. 2(b) & 2(e).
239 This example is a variation on the scenarios discussed in "Panel Discussion: Witness for the Prosecution: Successful Impeachment Strategies" (Criminal Lawyers' Association Annual Convention and Education Programme, Toronto, 21-22 November 1997), online: QL (OCLARP/1997-019) at paras. 75–128.

4.  All Canadian rules of professional conduct permit lawyers to reveal confidential information where necessary to defend against an allegation of wrongdoing. These rules arguably are drafted broadly enough to encompass release for the purpose of meeting an anticipated allegation and perhaps also an allegation made by a third party. In any event, however, information can be disclosed only to the extent truly necessary to defend the lawyer's legitimate interests (section E).

5.  Ethical rules in this country also permit a lawyer to disclose confidential information where necessary to establish or collect fees (section F).

6.  The future-harm exception permits disclosure of client confidences where necessary to protect the public from serious harm. Because there are a number of variations on the future-harm exception found in Canadian rules of professional conduct, counsel must determine the particular content of the rule applicable in his or her jurisdiction (section G(1)).

7.  The leading judicial ruling regarding future-harm is the Supreme Court of Canada's decision in *Smith* v. *Jones*. The Court's so-called public-safety exception applies where "the facts raise real concerns that an identifiable individual or group is in imminent danger of death or serious bodily harm." This decision relates to legal-professional privilege and the common law duty of confidentiality. It does not necessarily override the validity of ethical rules that adopt a wider exception for anticipated future-harm, a fact that may lead to confusion and present counsel with difficult choices (sections G(2) & (4)).

8.  A number of observations can be made regarding Canadian future-harm exceptions to the ethical duty of confidentiality:

    a.  Many rules of professional conduct only apply to future-harm that constitutes a crime. Ontario's future-harm exception is alone in containing no such requirement (section G(3)).

    b.  In British Columbia and Ontario, as well as *Smith* v. *Jones*, the standard for deciding whether confidential information may be released focuses upon "death or serious bodily harm." *Smith* v. *Jones* and the Ontario exception both suggest that "serious bodily harm" includes psychological harm that substantially interferes with health or well-being. It remains to be seen just how far this notion of harm extends (section G(4)).

    c.  The future-harm exception does not encompass the revelation of past acts. Yet where a harmful action is ongoing, and the disclosure of confidential information can work to prevent damage, the exception may apply (section G(5)).

  d.  A crucial limit upon the operation of future-harm exceptions is that disclosure must be necessary to prevent the harm in question (section G(6)).

  e.  Prior to releasing client secrets under the exception, a lawyer must confer with the client where circumstances permit. It may be that the harm can be averted by remonstration, or that the lawyer will conclude that his or her fears are misplaced (section G(7)).

  f.  It has been suggested that, where practicable, a lawyer obtain permission of the court prior to releasing confidential information under a future-harm exception (section G(9)).

9.  Many future-harm exceptions contain an element of discretion for the lawyer. Factors that a lawyer may wish to take into account in exercising a discretion include: probability that harm will occur, type and extent of harm, immediacy of harm, role of the client in creating threatened harm, role of the lawyer in creating threatened harm, impact of disclosure on the client, impact of disclosure on the lawyer's practice, reliance on the lawyer by the person who may be harmed, impact of lawyer's ultimate decision upon the legal system, and the lawyer's personal views (section G(8)).

10. A few jurisdictions have adopted, in addition to a future-harm exception, independent exceptions aimed at preventing particular types of harm, including any "dangerous situation" at a court facility or damage to the "national interest." We have difficulty in understanding why these *ad hoc* exceptions are necessary, provided that the jurisdiction employs a well-crafted future-harm exception (section H).

11. There exists an undisputed crime-fraud exception to legal-professional privilege for client-lawyer communications that are in themselves criminal or are knowingly made for the purpose of obtaining legal advice to facilitate the commission of a crime. However, in our view there is no comparable crime-fraud exception applicable to the ethical duty of confidentiality (section I).

12. A problem of particular difficulty arises where a lawyer learns that he or she has been unwittingly used by a dishonest client to commit or further a crime. A number of approaches to this conundrum are examined in the text above. At the end of the day, it may be that a lawyer has little in the way of options, other than refusing to commit any further improprieties and withdrawing from the representation (section J).

13. An unquestioned duty owed by all lawyers is not to mislead the court. This duty can apply in a myriad of situations and often will involve reacting to a client's improper attempt to evade conviction. Rectifying the problem may put confidential client information in jeopardy of being revealed (section K).

14. Where the court has not yet been misled, but the lawyer fears that such an eventuality will occur, the first step is to take all reasonable measures to avoid the deception. Where a client cannot be dissuaded from a deceptive plan, counsel may have the option of withdrawing from the case. Certainly, the lawyer cannot participate or aid in the plan. Generally, however, counsel should not divulge confidential information as a means of preventing the anticipated falsehood (section K(1)).

15. Where the court has already been misled, counsel's options are somewhat different. There is still a duty to attempt to persuade the client to consent to correcting the deception, and withdrawal may also remain an alternative. Disclosure of the problem, including the revelation of confidences, may be acceptable as a last resort in counsel's attempt to rectify the falsehood (section K(2)).

16. In some cases, counsel learns of the deception only after a matter has concluded. In Canada, the rules of professional conduct do not appear to impose any endpoint to counsel's obligation to rectify the deception. In contrast, American ethical rules tend to impose a remedial duty only until the point that the matter concludes (section K(3)).

## FURTHER READINGS

ARMSTRONG, K., "The Duty of Confidentiality and the Child Beating Client: An Ethical Conundrum" (1996) 13 Can. Fam. L.Q. 49

DODEK, A., "Doing Our Duty: The Case for a Duty of Disclosure to Prevent Death or Serious Harm" (2001) 50 U.N.B.L.J. 215

DODEK, A., "The Public Safety Exception to Solicitor-Client Privilege" (2000) 34 U.B.C. L. Rev. 293

FORBES, S., "Developments in the Law of Evidence: The 1998-1999 Term" (2000) 11 Supreme Court L.R. 411

HALL, J., *Professional Responsibility of the Criminal Lawyer*, 2d ed.(New York: Clark Boardman Callaghan, 1996)

HAZARD, G., & W. HODES, *The Law of Lawyering: A Handbook on the Model Rules of Professional Conduct*, 2d ed. (Englewood, N.J.: Prentice Hall, 1993)

HUTCHINSON, A., *Legal Ethics and Professional Responsibility* (Toronto: Irwin Law, 1999)

KAUFMAN, A., *Problems in Professional Responsibility*, 3d ed. (Boston: Little, Brown, 1989)

KAPOOR, A., "Public Safety and Private Communications: Keeping Up With the Jones'" Kapoor's Criminal Appeals Review 1 (7 May 1999), online: QL (KCAR 1999/003)

LAYTON, D., "The Pre-Trial Removal of Counsel for Conflict of Interest: Appealability and Remedies on Appeal" (1999) 4 Can. Crim. L. Rev. 25

LAYTON, D., "The Public Safety Exception: Confusing Confidentiality, Privilege and Ethics" (2001) 6 Can. Crim. L. Rev. 209

LUNDY, D., G. MACKENZIE & M.V. NEWBURY, *Barristers and Solicitors in Practice*, looseleaf (Markham, Ont.: Butterworths, 1999)

MACKENZIE, G., *Lawyers and Ethics: Professional Responsibility and Discipline* (Toronto: Carswell, 1993)

MANES, R. and M. SILVER, *Solicitor-Client Privilege in Canadian Law* (Toronto: Butterworths, 1993)

MCWILLIAMS, P., *Canadian Criminal Evidence*, 3d (Aurora: Canada Law Book, 1999)

MEWETT, A. & P. SANKOFF, *Witnesses* (Toronto: Carswell, 1999)

MORSE, J. & A. CASEMORE, "Doctor-Patient Confidentiality: To Disclose or Not to Disclose" (2000) 22 Advocates Q. 312

MOSTELLER, R., "Child Abuse Reporting Laws and Attorney-Client Confidence" (1992) 42 Duke L.J. 203

NILSEN, E., "Disclose or Not: The Client with a False Identity" in R. Uphoff, ed., *Ethical Problems Facing the Criminal Lawyer: Practical Answers to Tough Questions* (Chicago: American Bar Association, 1995) c. 15

NOCTOR, C., "Legal Professional Privilege and the Public Safety Exception" (1999) 17 Ir. L. T. 230.

ORKIN, M., *Legal Ethics: A Study of Professional Conduct* (Toronto: Cartwright, 1957)

PODGER, E., "Form 8300: The Demise of Law as a Profession" (1992) 5 Geo. J. Legal Ethics 485

RENKE, W., "Secrets and Lives — The Public Safety Exception to Solicitor-Client Privilege: *Smith v. Jones*" Case Comment (1999) 37 Alta. L. Rev. 1045

ROSS, S., *Ethics in Law: Lawyers' Responsibility and Accountability in Australia* (Sydney: Butterworths, 1998)

ROTMAN, L., "Balancing the "Scales of Justice": Fiduciary Obligations and *Stewart c. C.B.C.*" (1999) 78 Can. Bar Rev. 445

RUSSELL, I., "Cries and Whispers: Environmental Hazards, Model Rule 1.6, and the Attorney's Conflicting Duties to Clients and Others" (1997) 72 Wash. L. Rev. 409

SKURKA, S., & J. STRIBOPOULOS, "Professional Responsibility in Criminal Practice" in Law Society of Upper Canada, *42nd Bar Admission Course, 2000, Criminal Procedure Reference Materials* (Toronto: Law Society of Upper Canada, 2000) c. 1

SOPINKA, J., S. LEDERMAN & A. BRYANT, *The Law of Evidence in Canada*, 2d ed. (Toronto: Butterworths, 1999)

TALLEY, W., "Setting the Record Straight: The Client with Undisclosed Prior Convictions" in R. Uphoff, ed., *Ethical Problems Facing the Criminal Lawyer: Practical Answers to Tough Questions* (Chicago: American Bar Association, 1995) c. 14

WATT, D., *Watt's Manual of Criminal Evidence* (Scarborough, Ont.: Carswell, 1999)

WILLIAMS, B., "Some Secrets Are Not Worth Keeping" [1998] Crim. L. Bull. 1

WOLFRAM, C.W., *Modern Legal Ethics* (St. Paul: West, 1986)

# CHAPTER 6

# CONFLICT OF INTEREST

## A. INTRODUCTION

A conflict of interest occurs whenever a lawyer is placed in a position where loyalty to a client is compromised. There are an inexhaustible number of situations in which a conflict problem can arise. The conflicting interests may involve current, former, or prospective clients, or sometimes even third parties with whom a client-lawyer relationship was never established or contemplated. A lawyer's loyalty may also be compromised by his or her own interest or the interest of an affiliated lawyer. Categorizing scenarios according to the type of conflict raised is a helpful way to address the ethical and legal obligations of criminal counsel in this area. A discussion of any particular scenario, however, is incomplete without examining the principles that make conflict avoidance so important, as well as the professional-conduct standards, common law rules, and constitutional guarantees that are derived from and reflect these principles.

## B. BASIC PRINCIPLES

The client-lawyer relationship is based on the highest of trusts, where the lawyer's loyalty is unquestioned.[1] The duty to be loyal, born of the fiduciary relationship between counsel and client, must guide and inform every aspect of the lawyer's dealing with a client, and it leads to important component duties such as the duty of confidentiality. As we shall see, the duty of confidentiality is particularly important in the realm of conflict of interest. Yet a threat to confidentiality is not a *sine qua non* to the existence of a conflict problem. The leitmotif of conflict of interest is the broader duty of loyalty. Where the lawyer's duty of loyalty is compromised by a competing interest, a conflict of interest will exist even where there is no possibility that confidential information will be misused.[2]

The importance of loyalty to the lawyer-client relationship is underlined by the adversarial nature of the criminal justice system. An adversarial system gives litigants the responsibility and right to present their own cases and to challenge the evidence and arguments of their opponents. As agents for the litigants, lawyers operate within this adversarial setting, making loyalty towards the client absolutely essential. Failure to provide loyal service may harm the client's ability to exercise important constitutional rights and can also operate to undermine the reliability of the system. Consequently, the duties that are necessary for the existence of a healthy client-lawyer relationship are, by extension, important parts of the entire administration of justice. Given that the client-lawyer relationship is central to the operation of our justice system, the protection and promotion of the relationship by members of the profession and the courts not only advances the interests of each individual client but also bolsters the integrity of the entire system.

Placing a lawyer in a position where he or she must simultaneously serve conflicting interests is thus not only inimical to the duty of loyalty demanded of every lawyer for the benefit of each client but also undermines the well-being of the justice system as a whole.[3] Accordingly, two related but distinct concerns lie at the heart of the general prohibition against conflict of interest: harm to the client and harm to the administration of justice. These concerns are reflected in the rules of professional conduct, common law precepts, and constitutional guarantees pertaining to conflict of interest.

---

1   The principles articulated in this section have already been discussed elsewhere. For a fuller discussion, with case law citations, see section D, "The Rationale for Defending One Known to be Guilty," in chapter 1, and section B, "Rationale," in chapter 4.

2   This point is expanded upon below in the discussions accompanying notes 40 & 72–77.

3   See, for example, *MacDonald Estate* v. *Martin*, [1990] 3 S.C.R. 1235 at 1244 [*MacDonald Estate*]; *R.* v. *Robillard* (1986), 28 C.C.C. (3d) 22 (Ont. C.A.) [*Robillard*].

## C. RELATED RULES OF PROFESSIONAL CONDUCT

A number of the rules of professional conduct emphasize the principles underlying the proscription of conflict of interest. In particular, all provincial governing bodies and the CBA have adopted a rule specifically concerning conflict of interest, which evinces a strong concern for the preservation of the client-lawyer relationship.[4] For instance, the CBA Code defines a conflicting interest as "one that would be likely to affect adversely the lawyer's judgment or advice on behalf of, or loyalty to a client or prospective client."[5] Included in the Code's definition are the financial and other interests of the lawyer and any partners or associates of the lawyer, as well as the duties and loyalties of the lawyer to any other client (such as the obligation to communicate information).[6] The CBA Code also states that the lawyer shall not advise or represent both sides of a dispute and, save after adequate disclosure and with the consent of the clients, should not act in a matter where there is likely to be a conflicting interest.[7] Furthermore, a lawyer is expressly prohibited from acting against a former client in the same or a related matter, and is likewise forbidden from taking a position where he or she might be tempted or appear to be tempted to breach the duty of confidentiality owed to a former client.[8]

Clearly, the rationale for rules of professional conduct that address conflict of interest is that the client's interests may be seriously impaired unless the lawyer's judgment and ability to act on the client's behalf are as free as possible from compromising influences.[9] However, these rules recognize that a conflict of interest is not always fatal from the client's point of view but rather may be subservient to other factors such as the availability of another lawyer of comparable expertise and experience, the extra cost, delay, and inconvenience involved in engaging another lawyer, and a new lawyer's unfamiliarity with the client

---

4   See, for example, CBA Code ch. V (conflict of interest between clients), and ch. VI (conflict involving the lawyer's own interest); Ont. r. 2.04; Alta. ch. 6; B.C. ch. 6–7; and Man. ch. 6–7.

5   CBA Code ch. V, comm. 1. Compare the more matter-of-fact statement of principle used in Alberta: "In each matter, a lawyer's judgment and fidelity to the client's interests must be free from compromising influences" (ch. 6).

6   See CBA Code ch. V, comm. 3, and ch. VI.

7   See CBA Code ch. V, Rule.

8   See CBA Code ch. V, comm. 8.

9   See CBA Code ch. V, comm. 2.

and the client's affairs.[10] Hence, where there is full disclosure of the conflicting interest, the lawyer may continue to act with the client's consent, though the lawyer should guard against acting for multiple clients where it is reasonably obvious that an issue contentious between them may arise or where their interests, rights, or obligations will diverge as the matter progresses.[11]

Numerous other rules of professional conduct reflect the concerns raised whenever a lawyer finds himself or herself in a conflict on interest.[12] For instance:

1. **Integrity**: Lawyers are required to discharge with integrity all duties owed to client, the court, the public, and other members of the profession, as stipulated by Chapter I of the CBA Code. Integrity is the fundamental quality of a lawyer,[13] representing a key element of each rule of professional conduct, and vis-à-vis the client finds expression in absolute trustworthiness.[14] Trustworthiness, or loyalty, is seen to be the essential element of the client-lawyer relationship.[15]

2. **Confidential information**: A lawyer has a duty to hold in strict confidence all information concerning the business and affairs of the client acquired in the course of the professional relationship.[16] In particular, the information cannot be used for the benefit of the lawyer or a third party, or to the detriment of the client,[17] and this duty persists even after the demise of the professional relationship.[18]

3. **The lawyer as advocate**: When acting as advocate the lawyer must, *inter alia*, represent the client resolutely, honourably, and within the limits of the law. The duty to the client is to raise every issue, advance every argument, and ask every question, however distasteful, which the lawyer thinks will help the client's case, and to endeavour to obtain for the client the benefit of every remedy or defence available at law.[19]

---

10    See CBA Code ch. V, comm. 4.
11    See CBA Code ch. V, comms. 4 and 5.
12    See the discussion in P. Perell, *Conflict of Interest in the Legal Profession* (Toronto: Butterworths, 1995) at 2–4.
13    See CBA Code, ch. I, comm. 2.
14    See CBA Code, ch. I, comm. 1.
15    See CBA Code, ch. I, comm. 1.
16    See for example, CBA Code ch. IV, Rule.
17    See CBA Code ch. IV, Rule, comms. 5–7.
18    See CBA Code ch. IV, comm. 4.
19    See CBA Code, ch. IX, Rule, comms. 1, 10, & 15.

4. **The lawyer and the administration of justice**: The lawyer should encourage public respect for and try to improve the administration of justice. Judicial institutions will not function effectively unless they command the respect of the public, and constant efforts must be made to improve the administration of justice and thereby maintain its respect in the eyes of the public.[20]

Each of these rules integrally engages the lawyer's duty of loyalty to the client and is potentially jeopardized in cases where a conflict arises.

## D. COMMON LAW

The rules of professional conduct, while not constituting a statutory code, have been afforded close attention by the courts in determining the policy concerns and general principles that impact on conflict of interest.[21] It is thus not surprising that courts have recognized a common law prohibition against counsel acting while in a conflict of interest, as well as the jurisdiction to remove conflicted counsel from the record.[22]

**Observation**: While the rules of professional conduct will be given significant weight in the exercise of the court's inherent jurisdiction to disqualify counsel for a conflict of interest, compliance with such rules does not necessarily mean that no conflict exists.[23]

## E. CONSTITUTIONAL RIGHTS TO EFFECTIVE COUNSEL AND COUNSEL OF CHOICE

In criminal cases, the justification for prohibiting counsel from representing an accused while labouring under a conflict takes on constitu-

---

20  See CBA Code, ch. XIII, Rule & comm. 1.
21  See, for example, *MacDonald Estate*, above note 3 at 1244–46; *Gainers Inc.* v. *Pocklington* (1995), 125 D.L.R. (4th) 50 at 53 (Alta. C.A.), leave to appeal to S.C.C. refused 130 D.L.R. (4th) vii (note) (S.C.C.); and *Stewart* v. *Canadian Broadcasting Corp.* (1997), 150 D.L.R. (4th) 24 at 107–08 & 115 (Ont. Gen. Div.) [*Stewart*].
22  See *MacDonald Estate*, above note 3 at 1245.
23  This observation is implicitly supported by *MacDonald Estate*, above note 3 at 1245–46. See also *R.* v. *Dix* (1998), 218 A.R. 18 at 25 (Q.B.) [*Dix*]; and *Stewart*, above note 21 at 115.

tional dimensions. By definition, where counsel for the accused has an actual conflict of interest, the client suffers through representation by an advocate whose loyalty is suspect. In such circumstances, and no matter how competent the conflicted lawyer, the accused has not been provided with effective counsel, which is itself a denial of fundamental justice and a violation of the *Canadian Charter of Rights and Freedoms*.[24] We thus see the important interface between conflict of interest and the right to effective counsel. A lawyer can render effective assistance only when he or she gives the accused's cause the undivided loyalty which is a prerequisite to proper legal representation.[25] Failure to do so means that the adversary system cannot function properly, the appearance of fairness suffers, and the reliability of the verdict is called into question.[26]

A conflict-of-interest problem may also implicate an accused person's right to counsel of choice. This right has been recognized at common law as fundamental, is by implication entrenched in section 10(b) of the *Charter*, and most likely is among the principles of fundamental justice protected by section 7 of the *Charter*.[27] The rationale underlying the right to counsel of choice is inextricably bound up with many of the same concerns that justify the general prohibition against a lawyer acting while under a conflict of interest. The loyalty and confidentiality owed a client by counsel can flourish only in a setting where counsel enjoys the client's full trust. This relationship of trust by its nature has a special personal quality and will thus be most sedulously fostered in a setting where the client can choose his or her own lawyer.[28] Additionally, an accused has a constitutional right to present his or her own case to the trier of fact, a right that is derived from a

---

24  Part I of the *Constitution Act, 1982*, being Schedule 8 to the *Canada Act 1982* (U.K.), 1982, c. 11 [*Charter*]. See, for example, *R. v. Silvini* (1991), 68 C.C.C. (3d) 251 (Ont. C.A.) [*Silvini*]; *R. v. W.(W.)* (1995), 100 C.C.C. (3d) 225 (Ont. C.A.) [*W.(W.)*]; and *R. v. White* (1997), 114 C.C.C. (3d) 225 at 261–64 (Ont. C.A.), leave to appeal to S.C.C. refused (1977), 117 C.C.C. (3d) vi (S.C.C.) [*White*]. Leading right-to-effective-counsel cases that do not deal with conflict of interest are discussed in section 1(2), "The Constitutional Right to Effective Legal Assistance," in chapter 8.

25  See *W.(W.)*, above note 24 at 235.

26  *Ibid.* at 234.

27  See, for example, *R. v. Speid* (1983), 8 C.C.C. (3d) 18 at 20 (Ont. C.A.) [*Speid*]; *Robillard*, above note 3 at 26; *MacDonald Estate*, above note 3 at 1243; and *W.(W.)*, above note 24 at 225. The leading case on the right to choice of counsel is currently *R. v. McCallen* (1999), 131 C.C.C (3d) 518 at 530-532 (Ont. C.A.). [*McCallen*].

28  See, for example, *McCallen*, above note 27 at 531.

desire to protect personal autonomy and dignity from unjustified state intrusion.[29] The choice of lawyer is an important part of the accused's presentation and thus falls within the scope of this *Charter* protection.

An appreciation of the interplay between the constitutional rights to the effective assistance of counsel and the choice of counsel is necessary when approaching any conflict-of-interest problem. Often these rights will combine to force the removal of a conflicted lawyer prior to or during trial. For example, an accused may decide that he or she wishes to retain new counsel (that is, to exercise the right to choose counsel) because a conflict-of-interest has arisen that, if permitted to continue, will fatally undermine the ability of existing counsel to provide loyal representation (thus infringing the right to be represented by effective counsel). These two rights can also work in tandem on appeal. If the trial judge in the example just given erroneously refuses to accommodate the accused's desire to retain new counsel,[30] the appeal court will find that the accused's rights to the effective assistance and choice of counsel have both been violated.

In other cases, the relative importance of the rights to choice of counsel and the effective assistance of counsel may differ significantly, and on occasion these rights may diverge or even clash. The Supreme Court of Canada has suggested as much by identifying the right to choice of counsel as a factor that may militate *against* removing counsel from the record because of a perceived conflict.[31] Suppose, for example, that the Crown is worried that a conflict-of-interest problem might lead to a post-conviction appeal based upon ineffective assistance at trial. The Crown brings an application to remove defence counsel because of this concern, yet the accused opposes the application by relying on the right to keep his or her counsel of choice.[32] Or consider an application to remove defence counsel who formerly represented a Crown witness.[33] The accused's right to effective counsel

---

29   See *R. v. Swain* (1991), 63 C.C.C. (3d) 481 at 504–06 (S.C.C.); and *McCallen*, above note 27 at 531–32.

30   An accused can always discharge counsel, even though the trial judge refuses to find that a disqualifying conflict exists: see section E, "General Prohibition Against Withdrawal," in chapter 11. In such a case, however, the judge will likely refuse to grant an adjournment to retain new counsel, and the accused may choose to continue with conflicted counsel (albeit under protest) rather than face a *pro se* trial.

31   See *MacDonald Estate*, above note 3 at 1243.

32   Be careful to note, however, that in this example the Crown is not asserting a constitutional right to the effective assistance of counsel.

33   See, for example, *Speid*, above note 27; and *Robillard*, above note 3. In such an instance, the witness may be asserting countervailing constitutional rights,

may be scarcely threatened by the spectre of conflict. Instead, the witness's claim to loyalty and confidentiality from former counsel comes up against the accused's right to counsel of choice. Similarly, an accused may attempt to disqualify counsel for a co-accused on the basis of a conflict-of-interest, and removal may be warranted even though the accused making the application is not relying on the right to choice of counsel or the right to the effective assistance of counsel.[34]

## F. THE TEST FOR CONFLICT OF INTEREST PRIOR TO OR DURING TRIAL

Where a conflict-of-interest issue is raised in a criminal proceeding, and all parties have had the opportunity to consider their respective positions, there are several potential resolutions. One possibility is that all present clients of the allegedly conflicted lawyer discharge counsel. Once the allegedly conflicted lawyer is no longer on the case, the issue is settled. A similar result may occur if, though discharge is contrary to the desire of a current client, the allegedly conflicted counsel is reasonably of the opinion that he or she cannot continue because of a conflict-of-interest and withdraws from the case.[35] Where, however, the lawyer's present client (or, in the case of multiple representation, at least one of his or her clients) wishes to continue the retainer, and counsel is prepared to do so, the court will have to decide where a disqualifying conflict-of-interest exists.[36] At this point, the question arises as to what test or standard of review should be applied.

The leading discussion of the standard to be applied by a trial judge in determining whether a conflict-of-interest requires the removal of counsel in a criminal matter is found in the Ontario Court of Appeal decision of *R. v. W.(W.)*, a multiple representation case in which Mr. Justice Doherty stated:

---

including a right to privacy, which together with concerns as to public confidence in the administration of justice may trump the right to counsel of choice.

34   The accused making the application would nonetheless likely be able to assert the *Charter* right to a fair trial, linked to a right to protect the confidentiality of communications with former counsel. This possibility is referred to, albeit briefly, in *R. v. Zwicker* (1995), 169 N.B.R. (3d) 350 (C.A.) [*Zwicker*].

35   See section G, "Discretionary Withdrawal by the Lawyer," in chapter 11.

36   Once raised, this issue must be considered and resolved by the court: see *R. v. Bilmez* (1995), 101 C.C.C. (3d) 123 (Ont. C.A.) [*Bilmez*].

Where the issue [of conflict of interest] is raised at trial, the court must be concerned with actual conflicts of interest and potential conflicts that may develop as the trial unfolds. In deciding whether counsel should be permitted to act for co-accused, trial judges must, to some degree, speculate as to the issues which may arise and the course the trial will take. The trial judges' task is particularly difficult since they cannot be privy to the confidential discussions which may have passed between the clients and counsel and which may reveal the source of potential conflicts. Given those circumstances, trial judges must proceed with caution and when there is any realistic risk of a conflict-of-interests they must direct that counsel not act for one or perhaps either accused.[37]

A key distinction made by Mr. Justice Doherty is between an actual conflict-of-interest and a conflict-of-interest that does not presently exist but may crystallize (*i.e.* become "actual") in the future. In the context of multiple representation of co-accused, W.(W.) held that an actual conflict-of-interest exists where a course of conduct dictated by the best interests of one accused would, if followed, be inconsistent with the best interests of the co-accused.[38] An actual conflict-of-interest will always result in the removal of counsel, because counsel simply cannot carry out his or her duty of loyalty to the client.

The breadth of the exclusionary test articulated in W.(W.) is widest at the point where the *potential* for an actual conflict to crystallize in the future may warrant removal — that is, where there is "any realistic risk" of the conflict in fact occurring. Striking upon "realistic risk" as the appropriate standard is reminiscent of the "possibility of real mischief" test adopted by the Supreme Court of Canada in the leading civil case on conflict-of-interest, *MacDonald Estate* v. *Martin*.[39] *MacDonald*

---

37  W.(W.), above note 24 at 238. See also R. v. *Chen* (2001), 53 O.R. (3d) 264 (S.C.J.) [*Chen*]. Contrast the approach taken in the earlier case of *Speid*, above note 27 at 20–21. Because *Speid* was heard as an interlocutory appeal, the court was placed in the position of viewing the conflict-of-interest question from the perspective of the trial judge, and put the test as follows: "In assessing the merits of a disqualification order, the court must balance the individual's right to select counsel of his own choice, public policy and the public interest in the administration of justice and basic principles of fundamental fairness. Such an order should not be made unless there are compelling reasons. This is clearly such a case and to do otherwise would result in real mischief or real prejudice": *ibid.* at 20–21.

38  See W.(W.), above note 24 at 239, where "course of conduct" is used in a broad sense to include actions, inactions, and advice of counsel.

39  *MacDonald Estate*, above note 3.

*Estate* dealt with a risk that confidential information held by a lawyer would be misused against a former client. Multiple-representation cases such as *W.(W.)*, and indeed many criminal conflict-of-interest cases, examine threats to counsel's duty of loyalty that do not necessarily concern confidential information.[40] Yet, while *MacDonald Estate* and *W.(W.)* concern somewhat different aspects of the duty of loyalty, both decisions make clear that contingent threats can be sufficient to merit disqualification.

The phrase "any realistic risk" seems consistent with the overall trend in Canadian conflict-of-interest cases to speak of possibilities rather than probabilities. Nevertheless, one is left with the obvious question, when is a risk realistic? The term "risk" is not normative but connotes a whole spectrum of possibilities or chances that an event (usually a loss) will occur in the future. The risk that the event will occur may be non-existent, or minuscule, or, more likely than not, highly likely, or absolutely certain, or any number of other measures of probability in-between. The qualifying words "any realistic" would seem to mean that there must be some evidentiary foundation from which risk can reasonably be said to flow. Mere conjecture and bare possibility is simply not sufficient to require the removal of counsel.[41] On the whole, however, "any realistic" risk cannot be said to require proof beyond a reasonable doubt, nor even proof on the balance of probabilities, that an actual conflict will arise. The standard suggested in *W.(W.)* is not terribly imposing, and it would seem that any conflict-of-interest scenario that could reasonably occur during the course of the trial will suffice to require the removal of counsel.[42]

---

40   Compare *MacDonald Estate*, *ibid.*, to the well-known multiple representation case of *Silvini*, above note 24. The concerns raised by *Silvini*, many of which are mentioned below in the discussion of multiple representation, could well involve confidential information. However, the tenor of the reasons in *Silvini* suggests that the court's concern lay mostly with the fact that counsel had divided loyalties in providing advice to his clients and during the trial was forced to take positions adverse to at least one client, regardless of whether confidential information would be misused.

41   See, for example, *McCallen*, above note 27 at 541; *R. v. Parsons* (1992), 72 C.C.C. (3d) 137 at 142 (Nfld. C.A.) [*Parsons*]; and *R. v. Rapai* (1992), 11 O.R. (3d) 47 at 55–56 (Prov. Div.).

42   Compare the test used to assess prejudice in right-to-effective-counsel cases, and especially the comments of Mr. Justice Doherty in *R. v. Joanisse* (1995), 102 C.C.C. (3d) 35 at 64 (Ont. C.A.), where the terms "realistic possibility" and "realistic probability" are said to mean the same thing. "Realistic possibility" does not require proof on a balance of probability, rather requiring only a showing that counsel's error had "any conceivable" impact on the reliability of the

The standard of "any realistic risk" adopted in W.(W.) represents a clear, if unarticulated, preference for avoiding mistrials and overturned decisions over the competing interest of the accused's right to counsel of choice. As discussed above, if the court is required to decide the conflict-of-interest issue, it must be that the client (or in the case of multiple representation, at least one client) wishes the allegedly conflicted counsel to continue. Let us assume that a client is not prepared to allow counsel to continue if an actual conflict arises, but simply takes the position that no actual conflict exists at present and articulates a strong preference that counsel stay on the record unless and until such an event occurs. By removing counsel at this preliminary stage, upon showing "any realistic risk" of conflict-of-interest, as opposed to an actual conflict, or even some other standard in-between, is to incur immediate and certain harm to the right to counsel of choice in order to avoid the possibility of future harm occasioned by the crystallization of a conflict-of-interest.

It would appear that, whatever the exact meaning of "realistic risk," it will be helpful for the trial judge to obtain some appreciation of the nature and strength of the Crown case in order to discern the course that the trial might take and hence assess the degree of likelihood that an actual conflict-of-interest will occur. For example, a weak Crown case may make it less likely that two co-accused will adopt antagonistic defences, and thus reduce the chances of a conflict arising. In contrast, a strong Crown case that encourages *mens rea* defences might force one accused to take the stand and adopt a position in his or her own defence that is detrimental to the co-accused. It is also possible, though less likely, that the implicated accused will be able and willing to indicate probable defences, providing further valuable information to the trial judge.[43] The scenarios may be complicated and numerous. Obviously, the trial judge cannot be presented with a dry run of the entire trial as part of the application to remove counsel, but the nature and strength of the Crown case, and the helpfulness of calling evidence on the point, are worth considering when counsel launches or faces an application for removal.

---

result. Ultimately, the term is said to encompass that degree of likelihood sufficient to undermine confidence in the verdict.

43   Tactical issues arise at this point, as does the possible applicability of the principle against self-incrimination. It has been suggested that there is an obligation to reveal the nature of the defence, but that such information can be provided during an *ex parte* and *in camera* portion of the proceeding: see D. Littlefield, "Silvini: Divided Loyalty" (1992) 9 C.R. (4th) 250 at 257; but *contra* see R. v. Kalenderian (1999), 41 W.C.B. (ed) 417 (Ont. Gen. Div.).

# G. MULTIPLE REPRESENTATION (REPRESENTING CO-ACCUSED)

The simultaneous representation of two or more accused presents one of the most common and dangerous conflict-of-interest dilemmas for defence counsel. Counsel must be wary of representing multiple accused, and should only do so after extremely careful consideration of the conflict-of-interest issue. By the same token, Crown counsel confronted with a case of multiple representation should make it a practice to address conflict-of-interest concerns promptly, at the least with defence counsel if not with the court. Trial judges would also do well to make formal inquiries whenever co-accused share a single counsel.

The danger arising from multiple representation is simply a function of the increased likelihood of conflicting demands on counsel's loyalty where he or she represents two clients in the same matter. It follows that the right to effective counsel is especially susceptible to harm in cases of multiple representation.[44] The potential for harm is underlined in Canadian rules of professional conduct, which tend to make express mention of the risk of conflict-of-interest where the counsel acts for two clients in the same matter. For instance, the CBA Code states that, "common multiple client situations where there is a real danger of divergence of interest arising between clients include the defending of co-accused."[45] Canadian courts clearly share this view.[46]

**Comparison**: The commentary to the ABA Model Rule 1.7(b) states that "the potential for conflict-of-interest in representing multiple defendants in a criminal case is so grave that ordinarily a lawyer should decline to represent more than one codefendant." The commentary goes on to allow, however, that multiple representation may be permissible if the lawyer reasonably believes that the representation will not be adversely affected and the clients consent after consultation.[47]

A number of commentators have viewed the dangers of multiple representation as sufficiently grave to warrant a blanket prohibition

---

44    See *Silvini*, above note 24 at 257; and *W.(W.)*, above note 24 at 235–36.

45    CBA Code ch. V, comm. 5, Footnote 5.

46    See, for example, *W.(W.)*, above note 24 at 235–36; and *R. v. Graff* (1993), 80 C.C.C. (3d) 84 at 88–89 (Alta C.A.), leave to appeal to S.C.C. refused (1993), 83 C.C.C. (3d) vi (S.C.C.) [*Graff*].

47    See ABA Rule 1.7(b), commentary. See also the cautious approach taken in the Third Restatement §129(1); and ABA Defense Standard 4-3.5(c).

against the practice.[48] Yet there are valid reasons why in some circumstances two or more co-accused may benefit from representation by the same counsel. As Canadian professional conduct rules frequently recognize, clients may value the expertise of a particular counsel, have a deep trust and confidence in counsel because of prior dealings, or wish to minimize costs by jointly retaining one lawyer.[49] It may also work to the advantage of co-accused to adopt a unified stance *vis-à-vis* the Crown and to present a solid, uniform defence to the trier of fact. It is certainly the case that representation by a single lawyer will advance this interest.[50] Moreover, an informed decision to share counsel necessarily invokes the constitutional right to choice of counsel.

**Example**: A husband and wife are both charged with importing narcotics, the allegation being that they jointly controlled a drug organization. The Crown case appears to be that they played equal roles in the criminal enterprise, and the key evidence against each accused comes from a police agent and a "mule" who cooperated with police after being arrested. Both accused have the same defence — they ran a legitimate importing business that must have been exploited, without their knowledge, by employees who were smuggling drugs. The two have a harmonious, long-standing relationship, and both appear quite able to make informed independent decisions. They can afford jointly to retain a single counsel but would be hard pressed to hire lawyers separately. Subject to full disclosure and discussion with the accused, and the provision of independent legal advice, this may be a case where multiple representation is acceptable.[51]

---

48   See, for example, G. Lowenthal, "Joint Representation in Criminal Cases: A Critical Appraisal" (1978) 64 Va. L. Rev. 939; P. Tague, "Multiple Representation and Conflicts of Interest in Criminal Cases" (1979) 67 Geo. L.J. 1075; J. Geer, "Representation of Multiple Criminal Defendants: Conflicts of Interest and the Professional Responsibility of the Defence Attorney" (1978) 62 Minn. L. Rev. 119; Note, "Developments in the Law: Conflicts of Interest in the Legal Profession" (1981) 94 Harv. L. Rev. 1244; and Littlefield, above note 43.

49   See, for example, Ont. r. 2.04(3) (commentary); CBA Code ch. V, comm. 4; and Alta. ch. 6, comm. 2.1.

50   See W.(W.), above note 24 at 235; and *Graff*, above note 46 at 88–89. As was said in *Glasser v. United States*, 315 U.S. 60 at 92 (1942): "Joint representation is a means of ensuring against reciprocal recrimination. A common defence often gives strength against a common attack."

51   A circumstance where relatives are jointly charged may especially lend itself to multiple representation, everything else being equal, because the danger of adversity arising is usually (though by no means always) less grave where close family members are concerned: see, for example, W.(W.), above note 24; and *R. v. Barbeau* (1996), 110 C.C.C. (3d) 69 (Que. C.A.) [*Barbeau*].

Because sharing a single lawyer may present valuable benefits to co-accused, and in certain circumstances the potential for adversity (and hence irreconcilable conflict-of-interest) may be quite low, the rules of professional conduct and courts have stopped short of imposing an absolute prohibition on multiple representation.[52] Defence lawyers who act for two or more co-accused must, however, "assume the heavy burden of ensuring that they are not placed in a position of representing interests which are or may be in conflict."[53] Moreover, it is clear that a lawyer cannot act for multiple accused where it is likely that an issue contentious between them will arise or their interests, rights, or obligations will diverge as the case progresses.[54] Nor should the arguments in favour of joint representation be blithely accepted in every case or over-idealized. It must not be forgotten, for example, that separate lawyers can work together to present a common defence to the jury, or that in the long run the costs and delay occasioned where a conflict-of-interest crystallizes during trial may wipe out any savings provided by sharing a single counsel.[55] Indeed, utilizing separate counsel who cooperate in the preparation of a defence avoids the possibility that the trier of fact, and in particular a jury, will assume that all accused are guilty by reason of association with a single lawyer. As for the right to counsel of choice, courts have repeatedly held that this constitutional guarantee does not always trump society's interest in the administration of justice and may be required to give way because of a conflict-of-interest problem.[56]

The issue for counsel and the courts becomes identifying whether the interests of clients may clash so as to preclude multiple representation. There is no magic in making such an inquiry. Counsel must carefully examine the potential course that the proceeding might take, in light of the anticipated Crown case and the possible defences available to the clients, and look carefully for realistic scenarios where his or her loyalty might be called into question. Examples of divided loyalties in the context of multiple representation are set out below.

---

52  See, for example, W.(W.), above note 24 at 235.
53  *Ibid.* at 235-236.
54  See, for example, CBA Code ch. V, comm. 5; and Ont. r. 2.04(6). Compare the less strident view taken in Alta. ch. 6, comm. 2.1; and B.C. ch. 6, comm. 2, 4, & 5.
55  As for the risk that separate counsel might refuse to cooperate, any significant dissension would simply suggest that the clients in fact had conflicting interests.
56  See, for example, *Speid*, above note 27 at 20; *Robillard*, above note 3 at 26; and *McCallen*, above note 27 at 532.

## 1) Plea Discussions

The obvious example of a conflict related to plea bargaining occurs where one client is offered immunity from prosecution or a light sentence in return for testimony against the other client (or perhaps merely "off the record" information that would harm the other client). However, counsel must not assume that plea bargaining raises no other conflict-of-interest dangers. For instance, while not actively seeking cooperation, the Crown may decide to call the client who pleads guilty as a witness at the other client's trial.

Indeed, any aspect of plea negotiations that can help one client but harm the other presents a conflict problem. Perhaps one client wishes to rely on the other, who is more articulate and has no record, to testify in support of a joint defence. An offer by the Crown that is attractive to the articulate client may thus be harmful to the other. Or take the case of an aggregate deal offered by the Crown, only available if accepted by all of the accused, which provides a more favourable result to one client than the other (even taking into account individual differences). Remember that, because the Crown has discretion in fashioning a plea arrangement, multiple accused may be competing for the best deal possible. If even one client is interested in the possibility of a plea, or is approached by the Crown regarding a plea, a conflict could arise.[57]

## 2) Pre-trial Applications

Many pre-trial applications focus on the exclusion of Crown evidence. If evidence is harmful to one client but helpful to the other, and there exists a reasonable prospect of excluding the evidence, a conflict arises. Non-evidentiary pre-trial applications can also present problems. It may be, for example, in the interest of one accused but not the other to gain severance.[58]

## 3) Attacking the Crown Case

The Crown case can be attacked in a number of ways, including making objections to evidence being put before the trier of fact and mounting challenges to the evidence of witnesses through cross-examination. Such attacks may help one client but hurt the other, perhaps because the evi-

---

57 Specific examples of conflict-of-interest in the context of plea discussions are canvassed in section T, "Conflict of Interest," in chapter 8.

58 See, for example, *R. v. McCaw* (1971), 5 C.C.C. (2d) 416 (Ont. C.A.); *Silvini*, above note 24 at 260; and *Chen*, above note 37 at 283.

dence is clearly favourable to one co-accused but unfavourable to the other.[59] Loyalty may be compromised in this way where: the statement of one accused hurts the other accused; one accused is able to shift blame to the other (the "cutthroat" defence); the accused have inconsistent defences; or one accused provides an exculpatory statement, potentially underlining the failure of the other accused to follow suit.

Furthermore, the clients may have had differing levels of responsibility or involvement in the alleged offence. In such a case, it might may be in one client's best interests to contrast his or her limited involvement with the more significant role played by a co-accused. Objections and cross-examination that take this tack run the risk of hurting the accused who is more substantially implicated by the evidence, while foregoing this strategy may harm the other accused.

## 4) Building an Affirmative Defence

Evidence called by the Crown can often be used to build an affirmative defence, and cross-examination of a Crown witness is sometimes undertaken with this purpose in mind. Where a defence can be furthered in this way by one client, but will harm the other, a conflict exists.

A defence can also be put forward by calling evidence once the Crown case has closed.[60] A conflict will arise in this respect whenever a witness favourable to one accused is unfavourable, or presents a realistic risk of harm, to the other. Some classic examples of inconsistent affirmative defences include a case where one accused argues alibi while the other relies on a *mens rea* defence, or where two or more accused put forward inconsistent alibis. Additionally, where all accused share a single, common defence, it may be that one accused is able to make use of an alternative defence. If this accused decides to present the alternative, the inability of the other accused to follow suit may be viewed adversely by the trier of fact.

## 5) Decision to Testify and Testimony of a Client

A key instance where an attempt to build a defence may lead to conflict-of-interest occurs at the point where the clients must decide whether to testify, and also with respect to the content of the testimony

---

59   See, for example, *Silvini*, above note 24 at 259; *R. v. Bullis* (1990), 57 C.C.C.
     (3d) 438 at 443 (B.C.C.A.) [*Bullis*] and *Chen*, above note 37 at 283.
60   See, for example, *Bullis*, above note 59 at 443.

itself.[61] The testimony of one client may harm the other, leading to a clash of interests in advising one or both clients whether to testify.[62] Similarly, one client may not want or need to testify, yet the other, who is inarticulate or has a bad record, may desire the former to take the stand in order to present a joint defence. Also, putting one client on the stand but not the other may unavoidably lead the jury to speculate about the silence of the non-testifying client, even though this adverse inference is impermissible. That is to say, the trier of fact may wonder whether the lawyer's decision to put one client on the stand but not the other reflects the lawyer's belief in the guilt of the non-testifying client.

Once one client takes the stand, an intractable problem arises if any element of the testimony is adverse to the other.[63] Counsel cannot cross-examine on the point without attacking his or her own client and thus breaching his or her duty of loyalty. By the same token, the failure to cross-examine the testifying client will constitute a breach of duty to the other client.

## 6) Closing Arguments

If one client testifies but the other does not, counsel cannot comment on the silence of the non-testifying client.[64] Nor can counsel comment on the fact that the evidence may be stronger against one client than the other.[65] Yet the failure to raise such points harms the defence of the client who would thereby benefit. In both instances, counsel's loyalty is thus compromised. In fact, any argument made on behalf of one client that even inferentially points to the other client's guilt, perhaps in so subtle a way as highlighting the absence of a corresponding argument for the latter, raises a possible conflict problem.

---

61    See, for example, *Silvini*, above note 24 at 259; *Bullis*, above note 59 at 443; and *Chen*, above note 37 at 283.

62    This argument was advanced in *R. v. Phalen* (1997), 160 N.S.R. (2d) 371 C.A.) [*Phalen*], where a single counsel represented three co-accused, including the appellant, on a charge of assault causing bodily harm. One accused testified to the effect that he and the appellant acted in self-defence. The trial judge relied in part on this testimony to find that the appellant used excessive force and was guilty of the charge. However, the court found that no actual conflict existed.

63    In *R. v. Le* (1993), 78 C.C.C. (3d) 436 at 440–41 (B.C.C.A.) [*Le*], the court applied the *Bullis* test (discussed below at 350–51) and found that the testimony of the two co-accused was not inconsistent.

64    The same goes for a failure to make a statement to the police.

65    See, for example, *Silvini*, above note 24 at 259; and *Bullis*, above note 59 at 443.

## 7) Sentencing

Taking account of the comparative roles played in the offence by jointly involved offenders is often important in arriving at a proportionate and just sentence. However, counsel who acts for two or more individuals convicted of an offence will have difficulty in accentuating or minimizing distinct roles without harming one or both clients. The same problem arises if the clients have markedly different criminal records, or have substantially divergent prospects for rehabilitation, or exhibit any number of other differences that may have an impact on sentencing.

## 8) Bail Hearings

The limited function of a bail hearing makes conflict-of-interest less likely, but the problem of divided loyalty may nonetheless arise. Comparisons available to counsel at a bail hearing may be helpful to one client but harmful to the other. By the same token, one client may want a separate bail hearing because his or her circumstances are much more favourable than those of the other, who is likely to be detained. Finally, even though a bail hearing will occur early on in proceedings, the possibility of plea discussions, with the associated conflict concerns, may exist at this point.

## 9) Preliminary Inquiries

As with a bail hearing, the limited function of a preliminary inquiry makes conflict-of-interest somewhat less of a problem. Yet even where committal is not in issue, a conflict can arise. For instance, the preliminary inquiry hearing will create a record that can be used at trial, most often through cross-examination but sometimes also for substantive purposes. The preliminary inquiry is thus important in laying a groundwork for attacking the Crown case and building a defence at trial, and to the extent that the clients' interests may clash in either regard, a conflict-of-interest can arise.

It may also be in the interest of one client to waive the preliminary inquiry in order to avoid the possibility of committal on additional offences, while the other client would be better served by running a preliminary inquiry. Along the same lines, one client may want to consider having a trial in provincial court (where such an option is available), while the other is better advised to take the matter to a higher court. Finally, the possibility of plea negotiations and the attendant conflict-of-interest problems may exist at the preliminary inquiry stage.

## 10) Conflicting Instructions

Even where the clients' interests seem totally congruent from a preliminary, objective standpoint, an irreconcilable conflict may arise because they disagree as to the proper course of action to be taken with respect to a particular aspect of the case. For instance, bringing a pretrial application or calling a certain defence witness may affect both clients in exactly the same way, yet the clients take inconsistent positions as to the best course of action. The clients' personalities and subjective priorities come into play in this respect, and counsel should attempt to forecast important strategic and tactical decisions to determine whether inconsistent instructions might arise.[66]

## 11)    Conclusion

The above examples highlight a leading hallmark of conflict-of-interest problems in the context of multiple representation: adversity of interest arises where clients have inconsistent defences or are implicated in the offence to varying degrees, and with adversity of interest comes conflicting demands on counsel's loyalty. Ultimately, the danger in taking a multiple-representation retainer is significant, and while doing so is not absolutely prohibited, spurning such retainers goes a long way towards avoiding conflict-of-interest problems.

As an important aside, note that a multiple-representation retainer, once taken on, does not necessarily give counsel the option of remaining on the record for only one accused in the event that, for whatever reason, the retainer with one or more co-accused comes to an end. Rather, continuing to act for an accused who is tried alongside former clients raises what is sometimes called the "successive representation" problem, which, as discussed immediately below in section H, may itself create an impermissible conflict-of-interest.

---

66   In this respect, Alta. ch. 6, comm. 2.1, advises counsel who is considering multiple representation to assess "the probability that the conflict or potential conflict will ripen into a dispute due to the respective positions *or personalities of the parties*, the history of their relationship or other factors" (emphasis added).

# H. SUCCESSIVE REPRESENTATION (FORMER CLIENTS)

Because there is a duty of loyalty, and hence confidentiality, owed to former clients, a conflict-of-interest can occur where counsel previously acted for an individual connected to the criminal matter. Two common instances where the duties owed to a former client may lead to a conflict problem arise where counsel previously represented a co-accused or a Crown witness. Less common but nonetheless potentially problematic are cases where defence counsel moves to the Crown law office, or vice versa.[67] An egregious examples of this conflict scenario is seen in *R. v. Zwicker*,[68] where counsel acted for an accused on a guilty plea and argued for a non-custodial sentence. The case was adjourned for a pre-sentence report, and during this hiatus counsel began working for the Crown. When the sentence hearing resumed, the same counsel appeared for the Crown and argued that his former client should receive a significant jail term.

In any of these cases, the successive representation scenario may expose both the present and former clients to harm if the retainer is allowed to continue. It is thus to the question of harm that we now turn.

## 1) Harm Potentially Caused by Successive Representation

The current client may have doubts as to the loyalty of his or her lawyer when the proper carriage of the case demands that counsel take a position even somewhat adversarial to a former client. For instance, obligations of confidentiality owed to the former client may constrain counsel in cross-examining a witness whom he or she previously represented (whether a Crown witness or a testifying co-accused). Or the current client may have concerns that counsel is reluctant to object to

---

67   See, for example, *R. v. Joyal* (1990), 55 C.C.C. (3d) 233 (Que. C.A.) [*Joyal*]; *R. v. Dobrotic* (1995), 162 N.B.R. (2d) 379 (C.A.); *R. v. Covington* (1999), 41 W.C.B. (2d) 39 (Ont. C.A.); *R. v. Foster* (1997), 34 W.C.B. (2d) 454 (B.C.C.A.) [*Foster*]; *R. v. Johnson* (1995), 29 W.C.B. (2d) 378 (B.C.S.C.) [*Johnson*]; *R. v. Stokes*, [1999] N.S.J. No. 170 (S.C.) [*Stokes*]; and *R. v. Lindskog* (1997) 117 C.C.C. (3d) 551 (Sask. Q.B.) [*Lindskog*].

68   Above note 34. An unusual variation is seen in *R. v. J.(G.P.)* (2001), 151 C.C.C. (3d) 382 (Man. C.A.), where counsel acted for the Crown on appeal after representing the complainant on a section 278.1 hearing at trial, and drew judicial censure as a result.

Crown evidence that is harmful to him or her but useful to a co-accused who is a former client.

As for the former client, he or she is perhaps most susceptible to harm, given that the retainer has come to an end and counsel has now, in the former client's view, taken on a new allegiance. Often the greatest fear for the former client is that confidential information will be improperly used.[69] The misuse of confidential information could occur in a myriad of ways. Counsel might cross-examine Crown witnesses in a manner designed to foreclose a defence that he or she knows, by virtue of confidences obtained through the prior retainer, will be used by a former client who is a co-accused. Crown evidence helpful to the co-accused could be objected to based on the same misuse of a confidence. One of the most serious risks that confidential information will be misused arises where the former client is a testifying co-accused or Crown witness who is exposed to cross-examination by counsel. Even if client-lawyer confidences are not in fact misused during cross-examination, the ex-client may be prone to his or her former lawyer's suggestions on cross-examination because of fear of misuse or because of familiarity and trust arising from the erstwhile relationship.

The above examples of harm to a former client involve the spectre of confidential information being misused. However, altogether apart from this possibility, counsel owes a broader duty of loyalty to a former client. As most rules of professional conduct suggest, a former client has a legitimate claim to expect counsel's loyalty to persist with respect to the subject matter of a retainer, even after the client-lawyer relationship has ended and even if there is little or no possibility that confidential information can be misused.[70] In such circumstances, courts are quite prepared to find that a reasonable member of the public would hold the integrity of the justice system in considerably less esteem if, despite the protests of the former client, the original lawyer was permitted to launch an all-out attack.[71]

---

69    See, for example, *Speid*, above note 27 at 22.

70    See, for example, CBA Code ch. V, comm. 8; Ont. r. 2.04(4); B.C. ch. 6, r. 7(b); and Sask. ch. V, comm. 8.

71    See, for example, *R. v. B.(B.P.)* (1992), 71 C.C.C. (3d) 392 at 400–01 (B.C.S.C.) [*B.(B.P.)*]; *R. v. Louie* (1992), O.J. No. 67 (Prov. Div.) (QL) [*Louie*]; *Silvini*, above note 24; *Speid*, above note 27; *R. v. DePatie* (1970), 2 C.C.C. (2d) 339 (Ont. C.A.) [*DePatie*]; and *Booth v. Huxter* (1994), 16 O.R. (3d) 528 (Div. Ct.) [*Booth*]. See also P. Perell, "*Drabinsky v. KPMG* and *Bolkiah v. KPMG*: Disqualifying Conflicts of Interest in the Legal, Accounting, and Consulting Professions in Canada and England" (2001) 24 Advocates' Q. 109 at 116–17.

**Comparison**: Most Canadian rules of professional conduct make clear that counsel may be prohibited from acting against a former client even where there is no risk that confidential information will be misused.[72] American ethical standards tend to take the same view.[73] However, the Alberta rule regarding former clients seems to focus solely on the misuse of confidential information,[74] and the rules in Australia and New Zealand take the same stance.[75]

"Material adversity" should be a key concept in identifying conflict-of-interest involving successive representation, because the potential for adversity is intimately linked to the risk of harm. Yet some rules of professional conduct instead stipulate that the prohibition against successive representation arises where counsel "acts against" the former client.[76] The meaning of the phrase "acting against" is open to different interpretations. It has been suggested that defence counsel who cross-examines a former client who is an adverse Crown witness is not "acting against" a former client, because the former client is not a party in the case and in particular is not an accused and hence faces no jeopardy in the proceedings.[77] It has also been held that "acting against" within the meaning of the ethical rules does not encompass counsel's broadcast activities that cause harm to a former client.[78] However, in our view this narrow interpretation of "acting against" should not be used to support a less stringent conflict-of-interest test where counsel is poised to cross-examine a former client turned Crown witness. The duty of loyalty owed to a former client is broad and should not be attenuated simply because the client is not a named party in a proceeding or does not face criminal sanctions. Where there is no real adversity between the former and present clients, however, conflict-of-

---

72   See the rules referred to in note 70, above.

73   See for example, ABA Model Rule 1.9; and Third Restatement §132.

74   Alta. ch. 6, r. 3 (but see r. 4 concerning transfer of counsel to another law firm, and especially comm. 4(c)(3), which prohibits acting against a former client even though no confidential information is held by counsel). See also ABA Defense Standard 4-3.5(d).

75   See S. Ross, *Ethics in Law: Lawyers' Responsibility and Accountability in Australia* (Sydney: Butterworths, 1998) at 349; and G. Dal Pont, *Lawyers' Professional Responsibility in Australia and New Zealand* (North Ryde, N.S.W.: LBC Information Services, 1996) at 185–87.

76   See Ont. r. 2.04(4).

77   See *Dix*, above note 23 at 29.

78   See *Stewart*, above note 21 at 115.

interest problems are less likely.[79] We therefore prefer the "materially adverse" terminology used in leading American codes.[80]

To sum up, the dangers associated with successive representation are clearly linked to circumstances where some aspect of counsel's duty of loyalty, including but not limited to the duty of confidentiality, is compromised. Accordingly, a conflict-of-interest will arise: (i) where counsel may be tempted to reveal confidential information obtained during the course of the retainer with the former client; *or* (ii) where counsel who has formerly represented a client in a matter is poised to represent another client in the same or any related matter, in which the former and present clients' interests are materially adverse.

## 2) Misuse of Confidential Information

Having said that a breach of the duty of loyalty can lead to a conflict-of-interest even where confidential information is not susceptible to misuse, the fact remains that the improper use of such information is often a key concern in cases of successive representation. How do courts assess the danger in this regard? The leading case on point is the decision of the Supreme Court of Canada in *MacDonald Estate* v. *Martin*. As already discussed, *MacDonald Estate* holds that a conflict-of-interest exists whenever there is a "possibility of real mischief" regarding the misuse of confidential information. *MacDonald Estate* goes further, however, in setting out rules and presumptions for determining when a possibility of real mischief exists. To begin with, in order to determine whether a disqualifying conflict-of-interest exists, one must ask whether the public, as represented by a reasonably informed person, would be satisfied that no use of confidential information will occur. In so satisfying this hypothetical person, two questions must typically be answered: (1) Did the lawyer receive confidential information attributable to a client-lawyer relationship relevant to the matter at hand? And is there a risk that any such information will be used to the prejudice of the former client?[81]

In answering the first question, *MacDonald Estate* states that the starting point is to determine whether there existed a previous client-lawyer relationship that is sufficiently related to the retainer on the matter before the court. If so, a court should infer that confidential information has passed unless the lawyer satisfies the court that no

---

79   See, for example, *R.* v. *Pryor* (1997), 34 W.C.B. (2d) 138 (N.B. Q.B.(T.D.)).

80   See ABA Model Rule 1.9; and Third Restatement §132.

81   See *MacDonald Estate*, above note 3 at 1259–60.

information was imparted that could be relevant.[82] In attempting to discharge this burden (termed "heavy" by Mr. Justice Sopinka, writing for the majority), the lawyer must not reveal the specifics of any confidential communication. Moreover, the degree of satisfaction necessary to justify a holding that no confidential information was communicated must be gauged from the perspective of the reasonably informed member of the public.[83]

As for the second question — pertaining to risk of prejudice to the client — *MacDonald Estate* holds that a lawyer with confidential information from a professional relationship sufficiently related to the matter in question simply cannot act against a former client. The prohibition is strict, for in the words of Mr. Justice Sopinka:

> No assurances or undertakings not to use the information will avail. The lawyer cannot compartmentalize his or her mind so as to screen out what has been gleaned from the client and what was acquired legitimately because it might be perceived to have come from the client. This would prevent the lawyer from adequately representing the new client. Moreover, the former client would feel at a disadvantage. Questions put in cross-examination about personal matters, for example, would create the uneasy feeling that they had their genesis in the previous relationship.[84]

Automatic disqualification is the mandated result, even where (as in *MacDonald Estate* itself) affidavits are sworn by the counsel concerned to the effect that confidential information will not be misused.[85] Such a conclusion is warranted because a reasonably informed member of the public would look askance at continued representation based on the assurances of the lawyers in whose financial interest it is to keep the case.[86]

---

82  Mr. Justice Cory, in a dissent joined by two of the seven judges, appears to take the view that the inference that confidential information has passed is irrebuttable: see *MacDonald Estate*, above note 3 at 1264–65.

83  *Ibid.* at 1260–61.

84  *Ibid.* at 1261.

85  On the facts of *MacDonald Estate*, counsel for one side in a civil dispute joined a firm that represented the former client's adversary, though she did not work on the file at her new firm. Lawyers in the new firm swore affidavits stating that the transferring lawyer had not shared her confidential knowledge with those colleagues actually working on the file.

86  See, however, the discussion in sections H(5), "The Use of Independent (Screened) Counsel," and M(2), "Screening," in this chapter, which details how lawyers may be able to get around this demanding view.

## 3) Existence of a Client-lawyer Relationship

Where counsel for an accused has had previous contact with a Crown witness or a co-accused, but was never retained, there may be a preliminary issue as to whether communications occurred in the context of a client-lawyer relationship. If there was no such relationship, no fiduciary duty exists and the attendant obligations of loyalty, and hence confidentiality, ordinarily cannot arise.[87] It is important to remember, however, that a client-lawyer relationship is formed as soon as a potential client has his or her first dealings with a lawyer in order to obtain legal advice, and does not in any way depend upon the existence of a formal retainer.[88]

On the other hand, by no means does every contact with a lawyer result in a client-lawyer relationship.[89] Such a relationship arises only where the exchange of information can be seen to have occurred for the purpose of obtaining legal advice.[90] The existence of this precondition is determined by adopting the perspective of a reasonable member of the public who is fully informed of the circumstances. The subjective belief of the person consulting the lawyer is thus not governing on the point.

**Example**: A Crown witness approaches defence counsel in order to obtain legal advice with respect to her involvement in the matter. She is immediately and clearly told by counsel that he cannot represent her because of the pre-existing retainer with the accused. Counsel nevertheless wants to obtain a witness statement, and to this end requests an interview, with the express stipulation that the communications are not taking place in the context of a client-lawyer relationship and attract no duty of confidentiality. The witness agrees, and an interview takes place. In this example, no client-lawyer relationship can reasonably be seen to exist, and any understanding to the contrary by the witness is irrelevant.[91]

---

87  This general proposition comes, however, with the caveat that a duty of confidentiality can sometimes be owed to a third party who was never a client or prospective client: see section I, "Joint Defences," in this chapter.

88  See section H(6), "Information Can be Confidential Even in the Absence of a Retainer," in chapter 4.

89  See, for example, *R. v. McCulloch* (1992), 73 C.C.C. (3d) 451 (Ont. Gen. Div.); and *R. v. Doucet* (1994), 89 C.C.C. (3d) 474 (Man. C.A.), aff'd (1995), 95 C.C.C. (3d) 287 (S.C.C.).

90  See *Descôteaux*, above note 38 at 481.

91  See, for example, *R. v. Bennett*, [1991] O.J. No. 2503 (P.D.); see also *R. v. Bilotta* (1999), 139 C.C.C. (3d) 183 at 183–87 (Ont. S.C.J.).

It warrants emphasis, however, that courts will not rely on technical and esoteric analyses to avoid finding that a client-lawyer relationship exists and thus permit counsel to escape a conflict problem.[92] Moreover, some rules of professional conduct impose a duty of care on a lawyer to ensure that an unrepresented person is not proceeding under the impression that his or her interests will be protected by the lawyer.[93]

## 4) Relevance of Confidential Information or Retainer to the Matter at Hand

*MacDonald Estate* notes that the confidential information need be "relevant to the matter at hand" in order to create a conflict. Relevance of the communication to the matter at hand is an important consideration in assessing whether a conflict-of-interest exists, for the greater the relevance the greater the likelihood that the communication may be used and/or revealed by counsel during the course of the proceeding. Even where the possible misuse of information is not in issue, it is important to assess the relevance of the retainer with the former client to the matter at hand. The closer the connection, the more likely that the lawyer will take a position materially adverse to a former client and hence compromise the duty of loyalty.

It is worth recalling that the lawyer who seeks to fight off a removal application is severely constricted in arguing that the subject matter of any implicated confidential information is not relevant to the matter at hand. As stipulated in *MacDonald Estate*, counsel cannot put information before the court in an attempt to rebut an assertion of relevance if to do so would reveal the specifics of a client-lawyer communication.[94] It is therefore likely that any reasonable assertion by the former client that relevant confidential information passed will be accepted by the court. However, in sharp contrast, it may be that a former client willingly reveals the contents of confidential communications, thereby

---

92   See, for example, CBA Code ch. VI, comm. 6, suggesting that a client-lawyer relationship will exist in certain cases where a person "might reasonably feel entitled to look to the lawyer for guidance and advice in respect of the transaction." Along these same lines, in *Bennett*, above note 91, the court noted that had counsel been slow or obscure in telling the witness that no client-lawyer relationship would be formed, the result might have been different.

93   See, for example, CBA Code ch. 5, comm. 12; Ont. r. 2.04(14); as well as the duty imposed by Alta. ch. 6, comm. 3.

94   *MacDonald Estates*, above note 3 at 1260–61.

demonstrating that the communications are not related to the case at hand. Suppose, for example, that a Crown witness was formerly represented by an associate of the accused's trial counsel. On a *voir dire* during a Crown application to remove counsel from the record because of a perceived conflict-of-interest, the witness testifies as to the complete (though brief) contents of the confidential conversation with the associate, clearly revealing the irrelevance of the communications to the subject matter of the current trial.[95]

Most criminal cases look at the subject matter of the communication in the context of potential conflict between the interests of the accused and a Crown witness formerly represented by counsel for the accused. Considerations of relevance naturally focus upon whether the subject matter of the previous and present retainers is the same or related. Will the subject matter of the previous retainer become relevant in the case at hand? Where the subject matter of the present and former retainer is the same or closely related, a finding of conflict is certainly much more likely.[96] Moreover, although the witness was represented on criminal charges totally unconnected to the case at hand, these charges may nonetheless form an important part of defence counsel's cross-examination on the issue of credibility, or there may be reason to believe that personal information will have passed between counsel and the former client that can be used in cross-examination.[97] In either instance, sufficient relevance is established. In other cases, courts have perceived the former retainer between counsel and the witness as unproblematic for a variety of reasons, including that the former retainer occurred in the distant past,[98] was brief in nature,[99] was

---

95    See *R. v. Cobb*, [1993] Q.J. No. 881 (S.C.) [*Cobb*].

96    See, for example, *DePatie*, above note 71; *Speid*, above note 27; *Robillard*, above note 3; *R. v. Atkinson* (1991), 68 C.C.C. (3d) 109 at 114–16 (Ont. C.A.), aff'd (1992), 76 C.C.C. (3d) 288 (S.C.C.); *B.(B.P.)*, above note 71; *R. v. Munro* (1990), 11 W.C.B. (2d) 659 (Ont. Prov. Div.) (same subject matter); and *R. v. S(A.)* (1996), 28 O.R. (3d) 663 at 668–69 (Gen. Div.) [*S.(A.)*] ("at least related in appearance").

97    See, for example, *R. v. Leask* (1996), 1 C.R. (5th) 132 (Man. Prov. Ct.) [*Leask*]; *S.(A.)*, above note 96.

98    See, for example, *R. v. Marr*, [1992] B.C.J. No. 1782 (S.C.); *R. v. K.(G.)* (1994), 25 W.C.B. (2d) 496 (Sask. Q.B.) [*K.(G.)*]; and *Johnson*, above note 67.

99    See, for example, *R. v. Dunn* (January 4, 1996), unreported decision of Phillips J. (Ont. Prov. Div.).

unrelated to any matter that could arise during trial,[100] or involved matters already known to the public.[101]

## 5) The Use of Independent (Screened) Counsel

It is sometimes suggested that a conflict arising out of successive representation can be avoided by using independent counsel at those points during the trial where the former and present clients' interests are adverse.[102] Using independent counsel in this way is most easily envisaged where the former client is a Crown witness and the site of adversity is easily delineated, for instance, during cross-examination of the former client. Of course, because the duty of loyalty owed to a former client requires counsel not just to refrain from taking an adverse position in same matter but also to protect all confidential information, the use of an independent counsel must involve employment of screening devices.[103] Since the potential efficacy of screening devices has been recognized by Canadian rules of professional conduct where a lawyer transfers from one firm to another, there is no reason why similar screening procedures cannot sometimes be effective in other circumstances concerning former clients and the risk of leaked confidential information.[104]

**Example**: Counsel A acts for a client charged with murder, and one week prior to trial receives disclosure that reveals a new Crown witness. The witness is a jailhouse informer formerly represented by both Counsel A and members of his firm on previous unrelated criminal matters. Immediately upon learning of the conflict problem, Counsel A hires an independent lawyer, Counsel X, to cross-examine the witness at trial, and swears an affidavit undertaking not to pass any confidential information on to this lawyer. All firm files related to the witness are sealed. All firm members, including support staff, swear an affidavit

---

100 See, for example, *Joyal*, above note 67 at 239; *Parsons*, above note 41; *R. v. Dafoe* (1996), 30 W.C.B. (2d) 273 (Ont. Gen. Div.); *R. v. Judge* (1997), 201 A.R. 186 (Prov. Ct.) [*Judge*]; *K.(G.)*, above note 98; *R. v. Cousins* (1998), 176 Nfld. & P.E.I.R. 1 (Nfld. T.D.) (counsel was however disqualified on other grounds); *R. v. Desimone* (1999), 41 W.C.B. (2d) 418 (Ont. Prov. Div.); and *R. v. Spence* (1996), 32 W.C.B. (2d) 125 (Ont. Gen. Div.) [*Spence*].
101 See, for example, *Spence*, above note 100.
102 See *Dix*, above note 23, especially at 33–34; and *R. v. Stephenson* (1999), 138 C.C.C. (3d) 562 (Ont. S.C.J.) [*Stephenson*].
103 See, for example, section M(2), "Screening," in this chapter.
104 See *Dix*, above note 23 at 27.

undertaking not to discuss confidential information received from the witness with one another or anyone else, including Counsel X. All firm members agree in writing that breach of the undertaking must be reported immediately to the Crown, and is grounds for dismissal from the firm. For her part, Counsel X undertakes in writing that she will not receive any confidential information from Counsel A or his firm regarding the witness, and will receive all disclosure relevant to the witness directly from the Crown. Finally, the client obtains independent legal advice from yet another lawyer, after which he provides a waiver that includes approval of the steps taken by Counsel A. In these circumstances, the screening measures may well operate to permit Counsel A to stay on the case.[105]

Even if screening devices can be employed, some courts have with good reason been reluctant to permit the use of independent counsel as a means of side-stepping a conflict-of-interest issue.[106] There may be a lingering concern that confidential information can be misused in ways other than the cross-examination of the former client. It may also be that, while confidential information can be insulated from misuse, employing independent counsel fails to answer adequately the concern that a lawyer should not take a position adverse to a former client regarding the same or a related subject matter. There are a myriad of points during the conduct of the defence when counsel can arguably be disloyal in exactly this manner, for example, by criticizing the former client during the defence opening, eliciting testimony from Crown witnesses that helps to attack the former client's credibility, calling witnesses who contradict the former client, or disparaging the ex-client in the closing to the trier of fact. Indeed, leaving specific examples aside, the general function of helping an accused who takes a position materially adverse to the former client can be seen as highly problematic in light of counsel's persisting duty of loyalty to ex-clients.

---

105 This example approximates the facts in *Dix, ibid.* As the *Dix* court appreciated, many other factors have an impact on the decision whether such screening measures are acceptable in the circumstances. For other cases that permit independent counsel to cross-examine a former client, see *Parsons* v. *Newfoundland (Minister of Justice)* (1999), 142 C.C.C. (3d) 347 (Nfld. C.A.); and *Stephenson,* above note 102.

106 See, for example, *Leask,* above note 96; *S.(A),* above note 97; and *R.* v. *Werkman* (1997), 6 C.R. (5th) 221 (Q.B.) [*Werkman*].

# I.  JOINT DEFENCES

Conflict of interest concerns may surface where two or more co-accused and their respective lawyers agree to share information in order to promote a common defence interest. We can examine the potential for conflict by considering an example. Suppose that Accused A and Accused B are jointly charged with murder and retain separate counsel. Counsel A and Counsel B decide to share information in pursuit of a joint-defence interest, and to this end they speak to each other's client and exchange information, legal memoranda, witness interviews, and so on. In spite of this extensive cooperation, at the close of the Crown case, Accused A abruptly abandons the common interest and adopts a cutthroat defence. Testifying on his own behalf, Accused A says that he saw Accused B on the night of the murder, and that Accused B was covered in blood and admitted to stabbing the deceased. Counsel B hears this testimony in disbelief, for in numerous joint-defence meetings, Accused A never once implicated her client. Moreover, Counsel B has a raft of information obtained under the joint-defence arrangement that she feels would be useful in cross-examining Accused A. As soon as Accused A finishes testifying, Counsel B jumps to her feet, ready to begin the cross-examination. She is cut off by Counsel A, who announces that he is bringing an application to disqualify her based on a conflict-of-interest.

This example roughly reflects the factual setting found in the well-known case of *R. v. Dunbar*,[107] although in *Dunbar* the lawyer representing the "turncoat" accused did not seek to disqualify co-counsel, nor did the Court of Appeal address this conflict-of-interest issue. Certainly, the disqualification application occurring in our example would be novel in Canada. Nevertheless, the example raises complicated conflict-of-interest issues that cannot by any means be dismissed outright. Let us examine these issues in more detail.

The argument in support of removing counsel is based upon the supposition that information exchanged under a joint-defence arrangement is confidential. To elaborate, joint-defence privilege has been applied in a number of Canadian cases, following the United Kingdom case of *Buttes Gas and Oil Co. v. Hammer (No. 3)*.[108] The main Canadian criminal law decision on point is *Dunbar* itself. Since the existence of confidentiality is a *sine qua non* of a privilege, it must be that the law similarly recognizes in Accused A a right to confidentiality arising out

---

107  (1982), 68 C.C.C. (2d) 13 (Ont. C.A.) [*Dunbar*].
108  [1980] 3 All E.R. 475 (C.A.).

the exchange of information with Accused B.[109] Consequently, Counsel B owes Accused A a duty not to reveal or misuse such information without Accused A's consent. However, this duty of confidentiality clashes with Counsel B's duty of loyalty to her client, the latter duty mandating that all available information be marshalled to attack the "turncoat" Accused A. The conflict between these duties is thus somewhat comparable to the conflict that arises where defence counsel possesses confidential information from a former client who is an adverse witness against a present client.[110] That is to say, Accused A faces harm by reason of the improper use of the information (like the former client in a successive-representation scenario), while Accused B may suffer if Counsel B is overly cautious in attempting not to breach confidentiality (like the current client in a successive-representation scenario). A strict application of the test in *MacDonald Estate* v. *Martin* to the joint-defence example would probably result in the disqualification of Counsel B.

Of course, *MacDonald Estate* sets out a test that is expressly based on the notion that confidential information has passed *which is attributable to a client-lawyer relationship*. Should information passing under a joint-defence arrangement be viewed in this way? There is Canadian authority suggesting as much.[111] Moreover, some rules of professional conduct have been judicially interpreted to the same effect. In particular, the CBA Code and Ontario rules pertaining to conflict-of-interest prohibit a lawyer who has acted for a client in a matter from thereafter acting not only against the client in the same or related matter but also against "persons associated with the client."[112] Since Counsel B's client is associated with Accused A for the purpose of promoting a common defence, it can be argued that this ethical prohibition covers any counsel who, by reason of communications passing during the preparation of a joint-defence, obtains confidential information from a co-accused who has separate representation.[113] If the interests of the co-accused become adverse, there is an argument that the potential for conflict-of-interest has arisen.

The argument in favour of disqualifying Counsel B is open to the criticism that the duty of confidentiality created when information is

---

109  See *Dunbar*, above note 107 at 36, as well as section D, "Comparison with Legal-Professional Privilege," in chapter 4.

110  See section H(2), "Misuse of Confidential Information," in this chapter.

111  See, for example, *Almecon Industries Ltd.* v. *Nutron Manufacturing Ltd.* (1994), 55 C.P.R. (3d) 327 (F.C.T.D.), aff'd (1994), C.P.R. (3d) 69 (F.C.A.) [*Almecon*].

112  CBA Code ch. V, comm. 8; and Ont. r. 2.04(4).

113  See *Almecon*, above note 111. See also the Third Restatement §132, comm. g(ii).

exchanged under a joint-defence arrangement does not equate with the panoply of duties arising under a client-lawyer relationship. Accordingly, Accused A should not be regarded as the equivalent of a former client of Counsel B. Moreover, the duty of confidentiality owed by Counsel B must be informed by the nature and scope of joint-defence arrangements. From the outset, any participating accused should recognize that he or she may be cross-examined by counsel for a co-accused, and that circumstances may alter so that adversity arises between parties to the arrangement. In this light, it seems fair to define the duty of confidentiality so as to permit Counsel B to take a position adverse to Accused A, even during the cross-examination of Accused A, as long as confidential information received from Accused A is not misused.

Moreover, permitting Counsel B to cross-examine Accused A does not necessarily run afoul of those rules of professional conduct that refer to "persons associated with a client." This language has not been adopted by a number of provincial governing bodies, but in any event it is best seen as promoting loyalty to counsel's current or former clients. Acting against a person closely connected to a client or former client in a related matter can be seen as an act of disloyalty to the client. Prohibiting such activity is understandable. In sharp and total contrast, however, it may be in a client's best interest to act against a former associate, and in such a case the prohibition should be inapplicable.[114] Interpreting the rules of professional conduct to create a broad ethical obligation that harms a current client is counter-intuitive and should be avoided in the context of joint-defence arrangements.

Without a doubt, however, the rules of professional conduct bear upon the obligation of loyalty owed by Counsel B to her own client. For instance, if Counsel B is to cross-examine Accused A, her client may have concerns that she will overcompensate to avoid revealing confidential information, to the detriment of the defence. This sort of concern is not restricted to the cross-examination of Accused A, and it could realistically apply to any circumstance in which Accused B was adverse in interest to Accused A. As a result, as soon as adversity between the two accused arises, Counsel B should fully discuss the matter with her client, and she should continue to act only if the client consents to her doing so.

---

114 Compare *S.(A.)*, above note 96, where the court rejected the blanket proposition that counsel owes an obligation of loyalty to an individual whom he or she calls as a witness in an earlier matter.

**Recommendation**: Given the murkiness of the law in this area and the instability of joint-defence arrangements, counsel should exercise care when speaking with co-accused or exchanging information with co-counsel. Where the sharing of information in pursuit of a common interest is in the client's interest, a written joint-defence agreement is probably a good idea. Such an agreement may operate to circumvent conflict-of-interest problems, in particular by expressly stating the expectations of the participating accused and the scope of the duty of confidentiality.

## J.  THIRD-PARTY PAYMENT OF FEES

An arrangement whereby a third-party pays some or all of a client's fees and disbursements will often raise the spectre of an impermissible conflict-of-interest. The obvious danger created by third-party payment, no matter the size or the proportion of the total fee paid, is that the lawyer will favour the interests of the third-party over those of the client. Any potential for adversity of interest between the client and a third-party payer of fees should thus trigger alarm bells for counsel. While professional-conduct rules in Canada by and large do not address the issue of conflict-of-interest and third-party payments, there is no doubt that this scenario easily fits within the general prohibition against conflict-of-interest and related guiding principles.

**Comparison**: The Alberta rules are unique among Canadian ethical guidelines, in so far as they discuss conflict-of-interest where counsel acts for the payer (that is, a multiple-representation scenario). However, the Alberta rules do not expressly mention how third-party payment might on its own cause a conflict-of-interest.[115] In contrast, third-party payment is identified as a conflict-of-interest problem in ABA Model Rule 1.8(f), which provides that a lawyer shall not accept compensation from a third-party unless the client consents after consultation, there is no interference with the lawyer's independence of professional judgment, and the client's confidences are protected.[116]

The funding of a young person's defence by his or her parents provides especially rich potential for conflict-of-interest.[117] The parents

---

115  See Alta. ch. 9, comm. 9.1 & 9.2.

116  See ABA Model Rule 1.8(f) (see also the related Model Rule 5.4(c)); and Third Restatement §134(1).

117  See also section M(2), "The Role of the Parent," in chapter 3.

may have a particular idea as to how the matter should be handled, one that clashes with the young person's interests. For instance, the parents may insist that the young person plead guilty regardless of a strong *Charter* argument. Or they may demand that all information received by counsel be relayed to them regardless of the young person's wishes to the contrary. Perhaps because of these sorts of concerns, the *Young Offenders Act* provides that:

> [i]n any case where it appears to a youth court judge or a justice that the interests of a young person and his parents are in conflict or that it would be in the best interest of the young person to be represented by his own counsel, the judge or justice shall ensure that the young person is represented by counsel independent of his parents.[118]

It is thus especially important to remember that professional obligations are owed to the young person, not the parents, where the parents are paying for counsel's services. Providing financial aid does not allow the parent to assume the position of instructing client, nor to exercise greater influence over counsel.

Concerns should also be raised where the client's legal expenses are to be paid in whole or part by a co-accused, an unindicted co-conspirator, or the alleged head of a criminal organization.[119] This sort of third party may fear that the accused will cooperate with the prosecution, and pressure counsel to prevent such an outcome. Or the third party may wish the matter to go to trial, despite the availability of a favourable plea bargain for the accused, in order to resolve a legal issue important to the third party.[120] In the United States, third-party fee arrangements involving alleged partners in crime have also exposed clients to harm in another way: the prosecution has subpoenaed defence counsel in order to obtain evidence of the payment, which is then used to show participation in a criminal conspiracy.[121]

Payment by a third party may raise conflict-of-interest issues, but such an arrangement can also provide the obvious benefit to the client of having the cost of legal representation paid by another. It is therefore proper to accept a third-party payment where the client gives a

---

118  *Young Offenders Act*, R.S.C. 1985, c. Y-1, s. 11(8).

119  See, for example, *R. v. Stork* (1975), 24 C.C.C. (2d) 210 (B.C.C.A.). A leading case in the United States covering this sort of situation is *Wood v. Georgia*, 450 U.S. 261 (1981) [*Wood*]. See generally Lowenthal, above note 48 at 950–61.

120  See, for example, *Wood*, above note 119 at 267–70.

121  See, for example, R. Roszkewycz, "Third Party Payment of Criminal Defence Fees: What Lawyers Should Tell Potential Clients and Their Benefactors Pursuant to (an Amended) Model Code 1.8(f)" (1994) 7 Geo. J. Legal Ethics 573.

fully informed consent, provided always that it is reasonably likely that counsel will be able to provide adequate representation to the client.[122] Another option is to have the third party lend or give the client money sufficient to cover legal fees. Frequently, however, the third-party will not be willing to cede all control over the financial aspects of the retainer, and the conflict problem therefore cannot be circumvented in this manner.

While payment of legal expenses under a legal aid or public defender plan falls within the rubric of third-party payments, institutional arrangements that insulate counsel from any persons or agencies whose interests are potentially adverse to the client should obviate the need for counsel to obtain a client's consent. However, where such arrangements are not in place or where, for any other reason, counsel feels that his or her loyalty to the client is being compromised, the matter must be addressed immediately.

**Recommendation**: It is always wise to discuss the terms of the retainer and the risk of conflict-of-interest with the third party, in addition to the client.[123] Although the third party is owed no duty of loyalty, failure to explain to the payer the preconditions upon which the retainer is accepted invites discord and upset down the road. Accordingly, the Alberta rule dealing with third-party payments states: "[T]he lawyer should be satisfied that the financially responsible party understands the significance of the characterization of the other party as sole client and, in particular, that the financially responsible party will have no right to request or receive confidential information regarding the matter."[124] Failure to take this step could lead to a disgruntled third-party refusing payment or seeking the return of the retainer on the ground that the limits imposed by the duty of confidentiality and conflict-of-interest concerns were never made clear.

**Caveat**: Even if the conflict issue is satisfactorily resolved, the lawyer's duty of confidentiality owed to the client cannot be breached by revealing such information to the third party. In general, confidential information can be released to the third party only where the client expressly consents.

---

122 See ABA Model Rule 1.8(f); and Third Restatement §134 & §122 (regarding consent).

123 Roszkewycz, , above note 121, states that this point is crucial, and the same tack is taken in Alberta: see Alta. ch. 9, comm. 9.2. However, the relevant provisions of the ABA Model Rules and Third Restatement do not require discussion with the third-party.

124 Alta. ch. 9 comm. 9.2.

A separate but related issue is whether a third party should ever be permitted to direct the course of the representation.[125] In particular, the third party may wish some control over how, and how much, money is spent.[126] Similarly, a third party with responsibility for the accused, such as a parent or care giver, may sometimes desire involvement in decisions that the accused, if more sophisticated or mature, would ordinarily make alone. In this latter case, there may even be no financial ties between the lawyer and third party, for example, when legal aid covers the retainer for the representation of a young person. If such a role is to be played by a third party, fully informed consent of the client is a mandatory precondition. Moreover, the direction permitted by a third party must "be reasonable in scope and character."[127] Directions that are clearly to the disadvantage of the client can never be countenanced.

# K.  LAWYER AS WITNESS

The objections associated with counsel appearing as a witness involve the potential for harm to both the client's interests and the interests of the opposing party. While the Canadian rules of professional conduct that specifically address the advocate-witness problem do not mention conflict-of-interest,[128] the general rules dealing with conflict remain relevant. In particular, counsel's role as a witness, or his or her interest in being or not being a witness, may clash with the duties owed to the client. For instance, if counsel's evidence will hurt the client's defence, providing testimony will at the least undermine the duty of loyalty. Counsel will also be in a conflict-of-interest where testimony, though favourable to a current client, is materially adverse to a former client with respect to the same or a substantially related matter.

**Complication:** An impermissible conflict-of-interest may exist even where the lawyer's testimony falls within one of the exceptions to the advocate-witness rule set out in the professional-conduct rules. Thus,

---

125  See ABA Model Rule 5.4(c); and Third Restatement §134(2).

126  Such is invariably the case in any Legal Aid or public defender scheme.

127  Third Restatement §215(2).

128  See, for example, CBA Code ch. X, comm. 5; Ont. r. 4.02; Alta. ch. 10, r. 10; B.C. ch. 8, r. 9–10; and Sask. ch. IX, comm. 5. Although conflict-of-interest is not mentioned, Alberta is one of the few jurisdictions where the applicable advocate-witness rule speaks in terms of a lawyer's objectivity being compromised: see Alta. ch. 10, comm. 10.

while uncontroverted testimony does not contravene the advocate-witness rule, where such testimony is adverse to a current or former client it surely raises a conflict-of-interest concern. It may also be that counsel has evidence helpful to a client but wishes to avoid testifying (perhaps to side-step damage to reputation, an attack on credibility, or, most obviously, loss of a retainer fee). A decision not to testify avoids contravention of the advocate-witness rule yet raises a real concern regarding conflict-of-interest.

Depending on the circumstances, consent by the client may be capable of satisfactorily curing the *conflict-of-interest* aspect of an advocate-witness problem (where the lawyer decides to testify, however, problems may still arise under the advocate-witness rule). If a conflict-of-interest issue is susceptible to being cured in this way, the consent should have the same effect regarding an affiliated lawyer.[129]

**Example**: Counsel attends at the police station to surrender a client. The police take a statement, which is subject to a possible challenge based on right to counsel and right to silence arguments. The events occurring in counsel's presence are somewhat contentious, and the facts as ultimately found by the court would affect any *Charter* challenge. Counsel's testimony would support the client's best interests. The chances of successfully keeping the statement out of evidence are quite modest; many lawyers would forego a *Charter* application, but to bring a challenge would not be clearly unreasonable. Counsel is of the view that a *Charter* application should not be brought. However, he has a personal stake in the decision. Choosing to testify runs the risk of disqualification under the advocate-witness rule (and thus loss of the retainer). Taking the stand will also subject the lawyer's credibility to attack. Given these facts, counsel's loyalties are potentially divided when it comes to advising the client whether or not to undertake the *Charter* challenge. Full disclosure, independent legal advice, and waiver from the client will probably cure the problem.

---

129 A number of Canadian professional-conduct rules state that where a lawyer who appears as a witness is precluded from acting on the case, affiliated lawyers are, "generally speaking," also precluded from acting: see, for example, CBA Code ch. IX, comm. 5; Alta. ch. 10, r. 10; and Sask. ch. IX, comm. 5. Other rules of professional conduct do not adopt this blanket prohibition regarding affiliated lawyers: see, for example, Ont. r. 4.02; and B.C. ch. 8, r. 9. In the United States, the latter position is adopted by ABA Model Rule 3.7 and the Third Restatement §108. For a discussion of the Canadian case law on point, see Perell, above note 12 at 79–85.

# L.  LAWYER'S FINANCIAL AND OTHER PERSONAL INTERESTS

There are many instances where counsel's financial or other interests come into conflict with the duty of loyalty to a client. Some have already been discussed.[130] The general approach must be to look-out for, and avoid, any situation where a decision must be made or action taken on behalf of the client that simultaneously affects the lawyer's own financial or other interests. Some instances where a conflict of this sort may arise are set out below.

## 1)  Counsel's Alleged Involvement in Facts Relevant to the Retainer

Counsel's alleged involvement in facts relevant to the retainer (whether correct or not) should always raise conflict-of-interest alarm bells, completely apart from any question of becoming a witness in the matter. In particular, counsel's self-interest in protecting his or her reputation can influence the retainer in a myriad of ways, including the cross-examination of Crown witnesses, decisions on whether and how to call a defence, and the substance of submissions to the judge or jury.

**Example**: An accused rejects a Crown offer to plead guilty on a number of charges in return for a forty-five-month sentence. In light of this decision, the charges are to be dealt with at two separate trials. On the day of the first trial, the Crown witnesses do not appear. Crown counsel tells the defence lawyer that he believes the witnesses were paid money not to show, and that he plans to have both the accused and defence counsel investigated for a possible obstruction of justice. Defence counsel is extremely worried at the prospect of being investigated. He is successful in persuading the accused to accept the Crown's proposal for a forty-five-month sentence, knowing that the obstruction allegation will likely be dropped as a result. In doing so, counsel discloses the Crown's suspicions to his client, but the client receives no independent legal advice. The plea is accordingly entered as part of a joint position.

---

130  See sections J, "Third-Party Payment of Fees," and K, "Lawyer as Witness," in this chapter. In a sense, however, counsel's financial interest will run counter to his or her loyalty to the client *whenever* a potential conflict arises, given that there is usually a monetary incentive to continue to act.

On the facts of this example, defence counsel faced a substantial conflict and should not have acted or advised regarding the plea absent full disclosure to the client and independent legal advice.[131]

## 2) Acting as a Surety

Acting as a surety creates a substantial risk of conflict-of-interest, for the lawyer's duty of loyalty can easily clash with the obligations owed to the court as a surety, as well as the monetary loss that may result if the client breaches his or her recognizance.[132]

## 3) Taking an Assignment of a Bail Deposit or Seized Funds

Counsel who takes an assignment of a bail deposit to cover payment of fees and disbursements runs into a problem similar to that faced by counsel who acts as a surety. Acquiring a property interest in deposited funds will give counsel a strong interest in seeing that the funds are not depleted by reason of the client breaching bail or absconding. As an example, a lawyer in this position may be less inclined to fight strenuously against a Crown application to revoke bail following conviction, or may be tempted to encourage a nervous surety to pull the bail.

In a similar vein, counsel who takes an assignment of funds that have been seized under proceeds of crime provisions has an interest in protecting his or her property interest. The client's best interests may dictate that the funds be relinquished to the Crown as part of a plea

---

131 This example roughly reflects the facts in R. v. Laperrière (1995), 101 C.C.C. (3d) 462 (Que. C.A.), rev'd (1996), 109 C.C.C. (3d) 347 (S.C.C.). The pleas were quashed by the Supreme Court of Canada. See also Lavallee v. Canada (A.G.) (2000), 143 C.C.C. (3d) 187 at 199–200 (Alta. C.A.). One of the worst examples of a lawyer imprudently accepting a retainer where his reputation was at risk is seen in R. v. Henry (1990), 61 C.C.C. (3d) 455 (Que. C.A.) [Henry], where defence counsel was allegedly involved in the offence upon which he represented the accused. See also the problematic behaviour of counsel in R. v. Joubert (1993), 69 C.C.C. (3d) 553 (B.C.C.A.). In R. v. Ma (1978), 44 C.C.C. (2d) 511 at 514 (Ont. C.A.), the court opined that a lawyer involved in the factual background of a case should generally not act as counsel on the appeal.

132 See CBA Code ch. XIX comm. 9. G. Trotter, The Law of Bail in Canada, 2d ed. (Toronto: Carswell, 1999) at 294, states that "[a] lawyer ought not to stand as the accused's surety," though without express reference to the conflict-of-interest problem. Counsel who imprudently take on this obligation invite grief even if the client is not adversely affected: see, for example, R. v. Bucchianico (1998), 85 N.S.R. (2d) 284 (Co. Ct.).

agreement or that the client willingly concede forfeiture at a sentencing hearing, in order to avoid a fine or in exchange for reduced jail time. Yet counsel who has an interest in the funds will obtain the greatest benefit from exactly the opposite result, and for this reason an assignment of such funds creates a dangerous conflict-of-interest problem.[133]

## 4) Contingency Fees

With the exception of Ontario, all Canadian jurisdictions permit contingency fees.[134] Yet several provinces prohibit contingency fees in criminal matters, a prohibition rooted, at least in part, upon conflict-of-interest concerns. To provide an example, the client may be best advised to plead guilty rather than face a trial, whether or not a plea agreement is available, and yet counsel who is to be paid only upon an acquittal has an interest in taking the case to trial. At trial, the same counsel may be less inclined to run a defence that leaves open the possibility of conviction for a lesser charge. While similar conflict-of-interest concerns arise in civil cases, it is sometimes said that the public interest in prohibiting contingency fees is greater in criminal matters because of the substantial jeopardy faced by the client and the greater societal importance of obtaining a fair outcome.

## 5) Publication or Literary Rights

A lawyer who acquires publication rights from a client has an incentive to conduct the proceedings so as to maximize the monetary value of the story. Pleading guilty may not advance the attraction of the book-buying public to the case, and the decision of a client not to testify may similarly dampen sales. Counsel may also be more likely to indulge in dramatic and unusual trial tactics, or keep some information away from the trial record in the hope that a "revelation" of new information in a subsequent book will increase interest.

Conflict of interest rules adopted by Canadian governing bodies do not directly address the issue of publication or literary rights. Our rules

---

133 See *R. v. Pawlyk* (1991), 65 C.C.C. (3d) 63 (Man. C.A.); and *R. v. Wilson* (1993), 86 C.C.C. (3d) 464 (Ont. C.A.). This issue is also discussed in sections S, "Possession and Laundering of Proceeds of Crime," and T, "Forfeiture of Fees," in chapter 10.

134 A more thorough discussion is provided in section H, "Contingency Fees," in chapter 10.

of professional conduct in Canada only discuss this issue inferentially, in respect of the use of confidential information by a lawyer in a literary work (prohibited absent consent).[135] However, the American position is to impose a blanket prohibition on such arrangements prior to the conclusion of representation of the client.[136] It is generally thought that the conflict-of-interest is so serious that such an arrangement can never be countenanced, not even where counsel obtains the fully informed consent of the client.[137]

## 6) Business Relations with a Client

The opportunity for a lawyer to have business dealings with a client is more likely to occur in non-criminal settings. Nonetheless, criminal lawyers should be wary of conflict-of-interest problems if such an opportunity arises. There are certainly circumstances particular to criminal proceedings that can leave counsel with an interest potentially adverse to the client who is also a business associate. For instance, it may be in counsel's interest to have the client plead guilty in order to minimize the possibility of jail and thus increase the ability to pay back a loan or continue with a joint business enterprise.

**Recommendation**: An appearance of impropriety can arise by virtue of business dealings with a client who is under investigation or charge. Such dealings may attract police or Crown attention, and under these circumstances the lawyer may have a personal interest in self-protection that is adverse to the best interests of the client. It is therefore prudent to avoid assiduously business dealings where there is any such risk.[138]

## 7) Sexual Relationship with a Client

The rules of professional conduct generally forbid sexually harassment[139] but do not address the conflict-of-interest concerns that can arise out of a sexual relationship with a client. Entering into a sexual

---

135  See, for example, CBA Code ch. IV, comm. 5, and Ont. r. 2.03(6).

136  See, for example, ABA Model Rule 1.8(d); Third Restatement §36(3); and ABA Model Code DR 5-1.04(B).

137  See ABA Defense Standard 4-3.4.

138  In *White*, above note 24 at 264, the Ontario Court of Appeal notes that the prudent defence counsel will not engage in any kind of business dealings, however minor, with a client.

139  See, for example, Ont. r. 5.03(2).

relationship with a client is nonetheless fraught with conflict-of-interest dangers.[140] The lawyer may act to prolong or shorten proceedings depending upon whether he or she wishes to continue with the relationship. A relationship that ends in acrimony could also lead the lawyer to act out of spite and revenge to harm the client's case. Conversely, the relationship may operate to skew the client's view of the case and consequently affect the instructions given. In such instances, the general rule prohibiting conflict-of-interest would apply.

# M. AFFILIATED LAWYERS: IMPUTATION OF CONFLICT OF INTEREST

There is a strong presumption that members of a law firm share confidential information.[141] Additionally, lawyers in a firm inevitably have contractual, business and personal ties. To take but one example, a fee received by one lawyer may well benefit all partners and associates in the firm. As a result, where a lawyer has an actual or potential conflict-of-interest, such conflict is normally imputed to every lawyer in the firm.[142]

## 1) Office-Sharing Arrangements

Lawyers who are not members of the same firm but are associated for the purpose of sharing certain common expenses may in some circumstances be treated as affiliated so as to impute a conflict-of-interest.[143] Like partners or associates in a firm, these lawyers may share

---

140 See Y. Levy, "Attorneys, Clients and Sex: Conflicting Interests in the California Rule" (1992) 5 Geo. J. Legal Ethics 649; D. Filipovic, "The Sex Police Cometh: Lawyer-Client Sexual Relationships" (1993) 31 Alta. L. Rev. 391. Criminal consequences may also arise: see *R.* v. *Matheson* (1999), 134 C.C.C. (3d) 289 (Ont. C.A.). For a case where defence counsel initiated a sexual relationship with a client, and was ultimately disbarred for doing so, see *Adams* v. *Law Society of Alberta*, [2000] 11 W.W.R. 280 (Alta. C.A.).

141 See *MacDonald Estate*, above note 3 at 1262.

142 See CBA Code ch. V, comms. 3 & 9; Ont. r. 2.04(5); *MacDonald Estate*, above note 3 at 1262; *Speid*, above note 27 at 21; *Werkman*, above note 106; *Stephenson*, above note 102 at 565; *R.* v. *Neil* (1998), 235 A.R. 152 (Q.B.) [*Neil*], rev'd on other grounds (2000), 266 A.R. 363 (C.A.); and *Chen*, above note 37 at 278–80.

143 See *Neil*, above note 142. See *Spence*, above note 100, where the argument that office-sharing equated with affiliation between partners or associates was rejected.

client confidences while discussing files with one another (whether inadvertently or otherwise).

Many Canadian governing bodies treat lawyers who share office space as though they were partners or associates in the same firm *for at least some conflict-of-interest purposes*. The Alberta rules define "lawyer" and "firm" so as to treat lawyers in office-sharing arrangements as members of a single firm for all conflict-of-interest purposes.[144] Ontario used to take the more common approach, expressly addressing the office-sharing issue only in the discrete context of conflicts arising as a result of the transfer of a lawyer between law firms.[145] However, the new rules of professional conduct adopted by the Law Society of Upper Canada no longer encompass office-sharing arrangements even in this limited sphere.[146] The CBA and certain other governing bodies adopt yet another approach. They speak of an interest of "a partner or professional associate" and also purport to encompass "a lawyer who is associated with the lawyer in such a manner so as to be perceived as practising in partnership or association with the first lawyer, even though in fact no such partnership or association exists."[147] The British Columbia rules are a little unusual, in that office-sharing arrangements are arguably seen not to raise a conflict problem provided that sufficient disclosure is provided to the client and no question of transfer between law firms arises.[148]

There is a good argument that the rationale supporting the treatment of office-sharing lawyers as associates can apply to create a conflict-of-interest concern even where office-sharing arrangements are not expressly encompassed by the rules of professional conduct. Criminal lawyers who share office space must therefore take concrete steps to reduce the risk of leaking confidences and always be on the look-out for conflict problems.[149]

Of course, certain office-sharing arrangements are less likely to present conflict-of-interest problems. Where the office is organized and operated so that confidential information is not shared and is kept physically secure from review by others, no possible risks to loyalty and confidentiality exist and conflict-of-interest problems should not

---

144 See Alta. Interpretation 4(j) & (n); and ch. 6, comm. G(1).
145 See former Ont. r. 29(1)(c). The old Ontario rules also stated that conflicting interests include an interest of "an associate" of the lawyer: see r. 5, comm. 3. See also new r. 2.04(1).
146 Ont. r. 2.05; as well as the definition of "law firm" in r. 1.02.
147 See, for example, CBA Code ch. V, comm. 9.
148 See B.C. ch. 6.1, 6.2, & 7.1–7.9.
149 See section M(2), "Screening," in this chapter.

be imputed.[150] Consider, for instance, a sharing arrangement where each lawyer has a separate office that is locked after business hours, files are similarly kept discrete and secure, computer systems are not networked, support staff are not shared, and a formal written agreement between the lawyers states that no client confidences will be shared. Even if all office-sharing arrangements are automatically treated as the *prima facie* equivalent of a partnership for every conflict-of-interest purpose, it is submitted that such steps should typically constitute an effective screen so as to rebut the imputation of leaked confidences. Oddly enough, in Alberta (the one Canadian jurisdiction that treats office-sharing arrangements in something approaching this manner) these screening procedures would appear to work in some circumstances (for example, transfer of a lawyer to a new law firm)[151] but not others (for example, representation of co-accused).

## 2) Screening

In *MacDonald Estate* v. *Martin*, Mr. Justice Sopinka was prepared to impute a conflict-of-interest to all lawyers working in the same firm, yet he also appeared willing to allow for continued representation where the firm to which a "tainted" lawyer transfers implements formal steps approved by the legal profession to prevent the passing of the problematic confidential information to other lawyers in the firm.[152] Subsequent to *MacDonald Estate*, the Federation of Law Societies of Canada, a collection of the various bodies governing the legal profession in Canada, adopted a "Rule with Respect to Conflicts of Interest Arising as a result of Transfers between Law Firms." This rule draws upon a CBA Task Force Report which has been adopted by the Federation's constituent bodies.[153] The general rule by which all members of a firm are treated alike for the purposes of a conflict issue may therefore be subject to modification where steps can be taken to "screen" the lawyer who possesses confidential information.

---

150  See Third Restatement §123, comm. (e).

151  See Alta. ch. 6, r. 4.

152  See *MacDonald Estate* above note 3, at 1261–63. Cory J., writing for the minority on this point, was of the view that the confidential information must be irrebuttably imputed to all other members of the firm in order to preserve public confidence in the administration of justice: see *ibid.* at 1271.

153  See, Canadian Bar Association Task Force, *Conflict of Interest Disqualification: Martin v. Gray and Screening Methods* (Ottawa: Canadian Bar Association, 1993) [*CBA Task Force Report*]; and (for instance), Ont. r. 2.05; Alta. ch. 6, r. 4; B.C. ch. 6, comm. 7.1–7.9; and Sask. ch. VA.

The most common conflict problem that is susceptible to screening is the transfer of a lawyer possessing confidential information regarding a former client to a firm that represents a client having an adverse interest. Screening measures may be physical, in the sense that materials related to the new firm's client are kept away from the tainted lawyer, who does not work on or discuss the case with anyone at the firm. Measures may also be non-physical, in that the new firm adopts and circulates a written policy outlining the screening steps taken, requires that firm members provide affidavits or undertakings setting out their adherence to the policy, and informs all affected clients (including former clients) of the conflict problem and the steps taken. Ultimately, the ability of a screening mechanism to alleviate a conflict problem depends upon whether a reasonable person fully informed of the facts would be satisfied that no use of confidential information would occur.[154]

**Caveat**: Screening will not solve every conflict problem. For instance, if not implemented immediately, screening is unlikely to prevent a reasonable perception that confidences have been divulged. Also, screening has not been endorsed by Canadian governing bodies to permit affiliated lawyers to work simultaneously for clients who are adverse in interest. As an example, even rigid screening will not permit Partners A and B to represent Co-Accused A and B where the co-accused are adverse in interest.

An issue especially relevant in the criminal law context is whether screening can ever be effective when applied to the small firms in which defence lawyers often practice. To put the matter another way, the viability of a screen may be open to question where the size of the firm prevents meaningful implementation. Where few lawyers practise in a physical space that makes it difficult to institute effective screening procedures, courts will be reluctant to conclude that there is no perception that confidential information may be misused. It has been argued that, for this reason, and also given the weighty public and constitutional interests in ensuring the effective assistance of counsel,

---

154 See *MacDonald Estate*, above note 3 at 1262; *Ford Motor Company of Canada Ltd. v. Osler, Hoskin & Harcourt* (1996), 131 D.L.R. (4th) 419 at 440 (Ont. Gen. Div.); and *Canada Southern Petroleum* v. *Amoco Canada Petroleum Co.* (1997), 144 D.L.R. (4th) 30 at 41 (Alta. C.A.), leave to appeal to S.C.C. refused (1997), 216 N.R. 159n (S.C.C.). See also the discussion of screening in *Chen*, above note 37 at 279–80.

screening measures should never be applied in criminal cases.[155] If this position seems too stringent, its underlying concerns are nevertheless valid, and courts should not condone screening mechanisms in criminal cases absent real satisfaction as to their effectiveness.[156]

The impact of screening measures may also operate differently where Crown counsel or public defenders are concerned. Both the Crown and public defender lawyer may work in large offices, where screening measures are easily initiated.[157] Moreover, Crown and public defender law offices usually have multiple locations, which may go some way to creating a natural screening mechanism. It has thus been recognized that a Crown or public defender office "may be able to demonstrate that, because of its institutional structure, reporting relationships, function, nature of work, and geography, relatively fewer 'measures' are necessary to ensure the non-disclosure of client confidences."[158] Of course, where screening measures cannot be effectively implemented, the Crown or public defender will have to refer conduct of the matter to outside counsel.[159]

## N. WAIVER

Canadian professional-conduct rules suggest that, at least in some circumstances, a conflict-of-interest can be waived. For instance, the CBA Code's guiding rule regarding conflict-of-interest states that the lawyer, *"save after adequate disclosure to and with the consent of the clients or*

---

155 See J. Hall, Jr., *Professional Responsibility of the Criminal Lawyer*, 2d ed. (New York: Clark Boardman Callaghan, 1996) at §13.4. See also *Chen*, above note 37 at 281, where the court observed that "in a small, three-person firm such as theirs [i.e. the partner lawyers who faced the conflict], adequate institutional measures are difficult to imagine."

156 The *CBA Task Force Report*, above note 153 at 81–83, does not take the view that screening can never be effective where small firms are concerned, although the report does recognize that small firms may be less amenable to screening. The report does not, however, specifically deal with the issue of screening a member of a small firm in a criminal case.

157 *Ibid.* at 83.

158 Ont. r. 2.05(3) & 2.05(10)(c). Another way to approach the problem is to say that imputation is not warranted to begin with: see Third Restatement §123, comm. d(iii). We do not, however, advocate exempting the Crown altogether from imputed conflicts, and prefer the position taken in *Stokes*, above note 67 at paras. 6–8, and Hall, above note 155 at §13.9, to that apparently taken in *Lindskog*, above note 67 at 562–64.

159 Ont. r. 2.05(10)(c).

*prospective clients concerned*, shall not act in a matter when there is or is likely to be a conflicting interest."[160] The question of waiver can arise in numerous different circumstances. The difficulties lie in determining whether the waiver has been properly obtained, and whether in some circumstances even a fully informed waiver will be insufficient to cure a conflict problem.

## 1) Waiving a Constitutional Right

The first hurdle to be cleared in assessing the efficacy of a waiver stems from the fact that a constitutional right is at stake. The accused whose *current* counsel faces a potential conflict risks harm to his or her right to effective counsel. The accused whose *former* counsel is acting for a co-accused may also be able to claim *Charter* protection where a conflict issue arises.[161] Even a witness who is not an accused will likely be able to assert a *Charter* right in the face of cross-examination by current or former counsel who acts for an accused.[162] In sum, whether the conflict problem concerns an accused or witness, or a current as opposed to former client, constitutional rights are engaged.

How does waiver operate with respect to a constitutional right? We can start by observing that there is no general prohibition against an individual waiving a *Charter* guarantee.[163] Not surprisingly, therefore, the possibility of a valid waiver has been recognized in the conflict-of-interest context.[164] As with the relinquishment of any constitutional right, the standard for waiver in the conflict-of-interest context is high, especially where an accused whose liberty is in jeopardy purports to make the waiver. In *R. v. Silvini*, the Ontario Court of Appeal empha-

---

160 CBA Code ch. V (emphasis added). See also CBA Code ch. V, comm. 4–6; Ont. r. 2.04(3), 2.04(6) & 2.04(9); and Alta. ch. 6, r. 2–5, 6(b), 7 & 9, plus associated commentaries, and especially comm. 2.2.

161 In particular, the sanctity of legal-professional confidentiality as a fundamental legal right may be threatened: see *R. v. McClure* (2001), 151 C.C.C. (3d) 321 at 329 (S.C.C.) [*McClure*].

162 Discussions as to how the *Charter* might apply in the third-party-production context are of interest regarding this point: see, for example, *R. v. O'Connor* (1995), 103 C.C.C. (3d) 1 at 17 & 53–57 (S.C.C.); *R. v. Mills* (1999), 139 C.C.C. (3d) 321 (S.C.C.); *McClure*, above note 161; and *M.(A.) v. Ryan* (1997), 143 D.L.R. (4th) 1 at 8–9 & 11–12 (S.C.C.).

163 See *R. v. Turpin* (1989), 48 C.C.C. (3d) 8 (S.C.C.) [*Turpin*].

164 See, for example, *Silvini*, above note 24 at 261; *Henry*, above note 131 at 471–74; *S.(A.)*, above note 96 (waiver by Crown witness if present would solve problem); *McCallen*, above note 27 at 540; *Booth*, above note 71 at 538–39; *R. v. Berrardo* (1994), 93 C.C.C. (3d) 571 (Que. S.C.).

sized the need for clear and unequivocal evidence "that the person is waiving the implicated right and is doing so with full knowledge of the purpose of the right and the effect of a waiver."[165] Not surprisingly, Canadian rules of professional conduct stress the need for fully informed disclosure as a basis for consent.[166] In Alberta, "consent" is expressly defined by the ethical rules to mean "fully informed and voluntary consent after disclosure."[167]

**Caution**: The potential for confusion or misunderstanding on the part of the accused in waiving the right to be represented by non-conflicted counsel is significant. Understanding the concepts involved and appreciating the possible course that a trial might take are rarely straightforward. For this reason, some American courts have adopted a detailed procedure, undertaken on the record, by which the purported waiver is expressed and examined.[168] If a waiver is to have its intended effect, counsel must make full disclosure to the client, and obtaining independent legal advice is highly recommended in all but the most obvious and minor cases.[169]

## 2) Instances Where Waiver Cannot Overcome the Conflict Problem

In some circumstances, a fully informed waiver by all affected parties will provide a complete answer to a conflict problem. However, such is not always the case. Society at large has an interest, altogether apart from that of an accused (or anyone else), in promoting the administration of justice by avoiding conflict-of-interest, especially where the reliability of a criminal verdict may be at stake.[170] Even where all clients and former clients whose interests are or may be in conflict expressly consent to continued representation by the implicated counsel, this societal interest has not necessarily been accommodated. In this regard, care must be taken not to assume that the accused has an independent constitutional right to waive a *Charter* guarantee such as the right to effective counsel or to a fair trial. The ability to waive a constitutional right does not equate with a constitutional right to be tried

---

165  *Silvini*, above note 24 at 261.
166  See the rules cited at note 160, above.
167  Alta. Interpretation 4(f), in conjunction with ch. 6, comm. 2.2 & 3.
168  See, for example, *United States v. Garcia*, 517 F.2d 272 at 278 (5th Cir. 1975).
169  Disclosure and independent legal advice are discussed below in sections O(1)–(5).
170  See *Robillard*, above note 3 at 26.

in a proceeding involving counsel who has an actual or potential conflict-of-interest.[171]

On the other hand, there is a constitutional right whose *affirmation* — as opposed to waiver — can potentially offset or override the societal interest in avoiding a conflict-of-interest: the accused's right to counsel of choice. However, this right can be asserted only by an accused who is currently represented by the implicated counsel (a former client's right to counsel of choice will never be at stake). More importantly, while the assertion of the right to counsel of choice in combination with a waiver may in some cases operate to justify counsel remaining on the case, this right is not absolute.[172] Courts have generally defined the *Charter* guarantee of representation by counsel of choice so as to recognize an exception or limit where conflict-of-interest arises.[173] Canadian rules of professional conduct also make clear that consent will not solve every conflict-of-interest problem.[174] Consequently, even where all interested individual parties have provided fully informed waivers, the right can be overridden by the need to prevent harm to the justice system as a whole.[175] This result is sensible, given that the right to counsel of choice, while important, is arguably only partly infringed by an order disqualifying counsel.[176] In sum, waiver is a possible solution to a conflict-of-interest problem short of disqualifying counsel, but it does not always provide a complete and satisfactory answer to the problem.

**Example**: A husband and wife are jointly charged with manslaughter. The Crown case is much stronger against the husband, including DNA evidence and an inculpatory confession to the police. The husband's

---

171  This point is made by the Supreme Court of Canada in *Turpin*, above note 163 at 26–29. *Turpin* dealt with the right to a jury trial, which was held not to encompass a right to waive the benefit of a jury trial. The logic in *Turpin* applies equally where the rights to effective counsel and privacy are implicated in the context of a conflict-of-interest problem.

172  See *Speid*, above note 27 at 20; *Robillard*, above note 3 at 26;and *McCallen*, above note 27 at 532.

173  See, for example, *McCallen*, above note 27 at 532.

174  See, for example, CBA Code ch. V, r. 5 and commentary; Ont. r. 2.04(6)(c); Alta. ch. 6, and in particular comm. 2.1; and B.C. ch. 6, r. 2.

175  See *Robillard*, above note 3 at 27–28; *McCallen*, above note 27 at 540; *Booth*, above note 71 at 538–39. See also the leading American case on point, *Wheat* v. *United States*, 486 U.S. 153 (1988).

176  While counsel of first choice is prohibited, the accused will still be permitted to retain another lawyer of his or her choice: see D. Layton, "The Pre-trial Removal of Counsel for Conflict of Interest: Appealability and Remedies on Appeal" (1999) 4 Can. Crim. L. Rev. at 54.

confession contains several comments that tend to exonerate the wife. Moreover, the wife has a possible alibi defence. The husband and wife wish to retain a single counsel, despite independent legal advice to the contrary, and sign a waiver to this effect. On this scenario, a single counsel's loyalties would be so severely divided that it is not reasonable to presume that he or she could provide adequate representation to one or both clients. Counsel rash enough to accept the retainer should therefore be disqualified despite the presence of a waiver.

As a final point, waiver can never cure a conflict-of-interest problem where counsel is personally of the view that he or she will be unable to provide effective representation to a client.[177] There may be cases where a conflict is not so severe as to require automatic disqualification, but nevertheless in the circumstances a particular counsel reasonably feels unable to provide effective representation. Counsel who has any such concern should not act on the case, regardless of whether an effective waiver has been or can be provided.

## 3) Possible Revocation of the Waiver

A waiver is arguably subject to revocation. For instance, an accused may be willing to waive the right to have separate counsel based on expected and explained contingencies but seek to withdraw the waiver when an unexpected conflict-of-interest scenario develops. A cautious accused may wish to phrase a waiver so as to provide expressly for revocation in certain circumstances.

Even where a waiver purports to be irrevocable, it is hard to envisage a court rejecting a revocation attempt by an accused who faces an actual and serious conflict-of-interest.[178] It is one thing to hold a waiver against an accused who seeks to argue denial of the right to effective counsel only following a conviction, but quite another to force a reluctant accused to proceed with ineffective counsel against his or her will during trial. Where an accused complains of an actual conflict-of-interest that impinges his or her right to a fair trial, it is our view that a prior waiver can have no effect. As an aside, however, a court may be more inclined to reject a revocation attempt made by a Crown witness, given that the witness presumably does not risk conviction as a result of the conflict.

---

177 See *R. v. Martin* (1989), 86 Nfld. & P.E.I.R. 246 at 247 (Nfld. S.C.); and the comments made in *Parsons*, above note 41 at 144.

178 See *contra*, *Parsons*, above note 41 at 143, where the court speaks of an irrevocable waiver.

Can a waiver be fashioned so as to prevent the possibility of revocation? Consider the case of Accused A, whose former counsel acts for the jointly charged Accused B. The Crown brings an application to disqualify Counsel B based on the fact of successive representation. Accused A wishes to waive any rights that he might have to force the disqualification of Counsel B. He is especially keen that Counsel B remain on the case, for there are common elements to the defences of the two co-accused, and counsel's exceptional familiarity with the matter and unrivalled excellence as an advocate will help Accused A to avoid conviction. If no confidential communications of any import passed between Accused A and former counsel, Accused A may want make specific disclosure of all confidences. Once disclosure has been made, the confidences are waived, and thus arguably lost forever. At least with respect to the misuse of confidential information, the waiver can be seen as irrevocable.[179] Moreover, because Accused A is a former client, there is no issue as to the conflict affecting the quality of representation received during the trial. However, even if confidential communications are seen to be irrevocably waived, Accused A could revoke waiver of the right not to have former counsel take an adverse position in the same or a related matter.

# O. DUTY OF COUNSEL TO ADDRESS THE CONFLICT PROBLEM AS SOON AS POSSIBLE

As we have seen, a conflict-of-interest can cause substantial harm to a client or clients and undermine the integrity of the administration of justice more generally. The lawyer who permits a conflict to develop or continue unchecked may also suffer. He or she may be removed from the record, forced to return fees paid or forego compensation for work already done, face a civil lawsuit by a disaffected client, and/or be exposed to disciplinary proceedings. It is thus crucial, from the per-

---

179 This example somewhat reflects the "confidence-waiving" revelations of a Crown witness in *Cobb*, above note 95 and bears even greater resemblance to the facts in *R. v. Sterling* (1993), 108 Sask. R. 243 (Q.B.), where an accused swore an affidavit detailing the specifics of his communications with former counsel. This option is not advisable where the communications could be used to harm the accused. There is also a real danger that such disclosure will open up the accused to unwanted cross-examination on the application to remove.

spective of the client, the administration of justice, and the lawyer, that a potential conflict be identified and dealt with as soon as possible.

## 1) Consultation with the Client

The first step in addressing a conflict issue is to inform the client of the problem. Disclosure to the client at the earliest opportunity is itself an ethical obligation derived from counsel's duties of loyalty and communication and must never be ignored or delayed.[180] Some conflicts, whether potential or actual, can be satisfactorily dealt with by making full disclosure and obtaining the client's consent to continue. Other conflicts may not be susceptible to such a solution. Regardless, disclosure is the initial task facing the lawyer who perceives a conflict problem, and it is expressly mandated by the rules of professional conduct.[181]

The information to be disclosed to the client will vary depending upon the circumstances of the case. As a general rule, counsel must be guided by the knowledge that no client can make an informed decision regarding a conflict issue without a full and accurate explanation of the material risks of continued representation. Those matters that should be discussed with the client include:

1. **The importance of avoiding a conflict**: Counsel should define the notion of a conflict-of-interest for the client, and explain why, in light of a lawyer's duties of loyalty and confidentiality, a conflict could have a negative impact on the quality of representation. It must also be made clear to the client that he or she has a constitutional right to be represented by a lawyer who has no conflict.

2. **The manner in which a conflict may arise**: The discussion should be wide-ranging, covering tactics and strategies at all stages of the retainer and how the conflict may affect or even foreclose certain options. Counsel should raise any conflict scenario that realistically may arise on the facts of the case, and provide concrete examples to help the client's understanding. Counsel must also take care to inform himself or herself as to the client's circumstances in order to ensure an accurate and realistic review of the possible conflict scenarios.

---

180 See, for example, *Henry*, above note 131 at 465 & 470.
181 See CBA Code ch. 5, comms. 4–5.

3. **Impact on confidentiality and privilege**: Counsel must take special care to explain how the duty of confidentiality and the evidentiary rule of privilege might operate. For example, two co-accused represented by a single counsel must be told clearly that no confidentiality can exist as between them, but that confidentiality and privilege generally exist in full force against the outside world unless the clients become adversaries in future proceedings.

4. **How a conflict could hurt the client in ways unrelated to the quality of representation**: In this respect, a client should be told of the financial cost, delay and any other harm that may occur if an intractable conflict is not dealt with immediately or crystallizes later on in proceedings.

5. **The possibility that a currently resolvable conflict will later become fatal**: The actual or potential conflict, though presently "non-fatal" by reason of the client's informed consent to continued representation, may in the future make representation impossible on any terms, and the client should be advised of this possibility. For instance, adversity between co-accused who jointly retain a lawyer may develop to the point where counsel cannot continue despite the consent of all clients concerned, or one of the clients may withdraw consent to have the lawyer act.

6. **Conflict involving another client**: If the conflict involves another client, it is important to canvas the nature of the relationship with that other client, including the length, number, and type of retainers. Further, a client should be told of any possibility that, in the future, the conflict may develop so that counsel continues to act only for the other client.

7. **Advantages of continuing with the retainer**: The client must be told of any potential advantages that come with keeping present counsel. The closeness and comfort of an existing relationship, counsel's familiarity with the client's case or circumstances, financial savings, special expertise held by the lawyer and/or the lawyer's firm, avoiding any delay and, where co-accused are involved, presenting an unified front to the trier of fact may all be implicated. In this regard, the client should be told of his or her constitutional right to counsel of choice.

8. **Independent legal advice**: Counsel must explain the role and importance of independent legal advice, even where the client appears uninterested in obtaining an opinion from an independent lawyer.

## 2) Consultation with a Former Client

There is a natural tendency to focus upon a current client or clients when considering disclosure obligations related to a conflict-of-interest issue. However, where the conflict affects a former client, counsel may wish to approach that ex-client to obtain consent to act for the current client. If the former client has counsel, contact should be made through such counsel. The former client should be informed of the implications of the current representation, the fact that the lawyer possesses confidential information regarding the former client, any measures that have or will be taken to guard against misuse of such information, and the former client's right to refuse consent.

**Warning**: In dealing with a conflict involving a former client, counsel must be especially careful not to disclose confidential information in the course of informing the current and former clients of the problem. The affected clients may consent to a limited relaxation of the duty of confidentiality for the purpose of explaining the conflict issue. In other cases, it may be possible to make adequate disclosure even absent a waiver of confidentiality. However, a lack of consent could conceivably make any disclosure of confidential information impossible, thus foreclosing the possibility of obtaining consent to continued representation.[182]

## 3) Disclosure and Office-sharing Arrangements

If a conflict problem involves an office-sharing arrangement, all pertinent facts concerning the organization of the office-sharing group must be disclosed. In this regard, the rules of professional conduct in British Columbia are unique. These rules expressly require that lawyers who share space, unless they have all agreed not to act for clients adverse in interest, disclose in writing to every client: that an office-sharing arrangement exists; the identity of the lawyers who are in the arrangement; and that the lawyers are free to act for other clients who are adverse in interest.[183] The British Columbia rules also recommend that, even where the lawyers have agreed *not* to represent clients adverse in interest, disclosure of the office-sharing arrangement be made.

---

182 See Third Restatement §122, comm. (c)(i).
183 See B.C. ch. 6, r. 6.2.

## 4) Written Waiver

Where after receiving full disclosure the client decides to continue the retainer, consent should be obtained in writing. Prudent counsel will use a consent specific to the client, detailing the nature of the disclosure and advice given. Furthermore, even if independent legal advice has been obtained, separate written consent is a good idea. The time involved in preparing and executing the consent will be minimal, given that counsel will have already made full disclosure and provided the client with preliminary advice. In addition, there is always the danger that counsel providing independent legal advice will make an error. In such a case, a separate written consent may protect counsel from fallout arising from the vitiated independent legal advice.

## 5) Independent Legal Advice

The value of independent legal advice lies in the fact that the client obtains an opinion from a lawyer whose loyalties are not at all suspect and who has no interest whatsoever in whether or not the retainer continues. Independent legal advice is not always required where an actual or potential conflict exists. However, such advice helps to ensure that the client understands the conflict issue and comes to an informed view as to his or her position. Unless conflict concerns can fairly be described as trifling, prudent counsel will thus encourage a client to obtain independent legal advice and, in some circumstances, will insist upon an independent opinion.[184]

In arranging for independent legal advice, counsel must not recommend a lawyer who is also potentially in a conflict, such as a partner or associate. In certain circumstances, it may be inappropriate even to suggest a lawyer who shares office space as a co-tenant.[185] Nor should counsel attempt to streamline matters by personally obtaining independent legal advice, which he or she then passes on to the client.[186] Acting as a conduit for independent legal advice in this man-

---

184 A good example of a case where independent legal advice should have been obtained is *Henry*, above note 131. A waiver absent such advice was found to be ineffective in *Robillard*, above note 3 (although the subsequent obtaining of independent legal advice still failed to cure the conflict).

185 See section M(1), "Office-sharing Arrangements," in this chapter, regarding the potential for some office-sharing arrangements to be viewed as akin to a firm of lawyers.

186 This risky approach was taken in *Barbeau*, above note 51, though ultimately without any obvious adverse effect.

ner could well render the advice useless, given that the opinion is filtered through the lawyer who may have a conflict. A lawyer should also avoid providing independent legal advice to two or more clients whose interests are in conflict, a good example being co-accused. To do so risks replicating the conflict problem and fatally undermining the advice, for the clients may well have adverse interests regarding how the conflict should be handled.

Counsel who provides independent legal advice must take the retainer seriously and not perfunctorily discharge the duty.[187] He or she has taken on a client-lawyer relationship with all of its attendant responsibilities. It is therefore crucial that such counsel become fully informed of all relevant facts and provide carefully considered advice as he or she would to any other client. Absent exceptional circumstances, counsel should also personally meet with the client, without original counsel or other affected individuals being present, and render a written opinion.

## 6)  Instances Where Counsel Should Not Act under Any Circumstances

Counsel can never act for two clients who are directly opposed in litigation, for the institutional interest in vigorous advocacy of each client's position overwhelms any consent.[188] In these sorts of cases, waiver by the affected clients cannot cure the conflict problem.[189]

Additionally, if counsel is reasonably of the view, after thorough discussion with the client and full consideration, that he or she cannot act without adverse impact upon the interests of the client, the retainer should immediately come to an end. A lawyer who in his or her own mind cannot be loyal to a client can never act, and all doubts in this respect should be resolved in favour of not representing the actual or potentially conflicting interest.[190]

---

187  See CBA Code ch. 3, comm. 12.
188  See Third Restatement §122, comm. (g)(iii); and ABA Model Rule 1.7.
189  See the discussion of waiver in section N(2), "Instances Where Waiver Cannot Overcome the Conflict Problem," in this chapter.
190  See ABA Model Rule 1.7(b)(1). See also Third Restatement §122(2)(c).

## 7) Meeting a Potential Client: Avoiding Conflict Problems in Advance

Because a duty of confidentiality can arise prior to the formation of a retainer, counsel who interviews a prospective client but goes no further may nonetheless be exposed to a conflict problem.[191] Counsel can avoid or minimize a conflict-of-interest problem by exercising caution in meeting with potential clients. Available options include: assiduously avoiding all contact with any individual whose interests appear to be in conflict with those of a current client; restricting the initial discussion to matters required for a conflict check, and making the check before going any further; asking the prospective client to waive confidentiality regarding the preliminary discussions; and, if a conflict is perceived, and the decision is made not to go forward with the retainer, immediately screening the lawyer who met with the potential client.[192]

## 8) Crown Attorney

Whenever a realistic potential for conflict is perceived, Crown counsel must raise the problem with defence counsel. When interviewing a witness, or perhaps even before, Crown counsel may want to inquire as to whether a client-lawyer relationship exists or existed with counsel for the accused. Moreover, even if no potential for conflict is readily apparent, Crown counsel faced with the multiple or successive representation of co-accused should canvas the conflict issue with defence counsel. Remember that confidential information or defence strategies to which Crown counsel is not privy almost certainly bear upon the conflict issue, and insisting on a clear and unequivocal waiver for all affected accused is the safest course.

## P. DUTY TO RAISE CONFLICT ISSUE IN COURT

Since criminal cases usually involve court appearances, the issue arises as to whether counsel has an obligation to raise or canvas a conflict issue with the court. Although counsel should try to resolve any conflict problem prior to the start of proceedings, it may be that a conflict

---

191 See section H(3), "Existence of a Client-lawyer Relationship," in this chapter.

192 This last option is obviously available only where the circumstances are susceptible to an effective screen.

issue arises without warning during trial. It may also be that counsel wants to make absolutely sure that a potential conflict is not of such a nature so as to require withdrawal, and to this end informs the court of the conflict issue and any steps taken to resolve concerns.[193] A conflict problem can be raised at any point in the proceeding, including during a preliminary inquiry, the trial proper, or on appeal.[194] Depending upon the context, a lawyer who raises a conflict issue may be required to comply with special rules of the court pertaining to applications to remove counsel from the record.[195]

**Opinion:** Because of the serious impact that a conflict-of-interest can have upon legal representation, and given the lawyer's obligations to foster public respect for the administration of justice, any counsel involved in a matter, or who has a client involved in a matter, is completely justified in drawing the attention of the presiding judge to a possible conflict-of-interest.

## 1)  Defence Counsel

Defence counsel who has any real concern as to whether a disqualifying conflict has arisen has a duty to alert the court.[196] Frequently, no one else will be aware of the problem, especially in cases that do not involve multiple representation. When a conflict problem arises during the course of an ongoing trial, this duty requires that defence counsel inform the court immediately. If counsel is uncertain as to whether a real problem has arisen, the prudent course is nonetheless to alert the court, if necessary asking for an adjournment to consider the matter, make full disclosure to any affected client or former client, and (if necessary) obtain independent legal advice. The potential problem may, when fully considered by counsel and client, turn out to present no difficulty, but it is best to make such a determination before continuing with the trial. Finally, it may be preferable for defence counsel not to

---

193  See, for example, *Werkman*, above note 106, where defence counsel sought direction from the court on the conflict issue.

194  See, for example, *Robillard*, above note 3 (raised at preliminary inquiry); *Bilmez*, above note 36 (raised at commencement of trial); v. *Dunbar*, above note 107 (raised during the case for one of the accused); and *Silvini*, above note 24 (raised on appeal).

195  *Chen*, above note 37 at 271, referring to Rule 25.04(1) of the Ontario Court of Justice *Criminal Proceedings Rules*, S.I./92-99.

196  Prior to doing so, counsel should take the steps described in section O, "Duty of Counsel to Address the Conflict as Soon as Possible," in this chapter, where practicable.

argue an application for his or her removal, and instead for the client to retain separate counsel for the purpose.[197]

**Caveat:** Regardless of the circumstances, defence counsel must always take care not to violate the client's confidence in explaining the nature of conflict to the court.[198]

## 2) Crown Attorney

The Crown attorney should be especially alert to conflict problems involving the accused. Allowing the conflict issue to go unchecked may lead to a mistrial or successful appeal and retrial, with the attendant waste of judicial resources. Moreover, the Crown shares with all counsel the duty to raise conflict issues with the court where necessary to maintain the integrity of the administration of justice. The Crown should act promptly in bringing the conflict matter to the court's attention.[199] However, Crown counsel must never use a conflict application as a tactical tool to get rid of or pressure defence counsel. To do so would be unprofessional, constitute a highly illegitimate attack on the accused's right to choice of counsel, and undermine public confidence in the criminal justice system.

## 3) Ability of Judge to Raise the Conflict-of-Interest Issue

There is no doubt that a trial judge can raise the conflict-of-interest issue of his or her own accord, for the court has an inherent jurisdiction to prevent harm to the administration of justice.[200] In fact, in some instances the judge may have a positive obligation to inquire into the possibility of a conflict, most especially where a single counsel appears for multiple clients.[201] Given the risks associated with multiple representation, and the ease with which such an inquiry can be made, placing such a duty upon the judge does not seem onerous.

---

197 See *Chen*, above note 37 at 284–85, noting that counsel "was put in the unhappy position of, in effect, defending his own actions and professional judgments." As the court noted, retaining separate counsel ensures that the client received independent legal advice.

198 See *MacDonald Estate*, above note 3 at 1260–61; and *White*, above note 24 at 264.

199 See *Chen*, above note 37 at 271.

200 See *MacDonald Estate*, above note 3 at 1245.

201 See *W.(W.)*, above note 24 at 235 (note 5); *Robillard*, above note 3 at 26; and *Henry*, above note 131 at 473.

The court also has an obligation to inquire into the propriety of counsel continuing to act once a conflict issue has been raised. Simply accepting the assurance of counsel that no conflict exists does not necessarily satisfy this obligation.[202]

**Comparison**: In the United States, Rule 44(c) of the *Federal Rules of Criminal Procedure* requires the court to inquire as to possible conflict problems in multiple-representation cases, and expressly states that the judge shall personally advise each defendant of his or her right to the effective assistance of counsel, including separate representation. "Unless it appears that there is good cause to believe no conflict-of-interest is likely to arise, the court shall take such measures as may be appropriate to protect each defendant's right to counsel."[203]

## 4) Raising the Conflict-of-Interest Issue in Court prior to Trial

The conflict issue can properly be raised prior to committal for trial. Such was the case in *R. v. Robillard*, where the Ontario Court of Appeal noted that a judge presiding over a preliminary inquiry may, pursuant to section 540(1)(k) of the *Criminal Code*, regulate the course of the inquiry in any way that appears to him or her to be desirable and not inconsistent with the *Code*. Within the scope of this power, stated the court, is the capacity, indeed the duty, to prevent counsel from placing himself or herself in a position of conflict-of-interest.[204]

Moreover, counsel undoubtedly has a duty as an officer of the court not to act in the face of a conflict-of-interest at all stages of a proceeding, and not just at the trial itself. Any concerns as to a possible conflict should therefore be drawn to the attention of the preliminary inquiry judge, or even the judicial official presiding at a bail hearing. Of course, because the purposes of the preliminary inquiry and bail hearing are different from those of the trial, it may be that a disqualifying conflict-of-interest, though a probable danger in the trial context, is not at all problematic at an earlier stage.[205] Thus, depending on the

---

202 See *Bilmez*, above note 36; and *Chen*, above note 37 at 272.

203 For a review of the case law and writings on Rule 44(c), see C. Wright, *Federal Practise and Procedure*, vol. 3A (St. Paul: West, 1982) at §731.

204 See *Robillard*, above note 3 at 26. See also *R. v. Greenwood* (1995), 26 W.C.B. 356 (Ont. Gen. Div.); *R. v. Li* (1993), B.C.J. NO. 2312 (C.A.) (QL) [*Li*]; and *Louie*, above note 71.

205 This is not to say that the possibility of a conflict at a bail hearing or preliminary inquiry is remote: see Littlefield, above note 43 at 260–61.

circumstances of the case, the matter of conflict may be left for the trial judge where no actual conflict can exist prior to trial.[206] In addition, by the trial stage in the proceedings, potential issues of conflict may have crystallized or, conversely, dissipated.[207] Naturally, these points have little relevance where a former client of defence counsel will testify at the preliminary inquiry as an adverse Crown witness and thus be subject to cross-examination by former counsel. In such a case, the conflict issue is likely fully matured, whether or not disqualification is necessary.[208]

## Q. THE APPELLATE CONTEXT

Following the decision of the Supreme Court of Canada in *R. v. Druken*,[209] it seems that an interlocutory proceeding, no matter how framed, cannot be brought to challenge a decision removing or refusing to remove counsel because of a perceived conflict. It is certainly clear that an accused can appeal a trial decision concerning conflict-of-interest only following his or her conviction.[210] This restriction accords with the general rule against interlocutory appeals, thought necessary in order to prevent a multiplicity of proceedings (with the attendant confusion, delay, and waste of resources).[211]

**Commentary**: Restricting the ability to mount an interlocutory challenge to a decision removing or refusing to remove counsel is open to

---

206  See, for example, *Laidlaw Environmental Services (Sarnia) Ltd.* v. *Ontario (Minister of Environment and Energy)* (1997), 32 O.R. (3d) 795 (Gen. Div.), where counsel was prohibited from acting in the portion of the hearing devoted to factual determinations, given that he would have to cross-examine former clients, but counsel's firm was nonetheless allowed to argue a *certiorari* application.

207  This approach is seen in *Li*, above note 204, where an application to disqualify counsel was dismissed at the preliminary-inquiry stage without prejudice to the same application being brought back on later in the proceedings.

208  See, for example, *Robillard*, above note 3; and *Judge*, above note 100.

209  (1998), 126 C.C.C. (3d) 1 (S.C.C.) [*Druken*].

210  Other methods of seeking interlocutory review may exist, for example, seeking *certiorari* to challenge the decision of an inferior court, but the tenor of *Druken*, above note 209, does not hold out much hope in this regard: see Layton, above note 176.

211  See, for example, *R. v. Mills* (1986), 26 C.C.C. (3d) 481 (S.C.C.); and *R. v. Meltzer* (1989), 49 C.C.C. (3d) 453 (S.C.C.).

criticism.[212] The usual policy grounds that justify prohibiting inter-locutory appeals are often absent or much diminished. In particular, allowing an interlocutory appeal may serve to speed up the trial process and avoid needless mistrials and retrials. For instance, where counsel has been erroneously disqualified, an expedited interlocutory appeal on this discrete point may serve to *reduce* delay that would oth-erwise be necessary to permit the accused to retain new counsel. Moreover, if the error cannot be addressed until after a conviction, cur-rent case law suggests that a retrial is the only remedy,[213] representing a substantial waste of resources.

## 1)  Standard of Review: Ineffective-Counsel Claim

The issue of conflict-of-interest may be raised for the first time on a post-conviction appeal, usually in the context of a claim that the appel-lant's right to effective counsel was infringed at trial. In this case, the appellant will presumably argue that he or she could not be expected to have raised the issue at trial, given the nature of the allegation that counsel was ineffective by reason of an alleged conflict.[214] Note also that a waiver absent independent legal advice may be ineffective.[215] However, where the alleged conflict does not involve the appellant's trial counsel — for instance, where counsel for the Crown or a co-accused formerly represented the appellant — failure to raise the mat-ter at trial, while not fatal, may be detrimental to the argument.[216]

When an appellant seeks to overturn a conviction on the ground of an alleged conflict-of-interest at trial, the standard applied by the

---

212 See Layton, above note 176.

213 See, for example, *McCallen*, above note 27 at 541–45.

214 See *Silvini*, above note 24 at 261.

215 See *Robillard*, above note 3. Conversely, in *White*, above note 24 at 261–64, the accused sought independent legal advice on the conflict issue during trial, and failure to act on the advice was understandably seen by the court as significant. A much more difficult case is *Henry*, above note 131, where the trial court expressly alerted the appellant to the conflict issue, yet no independent legal advice was obtained and trial counsel made less than full disclosure to the client. Also see *R. v. Samra* (1998), 129 C.C.C. (3d) 144 at 155 & 159–60 (Ont. C.A.) [*Samra*], dealing with the failure to object to the appointment of former counsel as *amicus curiae*.

216 See, for example, *Joyal*, above note 67 at 239–40; and *Foster*, above note 67. See also the comments made in *Lindskog*, above note 67 at 561.

appeal court differs from that utilized by a trial judge. In *R. v. W.(W.)*, Mr. Justice Doherty noted that, in contrast to the trial judge:

> [t]he appellate court looks backward at the completed trial. The court has the full trial record and may have further material detailing the circumstances surrounding the joint representation and the effects of that representation on counsel's ability to defend the appellant. Unlike the trial court, the appellate court is not concerned with prophylactic measures intended to avoid the potential injustice which may flow from compromised representation. Instead, the appellate court must determine whether counsel's representation was in fact compromised in such a way as to result in a miscarriage of justice. The concern on appeal must be with what happened and not with what might have happened. It makes no more sense to find ineffective representation based on the possibility of a conflict-of-interest, than it does to find ineffective representation based on the mere possibility of incompetent representation.[217]

Given the unique and discrete perspectives and roles of trial judge and appeal court, Mr. Justice Doherty concluded that the appellant alleging denial of effective counsel by reason of a conflict-of-interest at trial must demonstrate: an actual conflict-of-interest between the respective interests represented by counsel; and, as a result of a conflict, some impairment of counsel's ability to represent effectively the interests of the appellant.[218] Looking at a case of multiple representation, an actual conflict-of-interest was said by Doherty J., to exist where a course of conduct dictated by the best interests of one accused would, if followed, be inconsistent with the best interests of the co-accused.[219] It is thus necessary that the appellant point to a specific instance at trial where his or her interests diverged from those of the co-accused, requiring counsel to choose between clients.[220]

As for the question of demonstrating some impairment of counsel's ability to represent effectively the appellant's interests, it need not be shown that, but for the actual conflict, the result would have been different. Rather, it appears to be enough that the appellant point to a single instance where, when faced with such a conflict-of-interests,

---

217  *W.(W.)*, above note 24 at 239.
218  *Ibid.* at 237 & 239.
219  *Ibid.* at 239.
220  *Ibid.* at 240.

counsel chose the course of action detrimental to the interest of the appellant.[221] There is no need to show prejudice in terms of adverse impact on the verdict, because the result of actual conflict is viewed as a miscarriage of justice which cannot be cured by the proviso in section 686(1)(b)(iii).[222]

Given the "actual conflict equates with a miscarriage of justice" approach taken in W.(W.), Mr. Justice Doherty correctly noted that, in a case involving two co-accused represented by a single counsel, the existence of an actual conflict-of-interest will almost invariably result in adverse impact upon (and a new trial for) at least one of the accused. In an aside to this observation,[223] he cites R. v. Li as a case which demonstrates that the distinction between actual conflict and adverse impact may become more important where the conflicted interests are not those of two co-accused but rather involve the accused and a non-party.[224] In Li, the British Columbia Court of Appeal *appeared* to find two instances of actual conflict between the interests of the appellant and some non-party clients who were represented by the appellant's trial counsel in separate proceedings. Both instances of conflict saw trial counsel take decisions adverse to the interests of the appellant, and it is hard to understand why, as long as such a finding is made, the appellant should be treated differently simply because the party whose interests were favoured was not a co-accused. Surely the distinction that is to be made between "co-accused" cases and other cases of conflict is that in the latter instance the conflicted counsel may favour the interests of the appellant over those of the non-participant, in which case there has been no adverse impact on the effectiveness of the appellant's trial counsel.

Of course, the approach adopted in W.(W.) is not the only one logically possible but rather is the product of a policy choice that seeks a balance between the desire to avoid mistrials and retrials and the need to foster the right to counsel of choice. Other standards of review are theoretically available. In fact, in a case called R. v. *Bullis* the British Columbia Court of Appeal had earlier seemed to adopt a standard more favourable to the appellant seeking to overturn a conviction based on

---

221  *Ibid.* at 240–41.
222  *Ibid.* at 237 & 240–41.
223  *Ibid.* at 241.
224  *Li*, above note 204.

conflict-of-interest at trial, the standard being "an appearance of a conflict-of-interest" or "an apparent conflict-of-interest."[225] In W.(W.), Doherty J.A. refused to adopt this standard, however, for the reasons already discussed. Moreover, the British Columbia Court of Appeal, after subsequently reiterating the *Bullis* standard,[226] has implicitly accepted the W.(W.) approach in two later cases.[227]

The distinction drawn between the trial and appeal contexts by the Ontario Court of Appeal in W.(W.) appears both logical and workable, and it has been adopted in other cases.[228] The appeal court has the benefit of hindsight in determining whether a conflict-of-interest actually materialized, and it also may be working from a position of greater knowledge by reason of fresh evidence as to confidential communications between lawyer and client. The trial court arguably must cut a wider swath in preventing conflict-of-interest, by reason of a desire to avoid mistrial or retrial after appeal if a conflict actually crystallizes during the course of the trial (concerns that are moot from the perspective of the appeal court). However, one might ask whether W.(W.) can be faulted for failing to consider the possibility that the entire course of the trial can be substantially affected when even the *potential* for conflict arises. That is to say, it may be that counsel, albeit subconsciously, makes a myriad of subtle (perhaps even imperceptible) decisions which, when taken as a whole, direct the trial in a course that avoids "actual" conflict, to the disadvantage of an accused. While this criticism carries some weight, interests in finality of judicial proceedings and the need for a workable and realistic test for conflict-of-interest justify the distinction adopted in W.(W.). Even so, appeal courts must recognize that an actual conflict may arise by reason of trial counsel making decisions aimed at avoiding a position of conflict, and be prepared to apply W.(W.) in such circumstances.

## 2) Fresh Evidence

Appeal counsel making a claim of denial of the right to effective counsel must be cognizant of the role that may be played by fresh evidence. A conflict at trial is not always apparent on the face of the record.

---

225 *Bullis*, above note 59 at 441–42.

226 See *Le*, above note 63 at 441–42.

227 See *R.* v. *Quick* (1993), 82 C.C.C. (3d) 51 at 69–70 (B.C.C.A.); and *R.* v. *Dean* (1997), 39 B.C.L.R. (3d) 287 at 311 (C.A.) [*Dean*].

228 See, for example, *Graff*, above note 46 at 90; *Phalen*, above note 62 at 377; *Barbeau*, above note 51 at 80; *Dean*, above note 227; and *Samra*, above note 215 at 160–61.

Evidence not found in the transcripts may thus be necessary to prove the claim, and in some cases the appellant may find it necessary to divulge confidential information in support of this ground of appeal.

The test for the admission of fresh evidence that relates to an alleged conflict-of-interest at trial is not that stipulated by section 683(1) of the *Criminal Code* as interpreted by *R. v. Palmer*.[229] Instead of seeking to attack a factual or legal determination made during the trial, the appellant is attacking the validity of the trial process itself. Accordingly, in the conflict-of-interest context, an easier test for admissibility is appropriate, and fresh evidence is generally admitted because the issue can be much more fully canvassed if such information is available.[230]

Appellate counsel must be cognizant of the potential implications of submitting an affidavit that goes behind (and hence to an extent waives) client-lawyer confidentiality and privilege. The Crown may be able to respond by delving into formerly confidential and privileged matters on cross-examination of the appellant or by obtaining evidence from trial counsel. In *R. v. Li*,[231] the Crown obtained a direction from the British Columbia Court of Appeal to the effect that the appellant had waived legal-professional privilege by virtue of making allegations against his trial counsel. The Crown then obtained an affidavit from trial counsel that disclosed confidential information, including the revelation that the appellant had admitted to committing the offence with which he was charged.[232]

## 3) Denial of the Right to Choice of Counsel

A trial that proceeds with counsel who labours under an actual conflict is open to a claim of ineffective counsel. Where the accused is rebuffed in an attempt to discharge the conflicted counsel, he or she can also claim infringement of the right to counsel of choice. A different possibility sees trial counsel wrongfully discharged because of an erroneous determination that a conflict exists. In this latter case, the right to

---

229 (1980), 50 C.C.C. (2d) 193 (S.C.C.).
230 See *W.(W.)*, above note 24 at 232–34; *Barbeau*, above note 51 at 77–79; *Henry*, above note 131 at 457–58; and *Dean*, above note 227 at 303.
231 Above note 204.
232 See also *Dean*, above note 227, where trial counsel, attacked by the appellant for a perceived conflict-of-interest, revealed that the appellant instructed him to seek a plea agreement on a charge of manslaughter.

choice of counsel is alone implicated (that is, the right to effective counsel is not engaged).[233] It appears that the wrongful denial of the right to counsel of choice will automatically result in a new trial.[234]

# R. SUMMARY AND RECOMMENDATIONS

Our summary and recommendations regarding conflict-of-interest are as follows:

1.  A lawyer owes a duty of loyalty to the client that must not be compromised by competing interests (section B).
2.  Canadian rules of professional conduct invariably emphasize the importance of counsel avoiding conflict of interest and encourage dealing with such problems promptly and properly if they occur (section C).
3.  At common law, courts have a power to remove counsel from the record because of a conflict-of-interest (section D).
4.  Conflict of interest also implicates constitutional rights, including the right to the effective assistance of counsel and the right to choice of counsel (section E).
5.  Courts will remove counsel from the record owing to an impermissible conflict of interest where an actual conflict exists or there is "any realistic risk" of a conflict in fact occurring during the trial. The "realistic-risk" standard does not appear to be terribly imposing, and is arguably met whenever a conflict could reasonably occur during the course of the trial (section F).
6.  One of the most dangerous conflict-of-interest scenarios occurs where a single counsel represents two or more co-accused. Multiple representation is not *per se* prohibited by the ethical rules, in recognition that clients may have legitimate reasons for desiring representation by one counsel. But the lawyer who considers acting for two or more co-accused assumes a heavy burden of ensuring that he or she is not placed in a position of representing interests that are or may be in conflict (section G).

---

233  See, for example, *McCallen*, above note 27.
234  *Ibid.*

7. Conflict-of-interest problems can arise in a variety of contexts where multiple representation occurs. Danger areas include plea discussions, bringing pre-trial applications, attacking the Crown case, building an affirmative defence, advising the client(s) whether to testify, calling the client(s) to the stand, making closing arguments, taking a position on sentencing, and receiving instructions on any material aspect of the litigation. Conflict of interest may also occur during a bail hearing or preliminary inquiry, though the risks are somewhat reduced. In short, counsel faces the potential for conflict at almost every turn and must be perpetually vigilant in guarding against the problem (section H).

8. Counsel owes a former client a duty of loyalty with respect to the subject matter of the retainer, and must not reveal any confidential information obtained from the ex-client. Accordingly, a conflict-of-interest will arise: where counsel who has formerly represented a client in a matter is poised to represent another client in the same or any related matter in which the former client's and present client's interests are materially adverse; or where counsel may be tempted to reveal or use confidential information obtained during the course of the retainer with the former client (section H).

9. There is a potential for conflict-of-interest whenever counsel takes part in a joint-defence arrangement under which information and effort is shared among separately represented co-accused (section I).

10. An arrangement whereby a third-party pays some or all of a client's fees and disbursements will often raise the spectre of an impermissible conflict-of-interest. The concern can arise where parents pay for a young person's legal costs, and is especially great where money is paid by a co-accused, unindicted co-conspirator, or the alleged head of a criminal organization (section J).

11. A lawyer who may be a witness in a proceeding faces the potential for conflict-of-interest, even in cases where the decision is made not to testify (section K).

12. Any financial or other interest personal to the lawyer can lead to a conflict-of-interest where at odds with the duty of loyalty owed a client. For instance, a conflict may arise if the lawyer is allegedly involved in facts relevant to the matter at hand, or where counsel acts as a surety for a client or takes an assignment of a bail deposit or seized funds. Contingency fees also raise possible conflict problems, as does the acquisition of publication rights and business or sexual relations with a client (section L).

13. Where lawyers work in the same firm, there is normally an imputation of any conflict-of-interest involving one lawyer to all mem-

bers of the firm. This imputation arguably applies to office-sharing arrangements, absent measures sufficient to prevent the flow of confidential information within the working environment. However, an imputation may in some cases be avoided by "screening" the lawyer who possesses confidential information leading to a conflict (section M).

14. It is often possible to avoid a conflict-of-interest problem by obtaining an informed waiver from the affected client or clients. However, in some instances even a properly obtained waiver will not be sufficient to remedy the conflict, for instance, where the problematic representation threatens to undermine the integrity of the criminal justice process. It is also possible that a client will subsequently revoke a waiver, in essence resurrecting the conflict issue (section N).

15. Counsel has a duty to identify and address a conflict-of-interest problem in a prompt and efficient manner. The components of this duty include consultation with the affected client or clients, including any former client. Waiver, if considered by the client to be a valid option, should be obtained in writing. Independent legal advice is also a wise response to any perceived conflict, and it may be absolutely essential where the problem is serious (section O).

16. Because of the serious impact that a conflict-of-interest can have upon legal representation, and given the lawyer's obligations to foster public respect for the administration of justice, any counsel involved in a matter, or who has a client involved in a matter, is completely justified in drawing the attention of the presiding judge to a possible conflict-of-interest (section P).

17. It appears that a trial court's decision to remove or not remove counsel for a conflict of interest can be appealed only following the conclusion of the trial proceeding. Once the issue is raised on appeal, the standard for review is more demanding than that applied prior to or during the trial proceeding. To succeed, the client appealing a conviction must convince the appeal court that: an actual conflict of interest arose during the trial; and that, as a result of the conflict, there occurred some impairment of counsel's ability to represent effectively the interests of the appellant (section Q).

## FURTHER READINGS

CANADIAN BAR ASSOCIATION, TASK FORCE ON CONFLICT OF INTERESTS, *Conflict of Interest Disqualification: Martin v. Gray and Screening Methods* (Canadian Bar Association, Ottawa: 1993)

DAL PONT, G., *Lawyers' Professional Responsibility in Australia and New Zealand* (North Ryde, N.S.W.: LBC Information Services, 1996)

FILIPOVIC, D., "The Sex Police Cometh: Lawyer-Client Sexual Relationships" (1993) 31 Alta. L. Rev. 391

GEER, J., "Representation of Multiple Criminal Defendants: Conflicts of Interest and the Professional Responsibilities of the Defence Attorney" (1978) 62 Minn. L. Rev. 119

HALL, JR., J., *Professional Responsibility of the Criminal Lawyer*, 2d ed. (New York: Clark Boardman Callaghan, 1996)

LAYTON, D., "Conflict of Interest and Separately Represented Co-Accused" Defence Brief #61, July 9, 1999, www.crimlaw.org/def-brief61.html.

LAYTON, D. "Joint Defence Doctrine and Privilege" *Defence Brief* 58 (18 June 1999) online, http/www.crimlaw.org/defbrief58.html

LAYTON, D., "The Pre-Trial Removal of Counsel for Conflict of Interest: Appealability and Remedies on Appeal" (1999) 4 Can. Crim. L. Rev. 25

LEVY, Y., "Attorneys, Clients and Sex: Conflicting Interests in the California Rule" (1992) 5 Geo. J. Legal Ethics 649

LITTLEFIELD, D., "*Silvini*: Divided Loyalty" (1992) 9 C.R. (4th) 250

LOWENTHAL, G., "Joint Representation in Criminal Cases: A Critical Appraisal" (1978) 64 Va. L. Rev. 939

LUNDY, D., G. MACKENZIE, & M. NEWBURY, *Barristers and Solicitors in Practice* (Toronto: Butterworths, 1998)

MACKENZIE, G., *Lawyers and Ethics: Professional Responsibility and Discipline* (Toronto: Carswell, 1993).

MANES, R, & M. SILVER, *Solicitor-Client Privilege in Canadian Law* (Toronto: Butterworths, 1993)

MOORE, N., "Conflicts of Interest in the Simultaneous Representation of Multiple Clients: A Proposed Solution to the Current Confusion and Controversy" (1982) 61 Texas L. Rev. 211

NESSIN, R., "Conflicts and Confidences: Does Conflict of Interest Kill the Joint Defence Privilege? The Defence Viewpoint" (1992) 7:1 Criminal Justice 6

NOTE, "Developments in the Law: Conflicts of Interest in the Legal Profession" (1981) 94 Harv. L. Rev. 1244

PERELL, P., *Conflict of Interest in the Legal Profession* (Toronto: Butterworths, 1995)

PERELL, P., "Classifying Conflicts of Interest" (1994) 28 L. Soc. Gaz. 11

PERELL, P., "*Drabinsky* v. *KPMG* and *Bolkiah* v. *KPMG*: Disqualifying Conflicts of Interest in the Legal, Accounting, and Consulting Professions in Canada and England" (2001) 24 Advocates' Q. 109

ROSS, S., *Ethics in Law: Lawyers' Responsibility and Accountability in Australia* (Sydney: Butterworths, 1995)

ROSZKEWYCZ, R., "Third Party Payment of Criminal Defence Fees: What Lawyers Should Tell Potential Clients and Their Benefactors Pursuant to (an amended) Model Code 1.8(f)" (1994) 7 Geo. J. Legal Ethics 573

SEABE, P., "Conflicts and Confidences: Does Conflict of Interest Kill the Joint Defence Privilege? The Prosecution Viewpoint" (1992) 7:1 Criminal Justice 7

TAGUE, P., "Multiple Representation and Conflicts of Interest in Criminal Cases" (1979) 67 Geo. L.J. 1075

WOLFRAM, C., *Modern Legal Ethics* (St. Paul: West, 1986)

WRIGHT, C., *Federal Practise and Procedure* (St. Paul: West, 1982) Vol. 3A at §731

# CHAPTER 7

# CLIENT PERJURY

## A. INTRODUCTION

What should a defence lawyer do upon learning that a client intends to give false testimony or has already lied on the stand? The proper response to anticipated or completed client perjury is one of the most hotly debated issues in criminal law ethics.[1] Almost every commentator who addresses general ethical aspects of criminal law practice devotes special attention to the thorny problem of client perjury. Client perjury has become a paradigmatic scenario for examining defence counsel's sometimes conflicting duties, on the one hand of loyalty to the client, and on the other to maintain the integrity of the truth-seeking function of the criminal justice system. The impact of the perjury issue on broader questions of ethics, and the repercussions for those who take challenging positions, has been substantial. In the United States, a provocative conference address on the topic by Professor Monroe Freedman in 1966 led several appellate court judges, including soon-to-be Chief Justice of the Supreme Court Warren Burger, to seek Freedman's disbarment and academic dismissal.[2] Freedman's controversial writings on client perjury constituted an

---

1   By perjury, we mean the offence set out in s. 131 of the *Criminal Code*, R.S.C. 1985, c. C-46.

2   The judges' attempt was unsuccessful: see M. Freedman, *Lawyers' Ethics in the Adversary System* (New York: Bobbs-Merrill, 1975) at viii.

important impetus for the American Bar Association to launch a reconsideration of the Model Code and eventually, in 1983, to adopt the replacement Model Rules.[3]

The perjurious-client problem can often be seen as a particular instance of defence counsel's difficulty in representing the client who is known to be guilty.[4] The perjury issue will frequently arise where the client admits his or her guilt but nonetheless insists upon testifying falsely at trial in the hope of securing an acquittal. Yet the spectre of client perjury can loom even where counsel is in no position to conclude that the client is guilty. The client may contend that false testimony is crucial in order to bolster an otherwise valid defence.[5] The issue of client perjury is also discrete because it implicates the accused's constitutional right to testify on his or her own behalf. Finally, the unique and labyrinthine range of possible responses to anticipated or completed client perjury warrants an in-depth examination of the topic. The approach eventually taken will have an impact on (and thus derives from) one's preferred model of the client-lawyer relationship, and will inferentially influence a defence lawyer's approach to every stage of the criminal justice process.

## B. COMPETING PRINCIPLES

The principles that touch upon an attempted resolution of any client-perjury problem are by now largely familiar. Defence counsel owes the client a duty of loyalty, which includes obligations to keep secret all confidential information and to act as a competent advocate for the client's cause. A lawyer faced with anticipated or completed client perjury quickly recognizes the pull of the duty of loyalty. Any action that explicitly or implicitly reveals the planned or already executed falsehood by definition serves to expose client secrets and, in many instances, to undermine the client's defence. Loyalty militates against rushing into action that will harm the client.

---

3    See J. Burkoff, *Criminal Defense Ethics: Law and Liability*, rev. ed. (St. Paul: West, 1999) at p. 6–75ff.

4    A. Kaufman, *Problems in Professional Resonsibility*, 3d ed. (Boston: Little, Brown, 1990) at 152.

5    See, for example, *Nix* v. *Whiteside*, 475 U.S. 157 (1986) [*Nix*], where the accused told counsel that he believed the victim was carrying a gun, and insisted that he had killed in self-defence. The accused wanted to help along this defence by falsely testifying that he had seen a flash of metal in the victim's hand.

There are also closely associated constitutional principles that prevent counsel from improperly interfering with the client's defence. If defence counsel acts unreasonably to cause unfairness at the trial or compromise the reliability of the verdict, the right to the effective assistance of counsel has been infringed.[6] As well, the unjustified release of confidential information by counsel could be seen to violate the principle against self-incrimination.[7] Given counsel's role in extracting information from his or her client, any systemic elements that encourage or require defence counsel to disclose information emanating from the accused, which would otherwise be non-compellable, could be said to violate the principle against self-incrimination. Disclosure by a lawyer could also infringe the substantive guarantees underlying client-lawyer privilege and confidentiality.[8] Finally, counsel must be cognizant of the client's undisputed constitutional right to control the conduct of the defence and in particular to testify in his or her own defence.[9] Interventions that keep the client from the stand, or impede his or her free choice to testify, risk censure by the courts.

The power of these constitutional principles is undeniable, both reflecting and shaping every client-lawyer relationship and counsel's attendant ethical obligations. Yet a lawyer's allegiance to the client's cause is not without its limits, and the same can be said for an accused's constitutional rights. A central objective of the adversarial criminal justice system is the search for truth. Granted, the principle against self-incrimination serves to temper the truth-finding function of the system. But this principle operates to require only that the Crown prove its case without any compulsion of the accused. The principle against self-incrimination does not encompass the right to fabricate evidence in a criminal proceeding. It is also questionable whether the right of an accused to testify includes the knowing pres-

---

6   See, for example, R. v. B.(G.D.) (2000), 143 C.C.C. (3d) 289 (S.C.C.) [B.(G.D.)].
7   See, for example, R. v. S.(R.J.) (1995), 96 C.C.C. (3d) 1 (S.C.C.).
8   See, for example, Smith v. Jones (1999), 132 C.C.C. (3d) 225 (S.C.C.); and R. v. McClure (2001), 151 C.C.C. (3d) 321 (S.C.C.).
9   See, for example, R. v. Swain (1991), 63 C.C.C. (3d) 481 at 505–07 (S.C.C.); R. v. Brigham (1992), 79 C.C.C. (3d) 365 at 380–83, 390–91 (Que. C.A) [Brigham]; R. v. Delisle (1999), 133 C.C.C. (3d) 541 at 557 (Que. C.A.) [Delisle]; R. v. Taylor (1992), 77 C.C.C. (3d) 551 at 567 (Ont. C.A.); R. v. Smith (1997), 120 C.C.C. (3d) 500 at 507–08 & 510–11 (Ont. C.A.); and R. v. Clinton, [1993] 2 All E.R. 998 (C.A.). In the United States, see Nix, above note 5; and Rock v. Arkansas, 483 U.S. 44 (1987).

entation of false testimony.[10] Such action is an unacceptable subversion of the truth-finding process, and counsel's complicity must be avoided. The idea that participants in a criminal trial must not mislead the court consequently represents a limit on the lawyer's duty of loyalty to the client,[11] and almost certainly imposes analogous restrictions on the accused's constitutional rights.

The question becomes, how can the profession's ethical standards best accommodate the competing principles of loyalty to the client and solicitude towards the truth-finding function of the criminal justice system? If there are instances where the principles clash, which, as we shall see, is certainly the case when it comes to client perjury, which interest must give way? The answers to these questions are far from easy. Resolutions cannot be obtained by applying set rules, because our criminal justice system is based upon principles that are inherently contradictory. Tellingly, the rules of professional conduct in most Anglo-American-influenced legal systems are unable to offer much precise guidance. These rules are not totally blind to the problem, however, and deserve careful review.

## C. RELATED RULES OF PROFESSIONAL CONDUCT

The CBA Code, along with the ethical standards promulgated by most Canadian governing bodies, does not incorporate any provisions that specifically address the issue of client perjury. However, the general ethical guidelines relating to "The Lawyer as Advocate" are applicable because they include prohibitions and direction concerning misleading the court. We have already seen and discussed some of these guidelines in the context of confidentiality exceptions and the defence of the client known to be guilty.[12] Yet the CBA Code's main interdiction against misleading the court bears repeating at this juncture, as do the commentaries pertaining to remedial measures and withdrawal:

> Prohibited Conduct

---

10 See *Nix*, above note 5 at 173. This limitation on the right to testify has yet to be considered by Canadian courts. See also the discussion below in section F(4)(b), "Refusal to Call the Client as a Witness," in this chapter.

11 See, for example, section K, "Duty Not to Mislead the Court in chapter 5.

12 See section B, "Related Rules of Professional Misconduct," in chapter 1, and section K, "Duty Not to Mislead the Court," in chapter 5.

2. The lawyer must not, for example:

(b) knowingly assist or permit the client to do anything that the lawyer considers to be dishonest or dishonourable,

(e) knowingly attempt to deceive or participate in the deception of a tribunal or influence the course of justice by offering false evidence, misstating facts or law, presenting or relying upon a false or deceptive affidavit, suppressing what ought to be disclosed or otherwise assisting in any fraud, crime or illegal conduct.[13]

Errors and Omissions

3. The lawyer who has unknowingly done or failed to do something that, if done or omitted knowingly, would have been in breach of this Rule and discovers it, has a duty to the court, subject to the Rule relating to confidential information, to disclose the error or omission and do all that can reasonably be done in the circumstances to rectify it.[14]

Duty to withdraw

4. If the client wishes to adopt a course that would involve a breach of this Rule, the lawyer must refuse and do everything reasonably possible to prevent it. If the client persists in such a course the lawyer should, subject to the Rule relating to withdrawal, withdraw or seek leave of the court to do so.[15]

Since by committing perjury the client is misleading the court, and counsel typically plays an active role in calling the client to the stand, eliciting testimony, and making submissions based upon the resulting evidence, these commentaries are undoubtedly relevant.

---

13  CBC Code ch. IX, comm. 2(b) & (e) (footnotes omitted). To similar effect, see Ont. r. 4.01(2)(b) & (e); N.S. r. 14, Guiding Principles (b) & (e); Que. s. 4.02.01(c) & (e); and B.C. ch. 8, r. 2(b). New Brunswick's provisions do not track the CBA Code language but are more or less similar in substance: N.B. Part A, r. 2; and Part B, r. 1.

14  CBA Code ch. IX, comm. 3 (footnote omitted). To similar effect, see Ont. r. 4.01(5); and N.S. r. 14.2. As we will discuss below, New Brunswick adopts a different position, requiring withdrawal from the case and disclosure to the court where counsel learns of "fraudulent testimony participated in by his client": see N.B. Part B, r. 8.

15  CBA Code ch. IX, comm. 4 (footnote omitted). To similar effect, see Ont. r. 4.01(5) (commentary); and N.S. r. 14.3. Compare the distinct position in New Brunswick, which clearly mandates withdrawal whenever counsel learns that there has been a fraud participated in by the client: see N.B. Part B, r. 8.

Two Canadian governing bodies have chosen to address the client perjury issue more directly and expansively. The Law Society of British Columbia's *Professional Conduct Handbook*, chapter 8, provides as follows:

Offering to give false testimony

2.   Where a client advises the lawyer that the client intends to offer false testimony in a proceeding, the lawyer shall explain to the client the lawyer's professional duty to withdraw if the client insists on offering, or in fact does offer, false testimony.

3.   Where a client who has been counselled in accordance with Rule 2 advises the lawyer that the client intends to offer false testimony in a proceeding the lawyer shall, in accordance with chapter 10, withdraw from representing the client in that matter.

4.   A lawyer who withdraws under Rule 3 shall not disclose to the court or tribunal, or to any other person, the fact that the withdrawal was occasioned by the client's insistence on offering false testimony.

5.   A lawyer shall not call as a witness in a proceeding a person who has advised the lawyer that the witness intends to offer false testimony.

Inconsistent statements or testimony

6.   Mere inconsistency in a client's or witness's statements or testimony, or between two proffered defences, is insufficient to support the conclusion that the person will offer or has offered false testimony. However, the lawyer shall explore the inconsistency with the client or witness at the first available opportunity. If, based on that enquiry, the lawyer is certain that the client or witness intends to offer false testimony, then the lawyer shall comply with Rules 2 to 5. Otherwise, the lawyer is entitled to proceed, leaving it to the court or tribunal to assess the truth or otherwise of the client's or witness's statements or testimony.

Duty to Withdraw

7.   Where a client wishes to adopt a course prohibited by this Chapter, the lawyer shall do everything reasonably possible to prevent it.

8.   Where the client, notwithstanding the lawyer's actions under Rule 7, does anything prohibited by this chapter the lawyer shall, subject to Rules 2 to 5 and in accordance with chapter 10, withdraw from representing the client in that matter.

The Code of Professional Conduct promulgated by the Law Society of Alberta also offers extensive guidance regarding the question of client perjury, in the following rules and commentary to chapter 10:

Rule 14. A lawyer must not mislead the court nor assist a client or witness to do so.[16]

Commentary 14.2

Rule #14 — Misrepresentation by client or witness: A lawyer has a duty to refuse to offer evidence provided by a client or other person that the lawyer knows to be false based on personal knowledge or the client's admission. Rule #14 applies to oral and written testimony as well as to other evidence such as exhibits. For example, a lawyer may not tender an affidavit known by the lawyer to contain misrepresentations or untrue statements. If a client persists in instructions to use such evidence, the lawyer must withdraw in accordance with chapter 14, *Withdrawal and Dismissal.*

If it becomes apparent after the fact that evidence submitted by the lawyer is false, then Rule #15 applies.

When a client in a civil or criminal matter makes admissions to a lawyer, subsequent conduct of the case by the lawyer may be limited or restricted so as to avoid possible participation in perjury. For example, the client may clearly admit certain relevant and important facts. The lawyer, if satisfied that the admissions are true, may properly take objection to the jurisdiction of the court or the admissibility or sufficiency of evidence, and may otherwise attack the case of opposing parties, including the credibility of witnesses through cross-examination. It would be improper, however, to set up an affirmative case that is contrary to such admissions. For example, if a lawyer is satisfied that the client committed a crime, the lawyer would be prohibited from calling evidence in support of an alibi intended to show that the client could not have committed, or in fact did not commit, the crime.

Rule 15.    Upon becoming aware that the court is under a misapprehension as a result of submissions made by the lawyer or evidence given by the lawyer's client or witness, a lawyer must (subject to confidentiality — see Rule #7 of chapter 7) immediately correct the misapprehension.

16   See also Rule 20, prohibiting a lawyer from counselling or participating in the falsification of evidence; and Rule 24, which states that a lawyer must not counsel a witness to give evidence that is untruthful or misleading.

Commentary 15.1

Rule #15 — General: This rule is similar to Rule #2 in chapter 4, *Relationship of the Lawyer to Other Lawyers*. A lawyer has a duty to correct a misapprehension of the court arising from an honest mistake on the part of counsel or from perjury by the lawyer's client or witness. It may be a sufficient discharge of this duty to merely advise the court not to rely on the impugned information.

The principle of Rule #15 applies not only to statements that were untrue at the time they were made, but to those that were true when made but have subsequently become inaccurate due to a change in circumstance. For example, it may have been represented to the court that a personal injury plaintiff is permanently disabled. If, prior to judgment, the plaintiff's condition undergoes material improvement, the lawyer must, subject to confidentiality, convey this information to the court.

Even if a matter has been judicially determined, the discovery of an error that may reasonably be viewed as having materially affected the outcome may oblige a lawyer to advise opposing counsel of the error. This may be the case notwithstanding that the appeal period has expired, since another remedy may be available to redress the mistake in whole or in part.

Commentary 15.2

Rule #15 — "Subject to Confidentiality": This conclusion is the subject of a rule and commentary in ch. 7, *Confidentiality*. Briefly, if correction of the misrepresentation requires disclosure of confidential information, the lawyer must seek the client's consent to such disclosure. If the client withholds consent, the lawyer is obliged to withdraw.

Also take note of Rule 16 and the associated commentary.[17] Although dealing with counsel's possible response to questions from the court and not perjury, the Alberta Code strikes a similar balance between the need to maintain confidentiality and the prohibition against misleading the court.

In England and Wales, the bar has not adopted any express rules regarding client perjury, although its ethical standards do prohibit counsel from misleading the court.[18] The Law Society, by contrast, not

---

17   Alta. ch. 10, r. 16 & commentary.

18   See *Code of Conduct of the Bar of England and Wales*, General Council, Annex "H" (London: The Council, 1990), Written Standards for the Conduct of

only includes this sort of general prohibition but also addresses the specific issue of client perjury, providing that an advocate must decline to act further upon discovering a completed perjury.[19] A solicitor is apparently forbidden from making disclosure to the court absent the client's consent. As for anticipated perjury, the Law Society recommends that the lawyer "decline to act"[20] but offers no guidance in situations where withdrawing from the case is not possible.

The governing bodies in Australia also forbid counsel from misleading the court and typically join the Law Society in England and Wales in addressing the issue of client perjury from a remedial perspective.[21] If counsel learns of a completed perjury at any point before the end of proceedings, he or she must withdraw unless the client authorizes disclosure of the lie to the court.[22] Absent such authorization, or in the event that the case has concluded, the lawyer must *not* reveal the perjury to the court.[23] Where a client informs counsel of a plan to commit perjury in the future, the ethical guidelines typically adopted in Australia forbid counsel from making disclosure to the court.[24]

The major ethical codes operating in the United States uniformly forbid counsel from knowingly misleading the court. But on the particular issue of client perjury in a criminal case, there is no single preferred method of approach, and much confusion persists. For instance, the position taken by the ABA Model Code is maddeningly hard to discern. The Code arguably condones disclosure of intended client perjury but can apparently be interpreted so as to forbid disclosure of a client's completed perjury.[25] As for the ABA's Model Rules, the commentary to Rule 3.3 notes that the issue of client perjury "has been intensely debated" and that there is disagreement as to a lawyer's duty

---

Professional Work at §5.2. The standards applicable to barristers are discussed in D. Pannick, *Advocates* (Oxford: Oxford University Press, 1992) at 162–63 (in particular regarding the state of affairs prior to 1989).

19   See Law Society, *The Guide to the Professional Conduct of Solicitors*, 8th ed. (London: Law Society, 1999) at §21.01, §21.13, §21.20 & Annex 21F.

20   *Ibid.* at §21.13.

21   See, for example, New South Wales Barristers' Rules §32–34. The situation in Australia is reviewed in S. Ross, *Ethics in Law: Lawyers' Responsibility and Accountability in Australia* (Sydney: Butterworths, 1998) at 431–32.

22   See, for example, New South Wales Barristers' Rules §32.

23   *Ibid.*

24   See, for example, New South Wales Barristers' Rules §35.

25   For a detailed review of the ABA Model Code provisions, in all their complexity, see Burkoff, above note 3 at §6.5(c)(1); and Kaufman, above note 4 at 173–77.

where he or she is unable to convince the client not to undertake the perjury.[26] Ultimately, the Model Rules require disclosure where absolutely necessary to remedy a material falsehood occasioned by a client's completed perjury.[27] But the Rules' position regarding anticipated client perjury is more opaque, perhaps permitting disclosure as a preventative measure.[28]

The American Law Institute's Third Restatement includes a fairly detailed comment on client perjury as part of the rule on "False Testimony or Evidence."[29] The gist of this comment is that counsel has a strong duty to remonstrate with the client to abandon any planned perjury and the comment favours disclosure to the court where the client ignores such advice and actually commits perjury.[30] Where perjury is anticipated, and remonstration has failed, the Third Restatement seems not to countenance pre-emptory disclosure.[31] Finally, ABA Defense Standard 4-7.5(a) contains a typical proscription against knowingly offering false evidence. Prior to 1979, the Defense Standards additionally advocated what is frequently called the "narrative approach" to client perjury, and hence struck a balance quite favourable to the client's right of confidentiality.[32] However, the endorsement of a narrative approach has since been removed from the Standards. Footnote 1 to the present commentary on "Use of False Evidence" indicates that a separate standard relating to client perjury was considered for inclusion but not adopted for lack of consensus as to the appropriate approach. The Defense Standards are thus almost refreshing in their willingness to offer no position regarding client perjury, quite candidly admitting that no consensus exists as to the proper avenue of response.

---

26   See ABA Model Rule 3.3, comm. 7.

27   See ABA Model Rule 3.3, comm. 7–14. No study of the Model Rules is complete without reviewing ABA Comm. on Ethics and Professional Responsibility, Formal Op. 353 (1987); and the decision of the United States Supreme Court in *Nix*, above note 5 (both discussed at various points below).

28   See the discussion in F(4)(f), "Disclosure of the Indended Perjury," in this chapter.

29   Third Restatement §120, comm. "i."

30   *Ibid.*

31   *Ibid.*

32   See section F(4)(c), "Eliciting Testimony By Means of Free or Open Narrative," in this chapter.

# D. MONROE FREEDMAN AND THE LAWYER'S TRILEMMA

We have already alluded to Professor Monroe Freedman's controversial contribution to the legal profession's discussion of client perjury. Freedman's influence on the parameters of the debate is hard to overstate. It is thus worth reviewing his position in a little more detail.[33]

The centrepiece of Freedman's position lies in the so-called "trilemma" presented whenever a lawyer is confronted with client perjury. This trilemma derives from three competing ethical obligations. First, the lawyer is expected to acquire full knowledge of the case, a vital prerequisite to the competent representation of the client. Second, counsel must maintain all client confidences, an essential means of encouraging full disclosure by the client. Third, the lawyer has a duty to be candid with the court, and especially not to undermine the judicial process by perpetrating falsehoods. In Freedman's opinion, any proposed resolution to the client-perjury problem puts at least one of these three obligations at risk. Counsel can attempt to circumvent the problem entirely by striving never to acquire knowledge of the true facts from the client, but at significant cost to the duty of competence. If, instead, the lawyer discloses the client's intended or completed perjury, confidentiality suffers and clients will learn to refrain from being open with counsel. Finally, keeping the confidence secure and proceeding with a defence that utilizes the perjured testimony means that the lawyer is playing a role in misleading the court.

Freedman concedes that the trilemma yields to no simple solution, and professes that he has never been entirely comfortable with any response.[34] But his preferred approach, based on the great importance that he ascribes to client-lawyer confidentiality within an adversarial criminal justice system, is to adopt the following steps. The lawyer must start by attempting to dissuade the client from committing perjury. If the client is unswayed from the planned course of action, the lawyer can withdraw from the case, provided that the client suffers no attendant prejudice. However, in most cases prejudice cannot be

---

33  Freedman has written extensively on the subject. His best-known works include "Professional Responsibility of the Criminal Defence Lawyer: The Three Hardest Questions" (1966) 64 Mich. L. Rev. 1469; *Lawyers' Ethics in an Adversary System*, above note 2; and *Understanding Lawyers' Ethics* (New York: Matthew Bender, 1990).

34  See *Understanding Lawyers' Ethics*, above note 33 at 121.

avoided, and therefore withdrawal will not be an option. Accordingly, the lawyer must conduct the defence as though nothing is amiss, calling the client to the stand, bringing out the perjured testimony through examination-in-chief and re-examination, and relying on the perjury in closing argument.

The notion that a lawyer can sometimes knowingly lead and rely upon perjured evidence undoubtedly remains shocking to many lawyers, judges, academics and lay people. Few other commentators go so far as Freedman in protecting client-lawyer confidentiality. And, as we have seen, the rules of professional conduct in Canada, the United States, England, and Australia tend to be much less sanguine about counsel playing an active role in eliciting and relying upon perjured evidence.[35] Freedman's position is certainly the high-water mark of aggressive lawyering when it comes to the client-perjury problem.[36] Yet the force of his illuminating work persists, a valuable touchstone in assessing the suitability of any suggested response to client perjury.[37] We will therefore periodically return to Freedman's ideas as this chapter progresses.

# E.  OVERVIEW OF THE ISSUES AND ANALYTICAL FRAMEWORK

There are a number of issues that flow from the client-perjury problem, most of which can be examined by looking at the various options available to defence counsel in response. Remonstration with the client, withdrawal, calling the client as a witness, eliciting testimony, arguing

---

35   See the discussion in section C, "Related Rules of Professional Conduct," in this chapter.

36   In 1988, N. Lefstein, "Client Perjury in Criminal Cases: Still in Search of an Answer" (1988) 1 Geo. J. Legal Ethics 521 at 523–24, could note an irony in the fact that such a hotly debated position has never really been endorsed by any court or other commentator. Since Lefstein made this comment, however, Freedman's position has been supported in two well-argued academic articles: see J. Silver, "Truth, Justice, and the American Way: The Case Against the Client Perjury Rules" (1994) 47 Vand. L. Rev. 339; and N. Crystal, "Limitations on Zealous Representation in an Adversarial System" (1997) 32 Wake Forest L. Rev. 671.

37   Currently, the strongest proponent of Freedman's general view is Jay Silver: see Silver, above note 36. However, Silver rejects the notion that any trilemma exists, for he argues that: the pursuit of truth is actually harmed by any response other than proceeding normally; and that proceeding normally presents no real risk of subverting the truth-finding function of the criminal justice system.

before the trier of fact, and making disclosure to the court or Crown: when, if ever, is each of these options permitted, mandated, or forbidden? Another important aspect of the problem concerns the initial determination as to whether perjury is truly planned or has in fact already occurred. For ease of reference, we will discuss these issues by considering anticipated and completed client perjury separately.

# F.  ANTICIPATED CLIENT PERJURY

Often a lawyer will suspect that a client intends to commit perjury. Sometimes there will be plenty of time to consider and address the possibility. On other occasions, notably where the issue arises immediately before the client is scheduled to take the stand, the difficulty inherent in the client-perjury problem is compounded by the pressures and time constraints of the trial process.[38] Regardless, the lawyer must begin by considering the nature of his or her suspicions.

## 1)  Acquiring Knowledge that the Client Intends to Commit Perjury

We have already discussed the role of knowledge in the context of defending the client who is known to be guilty.[39] Assessing the nature of the lawyer's knowledge is equally important when it comes to client perjury. In either instance, counsel must determine whether the conduct of the defence — be it cross-examining a witness, eliciting testimony from the client, or arguing the facts to the jury — involves misleading the court. The applicable principles remain constant whether one is considering the defence of the guilty client or the prospect of client perjury.

The question of knowledge involves two different but closely related aspects of anticipated client perjury. First, the lawyer may know that a certain version of facts is false and, if recounted by the client, would constitute perjury. Second, the lawyer may know that the client steadfastly plans to testify to the false version of facts, the inten-

---

38   For a case where counsel appears to have been surprised by last-minute news of impending perjury, see *Sankar v. State of Trinidad and Tobago*, [1995] 1 All E.R. 236 (P.C.).

39   See section F, "Acquiring Knowledge that the Client is Guilty," in chapter 1.

tion being to mislead the court.[40] If the version of facts is not false, or the client does not plan to utilize the false facts in his or her testimony, the client-perjury problem never arises. In all other cases, what type or degree of knowledge will operate to place limits upon the conduct of the defence?

We can start by emphasizing that counsel should not jump to rash conclusions about a story's falsity or the client's nefarious intention.[41] The role of counsel in the adversary system is to act as the accused's advocate, not to assume the role of judge. The conduct of the defence must not be limited simply because defence counsel suspects that perjury will occur. Imposing such restrictions too quickly may work to impinge the client's constitutional rights, and where counsel's assumption that perjury will occur is erroneous, limiting the conduct of the defence may contribute to an unreliable verdict.[42]

Having reiterated the basic presumption against judging the client, we can move on to focus upon counsel's knowledge in relation to the possible falsity of a version of facts proffered by the client. Assume, for example, that the client tells counsel that he intends to testify that he was at home sleeping at the time of the crime. When can counsel be said to "know" that this alibi is false? The possible thresholds and their justifications have been reviewed in chapter 1.[43] Here, suffice it to say that counsel can be said to know that a version of events is false where he or she reasonably draws an irresistible conclusion of falsity from available information. Yet two caveats are necessary. First, a lawyer has a duty to ensure that the information underlying the conclusion is reliable. His or her determination must be based upon a careful investigation of all relevant facts.[44] Second, it is improper to use avoidance techniques as a means of cultivating ignorance and evading any ethical strictures associated with client perjury.[45]

---

40   It is worth stressing the "knowledge" of the client's intention can be a slippery concept: see section F, "Acquiring Knowledge that the Client is Guilty," in chapter 1. Some writers argue that knowledge of this sort can never be acquired: see Silver, above note 36 at 391.

41   See section F(1), "The Basic Presumption Against Judging the Client's Culpability," in chapter 1.

42   See section F(1), *ibid.*, and notes 45-46 and accompanying text, as well as the subsequent discussion of *Delisle*, above note 9.

43   See section F(2), "The Exception: Irresistible Knowledge of Guilt," in chapter 1.

44   Counsel's duties in this regard are described in section F(2), *ibid.*, and F(3), "A Common Example of Irresistible Knowledge of Guilt: The Confession," in chapter 1.

45   The problems with avoidance techniques are discussed in section F(4), "Avoidance Techniques: Restricting Client-lawyer Communications, Wilful

As a last point, one of the most common instances where counsel should twig to the possibility of client perjury occurs where the client has provided inconsistent statements.[46] But inconsistency, on its own, does not warrant a conclusion that the client plans to commit perjury. A client may quite legitimately have remembered additional facts or realized that an earlier version of events was incorrect.[47] Counsel must therefore refrain from equating inconsistency with planned perjury. Apposite in this regard is the approach taken by the British Columbia Professional Conduct Handbook, which advises counsel to explore the inconsistency with the client at the first available opportunity.[48] Only if the lawyer ascertains that the client intends to offer false testimony do the rules covering client perjury apply.

**Consultation with the Client:** As the preceding discussion of inconsistent statements intimates, counsel should discuss with the client any reasonable suspicion that perjury is being planned. Such a discussion is a necessary part of determining whether a proffered story is perjurious. Even where counsel cannot be said to possess irresistible knowledge that the client's version of events is false, the discussion may serve to dissuade the client from perjuring him or herself. In all cases, counsel must approach the issue with great sensitivity. Hasty, angry, or otherwise impolitic recriminations may strain or rupture the professional relationship, and do more harm than good.

## 2) Admonishing the Client to Tell the Truth

Once counsel comes to the firm conclusion that a client intends to commit perjury, the immediate reaction should be to attempt to dissuade him or her from pursuing such a course. Admonishing against perjury serves two purposes. First, counsel acts in the best interests of the client by providing advice concerning the possible harmful repercussions of advancing a perjurious defence. Even if the client is not particularly interested in the ethical niceties of the perjury problem, he or she will surely want to hear about the strategic considerations that

---

Blindness, 'Woodshedding,' and Viewing Guilt as Completely Irrelevant, in chapter 1.

46 An example where an eleventh-hour change in the client's story caused counsel concern is *Brigham*, above note 9 at 373.

47 See, for example, *Commonwealth v. Alderman*, 437 A.2d 36 at 39 (Pa. Super. 1981); *Johnson v. United States*, 404 A.2d 162 at 164 (D.C. 1979); and *Nix*, above note 5 at 190–91.

48 See B.C. ch. 8, r. 6.

typically make perjury a bad idea. Second, the administration of justice benefits whenever counsel is successful in convincing the client not to testify falsely. The court is not presented with false evidence, counsel remains free of complicity in any deception, and the attendant harm to the truth-finding process is avoided. For these reasons, it is widely accepted that defence counsel has a duty to remonstrate with the client against providing false evidence.[49] Even Monroe Freedman, who in certain circumstances condones counsel's participation in presenting false testimony from the client, recognizes that a lawyer must always try to dissuade the client from telling falsehoods on the stand.[50]

Depending upon the circumstances of the case, counsel's admonition should cover a number of points. Typically, the client must be told that:

1. perjury is a crime;
2. the prosecution will likely attack the perjured testimony, using cross-examination, reply evidence, and/or argument to the trier of fact (concrete examples should be provided if at all possible);
3. the perjury may well be discovered by the trier of fact, leading or contributing to the client's conviction;
4. once revealed, the bogus defence may cause the court to impose a harsher sentence than would otherwise be the case (there is divided authority as to whether, and how, the trial judge can utilize the offender's perjury in imposing sentence, but courts are apparently prepared to take account of perjurious testimony to negate or discount any suggestion that the offender is remorseful);[51]
5. the client's falsehood may also lead the authorities to lay a separate charge of perjury, with the attendant risk of an additional conviction and punishment; and

---

49  See, for example, CBA Code ch. IX, comm. 4; B.C. ch. 8, r. 2 & 7. In the United States, the major ethical guidelines are clearer in requiring remonstration: see ABA Model Rule 3.3, comm. 5 & 7; and Third Restatement §120, comm. "g."

50  See *Lawyers' Ethics in the Adversary System*, above note 2 at 120. But Silver, above note 36 at 418–19, argues that remonstration should be permitted only when required in the best interests of the client, from a tactical point of view. He contends that trying to dissuade the client from presenting perjury based on ethical considerations alone is improper.

51  See, for example, *R. v. Kozy* (1990), 58 C.C.C. (3d) 500 at 506–07 (Ont. C.A.); *R. v. Vickers* (1998), 105 B.C.A.C. 42 (C.A.); as well as C. Ruby, *Sentencing*, 5th ed. (Toronto: Butterworths, 1999) at §6.19–25; and R. Nadine-Davis & C. Sproule, *Canadian Sentencing Digest* (Toronto: Carswell, 1986) at 155.

6. defence counsel has an ethical duty not to mislead the court, and this duty may operate to permit or mandate remedial measures if the client does not change his or her mind.

The point just made concerning possible remedial measures deserves elaboration. The client must be advised as to exactly how an impending or completed perjury may limit the conduct of defence. Counsel must therefore be clear and precise in outlining the possible responses if the client remains impervious to the admonition. The responses available, and hence the content of this portion of the admonition, remain to be discussed below. At this juncture, however, we can say that a client should never be threatened with a response that counsel knows to be improper or has no intention of carrying out. Such an admonition would be duplicitous and might even operate to deny the client the effective assistance of counsel. Moreover, counsel must tread carefully in admonishing the client. Employing too heavy a hand may destroy the client's sense of trust in counsel, causing the relationship to break down completely. Similarly, counsel should make sure that the client does not misunderstand the warning and erroneously conclude that he or she will be subject to remedial measures even where the testimony is truthful.[52]

The close connection between admonishing the client and permissible remedial measures is demonstrated by the decision of the United States Supreme Court in *Nix v. Whiteside*.[53] Whiteside was charged with stabbing a drug-dealer to death. He told defence counsel that the killing was precipitated by his belief that the victim was about to shoot him with a gun. This belief was not based upon Whiteside having actually seen a gun, but the claim of self-defence was nonetheless feasible given the victim's reputation and comments and movements made just prior to the killing. Shortly before trial, however, Whiteside changed his story. He told his lawyers that the self-defence claim could not succeed unless he testified to having seen something metallic in the victim's hand: "If I don't say I saw a gun," said Whiteside, "I'm dead."[54]

---

52  Compare *R. v. Kennie* (1993), 121 N.S.R. (2d) 91 (S.C.A.D.), where the trial judge made comments to an unrepresented accused that, reasonably misconstrued, caused the accused to believe that he was not allowed to take the stand.

53  Above note 5.

54  The Supreme Court proceeded on the basis that this comment supported counsel's conclusion that Whiteside intended to commit perjury: see *Nix*, above note 5 at 162–63, 180 & 190. For a critique of this view, see Lefstein, above note 36 at 531–33.

Whiteside's counsel reacted to this last-minute revelation by trying to convince his client not to present false evidence.[55] The remonstration consisted of counsel telling Whiteside that the proposed testimony would be perjurious, and that the false assertion was not needed in order to establish a valid defence. Indeed, adding the bogus reference to seeing a metallic object could hurt the defence, given that the victim was not found in possession of a gun.[56] Counsel told his client that he would move to withdraw from the case if Whiteside insisted on going ahead with the lie. He also indicated that, in such an event, he would inform the court that the testimony was perjurious, and probably would be allowed to attempt to impeach the testimony.

Whiteside responded to counsel's advice and warning by agreeing not to testify falsely. The defence lawyer accepted this change of heart and took no further steps to prevent the previously anticipated perjury. This confidence in the client's sincerity was justified, for Whiteside took the stand and testified in chief without making mention of a metallic object. He even went so far as to admit in cross-examination that he did not see the victim holding a gun. The jury nevertheless found Whiteside guilty as charged, and he appealed on the ground that counsel's admonition operated to deny him a fair trial and the constitutional right to the effective assistance of counsel. In other words, Whiteside argued that he should have been allowed to present a perjurious defence.[57]

The opinion of the court dismissing Whiteside's appeal was written by Burger C.J., who recognized that counsel's first duty when confronted with proposed perjury is to try to dissuade the client from the unlawful course of conduct.[58] This assertion is not contentious.[59] Much more controversial was the Chief Justice's holding that defence counsel did not act improperly in threatening to withdraw and disclose the perjury to the court.[60] The Chief Justice also saw no problem in counsel making reference to impeaching the client's testimony.[61] In affirming the content of counsel's admonition, most especially regarding disclosure, the decision in Nix v. Whiteside has attracted considerable

---

55   The content of the admonition is found in Nix, ibid. at 161 & 179.

56   See G. Hazard & W. Hodes, The Law of Lawyering: A Handbook on the Model Rules of Professional Conduct, 2d ed. (Englewood, N.J.: Prentice Hall, 1993) at §3.3 (217).

57   See Nix, above note 5 at 162.

58   Ibid. at 169.

59   But see the argument made by Silver, discussed at note 50, above.

60   See Nix, above note 5 at 174.

61   Ibid. at 172–73 (note 7).

attention. Many writers have criticized the court's opinion[62] and have sought to limit the impact of the case by pointing out that Chief Justice Burger's remarks are mere dicta.[63] We will examine the solutions condoned by *Nix* v. *Whiteside* further below. For the moment, we merely use the case to illustrate how the propriety of counsel's admonition depends upon the legitimacy of the remedial responses proposed.

## 3) Client's Response to Admonition by Counsel

Defence counsel must carefully assess the client's response to an admonition against committing perjury. Only if the client is recalcitrant will counsel be justified in taking further remedial measures. Always keeping in mind the basic presumption against judging the client, counsel must not assume that the client will persist in the desire to testify falsely. It has thus been suggested that a lawyer can ordinarily assume that the client will heed the advice to avoid perjury, and that following an admonition the usual course is for counsel to proceed on this basis.[64] The validity of this assumption is perhaps greatest where the lawyer feels ethically able to disclose a *completed* perjury to the court, and tells the client as much. That is to say, the client who knows that the lawyer will reveal any falsehood is much more likely to abandon the intended perjury.

**Example:** Counsel represents X on a charge of aggravated assault. The case against X is strong, and X candidly tells her lawyer that she committed the offence. She also tells counsel that she nonetheless intends to take the stand and put forth a mendacious alibi. Counsel admonishes X to abandon the scheme, following which he applies to be removed from the record. Without more, this immediate attempt to withdraw is imprudent. Counsel is justified in taking remedial measures beyond admonition, whatever those measures may be, only where

---

62   See, for example, Lefstein, above note 36.

63   See, for example, D. Liskov, "Criminal Defendant Perjury: A Lawyer's Choice Between Ethics, the Constitution and the Truth" (1994) 28 New Eng. L. Rev. 881. While many writers take this view, the Third Restatement notes that, from the perspective of state and federal courts, *Nix* has settled most of the questions concerning client perjury: see Third Restatement §120, comm. i.

64   See T. McCarthy C. Brook, "Anticipated Client Perjury: Truth or Dare Comes to Court" in R. Uphoff, ed., *Ethical Problems Facing the Criminal Lawyer: Practical Answers to Tough Questions* (Chicago: American Bar Association, 1995) c. 11 at 157; and ABA Comm. on Ethics and Professional Responsibility, Formal Op. 353 (1987) at 8.

the admonition clearly fails and counsel can safely conclude that the client is recalcitrant.[65]

## 4) Remedial Measures Where the Client Cannot be Dissuaded

In those instances where the client refuses to jettison the perjury plan, the lawyer's task becomes much more difficult. What steps can be taken to avoid complicity in misleading the court without fatally undermining the duty of loyalty to the client? Possible options include withdrawal, refusing to call the client as a witness, adopting a neutral or passive role in eliciting the client's testimony, refusing to use perjured testimony in closing submissions, and disclosing the planned falsehood to the court or other third party. We will look at the possible merits and demerits of each of these options in turn.

### a)   Withdrawal

The CBA Code is unequivocal in providing that a lawyer should withdraw (or seek the leave of the court to do so) where the client persists in a course of conduct that involves dishonesty or deception upon the court.[66] Severing all connections with the client and the case certainly allows counsel to avoid having to make difficult choices concerning the best response to the anticipated or completed perjury. But withdrawal is not an easy panacea to the perjury problem, and there exist valid criticisms of the withdrawal option. Not unreasonably, several American commentators take the position that withdrawal is rarely the ideal response to anticipated client perjury.[67]

One of the most obvious weaknesses of the withdrawal option is that the perjury problem may merely be transferred to another lawyer. It is also possible that the client will have learned to be more circumspect in discussing his or her planned perjury, and as a result succeeds

---

65   This example is loosely based on the facts and decision in *State* v. *Jones*, 923 P.2d 560 (Mont. 1996).

66   See CBA Code ch. IX, comm. 4; B.C. ch. 8, r. 3; Alta. ch. 10, r. 14 & comm. 14.2. See also ABA Model Rule 3.3, comm. 7; and CBA Code ch. XII, comm. 4, pertaining specifically to withdrawal.

67   To varying degrees, this position is taken in J. Hall, Jr., *Professional Responsibility of the Criminal Lawyer*, 2d ed. (New York: Clark Boardman Callaghan, 1996) at §26(12); Lefstein, above note 36 at 525–27, 533; *Understanding Lawyers' Ethics*, above note 33 at 120; and Silver, above note 36 at 413–15.

with new counsel in passing off the false version of events as true.[68] Perhaps, however, this result is a lesser evil, for at least no lawyer is *knowingly* participating in the presentation of false evidence.[69] A different concern regarding withdrawal involves prospective harm to the client. Where withdrawal occurs shortly before or during the trial, the client may suffer prejudice in several forms. Significant extra cost may be incurred in hiring new counsel, or the accused may have difficulty in finding counsel on short notice. Also, where a mistrial is granted as a result of counsel's withdrawal, the resulting delay will prejudice the accused who is detained pending trial but utimately acquitted. On the other hand, where the withdrawal occurs well into the trial, and the court refuses to declare a mistrial, the accused may be forced to continue unrepresented.[70] (Even where a mistrial is granted, a valid systemic concern arises from the withdrawal option, related to the cost in terms of court and human resources.)

Prejudice can also occur where the withdrawal request implicitly alerts the judge or jury to the possibility of planned client perjury. For instance, an application to get off the record brought immediately before the accused is scheduled to testify will usually raise suspicions. The danger is especially great where the trial is by judge alone. Yet withdrawal during a jury trial may also create problems. The jury may grow suspicious of counsel's sudden disappearance, despite being admonished otherwise by the judge. Also, if the accused is convicted, the judge may decide to take the perjury into account on sentencing.[71] For these reasons, withdrawal may undermine the duty of confidentiality owed to the client. A final concern regarding the withdrawal option stems from the fact that counsel must obtain leave of the court to get off the record. Where the trial is about to begin or is already in progress, the court may refuse to allow counsel to withdraw.[72] In such a case, counsel has failed to extricate himself or herself from the perjury problem.

---

68   See, for example, *People* v. *Johnson*, 72 Cal. Rptr. 2d 805 at 812–813 (Ct. App. 1998), cert. denied (sub nom. *Johnson* v. *California*), 525 U.S. 914 (1998) [*Johnson*]; and *State* v. *Crenshaw*, 554 A.2d 1074 (Conn. 1989).

69   See M. Franck, "Letter to the Editor: Response to Lefstein" (1988) 2 Geo. J. Legal Ethics 585 at 587. This position is ridiculed as self-centred and anti-accused in Silver, above note 36 at 414.

70   See also the text accompanying note 170, below.

71   See note 51, above and accompanying text.

72   See section K, "Notice to the Court and Crown of Termination," in chapter 11. As noted, however, in some Canadian jurisdictions withdrawal may not require the leave of the court.

The weaknesses associated with withdrawal are illustrated by the recent murder case of *R. v. Jenkins*.[73] There, the accused was being cross-examined by the prosecutor when the court adjourned for the day. Upon resuming the next morning, defence counsel told the court that a matter had arisen requiring a further adjournment. Counsel eventually applied to withdraw from the case, on the ground that any continued participation would result in a deception of the court. The trial judge granted the withdrawal request, but consider some of the attendant problems. First, in applying to withdraw defence counsel released a good deal of confidential information, sufficient to support a strong inference that client perjury had occurred.[74] Second, although replacement counsel was standing by to take over the case, this option would likely be unavailable in most ongoing and lengthy trials. One also wonders whether replacement counsel could realistically hope to familiarize himself or herself with the case and provide competent representation on such short notice. Third, given the information released by withdrawing counsel, replacement counsel arguably was fixed with the knowledge that the defence being advanced was a fraud. It may be that no new counsel could ethically continue with the case.[75]

The potential weaknesses associated with withdrawal and exhibited in *Jenkins* can sometimes be minimized. As we have seen, the defence lawyer must start by doing his or her best to dissuade the client from committing perjury. A successful admonition will alleviate the need to consider withdrawal. Where the client persists in the plan to testify falsely, the feasibility of withdrawal depends upon timing and method. Where plenty of time remains prior to the trial, counsel will likely be able to withdraw without causing undue prejudice to the client. New counsel can be retained, and the mere fact of withdrawal will probably not raise suspicions of planned perjury. What about concerns that the problem is being transferred to another counsel, or that the client will learn from the experience and hide the planned perjury from the new lawyer? A possible partial solution would see withdrawing counsel make disclosure to the new lawyer, even where forbidden to do so by the client. Such action arguably falls within the future crime exception to the duty of confidentiality (albeit not in British Columbia, Ontario, Nova Scotia or perhaps Quebec) and minimizes

---

73   (2001), 152 C.C.C. (3d) 426 (Ont. S.C.J.) [*Jenkins*]. *Jenkins* involved both completed and anticipated perjury.

74   *Ibid.* at 434.

75   These and other problems make the withdrawal option as employed in *Jenkins* prone to serious deficiencies.

harm to the client by limiting disclosure to one who owes the client the same duty.[76] This option also serves to alert new counsel that he or she must be careful in handling the perjury problem, for feckless or reckless conduct of the trial may cause the original lawyer to make a formal complaint to the jurisdiction's applicable governing body. It may also be possible that former counsel will decide to inform the court of the perjury, if he or she is convinced that the new lawyer intends to present and rely upon the false evidence.[77]

The problem of maintaining a client's confidences when requesting the court's permission to withdraw is also subject to partial resolution. Most obviously, it is well accepted that counsel who withdraws from a case must not reveal confidential information.[78] Mentioning that the client intends to commit perjury, for instance, would violate the duty of confidentiality. But how can counsel justify withdrawal without revealing, at least implicitly, the nature of the disagreement with the client? This was a prominent problem facing withdrawing counsel in *Jenkins*, and he came very close to making express disclosure of the perjury, revealing that information received from the client part way through cross-examination meant that he would mislead the court if forced to present further defence evidence, cross-examine any reply witnesses or present a closing address (except to advance the most basic of principles).[79]

Rather than going so far as counsel in *Jenkins*, some writers have advocated the use of a sort of code, understood only by counsel and the court. "I would be forensically embarrassed if forced to continue with the retainer," the lawyer might say, and the judge and other counsel would know that planned perjury or other deception was the cause of the withdrawal.[80] This approach is disingenuous, for confidential information is undoubtedly released. It is better for the lawyer to indicate that the professional relationship has irreparably broken down.

---

76   See the discussion of this option, in the analogous context of the client who uses a false identity, in section K(1), "The Court Has Not Yet Been Misled," in chapter 5. See also the discussion in section F(4)(f), "Disclosure of the Intended Perjury," in this chapter regarding disclosure of an anticipated client perjury. The general issue of confidential information and successor lawyers is discussed in section M(3), "Successor Lawyers," in chapter 11.

77   See section F(4)(f), "Disclosure of the Intended Perjury," in this chapter.

78   See section M, "Confidentiality," in chapter 11.

79   See *Jenkins*, above note 73 at 434.

80   See, for example, D. Ipp, "Lawyers' Duties to the Court" (1998) 114 L.Q. Rev. 63 at 88; F. Schroeder, "Some Ethical Problems in Criminal Law" in Law Society of Upper Canada, *Representing an Arrested Client and Police Interrogation* (Toronto: R. De Boo, 1963) 87 at 92.

Crucially, the language used should be as nondescript as possible and thus equally appropriate in any circumstance where counsel seeks to withdraw from the case.[81] But the timing and context may inherently raise a suspicion of perjury, in which case the lawyer can do little to prevent the inference that the client is intending to lie on the stand. It has even been held by an American court that withdrawing counsel's statement, "I cannot state the reason," represented in the circumstances an unequivocal assertion that the client was planning a deception.[82]

Another Canadian case that illustrates the disclosure problem that can occur where counsel withdraws is *R. v. Pomeroy*.[83] There, the Crown finished calling its case, and defence counsel announced that there would be no defence evidence. After a brief recess, however, counsel addressed the court as follows:

> My Lord a matter has arisen over the dinner break in which I am obliged to address you. I spoke to my client, the accused, Mr. Pomeroy. I am finding myself in the position where I am not able to abide by my client's instructions because of ethical considerations. My application, therefore, at this time is to be relieved of my obligation as counsel in the conduct of this man's defence.
>
> I am instructed that the accused wishes to call evidence in his defence and specifically that he proposes to call himself in his own defence. I am not in a position to comply with those instructions.[84]

The Court of Appeal for Alberta found that defence counsel did not act improperly in explaining the reasons for withdrawal to the trial judge. However, this conclusion is questionable. Counsel's statement, though not as brazen as that proffered in *Jenkins*, indubitably led to the inference that the accused was about to commit perjury; indeed, the Court of Appeal expressly recognized this fact. The court's preferred response

---

81   Consider the following language, paraphrasing a suggestion by S. Skurka & J. Stribopoulos, "Professional Responsibility in Criminal Practice" in Law Society of Upper Canada, *42nd Bar Admission Course, 2000, Criminal Procedure Reference Materials* (Toronto: Law Society of Upper Canada, 2000) c. 1 at 15: "[T]here has been a disagreement on a fundamental matter, and I have lost the confidence of my client."

82   See *Lowery v. Cardwell*, 575 F.2d 727 at 729–31 (9th Cir. 1978); *United States v. Henkel*, 799 F.2d 369 at 370 (7th Cir. 1986), cert. denied 479 U.S. 1101 (1987) [*Henkel*]; *United States v. Scott*, 909 F.2d 488 at 492 (note 3) (11th Cir. 1990); *Maddox v. State*, 613 S.W.2d 275 at 283 (note 15) (Tex. Crim. App. 1980); and *State v. Berrysmith*, 944 P.2d 397 (Wash. Ct. App. 1997).

83   (1984), 15 C.C.C. (3d) 193 (Alta. C.A.) [*Pomeroy*].

84   *Ibid.*

was to hold that the trial judge was required to put this inference out of his mind, and that a failure to do so (as revealed in the judge's reasons) was grounds for a new trial. The better approach, in keeping with counsel's duty of confidentiality, is to minimize the possibility of any adverse inference by not revealing, or hinting at, the grounds for withdrawal. An insoluble conundrum is thus subject to a resolution that leaves something to be desired but is the best of a bad lot of choices.

This intractable problem of implied disclosure has been instrumental in leading Freedman to reject withdrawal as an option where the trial is to begin shortly or has already commenced.[85] On the other hand, the vast majority of commentators[86] and courts[87] accept withdrawal as a valid response for counsel who is faced with planned perjury. As we have seen, the CBA Code actually requires counsel whose admonitions fail to attempt withdrawal.[88] *Jenkins*, the only Canadian authority on point, staunchly supports the withdrawal option. In our view, withdrawal is an acceptable answer to anticipated perjury, especially where the application to get off the record can be brought well before trial and no confidences are breached. But as the trial approaches, the dangers associated with withdrawal loom much larger. Counsel who chooses to withdraw just before or during the trial must strive, to the extent possible, to avoid even the inference that the client is intending to commit perjury. He or she must also recognize that the request to get off the record may be denied, and thus be prepared to take alternative measures, if necessary, in the effort to address the client's perjurious scheme.[89] It may make sense to accompany an application to withdraw with the suggestion that the court appoint a new

---

85   See *Understanding Lawyers' Ethics*, above note 33 at 115. Some writers claim, incorrectly, that Freedman rejects withdrawal in all cases: see, for example, Liskov, above note 63 at 901.

86   In Canada, rare sceptics as to the propriety of withdrawal are B. Finlay, "The Conduct of Lawyers in the Litigious Process: Some Thoughts" in E. Gertner, *Studies in Civil Procedure* (Toronto: Butterworths, 1979) 15 at 27–28 (writing in the civil context); and A. Hutchinson, *Legal Ethics and Professional Responsibility* (Toronto: Irwin Law, 1999) at 158.

87   See, for example, *Nix*, above note 5 at 170 & 173–74; *Newcomb v. State*, 651 P.2d 1176 at 1182 (Alaska Ct. App. 1982); *Johnson*, above note 68 at 812; and *Shelton v. Georgia*, 426 S.E.2d 69 at 72 (Ga. Ct. App. 1992).

88   See CBA Code ch. IX, comm. 4; and ch. XII, comm. 4. To the same effect, see Skurka & Stribopoulos, above note 81 at 14.

89   For a case holding that counsel must continue with the retainer where a withdrawal application is denied, see *Florida Bar v. Rubin*, 549 So. 2d 1000 (Fla. 1989).

lawyer as *amicus curiae*.[90] Ultimately, these problems may lead counsel to choose to forego a request to withdraw, especially where the application is likely to be denied or the client will have trouble finding a new lawyer. Despite the apparent mandatory direction to the contrary found in the CBA Code, we believe that such a choice, reasonably made, is properly within the discretion of the lawyer.

One advantage of bringing an application to withdraw is that counsel has created a public record demonstrating an attempt to ward off complicity in client perjury. For better or worse, the attempt to withdraw promotes the lawyer's self-interest in avoiding repercussions arising out of subsequent false testimony. It might be thought that withdrawal thus offers some benefits even where there is no real possibility that the request will be granted by the court. Yet a withdrawal application should not be made merely because the lawyer wishes to make public his or her disapproval of the client's intention to commit perjury. The better course is to document carefully and fully all relevant circumstances, including all discussions with the client. Ideally, counsel will obtain written confirmation from the client as to the nature of the problem, the advice provided, and the client's refusal to change his or her course of action. Withdrawal may be a valid response to anticipated client perjury in some instances, but an application to get off the record should not be made for the sole reason that defence counsel wants to create a record of an attempt to address the perjury problem.

**Observation:** It may be that the withdrawal option is rendered moot by virtue of the client's decision to discharge counsel.[91] Another possibility is that the perjury issue creates an irremedial rupture in the client-lawyer relationship. In this latter instance, counsel has no choice but to bring a withdrawal application.[92]

### b)   Refusal to Call the Client as a Witness
If the lawyer decides not to withdraw, or a withdrawal application is rejected by the court, the question arises as to whether he or she can

---

90   See R. Peck, "Ethical Problems in Defending a Criminal Case: The Serbonian Bog" [1992] National Criminal Law Program at 11. For examples in the case law, see *Maddox*, above note 82 at 278–79; *State* v. *Trapp*, 368 N.E.2d 1278 (Ohio 1977). However, if withdrawing counsel is appointed as *amicus curiae*, conflict of interest and disclosure problems may arise: see *R.* v. *Samra* (1998), 129 C.C.C. (3d) 144 at 164–69 (Ont. C.A.).

91   See section D, "Discharge by the Client," in chapter 11.

92   See also section G, "Discretionary Withdrawal by the Lawyer," in chapter 11.

refuse to call the client as a witness. This response has several advantages. The CBA Code prohibits counsel from knowingly assisting or permitting the client to do anything dishonest and from knowingly participating in the deception of the court.[93] Facilitating the client's ruse by calling him or her to the stand and playing a role in eliciting testimony arguably runs afoul of this prohibition. Refusing to call the client as a witness undeniably works to prevent the perjury from occurring. To this extent, the option finds some implicit support in most Canadian ethical guidelines, which typically provide that "[i]f the client wishes to adopt a course that would involve a breach of this Rule, the lawyer must refuse and do everything reasonably possible to prevent it."[94] Most notably, the British Columbia ethical rules provide that "[a] lawyer shall not call as a witness in a proceeding a person who has advised the lawyer that the witness intends to offer false testimony."[95]

Yet there are obvious problems with any attempt to prevent a client from testifying. For one thing, an accused has a constitutional right to choose whether or not to take the stand as part of the defence.[96] Freedman has added that counsel violates the duty of confidentiality by barring the accused from the stand, given that he or she is using confidential information in order to block the desired defence and hence to harm the client.[97] Many commentators therefore conclude that impeding access to the witness stand is impermissible.[98] To the general chagrin of most of these commentators, however, *Nix* v. *Whiteside* strongly opines that the accused has no constitutional right to give perjured testimony, and firmly holds that the right to effective counsel is not violated where a lawyer intervenes to stop him or her from doing so.[99] The law in Canada is not clear on this point, but our courts may also decide that counsel's refusal to call the accused to the stand does

---

93  See CBA Code ch. IX, comm. 2(b) & (e).
94  See, for example, CBA Code ch. IX, comm. 4; and B.C. ch. 8, r. 7.
95  B.C. ch. 8, r. 5.
96  See the cases cited at note 9, above.
97  See *Understanding Lawyers' Ethics*, above note 33 at 135–36.
98  See, for example, C.W. Wolfram, *Modern Legal Ethics* (St. Paul: West, 1986) at §12.5; McCarthy & Brook, above note 64 at 162; and Skurka & Stribopoulos, above note 81 at 14.
99  See *Nix*, above note 5 at 173–74. Even so, the Supreme Court's decision does not purport to determine whether a lawyer *must* intervene in this way: see Hazard & Hodes, above note 56 at §3.3(213).

not violate any constitutional rights.[100] Even so, denying an accused the opportunity to testify may be too extreme a response, and infringe the right to the effective assistance of counsel, where the result is to prevent him or her from presenting other, *non-perjurious* testimony to the fact-finder. In such an instance, refusing to call the client as a witness prevents perjury but in addition deprives him or her of a valid defence. Finally, it has been argued that denial of the accused's right to testify, even if justified in certain cases, should never be permitted without a full inquiry by the court, and thus defence counsel has no business unilaterally making such a decision.[101]

Leaving aside any constitutional concerns, there are other problems that flow from counsel's refusal to allow the client to testify. The client may ignore the lawyer's interdiction and simply inform the court that he or she wishes to testify. At this point, the lawyer cannot physically intervene to stop the client. Making submissions to the court in an effort to obtain a ruling that the client cannot testify may be possible in theory, but only if one concludes that disclosure is acceptable as a last alternative.[102] In any event, counsel who finds himself or herself advancing a position in opposition to the client's publicly stated wishes should not continue to act on the case. Of course, counsel could move to withdraw, but such a request might be refused, and given the cir-

---

100  See, for example, *Vickers*, above note 51 at 46 (court suggests that there is no right to testify falsely); *R. v. Li*, [1993] B.C.J. No. 2312 at para. 59 (C.A.) (QL), leave to appeal to S.C.C. refused (1994), 178 N.R. 395 (S.C.C.) (court suggests that there is no right to testify falsely); *R. v. Fabrikant* (1995), 97 C.C.C. (3d) 544 at 572–74 (Que. C.A.), leave to appeal to S.C.C. refused (1995), 98 C.C.C. (3d) vi (S.C.C.) (right to testify waived by virtue of disruptive behaviour); *R. v. Braun* (1994), 95 C.C.C. (3d) 443 at 451 & 454–55 (Man. C.A.) (court prevents offender from testifying on sentencing); *R. v. Strauss* (1995), 100 C.C.C. (3d) 303 at 318 (B.C.C.A.); *R. v. Tsang* (1985), 27 C.C.C. (3d) 365 at 372–75 (B.C.C.A.); and *R. v. Calder* (1994), 92 C.C.C. (3d) 97 at 110, 126–27 (Ont. C.A.), per Labrosse J.A. and Doherty J.A., respectively, leave to appeal to S.C.C. refused (1994), 94 C.C.C. (3d) vii (S.C.C.), aff'd (1996), 105 C.C.C. (3d) 1 (S.C.C.).

101  See Lefstein, above note 36 at 537 & 550. This point is pushed even further in Silver, above note 36 at 368–92, who rejects *any* intervention by defence counsel on this basis. Silver contends, among other things, that defence counsel are frequently handicapped in applying ethical standards, by reason of class and race bias and self-interest.

102  Regarding which, see the discussion in section F(4)(f)k, "Disclosure of the Intended Perjury," in this chapter.

cumstances a withdrawal application would probably suggest that the client intends to commit perjury.[103]

### c)    Eliciting Testimony By Means of Free or Open Narrative

"Free or open narrative" refers to a special mode of eliciting the client's testimony. Counsel identifies the accused as the next witness, and conducts the examination-in-chief in the normal manner where the anticipated answers are not known to contain falsehoods. However, when it comes to eliciting testimony that counsel knows to be untrue, the conventional examination-in-chief is abandoned. Instead, the lawyer is confined to asking the client whether he or she wishes to make any additional statement concerning the case to the fact-finder. No guidance is provided by counsel in the form of follow-up questions. Assuming that the client's testimony contains false assertions, counsel is not permitted to rely upon the perjurious evidence in addressing the jury. It is not clear whether the narrative approach would permit counsel to make valid objections during cross-examination, but arguably such interventions are justified given that counsel is not thereby eliciting false testimony.

The strength of the narrative approach, according to proponents, is the ability to accommodate the competing principles at stake. The lawyer does not fatally undermine the duty of loyalty to the client, and the client's ability to testify is preserved. At the same time, counsel is distanced from participation in the perjury and to this extent is not complicit in misleading the court.[104] The leading source of support for the narrative approach is the 1971 first edition of the ABA Defense Function Standards.[105] But the ABA House of Delegates withdrew this option from consideration as part of a proposed second edition, and the current Standards contain no reference to the narrative approach.[106] A number of courts in the United States have accepted the

---

103 Nonetheless, an initial refusal to call the client as a witness, followed by an application to withdraw if the client insists on taking the stand, is consistent with Commentary 4 to Chapter IX of the CBA Code.
104 See Lefstein, above note 36 at 548.
105 See ABA Defense Standard 4-7.7(c), the full text of which is reproduced in Hall, above note 67 at §26.4.
106 See the discussion in the Third Restatement §120, reporter's note to comment "i." The narrative approach endorsed by the first edition was altered somewhat in the proposed (but rejected) second edition: see Lefstein, above note 36 at 542.

narrative approach as a valid response to anticipated client perjury,[107] however, and several respected commentators have followed suit.[108]

Yet, paradoxically, the strength of a compromise position is often the source of its weakness, and the narrative approach is no exception. Utilizing this method of examination has been criticized because the lawyer, though admittedly adopting a more passive role, is still knowingly facilitating the presentation of false evidence.[109] Conversely, narrative examination is open to attack because counsel's unusual approach may well signal to the judge and prosecution that the client is lying.[110] It is also not inconceivable that an astute jury would arrive at the same conclusion, especially after noticing that the lawyer's closing submissions make no reference to key testimony by the accused. In either case, confidentiality suffers in a way that may harm the client when it comes to the final determination as to guilt and the imposition of a sentence. Finally, and despite protestations by its proponents, adopting the narrative approach may cause as much damage to the client-lawyer relationship as would outright disclosure. As Wolfram observes, the narrative approach thus tries to have it both ways, in his view incoherently so, and ends up causing substantial harm to all of the principles at stake.[111] Wolfram's view is shared by the ABA Model Rules, which reject the narrative approach,[112] and appears to find support in the Supreme Court's decision in *Nix* v. *Whiteside*.[113]

A related potential problem arises from the prosecutor's possible objection to defence counsel's use of the narrative approach. Upon

---

107 See, for example, *Sanborn* v. *State*, 474 So. 2d 309 (Fla. Dist. Ct. App. 1985); *Commonwealth* v. *Jermyn*, 620 A.2d 1128 at 1130–31 (Pa. 1993), cert. denied 510 U.S. 1049 (1994); *Rubin* v. *State*, 490 So. 2d 1001 (Fla. Dist. Ct. App. 1986), review denied 501 So. 2d 1283 (Fla.), cert. denied 483 U.S. 1005 (1987); *State* v. *Layton*, 432 S.E.2d 740 at 754–55 (W. Va. 1993); *People* v. *Bartee*, 566 N.E.2d 855 at 857 (Ill. 1991) [*Bartee*]; and *Shockley* v. *State*, 565 A.2d 1373 at 1377 (Del. Super. Ct. 1989). See also Conn. Bar Ass'n Comm. on Professional Ethics, Op. 42 (1992).

108 Principal among these commentators is Lefstein, above note 36; and W. Brazil, "Unanticipated Client Perjury and the Collision of Rules, Evidence, and Constitutional Law" (1979) 44 Mo. L. Rev. 601.

109 See *Nix*, above note 5 at 170–71.

110 On the other hand, a main proponent of the narrative approach argues that this potential harm is helpful to counsel in seeking to dissuade the client from committing perjury: see Lefstein above note 36, at 546.

111 Wolfram, above note 98 at 661.

112 See ABA Model Rule 3.3, comm. 9.

113 In *Nix*, above note 5 at 170–71, Chief Justice Burger describes the narrative approach without providing any sign of approval.

observing that defence counsel is not eliciting testimony in the normal manner, the prosecutor might demur on the ground that there is no opportunity to object to inadmissible evidence prior to such evidence being heard by the trier of fact. The defence lawyer would then be in the awkward position of trying to explain the basis for proceeding by way of narrative, without breaching confidentiality. Arguably, however, the narrative form of questioning is a perfectly acceptable manner of proceeding. Asking an open-ended question does not necessarily breach any of the rules usually applicable to the proper conduct of an examination-in-chief. Moreover, given that the narrative approach will usually result in the client's version of events being presented in a less than organized and coherent manner, and may alert the trier of fact to the client's lies, few prosecutors may care to intervene. Yet, if an objection is made and upheld, defence counsel is in a terribly difficult position, forbidden to continue using the narrative method but equally loath to facilitate perjury by eliciting testimony in the normal manner. The proposed (but rejected) client-perjury provision in the second edition of the ABA Defense Standards attempted to resolve this problem by permitting the lawyer to "seek to avoid direct examination," meaning that a sustained objection by the prosecutor would allow defence counsel to engage in something closer to a normal examination-in-chief.[114]

While counsel who employs the narrative approach is not allowed to rely upon perjurious testimony in making his or her closing arguments, the trial judge is not necessarily in the same position. To the contrary, the judge may be under a positive obligation to present the accused's version of events to the jury as part of the charge.[115] In *R. v. Colpitts*,[116] counsel's closing conspicuously neglected to make mention of a key element in his client's testimony. While we do not know for certain that this tack was prompted by knowledge that the testimony was false, the hallmarks of client perjury were decidedly present. Assuming that counsel felt constrained by reason of a perjury, consider the outcome of the case. The trial judge followed counsel's suit, making no reference to the accused's potentially perjurious testimony in his charge. But the Supreme Court of Canada ruled that the judge erred in not doing so, and granted the appellant a new trial. This sort of result will be avoided where the appellant also raises the issue of coun-

---

114 See Lefstein, above note 36 at 542.
115 See, for example, *R. v. Bernier* (1993), 20 C.R. (4th) 353 at 360–62 (Que. C.A.); and *R. v. Caron* (1998), 126 C.C.C. (3d) 84 at 91–93 (Que. C.A.).
116 (1965), [1966] 1 C.C.C. 146 (S.C.C.).

sel's conduct at trial, because attacking the competence of counsel will typically waive lawyer-client privilege.[117] Consequently, the perjury problem will come into the open on appeal and will likely operate to prevent censure of the trial judge for failing to review the perjured evidence in the charge.[118]

### d)   Eliciting Testimony in the Normal Manner

As we have seen, Monroe Freedman is the prime exponent of the view that counsel should elicit and use perjurious testimony in the normal manner.[119] Freedman's view is also adopted in the American Trial Lawyer's Association ethical code and an opinion promulgated by the National Association of Criminal Defense Lawyers (both of which he helped to draft).[120] Most recently, this view has been adopted by Jay Silver in a comprehensive article addressing many aspects of the client-perjury problem.[121] Proceeding in this manner has the advantage of bolstering the client's right to testify and preventing any breach of counsel's duty of loyalty. Moreover, counsel is arguably not wilfully procuring perjured evidence, for he or she must have made good-faith efforts to dissuade the client from leading false testimony.[122] Silver goes so far as to propose that this approach best serves the goal of promoting truth in criminal proceedings, on the ground that perjury is almost always detected by the trier of fact and that counsel is particularly ill-equipped to determine whether proposed testimony is false.[123]

Most ethical codes firmly reject Freedman's approach.[124] In Canada, by virtue of commentaries 2(b) and 2(e) to Chapter IX, the

---

117 See, for example, *B.(G.D.)*, above note 6.

118 A different issue concerns the impact of defence counsel's silence on Crown counsel. Can the prosecutor whose closing follows that of defence counsel ask the jury to draw an adverse inference from defence counsel's failure to comment on certain important aspects of the client's testimony in the closing argument? In *State* v. *Long*, 714 P.2d 465 at 467 (Ariz. Ct. App. 1986), the prosecutor's request that the jury draw this inference was held to be improper.

119 See section D, "Monroe Freedman and the Lawyer's Trilemma," in this chapter.

120 See the ATLA Code Rule 1.2, including the associated examples; and NACDL Op. 92-2.

121 Silver, above note 36.

122 See *Understanding Lawyers' Ethics*, above note 33 at 122–23. However, compare the view taken by Silver, who rejects the notion that counsel should make efforts to dissuade the client apart from pointing out the tactical disadvantages of lying on the stand, Silver, above note 36 at 418–19.

123 Silver, above note 36 at 423.

124 In the United States, see ABA Model Rule 3.3, comm. 7; and Third Restatement §120.

CBA Code appears to forbid counsel from proceeding in the normal manner.[125] *Jenkins* also arrives at this conclusion, in so far as the withdrawal option is endorsed because counsel is forbidden from misleading the court.[126] The vast majority of academic commentators have shown a similar reluctance to accept the Freedman position.[127] At bottom, allowing counsel to lead and use false evidence consciously is seen to be too great an impingement upon the truth-finding function of the adversarial criminal justice system. The duty of loyalty simply does not extend to embrace such conduct, nor do the client's constitutional protections include the right to present false evidence affirmatively.[128] Proceeding in the normal manner is therefore not recommended for the lawyer who faces a client-perjury problem.

e)   **Permitting the Client to Offer Only Non-Perjurious Testimony**
Yet another approach is to call the client as a witness, but only for the purpose of testifying to facts that counsel does not know to be false. This option, less commonly presented as a viable response to anticipated client perjury, seeks to alleviate some of the criticisms directed at refusing to call the client as a witness, and it garners support from both the ABA Standing Committee on Ethics and Professional Responsibility and the Third Restatement.[129] For instance, the Third Restatement states: "If the client nonetheless insists on the right to take the stand, defense counsel must accede to the demand of the accused to testify. *Thereafter defense counsel may not ask the accused any question if counsel knows that the response would be false.*"[130] Yet restricting the client's testimony presents its own serious problems. It is quite probable that, once on the stand, the client will testify to those facts that he or she wishes, regardless of counsel's attempts to guide the examination in a particular direction. Moreover, even if the client can be restricted to providing non-perjurious testimony, the result will frequently be that no testimony whatsoever is offered regarding crucial aspects of the case. Such a failure will leave the fact-finder highly

---

125 See CBA Code ch. IX, comm. 2(b) & (e).
126 See *Jenkins*, above note 73 at 437.
127 For instance, none of the Canadian, English, or Australian writers mentioned in this chapter adopts Freedman's view.
128 See also the discussions in sections B, "Competing Principles," and F(4)(b), "Refusal to Call the Client as a Witness," in this chapter, regarding some of the constitutional rights at play.
129 See ABA Formal Op. 353 (1987), above note 64 at 8; and Third Restatement §120, comm. "i." See also *State* v. *Lowery*, 523 P.2d 54 (Ariz. 1974).
130 Third Restatement §120, comm. "i" (emphasis added).

unimpressed and may twig other trial participants to the client-perjury problem. Finally, there is no guarantee that the Crown will not delve into the problematic area in the course of cross-examination. Presumably, the client will respond by providing the false evidence, undermining the entire point of the exercise.

## f)    Disclosure of the Intended Perjury

The possibility that a lawyer may be required or permitted to disclose a client's intended perjury is highly controversial. Those who advocate disclosure of an intended perjury rely primarily on the point that counsel must not allow false evidence to skew the truth-finding function of the criminal justice system.[131] On this view, where revelation is necessary to prevent such an occurrence, all other attempts at prevention having failed, counsel must or may take this final remedial step. A somewhat different argument in favour of disclosure focuses upon the benefits to be derived from involving a neutral arbiter in the process. Depending upon the nature of the procedure governing the act of disclosure, a judge may be able to examine and assess the disagreement between counsel and client. Judicial intervention at this stage might conceivably serve to fashion a resolution to the problem, or even to discover that counsel's fears were entirely unjustified.

The arguments against disclosure are familiar. It is said, quite rightly, that disclosure represents a huge incursion against the duty of confidentiality normally owed to the client. Indeed, disclosing the intended perjury may require the revelation of a whole raft of confidential information, especially if the client disputes counsel's allegations and an evidentiary hearing is held. Clients may therefore react by refusing to be candid in their dealings with lawyers, with the result that the overall quality of representation suffers. Less candid dealing may actually cause the incidence of completed perjury to rise. Clients who fear disclosure are more likely to hide planned perjury from their counsel, with a resulting decrease in the likelihood that counsel can discover the plan and dissuade the client from its execution. As well, obvious harms to the client may arise from counsel's disclosure, including conviction at trial, a harsher sentence, and the laying of new criminal charges.[132] Counsel risks visiting these harms upon the client

---

131 See, for example, Franck, above note 69; and ABA Formal Op. 353 (1987), above note 64 at 6 & 8.

132 These harms become more or less likely depending upon the procedure under which disclosure is made, as well as the court's reaction to the information.

even where the latter responds to disclosure by deciding to abandon the intended perjury.

It is also important to remember that a client's intentions can be fluid and changing. There is always a possibility that the seemingly determined perjurer will abandon his or her plan upon taking the stand.[133] For this reason, the ability to disclose a *completed* perjury may be sufficient to address concerns that counsel must not participate in misleading the court. Disclosure after the fact still goes a long way to avoid harm to the truth-finding function of the trial process, and the threat of an immediate *ex post facto* revelation would probably discourage even the most determined client from going ahead with perjury.[134]

Do the ethical guidelines promulgated by the Canadian legal profession shed any light on the debate? At first glance, it appears that our rules of professional responsibility successfully avoid addressing the disclosure issue. The CBA Code stipulates that the lawyer confronted with intended perjury "must refuse and do everything reasonably possible to prevent it."[135] If the client persists, the Code provides that the lawyer should withdraw or seek the leave of the court to do so.[136] One could argue that the reference to "doing everything reasonable to prevent the perjury" (to paraphrase) includes making disclosure. But inferring a duty or license to take such drastic action seems too bold. In contrast, where perjury has been completed, the CBA Code expressly addresses the disclosure possibility.[137] Silence in the context of anticipated perjury militates at least slightly against reading the Code to require or allow disclosure. Moreover, where counsel seeks to withdraw, which is presented as an action of last resort, some ethical rules expressly forbid any reference to the client's planned perjury.[138] This prohibition makes sense only if there has been no prior disclosure of the problem. In this vein, the decision in *Jenkins* seems to reject dis-

---

133  See ABA Formal Op. 353 (1098), above note 64 at 8.

134  For a discussion on the merits and demerits of disclosing a completed perjury, see section G(3)(b), "Disclosure," in this chapter.

135  CBA Code ch. IX, comm. 4. See also B.C. ch. 8, r. 7.

136  *Ibid.* See also B.C. ch. 8, r. 2–3; and Alta. ch. 10, r. 14 & comm. 14.2.

137  However, the disclosure provision pertaining to completed perjury is not exactly a model of clarity: see section K(2)(c), "The Disclosure Issue and the CBA Code," in chapter 5, as well as section C, "Related Rules of Professional Conduct," in this chapter.

138  The clearest statement of this position comes in the British Columbia code: see B.C. ch. 8, r. 4. See also section H(7), "Duty Survives End of Retainer," in chapter 4, and section M, "Confidentiality," in chapter 11.

closure of both anticipated and completed client perjury, instead supporting the view that defence counsel must withdraw.[139] Moreover, the court in *Jenkins* appeared to accept that withdrawing counsel remained bound by the duty of confidentiality.[140]

The major American ethical codes are not much clearer. Divining the position of the ABA Model Code is almost impossible.[141] As for the ABA Model Rules, Rule 3.3 can certainly be read to condone disclosure of anticipated perjury as a last resort.[142] However, this interpretation has been rejected by a number of writers, who offer involved arguments as to why Rule 3.3 does not permit prophylactic disclosure.[143] It is also open to discussion whether the Third Restatement permits disclosure in advance of the client's perjury. The wording adopted by the American Law Institute is slightly different from that employed in Rule 3.3,[144] and the comments and reporter's note seem slanted against preventative disclosure.[145]

Despite the confusion regarding the propriety of disclosing anticipated client perjury, some American commentators feel that the Supreme Court has settled the issue in *Nix v. Whiteside*.[146] Yet a great many writers take issue with this view, for a number of reasons.[147] Certainly, interpreting *Nix v. Whiteside* as condoning disclosure made prior to the commission of perjury is open to question. For one thing, on the facts of the case, the warning given to the client by counsel appears to suggest only that a completed perjury will be disclosed to the court.[148] There is no definitive, unambiguous statement by the court to the effect that counsel acts ethically in choosing to disclose a perjury that is merely anticipated. Perhaps the closest that the court comes to such a statement is the comment by Burger C.J. that "[a]n

---

139 *Jenkins*, above note 73.

140 *Ibid.* at 429 & 434.

141 See section C, "Related Rules of Professional Conduct," in this chapter, especially the discussion at note 25 and accompanying text.

142 Most notably, this interpretation is taken in ABA Formal Op. 353 (1987), above note 64 at 8.

143 See, for example, McCarthy & Brook, above note 64 at 157.

144 The Third Restatement's reference to an exception to the ordinary rule of confidentiality appears applicable only where perjury has already occurred: see §120(2).

145 *Ibid.* (in particular, see comments "h" and "i" and the associated portions of the Reporter's Note).

146 See, for example, Hazard & Hodes, above note 56 at §3.3(213, 216–17 & 219).

147 See, for example, Hall, above note 67 at §26.7.

148 See *Nix*, above note 5 at 161, 172, & 174 (per Burger C.J.), as well as 179–80 (per Blackmun J.).

attorney's duty of confidentiality, which totally covers the client's admission of guilt, does not extend to a client's announced plans to engage in future criminal conduct."[149]

Coming to an unassailable conclusion regarding the American position is impossible. The intricacies and uncertainties involved in reading the major ethical codes and the decision in *Nix v. Whiteside* demonstrate only that the experience in the United States offers no clear guidance to Canadian lawyers. To this muddled backdrop, however, we must add consideration of the future-harm exception to the duty of confidentiality.[150] The notion that counsel can ethically make disclosure of a client confidence in order to prevent certain kinds of future-harm is well-established in both Canada and the United States, and has been discussed at length elsewhere.[151] On the wording of many Canadian future-harm rules, a lawyer has a discretion to reveal an intended perjury, regardless of whether withdrawal has been sought or granted. Disclosure is thus permitted in most cases of anticipated perjury, though typically never required.[152] Naturally, in deciding whether to exercise this discretion, counsel must keep in mind the advantages and disadvantages of revealing the client's planned falsehoods.[153] Given our view that counsel can permissibly disclose *completed* client perjury,[154] and the difficulty in ascertaining whether the client will really act to implement the perjurious plan, we believe that this discretion should generally not be exercised. The one limited circumstance where we view disclosure of anticipated perjury as permissible, though not required, involves revelation to new counsel for the client following withdrawal.[155]

**Comparison:** British Columbia, Ontario, Nova Scotia, and possibly Quebec have the narrowest future-harm exceptions of all Canadian

---

149  *Ibid.* at 174.
150  See section G, "Future Harm or Public Safety," in chapter 5.
151  See section G(1), "The Rules of Professional Conduct," in chapter 5. See also section K(1), "The Court Has Not Yet Been Misled," in chapter 5, discussing the possible disclosure of a client's intention to use a false identity.
152  Disclosure would be required only if the anticipated result would involve violence, and only then in certain Canadian jurisdictions (for example, Ontario and British Columbia never mandate disclosure). In New Brunswick, however, the ethical rules require disclosure in order to prevent any "serious crime." See generally, section G(1), "The Rules of Professional Conduct," in chapter 5.
153  For a discussion of the factors that should impact on counsel's exercise of the discretion, see section G(8), "The Lawyer's Discretion," in chapter 5.
154  See section G(3)(b), "Disclosure," in this chapter.
155  See the discussion in section F(4)(a), "Withdrawal," in this chapter.

jurisdictions. In the former two provinces, counsel is permitted (and never required) to disclose confidential information only where necessary to prevent a crime involving death or serious bodily harm.[156] It is thus unlikely that counsel in British Columbia and Ontario can ever rely upon the governing body's future-harm exception to justify disclosure of anticipated client perjury (however, what of the case where counsel represents a client who intends to testify falsely to the detriment of a co-accused in a trial where both are charged with first degree murder?). The same goes for counsel in Nova Scotia, where the future harm exception requires disclosure where necessary to prevent a violent crime.[157] In Quebec, there is arguably no future-harm exception at all, meaning that this exception cannot provide a basis for making disclosure.[158]

If counsel does decide to make disclosure of intended perjury, settling upon the mechanics of the revelation raises numerous problems. In a trial by jury, counsel could make disclosure to the judge and prosecutor, in the absence of the trier of fact.[159] It has also been suggested that disclosure could be made to the judge alone, without notifying the Crown attorney or perhaps even the client.[160] However, keeping the client in the dark is of dubious ethical validity. Taking action without the knowledge of the client is ordinarily a serious breach of the duty to keep the client informed. Moreover, counsel must remonstrate with the client prior to making disclosure, in the course of which the client must be warned as to possible remedial measures. Going behind the client's back in this way may also violate the accused's right to be present during the trial.[161] Finally, and leaving logistical problems aside, counsel may want to consider bringing an emergency application to a judge other than the trial judge.[162] Yet once the trial has started, obtaining an adjournment for such a purpose, without alerting the trial judge to the reason, may be difficult.

---

156 See B.C. ch. 5, r. 5.12; and Ont. r. 2.03(3).

157 N.S. ch. 5, r. 5.12.

158 See the discussion in section G(1), "The Rules of Professional Conduct," in chapter 5.

159 See *United States* v. *Long*, 857 F.2d 436 (8th Cir. 1988) [*Long*].

160 See *United States* v. *Litchfield*, 959 F.2d 1514 (10th Cir. 1992).

161 See s. 650(1) of the *Criminal Code*, above note 1; R. v. *Dunbar* (1982), 68 C.C.C. (2d) 13 (Ont. C.A.); R. v. *Vézina* (1986), 23 C.C.C. (3d) 481 (S.C.C.); and R. v. *Barrow* (1987), 38 C.C.C. (3d) 193 (S.C.C.).

162 This possibility is raised in *Long*, above note 159. See also C. Reiger, "Client Perjury: A Proposed Resolution of the Constitutional and Ethical Issues" (1985) 70 Minn. L. Rev. 121 at 151.

Once a judge has been informed of the anticipated problem, the client may indicate an intention not to offer the testimony in question. At this point, the possibility of perjury will be remote, and counsel can proceed to call the client to the stand (if the professional relationship has not been destroyed by the disclosure). But in other cases there may be a dispute as to whether the client indeed intends to offer false testimony. A judge may be forced to hold an evidentiary hearing on the issue, obviously in the continued absence of the jury.[163] However, if this route is taken, the defence lawyer risks being removed from the record by virtue of a conflict of interest and his or her probable role as a witness.[164] A valid concern is whether the accused will therefore go unrepresented at the hearing. Also, will the evidentiary hearing require a review of the entire case against the accused, including all information (much of it confidential) in the possession of defence counsel? A further conundrum arises if new counsel is appointed, and that counsel concludes that the accused is going to commit perjury at the evidentiary hearing.[165]

If the trial judge is unable to determine that the client is intent upon committing perjury, the client should be permitted to testify. But where the judge concludes that perjury will occur if the accused takes the stand, the next step is not immediately obvious. The judge will in effect face many of the options that initially bedevilled defence counsel. He or she may try to dissuade the client from carrying out the perjury, and, if unsuccessful, may rule that counsel can withdraw from the case. Or the judge might allow counsel to remain and have the accused testify in narrative form,[166] or adopt Freedman's view and encourage counsel to proceed in calling the client as though nothing is amiss.[167] Yet this latter result means that the client's confidence has been violated without achieving much in return (apart from the court's permission to elicit and rely upon false evidence). A much different approach would be to hold that the disclosed information is neither confidential nor privileged, and permit the Crown counsel to lead evi-

---

163 See, for example, *Long*, above note 159; *Butler* v. *United States*, 414 A.2d 844 (D.C. 1980); *Thornton* v. *United States*, 357 A.2d 429 at 432 (D.C. 1976); and *Witherspoon* v. *United States*, 557 A.2d 587 (D.C. 1989). Other courts have rejected the idea that a hearing is necessary: see, for example, *Bartee*, above note 107 at 857.

164 See ABA Model Rule 3.3, comm. 11.

165 See Liskov, above note 63 at 903.

166 See *Henkel*, above note 82; *Long*, above note 159 at 44; and *Commonwealth* v. *Mascitti*, 534 A.2d 524 at 528 (1987).

167 See *Understanding Lawyers' Ethics*, above note 33 at 127.

dence of the accused's plan and/or cross-examine the accused on the matter if he or she takes the stand. Similarly, the judge may favour warning the jury that the accused's testimony is false or must be carefully scrutinized.[168] Finally, it is conceivable that a judge, once convinced beyond a reasonable doubt that proposed testimony is perjurious, and having concluded that there is no constitutional right to present false evidence, will rule that the accused cannot testify.[169]

Another possible judicial response is to declare a mistrial, perhaps on the ground that counsel has been discharged or (with the court's permission) withdrawn. A mistrial might also be sought on the basis of a reasonable apprehension that the judge will misuse the information on sentencing, in the event that the accused is convicted.[170] An objection to the mistrial option is that an accused could derail proceedings and delay a feared conviction by repeatedly asserting a firm intention to lie on the stand. This problem can be partially alleviated by making the record from the first trial available if the perjury issue arises during the second proceeding, and ruling that the accused's actions represent waiver of the right to counsel. Yet any mistrial that comes late in the proceedings has a high cost in terms of wasted resources, and may cause harm to the client who is awaiting trial in custody, not to mention the course of justice where witnesses become unavailable or memories fade.

Until now, we have assumed that the perjury problem is disclosed during a jury trial. But the same issue can obviously arise when the accused is being tried by a judge alone. In this case, the problems associated with disclosure are more severe. Notably, the revelation can be made only to the trier of fact, with the result that subsequent prejudice to the accused is all but unavoidable.[171] For this reason, a mistrial may be the only valid course of action for the trial judge once the accused's planned perjury is revealed. Others have suggested that disclosure to the court, while permissible in a jury trial, can never be countenanced in a trial by judge alone.[172] Yet another option is to make disclosure to a judge other than the trial judge. Of course, if one takes the view that the disclosed information is not confidential or privileged, and on the

---

168 See Silver, above note 36 at 416.

169 See, for example, *R. v. Jeffries* (1995), 62 B.C.A.C. 218 (C.A.), leave to appeal to S.C.C. refused, [1996] S.C.C.A. No. 371 (QL) (S.C.C.).

170 See the text accompanying note 70, above.

171 See, for example, *Pomeroy*, above note 83.

172 See, for example, Third Restatement §120, comm. "i," suggesting that disclosure instead be made to the prosecutor, who in turn is not permitted to inform the judge of the matter. Also see the associated portion of the Reporter's Note.

particular facts can reasonably be viewed as consciousness of guilt, no problem arises.

Unfortunately, on most of these disclosure scenarios the perjury problem is merely foisted upon the trial judge. Granted, the duties that make counsel's handling of the problem so difficult are not replicated exactly in the judicial context. In particular, the judge does not owe the accused a duty of loyalty or confidentiality. But any solution implemented by the court will have to take account of counsel's duties, and there are also difficult constitutional issues to consider.[173] Indeed, because the court may be in no better position to solve the problem than is defence counsel, it has been argued that disclosure of anticipated perjury should be avoided.[174]

# G. COMPLETED CLIENT PERJURY

Several of the issues that we have canvassed in relation to anticipated perjury arise in much the same fashion with respect to perjury that has already occurred. Yet the difference in timing does lead to distinctions. For instance, dealing with completed client perjury focuses more closely upon remedial steps. Sometimes, however, the line between anticipated and completed perjury blurs. Consider defence counsel who, in the course of conducting an examination-in-chief of her client, is stunned to hear testimony that she unequivocally knows to be false. As the client waits on the stand for the next question, obviously preparing to tell a series of associated lies, counsel anticipates further perjury. The worst sort of problem has arisen: perjury is both completed and anticipated, and counsel is under pressure to continue with the client's examination at a crucial point in the trial.[175]

## 1) Acquiring Knowledge that the Client Has Committed Perjury

Knowledge that the perjury has occurred is a vital prerequisite to counsel taking any remedial action. We have discussed the importance and

---

173 See the discussion of these constitutional rights in section B, "Competing Principles," and section F(4)(b), "Refusal to Call the Client as a Witness," in this chapter.

174 See Lefstein, above note 36 at 538–41.

175 The same combination of completed and anticipated client perjury occurred in *Jenkins*, above note 73, where counsel apparently learned of the lies part way through cross-examination.

nature of counsel's knowledge in relation to anticipated perjury.[176] The principles generally remain the same when counsel is confronted with client perjury that has already taken place. It is worth emphasizing, however, that counsel should not jump to any conclusions without discussing the matter with the client. Especially in the case where the problematic testimony has taken counsel by surprise, it is important that counsel confront the client confidentially, if necessary obtaining an adjournment for the purpose.[177]

## 2) Admonishing the Client to Correct the Perjury

Once the defence lawyer knows that a perjury has occurred, he or she must seek to convince the client to correct the falsehood.[178] In doing so, counsel should make sure that the client understands the consequences of not agreeing to disclose the lie to the court. If the client is steadfast in refusing to retract the perjury, counsel must proceed to take appropriate remedial measures. The admonition to correct a perjury is thus analogous to the requirement that counsel attempt to dissuade a client from committing an anticipated perjury.[179]

It has been suggested that counsel can attempt to correct the perjury by asking further questions of the accused.[180] Such an approach does not constitute a knowing attempt to mislead the court, for the lawyer's purpose is to retract the falsehood. However, this tack is not generally recommended. Because counsel cannot be sure of the client's answers or reaction, the exercise will be difficult to control. Any harmful result, such as an angry verbal attack directed at counsel, or the revelation of confidential information, will take place in front of the fact-finder. The better approach, therefore, is to consult with the client in private. If the client is amenable to correcting the perjury, further questions can be asked, with counsel fairly secure in anticipating the client's responses.

---

176 See section F(1), "Acquiring Knowledge that the Client Intends to Commit Perjury," in this chapter.
177 The mechanics of an adjournment request are discussed below in section G(2), "Admonishing the Client to Correct the Perjury," in this chapter.
178 See CBA Code ch. IX, comm. 3.
179 With respect to which, see section F(2), "Admonishing the Client to Tell the Truth," in this chapter.
180 See B. Smith, *Professional Conduct for Lawyers and Judges* (Fredericton, N.B.: Maritime Law Book, 1998) c. 7, para. 58; and Hutchinson, above note 86 at 159.

A related point arises as to how, exactly, counsel can engineer a confidential meeting with the client without alerting the Crown counsel, judge, and/or jury that something has gone terribly wrong. It may be that the perjury is discrete, and counsel has no fear that further lies will be told. In this case, counsel can perhaps continue with the examination in the normal fashion and talk to the client at the next break in proceedings. Where the examination is almost over, however, counsel may have no choice but to request an adjournment.[181] The adjournment should be suggested without fanfare, as casually as possible. If counsel anticipates problems, it is prudent to make the request in the absence of the jury. It is also a good idea, if possible, to continue with at least a few innocuous questions before asking for a break. This delay lessens the chances that the requested adjournment will trigger suspicion that the accused has lied.

The difficulties in obtaining an adjournment are immeasurably increased where the lawyer predicts that further perjury is sure to occur. One option is to ask for an immediate adjournment. Another is to shift the questions to an unproblematic area, and then to make the request. A more daring avenue is to continue as though nothing is wrong, in effect embracing, at least for a time, the Freedman approach.[182] By the same token, counsel could decide to complete the examination on the areas of concern by utilizing the narrative method.[183] Given our position that disclosure of a completed perjury is required, we believe that counsel is best advised to cut short the examination as soon as possible, or in any event without eliciting further perjurious responses. Successful remonstration, it is to be hoped, can address the problem before it gets worse.

## 3) Remedial Measures Where the Client Refuses to Correct the Perjury

There are three main options available to the lawyer who, coming to know of a completed perjury, and despite admonition, is faced with a recalitrant client. First, counsel can attempt to withdraw from the case.

---

181 See *Law Society of Saskatchewan v. Segal*, [1999] L.S.D.D. No. 9 (QL) [*Segal*] (in the context of perjury committed during examination in discovery).
182 See section F(4)(d), "Eliciting Testimony in the Normal Manner," in this chapter.
183 See section F(4)(c), "Eliciting Testimony By Means of Free or Open Narrative," in this chapter.

Second, counsel can disclose the falsehood to the court or Crown counsel. Third, counsel can continue to act on the case as though nothing is amiss.

### a) Withdrawal

We have already discussed many of the issues surrounding withdrawal as a response to client perjury, though in the context of perjury that has yet to occur.[184] In the case of completed perjury, counsel by definition finds himself or herself in the midst of the trial. Such was the case in *Jenkins*, where defence counsel learned of the client's falsehoods part way through cross-examination by the Crown.[185] Attempting to withdraw will probably alert the other trial participants to the perjury problem, if only by inference. Moreover, a court may decide to refuse such a request. The viability of withdrawal as a "stand-alone" response to completed perjury is thus open to question. Perhaps for this reason, though possibly owing to inattentive drafting, the CBA Code apparently does not require counsel to withdraw in response to completed client perjury.[186] Yet withdrawal is seen by some commentators to be a valid potential response.[187] Moreover, several Canadian ethical codes do impose an obligation to withdraw, in particular Alberta, British Columbia, and New Brunswick.[188] The withdrawal option is also endorsed by the court's ruling in *Jenkins*.

### b) Disclosure

Many of the arguments for and against disclosure have been alluded to in the discussion concerning anticipated client perjury.[189] While the reasons for not revealing a perjury that is merely planned are fairly convincing, once the client has actually perpetrated the falsehood the

---

184  See section F(4)(a), "Withdrawal," in this chapter. As well, reference can be made to section K(2)(b), "Initial Responses: Remonstration and Withdrawal," in chapter 5.

185  See *Jenkins*, above note 73 at 428–29.

186  See CBA Code ch. IX, comm. 3. Contrast the language used where perjury is anticipated and admonition fails: CBA Code ch. IX, comm. 4. On the other hand, the rule specifically dealing with withdrawal seems to impose a mandatory duty to get off the record: CBA Code ch. IX, comm. 4.

187  See, for example, Peck, above note 90 at 11–12.

188  See B.C. ch. 8, r. 8; N.B. Part B, r. 8; Alta. ch. 10, r. 15 & comm. 15.2.

189  See section F(4)(f), "Disclosure of the Intended Perjury," in this chapter.

balance shifts somewhat in favour of disclosure. The possibility that counsel is overreacting, to the client's detriment, to a feared course of action dissipates. In our view, disclosure is therefore justified, and in fact mandated, where perjury has occurred and the client refuses to correct the falsehood.

Many Canadian commentators advocate the disclosure of a completed client perjury.[190] Yet, frustratingly, the CBA Code does not offer a clear view on the subject. Navigating one's way among the various interconnected provisions and footnotes found in the Code promises little more than an exercise in confusion.[191] Admittedly, it is possible to read the Code's provisions as requiring disclosure.[192] But the preferable approach would have been to offer straightforward guidance. In contrast, the ABA Model Rules and Third Restatement both expressly require counsel to make disclosure of a client's completed perjury.[193] New Brunswick also takes a firm position, unequivocally providing that counsel must disclose the perjury to the court.[194]

Other provincial governing bodies appear to reject disclosure as an alternative. In Alberta, the applicable rules prohibit disclosure absent the consent of the client.[195] The same stance is inferentially adopted by the British Columbia and Nova Scotia rules, neither of which makes any mention of a duty or discretion to make disclosure.[196] Accordingly,

---

190 See, for example, G. MacKenzie, *Lawyers and Ethics: Professional Responsibility and Discipline* (Toronto: Carswell, 1993) at §7.5 (15); Hutchinson, above note 86 at 159; Smith, above note 180 at para. 58 (though rather obliquely); and M. Orkin, *Legal Ethics: A Study of Professional Conduct* (Toronto: Cartwright, 1957) at 53–54. See also *Maryland Casualty Co.* v. *Roland Roy Fourrures Inc.*, [1974] S.C.R. 52 at 56 (suggesting that opposing counsel should be informed immediately regarding an untrue statement made by the client on examination on discovery); and *Segal*, above note 181 at paras. 28–32. *Contra*, Peck, above note 90 at 12; Skurka & Stribopoulos, above note 81 at 13; and Finlay, above note 86 at 30.

191 This taxing exercise is undertaken in section K(2)(c), "The Disclosure Issue and the CBA Code," in chapter 5.

192 See MacKenzie, above note 190 at §7.5 & §4.13; Hutchinson, above note 86 at 159; and Finlay, above note 86 at 28.

193 See ABA Model Rule 3.3(a)(4) & (b); and Third Restatement §120(2).

194 See N.B. Part B, r. 8.

195 See Alta. ch. 10, r. 15, read in conjunction with ch. 7, r. 7. *But* see also note 188, below. See also the discussion in section K(2)(d), "Disclosure: Looking Beyond the CBA Code," in chapter 5.

196 See B.C. ch. 8, r. 8; and N.S. ch. 11, r. 11.1 & 11.3.

in these jurisdictions, and despite our preference for a disclosure requirement, counsel must keep secret the client's falsehood. Finally, in *Jenkins* the court apparently accepted that counsel could not disclose a completed perjury by the client.[197] While the arguments for and against disclosure were given minimal attention, *Jenkins* does support the notion that disclosure is improper (or at least not required).[198]

### c)   Other Options

Some other options have been advanced that fall short of full disclosure of the perjury. In particular, it has been suggested that counsel can continue to conduct the case in the normal manner but make no reference to the false testimony in closing.[199] If counsel discovers the falsehoods in the course of direct examination, and further perjury is anticipated, this option could also entail shifting to the narrative method for the remainder of the client's testimony. A variation that, while still not the equivalent of full disclosure, involves a greater degree of revelation would have counsel expressly inform the court that the evidence should not be relied upon. This approach is suggested by the Alberta rules of professional conduct, which state that "[a] lawyer has a duty to correct a misapprehension of the court arising from an honest mistake on the part of counsel or from perjury by the lawyer's client or witness. *It may be sufficient discharge of this duty to merely advise the court not to rely on the impugned information.*"[200] As already noted, however, the Alberta rules arguably do not permit disclosure of a completed perjury, absent the client's consent.[201] It may be that the option set out in the text above is available only where the client agrees, or that the Alberta code does not view this course of action as breaching client-lawyer confidentiality. In any event, informing the court that no heed should be paid to the evidence certainly avoids the problem discussed above regarding *R. v. Colpitts.*[202]

---

197  See *Jenkins*, above note 73.
198  This aspect of the decision in *Jenkins* is open to criticism. In particular, it is hard to accept the court's conclusion that the client's confidences were not in fact violated by the withdrawing counsel.
199  See Peck, above note 90 at 11–12. This option is similar to that proposed by the Crown in *Jenkins*, above note 73.
200  Alta. ch. 10, r. 15, comm. 15.1.
201  See the discussion at note 195, above.
202  See section F(4)(c), "Eliciting Testimony By Means of Free or Open Narrative," in this chapter.

# H. PREVENTATIVE MEASURES (EARLY ADVICE TO THE CLIENT)

The risk of the perjury problem arising can be reduced if counsel makes clear to the client, at the outset of the relationship, a lawyer's role and responsibilities. Of course, it would be inappropriate, and likely fatal to the relationship, to accuse the client of perjurious plans without any basis in fact. But counsel should diplomatically explain not only the nature and operation of client-lawyer confidentiality and privilege but also possible limits on the lawyer's duties connected with the prohibition against assisting in the presentation of false evidence.[203] This approach has been criticized by those who view such counselling as an invitation not to inform the lawyer of planned perjury, and who fear that the client will in any event develop a distrust for the lawyer.[204] Yet surely openness in the client-lawyer relationship runs both ways. As long as counsel approaches the matter in a sensitive, non-accusatory way, it makes sense to give the client accurate information as to what a defence lawyer can and cannot do in representing an accused.[205]

# I. REASONABLE BELIEF THAT EVIDENCE IS FALSE

Both ABA Model Rule 3.3 and the Third Restatement provide that, where a lawyer reasonably believes that evidence is false, there is a discretion to refuse to offer the evidence.[206] While Canadian rules of professional conduct make no mention of a discretion based on counsel's reasonable belief that evidence is false, there is an initial attraction to recognizing a *limited* discretion in this regard. Because counsel does

---

203 See L. Pizzimenti, "The Lawyer's Duty to Warn Clients about the Limits on Confidentiality" (1990) 39 Cath. U. L. Rev. 441 at 457–63.
204 See Silver, above note 36 at 394–95; and Peck, above note 90 at 8. We certainly do not countenance counselling that is directed at avoiding knowledge of planned or executed perjury.
205 See R. Shadley & J. Godin, "Dealing with the Unethical Client" (1992), Federation of Law Societies of Canada National Criminal Law Program at 8; and Hutchinson, above note 86 at 159–60.
206 See ABA Model Rule 3.3; and Third Restatement §180(3).

not irresistibly know that the evidence is false, there can certainly be no unequivocal interdiction against offering the impugned evidence. But on further reflection, there are substantial arguments against taking extensive remedial measures based on a reasonable belief that perjury will occur. In a criminal case, such a belief is surely insufficient to justify withdrawal where the result would be to prejudice the client in any significant way. Refusing to call the client as a witness, adopting a narrative approach, and disclosure to the court are all also inappropriate. The accused's rights to the effective assistance of counsel and to testify in his or her defence are likely pre-eminent where counsel's suspicions fall somewhere short of actual knowledge.

In essence, we are therefore sceptical of adopting the ABA Model Rule/Third Restatement position in the context of reasonably suspected perjury by a criminal accused. Absent irresistible knowledge of perjury, we prefer something more akin to the Freedman approach, permitting a fairly limited ability to withdraw, and also the option of remonstrating with the client. From a practical point of view, counsel should always point out to the client any perceived weaknesses in a suspicious version of events.[207] It may well be a wise tactical decision not to advance such a version, and, upon considering the matter, the client will agree wholeheartedly.

# J. SUMMARY AND RECOMMENDATIONS

Client perjury, whether anticipated or completed, presents a lawyer with the daunting challenge of reconciling the competing duties of loyalty to the client and fidelity to the truth-finding function of the criminal justice system. The potential options available to counsel are varied and complicated, and commentators often disagree as to the propriety of any given course of action. Our recommendations for the lawyer who is confronted by client perjury are as follows:

**Anticipated Client Perjury**
1. Counsel must first determine that the client intends to mislead the court through the presentation of false testimony. A lawyer is fixed with such knowledge where he or she reasonably draws an irresistible conclusion of falsity from available information (section F(1)).

---

207 It would be improper, however, to threaten to disclose the suspected perjury, given that disclosure in such a case is not ethically permitted: see Liskov, above note 63 at 885.

2. Once counsel comes to the firm conclusion that a client intends to commit perjury, the immediate reaction should be to attempt to dissuade the client from pursuing such a course. The client should be informed of the serious adverse consequences that can flow from perjurious testimony, including the remedial responses available to counsel (section F(2)).

3. After the client has been admonished, counsel must assess whether the threat of perjury has been alleviated. A lawyer can ordinarily assume that the client will heed the advice to avoid perjury. Remedial measures should be taken only where circumstances show this assumption to be unwarranted (section F(3)).

4. There are a number of possible remedial measures open to counsel whose client insists upon committing perjury despite admonitions. However, continuing with the retainer as if nothing untoward has happened, in accord with the views of Professor Monroe Freedman, is not a viable response in Canada in light of the applicable rules of professional conduct (section F(4)(d)).

5. Other options for dealing with the client who refuses to abandon a plan to commit perjury include:

    a. withdrawal: Withdrawal can be an acceptable response to planned perjury, especially where the application to get off the record can be brought well before trial and no confidences are breached. But where the trial is imminent or has already commenced, withdrawal may involve severe prejudice to the client and perhaps lead to the inescapable inference that perjury is going to occur. In such a case, counsel may legitimately decide not to apply to withdraw (though the CBA Code suggests that a withdrawal application is mandatory). Finally, where counsel successfully withdraws from a case owing to anticipated perjury, disclosure to the accused's new counsel may be a valid course of action (section F(4)(a)).

    b. refusal to call the client as a witness: Refusing to call the client as a witness is generally an unsatisfactory response in light of the client's constitutional right to testify and associated practical problems (section F(4)(b)).

    c. free or open narrative: Under the free- or open-narrative approach, counsel merely asks the client whether he or she wishes to make a statement concerning the case to the trier of fact. No follow-up questions are asked, and counsel does not rely on any false testimony in making closing submissions. This approach has some appeal as a compromise but is subject to valid criticism based upon prejudice to the client and damage to the truth-finding function of the system (section F(4)(c)).

d. permitting the client to offer only non-perjurious testimony: In theory, a good response to the problem of anticipated perjury would be to permit the client to offer only evidence not known to be false. However, in practise this approach would be subject to sabotage by the client (knowingly) or Crown (unknowingly, in cross-examination) (section F(4)(e)).

e. disclosure: Disclosure of anticipated perjury may be possible under some Canadian rules of professional conduct, in particular pursuant to the discretion afforded lawyers to disclose confidential information in order to prevent future-harm. Given our view that counsel can permissibly disclose *completed* client perjury, and the difficulty in ascertaining whether the client will really act to implement the perjurious plan, we believe that any available discretion to make pre-emptory disclosure should generally not be exercised (section F(4)(f)).

## Completed Client Perjury

6. As in the case of anticipated perjury, counsel must begin by determining that the client has misled the court through the presentation of false testimony. A lawyer is fixed with such knowledge where he or she reasonably draws an irresistible conclusion of falsity from available information (section G(1)).

7. Once counsel comes to the firm conclusion that a client has committed perjury, the immediate reaction should be to attempt to persuade the client to correct the falsehood. Counselling the client on this point should include canvassing the serious adverse consequences that can flow from perjurious testimony, as well as counsel's possible remedial responses if the client refuses to correct the falsehood (section G(2)).

8. It may be difficult to remonstrate with the client without stopping proceedings or otherwise alerting the court and Crown that something is amiss regarding the client's testimony. The lawyer should make reasonable attempts not to call attention to the problem, but should not go so far as to elicit further false testimony in a misguided effort to protect the client (section G(2)).

9. Where the client refuses to correct the perjury, counsel must take remedial measures and cannot proceed in the normal fashion, as though nothing is wrong. The available remedial options include:

a. withdrawal: The problems potentially associated with withdrawal come to the fore where the client is in the middle of testifying. Attempting to extract oneself from the retainer will likely alert the court and Crown to the perjury and cause substantial harm to the accused. Moreover, the court may well refuse to permit withdrawal. Although several Canadian jurisdictions impose an obligation to attempt withdrawal, other remedial measures may be preferable (section G(3)(a)).

  b.  disclosure: In our view, disclosure is mandated where the perjury has occurred and the client refuses to correct the falsehood. However, some Canadian governing bodies arguably forbid disclosure absent the client's consent or are at least unclear on the point (section G(3)(b)).

  c.  limited closing submissions: It has been suggested that counsel can continue with the case in the normal matter, except that the perjurious testimony cannot be relied upon in closing submissions. There are other variations on this approach, some of which involve fairly implicit disclosure of the falsehood to the court (section G(3)(c)).

10. Where the client tells the truth during examination-in-chief, but commits perjury during cross-examination, counsel's response should be no different (chapter 5, section K(2)(a)(iv)).

11. In Canada, the remedial duty concerning completed client perjury contains no clear endpoint and appears to continue even after the case has concluded (chapter 5, section K(3)).

**Other Matters**

12. The rules of professional responsibility in Canada do not distinguish between material and non-material falsehoods in setting out prohibitions against counsel knowingly misleading a court and requiring remedial action where counsel learns that the court has already been misled. However, where counsel is otherwise afforded some discretion in responding to an anticipated or completed falsehood, lack of materiality may be an appropriate factor to consider (chapter 5, section K(2)(a)(v)).

13. It is advisable to make clear to the client, at the outset of the relationship, a lawyer's role and responsibilities. As long as counsel approaches the matter in a sensitive, non-accusatory way, it makes sense to give the client accurate information as to what a defence lawyer can and cannot do in representing an accused (section H).

14. In the United States, many rules of professional responsibility contain a discretion to refuse to offer evidence that the lawyer reasonably believes to be false. There may be sound tactical reasons for not offering such evidence, but given the client's constitutional

right to testify we are against recognizing such a discretion in Canada (section I).

15. Counsel has a duty to prevent misleading evidence from being presented in court even where the client does not believe that the evidence is inaccurate. The focus is upon counsel's knowledge regarding the falsity of the information, regardless of the fact that the client may be acting in good faith (chapter 5, section K(2)(a)(i)).

## FURTHER READINGS

APPEL, B., "The Limited Impact of *Nix v. Whiteside* on Attorney-Client Relations" (1988) 136 U. Pa. L. Rev. 1913

BLAKE, M., & A. ASHWORTH, "Some Ethical Issues in Prosecuting and Defending Criminal Cases" [1998] Crim. L. Rev. 16

BOWMAN, A., "Standards of Conduct for Prosecution and Defense Personnel: An Attorney's Viewpoint" (1966) 5 Am. Crim. L. Rev. 23

BRAZIL, W., "Unanticipated Client Perjury and the Collision of Rules, Evidence, and Constitutional Law" (1979) 44 Mo. L. Rev. 601

BURKOFF, J., *Criminal Defense Ethics: Law and Liability*, rev. ed. (St. Paul: West, 1999)

CRYSTAL, N., "Limitations on Zealous Representation in an Adversarial System" (1997) 32 Wake Forest L. Rev. 671

FINLAY, B., "The Conduct of Lawyers in the Litigious Process: Some Thoughts" in E. Gertner, ed., *Studies in Civil Procedure* (Toronto: Butterworths, 1979) 15

FORTUNE, W., R. UNDERWOOD, & E. IMWINKELRIED, *Modern Litigation and Professional Responsibility Handbook: The Limits of Zealous Advocacy* (New York: Little, Brown, 1996)

FRANCK, M., "Letter to the Editor: Response to Lefstein" (1988) 2 Geo. J. Legal Ethics 585

FREEDMAN, M., "Client Confidences and Client Perjury: Some Unanswered Questions" (1988) 136 U. Pa. L. Rev. 1939

FREEDMAN, M., *Lawyers' Ethics in the Adversary System* (New York: Bobbs-Merrill, 1975)

FREEDMAN, M., "Professional Responsibility of the Criminal Defence Lawyer: The Three Hardest Questions" (1966) 64 Mich. L. Rev. 1469

FREEDMAN, M., *Understanding Lawyers' Ethics* (New York: Matthew Bender, 1990)

HALL, J., *Professional Responsibility of the Criminal Lawyer*, 2d ed. (New York: Clark Boardman Callaghan, 1996)

GARCIA, A., "The Right to Counsel Under Siege: Requiem for an Endangered Right?" (1991) 29 Am. Crim. L. Rev. 35

HAZARD, G., "The Client Fraud Problem as a Justinian Quartet: An Extended Analysis" (1997) 25 Hofstra L. Rev. 1041

HAZARD, F., & W. HODES, *The Law of Lawyering: A Handbook on the Model Rules of Professional Conduct*, 2d ed. (Englewood, N.J.: Prentice Hall, 1993)

HOOLIHAN, J., "Ethical Standards for Defence Counsel" in Canadian Bar Association, *Studies in Criminal Law and Procedure* (Agincourt, Ont.: Canada Law Book, 1973)

HUTCHINSON, A., *Legal Ethics and Professional Responsibility* (Toronto: Irwin Law, 1999)

IPP, D., "Lawyers' Duties to the Court" (1998) 114 L.Q. Rev. 63

KAUFMAN, A., *Problems in Professional Resonsibility*, 3d ed. (Boston: Little, Brown, 1990) at 152

LEFSTEIN, N., "Client Perjury in Criminal Cases: Still in Search of an Answer" (1988) 1 Geo. J. Legal Ethics 521

LISKOV, D., "Criminal Defendant Perjury: A Lawyer's Choice Between Ethics, the Constitution and the Truth" (1994) 28 New Eng. L. Rev. 881

LUNDY, D., G. MacKENZIE, & M. NEWBURY, *Barristers and Solicitors in Practice* (Toronto: Butterworths, 1998)

MacKENZIE, G., *Lawyers and Ethics: Professional Responsibility and Discipline* (Toronto: Carswell, 1993)

McCARTHY, T., & C. BROOK, "Anticipated Client Perjury: Truth or Dare Comes to Court," in R. Uphoff, ed., *Ethical Problems Facing the Criminal Lawyer* (Chicago: American Bar Association, 1995) c. 11

NADINE-DAVIS, R., & C. SPROULE, *Canadian Sentencing Digest* (Toronto: Carswell, 1986)

ORKIN, M., *Legal Ethics: A Study of Professional Conduct* (Toronto: Cartwright, 1957)

"Panel Discussion: Problems in Advocacy and Ethics" in Law Society of Upper Canada, *Defending a Criminal Case* (Toronto: R. De Boo, 1969) 279

"Panel Discussion: Witness for the Prosecution: Successful Impeachment Strategies" (Annual Criminal Lawyers' Association Convention and Education Programme, 21-22 November 1997, Toronto) QL online (OCLARP/1997-019)

PANNICK, D., *Advocates* (Oxford: Oxford University Press, 1992)

PECK, R., "Ethical Problems in Defending a Criminal Case: The Serbonian Bog" [1992] National Criminal Law Program

PIZZIMENTI, L., "The Lawyer's Duty to Warn Clients About the Limits on Confidentiality" (1990) 39 Cath. U. L. Rev. 441

PYE, A., "The Role of Counsel in the Suppression of Truth" [1978] Duke L.J. 921

QUINN, J., N. KUBASEK, & M. BROWNE, "Resisting the Individulaistic Flavor of Opposition to Model Rule 3.3" (1995) 8 Geo. J. Legal Ethics 901

REIGER, C., "Client Perjury: A Proposed Resolution of the Constitutional and Ethical Issues" (1985) 70 Minn. L. Rev. 121

RHODE, D., & D. LUBAN, *Legal Ethics*, 2d ed. (Westbury, N.Y.: Foundation Press, 1995)

ROBINETTE, J., & G. MARTIN, "Problems in Litigation: A Symposium" (1953) 31 Can. Bar Rev. 503

RUBY, C., *Sentencing*, 5th ed. (Toronto: Butterworths, 1999)

RUTHERGLEN, G., "Dilemmas and Disclosures: A Comment on Client Perjury" (1991) 18 Am. J. Crim. L. 319

SCHROEDER, E., "Some Ethical Problems in Criminal Law" in Law Society of Upper Canada, *Representing an Arrested Client and Police Interrogation* (Toronto: R. De Boo, 1963) 87

SHADLEY, R., & J. GODIN, "Dealing With the Unethical Client" [1992] National Criminal Law Program

SILVER, J., "Truth, Justice, and the American Way: The Case *Against* the Client Perjury Rules" (1994) 47 Vand. L. Rev. 339

SKURKA, S. & J. STRIBOPOULOS, "Professional Responsibility in Criminal Practice" in Law Society of Upper Canada, *42nd Bar Admission Course, 2000, Criminal Procedure Materials* (Toronto: Law Society of Upper Canada, 2000) c. 1

SMITH, B., *Professional Conduct for Lawyers and Judges* (Fredericton, N.B.: Maritime Law Book, 1998)

WILKINSON, E., "'That's a Damn Lie!': Ethical Obligations of Counsel when a Witness Offers False Testimony in a Criminal Trial" (2000) 31 St. Mary's L.J. 407

WILLIAMS, J., "Client Perjury and the Duty of Candor" (1993) 6 Geo. J. Legal Ethics 1005

WOLFRAM, C.W., "Client Perjury" (1979) 50 S. Cal. L. Rev. 809

WOLFRAM, C.W., *Modern Legal Ethics* (St. Paul: West, 1986)

ZITRIN, R., & C. LANGFORD, *Legal Ethics in the Practice of Law* (Charlottesville, Va.: Michie, 1995)

# CHAPTER 8

# PLEA DISCUSSIONS

## A. INTRODUCTION

Aside from instances where the prosecution stays or withdraws all charges, every accused person shares a common experience: entering a plea of guilty or not guilty to a charge. A large majority of these accused, easily upwards of 60 percent, pleads guilty.[1] For this majority, the plea has an immediate and dramatic impact on the proceedings. A conviction is recorded, there is no trial on the issue of culpability, and the matter proceeds to sentencing. Deciding how to plead in response to a charge is thus the key decision for many, many accused, and not surprisingly the law accords the accused total freedom of choice in this regard. At the same time, however, defence counsel fre-

---

1    Statistics Canada does not track the proportion of accused that pleads guilty: see, for example, Canadian Centre for Justice Statistics, *The Juristat Reader: A Statistical Overview of the Canadian Justice System* (Toronto: Thompson Educational, 1999). Figures compiled by the Ministry of the Attorney General for Ontario, current to 1998, suggest that 75.5 percent of criminal cases are resolved prior to the day of trial, another 15.8 percent are resolved on the day of trial, and 8.7 percent proceed to trial: see Ontario Criminal Justice Review Committee, *Report of the Criminal Justice Review Committee* (Toronto: Queen's Printer, 1999) (Co-chairs: H. Locke, J.D. Evans, & M. Segal) [Criminal Justice Review Committee] at 56. Based on the available statistics, it has been said, *ibid.* at 55, that "the vast majority of criminal cases are resolved by way of guilty plea."

quently plays a central role in advising the accused with respect to the plea. A common and crucial aspect of counsel's role in this regard is participation in resolution discussions with the Crown, also sometimes known as plea discussions or plea bargaining.

Plea discussions, if properly conducted by defence counsel, thus involve respecting the client's freedom of choice in entering a plea, all the while fulfilling the lawyer's professional obligation to provide the client with competent advice. The very essence of the client-lawyer relationship is caught up in this mix and permeates any analysis of counsel's ethical duties when engaging in plea discussions. Counsel walks a fine line in undertaking plea discussions and advising the client. He or she must avoid adopting the role of the "player," who dominates the client and imposes a course of action without much regard for the client's wishes.[2] Nor should counsel act as a "double agent," who facilitates "assembly-lne justice" while appearing to help his or her clients.[3] No matter which pejorative moniker one uses to describe unprofessional behaviour during plea discussions, the underlying message is clear: the lawyer's duty is to support the client's freedom of choice through the provision of quality legal advice.

# B. TERMINOLOGY

We should discuss terminology, as well as some of the limits of our ethical inquiry, before going any further. A potentially confusing feature of the literature on plea discussions is the failure to articulate exactly what process is being studied. Moreover, certain phrases tend to raise the public's hackles, especially those employing the term "bargaining," and have thus taken on a distasteful meaning in some quarters. We will follow the lead of the Martin Committee and use the term "resolution discussions" to refer to "any discussions between counsel aimed at resolving issues that a criminal prosecution raises."[4] The

---

2   See A. Alschuler, "The Defence Attorney's Role in Plea Bargaining" (1975) 84 Yale L.J. 1179 at 1306.

3   See R. Uphoff, "The Criminal Defense Lawyer: Zealous Advocate, Double Agent, or Beleaguered Dealer?" (1992) 28 Crim. L. Bull. 419; and A. Blumberg, "The Practice of Law as Confidence Game: Organizational Cooptation of a Profession" (1967) 1 L. & Socy Rev. 15.

4   Ontario, Attorney General's Advisory Committee, *Report of the Attorney General's Advisory Committee on Charge Screening, Disclosure, and Resolution Discussions* (Toronto: Queen's Printer, 1993) (Chair: G. Arthur Martin) at 282 [*Martin Committee Report*].

scope of resolution discussions is very wide, encompassing not only negotiations concerning a possible plea of guilty but almost any other aspect of the criminal proceeding, including an agreement to admit evidence, the adoption of an informal discovery process, or the scheduling of the trial itself. The primary focus of this chapter is plea discussions, or plea negotiations, by which we mean "discussions directed toward a plea of guilty by the accused in return for the prosecutor agreeing to take or refrain from taking a particular course of action."[5] We are therefore confining ourselves to a particular aspect of resolution discussions.

We should add that, while our focus is upon instances where negotiations occur between lawyers for the defence and the Crown, many of the obligations discussed in this chapter apply equally to any circumstance where an accused is considering whether to plead guilty. That is to say, the bulk of the duties discussed in this chapter apply any time an accused person pleads guilty or considers doing so, whether or not plea discussions have occurred between the defence and the Crown. Also, our discussion at times includes circumstances where no charges have been laid or where counsel's aim is to have the case diverted.

## C. CONSTITUTIONAL AND OTHER LEGAL FACETS OF A GUILTY PLEA

It is worth looking more closely at the impact that a guilty plea can have upon an accused's constitutional and other legal rights, in order to understand better the great detriment that can flow from a hasty or ill-advised plea. When an accused pleads guilty, he or she is ostensibly admitting to the crime.[6] There will be no trial on the general issue of culpability, and the Crown is not required to make its case on a standard of proof beyond a reasonable doubt.[7] The accused no longer asserts the right to make full answer and defence (including the right

---

5    This definition is adapted from the Law Reform Commission of Canada, *Plea Discussions and Agreements* (Working Paper No. 60) (Ottawa: The Commission, 1989) at 40 (Recommendations 1 and 2).

6    See, for example, *R. v. Gardiner* (1982), 68 C.C.C. (2d) 477 at 514 (S.C.C.) [*Gardiner*]. The relationship between a plea of guilty and an admission of culpability is not completely straightforward and is discussed in much more detail in section M, "The Client Who Maintains Innocence," in this chapter.

7    See, for example, *R. v. Lucas* (1983), 9 C.C.C. (3d) 71 at 76 (Ont. C.A.) [*Lucas*]; *R. v. T.(R.)* (1992), 17 C.R. (4th) 247 at 252 (Ont. C.A.) [*T.(R.)*]; *R. v. C.(W.B.)*

to test the Crown case), abandons the rights to silence and non-compellability as a witness, and foregoes the presumption of innocence.[8] In short, a guilty plea operates to waive many of the most sacrosanct rights afforded an accused.

Flowing naturally from these observations is the proposition that the accused has complete control and freedom of choice over the decision as to whether to enter a guilty plea. This proposition is well established by Canadian case law[9] and commentary.[10] It also has constitutional dimensions, derived from the fundamental principle of justice that demands that an accused be permitted to control the conduct of the defence.[11] Counsel who improperly pressures the accused to plead guilty or not guilty, so as to negate this freedom of choice, has thus undermined an important constitutional right.[12]

It is apposite to mention several attributes of a guilty plea that are perhaps not so immediately obvious. A guilty plea may also be used in subsequent proceedings to the disadvantage of the offender, for instance, in civil litigation commenced by a victim, to attack credibility in a subsequent and otherwise unrelated criminal prosecution, or as similar fact evidence.[13] Moreover, the accused who pleads guilty will likely be prevented from challenging on appeal any adverse rulings that

---

(2000), 142 C.C.C. (3d) 490 at 508 (Ont. C.A.) [*C.(W.B.)*]; *Korponey* v. *Canada (A.G.)* (1982), 65 C.C.C. (2d) 65 at 74 (S.C.C.).

8   See *R.* v. *Adgey* (1973), 13 C.C.C. (2d) 177 at 182–83 (S.C.C.) (per Laskin C.J.C.) and 190 (per Dickson J.). In more serious cases, the accused who pleads guilty is also waiving the right to a jury trial.

9   See, for example, *R.* v. *Laperrière* (1996), 109 C.C.C. (3d) 347 (S.C.C.) [*Laperrière*], affirming the dissent of Bisson J.A. in (1995), 101 C.C.C. (3d) 462 at 470–71 (Que. C.A.); *R.* v. *Lamoureux* (1984), 13 C.C.C. (3d) 101 at 105 (Que. C.A.) [*Lamoureux*]. The many cases that elucidate the test to be applied where an appellant seeks to have a plea struck or withdrawn on appeal implicitly confirm this point, given that the plea must be voluntary and unequivocal: see the case law cited at note 19, below. In the United Kingdom, the right of an accused to decide how to plead in response to criminal charges is recognized in *R.* v. *Turner*, [1970] 2 All E.R. 281 at 285 [*Turner*].

10  See, for example, A. Hutchinson, *Legal Ethics and Professional Responsibility* (Toronto: Irwin Law, 1999) at 166; G. Arthur Martin, "The Role and Responsibility of the Defence Advocate" (1970) 12 Crim. L.Q. 376 at 387; D. Heather, "Pleas and Elections" in Law Society of Upper Canada, *Defending a Criminal Case*, Toronto: R. De Boo, 1969) 69; *Criminal Justice Review Committee*, above note 1 at 64–65; and *Martin Committee Report*, above note 4 at 284–85.

11  See *R.* v. *Swain* (1991), 63 C.C.C. (3d) 481 at 504–07 (S.C.C.) [*Swain*].

12  See the further discussion in section K(3), "Respect for the Client's Freedom of Choice," in this chapter.

13  See, for example, *R.* v. *C.(W.B.)*, above note 7 at 510.

occurred prior to the plea.[14] Perhaps most important, the ability to appeal the conviction following a guilty plea is greatly curtailed. A change of heart or dissatisfaction with the sentence meted out is not, on its own, sufficient.[15] The appellant must employ more compelling arguments to convince the appeal court to set aside the guilty plea, and the test for doing so is quite stringent.[16] Valid grounds for setting aside a guilty plea include: the plea was not voluntary, unequivocal, and informed; the judge failed to make an adequate inquiry before accepting the plea; the judge should not have accepted the plea in light of the factual inquiry; or the accused was denied constitutional rights during the course of the plea hearing itself. It has also been suggested that the appellant stands a better chance of success if he or she can point to a valid defence at trial.[17]

Finally, it is worth noting that a guilty plea resulting from poor legal representation may be set aside on appeal, where the right to the effective assistance of counsel has been violated.[18] This constitutional right has not been relied upon in the context of guilty pleas nearly so often in Canada as in the United States. The difference may be that Canadian courts have long recognized special rules relating to the validity of pleas, while ineffective-counsel arguments are a relatively recent development. In any event, appeal courts apply a demanding test in determining whether a new trial is warranted by reason of defence counsel's incompetence. There is a strong presumption of competence that works in favour of letting the conviction stand.[19] In

---

14  See, for example, *R. v. Fegan* (1993), 80 C.C.C. (3d) 356 at 359 (Ont. C.A.) [*Fegan*]; *R. v. Roberts* (1998), 106 O.A.C. 308 (C.A.) [*Roberts*]; and *R. v. Davidson* (1992), 110 N.S.R. (2d) 307 (S.C.A.D.). A possible method for preserving the right to appeal a prior adverse ruling, without the necessity for a full-blown trial, is discussed in section K(8), "A Possible Alternative: An Attenuated 'Fegan' Trial," in this chapter.

15  See, for example, *R. v. Antoine* (1984), 40 C.R. (3d) 375 (Que. C.A.), aff'd [1988] 1 S.C.R. 212; and *R. v. Lyons* (1987), 37 C.C.C. (3d) 1 at 53 (S.C.C.) [*Lyons*].

16  See for example, *Adgey*, above note 8 at 189; *Lyons*, above note 15 at 52–53; *R. v. Rajaeefard* (1996), 104 C.C.C. (3d) 225 at 230–31 (Ont. C.A.) [*Rajaeefard*]; *T.(R.)*, above note 7 at 252; *Lamoureux*, above note 9 at 104; *R. v. Hirtle* (1991), 104 N.S.R. (2d) 56 (S.C.A.D.).

17  See *R. v. G.(A.M.)* (1997), 36 W.C.B. (2d) 419 (B.C.C.A.), leave to appeal to S.C.C. refused (1997), 227 N.R. 290n (S.C.C.).

18  Cases where denial of the right-to-effective-counsel claims have been made include *R. v. Newman* (1993), 12 O.R. (3d) 481, 61 O.A.C. 267, 79 C.C.C. (3d) 394, 20 C.R. (4th) 370 (C.A.); *R. v. Roberts*, above note 14; *R. v. Armstrong* (1997), 33 W.C.B. (2d) 254 (Ont. C.A.).

19  See, for example, *R. v. B.(G.D.)* (2000), 143 C.C.C. (3d) 289 at 298 (S.C.C.)

the United Kingdom, it has been noted that appeal courts tend to accept trial counsel's version of events where the recollections of the appellant and trial counsel differ, and the same is probably true in Canada.[20] Even where the performance of the lawyer in representing the accused is markedly below the standard reasonably required of a competent counsel, the appeal will be allowed only where the appellant has thereby suffered prejudice.[21] Consequently, negligent representation by defence counsel with respect to a guilty plea does not necessarily lead to a remedy on appeal.[22]

# D. SOME BACKGROUND CONSIDERATIONS

There are several considerations that, while not strictly speaking concerned with lawyers' ethics, deserve mention as constituting an important part of the contextual background for any examination of plea discussions and guilty pleas.

## 1) Plea Discussions are Privileged

Communications between defence counsel and prosecutor during plea discussions are confidential and privileged.[23] Public policy encourages full and candid discussion between the parties, and what has been revealed during those discussions is not admissible at trial. However, there may be circumstances where the privilege is set aside, most particularly where the client later waives privilege by alleging a denial of the right to the effective assistance of counsel.

---

[*B.(G.D.)*]; *R. v. Joanisse* (1995), 102 C.C.C. (3d) 35 at 61 (Ont. C.A.), leave to appeal to S.C.C. refused (1997), 111 C.C.C. (3d) vi (S.C.C.); and *Newman*, above note 18 at 403.

20  See Justice Society, *Negotiated Justice: A Closer Look at the Implications of Plea Bargains* (London: Justice Society), 1993) at 14.

21  See, for example, *B.(G.D.)*, above note 19 at 298.

22  See, for example, *Roberts*, above note 14; and *B.(G.D.)*, above note 19 at 298.

23  See, for example, *R. v. Pabini* (1994), 89 C.C.C. (3d) 437 at 443 (Ont. C.A.), leave to appeal to S.C.C. refused (1994), 91 C.C.C. (3d) vi (S.C.C.); *R. v. Goland* (1999), 133 C.C.C. (3d) 251 (Ont. Prov. Div.); *R. v. Larocque* (1998), 124 C.C.C. (3d) 564 (Ont. Gen. Div.) (QL); *R. v. Lake*, [1997] O.J. No. 5447 (Gen. Div.) (QL); *R. v. Bernardo*, [1994] O.J. No. 1718 (Gen. Div.) (QL); and J. Sopinka, S. Lederman & A. Bryant, *The Law of Evidence in Canada*, 2d ed. (Toronto: Butterworths, 1999) at §14.202.

## 2) Judges Are Not Obligated to Conduct a Plea Inquiry

Canadian law does not require judges to conduct an inquiry into the accused's understanding of the nature and circumstances of a plea every time a guilty plea is entered.[24] Nevertheless, there may be circumstances where such a plea inquiry is required, for instance, where the circumstances suggest that the plea may be equivocal or involuntary.[25] Moreover, some judges engage in plea inquiries as a matter of course, even though not required to do so.[26] Indeed, the *Martin Committee Report* recommends that the judge always question the accused to ensure that the latter appreciates the nature and consequences of the plea, has voluntarily entered the plea, and (if applicable) understands that a joint submission is not binding on the court.[27] Counsel should therefore always canvas this possibility with the client, so that he or she is not taken by surprise during the plea process.

## 3) Plea Agreement is Not Binding on the Court

A plea agreement is not binding upon the court. While a judge should give serious consideration to a joint submission from counsel, he or she has a discretion to depart from the recommended sentence in the interests of justice.[28] The exact circumstances in which a court can

---

24   See, for example, *R. v. Brosseau* (1968), [1969] 3 C.C.C. 129 at 138–39 (S.C.C.) [*Brosseau*]; *Adgey*, above note 8 at 188; *Lamoureux*, above note 9 at 104; and *R. v. Hechavarria* (1999), 42 W.C.B. (2d) 301 (Ont. C.A.).

25   See for example, *R. v. K.(S.)* (1995), 99 C.C.C. (3d) 376 at 382 (Ont. C.A.) [*K.(S.)*]; and *Brosseau*, above note 24 at 137–38.

26   See for example, *R. v. Ceballo* (1997), 14 C.R. (5th) 15 at 17–18 (Ont. Prov. Div.) [*Ceballo*]. In the United States, detailed plea inquiries are required in federal courts (see C. Wright, *Federal Practice and Procedure*, 3d ed. (St. Paul: West, 1999); and Federal Rules of Criminal Procedure, Rule 11(c)) and also under state procedure (see W. LaFave, J. Israel, & N. King, *Criminal Procedure*, 2d ed. (St. Paul: West, 1999) at §21.4(c)).

27   *Martin Committee Report*, above note 4 at 317–23.

28   See, for example, *R. v. St. Coeur* (1991), 69 C.C.C. (3d) 348 at 355 (Que. C.A.); *R. v. Vaudreuil* (1995), 98 C.C.C. (3d) 316 at 322 (B.C.C.A.); *R. v. Rubenstein* (1987), 41 C.C.C. (3d) 91 at 94 (Ont. C.A.), leave refused (1988), 41 C.C.C. (3d) vi (S.C.C.); *R. v. Hoang* (2001), 153 C.C.C. (3d) 317 at 318–20 (Alta. C.A.); *R. v. Carder* (1995), 174 A.R. 212 at 213 (C.A.); *R. v. Pashe* (1993), 100 Man. R. (2d) 61 at 62–63 (C.A.); and *R. v. C.(G.W.)* (2000), 150 C.C.C. (3d) 513 at 519–23 (Alta. C.A.). Also see s. 606(4) of the *Criminal Code*, R.S.C. 1985, c. C-46, which gives the court a discretion as to whether a plea will be accepted to any other offence arising out of the same transaction (s. 606(4) is discussed in *R. v. Naraindeen* (1990), 80 C.R. (3d) 66 (Ont. C.A.)).

depart from a joint submission are not discussed in every case, but we favour the view of the *Martin Committee Report* that a judge should reject counsels' recommendation only where the proposed sentence "would bring the administration of justice into disrepute, or is otherwise not in the public interest."[29] This judicial power must be expressly brought to the attention of the client whenever a plea proposal is being considered.

## E. PLEA DISCUSSIONS AND AGREEMENTS: AN INTEGRAL PART OF THE SYSTEM

In the not too distant past, there was considerable controversy in Canada as to whether plea agreements should be employed in the ordinary course of the criminal justice process. Some commentators argued against plea agreements,[30] and the Law Reform Commission of Canada took this view in one of its working papers.[31] The respective advantages and disadvantages of plea discussions continue to spark debate today.[32] However, it is now generally accepted that discussion and agreement between defence counsel and the Crown on the matter of the accused's plea constitutes an important part of our justice system.[33]

---

29  *Martin Committee Report*, above note 4 at 327–30.

30  Most notably, see the influential article written by G. Ferguson & D. Roberts, "Plea Bargaining: Directions for Canadian Reform" (1974) 52 Can. Bar Rev. 497.

31  Law Reform Commission of Canada, *Criminal Procedure: Control of the Process* (Working Paper No. 15) (Ottawa: The Commission, 1975) at 45. To similar effect, see the Law Reform Commission of Ontario, *Report on Administration of Ontario Courts, Part II* (Toronto: Ministry of the Attorney General, 1973) at 119–25.

32  Concise and current overviews of the arguments and literature are provided in J. Palmer, "Abolishing Plea Bargaining: An End to the Same Old Song and Dance" (1999) 26 Am. J. Crim. L. 505 at 512–28.

33  See, for example, *R. v. Burlingham* (1995), 97 C.C.C. (3d) 385 at 400 (S.C.C.); *Fegan*, above note 14 at 361–62; *K.(S.)*, above note 25 at 382; and *Santobello v. New York*, 404 U.S. 257 at 260 (1971). Recent expressions of support for resolution discussions include Department of Justice, Research and Development Directorate, *Plea Bargaining and Sentencing Guidelines* (Research Report of the Canadian Sentencing Commission) by S. Verdun-Jones (Ottawa: Department of Justice, 1988); Canadian Sentencing Commission, *Sentencing Reform: A Canadian Approach* (Ottawa: Supply and Services, 1987) at 404–29; Nova Scotia, *Report of the Royal Commission on the Donald Marshall, Jr., Prosecution*, vol. 1 (Halifax: The Commission, 1989) (Chair: T.A. Hickman) at 244–46; *Martin Committee Report*, above note 4 at 281; and *Report of the Criminal Justice Review Committee*, above note 1, c. 6.

It is especially instructive to note that the Law Reform Commission of Canada has changed its view and now approves of plea negotiations.[34] Support for plea discussions within the legal profession is reflected in the rules of professional conduct proffered by the CBA and the various Canadian governing bodies.[35] Because of this widespread acceptance, our discussion will focus upon defence counsel's ethical responsibilities in the plea-negotiation process, and will not delve more deeply to consider whether such a process should occur in the first place.

It is nonetheless helpful to review briefly some of the reasons why an accused might wish to make a plea agreement with the Crown.[36] Only by appreciating the full scope of possible benefits for the accused can we understand the importance of counsel's role in the process and formulate appropriate ethical guidelines. Most obviously, the accused can obtain concrete concessions from the Crown in exchange for the plea, including a promise to recommend a particular sentence, the withdrawal of a charge, or an acceptable stipulation as to the facts upon which the plea will be based.[37] There are also other benefits, sometimes less concrete, that can flow from a plea agreement. The agreement will often lead to a much faster resolution of the case, minimizing the uncertainty and stress that accompany pending charges. Avoiding a trial will spare an accused substantial legal costs, where he or she retains a lawyer privately. An accused may also desire to admit guilt quickly and publicly as a genuine expression of remorse, and to make amends with a victim. The result may be a faster and more successful path towards rehabilitation. Finally, plea discussions arguably allow the accused, through counsel, to play an active role in the process and actually influence the outcome, to an extent not always matched at trial.[38]

---

34   See *Plea Discussions and Agreements*, above note 5.

35   See the discussion in section F, "Related Rules of Professional Conduct," in this chapter.

36   We are restricting ourselves to the benefits to be gained by an accused. The advantages of resolution discussions from the perspectives of the Crown and the system more generally are canvassed in the *Martin Committee Report*, above note 4 at 281–91.

37   The panoply of possible concessions is large, and S. Cohen & A. Doob, "Public Attitudes to Plea Bargainin" (1989–90) 32 Crim. L.Q. 85 at 86–87, set out fourteen areas that could conceivably form the subject of a plea-resolution agreement.

38   See S. Clark, "Is Plea Bargaining a Short Cut to Justice?" *Lawyers Weekly* (1 March 1985) at 4. This "empowerment" justification for plea bargaining is at odds with the view taken in M. McConville, "Plea Bargaining: Ethics and Politics" (1998) 25 J. L. & Soc'y 562. See also R. Weisberg, "The Impropriety of Plea Agreements: An 'Anthropological' View" (1994), 19 L. & Soc. Inquiry 145

Of course, there are also potential pitfalls that exist for the accused who wishes to discuss a possible plea agreement with the Crown. Many of these pitfalls arise out of defence counsel's inadequacies or mistakes. A lawyer may see the plea agreement as an opportunity to avoid the effort of preparing for a trial, and fail to notice or discover a valid defence. In the same vein, the retainer with counsel may provide for a block-fee payment, regardless of the outcome, and hence provide the lawyer with an incentive to have the client plead guilty. Other lawyers may seek to maintain a good relationship with prosecutors and judges, and so shy away from running trials or taking truly adversarial positions during plea discussions. These sorts of problems undermine counsel's duty of loyalty to the client, often to the client's significant detriment, and may constitute incompetent representation. The result can be excessive pressure or poor advice that leads the accused to plead guilty against his or her wishes or best interests. Constitutional rights may be too quickly waived, and valid defences may be foregone.

Ethical guidelines for defence counsel concerning plea discussions should strive to maximize the potential benefits to an accused, while avoiding the disadvantages that can flow from ineffective or otherwise sloppy representation. Loyalty and competence must be the hallmarks of the lawyer's function. With these beacon principles in mind, we can now turn to look at the rules of professional conduct.

## F.  RELATED RULES OF PROFESSIONAL CONDUCT

Given that plea agreements are commonly reached and generally accepted in the criminal justice system, and can afford substantial benefits to an accused, it is not surprising that Canadian ethical rules invariably address the topic of plea discussions. Many governing bodies have adopted the provision found in Commentary 12 to Chapter IX of the CBA Code, which reads as follows:

> Agreement on Guilty Plea
>
> 12.  Where, following investigation,
>     (a) the defence lawyer *bona fide* concludes and advises the accused client that an acquittal of the offence charged is uncertain or unlikely,

---

(noting that plea bargaining "is both more choice and less freedom" for the accused).

(b) the client is prepared to admit the necessary factual and mental elements,

(c) the lawyer fully advises the client of the implications and possible consequences of a guilty plea and that the matter of sentence is solely in the discretion of the trial judge, and

(d) the client so instructs the lawyer, preferably in writing,

it is proper for the lawyer to discuss and agree tentatively with the prosecutor to enter a plea of guilty on behalf of the client to the offence charged or to a lesser or included offence or to another offence appropriate to the admissions, and also on a disposition or sentence to be proposed to the court. The public interest and the client's interests must not, however, be compromised by agreeing to a guilty plea.[39]

The Alberta Law Society's Code of Professional Conduct, while generally to the same effect, warrants special mention, because the commentary to the applicable ethical rule emphasizes that "a plea agreement may not involve a misrepresentation to the court."[40] Additionally, the Alberta commentary stipulates that a plea agreement "is not considered a usual lawyers' undertaking," and that either the defence or prosecution may withdraw from the agreement prior to performance.[41]

In the United Kingdom, neither the Law Society nor the General Council of the Bar offers broad and comprehensive guidelines concerning plea discussions and agreements. However, the rules of professional conduct promulgated by both governing bodies do contain relevant provisions that pertain to guilty pleas more generally. For instance, barristers are directed to follow basic standards derived from the leading decision of *R. v. Turner* (probably the most frequently quoted Commonwealth case on the subject of defence counsel's obli-

---

39   CBA Code ch. IX, comm. 12. Footnote 24 to Commentary 12 makes reference to guidelines set out in *Turner*, above note 9 at 285, as well as two articles on the subject. The same provision is found in the rules of professional conduct adopted by numerous provincial governing bodies: see, for example, Sask. ch. IX, comm. 12; Man. ch. IX, comm. 12; Nfld. ch. IX, comm. 12. The applicable Ontario and Nova Scotia rules are quite similar to Commentary 12, though there are some distinctions, as will be discussed further below: see Ont. r. 4.01(8) & (9); and N.S. ch. 10, r. 10.8 & 10.9. The same can be said for British Columbia, though the provision is quite brief and hence less comprehensive: B.C. ch. 8, r. 20). In Quebec, the Code of Ethics of Advocates deals with the topic only in so far as s. 3.02.10 requires a lawyer to inform the client of any settlement offer.

40   Alta. ch. 8, r. 27 & commentary.

41   *Ibid.*

gations in relation to the client's plea).[42] According to these standards, a barrister should advise the client generally about the plea, if necessary expressing the advice in strong terms.[43] At the same time, however, barristers are told to make clear to the client that he or she has complete freedom of choice and is ultimately responsible for the plea.[44] More daring, at least from a Canadian perspective, is the approach taken with respect to the client who wishes to plead guilty despite protestations of innocence made to counsel. In this regard, the Law Society's rules provide:

> If the client wishes to plead guilty, but at the same time asserts the truth of facts which, if true, would or could lead to an acquittal, the solicitor should use his or her best endeavours to persuade the client to plead not guilty. However, if the client insists on pleading guilty, despite being advised that such a plea may or will restrict the ambit of any plea in mitigation or appeal, then the solicitor is not prevented from continuing to act in accordance with the client's instructions, doing the best he or she can. The solicitor will not, in mitigation, be entitled to suggest that the facts are such that the ingredients of the offence have not been established.[45]

The propriety of undertaking plea discussions, reaching a plea agreement and eventually entering a plea of guilty, where the client maintains his or her innocence, is addressed in detail below.[46]

---

42   *Turner*, above note 9 at 285. Since *Turner* was decided, the legal landscape in the United Kingdom has altered, with the statutory recognition of sentence discounts for guilty pleas: see the *Criminal Justice and Public Order Act 1994* (U.K.), c. 33, s. 48.

43   See General Council, *Code of Conduct of the Bar of England and Wales* (London: The Council, 1990) [*Bar Code of Conduct*], Annex "H" (Written Standards for the Conduct of Professional Work, Standards Applicable to Criminal Cases) §12.3 & §12.4. No comparable provision is found in the Law Society's rules of professional conduct, but presumably the *Turner* approach applies equally to solicitors.

44   *Ibid.*

45   Law Society, *The Guide to the Professional Conduct of Solicitors*, 8th ed. (London: Law Society, 1999) at §21.20(7). The Bar Code of Conduct rules are to similar effect on this point, if slightly less detailed, stating that "[w]here a defendant tells his counsel that he did not commit the offence with which is [sic] charged but nevertheless insists on pleading guilty to it for reasons of his own, counsel must continue to represent him, but only after he has advised what the consequences will be and that what can be submitted in mitigation can only be on the basis that the client is guilty": see *Bar Code of Conduct*, above note 43, Annex "H" at §12.5.

46   See section M, "The Client Who Maintains Innocence," in this chapter.

424 ETHICS AND CANADIAN CRIMINAL LAW

In the United States, the ABA Model Rules and the ALI Third Restatement have little to say regarding the discrete topic of plea discussions.[47] But the ABA Defense Standards provide a comprehensive examination of the topic.[48] Despite their length, it is worthwhile to set out fully the relevant provisions:

Standard 4-5.1 Advising the Accused

(a) After informing himself or herself fully on the facts and the law, defense counsel should advise the accused with complete candor concerning all aspects of the case, including a candid estimate of the probable outcome.
(b) Defense counsel should not intentionally understate or overstate the risks, hazards, or prospects of the case to exert undue influence on the accused's decision as to his or her plea.

Standard 4-5.2 Control and Direction of the Case

(a) Certain decisions relating to the conduct of the case are ultimately for the accused and others are ultimately for defense counsel. The decisions which are to be made by the accused after full consultation with counsel include:
(i)  what pleas to enter;
(ii) whether to accept a plea agreement; . . . .

Standard 4-6.1 Duty to Explore Disposition Without Trial

(a) Whenever the law, nature, and circumstances of the case permit, defense counsel should explore the possibility of an early diversion of the case from the criminal process through the use of other community agencies.
(b) Defense counsel may engage in plea discussions with the prosecutor. Under no circumstances should defense counsel recommend to a defendant acceptance of a plea unless appropriate investigation and study of the case has been completed, including an analysis of controlling law and the evidence likely to be introduced at trial.

Standard 4-6.2 Plea Discussions

---

47  However, both the Model Rules and the Third Restatement contain general principles of ethics that obviously bear directly upon the process of plea discussions, such as the duties of competence (see, for example, ABA Model Rule 1.1; and Third Restatement §16(2)) and communication (see, for example, ABA Model Rule 1.4; and Third Restatement §20).
48  ABA Defense Standards 4-5.1, 4-6.1, & 4-6.2.

(a) Defense counsel should keep the accused advised of developments arising out of plea discussions conducted with the prosecutor.

(b) Defense counsel should promptly communicate and explain to the accused all significant plea proposals made by the prosecutor.

(c) Defense counsel should not knowingly make false statements concerning the evidence in the course of plea discussions with the prosecutor.

(d) Defense counsel should not seek concessions favorable to one client by any agreement which is detrimental to the legitimate interests of a client in another case.

(e) Defense counsel representing two or more clients in the same or related cases should not participate in making an aggregated agreement as to guilty or nolo contendere pleas, unless each client consents after consultation, including disclosure of the existence and nature of all the claims or pleas involved.

The ABA's Criminal Justice Section has also adopted a separate package of standards that solely concern the subject of guilty pleas. Regarding defence counsel's ethical obligations, these "Pleas of Guilty" standards reflect the provisions just quoted from the Defense Function Standards.[49]

# G. EXPLORING THE POSSIBILITY OF A RESOLUTION WITHOUT A PLEA

Sometimes a lawyer will be retained prior to any charges being brought against the client. In such circumstances, a resolution of the case without a charge being laid is the most successful result that can be achieved. Prompt and effective negotiation with the authorities is crucial if such a resolution is to be reached. Accordingly, resolution discussions may be undertaken, and indeed mandated, even before a charge has been laid.[50] With necessary modifications as dictated by the circumstances, counsel taking part in such resolution discussions

---

49    See ABA Pleas of Guilty Standard 14-3.2.

50    See Ont. r. 4.01(8), which states that "*[b]efore a charge is laid* or at any time after a charge is laid, a lawyer for an accused *or potential accused* may discuss with the prosecutor the possible disposition of the case, unless the client instructs otherwise" (emphasis added). Section 717 of the *Criminal Code*, above note 28, formally provides for diversion under the moniker "alternative measures."

should be guided by the ethical duties and considerations reviewed in this chapter.

The same approach should be taken where, although charges have been laid, circumstances make diversion from the criminal justice system a real possibility. Depending upon the jurisdiction in question, the Crown may be open to diverting less serious criminal charges such as minor thefts and communicating for the purpose of prostitution. Thus, the ABA Standards relating to both the Defense Function and Pleas of Guilty provide that counsel should explore the possibility of an early diversion of the case from the criminal process, whenever the law, nature, and circumstances of the case permit.[51] In Canada, the broad duties of competence and loyalty to the client surely fix defence counsel with the same duty to explore a diversion resolution for the case.

# H. DUTY TO NEGOTIATE

Most Canadian rules of professional conduct do not expressly impose any obligation upon defence counsel to canvas the possibility of a plea agreement with the Crown.[52] However, as just noted, counsel owes the client basic duties of loyalty and competence. Given that a plea agreement may be in the best interests of the client, and that the final decision as to how to plead belongs to the client, it follows that counsel has a duty to negotiate, at least where there is a reasonable prospect that the client will thereby receive a benefit.[53] It can also be argued that the proper and efficient functioning of the criminal justice system militates

---

51   See ABA Defense Standards 4-6.1(a); snf ABA Pleas of Guilty Standard 14-3.2(e). It has been argued that Defense Standard 4-6.1(a) effectively imposes a duty on counsel to explore the possibility of diversion: see J. Hall Jr., *Professional Responsibility of the Criminal Lawyer*, 2d ed. (New York: Clark Boardman Callaghan, 1996) at §15:2.

52   Some governing bodies include a duty to make every reasonable effort consistent with the legitimate interests of the client to expedite litigation, which obviously bears on the issue: see, for example, CBA Code ch. III, comm. 6; N.S. ch. 10, r. (b); Alta. ch. 10, r. 2; and Ont. r. 2.02(2). But such a duty does not directly address the plea bargaining context.

53   See, for example, *Report of the Criminal Justice Review Committee*, above note 1 at Recommendation 6.9 and the associated discussion; and *Martin Committee Report*, above note 4 at 335ff. The duty to negotiate does not operate in all cases, however, as implicitly accepted in R. v. W.(W.) (1995), 100 C.C.C. (3d) 225 at 244 (Ont. C.A.) [W.(W.)].

in favour of counsel pursuing a plea arrangement, where not against the best interests or instructions of the client.[54]

Counsel may take the position that, in certain circumstances, plea discussions are distasteful and antithetical to the lawyer's personal convictions, and are to be avoided at all costs. The prime example would be the lawyer who refuses to act on behalf of a client who seeks a plea agreement in exchange for informing on or testifying against another individual.[55] Assuming that counsel is justified in taking such a position, it is imperative that the client be told of any such limitation at the commencement of the retainer.[56]

## I.  CONDITIONAL OR PRELIMINARY PLEA DISCUSSIONS

The CBA Code provides that plea discussions are properly undertaken only after counsel has investigated the case, come to a view regarding its merits, and provided full advice to the client, *and* the client has indicated a willingness to admit to the necessary factual and mental elements and instructs the lawyer to commence such discussions.[57] This statement on its face suggests that defence counsel should not engage in plea discussions with the prosecution prior to providing complete advice and obtaining instructions and admissions from the client.[58] However, the realities of criminal litigation demonstrate that

---

54  See the ethical rules cited at note 52, above. The *Martin Committee Report*, above note 4 at 335ff, is especially (though not exclusively) concerned with the efficient and proper functioning of the system. For this reason, the early commencement of resolution discussions is seen to be particularly important.

55  This stance is examined, and tentatively criticized, in D. Richman, "Cooperating Clients" (1995), 56 Ohio St. L.J. 69. See also I. Weinstein, "Regulating the Market for Snitches" (1999) 47 Buff. L. Rev. 563 at 593–94.

56  See the case of *United States* v. *Lopez*, 765 F. Supp. 1433 at 1438 (N.D. Cal. 1991), vacated 989 F.2d 1032 (9th Cir. 1993), amended and superseded 4 F.3d 1455 (9th Cir. 1993), where counsel provided the client with just such a warning, yet the retainer did not survive the client's subsequent decision to seek a cooperation agreement with the prosecution. See also *Brown* v. *Doe*, 2 F.3d 1236 at 1240 (2d Cir. 1993), cert. denied 510 U.S. 1125 (1994).

57  See CBA Code ch. IX, comm. 12.

58  Such an interpretation is noted, though not necessarily endorsed, by Doherty J.A. in *W.(W.)*, above note 53 at 244 (in relation to the former Ontario rule 10, comm. 12).

this requirement is unnecessary, unwieldy, and impractical.[59] As the commentary to ABA Defense Standard 4-6.2 observes:

> In many cases, it will be appropriate to make an early contact with the prosecutor to secure information concerning the charge. In the course of this contact, the possibility of reducing the charge or making a plea may arise and counsel may have an opportunity to advance the client's interest without making any disclosures concerning the defence. The client's consent ordinarily need not be sought and obtained before any approaches are made, as there will be occasions when some discussion, perhaps only of a tentative and preliminary nature, will occur before an opportunity arises to obtain the client's consent.[60]

Presumably for these reasons, the Ontario rules of professional conduct no longer follow the CBA Code's rigid approach, and instead expressly provide that "[b]efore a charge is laid or at any time after a charge is laid, a lawyer for an accused or potential accused may discuss with the prosecutor the possible disposition of the case, unless the client instructs otherwise."[61] The rules in Alberta, British Columbia, and Nova Scotia, though worded differently, are apparently to similar effect.[62]

The Ontario approach does not, however, give the lawyer *carte blanche* with respect to plea discussions. Several obvious restrictions apply to conditional or tentative discussions. First, absent proper preparation, advice, and instructions, counsel can only canvas the possibility of a plea with the Crown and is not permitted to reach a final plea agreement. Making an agreement without authority is highly improper and, among other things may create an impetus for defence

---

59  It is interesting to note that the bar admission materials used in Ontario prior to implementation of the new rules of professional conduct expressly told students that "the practice of most competent defence counsel" is to engage in conditional plea discussions with the prosecution — in other words, to ignore the position taken in the Professional Conduct Handbook: see S. Skurka & J. Stribopoulos, "Professional Responsibility in Criminal Practice," in Law Society of Upper Canada, *41st Bar Admission Course, 1999, Criminal Procedure Reference Materials* (Toronto: Law Society of Upper Canada, 1999) ch. 1 at §2.6 (11).

60  ABA Defense Standard 4-6.2 & commentary.

61  Ont. r. 4.01(8).

62  See Alta. ch. 10, r. 27; and B.C. ch. 8, r. 20, which place limits upon counsel with respect to a completed plea agreement (Alberta) or representation on a plea (British Columbia), and hence would appear not to place similar restrictions upon tentative plea discussions. The Nova Scotia rule is more in the style of the Ontario rule quoted in the text above: see N.S. ch. 10, r. 10.8.

counsel to pressure the client to accept the arrangement against the latter's will.[63] Second, even tentative discussions are improper where forbidden by the client (as expressly noted by the Ontario rule). Where counsel has good reason to believe that the client would disapprove of plea discussions taking place, the proper course is to avoid even tentative discussions absent reviewing the matter with the client.[64] Third, it is prudent for counsel to inform the Crown that the discussions are only tentative, making clear that any proposal is subject to the client's consideration and agreement. Frankness in this regard avoids misunderstandings and minimizes the possibility that defence counsel will be blamed, castigated, or mistrusted if the deal does not go through.

## J.  DUTY TO INVESTIGATE

Effective negotiations with the Crown and competent advice for the client require more than mere experience, instinct, or wisdom. Rules of professional responsibility typically impose upon counsel a general, but nonetheless highly relevant, duty to understand adequately the factual and legal elements of a case prior to providing advice to the client.[65] Accordingly, it is not surprising to find that, in the specific area of plea agreements, all Canadian ethical rules implicitly recognize an obligation to investigate a matter adequately, invariably countenancing plea discussions or agreements "following investigation" by the lawyer.[66] As G. Arthur Martin said: "[B]efore urging a defendant to plead guilty [counsel] should have conducted the same type of intensive investigation which a lawyer preparing for trial should undertake."[67] Absent such investigation, counsel is simply unable to provide the best possible advice to the client regarding the advantages and disadvantages of a proposed plea agreement. Similarly, failure to master the details of the case may weaken defence counsel's negotiating position with the Crown, leading to a bad or mediocre result for the client.

---

63   Respecting the dangers of overbearing pressure put on the client by counsel, see section K(3), "Respect for the Client's Freedom of Choice," in this chapter.

64   On this point, see also section M(1), "The Client Who Maintains Innocence but Later Abandons the Claim," in this chapter.

65   See, for example, CBA Code ch. III, comm. 1 & 3, pertaining to "Advising Clients"; and ch. II, on the subject of competence and quality of service.

66   See the rules cited at notes 39–41, above. One of the most thorough expressions of the duty to investigate in relation to plea agreements is found in ABA Defense Standard 4-6.1(b): see also ABA Pleas of Guilty Standard 14-3.2(b).

67   Martin, above note 10 at 387.

For these reasons, counsel is under an obligation to investigate thoroughly the circumstances of the case prior to entering into a plea agreement.

The amount of investigation required will vary from case to case but should reflect the degree of preparation normally expected of competent counsel. In ascertaining the type and extent of investigation, one must take into account the number and complexity of factual and legal issues, the strength and nature of the Crown case, the strategy favoured by counsel, and any information provided by the accused. With regard to this last factor, it is worth reiterating a point already made in relation to the defence of a client known by counsel to be guilty.[68] A client's confession may be false, mistaken, or irrelevant to the issue of whether there exists a valid defence to the charge. For instance, the client may be attempting to shift the blame from a third party by falsely admitting to a crime. Or a *Charter* argument may be available that works to deny the Crown evidence essential to obtaining a conviction. These and other examples demonstrate the importance of investigating the case fully even where the accused tells counsel that he or she is guilty.

As a final point, it is tempting for some lawyers to view a plea resolution as an easy route to dispose of a case. Also, fee arrangements may be structured in a way that provides counsel with greater financial benefit where the client pleads guilty. These temptations must be shunned. Certainly, the level of preparation that is normally reflected in counsel's public performance at trial may not be so obvious on a joint submission to plead guilty, especially where the charges are not serious and the case not complex. Inadequate service to the client may therefore be hidden from the Crown, judge, and other participants in the process. But lack of preparation can nonetheless come back to haunt counsel who skimps on preparation to the disadvantage of the client, in the form of a complaint to the professional governing body, civil proceedings for negligence, or attack on appeal.

# K.  DUTY TO ADVISE THE CLIENT

Inextricably entwined with counsel's preparation is the duty to provide advice to the client. After all, a main reason why counsel must become familiar with the facts and law surrounding the case, undertaking inde-

---

68   See section F(3), "A Common Example of Irresistable Knowledge of Guilt: The Confession," in chapter 1.

pendent investigation if appropriate, is to ensure that the client receives fully informed and competent advice. In many if not most cases, an accused relies heavily on counsel's advice in choosing how to plead. The quality of advice therefore has a direct bearing on the proper exercise of the client's constitutional right to decide how best to plead in response to criminal charges.[69]

Some accused are experienced participants in the criminal justice system, apparently quite confident and capable of making a sensible decision as to the proper plea, especially where the charges are minor. The "experienced" accused may inform counsel that he or she has already determined how to plead, and claim that any advice on the point is unnecessary. While the client's choice must be respected, counsel would be wrong to accede too easily to the request to dispense with the provision of advice. The better response is to emphasize to the client the importance of fully understanding the implications of a plea, and to review the considerations that might be relevant on the facts of the case. If the client persists in refusing even to receive advice, counsel is faced with a choice: either accept the client's instructions (in writing if at all possible) and proceed with the case, or seek to withdraw from the retainer.[70]

## 1) Canadian Rules of Professional Conduct

Canadian ethical codes usually contain several provisions that ground counsel's duty to provide competent advice with respect to a plea decision. First, there is the duty to deliver competent service to the client, which surely includes educating the client so that he or she can make informed decisions regarding the conduct of the case.[71] Indeed, the CBA Code includes in its list of behaviour that falls short of the requisite level of competence the "failure to keep the client reasonably informed" and the "failure to inform the client of proposals of settle-

---

69 The constitutional implications of a plea, whether guilty or not guilty, are discussed above in section C, "Constitutional and Other Legal Facets of a Guilty Plea. See also the discussion in section E, "Informing and Advising the Client," in chapter 3.

70 Regarding the advisability of obtaining written instructions, see section Q, "Written Instructions," in this chapter. As for the possibility of withdrawing from the case, see section U, "Withdrawal Because of Disagreement With the Client," in this chapter.

71 Ethical rules regarding the duty of competence are reviewed in section I(1), "Competence and the Rules of Professional Conduct," in chapter 3.

ment, or to explain them properly."[72] Second, the ethical rules contain a separate duty to be honest and candid when providing advice, a duty that typically makes reference to the need for competent and informed counselling.[73] For instance, the commentary to the relevant Ontario rule states that "[t]he lawyer's duty to the client who seeks legal advice is to give the client a competent opinion based on a sufficient knowledge of the relevant facts, an adequate consideration of the applicable law, and the lawyer's own experience and expertise."[74] Finally, the provisions dealing directly with plea discussions and agreements contain express reference to the need to provide an accused with advice. In this regard, we have already seen that the CBA Code accepts the ethical propriety of plea agreements where "the lawyer fully advises the client of the implications and possible consequences of a guilty plea."[75]

## 2)  Potential Factors to Cover with the Client

What advice should the lawyer give, once he or she is fully informed regarding the factual and legal issues at stake?[76] While the proper advice in each case is largely driven by the particular circumstances at hand, a number of factors must be considered by defence counsel and discussed with the client, including

1.  the merits of the case, including the strengths and weaknesses of any available defences;[77]
2.  the likelihood of a conviction following trial;[78]
3.  the consequences to the client if he or she loses after a disputed trial, including the maximum sentence, the probable range of sen-

---

72  See CBA Code ch. II, comm. 7(a) & (j).
73  See, for example, CBA Code ch. III, Rule; Man. ch. 3; N.S. ch. 4; Ont. r. 2.02; Sask. ch. III; Alta. ch. 9, Statement of Principle; B.C. ch. 1, r. 3(1); and N.B. Part C, r. 7.
74  See Ont. r. 2.02 (commentary).
75  CBA Code ch. IX, comm. 12(c).
76  For a viewpoint that most practising criminal lawyers would find utterly shocking, see G. Bradley, "Plea Bargaining and the Criminal Defendant's Obligation to Plead Guilty" (1999) 40 S. Tex. L. Rev. 65 (suggesting that counsel should advise the blameworthy client to plead guilty, as the proper moral choice that furthers the common good).
77  See, for example, *Lamoureux*, above note 9 at 105; *Boudreau v. Benaiah* (1998), 37 O.R. (3d) 686 at 723 (Gen. Div.) [*Boudreau*], appeal allowed in part (2000), 46 O.R. (3d) 737 (C.A.); and *R. v. Herbert* (1992), 94 Cr. App. R. 230 at 233 [*Herbert*].
78  See, for example, *Lamoureux*, above note 9 at 105.

tences and any relevant impact on personal life (for example, work, family, driving, international travel, firearms use);

4. any adverse impact associated with the trial process where guilt is disputed, including publicity and the stress and unpleasantness that may flow from a decision to testify;

5. the impact that a guilty plea has upon the trial process, including the waiver of many fundamental constitutional rights;[79]

6. the factual basis for a guilty plea, and the sentencing process in instances where disputed aggravating or mitigating facts are litigated by the parties;[80]

7. the benefits that might accompany a guilty plea, including concessions made by the Crown under a proposed plea agreement[81] but also pertaining to speedier resolution, stress reduction, and minimized cost to the client;

8. the plea of guilty as a beneficial factor on sentencing, including the heightened mitigation that often accompanies an early plea;[82]

9. the possible methods of indicating remorse, and commencing the process of rehabilitation, as well as any associated disadvantages, responsibilities, or benefits;

10. the impact of the accused's prior criminal record and any other personal circumstances (family, work, character, drug dependency, and so on) on the sentencing outcome;

11. the nature and range of penalties attendant upon a guilty plea, including any mandatory minimum penalty and the maximum possible penalty;

---

79 Canadian ethical rules expressly require full advice regarding the implications and possible consequences of a guilty plea: see, for example, CBA Code ch. IX, comm. 12(c). As for constitutional implications, see the discussion in section C, "Constitutional and Other Legal Facets of a Guilty Plea," in this chapter.

80 The rules of professional conduct usually provide that a client must be prepared to admit the necessary factual and mental elements of the offence charged, and hence implicitly require that counsel advise the client accordingly. Depending on the jurisdiction in question, this requirement is a precondition to counsel participating in plea discussions, entering into a final plea agreement, and/or representing an accused on the guilty plea itself: see, for example, CBA Code ch. IX, comm. 12(b); Ont. r. 4.01(9)(c); B.C. ch. 8, r. 20(a); and Alta. ch. 10, r. 27(b). See also the discussions in section M, "The Client Who Maintains Innocence," and N, "Agreed Statement of Fact," in this chapter.

81 Reviewing proposed benefits is implicit in the duty to advise as formulated by most Canadian ethical rules: see, for example, CBA Code ch. IX, comm. 12(c).

82 See C. Ruby, Sentencing, 5th ed. (Toronto: Butterworths, 1999) at §5.165–5.178.

12. if the circumstances warrant, parole and probation possibilities, long-term and dangerous offender designations, conditional sentences and property forfeiture;

13. any reasonably anticipated collateral consequences of a guilty plea, such as the impact of the plea on personal life, civil litigation, criminal charges in a foreign jurisdiction, and deportation proceedings;

14. the judge's power to ignore a joint submission in some circumstances;[83]

15. if the identity of the judge hearing the case is known, the judge's sentencing predilections;

16. the precise process involved in entering a plea, including the possibility that the judge will embark upon a plea inquiry;[84] and

17. the client's complete freedom of choice regarding the plea decision.[85]

## 3) Respect for the Client's Freedom of Choice

Diligent counsel will usually encounter no great difficulty in covering many of the topics set out in section K(2) with the client. The real challenge, however, often comes in providing a final opinion as to whether the client should plead guilty. While the pros and cons of pleading guilty usually involve considerations personal to the accused, defence counsel who studiously avoids giving an opinion on the matter is not doing the client any service.[86] Lawyers should offer such advice where possible, and they are given license to provide the opinion in "strong terms."[87] But on the other hand, it is improper to bully the client into accepting counsel's preferred option. Valid defences may be foregone, perhaps even leading to the conviction of an innocent person, and in any event it is improper to interfere with the client's freedom of choice regarding the plea. Counsel should also keep in mind the ethical pro-

---

83   According to most Canadian ethical rules, counsel is expressly required to inform the client of this power: see, for example, CBA Code ch. IX, comm. 12(c). Such advice is consistent with current Canadian law: see section D(3), "Plea Agreement is Not Binding on the Court," in this chapter.

84   See the discussion in section D(2), "Judges Are Not Obligated to Conduct a Plea Inquiry," in this chapter.

85   See, for example, *Boudreau*, above note 77 at 719.

86   See *Rajaeefard*, above note 16 at 235, stating that "a more experienced counsel likely would, and should, have advised his client not to plead guilty."

87   See, for example, *Lamoureux*, above note 9 at 105; *R. v. Conflitti* (1999), 27 C.R. (5th) 63 (Ont. Prov. Div.) [*Conflitti*]; and *Herbert*, above note 77 at 233. The phrase "strong terms" is taken from the decision in *Turner*, above note 9 at 285.

hibition against usurping the role of the court by acting as judge of the client's culpability.[88] For all of these reasons, the lawyer should not "exert undue influence on the accused's decision as to his or her plea."[89] At the end of the day, counsel must strive to provide competent advice yet fully respect the client's freedom of choice.

Where a client is particularly vulnerable, whether by reason of emotional fragility or especially trying circumstances, special care should be taken to ensure that his or her free will is not subjugated. In extreme cases, the accused may suffer from mental illness requiring drastic measures, including close consultation with family members, appointment of a litigation guardian, or a fitness hearing.[90] Counsel should also work hard to avoid placing the client in a position where the pressure to plead guilty is needlessly increased. Pressure of this type is created when a defence lawyer unjustifiably waits until the last minute to provide complete and candid advice on the issue of the plea. Granted, there will always be accused persons who assiduously avoid making a decision until the trial date, no matter the timing and content of advice received from counsel. But in many cases, a lawyer can at least minimize external pressure on the accused by providing full, honest, and accurate advice in a timely manner. Even where circumstances beyond the control of counsel or the accused result in sudden pressure to plead guilty, counsel may be able to alleviate the problem by requesting an adjournment.[91]

**Example:** Accused Y is charged with domestic assault. He protests his innocence and provides counsel with useful ammunition for the cross-examination of the complainant. However, advice provided by counsel leaves Y with the impression that a fair trial can never be expected on a domestic assault charge. Y strongly considers a guilty plea but makes no final decision prior to the trial. Nevertheless, Y's lawyer arrives at

---

88  See generally chapter 1, and in particular sections B, "Related Rules of Professional Conduct," and D, "The Rationale for Defending One Known to Be Guilty."

89  ABA Defense Standard 4-5.1(b).

90  See section L, "Client Under a Disability," in chapter 3.

91  In *Laperriere*, above note 9, also discussed in the text accompanying note 217, below, troubling information received from the Crown at the last minute created sudden uncertainty and pressure regarding the plea decision. Despite a suggestion by the Crown that the matter be adjourned for a short time to permit calm reflection by the accused, defence counsel pushed ahead with a guilty plea. The plea was subsequently quashed by the Supreme Court of Canada, on the basis of undue pressure from counsel and conflict of interest.

the trial date unprepared, in the expectation that Y will likely plead guilty. In trying to convince Y to enter a guilty plea, counsel admits that he is not ready for trial. Fearing that a conviction is certain in any event, Y responds by agreeing to plead guilty. In failing to prepare for the case, counsel has effectively denied Y the option of going to trial, and hence subjected Y to undue pressure to plead guilty.[92]

## 4) Clarence Darrow and the Leopold and Loeb Case

A dubious departure from the ethical duty to keep the client informed in a timely manner, and not to interfere unduly with the client's choice whether to plead guilty, is seen in the infamous Leopold and Loeb case.[93] The defendants were two young men from wealthy Chicago families who in 1924 kidnapped and killed a fourteen-year-old boy as part of their Nietzschean quest to commit the "perfect crime." They confessed their crimes upon being arrested, and, aside from the confessions, the police had accumulated convincing evidence of their guilt. Clarence Darrow, one of the leading American lawyers of the past century, was retained to act on behalf of the defendants.

Under the law then applicable in Illinois, Leopold and Loeb faced the death penalty if convicted, but a judge had the discretion to substitute a punishment of life imprisonment. Darrow felt that only two options were open to his clients. First, they could put forth an insanity defence, but Darrow concluded that this strategy had little chance of success in view of the evidence and strong public condemnation of the crime. The probable result would be conviction and the death penalty. The second option was to enter a plea of guilty and focus all energies on attempting to persuade the judge not to impose the death penalty. Darrow believed that this latter approach presented the only realistic possibility for his clients to avoid the hangman's noose.

---

92   See *Ceballo*, above note 26. For other cases where counsel placed significant last-minute pressure on the accused, or failed to make reasonable attempts to circumvent pressure, reference can be made to R. v. *Toussaint* (1984), 16 C.C.C. (3d) 544 (Que. C.A.); R. v. *Lodge* (1996), 31 W.C.B. (2d) 368 (Ont. Gen. Div.); *Boudreau*, above note 77; and R. v. *Beaney*, [1999] E.W.J. No. 1677 (C.A.) (QL) [*Beaney*].

93   For a discussion of the case, see K. Tierney, *Darrow: A Biography* (New York: Crowell, 1979); and I. Stone, *Clarence Darrow for the Defence* (Garden City, N.Y.: Doubleday, Doran, 1941). The Leopold and Loeb case also provides the inspiration for several movies, including *Rope* (Warner Bros.) 1948 (Director A. Hitchcock), *Compulsion* (Twentieth Century Fox) 1959 (Director: R. Fleischer), and *Swoon* (American Playhouse) 1991 (Director: T. Kalin).

The normal procedure in Chicago at this time would have been for Darrow to try to make a deal with the prosecutor.[94] However, Darrow believed that the prosecutor would never agree to forego the death penalty.[95] He also saw a tactical advantage in not broaching the subject in advance. Accordingly, Darrow decided to have his clients plead guilty at the last minute, without any advance notice to the prosecutor. Yet if this plan was to succeed, absolute secrecy was essential, a tall order given the keen interest of the press in this notorious case. In pursuit of his goal, Darrow took the extreme step of keeping his clients in the dark, leaving them with the impression that the case would be fought on the issue of insanity.

On the morning of the date set for trial, Darrow visited his clients, informing them for the first time that they would be pleading guilty. He apologized for the last-minute revelation but explained that secrecy demanded this tactic. Leopold and Loeb followed their lawyer's advice, entering guilty pleas, and, after a month of evidence and argument, were sentenced to life in prison. Darrow's approach must be seen in the unique context of the case, including his clients' relative youth and the extreme public antipathy to the crime, but most especially as a product of an earlier time. We have great difficulty accepting that counsel today would ever be justified in following a similar course. The duty to keep the client reasonably informed, to respect the client's freedom of choice in deciding how to plead, and the dangers of pressuring the client with eleventh-hour revelations, all militate against Darrow's strategy.

## L. DUTY TO COMMUNICATE INFORMATION RELEVANT TO THE PLEA DECISION AND SENTENCING PROCESS

Lawyers have an ethical duty to keep the client reasonably informed,[96] and they breach this duty where the client is not told of a proposal of settlement or the proposal is not properly explained.[97] Moreover, there is a related duty to keep the client informed in a prompt manner.[98]

94   See Tierney, above note 93 at 329.
95   *Ibid.*
96   See, for example, CBA Code ch. II, comm. 7(a).
97   See, for example, CBA Code ch. II, comm. 7(j).
98   See, for example, CBA Code ch. II, comm. 8.

These duties are commensurate with counsel's overarching obligations of loyalty and competency, and mean that a lawyer can almost never choose to shield a client from relevant developments that bear upon the decision whether to plead guilty or not.[99] Adhering to this standard of conduct is especially crucial in jurisdictions where plea discussions with the Crown and pre-trial conferences with a judge are routinely held in the absence of the accused.

It might be thought that counsel can occasionally decide not to pass on a plea proposal to the client, perhaps because the Crown's offer appears so clearly to fall short of the client's expectations or is probably not in the client's best interests. Maybe counsel is eager to proceed to trial, given the existence of a strong defence. Or a lawyer might view information received from the Crown as extremely tentative, little more than a hint that a plea agreement may be possible at some point in the future, and see no need to pass on the information to the accused. In all of these cases, however, counsel acts improperly in failing to communicate the information. The final decision as to the plea is the client's, and failure to provide all information relevant to this decision risks subverting the client's freedom of choice. Counsel may be entirely correct in feeling that the client will reject a plea proposal but the proposal must nonetheless be communicated.[100] Furthermore, the ambit of this duty extends beyond firm plea offers and tentative proposals, to encompass any information that reasonably bears upon the decision how to plead.

In the course of plea discussions, new information about the case may come to counsel's attention. This is less likely to happen after disclosure is made but nonetheless can occur at any point during the case. It is especially possible where some tentative plea discussions take place prior to disclosure by the Crown. Regardless, relevant information received by counsel often bears upon the strengths and weaknesses of the prosecution case. Counsel therefore has a duty to communicate this information to the client in order to help him or her arrive at an informed decision regarding the plea.

---

99   See, generally, K. Bystrom, "Communicating Plea Offers to the Client" in R. Uphoff, ed., *Ethical Problems Facing the Criminal Lawyer: Practical Answers to Tough Questions* (Chicago: American Bar Association, 1995) c. 7. But see section E(1), "A Possible Exception: Keeping Information from a Client," in chapter 3.

100  In New Brunswick, the Law Society's ethical rules stipulate that "the lawyer must obtain instructions from his client before rejecting an offer of settlement": N.B. Part C, r. 7).

Also note that counsel's duty to act as a conduit for relevant information operates in both directions. Where the client instructs counsel to take a particular position regarding the Crown's plea proposal, it is imperative that counsel does so promptly and accurately. Failure to convey acceptance of a plea proposal to the Crown certainly violates counsel's ethical obligations[101] and may constitute denial of the right to the effective assistance of counsel.[102]

As a final point, counsel must keep the client informed as to all events bearing upon the sentencing process. An extreme instance of counsel failing to do so is evident in *R. v. Watkins*.[103] There, defence counsel negotiated a plea agreement with Crown counsel and obtained the client's informed consent to the proposal. The matter was remanded for the purpose of taking the plea. At the next scheduled court date, defence counsel failed to appear. His explanation, subsequently provided to the court, was that an associate had been engaged to act for the client but apparently failed to appear.[104] However, counsel was forced to admit that the client was never told of this arrangement. The client had clearly expected his original counsel to act on the plea.[105] Failure to inform the client of the scheduling problem and to obtain the client's agreement to be represented by replacement counsel was improper.[106] The duty to keep the client informed regarding material events pertaining to the sentencing process was violated.

---

101  In addition to the ethical rules already mentioned, CBA Code ch. II states that counsel has failed to provide competent service where the client is informed that a particular step will be taken by a certain date, but the date is allowed to pass without follow-up information or explanation (comm. 7(e)), or where the lawyer fails to answer within a reasonable time a communication that requires a reply (comm. 7(f)).

102  See, for example, *Flores v. States*, 784 S.W.2d 579 at 581 (Tex. App.-Fort Worth 1980).

103  (2000), 149 C.C.C. (3d) 279 (Ont. C.A.).

104  *Ibid.* at 282.

105  *Ibid.* at 281–82.

106  *Ibid.* at 284. Note, however, that counsel's ethical lapse was not sufficent to justify the trial judge's criminal contempt order, given the deficiencies in the contempt hearing.

# M. THE CLIENT WHO MAINTAINS INNOCENCE

The client who maintains his or her innocence yet wishes to plead guilty presents a complex and difficult problem for defence counsel. Few other "hot" topics in the field of ethics and criminal law illustrate such diverse responses from the various Anglo-American nations. In examining this issue, we will thus look at the differing approaches taken in Canada, the United States, and United Kingdom, as well as the pertinent policy arguments. Along the way, we will review some of the various scenarios that may confront counsel. Crucial to a proper resolution of any scenario is the degree of likelihood that the client's protestations are accurate and the precise manner in which he or she wishes to enter the guilty plea.

## 1) The Client Who Maintains Innocence but Later Abandons the Claim

Most defence counsel have encountered many clients who express an interest in pleading guilty, all the while maintaining innocence. The large majority of these clients are guilty but simply have trouble admitting culpability, even in a confidential setting with counsel. Perhaps, given the nature of the crime, the client cannot confess guilt without confronting a terrible personal weakness or alienating family and friends. Other clients exhibit an initial braggadocio in talking to counsel, especially early on in the case when Crown disclosure is not yet available and the professional relationship is just beginning. They may feel that counsel will work harder on the case if under the belief that the charge is totally unfounded. Still others, after months of trying, may actually convince themselves of facts that, while supporting innocence, never actually happened. Whatever the reason, the client who maintains innocence despite being guilty often changes his or her tune as the process unfolds.

For such a client, it may be permissible to participate in plea discussions with the Crown even while guilt is being denied. However, counsel should first obtain express instructions from the client. While a lawyer need not always receive instructions prior to undertaking plea discussions,[107] protestations of innocence represent a warning sign that the client may not be amenable. Accordingly, the better course is to

---

107 See section I, "Conditional or Preliminary Plea Discussions," in this chapter.

clear the discussions with the client in advance.[108] Indeed, the client's consent to counsel participating in plea discussions may be an initial step on the road towards a legitimate acknowledgment of guilt. Once the client has abandoned the claim of innocence, the finalization of a plea agreement and representation on a guilty plea is no longer problematic.

## 2)  The Client Who Maintains Innocence and Never Abandons the Claim

Rarer, but immensely more contentious, is the scenario where a client protests innocence and never abandons the claim yet desires to plead guilty. Any one of several possibilities may underlie the client's position. First, the client might be guilty but simply persist in denying culpability for some or all of the reasons just mentioned. Second, there may be a valid question as to whether the client is guilty, even though he or she admits facts from which a jury could conceivably convict. A good example is the accused who asserts self-defence or mounts a *mens rea* defence. Third, and most troubling, the client may indeed be innocent but nonetheless decide to accept responsibility for a crime that he or she did not commit.

There may be understandable practical reasons for an accused to contemplate a guilty plea even where he or she has a legitimate defence or is actually innocent. The accused may wish to protect a third party who is the real culprit, for instance, a spouse or child. Maybe the publicity, stress, and/or cost of a trial is so daunting that the accused is willing to give up a strong defence or admit guilt falsely as an avoidance measure. A guilty plea may also prove attractive to the accused who desires a fast and relatively certain conclusion to proceedings. Still other accused individuals, lacking in self-confidence, may buckle to pressure from the police, Crown, or defence counsel who mistakenly believe him or her to be guilty.

Perhaps the greatest impetus for pleading guilty, despite having a valid defence or being innocent, is the discount in sentence that usually accompanies a guilty plea. This discount can be extremely attractive where the Crown case appears strong and any possible defence

---

108 We glean support for this position from the comments of Doherty J.A. in *W.(W.)*, above note 53 at 244. On the other hand, we see no ethical bar to pursuing plea discussions where instructions to do so are obtained from the client, simply because the client is currently refusing "to admit the necessary factual and mental elements."

suffers from inherent weaknesses (witnesses may be uncooperative or unavailable, the accused may make a terrible witness or have an extensive criminal record, and so on). In relatively minor cases, an accused with a lengthy prior record may have no chance of obtaining bail, and recognize that the delay prior to trial will far exceed any discounted sentence handed out on an early plea.

As we shall see, the client who maintains innocence and adamantly refuses to admit guilt publicly in court, yet simultaneously wants to plead guilty, presents counsel with no real problem. Under current Canadian law, the court would not accept a guilty plea from this client, because the requisite admission of guilt is lacking.[109] Entering a guilty plea is simply not a viable option. The tougher predicament occurs where the client is quite willing to plead guilty and admit to blameworthy facts in court, but all the while asserts innocence in the confidential setting of the client-lawyer relationship. It is this latter scenario that presents the difficult ethical problem.

## 3) The Position in Canada

Most Canadian rules of professional conduct are not entirely comprehensible on the subject of guilty pleas by those who maintain innocence. The usual text of these rules provides that, before counsel can commence plea discussions and/or conclude a plea agreement, "the client must be prepared to admit the necessary factual and mental elements."[110] Some observers take this wording to mean that counsel cannot represent an accused on a guilty plea where the client maintains his or her innocence.[111] However, this conclusion is not necessarily compelled by the language of the rules. For one thing, the rules by their own terms often apply only to plea discussions or plea agreements. It is thus arguably open to counsel to proceed with the guilty plea of a client who maintains innocence in the absence of any such discussion or agreement.[112] Moreover, some of the rules are worded so as to require only that the accused "be prepared to admit" the necessary fac-

---

109 See the cases cited at note 116, below.

110 CBA Code ch. IX, comm. 12(b); Sask. ch. IX, comm. 12(b); Man. ch. IX, comm. 12(b); Nfld. ch. IX, comm. 12(b); Alta. ch. 10, r. 27(b); N.S. ch. 10, r. 10.8(c); Ont. r. 4.01(9)(c); and B.C. ch. 8, r. 20(a).

111 See, for example, K.(S.), above note 25 at 382, commenting on the relevant provision in the Law Society of Upper Canada's now obsolete Professional Conduct Handbook (r. 10, comm. 12).

112 This argument could be made in those jurisdictions that follow the wording of the CBA Code. However, it is not available in British Columbia or Alberta,

tual and mental elements of the offence. The phrase "be prepared to admit" could be taken to require only that an accused make a public admission during the sentencing proceeding, without necessitating that the admission be genuine. On this interpretation, counsel could knowingly allow the privately defiant accused to plead guilty, and the plea would be accepted as long as the court did not find out.[113]

But the better view of the Canadian ethical rules is that counsel is forbidden from representing the accused who maintains innocence on a guilty plea in at least one case: *where the result will be to mislead the court*. This conclusion is supported by the general prohibition against a lawyer attempting to deceive the court, and it would apply to the client known by counsel to be innocent.[114] A question remains, however, concerning the client who maintains innocence in circumstances where the lawyer does not believe the claim or is unsure. Consider, for example, the client who maintains innocence yet on counsel's careful assessment of the evidence is probably guilty. In this instance, counsel does not believe that the accused is innocent, and therefore permitting him or her to enter a guilty plea and admit to facts that establish culpability arguably does not constitute an intentional deception on the court. If anything, it is counsel who is likely being misled by the client, and the court that is receiving the true admission of guilt. The terminology used by many Canadian ethical codes encourages this response to our hypothetical example. The client need only be "prepared to admit the necessary factual and mental elements," presumably meaning that it is sufficient if he or she is ready to make the admission in court, regardless of what counsel has been told in confidence.[115] As long as counsel is not knowingly misleading the court, there is nothing unseemly about acting for the client on the guilty plea.

Yet this argument appears to find little favour in the case law. Canadian courts have consistently ruled that an accused who pleads guilty must admit facts sufficient to ground a conviction, and in particular have tended to view a guilty plea as exactly commensurate with

---

where the rules apply to guilty pleas more generally and are not confined to plea discussions and/or agreements.

113 This argument is available only on the wording used in the jurisdictions that follow the CBA Code's language. It cannot be made on the wording of the ethical codes in Alberta, British Columbia, or Nova Scotia.

114 See, for example, CBA Code ch. IX, comm. 2(b) & (e).

115 This approach is discussed in more detail in section M(7), "A Possible Solution," in this chapter.

an admission of culpability.[116] Where the accused equivocates, or refuses to admit the facts, or attempts to put forth facts that would constitute a valid defence, the plea is rejected, struck, or overturned on appeal.[117] Moreover, there is authority suggesting that the court has been misled whenever an accused pleads guilty and admits to culpable facts while simultaneously denying all responsibility for the offence to counsel.[118] On this view, a guilty plea must be heartfelt and genuine, a sincere acceptance of moral blame. The impermissible deception comes not from any inaccuracy in counsel's portrayal of the facts surrounding the offence but from helping the client to present a disingenuous expression of remorse.

Perhaps, then, a good deal of the concern over the client who maintains innocence flows from a belief that the guilty plea should constitute an *authentic* acceptance of culpability. We see strong hints of this belief in the leading case of *R. v. K.(S.)*,[119] where the accused young person was charged with numerous sexual offences. Following the close of the prosecution case, defence counsel worked out a resolution with the Crown, under which the accused would plead guilty to several minor counts in exchange for the more serious counts being dropped. The accused had always maintained his innocence, and he continued to do so in discussions with his lawyer pertaining to the plea agreement. Counsel responded by advising the accused that "criminal courts do not necessarily deal in truth, but they deal in evidence."[120] The accused pleaded guilty, and counsel admitted to an agreed statement of facts on behalf of the client.

At a meeting with a probation officer in preparation for a pre-disposition report, the accused's protestations of innocence continued and became known to the judge. The judge proceeded with the sentencing regardless, and there was no attempt by the accused to withdraw the plea. An appeal was subsequently launched. In holding that the guilty pleas should be set aside, the court observed:

---

116 See, for example, *K.(S.)*, above note 25 at 382; *Adgey*, above note 8 at 189; *Lucas*, above note 7 at 75; *Newman*, above note 18 at 400–01; *R. v. M.(G.O.)* (1989), 51 C.C.C. (3d) 171 (Sask. C.A.); *R. v. Jawbone* (1998), 126 Man. R. (2d) 295 (C.A.); *R. v. Yarlasky* (1999), 140 C.C.C. (3d) 281 at 282 (Ont. C.A.); and *R. v. Tennen* (1959), 122 C.C.C. 375 at 381–83 (Ont. C.A.).

117 See, for example, O. Fitzgerald, *The Guilty Plea and Summary Justice: A Guide for Practitioners* (Toronto: Carswell, 1990) at 34–37 & 105.

118 See *K.(S.)*, above note 25, discussed in the text immediately below.

119 Above note 25.

120 *Ibid.* at 379.

This case presents a graphic example of why it is essential to the plea bargaining process that the accused person is prepared to admit to the facts that support the conviction. The court should not be in the position of convicting and sentencing individuals, who fall short of admitting the facts to support the conviction unless that guilt is proved beyond a reasonable doubt. Nor should sentencing proceed on the false assumption of contrition. That did not happen here, but worse, the sentence became impossible to perform. Plea bargaining is an accepted and integral part of our criminal justice system but must be conducted with sensitivity to its vulnerabilities. A court that is misled, or allows itself to be misled, cannot serve the interests of justice.[121]

In other words, false contrition is in itself misleading and unacceptable. On this view, counsel probably cannot act on a guilty plea where the client, though fully prepared to admit culpability in court, denies guilt within the confidential context of the client-lawyer relationship.

## 4) The Position in the United Kingdom

We have already noted that lawyers in the United Kingdom are permitted by the applicable rules of professional conduct to proceed with a guilty plea despite the client's private assertions of innocence.[122] Before doing so, however, counsel must advise the client as to the consequences of the plea, and make clear to the client that submissions on sentencing can be made only on the basis that the client is guilty.[123] It has also been suggested that lawyers have a duty to advise the client against pleading guilty.[124] Interestingly, the ethical rules in the United Kingdom expressly forbid barristers from withdrawing on the ground that the client plans to plead guilty while maintaining his or her innocence to counsel.[125]

The position taken by the United Kingdom's ethical rules has been condoned by the courts in that country. The leading case in this regard

---

121 *Ibid.* at 382 (emphasis added).

122 See the text accompanying notes 42–44, above.

123 *Ibid.*

124 See *The Guide to the Professional Conduct of Solicitors*, above note 45 at §21.20(7), as well as U.K., H.C., Home Affairs Committee, *Report of the Royal Commission on Criminal Justice* (London: HMSO, 1993) (Chair: R.G. Runciman) at 111.

125 See *Bar Code of Conduct*, Annex "H" above note 43 at §12.5 (the *Guide to the Professional Conduct of Solicitors* does not impose the same dictate).

is *R. v. Herbert*,[126] decided by the Court of Appeal for England and Wales in 1991. Herbert was jointly charged with two others, including his wife, of narcotics offences. After the trial had started, counsel for Mrs. Herbert worked out a conditional plea agreement with the Crown. Under the agreement, the Crown would drop the charges against Mrs. Herbert in exchange for a guilty plea by her husband. This proposal was communicated to Herbert, who agreed to change his plea, though continuing to maintain his innocence to counsel. Herbert's lawyer followed the applicable rule of professional conduct to the letter, advising Herbert that if he was truly not guilty, the best course was to continue contesting the case. Counsel also told Herbert that a jail term was likely on a plea of guilty. Herbert nevertheless changed his plea. The Crown offered no further evidence against the wife, and the judge sentenced Herbert to five and a half years' imprisonment. In dismissing Herbert's conviction appeal, the Court of Appeal referred to paragraph 12.5 of the bar's Code of Conduct[127] and held that defence counsel had behaved properly. In the Court's opinion, Herbert had received complete and conscientious advice and had exercised his own free will in entering the plea.[128]

The ethical rules and legal precedent in the United Kingdom have embraced a position that expressly permits counsel to act on a guilty plea in spite of the client's assertions of innocence outside the courtroom.[129] But does the United Kingdom approach go further and permit lawyers to present and rely upon facts surrounding the offence that are known to be false? This extreme position, epitomized by the guilty plea of a true innocent, requires a lawyer to lie to the court as a means of protecting the plea. Certainly, counsel in the United Kingdom are subject to a general prohibition against misleading the court.[130] Moreover, the judiciary in the United Kingdom may not be entirely comfortable

---

126  Above note 77. To similar effect, see *Beaney*, above note 92, where the court seems to accept the validity of the ethical rule (although the appellants' guilty pleas were overturned).

127  *Herbert*, above note 77 at 232 (mistakenly cited as paragraph "2.5"). For the full text of paragraph 12.5, see note 44, *ibid.*

128  *Ibid.* at 233–34.

129  The *Herbert* approach has, however, drawn criticism: see, for example, McConville, above note 38 at 566–72. Contrast the view taken in the *Report of the Royal Commission on Criminal Justice*, above note 124 at 110–11, which takes solace from the assumption that the true innocent will only rarely plead guilty, the more common situation being the guilty client who falsely protests innocence.

130  See, for example, *Bar Code of Conduct*, above note 93 at §202 & Annex "H," §13.3. It has been argued, however, that paragraph 12.5 actually operates as an

with applying the *Herbert* approach to the case of the true innocent. On the facts recited by the court in *Herbert* itself (and despite the somewhat optimistic advice given by counsel regarding the merits of the case), the prosecution evidence seemed strong and the accused's exculpatory explanations largely unconvincing.[131] It is highly probable that the appeal court had no real doubt that Herbert was truly guilty. It is one thing to condone counsel acting on a guilty plea where the accused faces a strong Crown case and protestations of innocence are likely disingenuous. It is quite another to permit counsel to act where a true innocent is insistent on pleading guilty and the lawyer is being asked to advance facts that he or she knows to be false. This latter situation was not squarely faced by the court in *Herbert*. In short, the United Kingdom position is not necessarily so extreme as some might think.[132]

## 5) The Position in the United States

In the United States, the leading case regarding the client who wishes to plead guilty but maintains innocence is *North Carolina v. Alford*.[133] The defendant was charged with first-degree murder arising out of a shooting death and faced the possibility of execution if convicted after a trial. Under the law as it then stood, however, the maximum penalty was life imprisonment if the accused pleaded guilty. The prosecution case was strong, and the defendant pleaded guilty to second-degree murder, with the prosecutor's consent. The prosecutor called several witnesses on the plea hearing, all of whom provided evidence in support of Alford's guilt. Yet, when given an opportunity to speak before the court, Alford protested his innocence, stating that the plea was

---

exception to the general prohibition against misleading the court: see McConville, above note 38 at 566–72.

131 *Herbert*, above note 77 at 231–32.

132 This interpretation of paragraph 12.5 and *Herbert* does not elide all criticism of counsel who acts on a guilty plea where the client maintains innocence. Objections can still be made on the ground that the guilty plea is being falsely presented as an act of contrition: see M. McConville & L. Bridges, "Pleading Guilty Whilst Maintaining Innocence" (1993) 143 New L J. 160 at 161, as well as the discussion of *K.(S.)* in section M(3), "The Position in Canada," in this chapter.

133 400 U.S. 25 (1970) [*Alford*]. For more recent cases discussing the *Alford* plea, see *United States v. Tunning*, 69 F.3d 107 (6th Cir. 1995) [*Tunning*]; and *United States v. Fuentes-Mendoza*, 56 F.3d 1113 (9th Cir. 1995). It is unclear exactly how often *Alford* pleas are entered: see W. Pizzi, "Accepting Guilty Pleas from 'Innocent' Defendants?" (1996) 146 New L.J. 997 at 998.

entered only in an effort to ensure that he did not receive the death penalty.

On appeal, the Supreme Court held that the plea was valid, given that it represented a voluntary and intelligent choice among the alternative courses of action open to the defendant.[134] The Court went on to observe:

> Here the State had a strong case of first-degree murder against Alford. Whether he realized or disbelieved his guilt, he insisted on his plea because in his view he had absolutely nothing to gain by a trial and much to gain by pleading. Because of the overwhelming evidence against him, a trial was precisely what neither Alford nor his attorney desired. Confronted with the choice between a trial for first-degree murder, on the one hand, and a plea of guilty to second-degree murder, on the other, Alford quite reasonably chose the latter and thereby limited the maximum penalty to a 30-year term. When his plea is viewed in light of the evidence against him, which substantially negated his claim of innocence and which further provided a means by which the judge could test whether the plea was intelligently entered, see *McCarthy* v. *United States, supra*, at 466–467 (1969), its validity cannot seriously be questioned. In view of the strong factual basis for the plea demonstrated by the State and Alford's clearly expressed desire to enter it despite his professed belief in his innocence, we hold that the trial judge did not commit constitutional error in accepting it.

There are several points to be gleaned from *Alford*. Foremost is the Court's holding that a trial judge can enter a conviction after a guilty plea, despite an accused's open refusal to admit guilt, provided that there exists a strong factual basis in support of a conviction. The Court emphasized that the requirement of "strong factual basis" serves to protect the innocent and ensure that guilty pleas are a product of a free and intelligent choice.[135] Yet the Court did not hold that an accused has a constitutional right to plead guilty while protesting innocence. To the contrary, it ruled that the federal government and any of the states can quite properly, by statute or otherwise, prohibit a conviction absent an admission of guilt by the accused.[136] In other words, a defen-

---

134  See *Alford*, above note 133 at 31.

135  *Ibid.* at 38 (note 10).

136  *Ibid.* at 38 (note 11). For state rulings that forbid *Alford* pleas see, for example, *People ex rel. Daley* v. *Suria*, 490 N.E.2d 1288 (Ill. 1986); *Patton* v. *State*, 517 N.E.2d 374 (Ind. 1987); and *State* v. *Clanton*, 612 P.2d 662 (Kan. Ct. App. 1980).

dant does not have an affirmative right to have a plea accepted in the face of a refusal to admit culpability. Finally, the Court in *Alford* certainly did not countenance counsel representing an accused who wishes to base a guilty plea upon facts known to be untrue. There is thus a good argument that the ambit of an *Alford* guilty plea does not extend to permit a knowing deception of the court through the presentation of inaccurate facts.[137]

In the United States, use is also made of the *nolo contendere* plea.[138] This plea, which is not available in Canada, allows the court to enter a conviction based upon the accused's assertion that he or she is not contesting the prosecution's case. *Nolo contendere* is thus an implied admission of guilt for the limited purpose of the particular proceeding at hand. It is often available only where the prosecutor consents, and in some states is restricted to certain offences or entirely prohibited.[139] The United States Supreme Court observed in *Alford* that implicit in the *nolo contendere* cases is a recognition that the constitution does not bar imposition of a prison sentence upon an accused who is unwilling to admit his guilt but who, faced with "grim alternatives," is willing to waive his trial and accept sentence.[140] The Court noted the similarities between the *nolo contendere* plea and the method of plea used in Alford's case, and reasoned that, given the acceptability of a conviction where the client does not admit guilt, and merely chooses not to contest the Crown case, the same should follow for a protestation of innocence.[141]

## 6)  Policy Arguments: The True Innocent

Having stirred up the pot by canvassing various approaches to the problem of the accused who protests innocence yet wishes to plead guilty, we will now focus more directly on the relevant policy argu-

---

137  See C.W. Wolfram, *Modern Legal Ethics* (St. Paul: West, 1986) at 591.

138  See Wright, above note 26; Federal Rules of Criminal Procedure, Rule 11(b); La Fave, Israel & King, above note 26 at §21.4(a); and Fitzgerald, above note 117 at 38–41 & 106–07.

139  For a catalogue of the restrictions in federal courts and the various states, see Wright, above note 26; Federal Rules of Criminal Procedure, Rule 11(b); and La Fave, Israel & King, above note 26 at §21.4(a).

140  *Alford*, above note 133 at 36.

141  *Ibid.* at 37. Remember, however, that the *Alford* and *nolo contendere* pleas are not interchangeable: see *Tunning*, above note 133 at 110–11. As a last point, note that there is yet another method of entering an equivocal plea in the United States, the so-called conditional plea, discussed briefly at note 167, below.

ments. In doing so, we will start by considering only the case of the accused who is, to counsel's knowledge, innocent; viz., the case of the true innocent. Is it ethical for counsel to participate in a guilty plea proceeding where the accused is a true innocent, assuming that the decision to plead is freely made and counsel has otherwise performed in a competent manner?

While the bulk of opinion in Canada is against permitting the true innocent to enter a guilty plea, there are arguments for the opposite view. The most aggressive approach would allow a lawyer to represent an accused on a guilty plea, all the while knowing that the accused is falsely confirming the accuracy of facts that are untrue. Counsel's obligation to carry out the client's instructions within the context of an adversarial process can be held up to support such participation in a guilty plea by the innocent accused. Counsel may be playing a supporting role in misleading the court, but this action ostensibly is justified in furtherance of the accused's constitutional right to choose freely whether or not to plead guilty. It could also be contended that counsel will have done his or her best to convince the accused not to plead guilty, and hence cannot be viewed as encouraging a misleading plea. Along similar lines, some lawyers may feel justified in taking part in the plea proceedings as long as the client, and not counsel, admits to the false facts, whereupon counsel will make no submissions that rely directly upon the inaccuracies.[142]

The approach just described bears a strong resemblance to Monroe Freedman's "damn the torpedoes" solution to the problem of a client who wishes to commit perjury.[143] It is perhaps less objectionable, because the result is to convict an accused who knowingly chooses such an outcome, as opposed to helping a guilty accused to mislead the court in order to escape a conviction. A less controversial approach, however, is to push for changes in the law that would recognize the legitimacy of the *nolo contendere* or *Alford* plea, in effect restructuring the basic rules of the plea proceeding so that the accused is not mis-

---

142 Presumably, counsel would not be permitted to submit that the accused had demonstrated remorse by virtue of the plea.

143 See section D, "Monroe Freedman and the Lawyer's Trilemma," and section F(4)(d), "Eliciting Testimony in the Normal Manner," in chapter 7. Yet on the specific question of a guilty plea by a true innocent, where the *prosecutor* holds a reasonable doubt as to the accused's culpability, Professor Freedman disparages the *Alford* option, arguing that the prosecutor should not proceed with the charge: see *Understanding Lawyers' Ethics* (New York: Matthew Bender, 1990) at 220–21.

leading the court.[144] In essence, this approach attempts to meet the "truth-based" arguments against permitting an innocent accused to plead guilty by expanding the notion of what a guilty plea encompasses, to include cases where the accused does not expressly admit moral culpability. On this view, the accused would not be misleading the court and the search for truth would less arguably be undermined.

If one could be absolutely sure that an innocent accused can never be convicted, these policy arguments would lose most of their steam. But the system cannot guarantee that miscarriages of justice do not occur. We must therefore concede that the "true innocent" may come out ahead by virtue of a guilty plea, despite being convicted of an offence that he or she did not commit. It has also been convincingly noted that forbidding a guilty plea by a true innocent will merely encourage clients to lie to counsel as the only means of securing the system's permission to plead guilty.[145]

Nevertheless, there are strong arguments for prohibiting counsel from representing an innocent client on a guilty plea. First, a central purpose of the criminal justice system is to identify and denounce the offender. Permitting the true innocent to plead guilty subverts this purpose, makes a mockery of the associated objectives of rehabilitation, deterrence and punishment, and undermines public confidence in the system. Second, a fundamental goal of the system is to ascertain the truth. This truth-seeking process is damaged whenever a court is persuaded to accept a guilty plea based upon facts that are inaccurate. Simply put, a fraud has been committed on the court. Third, although the accused has a right to decide how to conduct his or her defence, including complete freedom of choice regarding the plea to be entered, this right does not extend to permit the accused to mislead the court intentionally.[146] Fourth, our criminal justice system has expended a

---

144 See, for example, R. Shadley & D. Druckman, "The Client Who Maintains Innocence" [1998] National Criminal Law Program, Federation of Law Societies of Canada; F. Forsyth, "A Plea for Nolo Contendere in the Canadian Criminal Justice System" (1998) 40 Crim. L.Q. 243; and "Panel Discussion: Witness for the Prosecution: Successful Impeachment Strategies" (Criminal Lawyers' Association Convention and Education Programme, Toronto, 21-22 November 1997), QL (OCLA RP/1997-019) at paras. 386–87 (S. Cohen).

145 C. Shipley, "The *Alford* Plea: A Necessary But Unpredictable Tool for the Criminal Defendant" (1987) 72 Iowa L. Rev. 1063 at 1073, 1086 & 1089.

146 Even *Swain*, above note 11, the case that constitutionalizes the accused's right to control the conduct of the defence, allows that reasonable limits may be imposed under s. 1 of the *Canadian Charter of Rights and Freedoms*, Part I of the *Constitution Act, 1982*, being Schedule B to the *Canada Act 1982* (U.K.), 1982, c. 11: *ibid.* at 512–18.

great deal of energy, and suffered considerable anxiety, over the prospect of the wrongfully convicted, as attested to by the cases involving Donald Marshall, Guy Paul Morin, David Milgaard, and Thomas Sophonow. Mislabelling an individual as guilty, when he or she is truly innocent, runs counter to the basic principles that drive the system and can be viewed as a miscarriage of justice that rewards hypocrisy and fosters cynicism. Fifth, there are other situations where the law limits the accused's freedom of choice to waive important constitutional protections, for instance, the right to a jury trial and to be represented by counsel who is not labouring under a serious conflict of interest.[147] It is also a criminal offence to commit perjury, even though an accused has a constitutional right to testify.[148] The accused does not have an absolute right to eschew the protections of a trial, nor does he or she have untrammelled license to subvert the truth-finding function of the process. Rather, there are important societal interests that justify limiting the accused's freedoms.

## 7) A Possible Solution

We endorse a practical, and hence admittedly contentious, resolution to the problem of the accused who maintains innocence yet wishes to plead guilty. For the reasons just given, we reject the argument that counsel can participate in a guilty plea involving a "true innocent." To do so misleads the court and stretches the truth-finding function of the criminal justice system beyond the breaking point. But we take a different view where the accused maintains innocence in the face of a strong Crown case and where nothing about the plea involves counsel knowingly misleading the court. The accused may carefully and realistically ponder the pros and the cons of a trial, and in the end voluntarily and unequivocally decide to plead guilty. The risk of an unsuccessful trial falls on the client, not counsel, and the client should therefore be permitted some latitude to enter a guilty plea.

To elaborate, counsel should be permitted to act on a guilty plea, regardless of the client's protestations of innocence, provided that the following preconditions are met:

---

147   See, for example, *R. v. Turpin* (1989), 48 C.C.C. (3d) 8 (S.C.C.) (holding that an accused does not have a constitutional right to waive a jury trial); and *R. v. Robillard* (1986), 28 C.C.C. (3d) 22 (Ont. C.A.) (holding that an accused does not have a constitutional right to waive a serious conflict of interest).
148   See section F(4)(b), "Refusal to Call the Client as a Witness," in chapter 7.

1. Complete advice must be provided based upon a thorough review of the Crown disclosure and any other appropriate preparation or investigation.
2. The accused need be prepared to admit in court the facts sufficient to ground a conviction, for the purposes of the plea proceeding. This requirement may be met even though the accused refuses to concede to counsel in private that the facts are true.
3. Counsel must be satisfied that there is a strong factual basis for the guilty plea, meaning that a reasonable jury would likely convict on the evidence in the possession of the Crown.[149]
4. The client's instructions must be informed, voluntary, and unequivocal. Given that counsel is entering an ethical grey area, the instructions should be detailed and in writing.[150]
5. Counsel should otherwise be satisfied that the court is not being misled by virtue of the admissions to be made in court by the client. It may be improper for counsel to contend that the client's plea demonstrates remorse.[151]
6. Counsel is not required to represent a client on a guilty plea where the client protests innocence privately but is prepared to admit the facts in court. Rather, the defence lawyer should have a discretion in this regard. The lawyer who decides not to act on the guilty plea may be discharged by the client or withdraw from the case.[152]

This response gives credence to the many legitimate considerations that can compel a client to choose to plead guilty and respects the client's autonomy and freedom of choice in deciding how to plead. On the other hand, it does not go so far as to embrace the extreme case where a true innocent is subject to conviction or the court is otherwise being misled.[153]

---

149 The "strong factual basis" standard is obviously associated with the *Alford* guilty plea, but its exact meaning is the subject of debate in the United States. We do not wish to import that debate into our proffered guidelines, and believe that too low a standard militates against an ethical rule that permits counsel to represent the client who maintains innocence.
150 See also section Q, "Written Instructions," in this chapter.
151 Do not forget that other credits are associated with a guilty plea, including cost and time savings for the system and avoiding the inconvenience and trauma that testifying may cause a witness.
152 See section T, "Conflict of Interest," in this chapter, regarding withdrawal.
153 This overall approach is consistent with that ultimately suggested by Shadley & Druckman, above note 144 at 10. See also the comments made by the defence

We realize that our preferred approach comes perilously close to an endorsement of an *Alford* guilty plea, at least where counsel is confident that the accused is not a "true innocent." Moreover, we accept that Canadian law does not at present, and perhaps never will, accept the legitimacy of the *Alford* plea. Where an accused pleads guilty, while at the same time asserting innocence on the record, most Canadian judges will have no hesitation in striking the plea. The reasoning seen in *R. v. K.(S.)*, set out above, almost certainly mandates this result,[154] even where the accused simultaneously seeks to "admit the facts" for the purpose of the plea proceeding. If the accused is thereby prevented from pleading guilty, so be it. But the possibility that the guilty plea will not be accepted by the court does not necessarily mean that counsel's actions in participating in the plea are unethical.[155] We therefore draw a distinction between what the court may do (that is, reject the plea) and what counsel may do (that is, participate in the plea where the client is prepared to admit the facts in court but maintains innocence). To put the matter another way, we are suggesting something akin to the *Alford* approach but more within the context of the client-lawyer relationship.[156]

Our approach can more easily be appreciated by looking at the facts in *R. v. Hector*,[157] a recent decision of the Ontario Court of Appeal. There, the appellant was charged with three counts of first degree murder, as well as related offences. He accepted a plea agreement under which the Crown promised not to seek a dangerous-offender designation, dropped obstruction of justice charges against his wife, and allowed a one-hour visit with his wife following the plea. Hector appealed the convictions, however, on the ground that he had protested his innocence to counsel, and counsel should have refused to go ahead with the guilty plea (or at the least tried to convince the appellant to change his mind).

---

lawyer and Crown counsel in *Newman*, above note 17 at 399–400, set out more fully below in section N, "Agreed Statements of Fact," in this chapter.

154 See the quotation accompanying note 121, above.

155 The contrary view is taken in the *Martin Committee Report*, above note 4 at 295: "[I]t is also improper, in the Committee's view, for counsel to facilitate a guilty plea to proceed where an accused maintains his or her innocence, by withholding from the Court the fact that an accused person does not acknowledge guilt."

156 In some respects, our approach bears greater similarity to that taken in *Herbert*, above note 77, for United Kingdom law does not recognize a guilty plea made in the face of protestations of innocence. The client's refusal to admit culpability can occur only within the client-lawyer relationship and not in open court: see McConville, above note 38 at 568.

157 (2000), 146 C.C.C. (3d) 81 (Ont. C.A.) [*Hector*].

Fresh evidence on appeal revealed that Hector, an experienced criminal, initially did not comment to counsel on his guilt or innocence. He eventually asserted innocence after several meetings with his lawyer. Even so, the Crown disclosure revealed an extremely strong case against Hector, including adverse testimony by his brother, his possession of the murder weapon, and an alibi already proven to be false. Counsel asked Hector to provide an explanation for these compelling features of the Crown case, but Hector declined to do so. He also refused to permit the lawyer to retain a private investigator to investigate possible defences. Hector eventually signed written instructions to plead guilty, which included an agreed statement of facts, and did not raise any objections to the accuracy of these facts. Counsel provided complete and clear advice as to the consequences of a guilty plea, and emphasized that Hector must admit to the agreed statement of facts in court. Hector understood but appears never to have expressly told counsel that the statement of facts was true. Moreover, during the sentencing itself, while the agreed facts were being recited in court, Hector told counsel that he did not commit the crime and wanted to plead guilty without admitting to the facts. Counsel responded by stating that it was not possible to plead guilty while refusing to admit the facts in court, and that he had to choose between admitting guilt in public or having a contested trial. Hector told counsel to let the plea stand and the proceedings continue, and a conviction was eventually recorded.

The Court of Appeal in *Hector* conceded that defence counsel should be "concerned if his or her client does not expressly admit guilt before assisting in a plea arrangement."[158] However, Finlayson J.A. concluded that

> . . . the appellant in this instance was simply pushing his luck at the last minute. Even without the express instruction from his counsel that, by his pleas of guilty, he was agreeing that he shot and killed three persons, he could not possibly have thought that the court would permit him to plead guilty to murder and at the same time maintain that he did not commit the crimes. In any event he was told in unequivocal terms that "if you say you didn't kill them then we stop the plea proceedings right now and we have a trial." There can be no suggestion, in the context of the entire plea process, that this exchange tainted the appellant's plea.[159]

---

158 *Ibid.* at 85.
159 *Ibid.* at 88.

Mr. Justice Finlayson did not in any way criticize defence counsel for proceeding to a plea hearing even though the client had never expressly admitted guilt within the client-lawyer relationship. Nor did he admonish counsel for continuing with the plea after the client maintained his innocence to counsel during the sentencing itself. Finally, he did not disparage counsel in any way for the professed practice of routinely pleading clients guilty even though they maintained innocence in private.[160]

What if the trial judge in *Hector* had launched a plea inquiry, as a judge has every right to do? Suppose that, in response to this inquiry, Hector stated that he was only pleading guilty because a conviction after trial was probable, and this way he could at least receive some credit from the Crown for avoiding a futile trial. After further questioning by the court, also assume that Hector professed his innocence but at the same time was fully prepared to admit the facts worked out as part of the plea agreement, on the basis that the Crown could prove these facts beyond a reasonable doubt. In this hypothetical instance, Canadian case law suggests that the plea would be struck.[161] Yet we believe that counsel is not ethically precluded from participating in a guilty plea on the fictional scenario just recounted. Indeed, counsel in *Hector* appears to have taken this approach (though obviously without the knowledge of the trial judge) and did not attract the Court of Appeal's censure for doing so.

**Example I:** The client is charged with assault and admits to counsel that he grabbed the complainant by the arm and shouted at her loudly. After determining that the admitted facts do not present the possibility of any defence, counsel explains that such actions constitute an assault in law. The client cannot accept this conclusion and steadfastly maintains his innocence. In his view, an "assault" requires substantial injury, and thus he has committed no crime. Given these circumstances, counsel must take considerable care in advising the client, participating in plea discussions, taking instructions, concluding a plea agreement, and appearing on a guilty plea. However, at the end of the

---

160 Trial counsel asserted: "It is not unusual in my experience for a seasoned criminal charged with a serious offence, to profess their [sic] innocence even when the evidence indicates otherwise and they enter pleas of guilty. In my experience this has happened in every murder case I have handled. It's not uncommon for an accused to still profess their [sic] innocence even after they've had a trial by jury and been convicted": see *Hector, ibid.* at 86.

161 Compare, however, the approach taken by counsel in *Newman*, above note 18 at 399–400, apparently without any disapproval by the sentencing court.

day the client's protestations of innocence should not prevent counsel from acting on a plea of guilty.[162]

**Example II:** X is charged with murder arising out of a shooting, and his counsel works out an agreement whereby he will plead guilty to manslaughter in return for a ten- year sentence. Identity is not in issue, but X tells counsel that he firmly believed the victim had a gun and felt that "it was either him or me." No gun was ever found, and the deceased had no known propensity for violence. Counsel advises X that he may have a good chance at raising a reasonable doubt on self-defence grounds, and advises against pleading guilty. However, X is experienced in the ways of the justice system and has a lengthy criminal record. He is convinced that he will make a bad witness and will not be believed by the jury. Ultimately, he is adamant that he would rather receive a certain and limited sentence than risk a life sentence with limited parole eligibility after an unsuccessful trial. In our view, counsel can permit X to plead guilty as long as he is prepared to admit to facts upon which a trier of fact could legitimately base a conviction.[163]

**Strong Recommendation:** These difficult cases always require that counsel obtain detailed and clear instructions from the client. The client's protestations of innocence should alert counsel that an appeal, complaint to the professional governing body or civil suit may be launched down the road. Not to protect oneself in such circumstances is foolhardy.[164]

## 8) A Possible Alternative: An Attenuated "Fegan" Trial

In *R. v. Fegan*,[165] the Ontario Court of Appeal ruled that a guilty plea ordinarily forecloses the subsequent appeal of an adverse pre-trial ruling. However, the court offered the view that, at least on the facts at hand,[166] there may have been a way to preserve appeal rights without contesting the Crown's case. Specifically, a statement of facts could be

---

162 The case of *Conflitti*, above note 87, provides the basis for this hypothetical.

163 This example is a slight variation on that provided by Shadley & Druckman, above note 144 at 1.

164 Also see the discussion in section Q, "Written Instructions," in this chapter.

165 Above note 14.

166 The Court of Appeal noted that "what might be said against this practice is that not every case is suited to the vehicle of an agreed statement of facts": *ibid.* at 361.

offered by the Crown and its admissibility not be contested by the defence. The Crown could then close its case, and the accused offer no defence and make no submissions on the issue of guilt. The trial judge would convict the accused, provided that the statement of facts supported such a result. In *Fegan*, the court implied that even absent a guilty plea, this procedure would provide "powerful circumstances in mitigation of sentence."[167] It has been argued that this approach answers the policy concerns associated with the client who maintains innocence yet refuses to dispute guilt, for if "[the] trial turns out to be speedier than most because the defendant does not contest the government's case, the cause of efficiency will be served at the same time as public confidence is enhanced."[168]

## 9)  Disclosure to the Court

We have elsewhere dealt with the issue of counsel revealing falsehoods to the court, specifically in the contexts of possible confidentiality exceptions and the perjurious client.[169] The relevant considerations and issues need not be repeated. Suffice it to say that, given our conclusion regarding the impropriety of permitting the true innocent to plea guilty, and the ethical rules prohibiting any action that misleads the court, in extremely rare instances counsel may be under a duty to make disclosure of a completed falsehood against the wishes of the client.[170]

---

167  *Ibid.* at 360. In the United States, in addition to the *Alford* and *nolo contendere* pleas, there is a further equivocal plea option available to an accused in some jurisdictions, called a conditional plea. The conditional plea is similar to the option suggested in *Fegan*, but without the artifice: see La Fave, Israel, & King, above note 26 at §21.6(b)).

168  See A. Goldstein, "Converging Criminal Justice Systems: Guilty Pleas and the Public Interest" (1997) 31 Isr. L. Rev. 159 at 177.

169  See section K, "Duty Not to Mislead the Court," in chapter 5; and sections F(4)(f), "Disclosure of the Intended Party," and G(3)(b), "Disclosure," in chapter 7.

170  This position is taken by W. Burger, "Standards of Conduct for Prosecution and Defense Personnel: A Judge's Viewpoint" (1966) 5 Am. Crim. L. Rev. 11 at 15; and *Martin Committee Report*, above note 4 at 295. Burger appears to go further, however, advocating a duty to disclose for all clients who maintain innocence and not just the "true innocent." We do not share this expansive view.

# N. AGREED STATEMENTS OF FACT

Somewhat related to, yet distinct from, the client who maintains innocence is the client who is fully willing to plead guilty and admit culpability yet insists on denying certain aggravating facts alleged by the Crown. The usual situation is not that the client wishes to admit to facts that are inaccurate, but that he or she denies facts that the Crown may well be in a position to prove. This common scenario leads one to ask, can counsel act ethically in negotiating a plea agreement that accommodates the client's concerns? Moreover, can counsel proceed with the plea even where the client persists in the denials and the Crown refuses to soften its position?

In Alberta, the rules of professional responsibility expressly state that "a plea agreement may not involve a misrepresentation or misstatement of facts to the court."[171] As we have seen, most other governing bodies simply provide that the client must be prepared to admit the necessary factual and mental elements of the offence, and do not deal with the possibility that the facts might be inaccurate or misleading.[172] However, the Alberta approach appears merely to particularize a prohibition accepted in a more general way by all Canadian governing bodies: counsel is forbidden from participating knowingly in deceiving or otherwise misleading the court, no matter the context.[173] Let us examine this proposition as it relates to agreed statements of fact in the context of two cases, one from the United Kingdom and one from Canada.

In *R. v. Beswick*,[174] decided in 1995 by the Court of Appeal for England and Wales, the accused was charged with unlawfully causing grievous bodily harm. Crown witnesses were prepared to state that he had instigated and participated in a vicious assault against the complainant in a fish and chips shop, at one point kneeing the complainant in the nose and completely biting off part of his ear. Defence counsel and the prosecutor worked out a plea agreement to a reduced charge, including an agreed statement of facts. The statement of facts provided that Beswick was not an aggressor and had bitten the complainant's ear only in an excessive attempt to extract himself from the fight. The plea agreement unravelled on sentencing, partly as the result of the judge's

---

171 Alta. ch. 10, comm. 27.
172 See the rules cited at note 110, above.
173 See note 114, above, and the accompanying text.
174 (1995), [1996] 1 Cr. App. R. 427 (C.A.).

plea inquiries. Witnesses were consequently called on behalf of the Crown, and they testified to aggravating facts inconsistent with the statement of facts previously offered to the court. Beswick was given a stiff sentence, and he appealed.

Beswick's appeal counsel attacked the failure of the prosecutor to stand by the facts outlined in the original plea agreement. In dismissing this complaint, the court was extremely unimpressed with the agreed statement of facts that had initially grounded the plea, and commented:

> It is axiomatic that whenever a court has to sentence an offender it should seek to do so on a basis which so far as is relevant to the determination of the correct sentence is true. It follows from this that the prosecution should not lend itself to any agreement whereby a case is presented to the sentencing judge to be dealt with so far as that basis is concerned on an unreal and untrue set of facts concerning the offence to which a plea of guilty is to be tendered.[175]

While these observations are directly primarily at the conduct of the Crown, the court's general sentiments suggest a comparable disapproval where defence counsel knowingly presents false facts to the court. Naturally, defence counsel must *know* that the facts are false before this prohibition can apply.[176] As well, the standard of knowledge cannot be set too low, given that a defence lawyer is not responsible for upholding the public interest in the manner of a prosecutor.[177] We also see nothing wrong with defence counsel convincing the Crown to exclude contentious aggravating facts, as long as the wording of the agreed statement is carefully crafted.[178] Nonetheless, there are ethical limits to the form and content of the agreed statement of facts that counsel negotiates and places before the court.

---

175  *Ibid.* at 430. To similar effect, see the *Martin Committee Report*, above note 4 at 325.

176  See section F, "Acquiring Knowledge that the Client is Guilty," in chapter 1, and section F(1), "Acquiring Knowledge that the Client Intends to Commit Perjury," in chapter 7. There is no indication that defence counsel in *Beswick* agreed to facts that he knew to be false. More likely is that the client insisted that he had not played the role attributed him, despite the strong Crown case to the contrary. Defence counsel will usually be entitled to put forth an agreed statement of facts based on the client's assertions.

177  See section B(1), "Role as Minister of Justice," in chapter 12.

178  For instance, the wording of the statement, as well as counsel's submissions, may speak of facts that the Crown is in a position to prove and that the parties have agreed will form the basis of the sentencing. See also the *Martin Committee Report*, above note 4 at 323–27.

Let us turn to the case where counsel is unable to convince the Crown to tone down the statement of facts to something more agreeable to the client. This scenario is illustrated in *R. v. Newman*,[179] a 1993 decision of the Ontario Court of Appeal. There, counsel represented a client on serious drug charges. After plea discussions with the Crown, a tentative plea agreement was reached. The Crown provided a statement of facts that he proposed would form the factual basis of the plea in court. While prepared to admit facts sufficient to found a conviction, the accused balked at several aggravating aspects of the Crown's proposed facts. The disputed facts were based on the anticipated testimony of a police agent. Defence counsel's efforts to amend the agreed statement were in vain, but he ultimately concluded that the plea agreement was a good one for the accused, and went ahead with the sentencing. He apparently did not tell the client what the consequences of going ahead might be, nor did he make any attempt to contest the facts by way of a *Gardiner* hearing.[180]

At the sentencing hearing, the agreed statement of facts was presented to the court, signed by counsel on behalf of his client "subject to comment."[181] Defence counsel's subsequent submissions to the court took issue with some of the facts. The Crown interjected and stated that the agreed statement contained facts that both sides admitted could be proven beyond a reasonable doubt under the test articulated in *R. v. Gardiner*. Defence counsel agreed with this submission, and also accepted that the facts could be used by the court as the basis for a sentence, apart from whether the accused would admit or swear to the facts.[182] The court accordingly sentenced the accused based on these facts, and an appeal was launched alleging denial of the right to the effective assistance of counsel.

The Court in *Newman* dismissed the appeal, holding that defence counsel was competent and provided sound judgment as to the overall benefits of pleading guilty in the circumstances. Regarding counsel's acceptance of the agreed statement of facts, the court observed that

> there is no evidence on this record or in the proffered fresh evidence
> to indicate that the appellant was not fully aware of the contents of

---

179 Above note 18.

180 So named for the case of *Gardiner*, above note 6 where the Supreme Court of Canada held that aggravating facts, if disputed on sentencing, must be proved by the Crown based on evidence and on a standard of proof beyond a reasonable doubt.

181 *Newman*, above 18 at 399.

182 *Ibid.* at 399–400.

the agreed statement of facts and the fact that his counsel had been unsuccessful in modifying it.

As to the fresh evidence, it does not meet the criteria in R. v. *Stolar* (1988), 40 C.C.C. (3d) 1, [1988] S.C.R. 480, 62 C.R. (3d) 313 (S.C.C.). It is not relevant to the issue of reduction of sentence and it is totally inadequate as to the threshold issue of setting aside the plea of guilty. I agree with counsel for the Crown that if the appellant was putting forward what amounts to a plea of non est factum, it was incumbent upon him to swear in an affidavit that the matters set out in para. 5 of his trial counsel's affidavit [that is, the disputed aggravating facts] were not true and that he was prepared to testify to that effect with respect to all or at least some of them. I would go further and state that he would have to swear that he would not have pleaded guilty to such a statement of facts had it been available to him prior to his plea. I think that the appellant was simply trying to improve on his situation when he told his counsel that he would not agree to the facts enumerated in his defence counsel's affidavit. In my opinion he is still trying to do just that by taking issue with the agreed statement of facts after sentencing.[183]

The court thus did not find a denial of the right to the effective assistance of counsel, and it did not question counsel's approach to the plea. However, we are not so sanguine regarding counsel's actions. If a client steadfastly disputes facts that are insisted upon by the Crown as part of a proposed plea agreement, there are two options.[184] First, the client can reject the plea agreement, and go to trial if necessary. Second, the client can require that the Crown prove the contested facts on a *Gardiner* hearing, whether or not as part of a plea agreement. Counsel in *Newman* may not have caused the appellant any prejudice, but neither was he entirely forthcoming with the client. Indeed, counsel left the client with the incorrect perception that the aggravating facts would not be conceded during the plea. The ethical propriety of such a course of conduct is definitely open to question.

---

183  *Ibid.* at 404.

184  Where the client disputes the facts in private, but is prepared to admit them in court for the purposes of the plea, we believe that counsel should be guided by the considerations set out in section M(7), "A Possible Solution," in this chapter.

# O. THE "UNCERTAIN OR UNLIKELY" PROSPECT OF ACQUITTAL

The CBA and the majority of Canadian professional governing bodies permit a defence lawyer to commence plea discussions or enter into a plea agreement only where he or she "*bona fide* concludes and advises the accused client that an acquittal of the offence charged is uncertain or unlikely."[185] What restrictions, if any, does this provision impose? In one sense, acquittal is never absolutely certain. For the lawyer who takes this view, the provision does not really serve to limit the circumstances in which he or she can conduct plea discussions or finalize a plea agreement. Yet there may be instances where some lawyers will in good faith conclude that acquittal on the merits is indeed certain. Suppose that a witness crucial to the Crown case has died or disappeared, or evidence necessary to support a conviction was indisputably obtained by means of a *Charter* breach that mandates exclusion under section 24(2). In either case, can counsel negotiate a plea agreement?

We can begin by stating an obvious point: counsel who believes that an acquittal is certain should ordinarily attempt to convince the Crown to withdraw or stay the charge. It seems equally obvious that, barring unequivocal instructions to the contrary, a lawyer who reasonably entertains this belief should not participate in discussions with the Crown that are directed towards entering a guilty plea. To do so is not in the client's best interests and is at odds with the duties of loyalty and competence. In may be, however, that despite receiving complete and competent advice from counsel regarding the certain prospect of an acquittal, the client instructs counsel that he or she is guilty and wishes to enter a plea to this effect. This possibility is not as outlandish as might be thought. The accused may feel a genuine remorse for having done wrong, and wish to acknowledge guilt publicly as part of the process of rehabilitation and to make amends to the victim and society.

Where the client is in fact guilty, by which we mean that he or she committed the *actus reus* and *mens rea* of the offence, counsel should have no compunction about taking part in plea discussions, making a

---

185   See, for example, CBA Code ch. IX, comm. 12(a); Sask. ch. IX, comm. 12(a); Man. ch. IX, comm. 12(a); Nfld. ch. IX, comm. 12(a); and N.S. ch. 10, r. 10.8(a). The "uncertain or unlikely" requirement is not found in the provisions used in Alberta, British Columbia or Ontario: see Ont. r. 4.01(9); Alta. ch. 8, r. 27; and B.C. ch. 8, r. 20.

plea agreement, or representing the client on a guilty plea.[186] The objections that arise where an innocent client wishes to plead guilty are not applicable, for the court will not be misled and the truthfully admitted facts will be sufficient to support a conviction. Furthermore, the accused's constitutional right to choose whether or not to plead guilty means that counsel must comply with such instructions.

**Example I:** Accused X is charged with various *Controlled Drugs and Substances Act* offences arising out of a police raid on a marijuana "grow operation." The only evidence against X was obtained by means of the raid and would not have otherwise been located. The police learned of the grow operation by means of a statement by X, made during the course of an interview arising out of unrelated charges. X was not provided with his rights under section 10(a) and (b) of the *Charter* and was improperly induced to make the statement. Counsel for X carefully investigates the facts and the law relevant to the matter, and concludes that the statement will be excluded and an acquittal secured if a *Charter* application is brought. However, before the trial can occur, X embraces the tenets of a religious faith and instructs counsel to work out a fair plea-bargain agreement with the Crown. Counsel should be able to do so, and can undoubtedly take this course of action in Ontario, British Columbia and Alberta, where the rules do not contain an "uncertain or unlikely" requirement.[187]

**Example II:** A lawyer is approached by Y, the complainant in a serious domestic-assault case against her husband. Y informs the lawyer that she helped her husband in the sexual assault and killing of three young women. Partly motivated by a desire for revenge against her husband, but also because she can no longer live with the knowledge of what she has done, she asks the lawyer to approach the authorities in an effort to work out a plea agreement. Based on information obtained after extensive interviews with Y, counsel concludes that the police are unlikely ever to discover the role of Y and her husband in the crimes, and advises Y accordingly. Y nevertheless is adamant that the police or Crown be approached with a view to charges being laid and a guilty plea entered. The lawyer is permitted to accept these instructions and make contact with the authorities, followed by plea discussions.[188]

---

186 See *Martin Committee Report*, above note 4 at 299–300.

187 See *R. v. Goldhart* (1996), 107 C.C.C. (3d) 481 at 486 (S.C.C.), which provides the basis for this example.

188 This fact scenario is based on the case of Paul Bernardo and Karla Homolka. A plea agreement was reached with Homolka and caused sufficient public outcry that the Attorney General for Ontario commissioned a report on the matter: see

As a footnote, we observe that the Nova Scotia Law Society's ethical rules not only contain the "uncertain or unlikely" provision found in many Canadian rules but also provide that the defence lawyer can conclude a plea agreement only where he or she "*bona fide* believes that it is in the interests of the client to negotiate a plea with the prosecutor."[189] In our view, this reference to the interests of the client should not be taken to permit counsel to override the client's instructions on the issue of the plea. The best interests of the client are a vital consideration for counsel, but it is the client who determines which interests come first.

## P. ILLEGAL VERSUS UNPALATABLE BARGAINING

It is axiomatic that a lawyer is not permitted to commit any illegalities in the course of plea discussions or by virtue of a plea agreement. On the other hand, counsel may be asked by the client to approach the Crown with an offer to provide information in exchange for a particular plea agreement. Some counsel may find the proposal, though not illegal, to be highly unpalatable. For instance, there are defence lawyers who balk at representing a client who wishes to provide the Crown with evidence against a co-accused or other third party.[190] Another example would be the type of bargaining undertaken by Clifford Olsen, in essence offering to exchange bodies for money.[191] This sort of bargaining, if legal and in the best interests of the client, is not in our view unethical.

---

P.T. Galligan, *Report to the Attorney General of Ontario on Certain Matters Relating to Karla Homolka* (Toronto: Ontario Ministry of the Attorney General, 1996). On the facts of the Homolka plea negotiations, however, defence counsel could in no way be sure that the police would not otherwise obtain evidence against his client: *ibid.* at 62–63.

189 N.S. ch. 10, r. 10.8(b).
190 See section H, "Duty to Negotiate," in this chapter.
191 Clifford Olsen, one of Canada's most notorious serial killers, eventually revealed the location of the bodies of his victims in return for a large monetary payment received by his family. This deal was not negotiated by a lawyer. See also *Henderson* v. *State*, 962 S.W.2d 544 (Tex. Crim. App., en banc, Texas, 1997), cert. den'd 119 S. Ct. 212 (October 5, 1998), leave to amend petition den'd 119 S. Ct. 437 (November 2, 1998); related reference 977 S.W. 2d 605 (Tex. Crim. App. 1998), where counsel tried to negotiate a plea bargain under which the client would direct police to the location of the victim's body.

**Example:** Counsel is provided with physical evidence implicating her client in a murder. She quickly determines that the evidence must be turned over to the authorities, and that concealment would constitute an obstruction of justice. Nevertheless, she approaches the Crown in an effort to hand over the item in return for concessions on a guilty plea. This course of action is risky and demonstrates the fine line between illegal and legal bargaining. If counsel pushes too hard in the negotiating process, and suggests that the item will not be turned over to the authorities absent a satisfactory plea agreement, the Crown might conclude that counsel is obstructing justice.[192]

# Q. WRITTEN INSTRUCTIONS

Many of the Canadian rules of professional conduct suggest that counsel obtain instructions in writing, if possible, prior to commencing plea discussions or securing a plea agreement.[193] Some judges have also offered the opinion that prudent counsel will obtain written instructions regarding the plea.[194] If time permits, there is certainly no disadvantage to following this advice. The process of setting out the instructions in writing will serve to remind both counsel and the accused of the gravity of the decision, and will provide counsel with a contemporaneous record of events in case the client later challenges the plea. If counsel prefers not to obtain written instructions, the next best course of action is to make a contemporaneous written record setting out the advice given and the client's instructions, and to keep this record in the file. If time permits, counsel should also consider confirming the client's instructions in a letter to the client.[195]

---

192 This tightrope was walked, apparently absent any adverse result, by counsel who conducted the trial for Paul Bernardo. Counsel ultimately turned over the videotapes without concluding a plea agreement. For some details surrounding counsel's approach, see *R. v. Murray* (2000), 144 C.C.C. (3d) 289 at 307–08 & 321 (Ont. S.C.J.).

193 See, for example, CBA Code ch. IX, comm. 12(d); Sask. ch. IX, comm. 12(d); Man. ch. IX, comm. 12(d); N.S. ch. 10, r. 12(e); Alta. ch. 10, comm. 27. Governing bodies whose ethical rules contain no such recommendation include Alta. ch. 10, r. 27, Ont. r. 4.01(9); and B.C. ch. 8, r. 20.

194 See, for example, *Conflitti*, above note 87; *R. v. Snow* (2000), 46 W.C.B. (2d) 611 at para. 16 (Ont. C.J.); *R. v. Alessandro* (1997), 36 W.C.B. (2d) 414 at paras. 64–66 & 90 (Ont. Prov. Div.).

195 See Bystrom, above note 99 at 93.

**Advice:** In cases where there is a disagreement between counsel and the accused regarding the plea, or the accused is experiencing significant difficulty in reaching a decision, the lawyer should always protect himself or herself by making a written record of the advice given, the instructions received, and any other pertinent factors.[196]

**Observation:** In Ontario, the old Professional Conduct Handbook did not suggest that counsel should obtain instructions in writing, and in this respect it differed from the rules in most other jurisdictions.[197] The recently adopted rules of professional conduct have continued this position.[198] While the silence of the new rules on this point may accurately reflect the practice of many lawyers, the decision not to encourage written instructions as a valid aspirational goal is disappointing. We prefer the approach taken by those governing bodies whose rules urge counsel to receive plea instructions in writing.

# R. DUTY TO ACT FAIRLY RESPECTING THE CROWN

Defence counsel's overriding obligation is to further the best interests of the client. However, this obligation does not extend so far as to permit counsel to mislead or otherwise act in bad faith towards the prosecutor. Counsel has an ethical obligation to act in good faith with all persons with whom he or she has dealings in the course of representing the client,[199] and must not knowingly assist or permit the client to do anything that counsel considers to be dishonest or dishonourable.[200] Lawyers must therefore resist the temptation to play fast and loose with the truth in negotiating with the Crown.[201] Misleading information, if discovered, may provide a legitimate basis for the Crown to renounce

---

196 See ABA Defense Standard 4-5.2(b).

197 Ont. r. 10, comm. 12(d).

198 Ont. r. 4.01(9).

199 See, for example, CBA Code ch. XVI, Rule; Sask. ch. XVI, Rule; Man. ch. XVI, Rule; and Ont. r. 6.03(1).

200 See, for example, CBA Code ch. IX, comm. 2(b), (e), (f) & (g); Sask. ch. IX, comm. 2(b), (e), (f) & (g); Man. ch. IX, comm. 2(b), (e), (f) & (g); and Ont. r. 4.01(2)(b), (e), (f) & (g).

201 While Canadian rules of professional conduct do not expressly forbid counsel from misleading the Crown in the context of plea discussions, such a prohibition is found in ABA Defense Standard 4-6.2(c); and ABA Pleas of Guilty Standard 14-3.2(d).

a plea agreement[202] or to take a sterner position where an agreement has yet to be reached. Dishonest dealing may also expose the counsel to disciplinary action. Finally, defence counsel who is suspected of taking unfair advantage of the Crown will soon garner a bad reputation, to the detriment of all future clients.

**Caveat:** Defence counsel is not permitted to mislead the Crown during the course of plea discussions. But this limitation on counsel's conduct does not equate with a duty to disclose information to the prosecutor. Rather, counsel remains under a strict duty to maintain a client's confidences absent the client's consent to the contrary.

On a slightly different note, defence counsel is ethically bound to honour a resolution agreement made with the Crown, absent exceptional circumstances. The Martin Committee has noted that:

> The Committee views the duty of counsel to honour resolution agreements as simply a particular example of the duties of integrity and responsibility discussed in some detail at the outset of this Report. As such, honouring resolution agreements lies at the heart of counsel's professional obligations. Implicit support for the requirement that resolution agreements be honoured can be found in the decisions of the Ontario Court of Appeal in R. v. *Brown* (1972), 8 C.C.C. (2d) 227 and R. v. *Agozzino* (1970), 1 C.C.C. 380. Agreements reached following resolution agreements are also, in the Committee's view, in the nature of undertakings. The Law Society of Upper Canada's Rules of Professional Conduct, Rule 10, Commentary 8, states that undertakings given in the course of litigation, "must be strictly and scrupulously carried out."[203]

The Martin Committee's comments are undoubtedly relevant to defence counsel; however, they require some qualification, for they are made in the context of a discussion that focuses upon the obligations of the Crown.

We would qualify the Martin Committee's position, in so far as defence lawyers are concerned, in the following way. Defence counsel may be duty-bound to comply with the terms of a plea agreement, but where the client changes his or her mind prior to sentencing, there

---

202  R. v. *Obadia* (1998), 20 C.R. (5th) 162 (Que. C.A.); and R. v. *MacDonald* (1990), 54 C.C.C. (3d) 97 (Ont. C.A.).

203  *Martin Committee Report*, above note 4 at 312–13. See also R. v. *Morrison* (1981), 63 C.C.C. (2d) 527 (N.S. S.C.(A.D.)) [*Morrison*]; and R. v. *Crneck* (1980), 55 C.C.C. (2d) 1 (H.C.J.).

may be no choice but to abandon the agreement. To hold otherwise would effectively treat the plea agreement as an irrevocable waiver of the accused's constitutional right to plead not guilty, a proposition for which no case law exists in support. In the same vein, it is clear that an accused who pleads guilty is not precluded from appealing the fitness of the sentence even where the judge accepted a joint submission.[204]

**Comparison:** In contrast to the position taken by the Martin Committee, the commentary to the Alberta Code of Professional Conduct states that "an agreement between the prosecution and defence regarding the plea to be entered is not considered a usual lawyers' undertaking due to the policy considerations involved. Either party may withdraw from the agreement prior to performance, although the withdrawing party should afford the other party ample notice. However, once the agreed-upon plea has been entered by the defence, it is generally improper for the prosecution to attempt to repudiate the agreement of the parties."[205] While we agree that the accused should not be bound by a plea agreement prior to the plea being entered, absent exceptional circumstances, we prefer the Martin Committee's view of the Crown's obligations.

# S.  DUTY TO THE PUBLIC INTEREST

The CBA Code specifically provides that the public interest cannot be compromised by a guilty plea.[206] In Ontario, the rules of professional responsibility are worded differently, providing in a commentary that "the public interest in the proper administration of justice should not be sacrificed in the interest of expediency."[207] Still other governing bodies make no reference to the public interest in the context of plea agreements.[208]

---

204  See, for example, *R. v. Wood* (1988), 43 C.C.C. (3d) 570 at 574 (Ont. C.A.); and *R. v. Sriskantharajah* (1994), 90 C.C.C. (3d) 559 at 562–63 (Ont. C.A.). The Crown is also permitted to appeal from a joint submission, though in more limited circumstances: see *Morrison*, above note 203 at 530.

205  Alta. ch. 10, comm. 27.

206  See CBA Code ch. IX, comm. 12. See also Sask. ch. IX, comm. 12; Man. ch. IX, comm. 12; and N.S. ch. 10, r. 10.9.

207  See the commentary to Ont. r. 4.01(9).

208  See, for example, B.C. ch. 8, r. 20; and Alta. ch. 10, r. 27.

Defence counsel obviously has obligations in relation to the public interest. We have already discussed in detail the problems that can arise where an accused who is truly innocent wishes to plea guilty. It would also be against the public's interest to commit illegalities in the course of negotiating or implementing a plea agreement. However, the ethical rules should not be taken to go much further with respect to defence counsel's role in plea discussions and agreements. In particular, it is not in any way part of defence counsel's duty to determine whether or not a proposed agreement is too lenient, and for this reason to defer to the public interest by seeking a resolution less favourable to the accused. This sort of consideration is solely within the Crown's bailiwick,[209] and within the judge's once a plea agreement is presented to the court.[210] We therefore like the language used by the Law Society of Upper Canada, which refers to the public interest in a manner that largely accords with the duties of loyalty and competency owed by counsel to the accused.[211]

## T. CONFLICT OF INTEREST

Where an accused is considering whether or not to plead guilty, and defence counsel's loyalty to the client is compromised, say by virtue of the competing interests of another client or the lawyer's personal circumstances, there is a conflict of interest. As in any case, where the real

---

209 See, for example, *Martin Committee Report*, above note 4 at 300–05. Most of the factors discussed by the Martin Committee as bearing upon the public interest, such as the views of any victims and comity with the sentence received by a comparably situated co-accused, are not applicable to defence counsel. On the other hand, appeal counsel representing a convicted individual can certainly raise the public interest in attacking a plea agreement after the fact: see, for example, the cases cited at note 214, above. For a comprehensive discussion of the prosecutor's obligations, see F. Zacharias, "Justice in Plea Bargaining" (1998) 39 Wm. & Mary L. Rev. 1121.

210 The public interest is a factor that will always be considered by the trial judge in deciding whether to accept a joint submission: see section D(3), "Plea Agreement is Not Binding on the Court," in this chapter.

211 The Ontario approach seems to draw from Recommendation 50 of the Martin Committee and the associated commentary, which focuses on the duties of Crown counsel: see *Martin Committee Report*, above note 4 at 300–05.

possibility of a conflict arises, counsel is often precluded from continuing to act in the matter, or must at the least take prophylactic steps. If counsel decides to pursue the representation, and an actual conflict arises in relation to the client's guilty plea or sentence hearing, the result is susceptible to being overturned on appeal.

Where counsel for an accused has divided loyalties, plea bargaining can provide a classic example of conflict of interest. At every step in the process, whether undertaking negotiations with the prosecution, transmitting the substance of plea discussions to the client or advising the client as to the advantages and disadvantages of a plea proposal, counsel's loyalty is potentially compromised to the client's detriment. The danger is especially great in the context of multiple representation, given that co-accused rarely have exactly the same interest.[212] The ABA Defense Standards therefore aptly provide that counsel representing multiple co-accused should not participate in making an aggregate plea agreement unless each client consents after consultation, including disclosure of the existence and nature of all the claims or pleas involved.[213]

There are also less obvious systemic pressures that can subtly work to weaken or fray counsel's duty of loyalty to the client. These pressures are not generally discussed using the language of conflict of interest, yet undeniably they can undercut counsel's obligation to carry out plea discussions in the best interests of the client. For instance, the temptation to avoid the hard work and stress involved in preparing for and participating in a trial cannot be allowed to influence counsel's advice to the client regarding the decision to plead guilty or not guilty.[214] Scheduling problems can also lead a lawyer to favour improperly a plea resolution, hoping to free up time to work on other cases. It is not uncommon for some lawyers to develop a practice that is dependent upon trials collapsing by reason of last-minute guilty pleas, often serving to place unfair pressure upon the accused. Counsel must also resist promoting a plea agreement as a means of fostering a good working relationship with prosecutors and judges. In the long run, conducting plea negotiations with skill and integrity, always keeping

---

212 For elaboration on this point, see section G(1), "Plea Discussions," in chapter 6.
213 See ABA Defense Standard 4-6.2(e).
214 See D. Lynch, "The Impropriety of Plea Agreements: A Tale of Two Counties" (1994) 19 L. & Soc. Inquiry 115.

paramount the best interests of the client, will earn counsel the respect of most other participants in the criminal justice system.[215]

**Example I:** A lawyer represents three men who are accused of trafficking in narcotics. Accused X agrees to pay the lawyer's entire fee, including the fee for representation of his two co-accused. The lawyer subsequently concludes a plea agreement with the prosecutor, under which charges against Accused X will be dropped and the other co-accused will plead guilty with a joint recommendation for penitentiary time. The lawyer advises all three men to accept the deal, which is accordingly endorsed by the court. On these facts, the lawyer has a serious conflict of interest, for the plea arrangement that substantially benefits Accused X may actually be to the detriment of the other two clients.[216]

**Example II:** A lawyer represents Accused Y, who is charged with several offences. Y considers but rejects a prosecution proposal for a guilty plea, and the case is set for trial. On the day scheduled for trial, the Crown informs defence counsel that the police not only suspect that Y has attempted to bribe several witnesses, but believe that defence counsel knowingly participated in the attempt. The lawyer, fearing a full-scale police investigation, convinces Y to accept the original plea proposal, in the knowledge that the Crown will not pursue the bribery allegations. Given that counsel's loyalty to the client is at odds with her own best interests, an impermissible conflict of interest exists.[217]

**Example III:** Defence counsel represents two co-accused, A and B. The Crown suggests that she might be willing to accept a plea from A to a minor charge, with little or no jail time, in exchange for A's testimony against B. Defence counsel chooses not to pass on this information to A, who goes to trial and is convicted on all counts. Counsel's failure to communicate the potential for a plea agreement operates to the detri-

---

215  For a different view, see Lynch, *ibid.*

216  See *R. v. Stork* (1975), 24 C.C.C. (2d) 210 (B.C.C.A.). For a similar case, where financial incentives built into the retainer agreement led counsel to show little interest in a prosecution plea proposal, see *United States ex rel. Simon v. Murphy*, 349 F. Supp. 818 (E.D. Pa. 1972).

217  These facts represent a simplified version of the circumstances in *Laperrière*, above note 9, which is also discussed in section L(1), "Counsel's Alleged Involvement in Facts Relevant to the Retainer," in chapter 6.

ment of A, and the conflict of interest will likely result in a successful appeal.[218]

## U. WITHDRAWAL BECAUSE OF DISAGREEMENT WITH THE CLIENT

The ability of defence counsel to withdraw from a case in a given situation is often controversial, and is discussed more generally elsewhere.[219] Where counsel and a client fundamentally disagree as to the proper plea to enter, we believe that counsel can withdraw from the case provided that no undue harm is caused to the client. Indeed, if the disagreement is so profound that counsel feels unable to represent the client properly, withdrawal may be necessary. Keeping in mind that the client has a constitutional right to choose how to plead, and that this right is also given great solicitude within the client-lawyer relationship, the lawyer should avoid withdrawing in all but the most problematic cases.

**Warning:** Counsel should not blithely threaten withdrawal in an effort to convince a client to enter a particular plea. Such pressure unduly interferes with the client's freedom of choice and may lead to later recriminations against the lawyer.[220]

## V. SUMMARY AND RECOMMENDATIONS

The most common resolution of criminal cases in Canada is by means of a guilty plea, which operates as a waiver by the accused of fundamental constitutional rights. It is therefore important that counsel act loyally and competently in representing a client during plea discus-

---

218 See *Krahn* v. *Kinney*, 538 N.E.2d 1058 (Ohio 1989). The possibility that counsel for two or more co-accused acts improperly by failing to instigate plea discussions was noted in *W.(W.)*, above note 63 at 244, but rejected on the particular facts of the case. See also *R. v. Neil* (1998), 235 A.R. 152 (Q.B.), rev'd (2000), 266 A.R. 363 (C.A.), which involved the converse problem (counsel acting for one accused sought to exchange testimony against the co-accused for withdrawal of the charges, at the same time that a member of his firm represented the co-accused).

219 See chapter 11; and section F(4)(a), "Withdrawal," in chapter 7.

220 See *Beaney*, above note 92, where counsel forced a client to plead guilty by withdrawing from the case. The plea was struck on appeal and a new trial ordered.

sions, in concluding a plea agreement, and during the guilty plea itself. Our summary and recommendations regarding counsel's duties and considerations are as follows:

1. Where applicable, counsel should explore the possibility of resolving a matter prior to charges being brought and, even after charges are laid, should consider whether diversion from the criminal process is feasible (section G).
2. Counsel has a duty to negotiate in those instances where reaching a plea agreement might reasonably afford the client a benefit (section H).
3. It should not be improper to undertake preliminary plea discussions with the Crown prior to the accused receiving full and complete advice and indicating a willingness to admit to the necessary factual and legal elements. However, some Canadian rules of professional conduct appear to suggest otherwise (section I).
4. Similarly, counsel need not receive express instructions from the client prior to participating in plea discussions. But in those cases where counsel reasonably suspects that the client would oppose such discussions taking place, or in fact has instructed counsel not to undertake plea discussions, counsel should not canvas the possibility of a guilty plea with the Crown (section I).
5. A plea agreement should never be concluded without prior authorization by the client (sections F and K(3)).
6. A defence lawyer must thoroughly understand the factual and legal elements of the case, and undertake any necessary independent investigation, in order to provide complete and competent advice to the client regarding the plea decision (section J).
7. Clients typically rely upon counsel to provide advice on the issue of the proper plea. Counsel need therefore provide fully informed and competent advice. This advice can be communicated in strong terms but should not overwhelm the client's freedom of choice (section K).
8. It is imperative that counsel communicate all plea proposals to the client, no matter how tentative. Moreover, counsel should pass on any information that is reasonably relevant to the plea decision (section L).
9. Where the client maintains innocence yet desires to plead guilty, counsel is confronted with a particularly difficult ethical dilemma. There is much debate as to the proper course of action in such circumstances. In our view, counsel should never act on a guilty plea where he or she knows that the client is truly innocent. However,

where counsel is satisfied that there is a strong factual basis for the guilty plea, meaning that a reasonable jury would likely convict on the evidence in the possession of the Crown, counsel can participate in the client's plea. In such a case, it is advisable to obtain detailed written instructions (section M).

10. When putting an agreed statement of facts before the court, counsel should not include any fact known to be misleading (section N).

11. Where the client instructs counsel accordingly, it may be proper to participate in plea discussions even though acquittal is certain or highly likely (section O).

12. Counsel must never conduct plea discussions in an illegal manner, nor conclude a plea agreement that violates the law. It is not, however, improper to participate in plea discussions that counsel personally finds to be unpalatable (section P).

13. Obtaining written instructions from the client regarding the final plea decision is a good idea, and is especially prudent where the decision is contentious or the client rejects counsel's advice (section Q).

14. While defence counsel has an overarching duty to act in the best interests of the client, this obligation does not extend so far as to permit counsel to mislead or otherwise act in bad faith towards the Crown during plea discussions (section R).

15. There is a duty to the public interest that circumscribes defence counsel in conducting plea discussions and reaching plea agreements. The main component of this duty is satisfied where counsel scrupulously avoids taking any action that would mislead the court. However, defence counsel does not have any obligation to avoid plea agreements that are too lenient or otherwise overly favourable to the accused (section S).

16. Counsel must be vigilant in avoiding conflicts of interest that can jeopardize a client's interests concerning a plea discussion and/or agreement. The spectre of an impermissible conflict is especially great where counsel acts for two or more co-accused (section T).

17. In rare cases, where counsel and the client fundamentally disagree as to the proper plea to enter, it may be permissible for counsel to withdraw from the retainer (section U).

## FURTHER READINGS

Alschuler, A., "Implementing the Defendant's Right to Trial: Alternatives to the Plea Bargaining System" (1983) 50 U. Chi. L. Rev. 931

ALSCHULER, A., "The Defence Attorney's Role in Plea Bargaining" (1975) 84 Yale L.J. 1179

ACEVEDO, R., "Is a Ban on Plea Bargaining an Ethical Abuse of Discretion? A Bronx County, New York Case Study" (1995–96) 64 Fordham L. Rev. 987

BALDWIN, J., & M. McCONVILLE, *Negotiated Justice: Pressures to Plead Guilty* (London: Martin Robertson, 1977)

BLAKE, M., & A. ASHWORTH, "Some Ethical Issues in Prosecuting and Defending Criminal Cases" [1998] Crim. L. Rev. 16

BLUMBERG, A., "The Practice of Law as Confidence Game: Organizational Cooptation of a Profession" (1967) 1 L. & Soc. Rev. 15

BOTSFORD, J., "Conditional Guilty Pleas: Post-Guilty Plea Appeal of Nonjurisdictional Issues" (1978) 26 U.C.L.A. L. Rev. 360

BOWMAN, A., "Standards of Conduct for Prosecution and Defense Personnel: An Attorney's Viewpoint" (1966) 5 Am. Crim. L. Rev. 23

BRADLEY, G., "Plea Bargaining and the Criminal Defendant's Obligation to Plead Guilty" (1999) 40 S. Tex. L. Rev. 65

BRANNIGAN, A., & J. LEVY, "The Legal Framework of Plea Bargaining" (1983) 25 Can. J. Crim. 399

BURGER, W., "Standards of Conduct for Prosecution and Defense Personnel: A Judge's Viewpoint" (1966) 5 Am. Crim. L. Rev. 11

BURNETT, C., "Of Crime, Punishment, Community and an Accused's Responsibility to Plead Guilty: A Response to Gerard Bradley" (1999) 40 S. Tex. L. Rev. 281

BYSTROM, K., "Communicating Plea Offers to the Client" in R. Uphoff, ed., *Ethical Problems Facing the Criminal Lawyer: Practical Answers to Tough Questions* (Chicago: American Bar Association, 1995) c. 7

CANADIAN SENTENCING COMMISSION, *Sentencing Reform: A Canadian Approach* (Ottawa: Supply and Services, 1987) (Chair: J.R. Omer Archambault)

CARNS, T., & J. KRUSE, "Alaska's Ban on Plea Bargaining Re-evaluated" (1992) 75 Judicature 310

CHURCH, T., "In Defense of 'Bargain Justice'" (1979) 13 L. & Soc. Rev. 509

CLARK, S., "Is Plea Bargaining a Short Cut to Justice?" *Lawyers Weekly* (1 March 1985) 4

COHEN, S., & A. DOOB, "Public Attitudes to Plea Bargaining" (1989–90) 32 Crim. L.Q. 85

CRAIG, J., "Guilty Plea Revocation, Constitutional Waiver, and the *Charter*" (1997) 20 Dal. L.J. 161

DEPARTMENT OF JUSTICE, RESEARCH AND DEVELOPMENT DIRECTORATE, *Plea Bargaining and Sentencing Guidelines* (Research Report of the Canadian Sentencing Commission) by S. Verdun-Jones (Ottawa: Department of Justice, 1988)

FERGUSON, G., & D. ROBERTS, "Plea Bargaining: Directions for Canadian Reform" (1974) 52 Can. Bar Rev. 497

FERGUSON, G., "The Plea of Guilty and Plea Inquiries" [1995] National Criminal Law Program

FITZGERALD, O., *The Guilty Plea and Summary Justice: A Guide for Practitioners* (Toronto: Carswell, 1990)

FORSYTH, F., "A Plea for Nolo Contendere in the Canadian Criminal Justice System" (1998) 40 Crim. L.Q. 243

FREEDMAN, M., *Understanding Lawyers' Ethics* (New York: Matthew Bender, 1990)

GALLIGAN, P.T., *Report to the Attorney General of Ontario on Certain Matters Relating to Karla Homolka* (Toronto: Ontario Ministry of the Attorney General, 1996)

GOLDSTEIN, A., "Converging Criminal Justice Systems: Guilty Pleas and the Public Interest" (1996) 49 SMU L. Rev. 567 (also found at (1997) 31 Isr. L. Rev. 159)

GUIDORIZZI, D., "Should We Really 'Ban' Plea-Bargaining?: The Core Concerns of Plea Bargaining Critics" (1998) 47 Emory L J. 753

HALL, J., JR., *Professional Responsibility of the Criminal Lawyer*, 2d ed. (New York: Clark Boardman Callaghan, 1996)

HEATHER, D., "Pleas and Elections" in Law Society of Upper Canada, *Defending a Criminal Case* (Toronto: R. De Boo, 1969) 69

HENHAM, R., "Truth in Plea-Bargaining: Anglo-American Approaches to the Use of Guilty Plea Discounts at the Sentencing Stage" (2000) 29 Anglo-Am. L. Rev. 1

HOOLIHAN, J., "Ethical Standards for Defence Counsel" in Canadian Bar Association, *Studies in Criminal Law and Procedure* (Agincourt, Ont.: Canada Law Book, 1973)

HUTCHINSON, A., *Legal Ethics and Professional Responsibility* (Toronto: Irwin Law, 1999)

Justice Society, *Negotiated Justice: A Closer Look at the Implications of Plea Bargains* (London: Justice Society, 1993)

KING, N., "Priceless Process: Nonnegotiable Features of Criminal Litigation" (1999) 47 U.C.L.A. L. Rev. 113

LA FAVE, W., J. ISRAEL, & N. KING, *Criminal Procedure*, 2d ed. (St. Paul: West, 1999)

LAW REFORM COMMISSION OF CANADA, *Criminal Procedure: Control of the Process* (Working Paper No. 15) (Ottawa: The Commission, 1975)

LAW REFORM COMMISSION OF CANADA, *Plea Discussions and Agreements* (Working Paper No. 60) (Ottawa: The Commission, 1989)

LAW REFORM COMMISSION OF ONTARIO, *Report on Administration of Ontario Courts, Part II* (Toronto: Ministry of the Attorney General, 1973)

LYNCH, D., "The Impropriety of Plea Agreements: A Tale of Two Counties" (1994) 19 L. & Soc. Inquiry 115

MACKENZIE, G., *Lawyers and Ethics: Professional Responsibility and Discipline* (Toronto: Carswell, 1993)

MARTIN, G. ARTHUR, "The Role and Responsibility of the Defence Advocate" (1970) 12 Crim. L.Q. 376

MCCONVILLE, M., "Plea Bargaining: Ethics and Politics" (1998) 25 J. L. & Soc. 562

MCCONVILLE, M., & L. BRIDGES, "Pleading Guilty Whilst Maintaining Innocence" (1993) 143 New L.J. 160

MCCONVILLE, M., & C. MIRSKY, "The Skeleton of Plea Bargaining" (1992) 142 New L.J. 1373

ODIAGA, U., "The Ethics of Judicial Discretion in Plea Bargaining" (1989) 2 Geo. J. Legal Ethics 695

ONTARIO, ATTORNEY GENERAL'S ADVISORY COMMITTEE, *Report of the Attorney General's Advisory Committee on Charge Screening, Disclosure, and Resolution Discussions* (Toronto: Queen's Printer, 1993) {Chair: G. Arthur Martin)

ONTARIO, CRIMINAL JUSTICE REVIEW COMMITTEE, *Report of the Criminal Justice Review Committee* (Toronto: Queen's Printer, 1999) (Co.chairs: H. Locke, J.D. Evans, & M. Segal)

ORKIN, M., *Legal Ethics: A Study of Professional Conduct* (Toronto: Cartwright, 1957)

PALMER, J., "Abolishing Plea Bargaining: An End to the Same Old Song and Dance" (1999) 26 Am. J. Crim. L. 505

"Panel Discussion: Problems in Advocacy and Ethics" in Law Society of Upper Canada, *Defending a Criminal Case* (Toronto: R. De Boo, 1969) 279

"Panel Discussion: Witness for the Prosecution: Successful Impeachment Strategies" (Criminal Lawyers' Association Convention and Education Programme, 21-22 November 1997) QL online (OCLARP/1997-019)

PERRAS, D., "Plea Negotiations" (1979–80), 22 Crim. L.Q. 58 (also found at (1979–80) 44 Sask. L. Rev. 143)

PIZZI, W., "Accepting Guilty Pleas from 'Innocent' Defendants?" (1996) 146 New L.J. 997

RATUSHNY, E., "Plea-Bargaining and the Public" (1972) 20 Chitty's L.J. 238

*Report of the Royal Commission on the Donald Marshall, Jr., Prosecution* vol. 1 (Halifax: The Commission, 1989) (Chair: T.A. Hickman)

RICHMAN, D., "Cooperating Clients" (1995) 56 Ohio St. L.J. 69

RUBY, C., *Sentencing*, 5th ed. (Toronto: Butterworths, 1999)

SCHULHOFER, S., "A Wake-Up Call from the Plea-Bargaining Trenches" (1994) 19 L. & Soc. Inquiry 135

SCHULHOFER, S., "Plea Bargaining as Disaster" (1992) 101 Yale L.J. 1979

SCOTT, R., & W. STUNTZ, "A Reply: Imperfect Bargains, Imperfect Trials and Innocent Defendants" (1992) 101 Yale L.J. 2011

SCOTT, R., & W. STUNTZ, "Plea Bargaining as Contract" (1992) 101 Yale L.J. 1909

SHADLEY, R., & D. DRUCKMAN, "The Client Who Maintains Innocence" [1998] National Criminal Law Program

SHIPLEY, C., "The *Alford* Plea: A Necessary But Unpredictable Tool for the Criminal Defendant" (1987) 72 Iowa L. Rev. 1063

SILVERMAN, H. "Plea Bargaining" (1976), 24 Chitty's L.J. 78

SKURKA, S., & J. STRIBOPOULOS, "Professional Responsibility in Criminal Practice" in Law Society of Upper Canada, *42nd Bar Admission Course, 2000, Criminal Procedure Reference Materials* (Toronto: Law Society of Upper Canada, 2000) c. 1

SOPINKA, J., S. LEDERMAN, & A. BRYANT, *The Law of Evidence in Canada*, 2d ed. (Toronto: Butterworths, 1999)

STONE, I., *Clarence Darrow for the Defence* (Garden City, N.Y.: Doubleday, Doran, 1941)

TAPPER, C., *Cross and Tapper on Evidence*, 9th ed. (London: Butterworths, 1999)

TIERNEY, K., *Darrow: A Biography* (New York: Crowell, 1979)

U.K., H.C., HOME AFFAIRS COMMITTEE, *Report of the Royal Commission on Criminal Justice* (London: HMSO, 1993) (Chair: R.G. Runciman)

UPHOFF, R., "The Criminal Defense Lawyer: Zealous Advocate, Double Agent, or Beleaguered Dealer?" (1992) 28 Crim. L. Bull. 419

WEINSTEIN, I., "Regulating the Market for Snitches" (1999) 47 Buffalo L. Rev. 563

WEISBERG, R., "The Impropriety of Plea Agreements: An 'Anthropological' View" (1994) 19 L. & Soc. Inquiry 145

WENINGER, R., "The Abolition of Plea Bargaining: A Case Study of El Paso County, Texas" (1987) 35 U.C.L.A. L. Rev. 265

WOLFRAM, C.W., *Modern Legal Ethics* (St. Paul: West, 1986)

WRIGHT, C., *Federal Practice and Procedure*, 3d ed. (St. Paul: West, 1999)

ZACHARIAS, F., "Justice in Plea Bargaining" (1998) 39 W. & Mary L. Rev. 1121

# INCRIMINATING PHYSICAL EVIDENCE

"Counsel came so close to the edge of the precipice that just a gentle breeze could have pushed him over" — observation made by a trial judge in acquitting a lawyer on a charge of obstruction of justice for taking possession of incriminating physical evidence.[1]

## A. SETTING UP THE PROBLEM: *R. V. COFFIN* AND *R. V. MURRAY*

A classic ethics problem posed to law students and practitioners alike is the dilemma of the "smoking gun" or "bloody shirt." What is the proper response when a client brings a gun to his or her lawyer, confesses to using the weapon to commit a murder, and asks for help in handling this piece of damning physical evidence? This problem sets up a potential clash between some of counsel's most sacrosanct duties. On the one hand, counsel owes duties of loyalty and confidentiality to the client that militate against taking any action that might harm the client. Yet, at the same time, counsel bears an obligation to the admin-

---

1 See *R. v. Gérin*, unreported decision of the Quebec Provincial Court of Sessions of the Peace, Lessard J. [*Gérin*]. The original reads: "S'est dangerousement penché audessus d'un gouffre et qu'il n'aurait suffi que d'un zéphyr pour l'y faire chuter."

istration of justice that forbids him or her from actively interfering with the availability of incriminating physical evidence, and forbids any action that would serve to compromise its evidentiary value.

We can gain a greater appreciation of the issues at stake by looking at a concrete example in the form of *Reference re R. v. Coffin*,[2] a notorious case from Quebec that garnered much attention in the 1950s and 1960s. While not typically known as a "smoking gun" case, *Coffin* illustrates a lawyer's unfortunate involvement in concealing incriminating evidence. In 1954 Coffin was convicted of murdering one of three American tourists who were shot to death while visiting the Gaspé for a hunting trip. Two years later, he became the last person to be hanged in the province of Quebec. Movies, television series, and popular writings made the case a *cause célèbre*, and many people were left with a doubt as to Coffin's guilt.[3] Because of these doubts, a royal commission was established in 1963 to examine the investigation and prosecution of the case.

New evidence heard by the Coffin Commission cleared up a mystery that had previously surrounded the disappearance of the suspected murder weapon, and in so doing revealed actions by defence counsel that, by today's standards, were almost certainly unethical and illegal. At trial, the Crown contended that a man named Eagle had loaned a rifle to Coffin prior to the crime, and led evidence that this rifle could well have been used to kill one of the victims. Moreover, a police officer testified at trial that, acting on "precise information" (the nature of which he did not disclose and was not asked to reveal), he had searched unsuccessfully for the rifle in the vicinity of Coffin's camp. The Crown also led evidence suggesting that Coffin had made arrangements to dispose of the rifle prior to the police search of his camp.[4]

The fate of the rifle was undoubtedly relevant to the issue of guilt. Yet the failure of the trial record to provide a satisfactory answer to this factual question, as well as the police officer's strange reference to "precise information" connecting Coffin to the rifle, helped to fuel arguments in favour of Coffin's possible innocence. The Coffin Commission therefore heard new evidence concerning the rifle. This

---

2    The facts of the case are set out in a reference heard by the Supreme Court of Canada: see *R. v. Coffin* (1956), 114 C.C.C. 1 (S.C.C.) *Reference re R.* [*Coffin*].

3    See, for example, Hébert, *I Accuse the Assassins of Coffin* (Montreal: Les Éditions du Jour, 1964); and J. Belleveau, *The Coffin Murder Case* (Toronto: Kingswood House, 1956).

4    *Coffin*, above note 2 at 29–30.

evidence revealed that, after his arrest, Coffin gave instructions to a lawyer to get rid of the weapon. The lawyer, in the company of others, located and disposed of the rifle according to his client's direction.[5] Needless to say, this startling new evidence, coming years after the trial and execution, shed light on Coffin's involvement and his counsel's conduct. Clearing up the mystery of the rifle helped to alleviate concerns that Coffin may have been innocent. The evidence put before the Commission also revealed why, at trial, defence counsel had neither pressed the police officer to disclose the source of the "precise information" nor attacked the weight of this evidence on cross-examination: counsel knew that the information provided to the officer was true.[6] However, the Commission made no comment as to the propriety of counsel's actions in helping to move the rifle.[7]

More recently, the sorts of ethical issues raised by *Coffin* were publicly aired in the Ontario case of *R. v. Murray*.[8] The accused was a defence counsel who acted for Paul Bernardo in connection with two murder charges and a number of related offences. Bernardo had videotaped the gross sexual abuse of four of his victims, including the two murder victims, and later hid the videotapes in the ceiling of his house. Despite a seventy-one-day search of the premises, police did not locate these tapes. Bernardo, who was in custody at the time, directed his counsel to attend at the house once the police had finished the search, and to remove the videotapes. Counsel did so, after which he retained the tapes for seventeen months without disclosing their existence to the Crown, ostensibly for the purpose of springing the tapes on Karla Homolka, the key Crown witness, during cross-examination at trial.[9] Charges were ultimately brought against counsel, alleging that the concealment of the tapes constituted an attempt to obstruct justice. Although he was acquitted, counsel's conduct was subject to sharp criticism by the court. The judgment in *Murray* amply demonstrates that

---

5    See Quebec, *Rapport de la Commission d'Enquête Brossard sur l'affaire Coffin* vol. 2 (Montreal: La Commission, 1964) at 300–08 [*Rapport sur l'affaire Coffin*].

6    *Rapport sur l'affaire Coffin, ibid.* 362. For a discussion of the limitations placed on defence counsel when cross-examining a witness who is known to be telling the truth, see section K(1), "Cross-examining the Truthful Witness," in chapter 1.

7    The commission did criticize co-counsel for taking on the case, given his knowledge that the other defence lawyer had been involved in disposing of the rifle: see *Rapport sur l'affaire Coffin*, above note 5 at 307, 357 & 606–07.

8    (2000), 144 C.C.C. (3d) 289 (Ont. S.C.J.) [*Murray*].

9    While this purpose was put forward by the accused as part of his defence, the Crown alleged that he initially intended to withhold the videotapes from the trial process altogether. The court was sceptical of the accused's claim but ultimately gave him the benefit of the doubt.

the lawyer given an opportunity to handle physical evidence of a client crime frequently faces an ethical minefield.

While *Coffin* and *Murray* provide actual instances where the problem of incriminating physical evidence has arisen, the proper response by defence counsel is not always obvious. Some Canadian commentators who have recently examined lawyers' ethical duties with respect to handling incriminating physical evidence have complained about the serious lack of guidance provided by the governing bodies' rules of professional conduct.[10] Other writers have demonstrated that there is a lack of consensus as to the kinds of physical evidence to which special ethical obligations may attach, in particular whether physical evidence should include only the so-called "fruits or instrumentalities" of a client crime.[11] Given that the improper handling of incriminating physical evidence can lead to criminal charges (including contempt of court) and/or disciplinary proceedings against a lawyer, this area therefore cries out for clarification. Indeed, the handling of such evidence is a prime example of the type of ethical problem that could benefit from a specific code of professional conduct with respect to defence functions.[12]

## B. RELATED RULES OF PROFESSIONAL CONDUCT

Broadly speaking, the various Canadian rules of professional conduct take one of two approaches to the incriminating physical-evidence problem. The first approach is to provide little or no express guidance in the rules. For instance, the CBA Code offers almost nothing in the way of useful advice. The closest the Code comes to commenting directly on the issue is the following portion of the chapter dealing with "The Lawyer As Advocate":

---

10    See, for example, R. Shadley & S. Costom, "Handling Physical Evidence: The Defence Lawyer's Dilemma" [1998] National Criminal Law Program; and A. MacDonald & J. Pink, "Murder, Silence and Physical Evidence: The Dilemma of Client Confidentiality" (1997) 2 Can. Crim. L. Rev. 111 at 113. See also *Murray*, above note 8 at 320–21.

11    See the discussion in section K(1), "Fruits and Instrumentalities of a Crime," in this chapter.

12    See the call for such a code by G. Arthur Martin, "The Role and Responsibility of the Defence Advocate" (1970) 12 Crim. L.Q. 376 at 392–93.

Chapter IX

2.  The lawyer must not, for example

. . .

(e) knowingly attempt to deceive or participate in the deception of a tribunal or influence the course of justice by offering false evidence, misstating facts or law, presenting or relying upon a false or deceptive affidavit, *suppressing what ought to be disclosed or otherwise assisting in any fraud, crime or illegal conduct.*[13]

Most provincial governing bodies follow the CBA Code's cryptic lead, with rules that leave practising lawyers largely in the dark as to how best to respond when confronted with the incriminating physical-evidence problem.[14] It has been aptly noted, in reference to the CBA Code's approach, that "the rule provides no guidance as to the nature of evidence that 'ought to be disclosed'. It is of small help either to counsel or to clients who may believe that both their secrets and their evidence are safe with their lawyers."[15]

The second approach to the incriminating physical-evidence problem is to adopt a rule of professional conduct that addresses the issue in a direct and thoughtful manner. In Canada, only the Alberta rules can currently be said to come close to this approach, stating:

Chapter 10

20. A lawyer must not counsel or participate in:

. . .

(c) the destruction of property having potential evidentiary value or the alteration of property so as to affect its evidentiary value; or

---

13  CBA Code, ch. IX,, comm. 2(e) (emphasis added).

14  See, for example, Ont. r. 4.01(2); N.S. ch. 14, Guiding Principle (e); and Que. s. 3.02.01(e). British Columbia has no comparable provision, but a similar sort of vague guidance can be found in ch. 1, r. 1(1); ch. 2, r. 1; and ch. 8, r. 1(b). The fact that Canadian rules of professional conduct typically provide little guidance on the incriminating physical evidence issue does not mean that governing bodies have given no thought to the subject. For instance, the Law Society of Upper Canada's bar admission course materials have for many years included a discussion on this topic: see S. Skurka & J. Stribopoulos, "Professional Responsibility in Criminal Practice" in Law Society of Upper Canada, *42nd Bar Admission Course, 2000, Criminal Procedure Reference Materials* (Toronto: Law Society of Upper Canada, 2000) c. 1 at §4.5.

15  *Murray*, above note 8 at 320–21 (in the context of former Ont. r. 10, comm. 2(e), which essentially mimics CBA Code ch. IX, comm. 2(e)).

(d) the concealment of property having potential evidentiary value in a criminal proceeding.[16]

The Alberta rules also provide a commentary that elaborates on these guidelines as follows:

> Paragraph (c) is not intended to interfere with the testing of evidence as contemplated by the Rules of Court.
>
> Paragraph (d) applies to criminal matters due to the danger of obstruction of justice if evidence in a criminal matter is withheld. While a lawyer has no obligation to disclose the mere existence of such evidence, it would be unethical to accept possession of it and then conceal or destroy it. The lawyer must therefore advise someone wishing to deliver potential evidence that, if possession is accepted by the lawyer, it will be necessary to turn the evidence over to appropriate authorities (unless it consists of communications or documents that are privileged). When surrendering criminal evidence, however, a lawyer must protect confidentiality attaching to the circumstances in which the material was acquired, which may require that the lawyer act anonymously or through a third party.[17]

Ontario will soon join Alberta in providing guidelines for lawyers who receive physical evidence of a client crime, or are presented with the opportunity to do so. In late 2000, in the aftermath of the *Murray* decision, the Law Society of Upper Canada struck a special committee to study the issue and prepare a rule and commentary for inclusion in the Rules of Professional Conduct. The Committee has reported to Convocation, offering a draft rule and extensive explanatory commentary for consultation purposes.[18] Given that the Committee's proposals may well undergo significant revision, we will defer any further discussion in this chapter.[19]

Examples of even more detailed and considered approaches to the incriminating physical-evidence problem can be seen in the United States, where some highly respected bodies have adopted more adventurous guidelines. The American Law Institute's Third Restatement provides:

---

16   Alta. ch. 10, r. 20.

17   Alta. ch. 10, r. 20, comm. 20.

18   Law Society of Upper Canada, *Report to Convocation, Special Committee on Lawyer's Duties with Respect to Physical Evidence Relevant to a Crime* (Toronto: Law Society of Upper Canada, 2001) [*Special Committee*].

19   An early draft of this chapter was provided to the Committee and was used as the basis for some of the text in the proposed rule and commentary: see *Special Committee*, above note 18 at para. 7.

### §119 Physical Evidence of a Client Crime

With respect to physical evidence of a client crime, a lawyer:
(1) may, when reasonably necessary for purposes of the representation, take possession of the evidence and retain it for the time reasonably necessary to examine it and subject it to tests that do not alter or destroy material characteristics of the evidence; but
(2) following possession under Subsection (1), the lawyer must notify prosecuting authorities of the lawyer's possession of the evidence or turn the evidence over to them.[20]

The Third Restatement is sceptical of allowing a lawyer to return the evidence to the site from which it was originally taken, even if this step can be managed without destroying or altering material characteristics of the evidence. The text of the applicable rule does not acknowledge this option, while the associated commentary suggests that returning the evidence to the site will often result in its destruction or material alteration.[21]

The guidelines found in the Third Restatement, which appear to provide counsel with somewhat greater leeway than do the Alberta rules, are nonetheless more cautious than those found in the ABA Standards for Criminal Justice.[22] Defense Standard 4-4.6 is even more detailed and aggressive in approaching the issue:

### Standard 4-4.6 Physical Evidence

(a) Defense counsel who receives a physical item under circumstances implicating a client in criminal conduct should disclose the location of or should deliver that item to law enforcement authorities only: (1) if required by law or court order, or (2) as provided in paragraph (d).
(b) Unless required to disclose, defense counsel should return the item to the source from whom defense counsel received it, except as provided in paragraph (c) and (d). In returning the item to the source, defense counsel should advise the source of the legal consequences pertaining to possession or destruction of the item. Defense counsel should also prepare a written record of these events for his or her file, but should not give the source a copy of such record.

---

20  Third Restatement §119(1).
21  See Third Restatement §119(1) & comm. "c."
22  ABA Defense Standard 4-4.6. It is worth noting that the ABA Model Rules address the physical evidence issue only obliquely, much in the manner of the CBA Code: see ABA Rule 3.4(a).

(c) Defense counsel may receive the item for a reasonable period of time during which defense counsel: (1) intends to return it to the owner; (2) reasonably fears that return of the item to the source will result in destruction of the item; (3) reasonably fears that return of the item to the source will result in physical harm to anyone; (4) intends to test, examine, inspect, or use the item in any way as part of defense counsel's representation of the client; or (5) cannot return it to the source. If defense counsel tests or examines the item, he or she should thereafter return it to the source unless there is reason to believe that the evidence might be altered or destroyed or used to harm another or return is otherwise impossible. If defense counsel retains the item, he or she should retain it in his or her law office in a manner that does not impede the lawful ability of law enforcement authorities to obtain the item.

(d) If the item received is contraband, i.e., an item possession of which is in and of itself a crime such as narcotics, defense counsel may suggest that the client destroy it where there is no pending case or investigation relating to this evidence and where such destruction is clearly not in violation of any criminal statute. If such destruction is not permitted by law or if in defense counsel's judgment he or she cannot retain the item, whether or not it is contraband, in a way that does not pose an unreasonable risk of physical harm to anyone, defense counsel should disclose the location of or should deliver the item to law enforcement authorities.

(e) If defense counsel discloses the location of or delivers the item to law enforcement authorities under paragraphs (a) or (d), or to a third party under paragraph (c)(1), he or she should do so in the way best designed to protect the client's interests.[23]

Of particular interest, Defense Standard 4-4.6 exhibits minimal compunction about allowing counsel to return the item to the originating source, and condones counsel advising the client to destroy contraband evidence where there is no pending case/investigation and the destruction is clearly not in violation of any criminal statute.[24]

---

23    ABA Defense Standard 4-4.6.

24    ABA Defense Standard 4-4.6(d). This approach is looked at askance by the commentary to the Third Restatement §119, Reporter's Note (comm. "c"), we believe with good reason: see the discussion in section E(4), "Illegal Items," in this chapter, as well as note 42, below.

# C. BASIC ETHICAL PRINCIPLES: LOYALTY/CONFIDENTIALITY AND THE ADMINISTRATION OF JUSTICE

Determining the proper response to the incriminating physical-evidence problem requires an appreciation of several fundamental ethical obligations owed by lawyers to the client and court. These obligations aid us in navigating the complicated common law, statutory, and constitutional rules and principles that bear upon the problem.

## 1) Loyalty and Confidentiality

The lawyer faced with the option of taking possession of physical evidence of a client crime owes certain duties to the client. Notably, the client is owed a duty of loyalty, as well as the closely associated duty of confidentiality.[25] These duties are fundamental to counsel's role in the criminal justice system, their purpose being, among other things, to encourage individuals to seek legal advice and to be candid with their legal advisor (arguably resulting in the best possible legal representation). For this reason, the client's right to confidentiality has been afforded constitutional status and is reflected in the evidentiary rule of legal-professional privilege.[26] Taking any action that is against the client's interest with respect to the subject matter of the retainer, or that serves to reveal confidential information against the client's wishes, is *prima facie* unethical. Counsel who is faced with incriminating physical evidence of a client crime must therefore determine whether, and how, the obligations of loyalty and confidentiality are engaged.

## 2) Administration of Justice

While the lawyer's duties of loyalty and confidentiality are integral to providing a client with the best possible defence, these ethical duties are not absolute and inviolable. We have already seen instances where the duties are tempered by reason of important competing societal

---

25  For a fuller discussion of confidentiality and loyalty, see chapter 4.

26  See section D, "Comparison with Legal-Professional Privilege," and F, "Constitutional Principle," in chapter 4. The role of the privilege in relation to incriminating physical evidence is discussed at various points in this chapter, including section F, "Legal-Professional Privilege."

interests.[27] Thus, confidential information may be released to the authorities where necessary to prevent anticipated serious bodily harm, the justification being that the value of avoiding future harm outweighs the need for confidentiality.[28] Another policy concern that sometimes operates to modify or prevent the application of the duties of loyalty and confidentiality is the need to prevent the subversion of the administration of justice.[29] Counsel cannot therefore act in a manner that violates the law, whether statutory or in the form of a court order. Nor can a lawyer actively impede a police investigation.[30] The destruction or concealment of incriminating physical evidence certainly implicates these policy concerns. The question becomes, where is the line to be drawn between counsel's duty to the administration of justice and his or her duties to the client?

# D. LACK OF A DEFENCE-DISCLOSURE OBLIGATION AND THE PRINCIPLE AGAINST SELF-INCRIMINATION

The ethical duties of loyalty and confidentiality can be seen in conjunction with the traditional view that an accused has no obligation to disclose the nature of his or her defence, including the evidence to be relied upon at trial, to the police or the Crown.[31] This traditional view

---

27   See generally chapter 5.

28   *Ibid.* at section G, "Future Harm or Public Safety."

29   In this regard, and using the CBA Code as a general guide, the relevant rules of professional conduct include Chapter I ("the lawyer must discharge with integrity all duties owed to clients, the court, other members of the profession and the public"); Chapter IX (the lawyer must "represent the client resolutely, honourably and within the limits of the law"); and Chapter XIII ("the lawyer should encourage public respect for and try to improve the administration of justice").

30   See the discussion of the *Criminal Code*, R.S.C. 1985, c. C-46 provisions found below in section E, "Relevant *Criminal Code* Provisions," in this chapter.

31   See D. Watt, *Watt's Manual of Criminal Evidence* (Toronto: Carswell, 2000) at §25.01; and P. McWilliams, *Canadian Criminal Evidence*, 3d ed. (Aurora: Canada Law Book, 1999) at §28:10300. A leading case that stands for the general proposition that the defence does not have any disclosure obligation is *R. v. Peruta* (1992), 78 C.C.C. (3d) 350 (Que. C.A.), leave to appeal to S.C.C. refused (1993), 81 C.C.C. (3d) vi (S.C.C.) [*Peruta*]. See also *R. v. Stinchcombe* (1991), 68 C.C.C. (3d) 1 at 7 (S.C.C.) [*Stinchcombe*]; *R. v. P.(M.B.)* (1994), 89 C.C.C. (3d) 289 at 304–05 (S.C.C.) [*P.(M.B.)*]; and *R. v. Stone* (1997), 113 C.C.C. (3d)

represents the current law in Canada.[32] There are commentators who argue for the development of a carefully crafted defence-disclosure obligation, in essence constituting an "accelerated" disclosure of evidence that would in any case be revealed by the defence during the course of the trial.[33] Even if adopted by the courts, however, an "accelerated" disclosure obligation would probably not operate to cover incriminating physical evidence. Rather, evidence that is harmful to the defence would probably not fit within the parameters of the disclosure obligation envisaged by these commentators, for in most instances such evidence would not be introduced by the defence at trial.

It is also worth mentioning that a number of limited exceptions to the general rule against a defence-disclosure obligation are already well established. For instance, failure to make timely disclosure of an alibi may justify an adverse inference against the accused,[34] as may an accused's refusal to be examined by a prosecution expert after having raised a defence of mental disorder.[35] Also, some defence information may be revealed at a pre-trial conference or, of necessity, be provided in the form of notice of a *Charter* application,[36] or certain *Criminal Code* applications,[37] or a notice of intention to adduce records.[38] However, apart from these *ad hoc* exceptions, the basic principle against defence disclosure remains fairly firm in Canada.

The reasons often advanced for rejecting a general defence-disclosure obligation include the disparate resources of the Crown/police and accused and the more purely adversarial role accorded the defence

---

158 at 170–73 (B.C.C.A.), aff'd in part (1999), 134 C.C.C. (3d) 353 at 402–03 (S.C.C.).

32   See the sources cited at note 31, above.

33   See, for example, D. Tanovich & L. Crocker, "Dancing with Stinchcombe's Ghost: A Modest Proposal for Reciprocal Defence Disclosure" (1994) 26 C.R. (4th) 333.

34   See, for example, *R. v. Cleghorn* (1995), 100 C.C.C. (3d) 393 (S.C.C.).

35   See, for example, *R. v. Stevenson* (1990), 58 C.C.C. (3d) 464 (Ont. C.A.).

36   See, for example, *R. v. Charlebois* (2000), 148 C.C.C. (3d) 449 (S.C.C.); and *R. v. Kutynec* (1992), 70 C.C.C. (3d) 289 (Ont. C.A.).

37   See, for example, ss. 276 & 278.2 of the *Criminal Code*, above note 30, respectively relating to cross-examination of a complainant on sexual matters and production of a complainant's private records.

38   See, for example, s. 657.3(1) of the *Criminal Code*, *ibid.*, regarding expert reports, and ss. 26, 29, & 30 of the *Canada Evidence Act*, R.S.C. 1985, ch. C-5 regarding public, banking, and business records.

by our criminal justice system.[39] Related constitutional principles also support the absence of a defence-disclosure obligation. The right to silence and presumption of innocence, both examples of the overarching principle against self-incrimination, are important *Charter* guarantees that protect an accused's ability not to reveal information to the police or the Crown.[40] In many instances, defence counsel who keeps a client's confidences secret, and refuses to provide information to the police or prosecutor, is therefore acting in furtherance of the client's constitutional rights.

# E.  RELEVANT *CRIMINAL CODE* PROVISIONS

There are a number of *Criminal Code* provisions that bear upon the incriminating physical-evidence problem. Before looking at several of these provisions, and at the risk of stating the obvious, let us emphasize that counsel should never act so as to violate the criminal law. Such action exposes a lawyer to criminal prosecution, and governing bodies invariably prohibit members from acting illegally in the representation of a client.[41]

**Recommendation:**    The overriding guideline for counsel is that physical evidence should never be handled in a manner that infringes the *Criminal Code*, regardless of whether there exists an express prohibition on taking such action under the governing body's ethical rules.[42] To the extent that the criminal law is unclear, counsel should err on

---

39  See for example, *Stinchcombe*, above note 31 at 7; and *P.(M.B.)*, above note 31 at 304–05.

40  Broadly speaking, the principle against self-incrimination prohibits state action that forces an individual to furnish evidence against him or herself in a proceeding in which the State and individual are adversaries: see, for example, *R. v. Jones* (1994), 89 C.C.C. (3d) 353 at 367 (S.C.C.); *R. v. S.(R.J.)* (1995), 96 C.C.C. (3d) 1 at 25 (S.C.C.); and *R. v. Fitzpatrick* (1995), 102 C.C.C. (3d) 144 at 158 (S.C.C.). The link between this principle and more specific *Charter* guarantees, including the right to silence and presumption of innocence, is made in *Jones, S.(R.J.)* and *P.(M.B.)*, above note 39.

41  See, for example, the ethical rules found in the CBA Code, set out in note 29, above.

42  Or even, for that matter, an apparent acceptance of such conduct by the ethical rules. An illustration of the need to treat the criminal law as governing can be seen in the Third Restatement, insofar as the Reporter's Note warns that the ethical standard concerning contraband found in ABA Defense Standard 4-4.6 may conflict with criminal and civil statutes: see Third Restatement §119, Reporter's Note (comm. "c").

the side of caution and seek if at all possible to resolve the uncertainty without putting himself or herself at risk of prosecution.

It is also worth noting that *Criminal Code* provisions do not always provide clear-cut answers to the many issues thrown up by the incriminating physical-evidence problem. For one thing, these provisions typically make no special mention of the role of defence counsel. Yet a lawyer who acts in the *legitimate* furtherance of a client's constitutional rights presumably cannot be prosecuted for breaking the criminal law. Thus, the lawyer who advises his or her client not to provide a statement to investigating officers, or who destroys a privileged document, has not obstructed justice. To a certain extent, courts must take account of ethical principles and practices, as well as the accused's constitutional protections, in interpreting *Criminal Code* provisions.[43]

## 1) Possession of Property Obtained by Crime and Laundering the Proceeds of Crime

The *Criminal Code* prohibits the possession of any property when it is known that all or part of the property was obtained by or derived directly or indirectly from the commission of an indictable offence.[44] It is also a criminal offence to deal with any property, by any means, with the intent to conceal or convert that property, when it is known or believed that the property was obtained by or derived directly or indirectly from the commission of certain specified crimes.[45] Both offences provide for an exception where a peace officer, or person acting under his or her direction, takes steps for the purposes of an investigation or otherwise in the execution of the officer's duties.[46]

Neither the offence of possession of property obtained by crime nor laundering the proceeds of crime contains an exception for a lawyer who otherwise commits the offence in the course of representing a client.[47] Consequently, it is clear that counsel is never justified in

---

43  See, for example, *Murray*, above note 8 at 309.

44  For the exact scope of the prohibition see s. 354 of the *Criminal Code*, above note 30.

45  For the exact scope of the prohibition, including the applicable specified crimes, see ss. 462.3 & 462.31 of the *Criminal Code, ibid.* See also s. 341 of the *Code*, which makes it an offence to take, obtain, remove, or conceal anything for a fraudulent purpose.

46  See ss. 354(4) & 462.31(3) of *Criminal Code, ibid.*

47  See, for example, *United States v. Scruggs*, 549 F.2d 1097 (6th Cir. 1977), cert. denied 434 U.S. 824 (1977) [*Scruggs*] (counsel takes stolen money as a retainer). A rare example of a law that exempts lawyers who are acting in the

dealing with a client's property, where the property is proceeds of crime and counsel acts for the purpose of concealing or converting the property (or, indeed, for most any other purpose). Counsel would commit a criminal act by accepting a retainer when he or she knew that the money came from a bank robbery, or by placing stolen jewellery in a safety deposit box for the purpose of preventing its discovery by police. In these instances, the duty of confidentiality simply does not apply.

## 2) Obstructing Justice

It is a crime wilfully to attempt in any manner to obstruct, pervert or defeat the course of justice.[48] The phrase "course of justice" includes, but is not restricted to, the investigatory phase of a matter, and no prosecution need yet have been commenced.[49] It has been held that this offence encompasses any improper interference with the functioning of any part of the justice system.[50]

In *R. v. Murray*, the facts of which are set out above, the court held that counsel's action in concealing the videotapes had the tendency to obstruct justice in a number of respects. Specifically:

1. The tapes were secreted by the accused, putting them beyond the reach of the police who had failed to locate them, hence tending to obstruct the police in their duty to investigate the murders.[51]
2. The Crown's ability to conduct its case was hampered throughout by the absence of the videotapes, given that the tapes formed an integral part of the crime and were exceptionally detrimental to the defence.[52] Examples given of this negative impact on the prosecu-

---

legitimate preparation of a client's defence is seen in *Clark v. State*, 261 S.W.2d 339 at 347 (Tex. Crim. App. 1953) [*Clark*].

48   See ss. 139(1) & (2) of the *Criminal Code*, above note 30.

49   See *R v. Wijesinha* (1995), 100 C.C.C. (3d) 410 (S.C.C.), which holds that s. 139(2) of the *Criminal Code* applies to investigations carried out with a view to determine whether or not disciplinary proceedings should be taken by a professional governing body.

50   *Murray*, above note 8 at 312. See also leading cases such as *R. v. May* (1984), 13 C.C.C. (3d) 257 (Ont. C.A.), leave to appeal to S.C.C. refused [1984] 2 S.C.R. viii; and *R. v. Spezzano* (1977), 34 C.C.C. (2d) 87 (Ont. C.A.). *May*, *ibid.* at 260, speaks of "an act which has a tendency to pervert or obstruct the course of justice, and which is done for that purpose."

51   *Murray*, above note 8 at 312.

52   *Ibid.*

tion included the Crown's resolution offer to Bernardo and the deal struck with Homolka.[53]

3. Concealing the tapes also influenced the way new defence counsel approached the conduct of the case.[54]
4. Finally, hiding the videotapes had the potential to deprive the jury of admissible evidence.[55]

The court in *Murray* concluded that "[c]oncealment of the tapes had the potential to infect all aspects of the criminal justice system."[56] Counsel was nonetheless acquitted on the basis that he lacked the requisite *mens rea* by virtue of the general uncertainty surrounding the legality of temporarily concealing evidence.[57] Following the decision in *Murray*, however, any such uncertainty has dissipated. There can be little doubt that counsel who suppresses or conceals evidence so as improperly to interfere with the functioning of the justice system has committed an offence. Along the same lines, it would be an offence even temporarily to remove evidence of a crime for the purpose of preventing seizure by the police.[58] So, too, would an act of destruction of incriminating physical evidence contravene the law.[59]

---

53  *Ibid.*

54  *Ibid.*

55  *Ibid.*

56  *Ibid.* at 313.

57  For a strong argument that this result amounts to an unsupportable "mistake of law" defence, see L. Vandervort, "Mistake of Law and Obstruction of Justice: A 'Bad Excuse' . . . Even for a Lawyer" (2001) 50 U.N.B.L.J. 171. See also D. Stuart, "Annotation: *R. v. Murray*" (2000) 34 C.R. (5th) 290 at 292.

58  See, for example, *R. v. Akrofi* (1997), 113 C.C.C. (3d) 201 (Ont. C.A.) (a pawnbroker obstructed justice by disposing of stolen property after being told not to do so by the police); and *R. v. Lajoie* (1989), 47 C.C.C. (3d) 380 (Que. C.A.) (hiding a gun from the police constituted obstruction of justice). See also *Commonwealth v. Stenhach*, 514 A.2d 114 (Pa. Super. 1986), appeal denied 534 A.2d 769 (1987) [*Stenhach*] (lawyers hid a stock from the rifle used in a shooting, though the court ruled that the legislation used to prosecute the lawyers was impermissibly broad and vague).

59  See, for example, *R. v. Andruszko* (1978), 44 C.C.C. (2d) 382 (Ont. C.A.) (the accused was convicted of obstructing a peace officer by eating marijuana that was sought after by the police); and *R. v. Zeck* (1980), 53 C.C.C. (2d) 551 (Ont. C.A.) (the accused was convicted of removing and destroying parking tickets that had been placed on parked cars). Compare *R. v. Davis* (1996), 32 W.C.B. (2d) 423 (Ont. Prov. Div.) (Crown failed to prove that substance swallowed was contraband).

## 3) Being an Accessory After the Fact

The crime of accessory after the fact is made out where an accused is found to have known that a person was party to an offence and provided assistance for the purpose of enabling that person to escape justice.[60] Counsel therefore cannot deal with physical evidence in a manner intended to provide such assistance to the client. Conduct that has been held to constitute the crime of accessory after the fact (though not involving lawyers) includes:[61] obtaining and wetting paper in order that the murderer could wipe blood from the murder weapon and a jacket,[62] cleaning up blood and hiding the weapon,[63] disposing of clothing worn by an individual during a crime,[64] assisting in the disposal or concealment of a body,[65] and concealing or altering evidence.[66]

**Example:** A client tells counsel that he has committed an armed robbery, and is worried that the police consider him to be a prime suspect. He advises counsel that the weapon used in the robbery, as well as the proceeds, are hidden in his safety-deposit box. In order to avoid the possibility that the police will obtain a search warrant and find the items, the client asks counsel to take possession of the weapon and cash. Counsel must refuse this request. Being a party to the removal of the items from the client's safety-deposit box for the purpose of avoiding police detection would constitute the criminal offences of possession of the proceeds of crime, laundering the proceeds of crime, obstruction of justice, and accessory after the fact.[67]

---

60   See s. 23 of the *Criminal Code*, above note 30 (see also s. 463 of the *Code, ibid.*). For authority that the word "escape" as found in the provision should be read as "escape justice," see *R. v. Vinette* (1974), 19 C.C.C. (2d) 1 at 7 (S.C.C.) [*Vinette*].

61   The following list of examples is largely taken from C. Hill, "Accessory After the Fact" [1993] National Criminal Law Program at 7–8.

62   See *R. v. Gratton* (1971), 5 C.C.C. (2d) 150 (N.B.S.C.(A.D.)).

63   *R. v. Knuff* (1980), 52 C.C.C. (2d) 523 (Alta. C.A.).

64   *R. v. McVay* (1982), 66 C.C.C. (2d) 512 (Ont. C.A.); and *R. v. Waterfield* (1974), 18 C.C.C. (2d) 140 (Ont. C.A.).

65   *Vinette*, above note 60; and *R. v. George* (1934) 63 C.C.C. 225 (B.C.C.A.).

66   See *R. v. Levy* (1912), 7 Cr. App. R. 61 (C.C.A.).

67   This example is based on the facts in *In re Ryder*, 381 F.2d 713 (4th Cir. 1967) [*Ryder*], where counsel was disciplined for transferring stolen money and a gun from the client's safety-deposit box to his own. See also *Clark*, above note 47 (the court offered the view that a lawyer was an accessory by virtue of advising a client how to destroy or dispose of a murder weapon), and *State ex rel. Oklahoma Bar Ass'n v. Harlton*, 669 P.2d 774 (Okla. 1983) (counsel was an accessory after the fact insofar as he concealed a weapon with the aim of foiling the investigation and prosecution of his client).

# 4) Illegal Items

Counsel should scrupulously avoid taking possession of an item that is itself illegal, such as a controlled drug or prohibited weapon.[68] Counsel's possession of an illegal substance is not any less illegal because he or she is a lawyer. The only exception occurs if an illegal item is forced upon counsel, who continues with possession for the sole purpose of delivering the item to the authorities.[69] In any event, the lawyer who finds himself or herself in the unfortunate position of possessing a contraband item may be unable to rely upon legal-professional privilege to protect the client from exposure.[70]

Is it also permissible for counsel who is forced to take possession of a contraband item to destroy the item, or to advise the client to do so? We have already seen that ABA Defense Standard 4-4.6 permits counsel to advise a client to destroy an illegal item in certain limited circumstances, in particular where there is no pending case or investigation relating to the evidence.[71] Such action is extremely risky, however, even within the narrow confines contemplated by Defense Standard 4-4.6. The mere fact that the item has been foisted upon the unwilling lawyer should alert counsel to the real possibility that the police are investigating related matters. Destruction of the item may lead to the problems discussed below in section G(1). We are thus inclined to reject any notion that counsel can destroy (or advise the destruction of) contraband evidence.

# 5) Improper Advice Constituting a Criminal Offence

The wrong advice to a client can lead to criminal charges being laid against a defence lawyer, even where the lawyer never takes possession or control of the incriminating physical evidence. Encouraging a client

---

68 Aside from the well-known *Criminal Code* provisions that prohibit possession of such items, s. 104(1) of the *Code*, above note 30, provides that everyone commits an offence who, on finding a prohibited weapon, restricted weapon, or firearm that he or she has reasonable grounds to believe has been lost or abandoned, does not with reasonable dispatch deliver the item or report its finding to the proper authorities.

69 Presumably, counsel who takes possession in such circumstances can argue a lack of intent: see J. Hall, *Professional Responsibility of the Criminal Lawyer*, 2d ed. (New York: Clark Boardman Callaghan, 1996) at §23.12.

70 Regarding the possible non-applicability of privilege, see the discussion below at note 89 and accompanying text.

71 See the text accompanying note 23.

to destroy such evidence could make counsel a party to an offence or a member of a conspiracy.[72]

**Example:** X shoots and kills his ex-wife, after which he calls a lawyer. X tells the lawyer that he still has the gun and asks for advice as to what he should do. The lawyer tells X to get rid of the weapon immediately. This advice constitutes a criminal offence, and it does not matter that the lawyer at no time handled or saw the gun.[73]

# F.  LEGAL-PROFESSIONAL PRIVILEGE

Closely connected with the ethical duty of confidentiality is the rule of evidence concerning legal-professional privilege.[74] This privilege attaches to certain confidential communications that either pass between lawyer and client as part of the professional relationship or pass between the lawyer or client and third parties for the dominant purpose of litigation.[75] The importance of legal-professional privilege has resulted in it being accorded constitutional status by Canadian courts.[76] Moreover, the privilege is integral to several discrete constitutional rights, including the right to counsel, the right to the effective assistance of counsel, the privilege against self-incrimination, and the presumption of innocence.[77]

Given that the concept of confidentiality is central to legal-professional privilege, the scenario of incriminating physical evidence usually requires that counsel assess whether the evidentiary rule applies. In making such an assessment, however, counsel must always keep in mind that the ethical duty of confidentiality is not coterminous with the evidentiary rule of privilege.[78] The ethical obligation is broader, applying to prevent the revelation of information even where there is no question of any attempt to compel disclosure by legal process. The

---

72  See the *Criminal Code*, above note 30, s. 21 (aiding and abetting); s. 22 (counselling); s. 464 (counselling an offence that is not committed); and s. 465(1)(c) (conspiracy). Compare the controversial ABA Defense Standard 4-4.6(d), discussed in section E(4), "Illegal Items," in this chapter, which gives counsel some latitude to advise that a contraband item be destroyed by the client.

73  See *Clark*, above note 47 at 347.

74  See the discussion in section D, "Comparison with Legal-Professional Privilege," in chapter 4.

75  *Ibid.*

76  See the discussion in section F, "Constitutional Principles," in chapter 4.

77  *Ibid.*

78  See section D, "Comparison with Legal-Professional Privilege," in chapter 4.

ethical duty of confidentiality may also apply to information that would not be subject to privilege, such as information provided by a client to his or her counsel in the presence of a third party.

Legal-professional privilege thus has a role to play in relation to the physical-evidence scenario, albeit a carefully circumscribed one. Let us now turn to consider some of the ways in which the privilege does or does not, according to the circumstances bear upon the issue.

## 1) Client-lawyer Communications versus Pre-existing Physical Evidence

We can begin by dispensing with the idea that an item becomes privileged merely because it is placed in a lawyer's possession. If such were the case, clients could employ counsel as a clearing house for pre-existing incriminating evidence, thereby insulating the evidence from use of any sort by the prosecution and providing a blanket justification for counsel keeping the evidence.[79] Such evidence is not covered by legal-professional privilege because the privilege extends only to the protection of communications exchanged as part of the professional relationship.[80] The rifle in *Coffin*, or the videotapes in *Murray*, are not communications made for the purpose of obtaining legal advice, and so do not attract the protection of privilege.[81]

**Example:** A client arrives unannounced at her lawyer's office. She tells counsel that the police are looking to arrest her in connection with a major drug deal that occurred earlier in the day. The client then pres-

---

79   See the sources cited in chapter 4, note 23.

80   Authority for the proposition that legal-professional privilege covers only communications is indisputable. A particularly apt example is provided by *R. v. Gosselin* (1903), 7 C.C.C. 139 (S.C.C.), where observations of bloodstained clothing were held not to be communications and hence not privileged. Granted, the line between communications and observations of fact is not always clear: see J. Sopinka, S. Lederman, & A. Bryant, *The Law of Evidence in Canada*, 2d ed. (Toronto: Butterworths, 1999) at §14.53. In our view, an observation may be so inextricably caught up in a legitimate client-lawyer communication so as to be encompassed by privilege: see also the discussion section F(2), "Communications and Observations Concerning Pre-existing Physical Evidence," in this chapter.

81   See especially *Murray*, above note 8 at 313–14, holding that the privilege does not apply. We do not read *Murray* as endorsing a simplistic distinction between a communication and physical evidence, meaning that a physical item created to facilitate client-lawyer communication can attract the privilege: see section F(3), "Physical Evidence Created as Part of a Client-Lawyer Communication," in this chapter.

ents counsel with a cellphone that she says was used to coordinate the drug deal, and believes to have been tapped. She also provides him with a debt list that connects her to individuals whom she strongly suspects have already been arrested. Counsel and the client proceed to have a lengthy meeting to discuss matters. Near the meeting's end, the police arrive at the law office with a search warrant for the cellphone and debt list (among other things). While counsel may well be obligated to claim privilege over these items, it is probable that a court would find the privilege to be inapplicable.

## 2) Communications and Observations Concerning Pre-existing Physical Evidence

What about observations made by counsel pertaining to physical evidence of the crime, as opposed to the physical evidence itself? Can the prosecution force a defence lawyer to testify as to how he or she acquired incriminating physical evidence, or the inculpatory communications that accompanied his or her reception of the item? Answering this question requires an examination of the circumstances of the particular case, to see whether the actions or facts observed by counsel can reasonably be viewed as part of a client-lawyer communication. Statements made by the client while handing over incriminating physical evidence are likely to be privileged. Similarly, observations made by the lawyer as the result of a communicative act are arguably privileged, for instance, where the client rolls up his sleeve to reveal a hidden scar or opens his desk drawer to reveal a gun.[82]

Sometimes, instead of receiving physical evidence that implicates the client in a crime, counsel will receive information from the client as to the location of inculpatory physical evidence. Such information, though pertaining to physical evidence that is not in itself privileged, is provided to counsel as part and parcel of a communication made in the course of the professional relationship. Privilege therefore applies to the communication.[83] Going further still, privilege should also cover information obtained by counsel as a direct result of a client's communication.[84] Both of these points are illustrated in the famous case of *People* v. *Belge*, also known as the Lake Pleasant Bodies Case.[85] There,

---

82    See J. Strong, ed., *McCormick on Evidence*, 5th ed. (St. Paul: West, 1999) at 358.

83    See, for example, *Peruta*, above note 31.

84    *Ibid.*

85    *People* v. *Belge*, 372 N.Y.S.2d 798 (Co. Ct. 1975), aff'd 376 N.Y.S.2d 771 (App. Div. 1975); aff'd 359 N.E.2d 377 (N.Y. 1976) [*Belge*].

a client charged with murder told his lawyers that he had killed two other victims, and divulged the location of the corpses. The lawyers went to the site and photographed the bodies, but did not disclose their information to the authorities until their client's testimony at trial.[86] Public indignation followed the realization that the lawyers had withheld their information, and one of the lawyers was charged with interfering with burial rights and failure to give notice of death without medical assistance. The charges were dismissed, however, on the grounds that the knowledge acquired by the lawyers and the observations made at the burial site all fell within the attorney-client privilege.[87]

## 3) Physical Evidence Created as Part of a Client-Lawyer Communication

Physical evidence that is created as part of a client-lawyer communication will ordinarily be treated as confidential and subject to legal-professional privilege. A common example would be a summary of pertinent events written by the client for the use of his or her lawyer. Such a document cannot be disassociated from the confidential communication itself.[88]

**Example:** X is charged with kidnapping and murdering a baby, whose body has not been found. The police unsuccessfully press X to direct them to the location of the body. Counsel meets with the client, who tells her that the baby is dead and draws a map outlining the location of the body. This map is a piece of incriminating physical evidence, yet it falls within the legal-professional privilege, given that it was created

---

86  The accused revealed the information during his testimony-in-chief, in an attempt to rely upon an insanity defence.

87  See *Belge*, above note 85. See also *Wemark v. State*, 602 N.W.2d 810 (Iowa 1999); and *Sanford v. State*, 21 S.W.3d 337 (Tex. App.-El Paso 2000) [*Sanford*], both cases where defence counsel improperly breached confidentiality by revealing the location of physical evidence to the authorities (or in *Wemark*, causing the client to do so).

88  See, for example, *Descôteaux v. Mierzwinski* (1982), 70 C.C.C. (2d) 385 (S.C.C.) [*Descôteaux*] where, but for application of the crime-fraud exception, the privilege would have applied to encompass a document created during the course of a client-lawyer interview. See also *British Columbia (Securities Commission) v. Branch* (1995), 97 C.C.C. (3d) 505 at 524–25 (S.C.C.) [*Branch*]; and *Susan Hosiery Ltd. v. M.N.R.*, [1969] 2 Ex. C.R. 27 (Ex. Ct.). For a discussion of copies created by a lawyer, see note 129, below, and accompanying text.

as part of a client-lawyer communication. Counsel has a duty to protect the privilege and cannot turn over the map to the police.[89]

This example represents a variation on the facts in *Henderson* v. *State*.[90] On the true facts of the case, police suspected that the baby might be alive. Counsel informed them of the existence of the map, and a grand jury was convened to issue a subpoena requiring the lawyer to produce the map. Ultimately, an appeals court ruled that the map must be disclosed because it fell within the future-harm exception to legal-professional privilege (*not* because the privilege was inapplicable to begin with). This same issue also arose in the *Belge* case referred to above, albeit without any future-harm implications, in relation to a document created by the client for use by his lawyers. The New York Bar Association's Ethics Committee concluded that the document merely memorialized in writing a client-lawyer communication, and as a result was privileged.[91]

## 4) Litigation Privilege

Litigation privilege encompasses communications that pass between the lawyer or client and third parties for the dominant purpose of existing or anticipated litigation, as well as materials prepared by counsel or an agent for the dominant purpose of such litigation.[92] Corporeal items will often be covered by litigation privilege, such as a lawyer's note to file outlining strategy for the case or a videotaped "KGB" witness statement prepared by a private investigator.[93]

---

89   The same reasoning should apply regarding the map and written instructions created by Paul Bernardo to assist his lawyer in locating the hidden videotapes, leaving aside any argument that privilege was perhaps lost or inapplicable owing to a criminal purpose: see *Murray*, above note 8 at 293–94.

90   962 S.W.2d 544 (Texas, 1997), cert. den. 119 S. Ct. 212 (1998), leave to amend petition ref'd 119 S.Ct. 437 (1998), also discussed in section G(5), "The Need for *Future* Harm," in chapter 5, in notes 114–15 and accompanying text.

91   See Opinion, N.Y. State Bar Ass'n. Comm. on Professional Ethics (1978) 50 N.Y. St. Bar. J. 259.

92   See *General Accident Assurance Co.* v. *Chrusz*, 45 O.R. (3d) 321 at 330–31 [*Chrusz*], arguing that "litigation privilege" is justified as a means of fostering the privacy needed for counsel and client to prepare for litigation in an adversarial setting.

93   See, for example, *R.* v. *Perron* (1990), 54 C.C.C. (3d) 108 (Que. C.A.); *Peruta*, above note 31; *Smith* v. *Jones* (1999), 132 C.C.C. (3d) 225 at 231–33 [*Smith*] per Major J.; and Third Restatement §119 comment "a." The "KGB" procedure is described in *R.* v. *B.(K.G.)* (1993), 79 C.C.C. (3d) 257 (S.C.C.).

## 5) The Crime-fraud and Other Exceptions to Legal-professional Privilege

Where a client asks counsel to handle physical evidence in a manner that would constitute a criminal offence, legal-professional privilege does not apply. This result is dictated by the crime-fraud exception to the privilege, which applies to communications that are in themselves criminal or are made with the purpose of obtaining legal advice to facilitate the commission of a crime.[94] An important caveat, however, is that the crime-fraud exception applies only if the client knew or should have known that the intended conduct was unlawful.[95] Thus, good-faith consultations with a lawyer for the purpose of finding out whether a proposed action is legal will not run afoul of the crime-fraud exception. Furthermore, privilege will not be lost *vis-à-vis* client-lawyer communications where the lawyer unilaterally acts in a criminal fashion, without the knowledge or tacit support of the client. To hold otherwise would be to punish the client unfairly for the wrongs of the lawyer, and to lose sight of the fact that the privilege is the client's to waive or lose (not the lawyer's).

**Example I:** X is charged with murder, the allegation being that he shot the victim to death using .380 calibre bullets. While in pre-trial custody, X asks a lawyer to meet him at the jail. X reveals that the .380 calibre pistol used in the killing is hidden beneath the bed in his apartment, and insists that counsel help to retrieve and dispose of the weapon. Counsel explains that such steps would constitute a criminal offence, but X persists in his request. The interview ends with the lawyer unable to dissuade X, and X adamant that he will find someone else to help execute his plan respecting the gun. Given these facts, the communications between X and the lawyer are likely not privileged, for X has knowingly communicated with the lawyer for a criminal purpose.[96]

**Example II:** A lawyer receives a call from an old client. The client tells her that he has some stolen property and wishes to hand over the item to the police without risking criminal charges. He has no reason to believe that he is a suspect in regards to the property in question. The lawyer agrees to aid in the transfer of the property, and accordingly

---

94   See section 1(1), "The Crime-Fraud Exception to Legal Professional Privilege," in chapter 5.

95   See *R. v. Campbell* (1999), 133 C.C.C. (3d) 257 at 292–95 (S.C.C.).

96   See *State v. Taylor*, 502 So. 2d 537 at 539 (La. 1987) [*Taylor*]; and *Clark*, above note 47 at 346–47.

receives the item from the client. She then delivers the item to the police without revealing her client's name. It transpires that the client later becomes a suspect, and is charged, in connection with a break and enter and possessing the property in question. The Crown subpoenas the lawyer and seeks to learn the identity of her client. Given that possession of the property was illegal, there is an argument that the lawyer's actions constitute a crime and privilege therefore does not apply.[97]

Other exceptions may apply to render legal-professional privilege inapplicable. The public-safety exception could apply to displace the privilege where the client-lawyer communication leads to a reasonable fear on the part of counsel that disclosure is necessary to prevent serious bodily harm or death.[98] Another exception that might apply is the innocence-at-stake exception, which would operate to set aside the privilege where required in order to ensure the full answer and defence of a third party charged with a crime.[99]

## G. BEYOND THE PRIVILEGE: HANDLING INCRIMINATING PHYSICAL EVIDENCE

We have seen that the scope of legal-professional privilege rarely extends to encompass physical evidence. But having made this determination, the question remains as to whether counsel can alter, remove, keep, or otherwise handle such evidence. Let us consider the *Murray* case discussed above, where the lawyer was instructed by his client to retrieve and hold videotapes of the crimes. The lawyer's actions in taking possession of the videotapes did not bring these physical items within the protective ambit of legal-professional privilege. Simply put, the videotapes did not constitute a communication

---

97   See *Hughes* v. *Meade*, 453 S.W.2d 538 (Ky. 1970), where on similar facts attorney-client privilege was held not to apply. The court found that delivering the stolen property to the police was not an act in the professional capacity of the lawyer. This position should not, in our view, be extended to instances where possession of the property to be delivered is *not* in itself illegal. Moreover, the court's reasoning is open to the valid criticism that the scope of the legal-professional relationship is being too narrowly defined.

98   See *Smith*, above note 93 discussed extensively in section G(2), "The Decision in *Smith* v. *Jones*," in chapter 5.

99   See *R.* v. *McClure* (2001), 151 C.C.C. (3d) 321 (S.C.C.), as well as the discussion in section H(8), "Duty Survives Death of Client," in chapter 4.

between client and lawyer for the purpose of obtaining legal advice. Consequently, in the face of a valid search warrant or subpoena, the lawyer would have been forced to relinquish the tapes.

Yet, just because counsel cannot use the rules of evidence to block the authorities from taking possession of incriminating physical evidence, it does not necessarily follow that the duty of confidentiality owed to a client has no application.[100] It is indisputable, for instance, that counsel's obligation of confidentiality prevents him or her from revealing information concerning the items to third parties such as friends and family. But do the duties of loyalty and confidentiality, in conjunction with the duty to provide competent representation, permit counsel to handle the evidence physically? The answer depends upon the particular facts of each case, including counsel's purpose and manner in handling the evidence. Some factual scenarios are susceptible to a reasonably uncontentious analysis, while others present more difficulty.

## 1) Counsel Cannot Destroy Incriminating Physical Evidence

There is no doubt that a lawyer is prohibited both ethically and legally from destroying incriminating physical evidence. We have seen that such action would constitute a criminal offence and would also violate the rules of professional conduct.[101]

## 2) Counsel Cannot Conceal Incriminating Physical Evidence in Order to Avoid Detection by the Authorities

Counsel cannot be a depository for incriminating physical evidence that the client seeks to hide from the authorities. Taking possession of incriminating physical evidence in order to impair the authorities' accessibility to the item or items in any pending investigation or criminal case is illegal and unethical.[102] Moreover, counsel cannot take steps to aid in the concealment of incriminating evidence, even where

---

100 See section D, "Comparison With Legal-Professional Privilege," in chapter 4.

101 See sections B, C, and F, in this chapter. In support, see also *State ex rel. Sowers v. Olwell*, 394 P.2d 681 (Wash. 1964) [*Olwell*]; *Stenhach*, above note 58 at 123; and Skurka & Stribopoulos, above note 14 at §4.5.

102 See the authorities cited in note 101, above. See also *Murray*, above note 8 at 315.

such steps do not involve taking possession of the evidence.[103] For instance, a lawyer cannot retain a third party to seek out, remove, and hide incriminating evidence.

## 3) Counsel Should Not Take Possession of Illegal Evidence

To recap the discussion in section F(4), a lawyer should never voluntarily take possession of evidence that is in itself illegal.[104] If counsel cannot avoid taking possession of illegal evidence, he or she should promptly arrange to deliver the evidence to the police in a manner that protects the client's identity from being disclosed.[105]

## 4) Counsel Should Not Interfere with the Authenticity of Incriminating Physical Evidence

Counsel cannot handle an item so as to alter its evidential value, for instance, by wiping a client's fingerprints from the surface of a murder weapon. To do so is akin to destroying an aspect of the evidence. Going further still, it has been argued that counsel should not act so as to deprive the prosecution of the opportunity to observe the evidence in its original condition or location, where to do so might impede the prosecution's case. This position is examined in the well-known California case of *People* v. *Meredith*.[106] There, the client was charged with first-degree murder and robbery. He informed his initial counsel that the victim's wallet was in a trash can behind his home. This counsel retained a private investigator to find and retrieve the wallet, which was then examined and provided to the authorities. At trial, the prosecutor wanted to establish that the wallet had been found behind the defendant's home, a fact that would be highly damaging to the defence, and to this end called the private investigator as a witness.[107]

---

103  See, for example, *Clark*, above note 47 at 347. See also section E, "Relevant *Criminal Code* Provisions," in this chapter.

104  A possible exception is discussed in section G(6), "Counsel May Take Possession of Incriminating Physical Evidence Where Necessary to Prevent Serious Future Harm," in this chapter.

105  The proper manner to make disclosure is discussed in detail in section J, "Mode of Turning Over Incriminating Physical Evidence to the Police, The Crown, or the Court," in this chapter.

106  631 P.2d 46 (Cal. 1981) [*Meredith*].

107  At the preliminary hearing, both the investigator and the original counsel (by that time no longer on retainer) testified as prosecution witnesses: *ibid.* at 49.

The court in *Meredith* recognized that legal-professional privilege ordinarily covers observations made by a lawyer or the lawyer's agent in the course of investigating information provided by the client.[108] To hold otherwise, in the court's view, would have the pernicious effect of inferentially revealing the initial communication between counsel and client. On the other hand, if such observations are always protected by privilege, and counsel is permitted to remove or alter the condition of physical evidence, the prosecution is effectively barred from access to the item's full evidential import. Such a result might even encourage defence counsel to race the police to seize critical evidence.

*Meredith* resolved these conflicting policy concerns by holding that, in choosing to remove physical evidence, the defence lawyer forfeits the protection of privilege regarding the original location or condition of the evidence in question. In coming to this conclusion, the court also commented on the propriety of defence counsel removing or altering physical evidence in the first place. While tending towards the view that counsel should not, as a general rule, remove evidence, the court recognized that in some instances the examination or testing of the evidence may be important to the competent preparation of the defence case.[109] If we accept this approach (discussed further immediately below in section G(5)), then counsel's duties to the client give some leeway for the temporary handling of incriminating physical evidence. However, in taking such action, the lawyer sacrifices an element of legal-professional privilege and also risks becoming a witness.[110]

## 5) Possession for the Purpose of Examining or Testing Incriminating Physical Evidence

In some instances, there is little doubt that counsel should not voluntarily take possession of physical evidence (for example, where the evidence is itself illegal). But there are occasions where the issue is not so straightforward, among these being the case where counsel wishes to examine the item, and perhaps conduct scientific testing, in the rea-

---

108  *Ibid.* at 51, citing the early case of *State v. Douglass*, 20 W. Va. 770 at 783 (1882).

109  See *Meredith*, above note 106 at 53 (note 7).

110  Respecting the potential for counsel to become a witness, consider the facts in *Murray*, above note 8. By personally retrieving the videotapes from the hiding place, counsel ran a real risk of becoming a prosecution witness, and thereby being forced to give up the retainer (the prohibition against counsel acting as both advocate and witness is discussed in section K, "Lawyer as Witness," in chapter 6).

sonable hope that the item might be helpful to the defence case. In such an instance, might a lawyer be ethically and legally justified in keeping hold of physical evidence that implicates the client in a crime?

Some commentators, including several Canadian writers who have considered the issue, are of the view that a lawyer should always avoid voluntarily taking possession of incriminating physical evidence.[111] Holding evidence for the purpose of examination and/or testing is not seen to be a possible exception. A central argument in support of this position is that taking possession of such evidence places counsel at too high a risk of being charged with a criminal offence such as obstructing justice or accessory after the fact.[112] Where counsel is forced to take possession of physical evidence against his or her will, for instance, where the client brings an item to the lawyer's office unannounced and then leaves, these commentators typically recommend that the evidence be promptly handed over to the proper authorities.

But the counter-argument is that permitting counsel the ability to retain incriminating physical evidence in certain limited circumstances may encourage the client to seek competent legal advice. If lawyers are not given at least a narrow discretion to retain physical evidence, some clients will be inhibited from communicating information to a lawyer.[113] Moreover, where the physical evidence might reasonably be thought to advance a client's case, counsel may have a positive ethical duty to retain the evidence for examination and testing.[114] Several well-reasoned American cases have therefore recognized that counsel may on occasion legitimately take possession of physical evidence.[115]

---

111 See, for example, MacDonald & Pink, above note 10 at 133 (although the authors do not categorically foreclose the examination/testing option: *Ibid.* at 131–32); Skurka & Stribopoulos, above note 14 at §4.5; "Panel Discussion: Problems in Advocacy and Ethics" in Law Society of Upper Canada, *Defending a Criminal Case* (Toronto: R. De Boo, 1969) at 311; and Shadley & Costom, above note 10 at 5.

112 See MacDonald & Pink, above note 10 at 133. Professor Kent Roach has noted that many lawyers may therefore decide as a blanket policy to refuse to accept incriminating physical evidence, but he does not condone such an inflexible approach: see K. Roach, "Smoking Guns: Beyond the Murray Case" (2000) 43 Crim. L.Q. 409.

113 See N. Lefstein, "Incriminating Physical Evidence, the Defense Attorney's Dilemma, and the Need for Rules" (1986) 64 N.C. L. Rev. 897 at 927.

114 *Ibid.* at 931.

115 See, for example, *Meredith*, above note 106; *Olwell*, above note 101; *Stenhach*, above note 58; and *In re Ryder*, above note 67. See also *Clutchette* v. *Rushen*, 770 F.2d 1469 (9th Cir. 1985).

The propriety of a lawyer retaining such evidence is given some support in the leading Canadian case of *R. v. Murray*.[116] Mr. Justice Gravely notes, without adverse comment, that the ABA Defense Standards permit counsel to retain evidence for a reasonable time for examination and testing. He then observes that the accused in the case at hand could not be said to have fit within the scope of this standard. Consequently, Gravely J. seemed potentially open to the possibility of an "examination and testing" retention exception, although the matter did not fall to be decided on the facts in *Murray*.

As just noted, the ABA Standards for Criminal Justice expressly allow for counsel to retain physical evidence that implicates the client in a crime for a reasonable period of time, where defence counsel "intends to test, examine, inspect, or use the item in any way as part of defense counsel's representation of the client."[117] The Third Restatement takes a narrower approach but nonetheless permits a lawyer to retain physical evidence for the purpose of examination and testing.[118] In Canada, the Alberta rules of professional conduct expressly recognize that counsel can retain evidence for the purpose of testing.[119]

In our view, the arguments in favour of a limited ability to retain incriminating physical evidence are persuasive. We therefore adopt the position that counsel can take temporary possession of such evidence, where the evidence is not known by counsel to be in itself illegal, for the limited purpose of examining or testing the evidence.[120] As an aside, in our view counsel has no duty to inform the authorities that tests have been conducted on the evidence. Rather, the fact that such testing, if properly conducted, has occurred is covered by legal-professional privilege. Moreover, there is no general defence obligation to make disclosure to the authorities.[121]

Although we condone possession and retention of incriminating physical evidence for examination/testing purposes, the circumstances where counsel can take possession need be carefully delineated. First, there must be a legitimate reason to take the item. Possession and retention are only justified where reasonably necessary for the pur-

---

116 Above note 8 at 314. See as well the position taken by both Martin, above note 12 at 392; and Roach, above note 112.
117 ABA Defense Standard 4-4.6(c)(4).
118 Third Restatement §119(1).
119 See Alta. ch. 10, comm. 20.
120 The main template for our position is the Third Restatement §119.
121 See section D, "Lack of a Defence-Disclosure Obligation and the Principle Against Self-Incrimination," in this chapter.

poses of representation: that is, in order to prepare the defence.[122] Hiding the item from the police is *not* a valid reason. It also follows that a lawyer should never accede to a client's request to hold but not examine potentially incriminating physical evidence.[123] Second, counsel cannot examine or test the item in a manner that alters or destroys its material characteristics.[124] Such action would serve to deprive the prosecution of access to the item in its original state. Third, counsel must retain the item only for the time reasonably necessary to complete the examination or testing.[125] Keeping the item longer than necessary opens counsel up to the charge that he or she is improperly concealing the evidence. Fourth, and as already noted, counsel who removes incriminating physical evidence from its original location for a legitimate examination/testing purpose risks losing the protection of legal-professional privilege, at least with respect to the facts surrounding the item's location and condition.[126] He or she additionally risks becoming a witness.[127]

Overall, a lawyer must be conscious of the serious responsibility that he or she assumes in receiving incriminating physical evidence. As in any legally and ethically sensitive area, counsel must carefully consider the best course of action and fully document all steps taken. Given the controversy currently surrounding the issue of a lawyer taking possession of incriminating physical evidence, counsel is well advised to seek legal advice from senior colleagues or a professional governing body.

**Example:** X is charged with the murder of his wife. The day after his arrest, his children visit X in jail. X tells his children that he placed the clothes that he was wearing at the time of the killing in a closet in his home. The children thereafter meet X's lawyer at the house. The clothes are found in the closet and are covered in what appears to be

---

122 See Third Restatement §119. ABA Defense Standard 4-4.6(c)(4) is arguably of wider scope, insofar as the item can be used "in any way as part of defense counsel's representation of the client." "Reasonable necessity" is not, for instance, a precondition.

123 See Roach, above note 112.

124 See Third Restatement §119(1). ABA Defense Standard 4-4.6(c) seems to imply this restriction, given that a lawyer should retain the item "in a manner that does not impede the lawful ability of law enforcement authorities to obtain the item."

125 See Third Restatement §119; and ABA Defense Standard 4-4.6(c)(4).

126 See section G(4), "Counsel Should Not Interfere with the Authenticity of Incriminating Physical Evidence," in this chapter.

127 *Ibid.*

blood. In our view, counsel should not take possession of the clothing, given that his action in so doing may well deprive the police of the opportunity to locate the evidence, and there appears to be no reasonable possibility that possession of the evidence is necessary in order for counsel to prepare X's defence.[128]

The possibility that a lawyer can legitimately accept possession of incriminating physical evidence for the limited purpose of examination or testing leads to two final points. First, in certain instances the lawyer may wish to copy the evidence, especially when it comes in documentary form, and keep the copies for use in the legitimate preparation of the case. Such action is surely justified and may even be mandated by counsel's duties of loyalty and competence. Moreover, it is probable that privilege will attach to the copies, given that they are created as part of the legal-professional relationship.[129] A second point to be made is that counsel who properly decides to accept physically incriminating evidence for the purpose of examination or testing should advise the client of any restrictions imposed by the law and counsel's ethical obligations.[130] The client must be under no misapprehension as to counsel's duties, including the possibility that the item will eventually be delivered to the authorities.

## 6) Counsel May Take Possession of Incriminating Physical Evidence Where Necessary to Prevent Serious Future Harm

There is a well-recognized exception to the duty of confidentiality that applies where disclosure of otherwise confidential information is necessary to prevent serious future-harm.[131] For the same reason that a

---

128 This fact situation is borrowed from *R. v. Gérin*, above note 1, where counsel decided to take possession of the clothing. He eventually surrendered the clothing to the police, but only after satisfying himself that the client would successfully raise an insanity plea against the murder charge. As noted in note 1, above, counsel was later charged with obstructing justice based on his handling of the clothing, and only narrowly escaped conviction.

129 See *Branch*, above note 77 at 524–25; *Hodgkinson v. Simms* (1988), 55 D.L.R. (4th) 577 (B.C.C.A.); and *Chrusz*, above note 92 at 360–61 & 370.

130 See the discussion in section L, "Providing Advice to the Client," in this chapter, as well as Alta. ch. 10, r. 20, comm. 20(d). See also Roach, above note 112.

131 See section G, "Future Harm or Public Safety," in chapter 5.

lawyer's duties to the client may require modification where the spectre of future-harm arises, counsel should be permitted to take temporary possession of incriminating physical evidence where he or she "reasonably fears that return of the item to the source will result in physical harm to anyone."[132] The exact parameters of this ground for taking possession are open to debate along the lines seen in our discussion of future-harm and the duty of confidentiality.[133] It may be, however, that the propriety of possessing dangerous items, as opposed to releasing confidential information, is less problematic from the client's self-interested point of view. The risk that counsel's possession of an item will lead to the client being exposed to the authorities is often minimized by the residual application of legal-professional privilege: as we shall see, any obligation to turn over the item to the authorities is tempered by a duty not to reveal privileged matters (including the identity of the client).[134]

Where the incriminating physical evidence is itself illegal, counsel courts a serious risk in taking possession, despite the fact that possession is necessary to prevent a reasonably anticipated threat of serious future-harm. Granted, it is likely that counsel would not be prosecuted or disciplined for taking temporary possession in such circumstances. Yet some lawyers may justifiably adopt a cautious approach and absolutely refuse to take possession of contraband. Even so, in such circumstances the future-harm exception to the duty of confidentiality may nonetheless apply, meaning that the lawyer, despite refusing to accept the item, can reveal confidential information to the extent necessary to avert the anticipated harm.

## 7) Counsel May Take Possession of Incriminating Physical Evidence Where Given No Choice in the Matter

It is permissible for a lawyer to take possession of incriminating physical evidence where the item is provided against his or her will. To hold

---

132 ABA Defense Standard 4-4.6(c)(3).
133 See section G, "Future Harm or Public Safety," in chapter 5.
134 See the discussion in section J, "Mode of Turning Over Incriminating Physical Evidence to the Police, the Crown, or the Court," in this chapter.

otherwise would be to ignore practical realities and impose an ethical responsibility for events that are truly beyond counsel's control.

## 8) Counsel May Take Possession of Incriminating Physical Evidence Where He or She Reasonably Fears That the Evidence Will Otherwise be Destroyed

What should a lawyer do when he or she reasonably fears that incriminating physical evidence will be destroyed absent intervention? Where the anticipated destruction does not constitute a future crime, for instance, in the case of an unsuspecting landlord's demolition of a house containing an item secreted by the tenant, the impending destruction does not, without more, justify counsel taking possession.

The proper response may change where the evidence is likely to be illegally destroyed by a client or other source. One view is that counsel facing such a predicament is nonetheless best advised to take no action, apart from explaining to the client or source that the law prohibits the destruction of evidence. This approach would have the lawyer always refuse to take possession of the evidence. But an alternative approach, which we prefer, is to allow counsel to take or retain possession of incriminating physical evidence in order to prevent reasonably anticipated illegal destruction. This approach, best seen as permissive and not mandatory, would preserve the integrity of the item and avoid any suggestion that counsel had been complicit in an illegal act.

**Warning:** The lawyer who chooses not to take possession of incriminating physical evidence despite holding a reasonable fear that the item will be illegally destroyed must *genuinely* advise the client or other source against taking any action that would contravene the law. A nudge or a wink designed to let the client know that the "advice" should be ignored is unprofessional and possibly criminal. Moreover, counsel should document such advice, in writing signed by the client or other source if at all possible.

# H. PLACING LIMITS ON THE DURATION OF COUNSEL'S POSSESSION

Where counsel legitimately takes possession of incriminating physical evidence, whether willingly or not, there undoubtedly will come a time where he or she can no longer keep the item. That is to say, excessive retention constitutes illegal and unethical concealment and cannot be countenanced. The propriety of continued possession is closely linked to whether or not the facts supporting the legitimacy of the original possession persist. Often, the period during which a lawyer can retain possession is quite brief. For instance, taking possession of incriminating physical evidence in order to prevent reasonably anticipated future-harm does not justify retention of the item beyond the time necessary to make arrangements for safe and legal transfer to another source. Similarly, the lawyer who has incriminating physical evidence forced upon him or her must promptly make arrangements to give up possession.

Perhaps the trickiest situation arises where the physical evidence, though in part incriminating, can be used or explained away by the defence at trial. While it may be permissible to examine or test the item for defence purposes, should the item be retained after such steps are completed? In some cases, such as *Murray*, defence counsel has assumed that continued possession is justified as long as the item is ultimately revealed at trial.[135] In the same vein, consider the intriguing English murder case of Herbert Rowse Armstrong,[136] in which defence counsel located and kept a packet of arsenic that had been stored in the accused's home. The accused was alleged to have poisoned his wife using arsenic, and police had failed to locate the packet during a search of the house. On one view, the evidence was helpful to the Crown. Yet defence counsel used the evidence, revealed for the first time at trial, to support the contention that all arsenic purchased by the accused was properly accounted for and thus could not have been used to poison the deceased.

Counsel who follows the route taken by the lawyers in *Murray* and *Armstrong* flirts with grave danger. Given the court's analysis in *Murray*, withholding incriminating physical evidence can obstruct justice at many stages of the criminal justice process, including the pre-

---

135 See *Murray*, above note 8, where the court entertained a reasonable doubt in favour of the defence on this factual issue. Of course, the court in *Murray* went on to reject the argument that counsel could legitimately retain the videotapes until trial. We strongly agree with this aspect of the court's ruling.

136 See *R. v. Armstrong*, [1922] 2 K.B. 555. The reported case makes no mention of defence counsel's actions. For the fuller story, told with some flourish, see Young, "Herbert Rowse Armstrong" in H. Hodge, ed., *Famous Trials*, 2d series (Middlesex: Penguin Books, 1948).

trial stages.[137] Additionally, assuming that proper precautionary measures are taken, there may be no reason to believe that handing the evidence over to the authorities will detract from its relevance or value to the accused's defence. Relying on the element of surprise as a tactical advantage does not appear to constitute a valid justification for retaining incriminating physical evidence beyond the time needed for examination and/or testing.[138] Where counsel entertains a valid concern that an important tactical advantage will be lost by turning over the item to the police or Crown, an option might be to deliver the item to the court accompanied by an *ex parte* application for directions.[139] We therefore believe that counsel should give up possession of the evidence — whether to the police, the Crown, or the court — once a reasonable time for examination/testing has passed. It is worth adding that any artificial delay in examination/testing, engineered by counsel in the hope of gaining a tactical advantage over the prosecution, may constitute an obstruction of justice and should be avoided at all costs.

# I. RELINQUISHING POSSESSION OF INCRIMINATING PHYSICAL EVIDENCE

When the time comes for a lawyer in possession of incriminating physical evidence to relinquish possession, a question arises as to whom, and how, the evidence should be delivered.

## 1) Returning the Evidence to the Client or Other Source

One option is to return the item to the client or other source. A common argument against taking this step, however, is that the source may well respond by improperly hiding or destroying the item. The Alberta rules of professional conduct therefore seem to preclude any option other than turning the evidence over to the authorities, a position also taken by several Canadian commentators.[140] But a rule that invariably

---

137 See the discussion of *Murray* in section E(2), "Obstructing Justice," in this chapter.

138 *Ibid.*

139 See Roach, above note 112 at 410.

140 See Alta. ch. 10, comm. 20(d); MacDonald & Pink, above note 10 at 130–33; G. MacKenzie, *Lawyers and Ethics: Professional Responsibility and Discipline* (Toronto: Carswell, 1993) §7.3; Skurka & Stribopoulos, above note 14 at §4.5; E. Cherniak, "The Ethics of Advocacy" (1985) 19 L. Soc. Gaz. 145 at 147; and R. Fogl, "Sex, Lies and Videotape: The Ambit of Solicitor-Client Privilege in

requires counsel to turn over the item to the authorities may discourage the client from seeking legal advice, with the result that the client is more likely to keep the evidence to himself or herself in the first place. Allowing counsel to return the evidence to the client in certain circumstances makes it no less probable that the evidence will see the light of day, and has the advantage of ensuring that the client receives proper legal advice.[141]

We thus prefer the view, taken by ABA Defense Standard 4-4.6,[142] that a lawyer may return the evidence to the client or other source, provided that he or she does not harbour any reasonable fear that the item will consequently be destroyed or used to cause physical harm to anyone. Naturally, if return to the source is not possible, perhaps because a client has disappeared or is in custody, this option is foreclosed.[143]

In returning an item, the lawyer should advise the client (or anyone else to whom the evidence is being returned) of the legal consequences pertaining to the possession or destruction of the item.[144] Counsel should also prepare a written record of all communications and actions taken respecting the item, to be kept in his or her file. Ideally, a signed receipt, including acknowledgment of all legal advice provided, will be obtained.

## 2) Returning the Item to Its Original Location

Where a lawyer obtains incriminating physical evidence from its original location, the possibility arises of returning the item to that location. The arguments for and against allowing a lawyer to do so are similar to those already canvassed in section I(1). We thus conclude that counsel should be permitted to "return the evidence to the site from which it was taken, when that can be accomplished without

---

Canadian Criminal Law as Illustrated in R. v. Murray" (2001) 50 U.N.B.L.J. 187 at 200. See also Martin, above note 12 at 392 (seemingly in agreement). Murray, above note 8 at 314, notes the general prevalence of the view that counsel has a broad duty to turn the incriminating physical evidence over to the authorities.

141  See Lefstein, above note 113 at 929.

142  See ABA Defense Standard 4-4.6(c). The Third Restatement §119 appears to preclude this option.

143  See Murray, above note 9 at 315.

144  See, for example, Hitch v. Pima County Superior Court, 708 P.2d 72 at 78 (Ariz. 1985); and Morrell v. State, 575 P.2d 1200 at 1206 (Alaska 1978) [Morrell] (referring to the view of the Ethics Committee of the Alaska Bar Association, to the effect that the duty to advise extends to a third party from whom the lawyer receives the item).

destroying or altering material characteristics of the evidence."[145] The other caveats mentioned in section I(1) also apply. For example, return to the original site is precluded if anyone would thereby be exposed to a real threat of physical harm.

## 3) Turning over the Item to the Police, the Crown or the Court

We have identified some circumstances where, in our opinion, counsel is justified in returning the item to the client or other source or to the location from which it was initially removed. Where such action is not prudent or possible, however, counsel who finds himself or herself in possession of incriminating physical evidence has an ethical obligation to turn over the item to the police, the Crown, or the court. The justification for taking this step lies in the public interest in criminal investigations and in the need to prevent lawyers from acting to impede such investigations. This result has been supported in several American cases,[146] as well as the leading Canadian case of *R. v. Murray.*

In *Murray*, Mr. Justice Gravely observed that, given the circumstances of the case, the accused lawyer had no option but to turn the videotapes over to the prosecution (either directly or anonymously), to deposit the tapes with the trial judge, or to disclose their existence to the prosecution "and prepare to do battle to retain them."[147] Yet *Murray* leaves open the issue as to whether, in some instances, counsel enjoys a discretion in deciding whether to turn incriminating physical evidence over to the authorities. Indeed, Mr. Justice Gravely parenthetically questioned whether the obligatory turn-over duty advocated by many Canadian commentators is truly warranted.[148] The case thus provides some tentative support for counsel, in proper circumstances, deciding not to deliver the item to the authorities.

Some ethical rules, in particular Alberta's, mandate that counsel *always* turn over incriminating physical evidence to the proper authorities, and the weight of Canadian academic authority agrees.[149] The

---

145 ABA Defense Standard 4-4.6(c).
146 See, for example, *Olwell*, above note 101; *Morrell*, above note 144; *People v. Sanchez*, 24 Cal. App. 4th 1012 (1994); *State v. Carlin*, 640 P.2d 324 (Kan. Ct. App. 1982); and *People v. Nash*, 341 N.W.2d 439 (Mich. 1983) [*Nash*].
147 See *Murray*, above note 8 at 315.
148 *Ibid.* at 314.
149 See the discussion in section I(1), "Returning the Evidence to the Client or Other Source," in this chapter.

Third Restatement appears to follow suit.[150] A different approach is taken by ABA Defense Standard 4-4.6, which precludes turning over incriminating physical evidence to the authorities absent a requirement to do so by law or court order or in certain cases where contraband is involved.[151] We prefer a more permissive approach, providing counsel with some discretion in the matter, but would mandate disclosure to the police, the Crown, or the court in certain instances, including where:

1. The evidence cannot be returned to the source or original location without the risk of destruction or material alteration;
2. It is no longer possible to return the evidence to the source or original location;
3. The evidence cannot be returned to the source or original location without incurring a real risk of physical harm to anyone; or
4. The evidence is in itself illegal.

## J. MODE OF TURNING OVER INCRIMINATING PHYSICAL EVIDENCE TO THE POLICE, THE CROWN, OR THE COURT

Turning over incriminating physical evidence to the police, the Crown, or the court can cause obvious harm to the client. For example, if counsel provides a murder weapon to the police, and the client's fingerprint is on the weapon, this fact will likely be important to the prosecution case. Such damage to the client's interests may be unavoidable; certainly, counsel cannot remove the fingerprint from the weapon prior to turning the item over to the authorities. On the other hand, there are rules of law and practical steps that can minimize the deleterious effects to the client. In particular, and as we have already seen, delivering incriminating physical evidence to the authorities does not totally extinguish the application of legal-professional privilege and the duty of confidentiality.[152] Rather, the source of the item and the circumstances surrounding its delivery to counsel will often remain priv-

---

150  See Third Restatement §119(2).
151  See ABA Defense Standard 4-4.6(a).
152  See the discussion in section F, "Legal-Professional Privilege," in this chapter.

ileged.[153] Counsel's duty to maintain confidentiality and prevent the loss of privilege thus requires that the evidence in question be provided to the authorities without revealing any more information than is necessary. Also, counsel must oppose any efforts by the Crown to obtain information surrounding the item, if that information can be reasonably seen as privileged.[154]

How might incriminating physical evidence best be delivered to the police, the Crown, or the court? Consider the Michigan case of *People* v. *Nash*,[155] where the lawyer simply chose to inform the prosecution that he was in possession of evidence relevant to the case. The prosecution responded by obtaining a search warrant to search the lawyer's premises. At trial, the jury was told that the incriminating evidence had been located at the accused's lawyer's office. On appeal, the court held that legal-professional privilege operated to prevent the prosecution from leading evidence concerning the location of the physical item.[156] This result is correct. Yet the whole issue could have been avoided, or at least made less likely to arise, if independent counsel was retained to turn over the evidence. Such counsel would be provided with only the bare essentials necessary to permit him or her to make delivery to the police, the Crown, or the court. This approach minimizes the possibility of accidental disclosure and makes it clear that privilege is not being waived. A variation is to have an officer of the applicable professional governing body make the delivery.[157] Yet another option is to provide the item to the police by means of an anonymous delivery. This latter approach is arguably problematic, however, for it prevents the court from determining whether privilege properly applies, and if so to what extent, and also precludes the court from determining whether counsel acted properly in handling the evidence.[158]

---

153 However, extreme caution must be taken where counsel possesses evidence that is in itself illegal. Our position is that counsel should never knowingly accept such contraband: see section G(3), "Counsel Should Not Take Possession of Illegal Evidence," in this chapter. But where possession is mistakenly accepted, or cannot be avoided, it may be that privilege does not apply: see the discussion above in notes 69 & 89, above, and accompanying text.

154 See section K, "Duty to Warn Client," in chapter 4.

155 Above note 146.

156 For a similar approach, see *State* v. *Green*, 493 So.2d 1178 (La. 1986); *Morrell*, above note 144; and *Sanford*, above note 87.

157 With the respect to the option of disclosure to the court, see *Murray*, above note 8 at 315.

158 See Lefstein, above note 113 at 936–37.

It cannot be emphasized enough that a lawyer turning evidence over to the police, the Crown, or the court has an ethical duty not to disclose more than is necessary. An example of how *not* to deliver evidence to the police is seen in the New York case of *People* v. *Cassas*.[159] The accused informed a lawyer that he had shot and killed his wife at their home, and that the gun was currently beside his wife's body. The lawyer accompanied the client to the police station, where he told the police: "I brought my client to surrender. I believe he shot his wife. You'll find the gun in the room. It will have my client's prints on it." The police arrested the client and recovered the gun from the client's house. The lawyer's approach is open to criticism, for he revealed a substantial amount of information to the police, beyond simply informing them that a death had occurred.[160]

# K. SCOPE OF PHYSICAL EVIDENCE COVERED BY THE ETHICAL AND LEGAL RULES

Precisely what type of physical evidence is subject to a possible ethical and legal prohibition against unjustified possession by counsel? The question arises, for instance, as to whether the prohibition and associated duties discussed to this point are restricted to the "fruits and instrumentalities" of a crime. Also, does the prohibition extend beyond evidence that inculpates the client (that is, to exculpatory evidence). It is also sometimes suggested that the physical evidence rule should not apply to documents. We will look at each of these areas in turn.

## 1) Fruits and Instrumentalities of a Crime

Some commentators have restricted the scope of the rules pertaining to physical evidence to the "fruits or instrumentalities" of a crime, which we take to mean those items that are used in the commission of an offence or obtained during the course of the offence.[161] However, rules of professional conduct that deal with the issue of physical evidence

---

159 622 N.Y.S.2d 228 (1995).

160 As it turned out, the Court of Appeals for New York held that counsel's statement could not be used against the client, and did not constitute waiver of privilege, for there was no indication that the client authorized the comments.

161 This restrictive view is taken in MacKenzie, above note 140 at 7–9, where reference is made to apparent instrumentalities and apparent products of a crime. See also Fogl, above note 140 at 200. For a leading case in which the court uses the phrase "fruits or instrumentalities," see *Ryder*, above note 67.

typically do not so limit counsel's ethical obligations,[162] and several leading American cases appear to eschew such a restriction.[163] Nor is there any rational reason for constraining counsel's obligations in this way.[164] Evidence that reveals a motive, connects the client to the victim in a material way, or constitutes inculpatory post-offence conduct is often *not* the instrument or product of a crime. Yet destroying or concealing such evidence to prevent its use by the prosecution comes up against the policy arguments raised above[165] and certainly leaves counsel open to charges of obstructing justice.

## 2) Documentary Evidence

It is worth emphasizing that a document implicating a client in a crime attracts the same ethical obligations that govern counsel who is faced with any other kind of incriminating physical evidence. There is no special attribute that justifies treating documents differently.[166] A document can be integrally related to the commission of a crime — consider a cheque forged by the client in order to defraud her employer, or the bank documents that track a client's attempts to launder drug proceeds. Counsel who destroys or conceals these sorts of documents to prevent their use by the prosecution, or who advises a client to do so, has obstructed justice just as surely as if he or she had taken the same steps with respect to a knife used in a robbery. As we have seen, however, a document that is created as part of a client-lawyer communication and therefore privileged is not treated in the same way.[167] Barring waiver or the application of an established exception to privilege, such a document cannot be used as evidence against the client, and can properly be kept secret or even destroyed by counsel.[168]

---

162 See, for example, Alta. ch. 10, r. 20; CBA Code ch. IX, comm. 2(e); ABA Model Rule 3.4(a); Third Restatement §119; and ABA Defense Standard 4-4.6.

163 See, for example, *Morrell*, above note 144; and *Carlin*, above note 146.

164 This point is made convincingly by MacDonald & Pink, above note 10 at 124.

165 See section C(2), "Administration of Justice," in this chapter.

166 While not absolutely clear on the point, MacKenzie, above note 140 at 7–9, can be read to say that documents are not covered by the rules applicable to physical evidence. If this reading is correct, we disagree, and draw support from several American commentators including G. Hazard, "Quis Custodiet Ipsos Custodes?" (1986) 95 Yale L.J. 1523 at 1532; and Lefstein, above note 113 at 898 & 926.

167 See section F(3), "Physical Evidence Created as Part of a Client-Lawyer Communication," in this chapter.

168 An example of such a document being subject to an established exception is seen in *Murray*, above note 8, where written instructions provided by Bernardo to Murray almost certainly came within the full answer and defence exception (see R. v. *Murray* (2000), 144 C.C.C. (3d) 322 (Ont. S.C.J.)).

**Example:** X meets counsel to discuss a police investigation in which he is suspected of defrauding investors in a phoney mortgage scheme. In anticipation of the meeting, X prepares a detailed written summary of events for the lawyer. X also brings the lawyer a number of documents that were created as part of the allegedly fraudulent transactions. All of the documents, including X's written summary, suggest that X has knowingly participated in a fraud. However, all of the documents need not be treated the same by counsel. The written summary was created for the purpose of obtaining legal advice, and is privileged. The authorities have no right to seize or use the privileged document, and hence counsel can keep it. In contrast, the transactional documents are not privileged and fall within counsel's obligations concerning incriminating physical evidence.

### 3)  Purely Exculpatory Physical Evidence

The Alberta ethical rules, which alone among the current Canadian rules deal expressly with the issue of physical evidence, are not clearly limited to evidence that incriminates the client. Rather, a lawyer is directed not to destroy evidence having "potential evidentiary value," to alter property so as to affect its "evidentiary value," or to conceal property having "potential evidentiary value in a criminal proceeding."[169] The same sort of inclusive language is used in ABA-influenced codes of professional conduct.[170]

Yet a different approach is taken in the Third Restatement, where an express distinction is made between evidence of a "client crime" and other physical evidence. Evidence of a client crime is subject to special rules that limit a lawyer in his or her handling of the item.[171] A similar approach is seen in ABA Defense Standard 4-4.6, which is limited to "circumstances implicating a client in criminal conduct."[172]

There are several arguments in favour of a rule that covers all relevant evidence, whether inculpatory or purely exculpatory. First, an analogy can be drawn to the search-warrant and subpoena powers in the *Criminal Code*, neither of which is limited to inculpatory evi-

---

169 See Alta. ch. 10, r. 20, as well as the associated commentary.
170 See, for example, ABA Model Rule 3.4(a), which applies to material having "potential evidentiary value."
171 See Third Restatement §119. The obligations of lawyers in dealing with evidence other than evidence of client crimes are set out in a separate section of the Restatement: see Third Restatement §118.
172 See ABA Defense Standard 4-4.6(a).

dence.[173] Second, it is often difficult to determine whether evidence is inculpatory or exculpatory, and in many instances the same evidence may be useful to both the prosecution and the defence. A rule that applies to all material evidence thus simplifies matters. Finally, there is arguably no harm to the client if purely exculpatory evidence is made subject to the same obligations that govern the handling of incriminating physical evidence. By definition, purely exculpatory evidence cannot harm the client even if disclosed to the authorities.

On the other hand, no judicial precedent in Canada or the United States suggests that counsel is limited in handling purely exculpatory physical evidence.[174] Moreover, destruction of such evidence, or what is much more likely, concealment until trial, does not raise the possibility that counsel is complicit in hiding evidence of a crime. The policy concerns related to the administration of justice are consequentially much less prominent, leaving the accused's constitutional rights to prevail.[175] The better view, subject to any authority to the contrary, is thus to place no restrictions on counsel's handling of purely exculpatory evidence. The usual restrictions will, however, apply to any items that can reasonably be seen as wholly or partially incriminating. Counsel must be extremely careful not to destroy or conceal such evidence improperly, and should err on the side of caution in this regard.

## L.  PROVIDING ADVICE TO THE CLIENT

Where an investigation or charge is pending against the client, and the client brings incriminating physical evidence to the lawyer, it is important that counsel provide sound advice. Various hints and recommen-

---

173 See ss. 487(1) & 698 of the *Criminal Code*, above note 30, as well as *Canadianoxy Chemical Ltd.* v. *Canada (A.G.)* (1999), 133 C.C.C. (3d) 426 at 433–36 (S.C.C.).

174 Some commentators state that no obligation arises with respect to such evidence: see, for example, MacDonald & Pink, above note 10 at 131. But most do not even address the possibility, simply assuming that only incriminating evidence is covered.

175 See the discussion in section D, "Lack of a Defence-Disclosure Obligation and the Principle Against Self-Incrimination," in this chapter. Less clear, however, is the case in which the evidence in question, though wholly exculpatory with reference to counsel's client, nonetheless incriminates a third party.

dations have been made above in this regard, but, by way of elaboration and summary, the following guidelines may be helpful.

When presented with incriminating physical evidence, counsel should fully advise the client as to the applicable ethical duties and legal rules and how these duties and rules affect the client's case. Among other things, the client should be informed that:

1. Counsel cannot be used as a means of destroying or concealing the evidence, nor can counsel alter or in any way tamper with the physical integrity of the evidence.
2. Any communications knowingly made for the purpose of improperly destroying or concealing the evidence are not covered by legal-professional privilege.
3. Counsel can take possession of incriminating physical evidence only in limited circumstances, and even then only temporarily.
4. The police or the Crown can successfully seize the evidence by means of a valid search warrant, regardless of whether the evidence is held by the client or lawyer.
5. If the evidence is left with counsel, he or she may ultimately be required to turn it over to the authorities. The potential advantages and disadvantages in doing so should be canvassed with the client. For instance, the operation of legal-professional privilege should be explained. It may be that the client prefers that the item be turned over to the police, once he or she understands that privilege will have some application.[176]
6. If the client chooses to keep the evidence, he or she cannot alter or tamper with the evidence in any way. Such improper steps not only risk attracting separate criminal charges, but may also constitute evidence against the client in the predicate investigation or prosecution.

In dealing with an incriminating physical-evidence problem, a lawyer should always be aware of the possibility that the client will later inform the police of the matter,[177] or that the police will otherwise discover some or all of the pertinent facts.[178] To protect against allega-

---

176 From the client's point of view, privilege may provide significant protection, especially when compared with the downside of later being found in possession of the incriminating evidence (for example, after the execution of a search warrant or a search incident upon arrest).
177 See, for example, *Scruggs*, above note 47, where the client ended up testifying against his former lawyers at their criminal trial.
178 In *Stenhach*, above note 58, the information was revealed during the examination of a private investigator, while in *Taylor*, above note 96, the police learned

tions of impropriety, including those made by a client, the lawyer should treat the client at arm's length and fully document all events as they occur.

# M. SUMMARY AND RECOMMENDATIONS

Given the complicated nature of this issue, it is helpful to summarize the approach that counsel should take when confronted by physical evidence that incriminates a client. As a caveat, it must be remembered that reasonable opinion is divided regarding certain aspects of the incriminating-physical-evidence scenario. The following summary represents an overview of our preferred approach.

1. A classic ethics problem concerns the dilemma of the "smoking gun" or "bloody shirt" brought to a lawyer by a client. On the one hand, counsel owes duties of loyalty and confidentiality to the client that militate against taking any action that might harm the client. Also, there is no general defence obligation to provide disclosure to the Crown or the police. Yet, at the same time counsel bears an obligation to the administration of justice that prohibits active interference with the availability of incriminating physical evidence. In fact, a mishandling of incriminating physical evidence by counsel risks attracting criminal charges (sections A, C, D, & G).
2. Few Canadian rules of professional conduct provide express guidance to the lawyer who is presented with incriminating physical evidence. Alberta is the sole jurisdiction that addresses the issue in a direct manner, and Ontario is currently considering adopting an ethical rule and commentary on point (section B).
3. Physical evidence is generally not protected by the duty of confidentiality or legal-professional privilege (section F(1)).
4. The identity of the source of the physical evidence and the act of delivery itself are likely confidential and privileged, provided that this information can be seen as an integral part of a communication made for the purpose of obtaining legal advice. However, where the evidence is moved or handled so as to affect its authenticity or deprive the police of the opportunity to locate the evidence, the original condition and location of the evidence may not be covered by privilege (sections F & G).

---

of counsel's handling of incriminating physical evidence from a confidential informer.

5. Defence counsel may keep possession of incriminating physical evidence for a reasonable length of time only for certain limited purposes, such as:
   a) to examine or test the evidence;
   b) to avoid serious future-harm;
   c) to prevent the destruction of the evidence; or
   d) to make arrangements for the proper divestment of the evidence, where the item has been forced upon counsel against his or her will (section G).
6. In all other circumstances, counsel should not take possession of incriminating physical evidence. Moreover, even where a lawyer can legitimately handle such evidence, he or she must carefully consider the risks involved before taking action (section G).
7. Once the purpose for which the incriminating physical evidence has been retained is exhausted, counsel must divest himself or herself of the item (section H).
8. Counsel can return the physical evidence to the source, or to the site from which the evidence was originally obtained, where he or she does not harbour any reasonable fear that the item will thereby be destroyed or used to cause physical harm to anyone (section I).
9. In all other circumstances, counsel must turn over the incriminating physical evidence to the proper authorities, such as the police, the Crown, or the court. In taking this step, counsel must strive to protect the client's confidences and preserve legal-professional privilege. Usually the preferable route is to retain independent counsel to turn over the item (sections I & J).
10. The above guidelines should apply to all incriminating physical evidence and not only to the so-called "fruits and instrumentalities" of a crime. Documentary evidence also falls within the ambit of the guidelines. However, comparable restrictions need not be placed upon counsel's handling of purely exculpatory evidence (section K).
11. When presented with incriminating physical evidence, counsel should fully advise the client as to the applicable ethical duties and legal rules and how these duties and rules affect on the client's case. A list of possible topics to canvas with the client is set out in the text above (section L).

## FURTHER READINGS

ARMSTRONG, D., "Confidentiality: The Future Crime — Contraband Dilemmas" (1983) 85 W. Va. L. Rev. 929

BURKOFF, J., *Criminal Defense Ethics: Law and Liability*, rev. ed. (St. Paul: West, 2000)

CHERNIAK, E., "The Ethics of Advocacy" (1985) 19 L. Soc. Gaz. 145 at 147

COSTOM, S., "Disclosure by the Defence: Why Should I Tell You?" (1996) 1 Can. Crim. L. Rev. 73

DASHJIAN, M., "*People* v. *Meredith*: The Attorney-Client Privilege and the Criminal Defendant's Constitutional Rights" (1982) 70 Cal. L. Rev. 1048

DAVISON, C., "Putting Ghosts to Rest: A Reply to the Modest Proposal for Defence Disclosure of Tanovich and Crocker" (1995) 43 C.R. (4th) 105

FOGL, R., "Sex, Laws and Videotape: The Ambit of Solicitor-Client Privilege in Canadian Criminal Law as Illuminated in *R. v. Murray*" (2001) 50 U.N.B.L.J. 187

FORTUNE, W., R. UNDERWOOD, & E. IMWINKELRIED, *Modern Litigation and Professional Responsibility Handbook: The Limits of Zealous Advocacy* (New York: Little, Brown, 1996)

FRYE, S., "Disclosure of Incriminating Physical Evidence Received from a Client: The Defense Attorney's Dilemma" (1981) 52 U. Colo. L. Rev. 419

GRAFFEO, J., "Ethics, Law, and Loyalty: The Attorney's Duty to Turn Over Incriminating Physical Evidence" (1980) 32 Stan. L. Rev. 977

HALL, J., *Professional Responsibility of the Criminal Lawyer*, 2d ed. (Deerfield, Ill.: Clark Boardman Callaghan, 1996)

HAZARD, G., "Quis Custodiet Ipsos Custodes?" (1986) 95 Yale L.J. 1523

HAZARD, G., & W. HODES, *The Law of Lawyering: A Handbook on the Model Rules of Professional Conduct*, 2d ed. (Englewood, N.J.: Prentice Hall, 1993)

HILL, C., "Accessory After the Fact" [1993] National Criminal Law Program

HUTCHINSON, A., *Legal Ethics and Professional Responsibility* (Toronto: Irwin Law, 1999)

JACOBSON, N., "Is Silence Really Golden?" (1989) 3 Geo. J. Legal Ethics 377

LAW SOCIETY OF UPPER CANADA, *Report to Convocation: Special Committee on Lawyer's Duties with Respect to Physical Evidence Relevant to a Crime* (Toronto: Law Society of Upper Canada, 2001)

LEFSTEIN, N., "Incriminating Physical Evidence, the Defense Attorney's Dilemma, and the Need for Rules" (1986) 64 N.C. L. Rev. 897

MACDONALD, A. & J. PINK, "Murder, Silence and Physical Evidence: The Dilemma of Client Confidentiality" (1997) 2 Can. Crim. L. Rev. 111

MACKENZIE, G., *Lawyers and Ethics: Professional Responsibility and Discipline* (Toronto: Carswell, 1993)

MARTIN, G. ARTHUR, "The Role and Responsibility of the Defence Advocate" (1970) 12 Crim. L.Q. 376

MAUDE, B., "Reciprocal Disclosure in Criminal Trials: Stacking the Deck Against the Accused, or Calling Defence Counsel's Bluff?" (1999) 37 Alta. L. Rev. 715

MCKINNON, G., "Accelerating Defence Disclosure: A Time for Change" (1996) 1 Can. Crim. L. Rev. 59

MCWILLIAMS, P., *Canadian Criminal Evidence*, 3d ed. (Aurora: Canada Law Book, 1999)

O'CONNOR, E., "Fruits of the Attorney-Client Privilege: Incriminating Evidence and Conflicting Duties" (1965) 3 Duq. L. Rev. 239

NOTE, "Legal Ethics and the Destruction of Evidence" (1979) 88 Yale L.J. 1665

NOTE, "The Right of a Criminal Defense Attorney to Withhold Physical Evidence Received from His Client" (1970), 38 U. of Chi. L. Rev. 211

PACIOCCO, D. & L. STUESSER, *The Law of Evidence*, 2d ed. (Concord: Irwin Law, 1999)

"Panel Discussion: Problems in Advocacy and Ethics" in Law Society of Upper Canada, *Defending a Criminal Case* (Toronto: De Boo, 1969) 279

PROULX, M., "Defence Disclosure and the Search for Truth" (1994) National Criminal Law Program, Federation of Law Societies of Canada

QUIGLEY, T., *Procedure in Canadian Criminal Law* (Toronto: Carswell, 1997)

QUEBEC, *Rapport de la Commission d'Enquête Brossard sur l'affaire Coffin* (Monteal: La Commission, 1964)

ROACH, K., "Smoking Guns: Beyond the Murray Case" (2000) 43 Crim. L.Q. 409

SALTZBURG, S., "Communications Falling Within the Attorney-Client Privilege" (1981) 66 Iowa L. Rev. 811

SCHIFF, S., *Evidence in the Litigation Process*, 4th ed. (Toronto: Carswell, 1993)

SHADLEY, R., & S. COSTOM, "Handling Physical Evidence: The Defence Lawyer's Dilemma" (1998) National Criminal Law Program

SKURKA, S., & J. STRIBOPOULOS, "Professional Responsibility in Criminal Practice" in Law Society of Upper Canada, *42nd Bar Admission Course, 2000, Criminal Procedure Reference Materials* (Toronto: Law Society of Upper Canada, 2000) c. 1

SOPINKA, J., S. LEDERMAN, & A. BRYANT, *The Law of Evidence in Canada*, 2d ed. (Toronto: Butterworths, 1999)

STRONG, J. ed., *McCormick on Evidence*, 5th ed. (St. Paul: West, 1999)

STUART, D., "Annotation: *R. v. Murray*" (2000) 34 C.R. (5th) 290

TANOVICH, D., & L. CROCKER, "Dancing with Stinchcombe's Ghost: A Modest Proposal for Reciprocal Defence Disclosure" (1994) 26 C.R. (4th) 333

TAPPER, C., *Cross and Tapper on Evidence*, 9th ed. (London: Butterworths, 1999)

TRAHAN, J., "A First Step Toward Resolution of the Physical Evidence Dilemma: *State v. Green*" (1988) 48 La. L. Rev. 1019

VANDERVORT, L., "Mistake of Law and Obstruction of Justice: A 'Bad Excuse' . . . Even for a Lawyer" (2001) 50 U.N.B.L.J. 171

WATSON, G., & F. AU, "Solicitor-Client Privilege and Litigation Privilege in Civil Litigation" (1999) 77 Can. Bar Rev. 315

WATT, D., *Watt's Manual of Criminal Evidence* (Toronto: Carswell, 2000)

WOLFRAM, C.W., *Modern Legal Ethics* (St. Paul: West, 1986)

YOUNG, F., "Herbert Rowse Armstrong" in H. Hodge, ed., *Famous Trials*, 2d series (Middlesex: Penguin Books, 1934)

YOUNG, H., "An Attorney in Possession of Evidence Incriminating His Client" (1968) 25 Wash. & Lee L. Rev. 133

# FEES AND DISBURSEMENTS

## A. INTRODUCTION

At one time, Roman barristers were not permitted to charge for their services. This restriction was eventually abandoned, yet in England barristers maintained the fiction that legal services were not provided to clients in exchange for compensation. According to this conceit, the barrister was a man of exceptionally high integrity, unsullied by base and quotidian concerns regarding money, and payment for services was anathema to the barrister's duties to the client and public. Granted, the client may have seen fit to reward the barrister with an honorarium in appreciation for a job well done. But the barrister was definitely not a tradesman, and he operated on a higher plane than individuals of other professions. As recently as 1969, the House of Lords relied on this view of the profession in observing that barristers could not sue clients for unpaid fees, given that the client-lawyer relationship was not contractual.[1] While the notion that a barrister's services are not exchanged for money is no longer maintained, the General Council of the Bar for England and Wales continues to embrace a rule of profes-

---

1    See *Rondel* v. *Worsley*, [1967] 3 All E.R. 993 at 1004 (H.L.) (Lord Morris), 1019–21 (Lord Pearce), 1033–35 (Lord Upjohn), & 1037 (Lord Pearson) [*Rondel*].

sional conduct that prohibits barristers from entering into contracts with clients.[2]

One of the main benefits that barristers receive from foregoing the legal right to enforce payment from clients is the ability to deflect conflict-of-interest allegations.[3] A barrister is not tempted to prefer self-interest in receiving payment over the client's best interests, so the argument goes, if he or she holds no legal right to receive payment. However, the view that barristers are not receiving a fee, and are prevented from recovering unpaid fees by "a rule of etiquette which has now hardened into a rule of law,"[4] is terribly antiquated. Certainly, the fiction has not been embraced in Canada and does not reflect the reality of criminal law practice in this country.[5]

# B. AN INHERENT CONFLICT OF INTEREST

It is often said that lawyers are engaged in both a profession and a business, in recognition that a steady flow of revenue is required for a lawyer to conduct a practice. The reality is that lawyers receive fees for their services in most cases, and the prospect of financial gain is an important facet of a lawyer's work. Yet this element of self-interest has the potential to clash with the lawyer's duties to the client and the administration of justice. It is to the advantage of the lawyer to receive the largest possible payment, while the client will often prefer exactly the opposite result (without, of course, detracting from the quality of services provided). The dangers are accentuated by the fact that clients are often in a poor position to evaluate the quality and cost-effectiveness of a lawyer's services. Moreover, clients may be in a vulnerable state, often desperate to avoid the serious consequences of a criminal conviction. Lawyers, skilled in a complex field and holding a monopoly over the provision of most legal services, are in a position of power over the client.

---

2   See General Council, *Code of Conduct of the Bar of England and Wales* (London: The Council, 1990) Annex "D" (Written Standards for the Conduct of Professional Work) at paras. 25 & 26. In practice, barristers employ clerks who negotiate the fee with a solicitor: see A. Boon & J. Levin, *The Ethics and Conduct of Lawyers in England and Wales* (Oxford: Hart, 1999) at 298.

3   Boon & Levin, above note 2 at 289.

4   *Rondel* above note 1 at 1004 (Lord Morris).

5   See *R. v. C.(D.D.)* (1996), 110 C.C.C. (3d) 323 at 326 (Alta. C.A.), leave to appeal to S.C.C. refused [1996] S.C.C.A. No. 453 (QL) [*C.(D.D.)*].

The potentially divergent interests of the lawyer and client on the matter of payment, and the vulnerability of many clients, taken together with the fiduciary duties owed a client by the lawyer, justify ethical standards that regulate the lawyer's actions in setting and collecting fees. Most rules of professional conduct that address the subject of legal expenses thus seek to accommodate the lawyer's legitimate need to receive a reasonable fee for services competently performed without unduly compromising duties to the client and administration of justice. Perhaps the most important component of the Canadian rules is the stipulation that fees be fair and reasonable. We therefore begin by looking at this primary ethical dictate.

## C. FEES MUST BE FAIR AND REASONABLE

Every governing body in Canada has adopted rules of professional conduct that pertain to legal expenses, and these rules invariably mandate that fees be "fair and reasonable."[6] This restriction on lawyers' fees implicitly recognizes that market forces cannot be relied upon as the sole determinant of the fees charged and collected. Most Canadian governing bodies also provide member lawyers with a number of factors that help to determine whether the "fair and reasonable" standard has been met.[7] These factors include but are not restricted to

1. time and effort required and spent;
2. difficulty and importance of the matter;
3. whether special skill or service has been required or provided;

---

6    See, for example, CBA Code ch. XI, Rule (a); Sask. ch. XI, Rule (a); Man. ch. 11 Rule (a); Nfld. ch. XI, Rule (a); Alta. ch. 13, Statement of Principle; N.S. ch. 12, Rule(a); Ont. r. 2.08(1); Que. s. 3.08.01; N.B. Part E , r. 1 (adding the comment that the fee "must be based on the nature and value of the services rendered"); and Yukon Part 1, r. 10.

7    See CBA Code ch. XI, comm. 1; Sask. ch. XI, comm. 1; Man. ch. 11, comm. 1; Nfld. ch. XI, comm. 1; Alta. ch. 13, r. 1; N.S. ch. 12, Guiding Principles; Ont. r. 2.08(2); Que. s. 3.08.02; and N.B. Part E, r. 1. The exact wording of these factors may vary depending on the jurisdiction. There is no analogous list of factors in British Columbia or the Yukon Territory. For cases where the courts review the criteria bearing on the reasonableness of a fee, see *Desmoulin (Committee of)* v. *Blair* (1994), 120 D.L.R. (4th) 700 at 704–06 (Ont. C.A.) [*Desmoulin*]; *Cohen* v. *Kealey & Blaney* (1985), 26 C.P.C. (2d) 211 at 215 (Ont. C.A.) [*Cohen*]; and *Cooper* v. *England*, [1994] 7 W.W.R. 345 (N.W.T.S.C.) [*Cooper*].

4. customary charges of other lawyers of equal standing in the locality in like matters and circumstances;

5. in civil cases, the amount involved, or the value of the subject matter;

6. in criminal cases, the exposure and risk to the client;

7. results obtained;

8. tariffs or scales authorized by local law;

9. such special circumstances as loss of other employment, urgency, and uncertainty of reward;[8]

10. any relevant agreement between the lawyer and client;[9]

11. reasonable office overhead;[10]

12. character of the retainer — whether it was casual or continuing;[11]

13. postponement of payment;[12]

14. urgency of concluding the matter or controversy;[13]

15. client's prior consent to the fee and the sophistication of that client;[14]

16. experience and ability of the lawyer;[15]

17. any estimate given by the lawyer;[16]

18. direct costs incurred by the lawyer in providing the services;[17]

19. responsibility assumed by the lawyer;[18] and

20. ability of the client to pay the fee.

As several Canadian codes state, following the lead of the CBA Code, "a fee will not be fair and reasonable and may be subject to disciplinary proceedings if it is one that cannot be justified in the light of all pertinent circumstances, including the factors mentioned, or is so dispro-

---

8    It has been held that "uncertainty of reward" refers to the reward to the lawyer and encompasses the risk of non-payment: see, for example, *Desmoulin*, above note 7 at 705.

9    In Nova Scotia, the language is altered slightly, and appropriately, to read "any reasonable agreement between the lawyer and the client": N.S. ch. 12, Guiding Principle (k).

10   This factor is listed only in Nova Scotia: see N.S. ch. 12, Guiding Principle (i).

11   This factor is listed only in New Brunswick: see N.B. Part E, r. 1(g)).

12   This factor is only mentioned in Ontario (Ont. r. 2.08(2), comm. (g)), and is recognized as a legitimate factor in *Desmoulin*, above note 7 at 706.

13   This factor is listed only in New Brunswick: see N.B. Part E, r. 1(h) and Ontario (Ont. r. 2.08(2), comm. (g).

14   This factor is listed only in Alberta: see Alta. ch. 13, r. 1(i).

15   This factor is listed only in Alberta and Quebec: see Alta. ch. 13, r. 1(f); and Que. s. 3.08.02(a) & (f). See also ABA Defense Standard 4-3.3(b).

16   This factor is only listed in Alberta: see Alta. ch. 13, r. 1(g).

17   This factor is only listed in Alberta: see Alta. ch. 13, r. 1(j).

18   This factor is only listed in Quebec: see Que. s. 3.08.02(e).

portionate to the services rendered as to introduce the element of fraud or dishonesty, or undue profit."[19]

As a tangential point, a differentiation between civil and criminal matters is adopted by those governing bodies that follow CBA Code, as reflected in items "5" and "6" set out above.[20] But not all governing bodies make this distinction, Alberta, British Columbia, Ontario, and New Brunswick being leading exceptions.[21] Indeed, the distinction is of questionable utility. Surely the factors attributed exclusively to civil or criminal cases by the CBA Code are not watertight. For instance, a criminal case can involve real concerns regarding "the amount involved, or the value of the subject matter" (for example, forfeiture proceedings, the prospect of a large fine). Conversely, a client involved in civil litigation, or any other non-criminal matter, may reasonably be prepared to link the fee paid to the degree of "exposure and risk" presented in the circumstances.

# D. FULL AND TIMELY DISCLOSURE TO THE CLIENT

A lawyer is a fiduciary and has a general duty to communicate with the client. It is thus important that all information relevant to the fee arrangement be disclosed to the client in a timely manner.[22] Accordingly, many rules of professional conduct go so far as to forbid the lawyer from charging any fee that is not fully disclosed.[23] Canadian rules also tend to prohibit hidden fees[24] and encourage full disclosure

---

19   CBA Code ch. XI, comm. 1; Sask. ch. XI, comm. 1; Man. ch. 11, comm. 1; Nfld. ch. XI, comm. 1; and N.S. ch. 12 guiding principles. This statement is probably unnecessary, given the blanket prohibition against fees that are not fair or reasonable, and is not found in Alberta, British Columbia, or New Brunswick.

20   CBA Code ch. XI, comm. 1.

21   See Alta. ch. 13, r. 1; Ont. r. 2.08(2) (commentary); B.C. ch. 9; N.B. Part E, r. 1.

22   See, for example, *Arctic Installation (Victoria) Ltd.* v. *Campney & Murphy* (1994), 109 D.L.R. (4th) 609 (B.C.C.A.) [*Arctic Installation*]; *Cooper*, above note 7 at 351.

23   See CBA Code ch. XI Rule(a); Sask. ch. XI Rule (a); Man. ch. 11 Rule (a); Nfld. ch. XI Rule (a); Alta. ch. 13, r. 2; B.C. ch. 9, r. 7; N.S. ch. 12, Rule(a) & comm. 12.1; Ont. r. 2.08(1); Yukon Rule 10. Alberta adds specific disclosure requirements regarding the separation of fees and disbursements (Alta. ch. 13, r. 4) and monies received in respect of party-and-party costs (Alta. ch. 13, r. 6).

24   See CBA Code ch. XI, comm. 7; Sask. ch. XI, comm. 7; Man. ch. 11, comm. 8; Nfld. ch. XI, comm. 7; Alta. ch. 13 Rule 8; B.C. ch. 9, r. 8-9; N.S. ch. 12, comm. 12.6–12.8; Ont. r. 2.08(2) (commentary); and N.B. Part E, r. 1. Among other

as a means of avoiding controversy relating to fees and disbursements.[25] The CBA Code and its progeny also forbid a lawyer from appropriating any funds of the client held in trust or otherwise under the lawyer's control absent express authority from the client, which in effect means that the client must provide consent based upon full disclosure.[26]

Full disclosure not only permits the client to assess the reasonableness of the fees. Additionally, it often influences the client's initial decision to hire counsel. Furthermore, the cost of undertaking a particular course of action, for instance, bringing a pre-trial application to exclude evidence, may determine the client's decision regarding strategic aspects of the case. Counsel should therefore not be shy about speaking frankly and providing full disclosure regarding all compensatory aspects of the retainer. It is not unseemly to discuss monetary matters, given the important role that financial reward plays in the client-lawyer relationship. To avoid the subject merely invites disagreements, disputes, and unpleasantness down the road.

## 1) Prior Dealings with a Client

Where the client and lawyer have had prior dealings, and it can reasonably be assumed that a fee arrangement is already in place based upon such dealings, counsel need not explain the arrangement in repetitive and unnecessary detail.[27] Also, an experienced client may not

---

things, the hidden-fee prohibition prevents counsel from receiving any compensation in connection with the employment from anyone other than the client, unless the client consents after full disclosure.

25   See CBA Code ch. XI, comm. 3; Sask. ch. XI, comm. 3; Man. ch. 11, comm. 4; Nfld. ch. XI, comm. 3; Alta. ch. 13, comm. G.1; and Ont. r. 2.08(2) (commentary). See also B.C. ch. 1, r. 3(10) and N.B. Part E, r. 1 (encouraging lawyers to avoid controversy regarding fees, but without mentioning full disclosure as an important means of doing so). This point is strongly made in the *Report of the Task Force on Systems of Civil Justice* (Ottawa: Canadian Bar Association, 1996) (Chair: E. Cronk) at 66–67 [*Report on Systems of Civil Justice*].

26   See, for example, CBA Code ch. XI, r. (b); Sask. ch. XI, Rule (b); Man. ch. 11, Rule (b); Nfld. ch. XI rule (b); Alta. ch. 13, r. 8; B.C. ch. 1, r. 3(8); Alta. ch. 13, r. 10; N.S. ch. 12, Rule (b); Ont. r. 2.08(11); and Yukon Part 1, r. 11. However, these rules often permit withdrawal of funds without the client's consent if authority to do so is provided by the governing body's rules. Such rules usually permit withdrawal from a trust account to pay fees after billing: see, for example, s. 14(8)(c), Reg. 708, R.R.O. 1990, passed pursuant to the *Law Society Act*, R.S.O. 1990, ch. L.8.

27   See Que. s. 3.08.05; ABA Defense Standard 4-3.3(e) & commentary (Communication of Fee Information).

require the same type of comprehensive review of financial arrangements as would be appropriate for an unsophisticated neophyte.[28]

## 2)  Estimates

Disclosure should include an estimate as to the total legal costs likely to be incurred.[29] This estimate must be global in nature, covering all fees, disbursements, and any applicable taxes. If an estimate is difficult to provide at the beginning of the retainer, the client may wish to receive regular interim accounts as a means of obtaining periodic updates as to costs. Other options include providing the client with an estimate as soon as the circumstances permit, and having the client authorize only an initial expenditure after which time the matter will be revisited.

**Caution:** Counsel should be wary of providing a binding promise regarding the total cost of fees and disbursements prior to gaining sufficient understanding of the circumstances of the case. A binding estimate provided rashly may come back to haunt the client and/or the lawyer, resulting in a fee that is too high or low.[30] Even in the case of a non-binding estimate, a lawyer is obliged to advise the client without delay of any developments that are likely to increase the fee beyond the estimate.[31]

## 3)  Basis for Calculating Fees and Disbursements

Whether or not an accurate estimate can be provided at the beginning of the relationship, the client should be informed regarding the basis upon which the legal costs will be calculated (for example, hourly rate, fixed fee, graduated fee, value-billing, and so on) and the manner of payment (for example, all or partially in advance to be held in trust, interim accounts to be provided, payment only after all work is com-

---

28  See, for example, *Equity Waste Management of Canada Corp.* v. *Halton Hills (Town of)* (1995), 22 O.R. (3d) 796 at 798–99 (Gen. Div.) (in the context of premium billing for corporate and sophisticated clients), but compare the more demanding position taken in *Swinton & Co.* v. *Perry* (1985), 69 B.C.L.R. 114 (Co. Ct.) [*Swinton*]; and *Arctic Installation*, above note 22.

29  See, for example, *Huda* v. *MacDonald & Associates*, [1995] 3 W.W.R. 623 (N.W.T.S.C.) [*Huda*]; *Re M. & T., Barristers & Solicitors* (1962), 40 W.W.R. 623 (Alta. S.C.T.D.) [*M. & T.*].

30  See *Huda*, above note 29, where counsel was held to an early estimate regarding legal fees for an impaired charge that proved to be unduly low.

31  See, for example, *Cohen*, above note 7 at 215.

plete, and so on). Moreover, most rules provide that a lawyer can charge interest on an overdue account only with the prior agreement of the client, unless otherwise permitted by law or local practice.[32] Counsel who intends on charging interest should thus provide notice to the client.[33]

## 4) Providing Accounts

In fulfillment of the disclosure obligation, counsel should habitually provide the client with a comprehensive accounting of the basis for the fees and disbursements charged, so that the client can confirm whether the charges are fair, reasonable and in accordance with the retainer agreement.[34] In the 1962 case of *Re M. & T., Barristers & Solicitors*,[35] the court noted that criminal lawyers do not customarily provide clients with detailed bills. This observation would not be warranted today. Granted, fixed-fee arrangements may lead some criminal lawyers to provide clients with a one-line summary of the work performed (for example, "To all services performed to date in relation to criminal matter"). In the fairly recent case of *Mullins v. Beneteau*,[36] for example, a block fee of over $47,000 was charged for one week of preliminary inquiry and one week of trial. The lawyer kept no dockets and did not even provide the client with an account (though the court held that the fee was reasonable). We do not believe that this opaque form of accounting is satisfactory. Fortunately, however, the welcome trend among criminal lawyers, though somewhat late in coming, is to provide accounts that itemize work done in considerable detail.

**Conclusion and Helpful References:** The guiding principle for counsel in making full disclosure is to provide information to the client concerning all aspects of the financial arrangements. Excellent discussions of the information that can, or should, be disclosed are provided in the

---

32  See, for example, CBA Code ch. XI, comm. 4; Sask. ch. XI, comm. 4; Man. ch. 11, comm. 5; Nfld. ch. XI, comm. 4; N.S. ch. 12, comm. 12.3; Ont. r. 2.08(2); and Que. s. 3.08.07. These rules typically provide that the interest charged must be reasonable.

33  See, for example, *Boerrichter v. Robertson* (1992), 98 Sask. R. 207 (Q.B.).

34  See, for example, *Re Toulany and McInnes, Cooper & Robertson* (1989), 57 D.L.R. (4th) 649 at 654 (N.S. S.C.(T.D.), leave to appeal to S.C.C. refused (1989), 92 N.S.R. (2d) 91 (S.C.A.D.); and *Cooper*, above note 7 at 353–55.

35  Above note 29.

36  [1996] O.J. No. 2784 at para. 34 (Gen. Div.) (QL).

Alberta Code of Professional Conduct and the CBA's *Report of the Task Force on Systems of Civil Justice*.[37]

## 5) Third-Party Payment

Not infrequently, third parties pay all or part of the cost associated with a retainer. While a lawyer does not normally stand in a fiduciary relationship to the third-party payor, and owes the third-party no general duty to communicate all relevant matters, Canadian rules of professional conduct often impose a limited-disclosure obligation.[38] Altogether apart from any obligations imposed by the professional governing bodies, prudent counsel will keep the third-party payor informed concerning the fees and disbursements to be paid under the retainer. At the same time, however, counsel must never release confidential information to the third-party absent the client's consent.[39] Also, where a third-party is paying any portion of legal costs, special concerns can arise regarding conflict of interest. These concerns must be discussed with the client and should also be mentioned to the third-party.[40] Finally, a lawyer must not approach a third-party for payment of fees without obtaining the prior permission of the client.[41] The client may quite reasonably view the lawyer's unilateral action as a betrayal or an improper revelation of confidential information, and conclude that the lawyer can no longer be trusted.

Counsel who is paid by a third-party should take special care to document the arrangement, and communicate with both the client and third-party regarding developments that bear upon legal costs. An overly carefree approach could lead to no payment at all, despite a competent and even successful defence. An illustration of the problem to be avoided is seen in *Shillington* v. *Foley*,[42] where counsel assumed that the young person's father was paying for legal services, but confirmed nothing in writing and never really clarified the arrangement

---

37  See Alta. ch. 13, comm. 2; and *Report of the Task Force on Systems of Civil Justice*, above note 25 at 67.

38  Most often, disclosure is required as a precursor to the consent of the third-party to a "hidden fee": see, for example, CBA Code ch. XI, comm. 7; Sask. ch. XI, comm. 7; Man. ch. 11, comm. 8; Nfld. ch. XI, comm. 7; Alta. ch. 13, r. 8; B.C. ch. 9, r. 8–9; N.S. ch. 12, comm. 12.8; Ont. r. 2.08(2) (commentary); and N.B. Part E, r. 1.

39  See section J, "Third-Party Payment of Fees," in chapter 6.

40  *Ibid.*

41  See ABA Defense Standard 4-3.3, commentary (Overreaching).

42  (1985), 45 Sask. R. 238 (Q.B.).

with the father. After the client was discharged at the preliminary inquiry, on a charge of murder no less, the father refused to pay. The court ruled that the lawyer could not recover from the father, having failed to prove any contract between the two parties.

Where a client relies on a legal aid plan to pay the lawyer, the obligation to keep the client fully informed regarding fees and disbursements persists.[43] In particular, any pertinent restrictions on the scope of work covered by the plan should be discussed with the client.[44] The legal aid plan may itself provide for disclosure to the client, in which case the lawyer must comply with such requirements.[45] The plan will also likely impose upon the lawyer an obligation to provide the plan with certain information concerning the case. These obligations should be carried out fully. Finally, given the fiduciary nature of the client-lawyer relationship, we believe that a lawyer has a duty to inform the client regarding the availability of a legal aid plan where the client might reasonably be thought to qualify for and have an interest in utilizing such a plan.[46]

# E. MISREPRESENTATION

Lawyers are ethically forbidden to mislead a client in almost all contexts.[47] It follows that lawyers are not permitted to mislead the client in an effort to set higher fees or collect amounts owed, not even where the fees are reasonable and payment is deserved. For instance, making a bogus claim that counsel can bribe a prosecutor or judge is highly improper, especially as the client is betrayed in a manner that suggests

---

43   The main types of legal aid plan in operation in Canada (judicare, staff system, or a combination) are discussed in *R. v. Brydges* (1990), 53 C.C.C. (3d) 330 at 348 (S.C.C.). It appears that counsel who represents a client covered by a legal aid plan has contractual relations with both the client and the plan: see D. Lundy, G. MacKenzie, & M. Newbury, *Barristers and Solicitors in Practice* (Toronto: Butterworths, 1998) at §13.11.

44   See B.C. ch. 9, r. 4. This is not to say, however, that clients who rely upon a legal aid plan are forced to accept service that is less than competent: see *R. v. B.(L.C.)* (1996), 104 C.C.C. (3d) 353 (Ont. C.A.)) [*B. (L.C.)*]

45   See, for example, *P. v. Legal Aid Society of Alberta* (1994), 121 D.L.R. (4th) 137 at 142 & 144 (Alta. Q.B.) [*Legal Aid Society of Alberta*].

46   See Que. s. 3.01.05; Man. ch. 11, comm. 3; and *Karpenic v. Kress* (1998), 128 Man. R. (2d) 32 (Q.B.).

47   There may be extraordinary exceptions, such as a falsehood necessary to prevent substantial bodily harm to a third party.

a corrupt system of justice.[48] The lawyer who artificially inflates the jeopardy faced by the accused, or exaggerates the complexity of the case, in an effort to increase fees has also acted improperly. Similarly, counsel should never pad fees for the purpose of charging the client an inflated amount (or indeed for any other purpose).[49]

## F. RETAINER AGREEMENT SHOULD BE IN WRITING

Counsel should always have the client sign a retainer agreement, or at least memorialize the retainer terms in a document provided to the client. A dispute over the terms of the retainer is much more easily resolved if the agreement is reflected in a written document. If a dispute over fees goes to litigation, the lawyer bears a heavy onus to show that the client agreed to the payment terms.[50] A signed retainer agreement goes a long way towards meeting this onus, although ambiguity in the written agreement will be resolved in favour of the client.[51] Finally, a comprehensive written review of financial matters relevant to the retainer may avoid disagreements in the first place, and serves to ensure (and confirm) that the client is fully informed.

Most Canadian rules of professional conduct do not require or even advise counsel to set out the arrangements regarding fees and disbursements in writing.[52] The British Columbia Professional Conduct Handbook mentions writing, but only regarding communications with the client pertaining to the limits of a pre-paid legal services plan.[53]

---

48 See ABA Defense Standard 4-3.3(c) & commentary (Implication that Fee Is for Other than Professional Services).

49 See Que. s. 4.02.01(w) (prohibiting counsel from claiming fees for unperformed or falsely described work). See also S. Chan, "ABA Formal Opinion 93-379: Double Billing, Padding and Other Forms of Overbilling" (1996), 9 Geo. J. Legal Ethics 611; and L. Lerman, "Lying to Clients" (1990), 138 U. Pa. L. Rev. 659 at 709–13, 749–53.

50 See, for example, *Swinton*, above note 28; and *Cooper*, above note 7 at 356.

51 See, for example, *Huda*, above note 29.

52 See, for example, CBA Code ch. XI; Sask. ch. XI; Man. ch. 11; Nfld. ch. XI; B.C. ch. 9, r. 8–9; N.S. ch. 12; Ont. r. 2.08. However, most provinces require that contingency-fee agreements be in writing: see, for example, N.B. Part E, r. 2; Yukon Part 1, r. 12; Law Society of British Columbia Rules, Part 12, r. 1060(a); Law Society of Saskatchewan Rules, Part 18, r. 1501(1); Manitoba, *Law Society Act*, R.S.M. 1987, ch. L100, s. 58(2); and Ontario, *Class Proceedings Act, 1992*, S.O. 1992, ch. 6, s. 32(1).

53 See B.C. ch. 9, r. 4.

New Brunswick has a general rule requiring written confirmation of any agreement between client and lawyer, which perhaps applies to the retainer agreement.[54] Alberta's code is a rare beacon of light in this regard, however, stating that "[a] lawyer must provide to the client *in writing*, before or within a reasonable time after commencing a representation, as much information regarding fees and disbursements as is reasonable and practical in the circumstances, including the basis on which fees will be determined."[55] For the reasons already given, we believe that lawyers in other jurisdictions are wise to follow the Alberta approach. The Canadian Bar Association is moving in the direction of recommending written confirmation of the retainer agreement, to be included in what is called an engagement letter.[56] Canadian courts have also urged counsel to memorialize retainer agreements in writing.[57]

## G. FLAT FEES, HOURLY RATES, AND OTHER COMPENSATORY METHODS

There are several general methods by which a lawyer's fees can be calculated. Criminal lawyers often charge fees on a block- or flat-fee basis, under which a total amount is set, to be paid regardless of the amount of time spent on the case. The other main fee arrangement is to charge the client by the hour for all work done. Block fees have the benefit of finality and simplicity for both parties. Hourly fees may be better attuned to proportioning the amount of work actually done to costs paid by the client. A graduated block-fee arrangement, sometimes called a "stair-step fee" is also possible, whereby block fees are paid at different stages of the case.[58] Furthermore, some lawyers charge on an

---

54  See N.B. Part E, r. 3.

55  Alta. ch. 13, r. 2 (emphasis added).

56  See *Report on Systems of Civil Justice*, above note 25 at 67.

57  See, for example, *Gorin* v. *Flinn Merrick* (1995), 138 N.S.R. (2d) 116 (C.A.); and *Swinton*, above note 28.

58  It has been argued that the graduated or block fee, while attractive in theory, provides too great an incentive for counsel not to win at the preliminary inquiry or on a pre-trial motion: see Perini, "Setting and Collecting Fees in Criminal Cases," above note  at 4. Yet this criticism would apply equally to all hourly-fee arrangements. Conversely, it could be argued that a graduated fee incorporates the objectionable elements of a contingency fee. However, ABA Defense Standard 4-3.3, commentary (Contingent Fees), sensibly observes that a gradu-

hourly basis for out-of-court preparation, plus a block fee for each day in court.

The relative advantages and disadvantages of the various methods of calculating fees depend upon many factors, few of which directly concern lawyers' ethics. In particular, aside from the special problems associated with non-refundable retainer payments and contingency fees, which are discussed below,[59] we see no ethical bar to lawyers accepting retainers that are based all or in part on block-fee payments. However, as with any payment for legal services, the block fee must be reasonable, and the client must understand and consent to the arrangement following a full explanation by the lawyer. In Quebec a lawyer "advertising lump-sum fees" is subject to particular ethical duties, which essentially amount to requiring fair and complete disclosure.[60] Moreover, a block fee does not provide counsel with a license to skimp on time spent preparing for trial.[61] As well, counsel would be wise to record all time spent on the file, even though fees are not calculated on an hourly basis, in case a dispute later arises regarding the reasonableness of the block fee.

Finally, if a block fee is envisioned, counsel should precisely set out the service to be provided. Consider the client and lawyer who enter into a written retainer agreement that runs as follows: "I hereby request that you act as my counsel at trial in respect of two charges under the *Controlled Drugs and Substances Act*. In consideration of your so doing I agree to pay your fee of $15,000." The client eventually pleads guilty without the need for a trial. Counsel insists that the entire amount of $15,000 has been earned. The client argues that the agreement provides for full payment only in the event of a contested trial. A court may well conclude that the agreement is ambiguous and resolve the uncertainty in favour of the client.[62]

---

ated fee "is not a contingent fee but merely an attempt to relate the fee to the time and service involved."

59  See section H, "Contingency Fees," and J, "Non-Refundable Fees," in this chapter.

60  See Que. s. 5.03.

61  See, for example, *B.(L.C.)*, above note 44 at 371, where the court suggests that counsel acted improperly in failing to visit the client in jail prior to trial because his block fee-based profit margin would suffer.

62  The facts in this example, and the suggested judicial resolution, generally follow the case of *Re Solicitor* (1967), [1968] 1 O.R. 45 (S.C. Masters/Registrars) (Assess. O.) [*Re Solicitor*].

## H. CONTINGENCY FEES

All Canadian jurisdictions except for Ontario accept the use of contingency fees,[63] by which is meant any arrangement where the lawyer risks non-payment of fees if the result is not favourable to the client.[64] Even in Ontario, contingency fees are allowed in the context of class proceedings.[65] Despite the widespread acceptance of contingency fees in civil matters in Canada and the United States, a number of jurisdictions expressly prohibit such fee arrangements in the criminal setting.[66] The ban on criminal contingency fees is often portrayed as, or assumed to be, close to universal. Such is not, however, the case. In fact, in Canada the significant majority of jurisdictions do *not* prohibit contingency fees in criminal cases. Only in Alberta, New Brunswick, and Ontario are criminal contingency fees expressly forbidden.[67]

Even in the provinces that forbid criminal contingency fees, for all intents and purposes criminal lawyers can probably work under contingency-like fee arrangements without fear of breaking the law or vio-

---

63   See, for example, Alta. ch. 13, r. 3; B.C. ch. 1, r. 3(7); Man. ch. 11, comm. 11; Sask. ch. XI, comm. 10; N.S. ch. 12, comm. 12.11; N.B. Part E, r. 2; and Yukon Part 1, r. 12. The CBA Code states that contingency fees are allowed except where prohibited by the laws of the jurisdiction in which the lawyer practices: CBA Code ch. XI, comm. 10. The statutory and ethical provisions bearing upon contingency fees in each province are set out in the Federation of Law Societies of Canada, *Contingent Fee Agreement* (Montreal: Federation of Law Societies of Canada, 1998).

64   This definition is taken from G. MacKenzie, *Lawyers and Ethics: Professional Responsibility and Discipline* (Toronto: Carswell, 1993) at 12-1. Overall, MacKenzie provides an extensive and thoughtful review of contingency fees in chapter 12 of his book.

65   See Ontario *Class Proceedings Act, 1992*, above note 52, ss. 32–33. The Law Society of Upper Canada has encouraged the government to permit contingency fees more generally, but without success to date. Note that the Rules of Professional Conduct in Ontario are currently worded so as to permit contingency fees if the *Solicitors Act*, R.S.O. 1990, ch. S.15, s. 28, is amended to this effect: see Ont. r. 2.08(4).

66   In the United States, see ABA Model Code DR 2-106(C); ABA Model Rule 1.5(d); ABA Defense Standard 4-3.3(f); and Third Restatement §47, all of which forbid contingency fees in criminal matters. Contingency fees are also frequently forbidden or restricted in family law matters: see, for example, Alta. ch. 13, r. 3.

67   See Alta ch. 13, r. 3; N.B. Part E, r. 2; Ontario *Solicitors Act*, above note 65, s. 28. See also the recommendations of the Ontario Civil Justice Review, *Task Force Report on the Ontario Civil Justice System* (Toronto: Ontario Civil Justice Review, 1996) at 148; and the Law Society of Upper Canada, *Report to Convocation: Joint Committee on Contingency Fees* (23 June 2000) at para. 5(a), to allow contingency fees but not in criminal or family matters.

lating rules of professional conduct. A lawyer who does not require a retainer payment in advance, to be applied against legal fees and disbursements, may reasonably have little or no expectation of payment if the client is convicted. Such is especially true where the client faces a substantial jail sentence if convicted, yet if acquitted will be able to pay legal expenses over time by virtue of ongoing employment. Slightly more contentious, though seemingly valid, is the charging of premiums. It would appear that a premium based on an excellent result in a criminal matter does not violate a general prohibition against contingency fees (although this assertion is more difficult to justify where a substantial proportion of the total fee paid is based on achieving the favourable result). It has also been noted that lawyers have an incentive to win cases, as a means to acquire good reputations and the associated financial rewards of attracting clients. In this extremely broad sense, there is a modest contingency element in all criminal-litigation files.

The reasons usually offered for barring criminal lawyers from taking contingency fees are ostensibly linked to particular features of the criminal justice system. For instance, it is often said that a contingency fee will encourage the lawyer to ignore plea-resolution possibilities and attempt to obtain an acquittal at all costs, in a single-minded effort to get paid. Or the lawyer might fail to lead evidence or forego an argument that involves conceding culpability to a lesser offence in order to avoid conviction on a more serious charge. Because the liberty of the accused is often in jeopardy in a criminal matter, this sort of conduct will have especially serious adverse impact on the client. Arguably, the client is also more vulnerable in the criminal context, by virtue of the jeopardy faced, and thus more susceptible to overreaching contingency-fee arrangements.[68] It has additionally been said that criminal lawyers will be tempted to suborn perjury and otherwise pervert the course of justice in an effort to win cases and collect fees. Yet a different objection to criminal contingency fees is that criminal proceedings by their nature make such arrangements unnecessary. Access to justice, a primary basis for permitting contingency fees in civil matters, is a diminished concern in the criminal setting, owing to legal aid programs and the constitutional right of an accused to legal representation

---

68    See P. Karlan, "Contingent Fees and Criminal Cases" (1993) 93 Colum. L. Rev. 595 at 625–29, though speaking primarily of the situation where the contingency fee is related to the result obtained by the lawyer on a negotiated guilty plea.

in complex cases. Similarly, there is often no property at stake in criminal cases, making contingency arrangements inapplicable.[69]

The arguments against permitting contingency arrangements in criminal matters are not exactly overwhelming.[70] First, other fee arrangements can provide counsel with a comparable incentive to subordinate the client's interests. The flat-fee retainer can be seen to reward the lawyer for not going to trial. Conversely, payment by the hour might serve as an incentive to take the case to trial and drag out the proceeding as much as possible. Contingency-fee arrangements are not unique in this regard. Second, a contingency-fee agreement can be structured to include a plea resolution. For instance, a graduated scale of payments, linking compensation to results at various points in the process, can be used to encourage counsel to work towards a plea resolution where appropriate. Third, it is manifestly unfair to suggest that criminal lawyers are somehow more prone to betray the client's interest, or the system's, than are their civil counterparts. Finally, the absence of a *res* from which recovery can be sought by the lawyer, and diminished access to justice concerns owing to the availability of legal aid, do not justify banning contingency fees in criminal cases.

Nevertheless, practically speaking, the unattractiveness of contingency-fee arrangements in criminal matters, from the defence lawyer's perspective, probably represents the main reason why retainers are not set up on this basis. The arguments that drive contingency fees in the civil setting relate in large part to ensuring access to justice for those who cannot otherwise afford legal representation. But these arguments carry much less weight in the criminal sphere. For one thing, in most cases there is no asset or reward to which defence counsel can look for payment if the client is acquitted.[71] Moreover, the accused who has no

---

69   More novel potential justifications for forbidding or regulating contingency fee arrangements in criminal matters are discussed by Karlan, *ibid.* at 613–32. For instance, she suggests that such arrangements may cause an adverse impact on innocent clients, who are in effect forced to subsidize the legal costs of guilty clients. She also alludes to the temptation of lawyers to take advantage of ignorant clients in assessing the likelihood of a particular result, and the systemic problems associated with a lawyer "judging" the client in an effort to assess the risk of conviction.

70   See Karlan, *ibid.*; C.W. Wolfram, *Modern Legal Ethics* (St. Paul: West, 1986) at 535–38; and P. Lushing, "The Rise and Fall of the Criminal Contingent Fee" (1991), 82 J. Crim. L. & Criminology 498 (all recommending that criminal contingency fees be allowed, though Karlan is more tentative).

71   A type of criminal case where contingency fees may make some sense is the forfeiture proceeding. In this instance, there is an asset, sometimes of substantial size, that a lawyer can look to for payment. Other assets from which payment

money to pay for legal services frequently qualifies for some sort of legal aid program. Finally, a substantial majority of accused persons end up being convicted of some offence. A retainer arrangement that makes the lawyer's payment largely dependent upon obtaining an acquittal is thus not feasible in many cases.[72]

Ultimately, we do not see any principled ethical bar to contingency fees that is particular to criminal cases. The more formidable impediment is the economic infeasibility of contingency fees from the defence lawyer's perspective. Nevertheless, in the rare case where a lawyer decides that a contingency fee may be a reasonable way of arranging payment for services provided, and the client is agreeable, it is important to review the law and ethical rules applicable in the particular jurisdiction. If, as is quite possible, contingency fees in criminal matters are illegal or prohibited by the governing body, counsel must not enter into a contingency arrangement.

# I. ADVANCE PAYMENTS TO BE HELD IN TRUST

The reasons why contingency fees are frequently an unattractive option for criminal lawyers in part explain why advance payments, to be held in trust, are so often required by counsel as a condition of taking on the case. Many clients have limited financial resources, and there is rarely any prospect of gaining access to an asset or rewards by means of successful litigation. Moreover, the accused in a criminal case is frequently a poor credit risk and may have little incentive to pay an account for legal costs regardless of whether the result at trial is favourable. Consequently, it is perfectly acceptable to require advance payment of fees and disbursements (to be held in trust pending completion of work and the rendering of an account). Obviously, the amounts billed for legal services must be reasonable and the client kept fully informed. In British Columbia, an added requirement is imposed,

---

can be obtained include insurance policies, civil suits for malicious prosecution, and literary rights. With respect to some of these assets, the successful lawyer may in any event acquire a lien in respect of legal costs, the most obvious example being assets that are saved from forfeiture.

72 Even if the lawyer is willing to take the risk in return for a high fee, the client may be unable or unprepared to pay such an amount.

namely, the lawyer must confirm the agreement regarding advance payment in writing and specify a payment date.[73]

It is a bit of a misnomer to refer to the money received in this fashion as an "advance payment," for the phrase incorrectly suggests that the retainer amount can be properly deposited directly to the lawyer's general account. Rather, it is important to emphasize that "advance payments" must be held in trust. Such trust deposits should not be moved to the lawyer's general account until fees have been earned and an account sent to the client,[74] nor can deposited amounts be paid to third parties in the form of disbursements until liability for the expenditure is incurred. It is improper, for instance, for a lawyer to bill the client for a substantial portion of the estimated total legal costs immediately upon receiving an advance retainer payment, unless the amount accurately reflects work actually done to date.

## J.  NON-REFUNDABLE FEES

Some lawyers treat monies received in advance of any work being done as non-refundable, meaning that the money is earned immediately upon receipt. Counsel will therefore keep the entire amount even where the case unexpectedly ends before much time or energy has been expended, or where the client discharges counsel early on in the retainer.[75] The question arises as to whether a lawyer can properly keep the entire amount, on the basis that the payment is non-refundable.

The main argument against non-refundable fees is that such arrangements impede the client's right to discharge counsel. The client who has paid a non-refundable fee may desist from firing a lawyer, despite having excellent cause to do so, because the result will be to waste money that would otherwise serve to ensure the provision of legal services.[76] The client-lawyer relationship is dependent upon a high level of trust and confidence. If the client is forced to continue with the relationship despite a lack of confidence, merely because the

---

73    See B.C. ch. 10, r. 6 (in the context of withdrawal).

74    See in particular Alta. ch. 13, r. 10 and Yukon Part 1, r. 11. See also the other rules mentioned at note 26, above.

75    The meanings given to various terms related to non-refundable fees, including special retainers, non-refundable retainers, and general retainers, are canvassed in *Wong v. Michael Kennedy, P.C.*, 853 F. Supp. 73 (E.D.N.Y. 1994) (a criminal case examining the propriety of a non-refundable retainer).

76    The reasons behind protecting the right of a client to discharge counsel at any time are also discussed in section D, "Discharge by the Client," in chapter 11.

financial cost of switching lawyers is oppressively high, the right to legal representation by counsel of choice is placed in jeopardy.[77] Non-refundable retainers may also raise concerns about the reasonableness of the client-lawyer financial arrangement.

On the other hand, there are reasons, of varying persuasiveness, why a lawyer might insist that all or a portion of a retainer not be returned to the client. Perhaps the client is retaining counsel in part so that the lawyer cannot be hired by another party with an interest in the same matter. The lawyer is thus giving up the opportunity to work for another client. Or the client may be hiring the lawyer to ensure the lawyer's availability at a certain future time, to be free to work on a case regardless of other professional obligations. Once again, the lawyer may wish to be fairly compensated for work that must consequently be turned away. Still other lawyers may desire to ensure that overhead costs, often greatest when opening a file, are entirely recouped, or desire some insurance against losing the case because of a conflict of interest not reasonably foreseen.

There is nothing inherently objectionable about a fee arrangement that reasonably compensates the lawyer for ensuring his or her availability, provided that certain preconditions are met. First, full disclosure to the client is especially important, and counsel must be precise and accurate in describing exactly how the retainer is to be earned. Absent a clear explanation, some clients may misunderstand the lawyer's intentions. Conversely, once made completely aware of the proposal, a client may refuse to agree. If, however, the client consents, a written record of the agreement is advisable.[78] Second, the arrangement must always accord with the requirement that legal fees be fair and reasonable.[79] Thus, a $50,000 non-refundable payment becomes unreasonable where the lawyer is forced to get off the record after spending only a few hours working on the case because of a conflict problem. Third, the retainer must not operate as a substantial bar to the client discharging counsel. In our view, this limit operates to

---

77   A case that stresses this problem in declaring that non-refundable retainers are always improper is *In re Cooperman*, 591 N.Y.S.2d 855 (App Div. 1993), appeal granted, stay granted 622 N.E.2d 299 (N.Y. 1993), aff'd 633 N.E.2d 1069 (N.Y. 1994).

78   In *Richmond v. Nodland*, 501 N.W.2d 759 (N.D. 1993), cert. denied 510 U.S. 869 (1993), counsel neglected to memorialize the non-refundable nature of the agreement in writing. He was fortunate, however, in that the client independently created a written record corroborating of the lawyer's version of events.

79   As Wolfram states, "no retainer should be non-refundable to the extent that it exceeds a reasonable fee": *Modern Legal Ethics*, above note 70 at 547.

ensure that the lawyer keeps only those monies that reasonably compensate for foregone opportunities and guaranteed availability.

Whenever a non-refundable retainer is agreed upon and paid by the client, counsel is well advised to keep track of all time spent on the file. If a dispute arises regarding the fees, and the client asks for a breakdown of the services provided, counsel will be able to comply. If the dispute leads to an assessment of the lawyer's account, the lawyer's records will help provide the basis for a just resolution. It is also possible that a court or assessment officer determines that payment should be based upon *quantum meruit*.[80] In such a case, the lawyer's detailed records will obviously provide important information.

**Caveat:** A client may wish to pay a fixed amount in exchange for the lawyer's promise to be available to perform legal services at an agreed price during a specific period. A criminal lawyer should refuse this sort of retainer where the client is essentially seeking to prearrange representation in case he or she is arrested in connection with a future crime. Accepting this general retainer may not unreasonably be viewed as participation in an ongoing criminal conspiracy.

# K. CONTRACT FOR LIMITED REPRESENTATION

A contract for limited representation involves the lawyer being retained for a discrete and restricted purpose, as opposed to the conduct of the entire case from start to finish. Sometimes the lawyer is expert in a particular area and is retained to conduct a specific portion of the case. A common instance is the lawyer who argues only a pretrial motion. Or a lawyer may accept a retainer for a bail hearing, without any assurance or understanding that he or she will subsequently continue with the representation. Another example of a limited-representation retainer occurs where the client wishes to hire a lawyer privately but will not be able to make sufficient payment to cover a full-blown trial. In this instance, the retainer agreement may provide that the lawyer can withdraw from the case at a certain predetermined stage, such as upon completion of the preliminary inquiry.

---

80   See, for example, *Olsen and Brown v. City of Englewood*, 889 P.2d 673 (Colo. 1995).

Limited retainers are ethically acceptable, provided that full disclosure is made to the client,[81] the fees charged are fair and reasonable, and the client is not being abused or unduly prejudiced by the arrangement. Furthermore, counsel should set out for the client the limits on representation in writing: "Any attempt by a solicitor to limit his/her retainer to a scope less than that required of a reasonably competent and diligent solicitor should be done in simple, concise and precise language reduced to writing. Any ambiguity in any such communication, whether it be written or oral, should be resolved against the solicitor."[82] Taking this precautionary step reduces the possibility of misunderstanding between client and counsel, and avoids an adverse finding against the lawyer if the matter requires resolution by a court.

Unless instructed otherwise, based on a valid reason, defence counsel should also make clear to Crown counsel and the court that the retainer is limited. In particular, the court should not be left with the incorrect impression that the lawyer will appear for the duration of the case, including the trial. In this respect, the British Columbia rules of professional conduct require that "a lawyer who acts for a client in a limited capacity only shall disclose promptly to the court and to any other interested person in the proceeding the limited retainer, in any case where failure to make disclosure would mislead the court or that other person."[83]

## L. UPDATING THE CLIENT AND MODIFYING THE FEE AGREEMENT

The duty to inform the client regarding the basis upon which a fee is to be charged must be ongoing. As the Alberta Code of Professional Conduct provides:

---

81  See ABA Model Rule 1.5, comm. 3.

82  See *ABN Amro Bank Canada* v. *Gowling, Strathy & Henderson* (1994), 20 O.R. (3d) 779 at 794 (Gen. Div.). See also *Carter* v. *Blake* (1982), 41 A.R. 418 (N.W.T.C.A.), where a lawyer failed to convince the court that a retainer covered only certain preliminary steps in preparing an appeal of the client's break-and-enter conviction.

83  B.C. ch. 10, r. 10. See also Que. s. 3.02.05. The same admonition is repeated in the case law: see, for example, the trio of Alberta cases, *R.* v. *Harrison* (1982), 67 C.C.C. (2d) 401 at 412–13 (Alta. C.A.), leave to appeal to S.C.C. refused (1982), 45 N.R. 540n (S.C.C.); *R.* v. *Le* (1994), 162 A.R. 4 at 5 (C.A.); and *C.(D.D.)*, above note 5 at 328.

> After initial fee consultations with the client, and in keeping with a lawyer's general obligation to maintain ongoing communication, the client must be kept advised of any developments affecting the current assessment (cf. Commentary 1(g)). Although there is no requirement that interim accounts be rendered, this practice is an excellent means of determining whether the most recent information provided by a lawyer remains valid while permitting the client to monitor legal costs as they accrue. A lawyer must confirm with the client in writing the substance of all fee discussions that occur as a matter progresses.[84]

Keeping the client informed as the matter progresses not only ensures that the client will be treated fairly by counsel. The practice also reduces the chances that misunderstandings will arise. Even if controversy regarding fees is unavoidable, prompt communication regarding financial matters almost always works to lessen the extent of the unpleasantness and disagreement.

Counsel who promptly keeps the client informed as to all matters bearing upon the retainer also avoids committing a cardinal sin: using the fact of an imminent or ongoing trial to pressure the client for payments. The client is especially vulnerable if the trial date is at hand, and counsel may desire to take advantage of this weakness in pressing for funds. Where such pressure is imposed to force a change in the retainer agreement, counsel's conduct is disloyal, breaches the fiduciary duty owed to the client, and hence is unethical.[85] Where the client is delinquent in paying overdue accounts or providing an agreed-upon advance payment, counsel's actions in pressing the client to honour the original agreement may be less problematic. It remains clear, however, that prudent counsel will not tempt fate by leaving the resolution of monetary matters to the court-house steps. The better approach is to settle retainer problems well before the trial and to make a timely application to withdraw if counsel is not willing to risk non-payment.[86]

It is also worth stressing that not every modification of the retainer agreement is forbidden. There may be good reason why the client and lawyer desire to alter the initial financial arrangement. Nevertheless,

---

84   Alta. ch. 13, comm. 2 (see also Alta. ch. 13, comm. 1(g)). See also CBA Code ch. XI, comm. 3; Sask. ch. IX, comm. 3; Man. ch. 11, comm. 4; Nfld. ch. IX, comm. 3; N.S. ch. 12, comm. 12.1; Ont. r. 2.08(2) (commentary).

85   See ABA Defense Standard 4-3.3 (commentary) Overreaching, stating that such conduct borders on extortion.

86   The topic of withdrawal for non-payment is discussed in section W, "Withdrawal," in this chapter.

modification at a minimum requires full disclosure to the client and the client's unpressured consent, and must not be unfair or unreasonable in the circumstances. Moreover, if the trial date is fast approaching, counsel would be wise to recommend that the client obtain independent legal advice on the matter, given that inequality of bargaining power and conflict concerns are often greatest once the trial is imminent.

# M. COST AWARDS AGAINST THE CROWN

Until fairly recently, the prospect of one party paying another's legal costs in criminal litigation was slim.[87] Cost awards have become more common of late, however, with the Crown sometimes being ordered to pay an amount towards defence legal expenses.[88] The general standard for obtaining such an award is demanding, and orders for costs represent the exception, not the rule. It appears, for instance, that the Crown must be guilty of at least some degree of misconduct or unacceptable negligence.[89]

Defence counsel should carefully assess whether an application for costs is warranted as having a reasonable prospect of success. If so, there is a duty to raise the matter with the client, who must decide whether to proceed with an application.[90] Where costs are recovered, they are the client's property subject to any reasonable agreement to

---

87   See *R. v. Pawlowski* (1993), 79 C.C.C. (3d) 353 at 356 (Ont. C.A.), leave to appeal to S.C.C. refused (1993), 83 C.C.C. (3d) vi (S.C.C.) [*Pawlowski*].

88   Costs can be awarded pursuant to the inherent jurisdiction of a superior court, and additionally under s. 24(1) of the *Canadian Charter of Rights and Freedoms*, Part 1 of the *Constitution Act, 1982*, being Schedule B to the *Canada Act 1982* (U.K.), 1982, c. 11 [*Charter*] on proof of a breach of the accused's constitutional rights: see for example, *R. v. Pawlowski*, above note 87 at 356–57; *R. v. Dostaler* (1994), 91 C.C.C. (3d) 444 (N.W.T.S.C.); *R. v. Pang* (1994), 95 C.C.C. (3d) 60 (Alta. C.A.); *R. v. Daigle* (1997), 162 N.S.R. (2d) 81 (S.C.), aff'd (1998), 165 N.S.R. (2d) 262 (C.A.) [*Daigle*]; and *R. v. McGillivary* (1990), 56 C.C.C. (3d) 304 (N.B.C.A.).

89   See, for example, *R. v. Robinson* (1999), 142 C.C.C. (3d) 303 (Alta. C.A.); and *R. v. Cole* (2000), 143 C.C.C. (3d) 417 (N.S.C.A.).

90   Notice should also be provided to the Crown, at least where costs are sought under s. 24(1) of the *Charter*, above note 88: see, for example, *Daigle* (S.C.), above note 88 at 91. A civil action for damages or other remedies may also arise from a *Charter* violation: see for example, *R. v. Simpson* (1994), 88 C.C.C. (3d) 377 (Nfld. C.A.), rev'd on other grounds (1995), 95 C.C.C. (3d) 96 (S.C.C.); and *Michaud v. Quebec (A.G.)* (1996), 109 C.C.C. (3d) 289 (S.C.C.)).

the contrary and the possibility of a lawyer's lien. It is therefore always necessary to provide the client with an accurate accounting regarding costs received from the Crown.[91] An interesting issue arises as to whether counsel and the client can agree upon a contingency-fee arrangement regarding a prospective cost award.[92]

# N. REFERRALS

Referrals are an important part of the typical criminal lawyer's practice. However, there are a number of ethical issues that arise regarding referrals. First, can a lawyer properly receive payment in return for referring a matter to another lawyer? Second, is payment to a non-lawyer who refers clients ethically permitted? Third, are there instances where a lawyer should not accept a referral under any circumstances, regardless of the fact that no money is being paid for the referral? We will address each of these questions in turn.

## 1)  Payment for Referrals Received from a Lawyer

Referral fees are amounts paid to a lawyer, not for work done in connection with a case but rather as a reward for referring the matter to a professional colleague. Traditionally, rules of professional conduct in Canada have looked askance at referral fees. The CBA Code and most governing bodies ostensibly prohibit referral fees unless the lawyer receiving the payment is rewarded in proportion to work done and responsibility assumed, and the client consents.[93] The role that shared "responsibility" might play under these rules is unclear. Arguably, the lawyer who locates a client can "share responsibility," while doing little or perhaps even no work on the file, and be paid a portion of the overall fee. It could be countered, however, that the conjunctive wording used in the CBA Code and other Canadian rules prohibits a "pure referral" situation, where the referring lawyer does absolutely no work on the case. The language used in New Brunswick is amenable to a

---

91    Compare the Alberta provision regarding party-and-party costs, which requires a full accounting to the client: Alta. ch. 13, r. 6).

92    Such an agreement should not be made without first establishing that there is no legal or ethical bar in the jurisdiction. See section H, "Contingency Fees," in this chapter.

93    See, for example, CBA Code ch. IX, comm. 6; Sask. ch. IX, comm. 6; Man. ch. 11, comm. 7; Nfld. ch. IX, comm. 6; N.S. ch. 12, comm. 12.5; Que. s. 3.05.15; Alta. ch. 13, r. 7; N.B. Part E, r. 1; and Yukon Part 1, r. 9.

more daring interpretation, for the disjunctive reference to "service or responsibility" implies that a pure referral is acceptable simply provided that the referring lawyer shares responsibility.[94] Yet, regardless of the meaning attributed to "responsibility," in larger firms a partner or associate may end up receiving compensation for work provided to an in-house colleague, and Canadian professional conduct rules expressly permit this sort of arrangement.[95]

Prohibiting referral fees is thought to avoid needless litigation arising out of fee-related disputes, and also holds at bay what has often been viewed as the unseemly commercialization of law practice.[96] But the prohibition definitely works to the disadvantage of small firms and sole practitioners, who are much less likely to possess expertise in-house. The lawyer in a larger firm can refer a matter to a colleague, safe in the knowledge that the financial benefits from the retainer will still be enjoyed by the entire firm. But the sole practitioner receives no similar benefit from referring a matter to outside counsel. The incentive therefore may be to keep the client, even where counsel is not especially well equipped to handle the matter, to the ultimate detriment of the client. From the client's perspective, referral fees can thus serve to help secure competent and cost-effective representation. Accordingly, preventing referral fees can work as a bar to the client finding the right lawyer for the particular case.

To maximize benefits for the client, and avoid unfairness for smaller firms, the Law Society of Upper Canada has recently approved referral fees in the following terms:

> Where a lawyer refers a matter to another lawyer because of expertise and ability of the other lawyer to handle the matter and the referral was not made because of conflict of interest, the referring lawyer may accept and the other lawyer may pay a referral fee provided that:
> (a) the fee is reasonable and does not increase the total amount of the fee charged to the client; and
> (b) the client is informed and consents.[97]

---

94   See N.B. Part E, r. 1.

95   See, for example, CBA Code ch. IX, comm. 6; Sask. ch. IX, comm. 6; Man. ch. 11, comm. 7; Nfld. ch. IX, comm. 6; N.S. ch. 12, comm. 12.5; and Alta. ch. 13, r. 7.

96   See G. Hazard & W. Hodes, *The Law of Lawyering: A Handbook on the Model Rules of Professional Conduct*, 2d ed. (Englewood, N.J.: Prentice Hall, 1993) at §1.5(601).

97   Ont. r. 2.08(8). The Ontario rule still prohibits payment of referral fees to non-lawyers: see Ont. r. 2.08(9), as well as section N(2), "Referral Fees Paid to Non-Lawyers," in this chapter.

This position, while relatively unique among Canadian governing bodies,[98] represents a logical approach to referral fees. An outstanding question, however, pertains to the ostensible cap on the total fee ("does not increase the total amount of the fee charged to the client"). If the referral process results in added value to the client, perhaps the cap can accommodate a corresponding increase in the total fee. In any event, it may be exceedingly difficult to determine whether a referral fee actually operates to exceed this cap.

## 2)   Referral Fees Paid to Non-Lawyers

Dividing fees among non-lawyers is forbidden by most Canadian rules of professional conduct.[99] Yet, despite the preclusion against paying referral fees to non-lawyers, it is obviously permissible for a lawyer to pay amounts to employees and contract workers in return for assistance regarding a case (as opposed to referring business) on a non-file specific basis.[100]

An egregious example of breaching the prohibition against referral fees paid to non-lawyers is found in *R. v. Wijesinha*,[101] where a lawyer routinely paid a police officer money in return for referring impaired and "over 80" cases. The scheme was revealed when the lawyer attempted to recruit a second police officer, who went "undercover" in collecting evidence as part of a police investigation. The referral arrangement was not in contravention of any criminal law, for the lawyer never suggested that the police officers or clients should pres-

---

98   The only other governing body that permits referral fees paid to other lawyers is the Law Society of British Columbia: see B.C. ch. 9, r. 3. In the United States, such fees are to some extent permitted by ABA Model Rule 1.5(e); and ABA Defense Standard 4-2.3 & 4-3.3(e). The Third Restatement §47 goes the furthest among the major American ethical codes in condoning referral payments to lawyers, since the division of fees between lawyers who are not in the same firm is permitted where the lawyers involved assume joint responsibility, the client gives informed consent, and the total fee remains reasonable.

99   See, for example, CBA Code ch. XI, comm. 8; Sask. ch. IX, comm. 8; Man. ch. 11, comm. 9; Nfld. ch. IX, comm. 8; Alta. ch. 13, r. 7; B.C. ch. 9, r. 2(a) & 6; Que. s. 3.05.14; N.S. ch. 12, comm. 12.9; Ont. r. 2.08(9); and Yukon Part 1, r. 9. See also ABA Defense Standard 4-2.3 (referral fees prohibited subject to certain exceptions covering payments to other lawyers) & 4-3.3(d) (division of fees with non-lawyers only condoned where permitted by applicable ethical codes of conduct).

100  See, for example, Alta. ch. 13, comm. 7; B.C. ch. 9, r. 6, n. 1; and N.S. ch. 12, comm. 12.9.

101  (1995), 100 C.C.C. (3d) 410 (S.C.C.).

ent false evidence. But the lawyer's governing body, the Law Society of Upper Canada, commenced an investigation upon learning of the referral arrangement. This investigation proved to be his downfall, for, in providing responding materials to the Law Society, the lawyer knowingly submitted false statutory declarations. He was discovered, charged with attempting to obstruct justice, and convicted, the sentence being fifteen months' incarceration. This case underlines the damage that can occur where a lawyer dissembles in an effort to cover up a breach of the rules of professional conduct. What began as a disciplinary infraction was transformed into a career-ending criminal conviction.

## 3) Non-paying Referrals and Conflict of Interest

Counsel must never accept referrals from any source where the result would be to compromise loyalties to the client, this regardless of the fact that no compensation or reward is paid to the referring individual.[102] The problem is a potential for conflict of interest.[103] Referrals from a Crown lawyer, court clerk, complainant, police officer or others do not invariably represent a disqualifying conflict of interest. However, where such referrals come with any modicum of regularity, and the referring party is a frequent participant in cases involving the defence lawyer, or where the referring party is materially involved in the client's case, serious conflict problems can occur. Where any hint of conflict arises, counsel should make full disclosure to the client, recommend that independent legal advice be obtained, and obtain a written waiver. In especially problematic cases, counsel may be best advised or forced to decline the retainer altogether.

**Example I:** A defence lawyer receives a referral from a law school friend who is now a Crown lawyer in another city. The Crown lawyer is recommending defence counsel to an acquaintance who requires legal representation in an impaired driving case. The two lawyers have little prospect of ever facing each other in a case, and none whatsoever in the matter at hand. With full disclosure and a written waiver, there is likely no problem in defence counsel taking on the case.

**Example II:** Let us change the example just given, so that the referral comes from a police officer, primarily as an expression of respect for

---

102 See ABA Defense Standard 4-2.3.
103 See chapter 6, especially section L, "Lawyer's Financial and Other Personal Interests."

counsel's abilities. Assume that the credibility of the officer and his colleagues is potentially at issue in the case. In this instance, the potential for conflict is not so easily rectified by disclosure to the client, independent legal advice, and waiver.

## O. APPORTIONING FEES AMONG CLIENTS AND DOUBLE-BILLING

Where counsel acts for two or more clients in respect of the same matter, the lawyer is under a duty to apportion the fees and disbursements equitably among the clients (in the absence of an agreement otherwise).[104] This obligation to apportion legal costs among clients equitably should also apply where work is done for the joint benefit of clients who are not represented in respect of the same matter. Even where the rules of professional responsibility do not expressly set out this duty, the lawyer's fiduciary obligations to the clients require equitable apportionment of fees and disbursements in the normal course.

It should go without saying that counsel must not bill a client for time spent working on another client's matter. The temptation arises where counsel is travelling or waiting in court in relation to a case and uses the opportunity to do research or review disclosure respecting a different matter. Double-billing for the lawyer's work is at best unethical and at worst fraudulent.

## P.  *PRO BONO* WORK AND WEALTHY CLIENTS

Most rules of professional conduct encourage lawyers to provide legal services for free, or at a reduced rate, where an impoverished client would otherwise be unable to obtain justice. In this vein, the CBA Code states: "It is in keeping with the best traditions of the legal profession to reduce or waive a fee in cases of hardship or poverty, or

---

104  See, for example, CBA Code ch. IX, comm. 5; Sask. ch. IX, comm. 5; Man. ch. 11, comm. 6; Nfld. ch. IX, comm. 5; N.S. ch. 12, comm. 12.4; B.C. ch. 9, r. 5; Alta. ch. 13, r. 7; and Ont. r. 2.08(6). See also *Canada Life Casualty Insurance Co.* v. *Pahl*, [1998] 3 W.W.R. 263 at 268 (Alta. Q.B.).

where the client or prospective client would otherwise effectively be deprived of legal advice or representation."[105]

Many criminal lawyers provide a substantial amount of work for clients at reduced rates and in so doing are heeding the aspirational goal of acting in the "best traditions of the legal profession."[106] The rationale behind *pro bono* work is that, as officers of the court and beneficiaries of a professional monopoly, lawyers have an obligation to provide a public service by ensuring access to the legal system.[107]

What about the converse situation, involving the client of considerable means? Some commentators believe that clients who manifest an ability to pay large legal fees can be charged a premium for this reason alone.[108] The justification offered for this sort of premium billing is that defence lawyers frequently provide work for clients who cannot afford to pay a full fee for work provided. The wealthy client is thus subsidizing the work done for the impoverished client. This "Robin Hood" approach to client billing is less attractive where legal aid plans provide coverage for all accused whose incomes fall below a certain level. But some governing bodies in Canada, namely, Alberta, British Columbia, and New Brunswick, expressly forbid counsel from billing wealthy clients at a higher rate.[109] The rules in these jurisdictions are

---

105 CBA Code ch. XI, comm. 2. See also Sask. ch. XI, comm. 2; Man. C. 11, comm. 2; Nfld. c. XI, comm. 2; N.S. ch. 12, comm. 12.2 (adding a reference to arranging for delayed payment of fees); B.C. ch. 1, r. 3(9); N.B. Part E, r. 1; and Ont. r. 2.08(2) (commentary) (adding that a lawyer should provide public-interest legal services and should support organizations that provide services to persons of limited means). Also relevant is CBA Code ch. XIII, comm. 5, which states that a lawyer may assist in making legal services available by participating in legal aid referral services. In the United States, see ABA Model Rule 6.1, which offers counsel a detailed outline of the minimum obligation expected (though not necessarily required).

106 For candid criticisms of Canadian ethical codes' failure to *require* counsel to take on work at reduced or no fees, and suggestions aimed at increasing access to legal system, see MacKenzie, above note 64 at 9-1–4; and A. Hutchinson, *Legal Ethics and Professional Responsibility* (Toronto: Irwin Law, 1999) at 83–86. Recommendations to increase *pro bono* work in the civil setting are contained in the *Report on Systems of Civil Justice*, above note 25 at 69–71. Admittedly, there can be problems associated with forced *pro bono* retainers, especially where substantial burdens are disproportionately placed upon certain lawyers.

107 See B. Dickson, "The Public Responsibilities of Lawyers" (1983) 13 Man. L.J. 175.

108 See the roundtable discussion in "Exploring the Labyrinth of Fee Setting" in American Bar Association, *How to Set and Collect Attorney Fees in Criminal Cases* (Chicago: American Bar Association, 1985) at 17–18.

109 See Alta. ch. 13, comm. 1; B.C. ch. 1, r. 3(9); and N.B. Part E, r. 1.

not exactly the same. Alberta says that a client's wealth is irrelevant to the calculation of the proper fee. New Brunswick precludes charging "a larger than ordinary fee" based on the client's ability to pay. British Columbia stipulates that ability to pay cannot justify a charge "in excess of the value of the service."

In other Canadian jurisdictions, the rules of professional conduct do not directly address the issue of charging wealthy clients at a higher rate. Yet the general disclosure rules pertaining to fees would likely require that the wealthy client be told that a premium is being charged, and why.[110] However, there is room to manoeuvre in this regard. A client of substantial means may be able to pay a fee that is fair and reasonable, while an impecunious client cannot. The unavoidable truth of the matter is that the wealthy client in effect helps to subsidize the poorer client. We see nothing wrong with this state of affairs, as long as the wealthy client is not charged an excessive amount. In this respect, note that the ABA Defense Standards list "the capacity of the client to pay the fee" as a valid factor to take into account in determining the amount of the fee in a criminal case (albeit without distinguishing between wealthy and impoverished clients).[111]

## Q. DISBURSEMENTS

Lawyers are occasionally cavalier about disbursements, perhaps because these expenditures do not result in any benefit for counsel. But clients tend not to distinguish so clearly between fees and disbursements, and reasonably so: both are necessary and real costs associated with legal representation. The CBA Code's rule covering legal costs is devoted almost entirely to the subject of fees.[112] However, there are some references made to disbursements. For instance, the lawyer should give the client an early and fair estimate of fees and disbursements.[113] In addition, the duty to apportion legal costs equitably between clients is expressly said to encompass fees and disbursements.[114] Finally, the CBA Code advises that, "so far as disbursements

---

110 See section D, "Full and Timely Disclosure to the Client," in this chapter.
111 See ABA Defense Standard 4-3.3(b).
112 CBA Code ch. XI.
113 See, for example, CBA Code ch. XI, comm. 3; N.S. ch. 12, comm. 12.1; and Ont. r. 2.08(2) (commentary).
114 See, for example, CBA Code ch. XI, comm. 5; B.C. ch. 9 rule 5; N.S. ch. 12, comm. 12.4; and Ont. r. 2.08(6).

are concerned, only *bona fide* and specified payments to others may be included. If the lawyer is financially interested in the person to whom the disbursements are made, such as an investigating, brokerage or copying agency, the lawyer shall expressly disclose this fact to the client."[115]

Canadian rules of professional conduct of a more recent vintage do not allow the topic of disbursements to recede into the background. In Ontario, the general rule pertaining to legal costs expressly requires that a disbursement be fair, reasonable, and disclosed in a timely fashion.[116] The Ontario rules also indicate that a statement of account delivered to the client must "clearly and separately detail the amounts charged as fees and as disbursements."[117] The Alberta Code of Professional Conduct provides that disclosure obligations apply to both fees and disbursements[118] and forbids a lawyer from charging as disbursements any amounts that have not been paid or are not required to be paid to a third-party on the client's behalf.[119] These newer rules are more open about counsel's fiduciary duty to ensure that disbursements are incurred only where reasonable[120] and with the client's express or implied consent.[121] If a lawyer entertains any doubt whatsoever regarding the client's approval of a disbursement, the proper course of action is to obtain instructions.

# R. REPORTING REQUIREMENTS, CONFIDENTIALITY, AND PRIVILEGE

A lawyer owes the client a duty of confidentiality that encompasses all information pertaining to legal fees and disbursements. This proposi-

---

115 See, for example, CBA Code ch. XI, comm. 7; B.C. ch. 9, r. 9; N.S. ch. 12, comm. 12.8. Note that this reference to disbursements seems directed to the problem of so-called "hidden fees." For a more general obligation to keep the client informed regarding disbursements (in the form of the phrase "all financial matters"), see N.S. ch. 12, comm. 12.6.

116 Ont. r. 2.08(1). See also the commentary to r. 2.08(2), which makes frequent reference to obligations regarding both fees and disbursements.

117 Ont. r. 2.08(5). To the same effect, see Alta. ch. 13, r. 4. The Alberta code specifies that internal office expenses such as photocopying and fax charges, from which the lawyer usually imposes a set charge that contains a profit component, should be itemized as a fee on the account.

118 Alta. ch. 13, r. 2.

119 Alta. ch. 13, r. 5.

120 Alta. ch. 13, comm. 5.

121 *Ibid.*

tion is straightforward. But the application of legal-professional privilege to fee information is another matter altogether and can be maddenly difficult to ascertain. The need to clarify the protective ambit of privilege is made more urgent by virtue of impending legislative changes that may require lawyers to disclose confidential information relating to legal expenses. In this respect, some of the relevant issues have been addressed in the United States over the past two decades, though not without engendering a great deal of acrimony between defence lawyers and agents of the federal government. The American experience, while obviously not binding or necessarily appropriate for use in Canada, is of interest in ascertaining the suitability of various responses to the problem of confidentiality, privilege, and reporting requirements.

## 1) Confidentiality, Privilege, and Legal Fees

Details surrounding legal fees and disbursements are confidential in the broadest sense and cannot be revealed to third parties absent the client's consent. But the ethical duty of confidentiality does not necessarily equate with the scope of legal-professional privilege.[122] Whether privilege applies to information regarding legal costs, so as to provide an effective shield against a subpoena or other legal compulsion, is a discrete issue entirely and is presently the subject of divided case law in Canada. The strong trend evident in the authorities, however, is that a lawyer's trust-account transactions do not ordinarily constitute communications between client and lawyer for the purpose of obtaining legal advice. Instead, such transactions represent bare acts or facts and accordingly attract no legal-professional privilege.[123] Case law to the contrary is typically found in the context of tax litigation, of slightly

---

122 See M. Proctor, "Privilege and Fee Agreements" (1996) 75 Mich. St. Bar J. 822. On the general distinction between confidentiality and privilege, see section D, "Comparison with Legal-Professional Privilege," in chapter 4.
123 For cases that draw this distinction, many of which arise in a criminal or quasi-criminal setting, see, for example, *United States of America* v. *Mammoth Oil Co.* (1924), 56 O.L.R. 307 at 317–18 (H.C.J.); *Ontario (Securities Commission)* v. *Greymac Credit Corp.* (1983), 41 O.R. (2d) 328 (Div. Ct.); *R. v. Joubert* (1992), 69 C.C.C. (3d) 553 at 569 (B.C.C.A.); *R. v. Tysowski*, [1997] 8 W.W.R. 493 at 498 (Man. Q.B.); *R. v. Leibel* (1993), 111 Sask. R. 107 at 109 & 112 (Q.B.); *Re Murphy* (1998), 229 A.R. 157 at 160 (Q.B.); *R. v. B.* (1995), 3 B.C.L.R. (3d) 363 at 372–73 (S.C.); *Nova Scotia Securities Commission* v. *W.* (1996), 152 N.S.R. (2d) 1 at 11 (S.C.); *Law Society of Prince Edward Island* v. *Prince Edward Island (A.G.)* (1994), 123 Nfld. & P.E.I.R. 217 at 221 (P.E.I. S.C.(T.D.)); and *Stevens* v. *Canada (Prime Minister)* (1998), 161 D.L.R. (4th) 85 (F.C.A.) [*Stevens*].

older vintage, and rarely engages in a principled review of the interests at stake.[124]

**Reminder:** Excluding trust transactions from the protective ambit of privilege does not mean that a lawyer is free to breach confidences with respect to such information, as we have already observed. Disclosure of non-privileged but confidential information is permissible absent the client's consent only where mandated by statute or court order (that is, supplying compulsion by legal process).[125]

Bare trust-transaction information is thus probably not covered by legal-professional privilege in many instances. Yet recent Canadian authority suggests that much other information pertaining to client-lawyer fee arrangements may be privileged. Consider the leading case of *Descôteaux* v. *Mierzwinski*, where the Supreme Court of Canada held that, but for the application of the crime-fraud exception, general financial information communicated to a lawyer as part of the process of finalizing the retainer agreement is usually privileged.[126] Indeed, because our courts have chosen to focus on the distinction between facts/acts (not privileged) and communications (privileged), much information passing between client and lawyer regarding fee arrangements arguably remains privileged.[127] In this vein, there is authority holding that privilege applies to encompass general financial information provided by the client,[128] accounts prepared for the client by the lawyer,[129] the nature and terms of the lawyer's retainer,[130] and many of

---

124 See, for example, *Cox* v. *Canada (A.G.)* (1989), 31 B.C.L.R. (2d) 172 (S.C.); *Re Helman and M.N.R.* (1971), 15 D.L.R. (3d) 753; as well as the discussion in D. Brindle, "Solicitor-Client Confidentiality and the Implications of the Proceeds of Crime (Money Laundering) Act and Regulation" (1994) 52 Advocate 545 at 552–54.
125 See section D, "Disclosure Required by Law," in chapter 5.
126 *Descôteaux* v. *Mierzwinski* (1982), 70 C.C.C. (2d) 385 at 401–04 & 413 (S.C.C.) [*Descôteaux*].
127 The most recent, comprehensive, and principled judicial discussion of the subject is found in *Stevens*, above note 123.
128 See, for example, *Descôteaux*, above note 126 at 401–04 & 413.
129 See, for example, *Stevens*, above note 123; *Legal Services Society* v. *British Columbia (Information and Privacy Commissioner)* (1996), 140 D.L.R. (4th) 372 (S.C.) [*Legal Services Society*]; and *Mutual Life Assurance Co. of Canada* v. *Canada (Deputy A.G.)* (1984), 42 C.P.C. 61 at 64 (Ont. H.C.J.).
130 See, for example, *Legal Services Society*, above note 129 at 378–79; and *British Columbia* v. *British Columbia (Information and Privacy Commissioner)* (1996), 31 B.C.L.R. (3d) 203 at 209 (S.C.).

a law firm's internal memos and communications relating to a client's assets.[131]

As a last point, remember that the crime-fraud exception may apply to communications pertaining to client-lawyer fee arrangements. Fee communications that are criminal in themselves or are made with the aim of effecting a criminal purpose fall within this exception and consequently are never protected by legal-professional privilege.[132] A lawyer who helps a client to launder money, unknowingly or not, will therefore likely find that all communications with the client, including the terms of the retainer and the legal accounts, are compellable upon a *prima facie* showing that the crime-fraud exception applies. It has even been argued that the payment of legal fees, whether or not using proceeds of crime, can constitute a pre-planned facet of an ongoing criminal conspiracy. If this more daring contention is supported by the evidence, and accepted by a court, legal-professional privilege will be supplanted.[133]

## 2) Statutory Reporting Requirements in Canada

The applicability of privilege to financial arrangements between counsel and client will almost certainly be subject to intense scrutiny by our courts in the near future, the result of mandatory requirements imposed by the federal government under the recently enacted, but only partially proclaimed, *Proceeds of Crime (Money Laundering) Act*.[134] Integral to the reporting scheme will be new regulations that have yet

---

131 See, for example, *Playfair Developments Ltd.* v. *Deputy M.N.R.* (1985), 85 D.T.C. 5155 (Ont. H.C.) (although the case also espouses a narrow view of the privilege based on the particular language of the taxation legislation being interpreted).

132 See, for example, *R.* v. *Campbell* (1999), 133 C.C.C. (3d) 257 at 291–95 (S.C.C.).

133 See the discussions in *United States* v. *Hodge and Zweig*, 548 F.2d 1347 at 1354 (9th Cir. 1977); and *In re Grand Jury Proceedings*, 600 F.2d 215 at 219 (9th Cir. 1979). However, in Canada legal fees can in limited circumstances be paid to counsel using proceeds of crime if a court order is obtained pursuant to s. 462.34 of the *Criminal Code*, R.S.C. 1985, c. C-46: see section S(4), "A Crucial Exception: The Section 462.34 Order for Legal Expense," in this chapter.

134 S.C. 2000, ch. 17 [*Proceeds of Crime Act*] (only partly in force as of 5 July 2000, pursuant to S.I./2000-55, so that for the time being parts of the predecessor Act remain in effect).

to be published and implemented. The Federal government has, however, recently published draft regulations for consultation purposes.[135]

The reporting requirements apply to lawyers and have two general prongs pertaining to record keeping and reporting.[136] First, a person to whom the Act and associated regulations apply must keep records regarding every transaction involving the receipt of $10,000 *cash* or more.[137] "Cash" is defined as "coins referred to in section 7 of the *Currency Act*, notes issued by the Bank of Canada pursuant to the *Bank of Canada Act* that are intended for circulation in Canada and coins or bank notes in the currency of other countries."[138] Second, and in addition, the Act creates two distinct reporting requirements. To begin with, a lawyer must report every financial transaction reasonably suspected to relate to the commission of a money-laundering offence.[139] The report is made to the Financial Transactions and Reports Analysis Centre of Canada (FINTRAC)[140] and is not restricted to cash transactions. As well, a lawyer must make reports regarding certain transactions prescribed by regulations passed pursuant to the new legislation.[141] This reporting obligation has not yet been fleshed out in the regulations, but the draft consultation regulations suggest that it may turn out to encompass the cash transactions of $10,000 or more that currently require a lawyer to keep records under the Act.[142]

---

135 See *Proceeds of Crime (Money Laundering) Regulations, 2000*, C. Gaz. 2001.1.532 [*Draft Proceeds of Crime Regulations*] (released 17 February 2001 for a ninety-day public comment period).

136 To be completely accurate, the new *Proceeds of Crime Act*, above note 184, has three general prongs of attack. The third area – not dealt with here – covers the import/export of money into and out of Canada: see Part II of the *Act*).

137 *Ibid.* at ss. 5 & 6 (not in force, require proclamation); and *Proceeds of Crime (Money Laundering) Regulations*, S.O.R./93-75, s. 4 [*Proceeds of Crime Regulations*] (currently in force, but due to be replaced by new regulations passed under the *Proceeds of Crime Act*, above note 134).

138 *Proceeds of Crime Regulations*, above note 137, s. 1 (currently in force but due to be replaced by new regulations passed under the Act). See also *Draft Proceeds of Crime Regulations,* above note 135, s. 1(2).

139 See ss. 5 & 7 of the *Proceeds of Crime Act*, above note 134 (not in force, require proclamation); and *Draft Proceeds of Crime Regulations,* above note 135, s. 11.

140 See ss. 5 & 7 of the *Proceeds of Crime Act*, above note 134 (not in force, require proclamation). FINTRAC is created by s. 41 of the *Act* (in force 5 July 2000, S.I./2000-55).

141 See s. 9 of the *Proceeds of Crime Act*, above note 134 (not in force, requires proclamation).

142 See *Draft Proceeds of Crime Regulations*, above note 135, ss. 31–33.

FINTRAC, to which all reports are made, has a statutory obligation to analyse and assess all information received under the Act.[143] If FIN-TRAC consequently determines that reasonable grounds exist to suspect that the information would be relevant to investigating or prosecuting a money-laundering offence, it must disclose the information to the appropriate police force or other investigative agency.[144] The ultimate effect of the reporting obligations, taken in conjunction with the duties and powers of FINTRAC, is thus to expose clients to the potential for investigation and prosecution by virtue of information disclosed by their lawyers.

## 3)  Privilege and the Statutory Reporting Requirements

How does this latest version of the *Proceeds of Crime (Money Laundering) Act* affect legal-professional privilege? The answer to this question is not yet clear. Section 11 of the Act, a new facet of the legislation that was not included in the predecessor statute, provides an exemption for "any communication that is subject to solicitor-client privilege."[145] Moreover, the regulations *currently* in operation (though due to be replaced) contain an express exception for money received for legal expenses and bail monies.[146] The recently published draft consultation regulations retain this exception.[147] This exception regarding legal expenses represents a huge concession to criminal lawyers. Indeed, exempting legal fees renders the Act of reduced concern to lawyers practising criminal litigation, because defence counsel do not usually handle large sums of money on behalf of clients other than (sometimes) in the form of legal fees.

If, contrary to present indications, legal expenses are not exempt from reporting requirements, criminal lawyers will be placed in a potential bind. There is no single approach that would guarantee the full satisfaction of the duty of confidentiality and mandatory statutory reporting obligations regarding legal expenses. Nevertheless, counsel should consider taking the following steps if reporting requirements do not exempt legal fees and disbursements:

---

143  See s. 54(c) of the *Proceeds of Crime Act*, above note 134 (in force 5 July 2000, S.I./2000-55).

144  *Ibid.*, ss. 55(4) & (5) (not in force, requires proclamation).

145  *Ibid.*, s. 11 (not in force, requires proclamation).

146  See *Proceeds of Crime Regulations*, above note 137, s. 4(3)(a).

147  See *Draft Proceeds of Crime Regulations*, above note 135, ss. 31(a), exempting funds "received or paid in respect of professional fees, disbursements, expenses or bail."

1. The client or third-party payor should be informed in advance of the reporting law. It may be an offence to disclose to the client that a "suspicious transaction" has been reported to FINTRAC, at least where disclosure is made with intent to prejudice a criminal investigation (whether or not the investigation has begun).[148] Yet the lawyer who warns the client regarding the reporting requirement *in advance* of accepting money may well avoid violating this prohibition.

2. The lawyer should not accept any cash payment that he or she reasonably suspects to be proceeds of crime.

3. In addition to refusing suspicious funds, the lawyer should decline to give the client or third-party any advice regarding investing, depositing or spending the money. Doing so risks making counsel a party to a proceeds-of-crime or money-laundering offence.

4. If the lawyer is satisfied that the payment is not proceeds of crime, and accepts the payment, adherence to the reporting law is necessary.[149] However, legal challenge to the reporting requirements should first be considered, where not frivolous.

Of course, if the statutory regime eventually excludes legal expenses from its ambit, as appears quite likely, the criminal lawyer's dilemma is largely avoided. However, even if legal expenses are excluded, counsel must adhere to the ethical and legal prohibitions regarding proceeds of crime, described below in section S.

As a final point, it is crucial to keep in mind that the new regulatory regime regarding money laundering is not yet finalized, and will likely be implemented gradually over the next couple of years. All Canadian lawyers must keep abreast of any developments concerning this regime, as well as case law bearing on its interpretation and constitutional validity. As well, lawyers must be cognizant of how the new legal requirements impact upon ethical duties set out in applicable rules of professional conduct. Some provincial law societies have already issued advisory papers on this topic.[150] It is not going too far to

---

148 See *Proceeds of Crime Act*, above note 134, s. 8 (not in force, requires proclamation).

149 A number of similar recommendations are found in *United States* v. *Monnat*, 853 F. Supp. 1301 (D. Kan. 1994), related reference 853 F. Supp. 1304 at 1307 (D. Kan. 1994) [*Monnat*].

150 See, for example, Law Society of Upper Canada, Advisory Services, *Proceeds of Crime (Money Laundering) Act and the Rules of Professional Conduct* (Toronto: Law Society of Upper Canada, 2001). See also Lawyers' Professional Indemnity Company, *Managing Your Obligations Under the Proceeds of Crime Legislation*, Version #1 (17 May 2001).

suggest that no Canadian statutory initiative has ever carried such potential for substantial impact upon the function of lawyering.

## 4) The American Experience: A Brief Overview

In the United States, the Internal Revenue Service (IRS) has for some time imposed reporting requirements that cover all cash receipts exceeding $10,000, often colloquially known by the name of the IRS form used for reporting, called a Form 8300.[151] The Form 8300 obligations thus approximate one of the reporting duties currently imposed by our *Proceeds of Crime (Money Laundering) Act*. However, unlike the current state of affairs in Canada, cash payments received by American lawyers for legal expenses are not exempt from the Form 8300 reporting requirement. Consequently, from the inception of the Form 8300 obligations, the applicability of legal-professional privilege and the constitutionality of the IRS requirements were of intense interest to defence lawyers seeking to uphold client-lawyer confidentiality regarding fees.

After considerable litigation involving Form 8300, it can safely be said that American law does not generally recognize any privilege pertaining to legal expenses and associated financial matters.[152] Courts in the United States have held that the fact of payment, the form the payment takes, and the identity of the payor are not usually privileged, and they have simultaneously upheld the constitutionality of Form 8300 reporting requirements.[153] Yet, despite extensive American authority to this broad effect, the privilege does appear to apply in certain limited "special circumstances."[154] Prime among these circumstances, for our

---

151 The case law and commentary regarding Form 8300 is voluminous and involved. For helpful overviews in sources that are frequently updated, see J. Hall, *Professional Responsibility of the Criminal Lawyer*, 2d ed. (New York: Clark Boardman Callaghan, 1996) c. 8; and J. Burkoff, *Criminal Defense Ethics: Law and Liability*, rev. ed. (St. Paul: West, 2000) at §11:9.

152 The leading cases in this regard include *United States* v. *Goldberger and Dubin P.C.*, 935 F.2d 501 (2d Cir. 1991); *United States* v. *Ritchie*, 15 F.3d 592 (6th Cir. 1994), cert. denied 513 U.S. 868 (1994); *United States* v. *Leventhal*, 961 F.2d 939 (11th Cir. 1992); *United States* v. *Sindel*, 53 F.3d 874 (8th Cir. 1995) [*Sindel*]; *United States* v. *Blackman*, 72 F.3d 1418 (9th Cir. 1995); *Ralls* v. *United States*, 52 F.3d 223 (9th Cir. 1995); *Monnat*, above note 149; *In re Grand Jury Subpoenas*, 123 F.3d 695 (1st Cir. 1997); and *Lefcourt* v. *United States*, 125 F.3d 79 (2d Cir. 1997), cert. denied 524 U.S. 937 (1998). However, attorney-client privilege is given some credence in certain special circumstances, as described in the text accompanying notes 154–55.

153 See the cases cited at note 152, above.

154 See Hall, above note 151 at §§33–36.

purposes, is the case where the fee information in question relates to a pending criminal matter.[155] Nevertheless, attorneys are still required to inform the IRS that privilege is being claimed, and why. Also, once the criminal case has concluded, the privilege dissipates, and the fee information is no longer exempt from disclosure.

Even before the state of the law in the United States became clear, in the early to mid-1990s, some ethics committees held that member lawyers may or must comply with the IRS reporting requirements.[156] Other committees took a different view, initially suggesting that the ethical and legal duties of confidentiality prevented members from disclosing fee information without the client's consent, in spite of the Form 8300 mandate.[157] However, these latter opinions were released prior to the leading court judgments upholding the constitutional validity of the IRS reporting provisions, and have thus been overtaken by events. Consequently, where an attorney determines that legal-professional privilege does not apply, American ethical rules do not justify non-compliance with statutory reporting requirements. Indeed, the National Association of Criminal Defense Lawyers, which initially supported an aggressive approach that precluded compliance with Form 8300 absent the client's consent, has since altered its position and now condones disclosure where the member attorney determines that privilege is not applicable.[158]

In Canada, the constitutional validity of reporting legislation, and the inapplicability of legal-professional privilege, *if supported by clear judicial authority*, would lead to the same result. Our rules of professional conduct invariably require disclosure of otherwise confidential information, including information pertaining to fees, where required

---

155 See, for example, *Sindel*, above note 152; *United States* v. *Gertner*, 873 F. Sup. 729 (D. Mass.), aff'd 65 F.3d 963 (1st Cir. 1995).

156 See, for example, Federal Court Committee on Attorney Conduct, contained in an appendix to *Monnat*, above note 149; and Committee on Rules of Professional Conduct of the Arizona State Bar, Opinion 3 (1987).

157 See, for example, State Bar of Wisconsin, Wis. Formal Op. E-90-3 (1990); Chicago Op. No. 86-2 (1988) (published in Berman, "The Attorney/Client Privilege and the IRS: Assessing the Currency Transaction Reporting Regulations" (June 1989) Ill. B.J.); Ohio Bd. of Comm'rs on Griev. and Disc., Op. 94 (1990); and NACDL Ethics Advisory Comm. (July 1990) Formal Op. 1 (1990), published in 37 The Champion, mentioned in (29 Jan. 1992) Laws Man. on Prof. Conduct (ABA/BNA), Current Reports 439.

158 See M. Weinberg, "*Lefcourt* Decision Requires Reassessment of NACDL 8300 Ethics Opinions" (Nov. 1997) The Champion 8. See also *Office of Disciplinary Counsel* v. *Massey*, 687 N.E.2d 734 (Ohio 1998); and *In re Mitchell*, 456 S.E.2d 396 (S.C. 1995).

by law.[159] On the other hand, it is by no means crystal clear that our courts will adopt the American position. It already appears, for example, that Canadian law is more willing to apply privilege to communications surrounding the financial arrangements between client and lawyer (if not to the bare financial transactions themselves). Ultimately, the American experience is of interest to Canadian lawyers, courts, and commentators grappling with the problem of privilege and reporting requirements. Whether our courts will follow suit, however, is quite a different matter.

# S.   POSSESSION AND LAUNDERING OF PROCEEDS OF CRIME

Closely related to the issues of confidentiality, privilege, and statutory reporting requirements is the topic of proceeds of crime and money laundering. There is obviously a prohibition against counsel demanding or receiving an illegal fee or otherwise engaging in any crime by virtue of receiving a fee.[160] Ethically, the general principle in this regard is thus quite straightforward. The problem for criminal counsel lies in trying to ascertain the exact parameters of impermissible conduct, and in particular determining whether an asset offered up to pay legal costs in fact represents the proceeds of a crime.

## 1)   A Statutory Overview

Let us start by providing a brief overview of the most relevant statutory provisions. There are a number of federal statutes that criminalize individuals who handle the proceeds of crime.[161] These statutes make it an offence simply to possess proceeds of crime.[162] "Proceeds of crime" is defined in an extremely wide manner, to include any property obtained

---

159  See section D, "Disclosure Required by Law," in chapter 5.

160  Canadian rules of professional responsibility uniformly forbid counsel from participating in illegal activities: see, for example, CBA Code ch. III, comm. 7. ABA Defense Standard 4-3.3(a) specifically sets out this prohibition in connection with a lawyer's fees.

161  Including the *Criminal Code*, above note 133; the *Controlled Drugs and Substances Act*, S.C. 1996, c. 19; the *Excise Act*, R.S.C. 1985, c. E-14; and the *Customs Act*, R.S.C. 1985, c. 1 (2nd Supp.).

162  See s. 354 of the *Criminal Code*, above note 133; s. 8(1) of the *Controlled Drugs and Substances Act*, above note 161; s. 126.1 of the *Excise Act*, above note 161; and s. 163.1 of the *Customs Act*, above note 161.

or derived directly or indirectly from (usually) certain specified criminal offences.[163] The specified offences, referred to as "enterprise crime offences" and "designated substance offences," cover a great many criminal acts.[164] The offence of laundering is different from the criminal act of possession of proceeds of crime but is certainly closely related. Laundering occurs where proceeds of crime are handled with an intent to conceal or convert.[165] The *actus reus* of laundering covers a broad range of activities, including dealing in any manner or by any means with proceeds of crime.[166] The *mens rea* for the offence is satisfied where an individual knows or believes that the property was thus obtained or derived, and handles the property with intent to conceal or convert.[167]

Given the robust reach of the criminal prohibitions against possession of proceeds of crime and laundering, there is no doubt that counsel who accepts payment knowing that the money (or any other asset) is derived from a crime is committing a criminal offence. Handling or hiding proceeds of crime can also constitute other offences, such as obstruction of justice, accessory after the fact, and conspiracy.[168] To avoid being charged with these or other offences, counsel must never receive or deal in any way with funds that he or she knows are obtained from the commission of a criminal act. Moreover, the doctrine of wilful blindness may operate to impose knowledge upon counsel, and so ignoring plain facts in proceeding to accept the retainer is not an acceptable course of action.[169]

---

163 See, for example, the definition provided by s. 462.3 of the *Criminal Code*, above note 133. Specified offences are set out in all proceeds of crime legislation except for the general offence of possession of proceeds of crime set out in s. 354 of the *Code*. Accordingly, an offence is committed under s. 354 regardless of the type of crime from which the proceeds are derived: see *R. v. Hayes* (1995), 104 C.C.C. (3d) 316 at 321 (Que. C.A.) [*Hayes*].

164 See s. 462.3 of the *Criminal Code*, above note 133.

165 See s. 462.31 of the *Criminal Code*, above note 133; s. 9(1) of the *Controlled Drugs and Substances Act*, above note 161; s. 163.2 of the *Customs Act*, above note 161; and s. 126.2 of the *Excise Act*, above note 161.

166 See *Hayes*, above note 163 at 321.

167 *Ibid.* at 321; and *R. v. Tejani* (1999), 138 C.C.C. (3d) 366 (Ont. C.A.), leave to appeal to S.C.C. refused [1999] S.C.C.A. No. 509 (QL).

168 See, for example, *Criminal Code*, above note 133, s. 139 (obstructing justice); s. 23 (accessory after the fact) and s. 465(1)(c) (conspiracy).

169 See the discussion of wilful blindness in section F(4), "Avoidance Techniques: Restricting Client-Lawyer Communications, Wilful Blindness, 'Woodshedding', and Viewing Guilty as Completely Irrelevant," in chapter 1, as well as *Hayes*, above note 163 at 325. In *United States v. Moffitt, Zwerling & Kemler, P.C.*, 83 F.3d 660 (4th Cir. 1996) [*Moffitt*], the court strongly suspected that counsel and

**Example I:** Client X is charged in connection with the theft of numerous fully loaded tractor-trailers, none of which was recovered, and visits a lawyer to arrange for representation. X candidly admits the crime and states that the substantial legal costs will be paid by his mother. X's mother is sitting in the waiting room with her chequebook. Counsel speaks to her briefly and learns that she has no assets except for the retainer amount that sits in her bank account. Further questioning determines that the money came from X, obtained through the sale of the stolen trucks and goods. Counsel cannot take the money from X's mother, since it is derived from a crime.

**Variation:** Alter the above example so that X's mother owns a house and has arranged to obtain money for her son's legal costs from a bank by placing a first-mortgage on the property. A trust cheque from the mother's real estate lawyer will be provided to defence counsel. X informs counsel that he bought the house using proceeds from the sale of shares in a reputable, publicly traded company. He adds that these shares were purchased using some money from his legitimate employment but were substantially financed using proceeds from the crime. Because proceeds derived indirectly from crime are covered by the provisions pertaining to laundering and possession of proceeds of crime, counsel cannot accept the proposed retainer. At the end of the day, receiving a fee from a third-party may be a totally valid method of eliding proceeds-of-crime concerns, but only if there is no reason to believe that the third-party's funds are directly or indirectly derived from crime.

**Example II:** Counsel receives $100,000 in cash stuffed in a cracker box, to be used for fees. The client refuses to indicate the source of the money. Receiving these funds is extremely foolhardy, given the law regarding proceeds of crime.[170]

---

the client "were engaging in some sort of wink and nod ritual whereby they agreed not to ask – or tell – too much" regarding the origin of retainer funds. The court found that facts known to the law firm at the time the retainer was accepted, taken in conjunction with what the firm declined to inquire about, constituted reasonable cause to know that the retainer was subject to forfeiture.

170 These facts are loosely taken from *Moffitt, ibid.* The court held that counsel's acceptance of $103,000 in cash was not reasonable in the circumstances, given the strong indicia that the money was proceeds of crime.

## 2) Due Diligence

Counsel must clearly not succumb to wilful blindness, but does a lawyer bear a further ethical obligation to perform due diligence in relation to a proposed retainer? In our view, counsel must strive to avoid receiving proceeds of crime in the first place. Any reasonable suspicion that retainer funds are proceeds of crime should cause counsel to refuse the retainer, absent a satisfactory explanation by the client. Moreover, the client's explanation should be set out in writing, whether or not it is accepted by the lawyer. Cases that are close to the line should spur counsel to seek legal advice from senior and experienced counsel, preferably in writing, and perhaps also to obtain advice from the applicable professional governing body. Where counsel realistically suspects that funds are derived from crime, a further precautionary option is to retain independent counsel to conduct an investigation.[171] Some lawyers might view these sorts of measures as inappropriate, given the implicit lack of trust shown in the client and the unavoidable adversarial element that seems at odds with a normal client-lawyer relationship. Others may feel that too intrusive and demanding an inquiry unduly interferes with the client's right to retain counsel of choice. Ultimately, counsel must take these valid countervailing concerns into account in deciding upon the proper course of action, but not as a disingenuous justification for accepting a retainer reasonably suspected to be proceeds of crime.

## 3) Proceeds Problems Arising after a Retainer is Received

Counsel may quite properly accept a retainer payment, there being no alarm bells suggesting that the money represents proceeds of crime, only to receive subsequent information pointing to the criminal origins of the money. The Law Society of British Columbia has provided guidance to counsel in this position, at least in respect of money known to be proceeds of crime. The Law Society's Proceeds of Crime Subcommittee has formulated the following standards of conduct:

---

171 See J. Bascom, *The Proceeds of Crime and Money Laundering: Information for Alberta Lawyers*, ("How to Identify the Money Launderer"), online: http://www.lawsocietyalberta.com/pubs_policies_reports/money-laundering.asp.

What course of action should a member take upon learning that funds held in his or her trust account constitute the proceeds of crime?

Clearly, the member is liable to prosecution for the offence of laundering if he or she returns the property to the client, transfers it to another member's trust account on the direction of the client, or distributes it to other parties such as conveyancing vendors or estate beneficiaries.

On the other hand, the member may put himself or herself at risk under the proceeds of crime legislation by continuing to hold the property in trust, unless the member takes proper and adequate steps to safeguard his or her position.

Upon learning that funds held in trust are proceeds of crime the member should promptly:

(1) retain counsel knowledgeable about the proceeds of crime legislation, disclose to that counsel his or her state of knowledge respecting the funds, and confirm that information in writing. This action is important for two reasons. First, it evidences an intention by the member to retain the funds in the public interest (until entitlement to the funds is determined by a court), thus negativing the criminal intent. Second, the lawful options available to the member may vary, depending on the circumstances of the case, and the member needs legal advice from a colleague knowledgeable in the legislation.

(2) advise the client that the member is holding the funds in trust and that they will be released from trust only by court order.[172]

These guidelines offer a cautious plan of action that focuses on protecting counsel's legitimate self-interest in avoiding complicity in a criminal act. They can be criticized, insofar as the proper course of conduct is left largely to the "counsel knowledgable about proceeds of

---

172 Law Society of British Columbia, Proceeds of Crime Subcommittee, *The Impact of the Proceeds of Crime Legislation on the Practice of Law in British Columbia* (August 1990) 7 Benchers' Bull. Supp.. This same report has been endorsed by the Nova Scotia Barristers' Society, *A Special Report to Members: The Impact of Proceeds of Crime Legislation on the Practice of Law* (1991), 17 N.S.L. News 45. See also the guidelines set out in Bascom, above note 171 at Part VI ("The Effect of Proceeds of Crime Legislation and Money Laundering Legislation on the Profession"). The Law Society of Upper Canada is currently working on a set of guidelines pertaining to this topic.

crime legislation," without much more guidance. It is probably safe to say, however, that upon determining that the funds are proceeds of crime, counsel is bound to comply with the ethical duties regarding incriminating physical evidence.[173]

## 4) A Crucial Exception: The Section 462.34 Order for Legal Expenses

There is an important exception to the general prohibition against counsel receiving proceeds of crime, or potential proceeds of crime, as payment for legal expenses. Under section 462.34 of the *Criminal Code*, any person with an interest in property that has been seized or restrained in the course of a criminal investigation may apply to a judge for an order that all or a portion of the property be applied towards, among other things, reasonable legal expenses. Individuals whose legal expenses can be covered include a person who was in possession of the property at the time of seizure or restraint, or any person who in the judge's opinion has a valid interest in the property and the dependants of such person.[174] Note that, pursuant to recent amendments, money seized under the general search-and-seizure provisions of the *Criminal Code* or *Controlled Drugs and Substances Act*, and not just Part XII.2 of the *Criminal Code*, can also be the subject of an order permitting its use for reasonable legal costs.[175]

The details pertaining to the court-sanctioned use of seized property to defer legal costs are complicated and require a careful review of the legislation and case law. Central to our discussion here, however, is the basic role of section 462.34, which in essence provides "judicial money laundering" for the purpose of paying lawyers. Where so countenanced by court order, we see no general ethical bar to counsel accepting potential proceeds of crime as payment for legal services.

**Comparison:** In the United States, the proceeds-of-crime legislation does not include any exception allowing lawyers to receive forfeitable funds to pay legal fees, a position that has been upheld by the Supreme Court.[176] Many American defence lawyers have responded with anger

---

173 See chapter 9, including section E, "Relevant Criminal Code Provisions."

174 See s. 462.34(4)(c) of the *Criminal Code*, above note 133.

175 See s. 462.341, *ibid.*, reversing the impact of cases such as *R. v. Gaudreau* (1994), 90 C.C.C. (3d) 436 (Sask. C.A.).

176 See *Caplin and Drysdale, Chartered v. United States*, 491 U.S. 617 (1989) [*Caplin*]; and *United States v. Monsanto*, 491 U.S. 600 (1989). Important in understanding the complex American position are the Department of Justice

and incredulity to this state of affairs, and some have pushed the boundaries of ethical conduct in response. Consider, for instance, the extremely candid and aggressive advice given by John Wesley Hall, Jr., one of the leading American writers on criminal law and ethics: "If it [that is, a proposed retainer] is potentially a forfeitable asset: (a) remain as ignorant as you dare about the source of funds without shutting your eyes to the obvious, (b) receive the funds as early as possible before the government puts anyone on notice of forfeitability, and (c) spend it promptly." Hall's advice has the lawyer walking exceedingly close to the line of wilful blindness, and counsel who acts pursuant to this approach risks attracting criminal charges. Given the potential applicability of section 462.34 of the *Criminal Code*, and the fairly comprehensive legal aid plans in place in many Canadian provinces, Hall's view is hard to justify in this country.

## T.  FORFEITURE OF FEES

The *Criminal Code* and other criminal statutes provide that proceeds of crime, or their derivatives, can be forfeited to the government.[177] A forfeiture proceeding is usually preceded by seizure or restraint of the property under the applicable legislation.[178] Where the prosecution proves that the accused has been convicted of an enterprise-crime offence,[179] the Crown can keep the property upon showing on a balance of probabilities that the property is proceeds of crime and the offence was committed in relation to that property.[180] If the accused is not convicted of a predicate enterprise-crime offence, the Crown can nonetheless obtain a forfeiture order upon demonstrating on proof beyond a reasonable doubt that the property is proceeds of crime.[181]

---

Guidelines, which soften somewhat the impact of the legislation and the leading Supreme Court decisions: see Hall, above note 151 at §7:31 & §7:29A.

177  See s. 462.37 of the *Criminal Code*, above note 133; s. 19.3 of the *Controlled Drugs and Substances Act*, above note 161; s. 163.3(1) of the *Customs Act*, above note 161; and s. 126.3 of the *Excise Act*, above note 161.

178  See *Criminal Code*, above note 133, s. 462.32 (seizure); s. 462.33 (restraint); and the incorporating provisions of the *Controlled Drugs and Substances Act*, above note 161, s. 23.

179  As already noted, this term is defined in the legislation to encompass a broad spectrum of criminal activity: see s. 462.3 of the *Criminal Code*, above note 133.

180  *Ibid.*, s. 462.37(1).

181  *Ibid.*, s. 462.37(2).

The potential forfeiture of a client's property may create problems for the lawyer, given that the assets forfeited might otherwise be available in order to pay legal costs. What is more, the proceeds-of-crime provisions permit the court to order a fine in lieu of forfeiture where property otherwise subject to forfeiture has been transferred to a third-party. Where the individual is unable to pay such a fine, jail becomes a real possibility, for the *Criminal Code* provides that the court *shall* order a term of imprisonment in default of payment at a stipulated rate, consecutive to any other jail term.[182] Given this forfeiture scheme, the payment of legal fees by the client, instead of waiting for the outcome of a forfeiture hearing, can directly lead to the imposition of a fine or jail time. Counsel's interest in receiving fees paid out of possible proceeds of crime is thus potentially at odds with the client's interest in avoiding a fine or jail.[183]

The danger of conflict is perhaps greatest where a client seeks to obtain a section 462.34 court order permitting the use of seized or restrained property to pay legal expenses. In such a case, the lawyer can reasonably assume that the prosecution will be seeking a forfeiture order in respect of the property. It is open to counsel to argue that the use of seized funds to pay for legal costs is entirely legitimate, and hence the court should not exercise its discretion under section 462.37(3) of the *Criminal Code* to impose a fine in lieu of forfeiture.[184] Yet we believe that the client should always receive independent legal advice and waive any conflict of interest prior to counsel seeking to employ seized or restrained funds for paying legal costs.[185] Indeed, it is wise to retain separate counsel to conduct the section 462.34 application.

As a last point, proceeds-of-crime legislation provides that a transfer of seized or restrained property to a third-party is voidable, and

---

182  *Ibid.*, s. 462.37(4).

183  In *Moffitt*, above note 169, the court appeared inclined to accept the client's allegation that defence counsel refused to partake in plea discussions because the prosecutor would likely insist that monies paid to the law firm for fees be forfeited. If true, such behaviour by counsel was unethical.

184  See *R. v. Gagnon* (1993), 80 C.C.C. (3d) 508 (Alta. Q.B.).

185  In *R. v. Pawlyk* (1991), 65 C.C.C. (3d) 63 (Man. C.A.), the court refused to countenance an order permitting use of the seized funds to pay legal costs for exactly this reason. However, in *R. v. Wilson* (1993), 86 C.C.C. (3d) 464 at 479–80 (Ont. C.A.) [*Wilson*], the court recognized that Parliament condoned the possibility that payment to the lawyer would ultimately result in a fine or prison time. See also *R. v. Thomas* (2001), 158 C.C.C. (3d) 94 (Ont. C.A.), where the court upheld the trial judge's decision to pay a portion of the forfeitable proceeds to defence counsel and the Ontario Legal Aid Plan.

subject to being set aside by court order, unless the transfer was for valuable consideration to a person acting in good faith and without notice.[186] The lawyer who takes an assignment of property knowing that the Crown intends to seek forfeiture cannot later claim to be a third-party without notice. Indeed, under these circumstances, the client arguably has only a contingent (and therefore limited) interest to give, apart from that made possible by s. 462.34 of the *Criminal Code*.[187] Consequently, the lawyer who attempts a transfer outside of the section 462.34 procedure risks receiving nothing if, at the conclusion of the case, the property is forfeited. Because of this risk of non-payment, an assignment of property that is subject to possible forfeiture approximates a contingency-fee arrangement. That is to say, the lawyer will hold a valid property interest if the forfeiture claim is defeated but otherwise will receive nothing.[188] Such an arrangement may be unethical and illegal, depending upon the contingency-fee rules applicable in the particular jurisdiction.[189]

## U. REFUSAL TO HAND OVER THE FILE OWING TO UNPAID LEGAL COSTS

Canadian rules of professional conduct recognize that, upon termination of the retainer, a lawyer can acquire a possessory lien over the file in respect of unpaid fees and disbursements.[190] Such a lien, sometimes called a retaining or general lien, is created at law.[191] A lien may not arise, however, where counsel is discharged for valid cause or withdraws without good reason.[192] Moreover, counsel is advised by the ethical rules not to enforce the lien "if to do so would prejudice materially

---

186  See s. 462.4 of the *Criminal Code*, above note 133.

187  See *Wilson*, above note 185 at 476–77.

188  This concern is raised by Justice White in *Caplin*, above note 176 at 632–33 (note 10), but is best expressed in the dissenting opinion of Brennan J., at 649.

189  See section H, "Contingency Fees," in this chapter.

190  See, for example, CBA Code ch. XII, comm. 11; Sask. ch. XII, comm. 11; Man. ch. 12, comm. 11; and Ont. r. 2.09(9) (commentary).

191  See, for example, *Linauskas v. Linauskas (No. 2)* (1998), 38 O.R. (3d) 113 at 117 (Gen. Div.); and *Appleton v. Hawes* (1990), 46 C.P.C. (2d) 107 at 110–11 (Ont. Gen. Div.) [*Appleton*].

192  See, for example, *Appleton*, above note 191 at 110–11.

the client's position in any uncompleted matter."[193] We tend towards the view that counsel in a criminal matter should never refuse to hand over a file in an ongoing case based on unpaid legal costs.[194] The possibility of an adverse impact on the client's reputation and liberty is in many instances too severe to justify such action. Certainly, delivery of the file should never be refused where the materials are needed to permit the client to instruct a new lawyer.[195] In cases where no real prejudice will result if the file is withheld, counsel may consider asking the former client to pay the disputed amount into court, or to a neutral third-party, in exchange for release of the file, the idea being to settle the fee dispute in the future.[196]

**Example:** The client provides counsel with an original receipt that helps to establish her location at the time of the offence, and hence is important support for an alibi. Counsel is later discharged without cause, at which time the client refuses to pay substantial outstanding legal fees. A retaining lien *prima facie* exists over the file, yet it is clear that the client will suffer serious prejudice if the receipt is not returned. It would therefore be unethical to claim a lien over the receipt.

# V. CONFLICT OF INTEREST

The potential for conflict of interest can arise in a number of ways concerning lawyer's fees. The real problem occurs whenever the lawyer's financial interests in conducting the case reasonably appear to be at odds with the best interests of the client. Some of the more common conflict-of-interest problems that can arise in the context of legal fees

---

193 See the rules cited at note 190. This restriction may also be applied by courts in deciding that a lien cannot be claimed: see *Collison v. Hurst*, [1946] 4 D.L.R. 27 at 34–35 (Ont. H.C.J.).

194 See *People v. Altvater*, 355 N.Y.S.2d. 736 (Sup. 1974). See also Wolfram, above note 70 at 560–61, who says that lawyers should never rely on retaining liens; and Ontario Law Reform Commission, *Report on the Solicitors Act* (Toronto: Ministry of the Attorney General, 1973) at 37–38, which recommends abolishing the lien, on the grounds that it represents an unjustified impediment to a client discharging counsel and an unwarranted interference with the orderly progression of litigation.

195 Other instances where reliance on a lien is of dubious legitimacy are set out in *Miller v. Paul*, 615 P.2d 615 (Alaska 1989). Regarding files held by trial counsel who is the subject of an ineffective counsel claim on appeal, see section P, "Right to Effective Assistance of Counsel Claims on Appeal," in chapter 11.

196 See, for example, *Re Bannan* (1921), 59 D.L.R. 625 (Alta. S.C.(A.D.)).

are discussed elsewhere, and include payment of all or a portion of a fee by a third-party, the assignment of media or publication rights to counsel by the client, contingency fees, referrals, and payment from a bail deposit or seized assets alleged to be proceeds of crime.[197]

**Example:** A client owes his lawyer $20,000 for services rendered in respect of serious sexual-assault charges. He wishes to pay the lawyer by transferring title in a piece of land. Assuming that the lawyer's account is reasonable, conflict-of-interest problems must be addressed. In particular, the client and lawyer have potentially divergent interests regarding the valuation of the property to be transferred. The lawyer should therefore inquire into the possibility of the client selling or mortgaging the property in order to pay the fees. If this option is not acceptable, it is imperative that the client receives independent legal advice before transferring the property to counsel.[198]

# W. WITHDRAWAL

Withdrawing for non-payment of fees is generally possible in criminal cases, although case law suggests that Alberta lawyers face a blanket prohibition against ending a retainer owing to non-payment.[199] In those jurisdictions where withdrawal for non-payment is permitted, lawyers must exercise considerable care in attempting to end an ongoing retainer for this reason. Professional-conduct guidelines, rules of criminal procedure and case law all place limits on counsel's ability to withdraw by reason of failure to pay legal fees, and these limits are especially strict where the trial has commenced or is imminent.[200]

---

197  See sections N(3) and T in this chapter, as well as chapter 6, especially sections J, L(4), L(5), & L(3).
198  This example is based on the case of *Karpinsky Estate v. Hogue* (1995), 105 Man. R. (2d) 167 (Q.B.), where the client did in fact receive independent legal advice. Such advice may also be needed where a lawyer takes property from a third-party as security: see *Wilder v. 337236 Alberta Ltd.* (1998), 224 A.R. 306 (Q.B.), rev'd in part (2000), 250 A.R. 258 (C.A.).
199  See *C.(D.D.)*, above note 5.
200  See generally section I, "Non-Payment of Fees or Unreasonable Financial Burden," in chapter 11.

# X.  REVIEWING FEES

Standards of professional conduct are geared to protect the vulnerable client from overcharging by lawyers, but in addition there must be an accessible forum for reviewing and resolving fee disputes. One possibility is for the client to complain to the governing body, which can launch an investigation and undertake disciplinary proceedings against a lawyer who acts unethically in setting or collecting fees. The more usual method of review, however, is to assess the amounts charged before a judicial officer.[201] The New Brunswick rules discuss the ability of a client to have an account reviewed, and add that the failure of a lawyer to tax a bill when required by a client constitutes professional misconduct.[202] Also of interest is a provision found in the Yukon, providing that, in the event that the amount of fees or disbursements charged by a lawyer is reduced on a taxation, the lawyer shall immediately repay the monies to the client.[203]

Not surprisingly, the criteria bearing upon an assessment are similar to those factors that determine whether a fee is ethical according to the "fair and reasonable" standard utilized by most governing bodies.[204] Moreover, the relevant factors are the same for both civil and criminal matters.[205] As the presiding judicial officer acerbically noted in *Re Solicitor*:

> [T]he nature of [criminal lawyers'] legal services cannot be invested with an aura of forensic black magic. Their duty to their clients is basically that of any other solicitor and the services they are required to render are fundamentally those expected of an advocate in any other field of law. And, in my opinion, the broad basis upon which their fees should be calculated is the same as in the case of other solicitors.[206]

---

201 For comprehensive discussions concerning review of a lawyer's account, see MacKenzie, above note 64 at §25.5(a); B. Smith, *Professional Conduct for Lawyers and Judges* (Fredericton, N.B.: Maritime Law Book, 1998) c. 2, paras. 68–70; and Lundy, MacKenzie & Newbury, above note 43, c. 13.

202 See N.B. Part E, r. 1.

203 See Yukon Part 1, r. 14.

204 See section C, "Fees Must Be Fair and Reasonable," in this chapter. For example, in *Duerinckx* v. *McNeill* (1997), 122 Man. R. (2d) 158 (Q.B.), the assessment of a criminal account was conducted based upon the "fair and reasonable" factors set out in the Manitoba Code of Professional Conduct.

205 See *Re Solicitor*, above note 62.

206 *Ibid.* at 47.

In Ontario, the rules of professional conduct urge lawyers to inform clients of the right to have a disputed account assessed.[207] This duty is surely applicable in all Canadian jurisdictions, whether or not expressly stipulated by the rules of professional conduct, given the lawyer's basic fiduciary duty to the client. Indeed, the CBA's *Report of the Task Force on Systems of Civil Justice* suggests that lawyers inform the client of avenues of redress at the beginning of the retainer.[208]

**Restriction:** It is improper for a lawyer to require that a client waive all rights to assess legal fees. Moreover, it is unlikely that a court would uphold such an agreement.[209]

# Y.  SUMMARY AND RECOMMENDATIONS

Our summary and recommendations regarding fees and disbursements are as follows:

1.  The reality of the legal profession is that lawyers usually provide services in return for payment and hence operate businesses that require revenue for survival. However, the receipt of fees by the lawyer, who acts in a fiduciary capacity towards the client, represents an inherent conflict of interest vis-à-vis the client. The goal of most ethical rules in respect of legal fees is thus to alleviate the resulting potential for danger to the client (sections A & B).
2.  All fees charged to the client must be fair and reasonable (section C).
3.  The retainer agreement and any related financial arrangements with a client must be preceded by full and timely disclosure by the lawyer. Disclosure obligations are not obviated simply because payment of legal expenses is made by a legal aid plan or other third-party, although third-party involvement may raise special disclosure issues (section D).
4.  It is unethical for a lawyer to misrepresent any matter to the client in connection with fee and disbursement arrangements (section E).
5.  It is highly advisable to set out the retainer agreement in writing, the better to avoid later controversy and ensure full disclosure to the client (section F).
6.  There are many methods of calculating a fair and reasonable fee, including flat fees, hourly rates, and graduated payments. A broad

---

207  See, for example, Ont. r. 2.08(2) (commentary).
208  *Report on Systems of Civil Justice*, above note 25 at 67.
209  See, for example, *Legal Aid Society of Alberta*, above note 45 at 144.

range of compensatory arrangements is acceptable, provided that the overall fee is fair and reasonable and full disclosure is made to the client (section G).

7. Contingency fees in criminal matters are prohibited in Alberta, New Brunswick, and Ontario but seem to be permissible in other Canadian jurisdictions. Contingency fees in the criminal setting are frequently regarded as ethically dubious. This criticism may well be overblown. Regardless, defence counsel should take special care to ascertain the ethical and legal ramifications in his or her jurisdiction before entering into a contingency agreement with a client (section H).

8. It is common for criminal defence lawyers to require an advance payment from clients. Such a requirement is ethically permissible and often represents sound business practice. However, the lawyer cannot bill the client in respect of advance payments unless services have been provided under the retainer agreement and an account has been rendered, and as always, any fees charged against the advance payment must be fair and reasonable (section I).

9. Non-refundable fees are generally to be avoided. In our view, a lawyer may legitimately charge a client for guaranteeing availability to take on a case or for the lost opportunity to accept other retainers. To this extent, the fee can perhaps be seen as earned without the lawyer providing any concrete services. But any such arrangement requires the client's consent following full disclosure. Moreover, the arrangement cannot serve to impede unduly the client's right to discharge counsel at any time (section J).

10. A contract for limited representation is permissible in a criminal case. The lawyer who accepts a limited retainer must ensure that the client fully understands the resulting restrictions on the representation. There may also be an obligation to inform the court and Crown counsel of any such restrictions (section K).

11. As a client-lawyer relationship progresses, the lawyer must keep the client informed as to any developments that have an impact on the financial arrangements. If the lawyer wishes to modify the original retainer agreement, it is imperative that no undue pressure be applied to the client. In particular, a lawyer should not use the fact of an imminent or ongoing trial to pry extra funds from a vulnerable client (section L).

12. In fairly exceptional circumstances, a client may have an opportunity to recover legal costs from the Crown. Counsel has a duty to inform the client whenever a cost award is a reasonable possibility,

so that the client can determine whether to bring an application for recovery (section M).

13. Referral fees paid to other lawyers are ethically permissible in Ontario and British Columbia, provided that certain preconditions are met. In other Canadian jurisdictions, such fees are generally prohibited. By contrast, referral fees paid to non-lawyers are forbidden in every Canadian jurisdiction. Finally, even where no fee is paid in connection with a referral, a lawyer must refrain from accepting the referred matter if insurmountable conflict-of-interest concerns arise (section N).

14. A lawyer who does work that simultaneously benefits two or more clients must apportion the related fees equitably among the clients, absent the agreement of all affected clients to the contrary (section O).

15. Lawyers are encouraged by the rules of professional conduct to provide legal services for free, or at a reduced rate, in order to ensure that deserving individuals and causes receive access to justice. As for wealthy clients who have no difficulty paying for legal services, some governing bodies expressly forbid charging a higher fee (Alberta, British Columbia, and New Brunswick). However, in practice, wealthy clients end up subsidizing legal services provided to clients who cannot afford to pay the lawyer's ordinary fee rate. We see nothing wrong with this outcome, provided that no client is misled or charged an otherwise unreasonable or unfair fee (section P).

16. Disbursement expenditures must be fully explained to the client and require the client's consent. The principles of fairness, reasonableness and full disclosure that apply to fees are equally applicable to disbursements (section Q).

17. All financial arrangements between client and lawyer are confidential. However, legal-professional privilege may not apply with respect to every such arrangement, especially acts that cannot easily be classified as "communications." In particular, it appears that bare trust transfers are generally not protected by privilege (section R).

18. Canadian lawyers are subject to reporting requirements set out in the *Proceeds of Crime (Money Laundering) Act*, mandating that specified information be provided to the Financial Transactions and Reports Analysis Centre of Canada (FINTRAC). These reporting requirements are in the process of being revamped and hold the potential to necessitate the disclosure of at least some information that would otherwise be confidential (though not privileged). Counsel must carefully review the *Act* and its accompanying regulations, as well as the law regarding legal-professional privilege, in

ascertaining whether any information must be provided to FIN-TRAC. In addition, the client must be warned in advance of any potentially applicable reporting obligations (section R).

19. Subject to the statutory exception set out in section 462.34 of the *Criminal Code*, discussed below, counsel cannot knowingly accept proceeds of crime in payment of legal expenses. Contravening this cardinal rule risks prosecution and conviction for possession of proceeds of crime and/or laundering, not to mention disciplinary action by the governing body and loss of the fees in question. We believe that counsel should take reasonable steps to dispel any real suspicion that legal expenses are being paid using proceeds of crime (section S).

20. The one instance where counsel can accept payment in the form of property that may be proceeds of crime is set out in section 462.34 of the *Criminal Code*. This provision permits a client to use seized or restrained assets for the payment of reasonable legal expenses, provided that a court order to this effect is obtained (section R).

21. Proceeds of crime may be subject to forfeiture to the government. The client can be fined or imprisoned if assets determined to be proceeds are no longer available for forfeiture. It is also possible that the court will void an assignment of seized or restrained assets. Consequently, counsel must take care not to accept potentially for-feitable assets as payment for legal expenses, even pursuant to a section 462.34 court order, absent proper precautions relating to conflict of interest (section T).

22. Where counsel is discharged or withdraws, and is owed money by the client, a retaining lien can arise over the file. However, it is improper to enforce such a lien where the result would be material prejudice to the former client's case. In our view, criminal defence counsel should only rarely, if ever, claim a retaining lien over the file (section U).

23. The potential for an unacceptable conflict of interest is inherent in many fee arrangements. Counsel must be attuned to the dangers in this regard and take appropriate precautionary steps where neces-sary (section V).

24. Withdrawal for non-payment of fees is frequently permissible but is usually precluded once the trial commences or is imminent (sec-tion W).

25. A client who is dissatisfied with the financial aspect of a retainer can seek redress through a number of channels. A common option is to assess the lawyer's account. Where a disagreement arises con-

cerning legal expenses, the lawyer has a duty to inform the client of the availability of the assessment procedure (section X).

## FURTHER READINGS

AMERICAN BAR ASSOCIATION, *How to Set and Collect Attorney Fees in Criminal Cases* (Chicago: American Bar Association, 1985)

ANDERSON, J., "Court-Appointed Counsel: The Constitutionality of Uncompensated Conscription" (1990) 3 Geo. J. Legal Ethics 503

ANDERSON, R., & W. STEELE, "Ethics and the Law of Contracts Juxtaposed: A Jaundiced View of Professional Responsibility Considerations in the Attorney-Client Relationship" (1991) 4 Geo. J. Legal Ethics 791

AXELROD, D., & S. HARRIS, "The Perils of Getting Paid in Cash" (Winter 1989) 4 Criminal Justice 6

BALLMAN, B., "Amended Rule 6.1: Another Move Towards Mandatory Pro Bono? Is that What We Want?" (1994) 7 Geo. J. Legal Ethics 1139

BASCOM, J., *The Proceeds of Crime and Money Laundering: Information for Alberta Lawyers*, online: http://www.lawsocietyalberta.com/-pubs_policies_reports/money-laundering.asp

BOON, A., & J. LEVIN, *The Ethics and Conduct of Lawyers in England and Wales* (Oxford: Hart, 1999)

BRICKMAN, L., & L. CUNNINGHAM, "Non-refundable Retainers: Impermissible Under Fiduciary, Statutory and Contract Law" (1988) 57 Fordham L. Rev. 149

BRICKMAN, L., & L. CUNNINGHAM, "Non-refundable Retainers: A Response to the Critics of the Absolute Ban" (1995) 64 U. Cinn. L. Rev 11

BRINDLE, D., "Solicitor-Client Confidentiality and the Implications of the Proceeds of Crime (Money Laundering) Act and Regulation" (1994) 52 Advocate 545

BRUCKER, T., "Money Laundering and The Client: How Can I Be Retained without Becoming a Party to an Offence" (1997) 39 Crim. L.Q. 312

BURKOFF, J., *Criminal Defense Ethics: Law and Liability*, rev. ed. (St. Paul: West, 2000)

CANADIAN BAR ASSOCIATION, *Report of the Task Force on Systems of Civil Justice* (Ottawa: Canadian Bar Association, 1996) (Chair: E. Cronk)

CHAN, S., "ABA Formal Opinion 93-379: Double Billing, Padding and Other Forms of Overbilling" (1996) 9 Geo. J. Legal Ethics 611

DICKSON, B., "The Public Responsibilities of Lawyers" (1983) 13 Man. L.J. 175

FEDERATION OF LAW SOCIETIES OF CANADA, *Contingent Fee Agreements* (Federation of Law Societies of Canada, Montreal 1998)

GERMAN, P., *Proceeds of Crime* (Toronto: Carswell, 1998)

HALL, J., *Professional Responsibility of the Criminal Lawyer*, 2d ed. (New York: Clark Boardman Callaghan, 1996)

HAZARD, G., & W. HODES, *The Law of Lawyering*, 2d ed. (Englewood, N.J.: Prentice Hall, 1993)

HUTCHINSON, A., *Legal Ethics and Professional Responsibility* (Toronto: Irwin Law, 1999)

KARLAN, P., "Contingent Fees and Criminal Cases" (1993) 93 Colum. L. Rev. 595

LAW SOCIETY OF BRITISH COLUMBIA, PROCEEDS OF CRIME SUBCOMMITTEE, *The Impact of the Proceeds of Crime Legislation on the Practice of Law in British Columbia* (August 1990) 7 Benchers' Bull. Supp.

*Law Society of Upper Canada, Report to Convocation: Joint Committee on Contingency Fees* (Toronto: Law Society of Upper Canada, 2000)

LERMAN, L., "Lying to Clients" (1990) 138 U. Pa. L. Rev. 659

LUNDY, D., G. MacKENZIE, & M. NEWBURY, *Barristers and Solicitors in Practice* (Toronto: Butterworths, 1998)

LUSHING, P., "The Rise and Fall of the Criminal Contingent Fee" (1991) 82 J. of Crim. L. & Criminology 498

MacKENZIE, G., *Lawyers and Ethics: Professional Responsibility and Discipline* (Toronto: Carswell, 1993)

McKINNON, A., "Analytical Approaches to the Non-Refundable Retainer" (1996) 9 Geo. J. L. & Ethics 583

NOVA SCOTIA BARRISTERS' SOCIETY, *A Special Report to Members: The Impact of Proceeds of Crime Legislation on the Practice of Law* (1991) 17 N.S.L. News 45

ONTARIO CIVIL JUSTICE REVIEW, *Task Force Report on the Ontario Civil Justice System* (Toronto: Ontario Civil Justice Review, 1996)

PITTMAN, A., "Money Laundering: A Challenge for Canadian Law Enforcement" (1998) 41 Crim. L.Q. 238

PROCTOR, M., "Privilege and Fee Agreements" (1996) 75 Mich. St. Bar J. 822

ROSS, W., "The Ethics of Hourly Billing by Attorneys" (1991) 44 Rutgers L. Rev. 1

SALVESON, D., "The Mandatory Pro Bono Service Dilemma: A Way Out of the Thicket" (1997) 82 Mass. L. Rev. 197

SMITH, B., *Professional Conduct for Lawyers and Judges* (Fredericton, N.B.: Maritime Law Book, 1998)

STORROW, M., & L. BATTEN, "The New Proceeds of Crime Legislation or 'Caveat Avocatus'" (1991) 49 Advocate 53

TOLLEFSON, C., "Forfeiting The Right to Counsel?" (1994) 25 C.R. (4th) 257

WEINBERG, M., "*Lefcourt* Decision Requires Reassessment of NACDL 8300 Ethics Opinions" (Nov. 1997) The Champion 8

WELLE, L., "Power, Policy, and the Hyde Amendment: Ensuring Sound Judicial Interpretation of the Criminal Attorney's Fees Law (1999) 41 Wm. & Mary L. Rev. 333

WOLFRAM, C., *Modern Legal Ethics* (St. Paul: West, 1986)

# CHAPTER 11

# TERMINATION OF THE CLIENT-LAWYER RELATIONSHIP

## A. INTRODUCTION

Termination of a client-lawyer relationship can occur in a number of ways. But the most familiar forms of termination are discharge by the client and withdrawal by the lawyer. While both discharge and withdrawal are dealt with in this chapter, the primary focus is upon the circumstances where a lawyer can properly withdraw from a case, and the duties associated with withdrawal. Ideally, a number of different interests should be accommodated by rules of ethics that govern withdrawal. First, the fiduciary nature of the client-lawyer relationship, with attendant duties of competence, loyalty, and communication, requires that counsel act in the client's best interests. As far as possible, the client should receive competent and continuing representation, without undue delay or excessive cost occasioned by termination. Second, lawyers are bound by demanding professional standards in the conduct of the client's defence. There are ethical obligations not to breach the law, mislead the court or otherwise undermine the administration of justice in representing a client. Withdrawal may be the only method by which these obligations can be met. Third, society at large and participants in the criminal justice process other than the accused and defence counsel have an interest in ensuring reasonably efficient and prompt proceedings that promote a fair and just outcome.

In light of these diverse but interconnected interests, counsel is not permitted to terminate the client-lawyer relationship at will. Rather, withdrawal must be for good cause, with appropriate notice to the client. In instances where withdrawal is justified, the lawyer must extricate himself or herself from the case with a minimum of prejudice to the former client.

It could be argued, with convincing reference to the rules of professional conduct and case law, and despite the occasional judicial comment to the contrary, that lawyers are in fact given considerable latitude to withdraw from a case. Certainly, counsel who does not wait until the last minute to abandon a client prior to trial can choose from a panoply of grounds in engineering withdrawal, and there may be little that a client can do in response. Moreover, at the end of the day few clients will be keen to keep a lawyer who has no interest or inclination to continue with the case. These musings, though somewhat cynical, inarguably contain a kernel of validity and highlight the need for lawyers to exercise fair judgment and exhibit respect for the client and the proper administration of justice in considering the withdrawal option. Lawyers would also do well to think ahead by considering difficulties that might lead to withdrawal before accepting a case in the first place.[1]

Lawyers are not often exposed to complaint or censure for inappropriately withdrawing from a case. It is possible, however, for a dissatisfied former client to launch a disciplinary complaint or sue the lawyer civilly for negligence, breach of fiduciary duty or breach of contract. The issue of the former lawyer's conduct may also be raised by the abandoned client in seeking an adjournment or basing an appeal on a denial of the right to the effective assistance of counsel. Finally, a lawyer who disobeys a court order to continue with a case may be cited for contempt. The prospect of being subjected to such inquires or challenges provides an incentive for lawyers to exercise the withdrawal option with appropriate care and caution.

## B.  ONTARIO'S SPECIAL RULES FOR WITHDRAWAL IN CRIMINAL CASES

The Law Society of Upper Canada is alone among Canadian governing bodies in providing members with several rules applicable specifically

---

1    This point is closely related to the question of whether a lawyer is obliged to accept, or refuse, a proffered retainer: see chapter 2.

to withdrawal in criminal proceedings.[2] While most other governing bodies have general rules that apply in a similar manner to civil and criminal cases, Ontario's unique provisions show substantial appreciation for the particular problems that can arise where counsel seeks to withdraw in a criminal case. The Law Society's rules and the associated commentary are thus worth setting out in full:

> 2.09(4) Where a lawyer has agreed to act in a criminal case and where the interval between a withdrawal and the trial of the case is sufficient to enable the client to obtain another lawyer and to allow such other lawyer adequate time for preparation, the lawyer who has agreed to act may withdraw because the client has not paid the agreed fee or for other adequate cause provided that the lawyer:
>
> > (a) notifies the client, preferably in writing, that the lawyer is withdrawing because the fees have not been paid or for other adequate cause;
> >
> > (b) accounts to the client for any monies received on account of fees and disbursements;
> >
> > (c) notifies Crown counsel in writing that the lawyer is no longer acting;
> >
> > (d) in a case when the lawyer's name appears on the records of the court as acting for the accused notifies the clerk or registrar of the appropriate court in writing that the lawyer is no longer acting.
>
> *Commentary*: A lawyer who has withdrawn because of conflict with the client should not indicate in the notice addressed to the court or Crown counsel the cause of the conflict or make reference to any matter that would violate the privilege that exists between lawyer and client. The notice should merely state that the lawyer is no longer acting and has withdrawn.
>
> 2.09(5) Where a lawyer has agreed to act in a criminal case and where the date set for trial is not far enough removed to enable the client to obtain another lawyer or to enable another lawyer to prepare adequately for trial and an adjournment of the trial date cannot be obtained without adversely affecting the client's interests, the lawyer who agreed to act may not withdraw because of non-payment of fees.

---

2    Some other governing bodies make brief reference to criminal matters in dealing with withdrawal, whether expressly or otherwise: see, for example, B.C. ch. 10, r. 8(c) and note 1; N.B. Part C, r. 6; N.S. ch. 11, note 5; CBA Code ch. XII, note 4; Man. ch. XII, note 4; and Sask. ch. XII, note 4. But none has an extensive rule or rules in the manner of the Law Society of Upper Canada.

2.09(6) Where the lawyer is justified in withdrawing from a criminal case for reasons other than non-payment of fees and there is not sufficient interval between a notice to the client of the lawyer's intention to withdraw and the date when the case is to be tried to enable the client to obtain another lawyer and to enable such lawyer to prepare adequately for trial, the first lawyer, unless instructed otherwise by the client, should attempt to have the trial date adjourned and may withdraw from the case only with the permission of the court before which the case is to be tried.

*Commentary*: Where circumstances arise that in the opinion of the lawyer require an application to the court for leave to withdraw, the lawyer should promptly inform Crown counsel and the court of the intention to apply for leave in order to avoid or minimize any inconvenience to the court and witnesses.

These rules and commentary provide an excellent guide for counsel in other provinces, assuming that the applicable governing body has not adopted rules that are inconsistent.

## C. RULES OF THE COURT

Some provincial justice systems have adopted rules of criminal procedure that bear upon the withdrawal issue, thus providing yet another layer of potential obligations for counsel. For instance, the Ontario *Criminal Proceedings Rules* provide guidelines for counsel seeking to get off the record in a criminal matter.[3] Among other things, the *Rules* provide that the application for withdrawal must be made "as soon as is reasonably practicable and sufficiently in advance of the scheduled date of trial to ensure that no adjournment of the proceedings will be required for such purpose."[4] The *Rules* also set out requirements pertaining to notice to the prosecutor and court and to the contents of the affidavit filed by or on behalf of the accused.[5] Slightly less detailed, though to similar effect, are the *Rules of Practice of the Superior Court of the Province of Quebec, Criminal Division*, requiring leave of the court if withdrawal is sought within fourteen days preceding the opening of

---

3   Ontario Court of Justice, *Criminal Proceedings Rules*, S.I. 92/99, made pursuant to the authority of s. 482 of the *Criminal Code*, R.S.C. 1985, c. C-46, and s. 70 of the Ontario *Courts of Justice Act*, R.S.O. 1990, ch. C.43.

4   *Criminal Proceedings Rules*, above note 3, r. 25.02.

5   *Ibid.*, r. 25.03 & 25.04, respectively.

term or during the court term,[6] and *Rules of Practice of the Court of Quebec, Penal and Criminal Jurisdiction*, requiring leave of the court to withdraw where a lawyer "has appeared on behalf of an accused who is awaiting trial."[7] A lawyer who is considering withdrawal should determine whether any rules of the court apply, and make sure to comply with such rules in bringing the client-lawyer relationship to an end.

# D. DISCHARGE BY THE CLIENT

The client has an absolute and unreviewable power to discharge counsel at any time.[8] The rationale behind this rule is that the client-lawyer relationship is based on confidence and trust and has an impact upon the ability to make full answer and defence. If the client loses confidence in counsel, for whatever reason, his or her representation is likely to suffer. Moreover, there is a strong sense that individual autonomy and dignity demands respect for the client's decision to reject a particular lawyer in favour of retaining new counsel or going it alone.[9] In short, the client must have unfettered freedom to discharge counsel.[10]

Where the client discharges his or her lawyer, it matters not that the trial is under way, nor that the client may suffer prejudice as a result, nor indeed that the client has no articulable reason for firing

---

6    See *Rules of Practice of the Superior Court of the Province of Quebec, Criminal Division*, S.I./74-53 (Part III — Counsel).

7    *Rules of Practice of the Court of Quebec, Penal and Criminal Jurisdiction*, S.I./81-32, c. 9, s. 37.

8    See, for example, CBA Code ch. XII, comm. 1; Man. ch. XII, comm. 1; Sask. ch. XII, comm. 1; Alta. ch. 14, comm. G.1; N.S. ch. 11, comm. 11.1; Ont. r. 2.09(1) (commentary); and N.B. Part C, r. 6. For judicial authority to this effect see, for example, *R. v. Spataro* (1972), 7 C.C.C. (2d) 1 at 4 & 12 (S.C.C.) (the latter per Spence J. in dissent, though not on this point); *McQuarrie Hunter* v. *Foote* (1982), [1983] 2 W.W.R. 283 at 285–86 (B.C.C.A.); *R. v. C.(D.D.)* (1996), 110 C.C.C. (3d) 323 at 325 (Alta. C.A.), leave to appeal to S.C.C. refused [1996] S.C.C.A. No. 453 (QL) [*C.(D.D.)*]; and *R. v. Dunbar* (1982), 68 C.C.C. (2d) 13 at 46–49 (Ont. C.A.). An exception might apply where the client is mentally incompetent: see section L, "Client Under a Disability," in chapter 3.

9    See, for example, *R. v. Swain* (1991), 63 C.C.C. (3d) 481 at 504–06 (S.C.C.) [*Swain*]; and *R. v. McCallen* (1999), 131 C.C.C. (3d) 518 at 530–32 (Ont. C.A.) [*McCallen*].

10    This freedom cannot be unduly constrained by agreement between the client and lawyer. The Third Restatement §31, comm. "d" therefore notes that a client and lawyer cannot validly enter a contract forbidding the client to discharge the lawyer.

counsel. Moreover, the discharge is not dependent upon reasonable or any notice to the lawyer. What is more, a lawyer cannot be forced upon a reluctant accused. Where the accused discharges counsel during a trial, the court cannot therefore insist that counsel nevertheless continue with the representation.[11] Nor can the lawyer continue to act of his or her own accord.

In this latter respect, an intriguing ethical problem has occasionally occurred in the United States, where counsel for a condemned client has been discharged upon the client deciding not to contest a death sentence. It has happened that counsel persists in making representations to the court, even launching court proceedings, despite having been discharged.[12] Given our views on the decision-making authority enjoyed by the client, including the decision to fire counsel and not to pursue all available avenues of legal redress, we disagree with counsel who attempts to act for a client following discharge. We prefer the view taken in the Third Restatement, which expressly forbids a discharged lawyer from continuing to act on the case.[13]

Where a client informs counsel that the latter is discharged, and the trial is imminent or under way, counsel should make sure that the client understands the jeopardy faced if the court refuses to grant an adjournment.[14] The client should be under no illusions that an

---

11 See, for example, *R. v. Vescio* (1948), 92 C.C.C. 161 (S.C.C.); *Swain*, above note 9 at 505–06; *R. v. Taylor* (1992), 77 C.C.C. (3d) 551 at 567 (Ont. C.A.); *R. v. Romanowicz* (1999), 138 C.C.C. (3d) 225 at 237 (Ont. C.A.); *R. v. Bowles* (1985), 21 C.C.C. (3d) 540 at 543 & 545 (Alta. C.A.); *R. v. Fabrikant* (1995), 97 C.C.C. (3d) 544 at 555 (Que. C.A.), leave to appeal to S.C.C. refused 98 C.C.C. (3d) vi (S.C.C.); *R. v. Mian* (1998), 133 C.C.C. (3d) 573 at 575–76 (N.S.C.A.); and *Sherman* v. *Manley* (1978), 85 D.L.R. (3d) 575 at 579–80 (Ont. C.A.). The possibility that willing counsel will continue in the role of *amicus curiae* is another matter: see *R. v. Samra* (1998), 129 C.C.C. (3d) 144 at 152–59 (Ont. C.A.), leave to appeal to S.C.C. refused (1999), 239 N.R. 400n (S.C.C.); and *R. v. S.(M.)* (1996), 111 C.C.C. (3d) 467 at 473–74 (B.C.C.A.), leave to appeal to S.C.C. refused (1997), 113 C.C.C. (3d) vii (S.C.C.). The converse is not necessarily true: *i.e.* a reluctant lawyer may be forced upon a willing accused: see section L, "Leave of the Court to Withdraw," in this chapter.

12 See, for example, *Red Dog* v. *State*, 620 A.2d 848 (Del. 1993), related reference 625 A.2d 245 (Del. 1993) (where there is some uncertainty as to whether counsel was discharged, but see the client's comments at 620 A.2d 848 at 853) and the discussion in R. Zitrin & C. Langford, *Legal Ethics in the Practice of Law* (Charlottesville: Michie, 1995) at 212–16.

13 See Third Restatement §33(2)(b).

14 See ABA Model Rule 1.16, comm. 5.

adjournment is automatic.[15] Where the client is adamant in the decision to effect a discharge, counsel has no choice but to accede. Whenever counsel is irrevocably discharged, the safest reaction is to confirm the discharge and the client's reasons in writing. The purpose is not to disparage the client's decision but to set out fairly the circumstances to prevent misunderstanding and/or later recriminations. Counsel must refrain from seeking revenge for an unjustified discharge and must take reasonable measures to mitigate any adverse impact for the client.[16] Generally speaking, the same duty to mitigate prejudice to the client that applies upon withdrawal by counsel operates in the case of discharge by the client.[17]

# E.  GENERAL PROHIBITION AGAINST WITHDRAWAL

Lawyers do not have the same untrammelled freedom as clients in ending the professional relationship.[18] Most Canadian rules of professional conduct dealing with withdrawal adopt the proposition that a lawyer owes the client a general duty *not* to withdraw services absent good reason and sufficient notice.[19] This starting point is justified by reason

---

15    For cases where a client discharged counsel just prior to or during trial, and then was refused an adjournment see, for example, *R. v. Pomeroy* (1984), 15 C.C.C. (3d) 193 (Alta. C.A.); *R. v. Mitchell* (1981), 28 C.R. (3d) 112 (B.C.C.A.); *R. v. MacDonald* (1981), 50 N.S.R. (2d) 207 (S.C.A.D.), leave to appeal to S.C.C. refused (1982), 53 N.S.R. (2d) 290n (S.C.C.); and *R. v. Richard* (1992), 55 O.A.C. 43 at 45–46 (C.A.). See also the general comments made by Griffiths J.A. in *R. v. McGibbon* (1988), 45 C.C.C. (3d) 334 at 346 (Ont. C.A.).

16    See ABA Model Rule 1.16, comm. 9.

17    See, for example, ABA Model Rule 1.16 comment 9. Canadian rules of professional conduct typically view discharge as a form of withdrawal (see, for example CBA Code ch. XII, comm. 4), and thus presumably require reasonable mitigation by the discharged lawyer. The rules in Alberta are especially clear on this point: see Alta. ch. 14, r. 3).

18    See, for example, CBA Code ch. XII, comm. 1; Man. ch. XII, comm. 1; Sask. ch. XII, comm. 1; B.C. ch. 10, r. 3; Alta. ch. 14, Statement of Principle; N.S. ch. 11, Rule; Ont. r. 2.09(1) (commentary); N.B. Part C, r. 6; and Yukon Part 1, r. 21.

19    See, for example, CBA Code ch. XII, Rule; Man. ch. XII, Rule; Sask. ch. XII, Rule; Alta. ch. 14, Statement of Principle; N.S. ch. 11, Rule; Ont. r. 2.09(1); Que. s. 3.03.04 & s. 4.02.01(j); N.B. Part C, r. 6; and Yukon Part 1, r. 21. To similar effect, in England and Wales, see Law Society, *The Guide to the Professional Conduct of Solicitors*, 8th ed. (London: Law Society, 1999) §12.20; General Council, *Code of Conduct of the Bar of England and Wales* (London: The Council, 1990), r. 506 and Annex "H" (Written Standards for the Conduct of

of the lawyer's fiduciary duty to the client. Loyalty demands that the lawyer be restricted from taking any action that will harm the client's interests absent good cause. Consequently, even where there is substantial leeway in choosing whether or not to represent a client in the first place,[20] a lawyer's control over the continuation of the relationship is significantly curtailed from the point of being retained forward. In particular, and as we have seen, the lawyer's knowledge that a client is guilty neither requires nor justifies putting an end to the retainer.[21] Nor can counsel end the professional relationship because he or she feels that the accused is destined to lose.[22] It is also improper for a lawyer to withdraw from a case because of dissatisfaction or frustration with a judge's ruling.[23] Nevertheless, it has been suggested that withdrawal in reaction to an adverse ruling may be an acceptable course of action in the rare and extreme case, apparently where the ruling prevents a fair trial and interferes with counsel's ability to represent the client.[24]

**Example:** A lawyer is retained by a client to provide a defence in an extortion case. The client has an unpleasant countenance and is intensely disliked by the lawyer. However, this dislike is not so deeply founded that counsel cannot perform the proper duties of competent

---

Professional Work, Standards Applicable to Criminal Cases) at §4.2. British Columbia is a notable exception, insofar as a lawyer can withdraw for any reason provided that the client suffers no unfairness and withdrawal is not done for an improper purpose: see section H, "British Columbia's Residual Right to Withdraw," in this chapter. American codes tend to provide counsel with even more leeway in withdrawing, which is not surprising given the latitude accorded attorneys in refusing to accept a retainer: see chapter 2.

20   See chapter 2.

21   See section G, "Accepting or Continuing with the Retainer of a Client Known to Be Guilty," in chapter 1.

22   Consider, however, the case where the client insists on counsel conducting the defence in a manner that is destined to forgo a reasonable chance of acquittal. Counsel may be permitted to withdraw in such circumstances, but the reason would lie in a determination that there had been a fundamental breakdown in the client-lawyer relationship: see section I, "A Client's Insistence that the Lawyer Act Incompetently," in chapter 3.

23   See, for example, *R. v. Swartz* (1977), 34 C.C.C. (2d) 477 at 481–82 (Man. C.A.) [*Swartz*]; *R. v. Gillespie* (2000), 35 C.R. (5th) 340 (Man. Q.B.) [*Gillespie*] (application to withdraw following adverse ruling termed "suspicious"). For an atrocious example of counsel leaving a client in the lurch by withdrawing in response to a clash with the trial judge, in a murder trial at that, see *Dunkley* v. R. (1994), [1995] 1 All E.R. 279 (P.C.) [*Dunkley*].

24   See *Swartz*, above note 23 at 482.

defence counsel. Accordingly, counsel should remain on the case barring reasonable cause to withdraw or the client's consent.[25]

At the beginning of the client-lawyer relationship, counsel should consider expressly identifying in the retainer those conditions under which withdrawal will be permitted. Given the fiduciary nature of the relationship, and the duty to act in the client's best interests, it is unlikely that the client can "contract out" of *all* protections otherwise provided by the law. It would, for instance, be unethical to provide for unilateral withdrawal by the lawyer without cause in a retainer agreement. But a lawyer can surely lay out the groundwork for a reasonable right to terminate, and include provisions covering notice.[26]

Another matter that counsel should consider covering in a written retainer agreement is the natural end point of the relationship.[27] In this respect, since ambiguous contracts are construed to the advantage of the client, clearly demarcating the end point of the retainer is a good idea.[28] Most clients realize that the trial lawyer is not bound to continue on with an appeal, but such is not always the case. A trickier area concerns post-trial matters with respect to which the client could frequently benefit from a lawyer's help. Criminal lawyers are in many instances requested to assist clients in working out problems at penal institutions or in following up on rehabilitation efforts. Some counsel simply refuse to accept any responsibility for undertaking this "post-retainer" work. Many others aid the client without giving much thought to whether or not a formal retainer continues to exist.

When the relationship does come to an end, a reporting letter to the client is always a good idea. If the client is expressly informed that the relationship has ended, the possibility of misunderstanding and

---

25   In Australia, some rules of professional conduct expressly forbid counsel from withdrawing owing to a dislike of the client: see, for example, Western Australia, *Professional Conduct Rules*, r. 12.3; and Tasmania, *Bar Association Professional Conduct Guidelines*, para. 18. Counsel in British Columbia may be able to withdraw on the facts of this hypothetical, however, provided that the client suffers no "unfairness": see section H, "British Columbia's Residual Right to Withdrawal," in this chapter.

26   See, for example, the Third Restatement §32, comm. "h(i)" & "i" permitting agreement on withdrawal where the client's consent is informed but never where the arrangement works to impair the quality of the representation.

27   See *R. v. Williams* (1897), 3 C.C.C. 9 (Ont. H.C.J.) (the authority of a lawyer to act is *prima facie* terminated following an accused's acquittal). For a case where trial counsel filed a notice of appeal following a conviction, and was permitted to withdraw given the subsequent refusal of legal aid, see *R. v. Dorion* (1978), 40 C.C.C. (2d) 549 at 553 (Man. C.A.) [*Dorion*].

28   Third Restatement §31, comm. "h."

continued reliance, to the detriment of the client and counsel, is alleviated.

## F. MANDATORY WITHDRAWAL BY THE LAWYER

We have just seen that Canadian lawyers have a duty to continue the retainer absent good justification for termination. Conversely, however, there are instances where withdrawal is mandated, leaving the lawyer with no choice in the matter. Some rules of professional conduct simply state that withdrawal is obligatory in certain circumstances, and go on to provide what appears to be a non-exhaustive list of examples.[29] Other governing bodies purport to itemize all of the grounds that impose upon a lawyer the duty to end the relationship.[30] Examples provided in Canadian rules of professional conduct, culled from both the exhaustive and non-exhaustive types of rule, include:

1. discharge by the client;[31]
2. instructions by the client to take action inconsistent with the lawyer's duties to the court;[32]
3. the client is guilty of dishonourable conduct in the proceedings;[33]
4. instructions by the client intended solely to harass or maliciously injure another person;[34]
5. persistence by the client in pursuing a futile or vexatious proceeding;[35]

---

29   See, for example, CBA Code ch. XII, comm. 4; Man. ch. XII, comm. 4; Sask. ch. XII, comm. 4. Nova Scotia is especially direct in stating that the instances cited are merely examples: N.S. ch. 11, comm. 11.1.
30   See, for example, B.C. ch. 10, r. 1; Alta. ch. 14, r. 2; and Ont. r. 2.09(7).
31   See, for example, CBA Code ch. XII, comm. 4; Man. ch. XII, comm. 4; Sask. ch. XII, comm. 4; B.C. ch. 10, r. 1(a); Alta. ch. 14, Statement of Principle; Ont. r. 2.09(7)(a); N.B. Part C, r. 6; and Yukon Part 1, r. 21.
32   See, for example, CBA Code ch. XII, comm. 4(a); Man. ch. XII, comm. 4(a); Sask. ch. XII, comm. 4(a); B.C. ch. 10, r. 1(b); N.S. ch. 11, comm. 11.1(a); Ont. r. 2.09(7)(b); N.B. Part C, r. 6; and Yukon Part 1, r. 21.
33   See, for example, CBA Code ch. XII, comm. 4(b); Man. ch. XII, comm. 4(b); Sask. ch. XII, comm. 4(b); Ont. r. 2.09(7)(c); and N.S. ch. 11, comm. 11.1(b).
34   See, for example, CBA Code ch. XII, comm. 4(b); Man. ch. XII, comm. 4(b); Sask. ch. XII, comm. 4(b); B.C. ch. 10, r. 1(c); N.S. ch. 11, comm. 11.1(b) (adding a reference to injury to another person's property); Ont. r. 2.09(7)(c); N.B. Part C, r. 6; Yukon Part 1, r. 21.
35   See Que. s. 3.03.04(d).

6. instructions by the client to take action that the lawyer knows will result in assisting the client to commit a crime or fraud;[36]
7. the lawyer's continued employment will clearly lead to a breach of the rules;[37]
8. conflict of interest;[38]
9. the lawyer has insufficient expertise and knowledge, or other infirmities, that prevents him or her from competently handling the matter;[39] and
10. the lawyer is unable to provide services with reasonable promptness.[40]

Not all of these grounds are found in every Canadian governing body's rules. Some of the grounds overlap with others and are perhaps rendered otiose by virtue of broader companion grounds. But the linchpin guiding principle is indisputable, mandating withdrawal where continued representation will necessarily compromise service to the client or involve the lawyer in violating legal or ethical duties. Also, once the standard for mandatory withdrawal is met, the fact that the client will suffer prejudice by reason of termination of the retainer becomes irrelevant.

In considering whether withdrawal is obligatory, counsel must carefully assess the surrounding circumstances. Because the consequence of withdrawal can be severe for the client, such action should not be taken lightly. The lawyer who apprehends a possible duty to end the relationship must ensure that he or she is in possession of all relevant facts. There is also an issue relating to the precise nature of a lawyer's knowledge regarding anticipated client misbehaviour. What

---

36 See Alta. ch. 14, r. 2(b); and Que. s. 3.03.04(c).
37 See, for example, CBA Code ch. XII, comm. 4(c); Man. ch. XII, comm. 4(c); Sask. ch. XII, comm. 4(c); Alta. ch. 14, r. 2(a); Ont. r. 2.09(7)(d); and N.S. ch. 11, comm. 11.1(c).
38 See, for example, CBA Code ch. XII, Rule; Man. ch. XII, Rule; Sask. ch. XII, Rule; B.C. ch. 10, r. 1(d); Alta. ch. 14, r. 2(d); N.S. ch. 11, comm. 11.1(c); N.B. Part C, r. 6; Yukon Part 1, r. 21; and Que. s. 3.03.04(e).
39 See, for example, CBA Code ch. XII, comm. 4(d); Man. ch. XII, comm. 4(d); Sask. ch. XII, comm. 4(d); B.C. ch. 10, r. 1(e); Alta. ch. 14, r. 2(c); N.S. ch. 11, comm. 11.1(d); Ont. r. 2.09(7)(e); N.B. Part C, r. 6; and Yukon Part 1, r. 21. For a rare case where physical limitations, of an admittedly vague sort, were put forward as a basis for seeking leave to withdraw, see *R. v. Laframboise* (1998), 224 A.R. 24 (Q.B.) (application denied, but the accused later discharged counsel).
40 See Alta. ch. 14, r. 2(c). The promptness factor is really a subset of the broader obligation to withdraw where the lawyer is not competent to act, given that competent service includes prompt service.

standard must be met to mandate withdrawal or, to look at the problem more from the client's perspective, what degree of uncertainty will justify staying on the case?[41] The Alberta rule speaks of the lawyer "knowing" that a crime or fraud will occur.[42] This standard has already been discussed in the context of the client known to be guilty and the perjurious client.[43]

Even assuming that counsel can be said to "know" that an illegality will occur, if the client insists on unethical behaviour can counsel simply refuse to carry out the offending instructions? If so, is withdrawal no longer mandated? The risk of the illegality occurring by virtue of the lawyer staying on the case is zero, given that the lawyer must refuse to act as directed.[44] The more likely scenario may be that the client fires the uncooperative lawyer. The client's persistent instructions may also lead the lawyer to view the relationship as irrevocably ruptured, hence permitting optional withdrawal.[45] Resolving this issue is difficult, but we are inclined to the view that counsel should withdraw rather than simply override the client's improper instructions.[46] Moreover, it is imperative that the matter be discussed with the client prior to withdrawing where at all possible. Upon learning of a particular problem, the client might quite readily agree to abandon the troublesome instructions.[47]

On the other hand, the grounds that mandate withdrawal generally involve a substantial threat to the administration of justice, and perhaps also to the best interests of the client (as in the case of an unwaivable conflict of interest or counsel's incompetence). The lawyer's interest in self-protection may also be implicated, for example, where remaining on the case may invite allegations of complicity in client fraud. For these reasons, on occasion the lawyer may have to act quickly, in extreme cases perhaps even withdrawing absent notice to the client, to avoid knowingly violating the rules of ethics.[48]

---

41   These issues are addressed in G. Hazard & W. Hodes, *The Law of Lawyering*, 2d ed. (Englewood, N.J.: Prentice Hall, 1993) at §1.16(202).

42   See Alta. ch. 14, r. 2(b).

43   See section F, "Acquiring Knowledge that the Client is Guilty," in chapter 1 and section F(1), "Acquiring Knowledge that the Client Intends to Commit Perjury," in chapter 7.

44   See C.W. Wolfram, *Modern Legal Ethics* (St. Paul: West, 1986) at 552.

45   See section G, "Discretionary Withdrawal by the Lawyer," in this chapter.

46   Our position is explained in section H, "Instructions that Require Unethical Conduct from the Lawyer," in chapter 3.

47   See, for example, CBA Code ch. XII, comm. 4(a); Sask. ch. XII, comm. 4(a); Man. ch. XII, comm. 4(a); Alta. ch. 14, comm. 2.

48   See Alta. ch. 14, comm. 2.

# G. DISCRETIONARY WITHDRAWAL BY THE LAWYER

Just as Canadian rules of professional conduct often categorize those circumstances where withdrawal is obligatory, so, too, do the rules set out instances where a lawyer is permitted, but not required, to terminate the retainer.[49] The grounds that may justify withdrawal, selected from the various Canadian rules, include:

1. serious loss of confidence between client and lawyer, going to the basis of the relationship;[50]
2. the lawyer has been deceived by the client;[51]
3. the client refuses to accept and act upon the lawyer's advice on a significant point;[52]
4. the client's conduct in the matter is dishonourable or motivated primarily by malice;[53]
5. the client is persistently unreasonable or uncooperative in a material respect;[54]
6. the client fails after reasonable notice to provide funds on account of fees or disbursements, contravening an agreement made with the lawyer;[55] and
7. inability to locate the client or obtain adequate instructions.[56]

---

49  See, for example, CBA Code ch. XII, comm. 5; Sask. ch. XII, comm. 5; Man. ch. XII, comm. 5; B.C. ch. 10, r. 2; N.S. ch. 11, comm. 11.3; Alta. ch. 14, r. 1; Ont. r. 2.09(2).

50  See, for example, CBA Code ch. XII, comm. 5; Sask. ch. XII, comm. 5; Man. ch. XII, comm. 5; B.C. ch. 10, r. 2; N.S. ch. 11, comm. 11.3; Alta. ch. 14, r. 1(e); Ont. r. 2.09(2); and Que. s. 3.03.04(a).

51  See, for example, CBA Code ch. XII, comm. 5; Sask. ch. XII, comm. 5; Man. ch. XII, comm. 5; B.C. ch. 10, r. 2(a); N.S. ch. 11, comm. 11.3; Ont. r. 2.09(2) (commentary); and Que. s. 3.03.04(b).

52  See, for example, CBA Code ch. XII, comm. 5; Sask. ch. XII, comm. 5; Man. ch. XII, comm. 5; B.C. ch. 10, r. 2(c); N.S. ch. 11, comm. 11.4; and Ont. r. 2.09(2) (commentary).

53  See Alta. ch. 14, r. 1(b).

54  See Alta. ch. 14, r. 1(c).

55  See, for example, CBA Code ch. XII, comm. 6; Sask. ch. XII, comm. 6; Man. ch. XII, comm. 6; N.S. ch. 11, comm. 11.6; Alta. ch. 14, r. 1(a); and Ont. r. 2.09(3). See also section I, "Non-Payment of Fees or Unreasonable Financial Burden," in this chapter.

56  See, for example, B.C. ch. 10, r. 2(b) (only covering refusal by the client to provide instructions); N.S. ch. 11, comm. 11.5; and Alta. ch. 14, r. 1(d). See also section K, "The Lawyer Is Unable to Obtain Instructions," in chapter 3.

Some of these justifications are also found in the list provided in section F, regarding mandatory withdrawal. This repetition is the result of different grounds embraced by different governing bodies. For instance, dishonourable conduct in the proceedings by the client mandates withdrawal under the CBA Code, yet the Alberta rules provide that a client's dishonourable conduct allows a lawyer the discretion to withdraw.[57] It is thus important for a lawyer considering withdrawal to review the ethical rules applicable in his or her province.

As the rules generally recognize, the justifications for discretionary withdrawal provide examples of instances where the central components of trust and confidence that are so essential to an effective client-lawyer relationship have substantially eroded and the relationship is possibly dysfunctional. There may also be an element of self-protection evident in the decision to withdraw, the lawyer legitimately desiring to terminate the relationship to avert a real possibility of being blamed for past or future illegality. This concern would be evident, for example, if the lawyer discovered that the client was intent on committing perjury or had used the lawyer's services to track down and intimidate or bribe a witness.

It is worth emphasizing that no Canadian rule of professional conduct purports to provide an exhaustive list of situations where withdrawal is permitted. That is to say, the wording of all of the rules is, to varying extents, open-ended. Some rules, such as those adopted in New Brunswick and Yukon Territory, permit withdrawal whenever the lawyer has "good cause," without specifying what factors will meet this standard.[58] Others, based on the CBA Code's wording, say that permissive withdrawal will, "as a rule," arise only where there has been a serious loss of confidence between client and counsel.[59] Perhaps the narrowest delineation of cases where discretionary withdrawal is permitted is found in Ontario, where the justifying cause must pertain to a serious loss of confidence between the lawyer and client.[60] Once again, we stress that counsel considering withdrawal must therefore begin by consulting the rule applicable in his or her jurisdiction.

The more restrictive rules pertaining to discretionary withdrawal, such as Ontario's, focus on a breakdown in confidence. Yet there may be other circumstances where withdrawal is advisable, despite the

---

57   Compare CBA Code ch. XII, comm. 5 with Alta. ch. 14, r. 1(b).
58   See N.B. Part C, r. 6; and Yukon Part 1, r. 21.
59   See CBA Code ch. XII, comm. 5; Sask. ch. XII, comm. 5; Man. ch. XII, comm. 5; and N.S. ch. 11, comm. 11.3.
60   See Ont. r. 2.09(2).

absence of any distrust or disagreement between lawyer and client. For instance, suppose that several accused are charged together, and two or more defence counsel simply cannot get along. Where one counsel feels strongly that an inability to work with co-counsel could cause the client's defence to suffer, withdrawal is perhaps not only permissible but necessary.[61] It can also be argued that counsel is allowed to withdraw from the case whenever granted informed permission to do so by the client.[62] Furthermore, there is some support for the idea that a lawyer can withdraw from the case even where the client opposes such action, provided that the client suffers no material adverse impact.[63] This particular possibility will be considered in detail as part of the discussion of the "residual" right of withdrawal established in British Columbia (see section H, below). Speaking more generally, however, these examples do not fit comfortably within the rules permitting (or mandating, for that matter) withdrawal in many Canadian jurisdictions. There is thus reason to favour a more flexible approach to the problem.

How is counsel to exercise the discretion typically inherent in those ethical rules that permit withdrawal? The following factors are surely among those relevant to a lawyer's considerations:

1.  It is necessary to determine the extent to which the problem undermines the "very basis" of the relationship.[64] The lawyer and client may have a huge disagreement regarding a matter relevant to the case, but without any continued adverse impact on the integrity of the relationship. The lawyer must ascertain whether the relationship can properly function to the continued benefit of the client.

2.  If there is a serious rift in the relationship, counsel should consider whether the problem can be repaired. It may be, however, that the effort and time required to do so is too daunting or impractical in the circumstances or stands little chance of permanent success.

---

61  Serious friction between co-counsel as a legitimate justification for withdrawal is recognized in the ABA Model Code DR 2-110(C)(3). No Canadian rule addresses this issue. It may well be that a client will discharge counsel upon being informed of the difficulty.

62  See ABA Model Code DR 2-110(C)(5); and Third Restatement §32(3)(c). Certainly, discharge by the client requires withdrawal under Canadian rules. But consent and discharge are not necessarily the same thing.

63  This possibility is countenanced by ABA Model Rule 1.16(b) and Third Restatement §32(3)(a), yet is not provided for by the ABA Model Code.

64  To use the language found in CBA Code ch. XII, comm. 5.

3. The prejudicial impact that termination of the retainer will have on the client must be taken into account.[65] In some circumstances, withdrawal unavoidably amounts to an implicit breach of confidentiality that may harm the client. In other instances, the client is unable to obtain a new lawyer by virtue of an ongoing trial or prohibitive cost. In almost every case, withdrawal will cause the client some harm in the form of time lost, added cost, and/or stress. It may be that the withdrawing lawyer can mitigate such harm by refunding fees or helping to find a new lawyer, but such is not always possible.

4. The lawyer must avoid submitting to a temptation to terminate the retainer where, though perhaps justified on the facts, the real reason for wishing to end the relationship is extraneous to any proper consideration. A desire to escape from what appears to be an insurmountable Crown case, to ease the pressures of a busy practice, or to attend an important social engagement is not a valid factor.[66]

As in the case where withdrawal is mandatory, the lawyer considering optional withdrawal has a duty to discuss the matter with the client in an effort to repair the damaged relationship, and in any event to inform the client of the decision to withdraw.[67] Moreover, given that withdrawal is permitted, not required, where feasible the proper course in mitigating prejudice to the client may be to continue to act until new counsel is retained.[68]

**Prohibition:** Counsel should never threaten withdrawal as a means of forcing the client to make an unpalatable or rushed decision.[69] Granted, there will be instances that demand quick action, and where appropriate the client must be told that withdrawal may be the lawyer's response. But ending the professional relationship should not be used as a brickbat to make the client bow to counsel's dictates.

---

65 See Third Restatement §32(4), which provides that a lawyer may not exercise his or her discretion to withdraw "if the harm that withdrawal would cause significantly exceeds the harm to the lawyer or others in not withdrawing." However, this restriction applies only to certain specified grounds of optional withdrawal (client insists on repugnant or imprudent action, breach of contract including failure to pay fees, irreparable breakdown, and "other good cause").

66 See Que. s. 4.02.01(j).

67 See, for example, CBA Code ch. XII, Rule & comm. 7; Sask. ch. XII, Rule & comm. 7; Man. ch. XII, Rule & comm. 7; B.C. ch. 10, r. 8(a); N.S. ch. 11, Rule & comm. 11.7; Alta. ch. 14, comm. 1; Ont. r. 2.09(1) & commentary.

68 See Alta. ch. 14, comm. 1.

69 See CBA Code ch. XII, comm. 5; Sask. ch. XII, comm. 5; Man. ch. XII, comm. 5; N.S. ch. 11, comm. 11.4; and Ont. r. 2.09(2) (commentary).

As a last point, we believe that in extreme cases, where the client-lawyer relationship has totally broken down, leading to outright hostility and an utter and irreconcilable lack of trust, the discretion to withdraw begins to shade into a mandatory duty to terminate. Surely, counsel cannot be expected or allowed to continue acting for the client in such circumstances, given the detrimental effect on the client's constitutional rights and the administration of justice. Undoubtedly, a terribly malfunctioning client-lawyer relationship will quite often cause the client to discharge the lawyer. But where this step is not taken, there is a good argument that the lawyer must withdraw, especially where resulting adverse impact to the client is negligible or manageable. Indeed, an excellent case can be made that an extreme rupture to the client-lawyer relationship makes pursuing the representation improper under various rules of professional conduct (pertaining to loyalty, competence, integrity, and so on), and hence mandates withdrawal because continued employment will clearly lead to a breach of the rules.[70]

**Example I:** Part way through the trial, the accused absconds. Counsel applies to withdraw. This course of action is justified, and perhaps even mandated, because the lawyer is unable to obtain instructions.[71]

**Example II:** Counsel is retained by a client who relentlessly insists, from the first meeting onwards, that he testify as part of the defence. Counsel eventually concludes that testifying will undermine any prospect of acquittal, and following the close of the Crown case he strongly advises against the client taking the stand. The client nonetheless persists in his desire to testify. If the difference of opinion between counsel and the client is so severe that the integrity of the client-lawyer relationship has been destroyed, counsel may seek leave of the court to withdraw.[72] But such a step should not be lightly taken, given the possible (though incorrect) adverse inference that the client is about to

---

70    See the rules cited at note 37, above, and accompanying text.

71    See *R. v. Garofoli* (1988), 41 C.C.C. (3d) 97 at 143 (Ont. C.A.), rev'd on other grounds (1990), 60 C.C.C. (3d) 161 (S.C.C.), where the court comes close to saying that a lawyer for an absconding accused has a right to withdraw. See also section K, "The Lawyer is Unable to Obtain Instructions," in chapter 3.

72    See *R. v. Brigham* (1992), 79 C.C.C. (3d) 365 at 380–83 (Que. C.A.), upon which this example is loosely based. See also *R. v. Steele* (1991), 63 C.C.C. (3d) 149 at 160 (Que. C.A.) [*Steele*]; and "Panel Discussion: Problems in Ethics and Advocacy" in Law Society of Upper Canada, *Defending a Criminal Case* (Toronto: R. De Boo, 1969) 279 at 284 ["Panel Discussion"].

commit perjury and the difficulty that the client may have in completing the case without the help of counsel.[73]

## H. BRITISH COLUMBIA'S RESIDUAL RIGHT TO WITHDRAW

In British Columbia, the Law Society's rules not only provide for mandatory and optional withdrawal but also create a so-called "residual right to withdraw."[74] British Columbia's residual category creates something not seen in other Canadian jurisdictions: a broad ability of the lawyer to withdraw from a case, without the need for any particular justification (such as a breakdown in the client-lawyer relationship or a real threat to the administration of justice). This residual right to withdraw is similar to the approach seen in ABA Model Rule 1.16(b) and the Third Restatement §32(3)(a). Both American codes allow an attorney to withdraw for any reason whatsoever where there is no "material adverse effect on the interests of the client."[75]

As the text of the British Columbia rules makes obvious, however, the residual right to withdraw is tempered by important limits. Counsel can withdraw only where to do so is not "unfair to the client" and where the withdrawal is not done for an "improper purpose."[76] The rules go on to flesh out the meaning of both limitations. Unfairness to the client depends on the circumstances of each case, but normally includes consideration of whether withdrawal will require the client to have new counsel repeat some or all of the same work again, or leave the client with insufficient time to retain new counsel who can adequately prepare for the case.[77] Impropriety of purpose is also said to depend on the circumstances of the case, but examples of improper grounds for withdrawal include the taking of such action to delay court proceedings or to assist the client in effecting an improper purpose.[78]

**Example:** Through inadvertence, or because of an unexpected development in the case, the client's trial is scheduled to conflict with coun-

---

73   See section F(4)(a), "Withdrawal," in chapter 7.

74   B.C. ch. 10, r. 3.

75   An ability to withdraw, provided only that the client will not suffer adverse consequences, is not granted by the ABA Model Code.

76   B.C. ch. 10, r. 3.

77   See B.C. ch. 10, r. 4.

78   See B.C. ch. 10, r. 5.

sel's vacation. Or perhaps after taking on a case the lawyer learns that she can act for a rich client in a lengthy matter that will demand substantial time commitments and require shedding a few "small" clients. In British Columbia, counsel can apparently withdraw from the case if the client suffers no prejudice. Assuming that there is no material financial disadvantage, and no problem in finding another lawyer, the client's lack of consent is irrelevant. In Ontario, by contrast, withdrawal would not be permitted. The same conclusion is probably justified for any Canadian jurisdiction that prohibits withdrawal absent "good cause."[79]

# I.  NON-PAYMENT OF FEES OR UNREASONABLE FINANCIAL BURDEN

Non-payment of fees is frequently a major concern for criminal lawyers, whose clients are often unemployed or under-employed, incarcerated, or otherwise financially disadvantaged. Full payment in advance is nothing more than an unattainable aspiration in many cases, and counsel is left with no alternative but to accept partial payments of a piecemeal nature. Where, for any one of a number of reasons, the client has substantially defaulted in paying the agreed-upon amounts, the issue of prematurely ending the retainer arises. But withdrawal is not always the proper response. The CBA Code states that "[f]ailure on the part of the client after reasonable notice to provide funds on account of disbursements or fees will justify withdrawal by the lawyer unless serious prejudice to the client would result."[80] The key here is that the client must not suffer any serious prejudice.[81] In Alberta, the rules are perhaps less onerous for the lawyer, stating that the lawyer "ought to seriously consider continuing to act" if the default is minor, the amount of work remaining to be done is minimal, or the client would be placed in peril as a result of withdrawal.[82] In our view, the sterner position taken in most other provinces is preferable, under which serious prejudice to the client operates to preclude ending the

---

79  See the rules cited at note 19, above, and accompanying text.

80  CBA Code ch. XII, comm. 6. See also Sask. ch. XII, comm. 6; Man. ch. XII, comm. 6; N.S. ch. 11, comm. 11.6; Ont. r. 2.09(3), 2.09(4), & 2.09(5) (the latter two rules pertaining specifically to criminal matters); and B.C. ch. 10, r. 7.

81  See also M. Pasano, "Permanent Appearance Rules: A Concern for Continuity Imperils Criminal Defense Work" (1993) 7 Crim. Just. 8.

82  See Alta. ch. 14, comm. 1.

retainer. Other Anglo-American jurisdictions tend to adopt the CBA Code's approach, permitting withdrawal where the client fails to make agreed-upon payments, provided that undue prejudice does not occur.[83]

The typical instance where unacceptable prejudice would result, and where withdrawal is therefore improper, sees counsel wait until the trial is about to begin or has already started before attempting to extricate himself or herself from the retainer.[84] In most cases of this sort, the client will not be able to retain and instruct replacement counsel in time to ensure competent representation at trial. An adjournment might be a satisfactory answer, but only where permitted by the court and not adverse to the client's interests.[85] The bottom line is that failure to pay fees justifies withdrawal only where the client will not suffer substantial adverse impact.

**Example:** Counsel is retained privately under a flat-fee arrangement to defend the client on a fraud charge, with the trial expected to last two weeks. The case is fairly complex, and the prosecution evidence involves substantial documentation. In preparing for the case, defence counsel begins to suspect that the retainer provides woefully insufficient compensation for the work required. The day before the trial is to commence, he asks the client for further funds. On this scenario, counsel has only himself to blame for badly underestimating the fee required, and especially for leaving the matter of an extra payment to the last minute. Moreover, the late request puts intense pressure on the client, who will almost certainly fear a substandard performance absent an infusion of funds. On these facts, counsel was wrong to make the request. In other circumstances, a request might be permissible. For instance, counsel would not be acting improperly in making the request in a low-key way, where independent legal advice was offered to the client, counsel had good reason to believe that the added pay-

---

83  See, for example, *The Guide to the Professional Conduct of Solicitors*, above note 19 at §14.01(2); ABA Model Rule 1.16(b)(4); ABA Model Code DR 2-110(c)(1)(f); and Third Restatement §32(3)(g).

84  This scenario is explicitly dealt with, and withdrawal generally forbidden, by Ont. r. 2.09(5). For an example of counsel withdrawing at the last minute for non-payment of fees, without adverse comment by the court, see *R. v. Hazlewood* (1994), 42 B.C.A.C. 44 (C.A.).

85  See Ont. r. 2.09(5), implicitly allowing for withdrawal accompanied by an adjournment, yet only where not contrary to the client's interests. To the same effect, see *R. v. Chevarie* (1996), 185 A.R. 318 (Q.B.) (though perhaps no longer good law in Alberta following the decision in *C.(D.D.)*, above note 8).

ment would not represent a significant financial burden for the client, and the client was given as much notice as possible.

There is judicial authority suggesting that, once on the record, counsel in a criminal case is *never* allowed to withdraw because of non-payment of fees, not even where the accused is exposed to no undue prejudice as a result. This stern position is set out in *R. v. C.(D.D.)*, where the Alberta Court of Appeal stated that counsel will be granted permission to withdraw for cause or with the client's consent, but opined that cause does not include non-payment of fees.[86] We strongly believe that this position goes too far. Counsel should not be obligated to stay on the case where the client has substantially breached a contractual obligation to pay legal costs, reasonable warning that withdrawal will occur is provided, and the client is not exposed to serious prejudice by reason of withdrawal. Naturally, there are other considerations that bear upon the matter, related to the efficient running of the criminal justice process. But where these considerations also do not weigh against permitting withdrawal for non-payment, the proper course should be to allow counsel to terminate the relationship, as countenanced by those Canadian rules of professional conduct that address the matter.[87] In this vein, the Ontario Court of Appeal has recognized that counsel may withdraw for non-payment of fees.[88] The court did not mention *C.(D.D.)*, and was speaking in hypothetical terms, but its position is sensible and finds support in the Law Society of Upper Canada's then (and now) current rules of professional conduct.

Even where the accused will suffer no real prejudice, the failure to pay fees should not be used to justify immediate withdrawal in every case. For one thing, the client's delinquency should be substantial and serious.[89] Being a few days late with a payment, or paying only 95 percent of the required amount, will probably not represent a sufficient

---

86   *C.(D.D.)*, above note 8 at 324. In fairness, the Alberta Court of Appeal may not have intended to embrace a blanket prohibition against withdrawal for non-payment. Rather, on the facts of the case, the court clearly felt that withdrawal would have caused unacceptable harm to the administration of justice, hence justifying refusal to grant leave.

87   See the rules set out at note 80, above. Our view is shared by M. Rauf, "Must the Court Consent to Defence Counsel Withdrawing for Non-Payment of Fees?" (1996) 3 C.R. (5th) 46 at 59.

88   See *R. v. Chatwell* (1998), 122 C.C.C. (3d) 162 at 166 (Ont. C.A.), appeal as of right quashed (1998), 125 C.C.C. (3d) 433 (S.C.C.).

89   This requirement is not set out in any Canadian rules but is alluded to in a commentary to the applicable Alberta provision: see Alta. ch. 14, comm. 1(a).

breach of the agreement to justify terminating the relationship. Moreover, counsel should ensure that the client understands that a breach has occurred before rushing to the worst conclusions and taking action to end the relationship. The client may quite legitimately have forgotten about a payment deadline or reasonably misunderstood the lawyer's expectations. In any event, the lawyer should also provide warning of possible withdrawal to allow the client an opportunity to correct the failure to pay. Further, where the default is substantial, but counsel has allowed the delinquency to continue for a long time and the matter is almost completed, withdrawal may be inappropriate.[90] Finally, where the failure to pay is the result of penury, counsel should consider staying on the case in a *pro bono* capacity or granting the client more leeway in scheduling payments.[91]

**Advice:** Where the client has failed to pay under a retainer agreement, and counsel is with good reason determined to do no more work on the case, the proper course is to make a definitive break. Simply failing to provide any further service, without notice to the client, is unacceptable. This sloppy response may cause serious harm to the client, and the lawyer could end up being forced to act in the case because the trial date, initially well in the future, is allowed to become imminent.

As a final point, in the United States the ABA Model Rules go especially far in terms of allowing withdrawal based upon financial grounds. A lawyer can withdraw from a case not merely because the client has failed to live up to his or her end of the retainer agreement. According to the Rules, withdrawal is also permitted where continued representation "will result in an unreasonable financial burden on the lawyer."[92] Thus, counsel can conceivably withdraw where the problem stems from an unexpected turn of events that increases the work required, or where the lawyer has simply made a mistake in estimating the proper fees. Canadian rules do not expressly provide so broad a scope for withdrawal owing to financial miscalculation,[93] and we believe that counsel must bear the brunt of a failure to estimate properly the work required to conduct a case. There is nothing wrong with

---

90  See Alta. ch. 14, comm. 1(a).

91  *Ibid.*

92  ABA Model Rule 1.16(b)(5).

93  One might ask whether the residual right of withdrawal found in British Columbia is broad enough to permit withdrawal owing to an unreasonable financial burden. Also, does the ability to withdraw "for good cause," as set out in many Canadian rules, conceivably permit withdrawal to avoid an unreasonable financial burden on the lawyer: see the related discussion at note 95, below.

asking the client to amend the agreement,[94] or better yet with drafting the original retainer agreement so that subsequent events will trigger adjustments to the payment amount and schedule. But the lawyer cannot unilaterally shirk his or her duties to the client by breaching the contract and ignoring the obligations of a fiduciary.[95]

# J. NOTICE TO CLIENT OF WITHDRAWAL

The lawyer has a duty to inform the client of his or her intention to withdraw, and the notice must be "appropriate in the circumstances."[96] This obligation is part and parcel of the broader duty to keep the client informed regarding all matters relevant to the representation.[97] It also flows from the duty of loyalty, which requires counsel to act with the best interests of the client in mind. Withdrawal can have a devastating impact on the client, including a negative impact on the ability to make full answer and defence, so counsel must take all reasonable measures to avoid prejudice to the client. In particular, notice allows the client to act expeditiously in arranging for new counsel.

The CBA Code elaborates upon the concept of appropriate notice, stating: "No hard and fast rules can be laid down as to what will constitute reasonable notice prior to withdrawal. Where the matter is covered by statutory provisions or rules of court, these will govern. In other situations the governing principle is that the lawyer should protect the client's interests so far as possible and should not desert the client at a critical stage of a matter or at a time when withdrawal would

---

94 However, attempting to amend financial arrangements to the lawyer's benefit is risky, as noted in section L, "Updating the Client and Modifying the Agreement," in chapter 10.

95 The Third Restatement §32, which closely follows the ABA Model Rules in setting out the circumstances where a lawyer must or may withdraw, does not include an express provision for withdrawal where the case develops into an unreasonable financial burden for the lawyer. This ground might conceivably fit within the basket clause that permits withdrawal for "other good cause," but the Third Restatement is not enamoured with such a possibility: see Third Restatement §32, comm. "m".

96 See, for example, CBA Code ch. XII,Rule, comm. 4 & 7; Sask. ch. XII, Rule, comm. 4 & 7; Man. ch. XII, Rule, comm. 4 & 7; N.S. ch. 11, Rule, comm. 11.2 & 11.7; Ont. r. 2.09(1); Yukon Part 1, r. 21; and N.B. Part C, r. 6(b). See also *Gillespie*, above note 23 at 342.

97 See, for example, CBA Code ch. II, comm. 7(a).

put the client in a position of disadvantage or peril."[98] Most Canadian governing bodies adopt this same language.[99]

Contrast the different language used in British Columbia, where the rule applicable to notice reads as follows:

> Upon severance or withdrawal, the lawyer shall forthwith:
> (a) notify the client in writing, stating:
>> (i) the fact that the lawyer has severed the solicitor-client relationship or has withdrawn as counsel,
>> (ii) the reasons, if any, for the severance or withdrawal, and
>> (iii) in the case of litigation, that the client should expect that the hearing or trial will proceed on the date scheduled and that the client should retain new counsel promptly.[100]

This provision is distinct from the CBA Code's approach in two major respects. First, the British Columbia rule is much more focused on concrete procedures and rather less concerned with articulating a general defining principle. Second, the notice requirement appears to arise only subsequent to counsel terminating the relationship. Both of these points represent deficiencies in the British Columbia approach. A general guiding principle is important, whether or not accompanied by recommendations as to specific steps that should be taken. Moreover, *prior* notice, so clearly required by most other Canadian rules, is surely mandated by the lawyer's duties of loyalty and communication. In our view, altogether apart from the language of the rules, lawyers in British Columbia are obligated by their fiduciary duties to provide the client with appropriate advance notice of withdrawal.

While the British Columbia provision regarding notice is lacking in some respects, the requirement that the client be informed of withdrawal in writing is commendable. Written notice is advisable, in our view, as a method of reducing the possibility of misunderstanding and protecting both the client and the lawyer if a dispute later arises as to the circumstances surrounding withdrawal.[101] The British Columbia rule is also to be commended in stipulating a particular content for the

---

98   CBA Code ch. II, comm. 7(a).

99   See, for example, Sask. ch. XII, comm. 7; Man. ch. XII, comm. 7; N.S. ch. 11, comm. 11.7 & 11.8; and Ont. r. 2.09(1) (commentary). In Alberta, New Brunswick, and Yukon Territory, the language of the rule is different, but the need for advance reasonable notice is made equally clear: see Alta. ch. 14, r. 1 & 2; N.B. Part C, r. 6; and Yukon Part 1, r. 21.

100   B.C. ch. 10, r. 8.

101   An American case espousing the view that written notice is prudent, though not required, is *Trumbull County Bar Ass'n* v. *Donlin*, 666 N.E.2d 1137 (Ohio 1996).

notice. It is in the client's best interests that notice set out the reasons for withdrawal and also include a clear direction to retain replacement counsel promptly and not to assume that an adjournment will be granted.

Is advance notice required in every case, regardless of the circumstances? Probably not. Most governing bodies specify that notice must be appropriate "in the circumstances" and hence seem to recognize the possibility that notice might not be necessary on the special facts of a particular case.[102] If the client cannot be found, for instance, and counsel's reasonable efforts to make contact are futile, the lawyer surely can dispense with notice.[103] There may also be circumstances where notice places the lawyer or a third party in serious jeopardy. The lawyer who determines that disclosure to the authorities is necessary in order to prevent imminent risk of serious bodily harm, and chooses to withdraw from the case as a result, may reasonably conclude that advance notice to the client will act as a warning that permits the client to cause the harm unimpeded.[104]

# K.  NOTICE TO THE COURT AND CROWN OF TERMINATION

While the client must be provided with notice of withdrawal, where reasonable in the circumstances, the matter of notice is not so obvious with respect to other parties involved in the criminal justice process. Some ethical rules make no mention of any duty to inform the court or the Crown of the fact of discharge or an intention to withdraw.[105] The CBA Code and its progeny merely state that "the lawyer must comply with all applicable rules of court as well as local rules and practice."[106] Civil rules often require that notice be given to the court and an opposing party where a lawyer seeks to get off the record. But not all

---

102  See in particular CBA Code ch. XII, Rule & comm. 7; Sask. ch. XII, Rule & comm. 7; Man. ch. XII, Rule & comm. 7; N.S. ch. 11, Rule & comm. 11.7 & 11.8; Ont. r. 2.09(1) & commentary; and Yukon Part 1, r. 21.

103  This problem is discussed in Alta. ch. 14, comm. G.3.

104  See section G(7), "Duty to Confer with the Client," in chapter 5.

105  See, for example, N.B. Part C, r. 6; and Yukon Part 1, r. 21.

106  See, for example, CBA Code ch. XII, comm. 3; Sask. ch. XII, comm. 3; Man. ch. XII, comm. 3; and N.S. ch. 11, Guiding Principle 3. As well, note 3 to Commentary 2 of the CBA Code mentions that provincial rules of court provide for giving notice of a change of solicitors and for making applications for leave to withdraw.

Canadian provinces possess comparable rules for criminal cases.[107] One could conceivably read the reference to "notice appropriate in the circumstances" as inferentially requiring notice to certain third parties. However, this interpretation is open to debate.

In contrast, the newer rules of professional conduct, evident in Alberta, British Columbia and Ontario, tend to impose upon counsel an express obligation to notify the court or the Crown of counsel's withdrawal.[108] This obligation is well warranted as a means of minimizing systemic disruption (delay and confusion) and as a professional courtesy to the court and Crown counsel. There is often an appreciable benefit to the client as well. Thus, for example, the Crown lawyer who knows about a withdrawal will not mistakenly send disclosure to the former lawyer. Similarly, the judge who learns of withdrawal can ensure that the accused is aware of the need to retain new counsel and, if requested, can consider the appropriateness of an adjournment or any other necessary response.

There may be instances, however, where notice to the court or Crown is not required, and the rules in Alberta, British Columbia and Ontario to varying degrees recognize such a possibility. Where the lawyer's name does not appear on the court records as representing the accused, notice to the court may not be necessary.[109] Also, the defence lawyer who withdraws early in the case, where there is no assigned Crown and new counsel is promptly retained, may reasonably decide not to notify the Crown law office, at least in Alberta.[110] By contrast, the plain wording of the British Columbia and Ontario rules suggests that defence counsel must always inform the Crown law office in writing that withdrawal has occurred.[111]

**Recommendation:** Counsel in Ontario and British Columbia are required to inform the Crown law office in writing where the retainer has ended. Notification seems unnecessary, from a practical perspective, where counsel is discharged or withdraws early in the case, prior to any court appearance or interaction with the Crown. In most other

---

107 See section D, "Discharge by the Client," in this chapter. Note that the Ontario *Rules of Civil Procedure*, r. 15.04, requires notice to the court and Crown.

108 See Alta. ch. 14, comm. G.3; B.C. ch. 10, r. 8; and Ont. r. 2.09(4). See also the Third Restatement §33(2)(b), which requires that the lawyer whose representation ends "give reasonable notice, to those who might otherwise be misled, that the lawyer lacks authority to act for the client."

109 See B.C. ch. 10, r. 8(b); and Ont. r. 2.09(4)(d).

110 See Alta. ch. 14, comm. G.3.

111 See B.C. ch. 10, r. 8(c) ("notify in writing all other parties, including the Crown where appropriate"); and Ont. r. 2.09(4) & (6) & commentary.

cases, however, notice to the Crown is advisable. Such notification is a matter of professional courtesy and tends to help in the general administration of justice. It also acts as a protection for the withdrawing lawyer in the event that the former client or another party later alleges that counsel remains on the case.

**Caution:** Notice to the court and/or Crown must never reveal legal-professional confidences, absent the client's consent or the application of a recognized exception to the duty of confidentiality.[112]

# L.  LEAVE OF THE COURT TO WITHDRAW

One of the most debated issues in Canada concerning withdrawal in criminal matters is whether counsel must obtain leave of the court before terminating the client-lawyer relationship, independent entirely of any applicable ethical obligations that may restrict the lawyer's actions. There are valid reasons why, once counsel has committed to the retainer on the record, the court should enjoy a degree of supervisory power over withdrawal. First, the withdrawal of counsel can lead to significant administrative problems. The trial may need to be postponed, other matters rescheduled, witnesses called off, preparations forestalled, and so on. Society has an interest in expeditious justice and in maintaining an efficient criminal justice process.[113] Providing the court with some supervisory power over counsel's decision to withdraw can help to ensure that these interests are protected. Second, withdrawal frequently puts the lawyer's interests in sharp juxtaposition to the client's. Within reason, the client has a right to legal representation by counsel of choice.[114] It makes sense for the court to make inquiries to ensure that the client is being treated fairly by counsel and does not face undue prejudice if withdrawal is effected.

In Ontario, the rules of professional conduct impose an ethical obligation upon counsel to seek leave where "there is not a sufficient interval between a notice to the client of the lawyer's intention to withdraw and the date when the case is to be tried to enable the client to obtain another lawyer and to enable such lawyer to prepare adequately for trial."[115] The Ontario rules also state that counsel facing such cir-

---

112  See section M, "Confidentiality," in this chapter.
113  See, for example, *C. (D.D.)*, above note 8.
114  See, for example, *McCallen*, above note 9 at 532.
115  Ont. r. 2.09(6).

cumstances should seek an adjournment on behalf of the client, unless instructed otherwise.[116] While no other Canadian ethical rules specify that leave to withdraw is required, other governing bodies usually require that counsel comply with the local law on this point.[117] We agree that leave should be sought as provided for in the Ontario rules.

Arguably, however, lawyers in British Columbia do not require leave of the court to withdraw. Certainly, the rules of professional conduct in that province do not impose this precondition.[118] More important, the leading case on point in that province, *Leask* v. *Cronin*,[119] appears to hold that counsel has almost free reign in withdrawing. There, the trial was under way when defence counsel informed the court that he was withdrawing, the reason given being that the accused had failed to provide instructions. The problem appears to have been that the client missed a number of appointments, with the effect that counsel's preparations were hampered, and failed to provide information necessary to decide what witnesses to call for the defence.[120] After ascertaining that the client was content to have counsel continue in the matter, the trial judge declined to permit withdrawal. Defence counsel then refused to participate in the cross-examination of the next Crown witness, and was cited in contempt. Counsel brought an application for prohibition. The British Columbia Supreme Court allowed the application, opining that lawyers often seek leave to withdraw as a courtesy

---

116 See Ont. r. 2.09(6).

117 See, for example, CBA Code ch. XII, comm. 3; Sask. ch. XII, comm. 3; Man. ch. XII, comm. 3; and N.S. ch. 11, Guiding Principle 3. In the United States, ABA Model Rule 1.16(c) (and comm. 3) and Third Restatement §32(5) note that counsel is not permitted to withdraw absent leave of the court. The Privy Council has also held that leave of the court is required to withdraw in a criminal case: see *Dunkley*, above note 23 at 286 ("the trial judge should only permit withdrawal if he is satisfied that the defendant will not suffer significant prejudice thereby").

118 B.C. ch. 10, r. 8, note 1 cites *Leask* v. *Cronin* (1985), 18 C.C.C. (3d) 315 (B.C.S.C.) [*Leask*], as setting out the law court in this regard. *Leask* v. *Cronin* is discussed in the text below.

119 Above note 118.

120 *Ibid.* at 320. This interpretation of the case is adopted by commentators yet may be overly generous to defence counsel. Given the interjections by the accused and the court's expressed willingness to grant an adjournment to facilitate counsel's preparation, one cannot help but suspect that the main impetus for withdrawal was the client's failure to pay legal fees.

to the court while in reality a judge has no discretion in the matter and must accept counsel's decision.[121]

*Leask* v. *Cronin* must be compared to *R.* v. *C.(D.D.)*, a decision of the Alberta Court of Appeal already alluded to on the subject of withdrawal for failure to pay fees. The accused retained counsel, who appeared on the matter and set dates for a two-week trial. Roughly one month before the trial was scheduled to begin, counsel determined that the client was unable to pay the agreed-upon legal costs. An attempt to obtain legal aid failed. Three weeks prior to the trial date, counsel brought an adjournment application, but the matter was not heard until a mere two weeks before the trial was to start. By this time, an adjournment was almost certain to result in an inability to use the lost court time for other matters.[122] The judge hearing the application not only refused the request for the adjournment but also declared that leave to withdraw, required if counsel wished to get off the case, was denied.

On appeal, counsel for the accused argued that, while there may be ethical obligations that restrict withdrawal, which can be regulated and enforced by the governing body, a court has no power whatsoever to interfere with a lawyer's decision to withdraw. The Alberta Court of Appeal wholeheartedly rejected this argument. The court stressed that a lawyer owes duties not just to the client but also to the court, and that the court has the power to ensure that such duties are respected.[123] These duties to the court were seen to include continuing to act for the client absent judicial permission to withdraw or the client's consent.[124] Withdrawal would be permitted by the court only for good cause, and good cause was not seen to include non-payment of agreed-upon legal fees.

The Alberta Court of Appeal concluded, however, by noting that the power to grant or deny leave to withdraw must not be exercised unreasonably by the court. Rather, the judge hearing the application must consider whether the time scheduled for trial can be usefully employed for other cases. The judge should also consider other potential prejudices to the administration of justice, including harm done to

---

121  *Ibid.* at 324–25. To similar effect, see *Luchka* v. *Zens* (1989), 37 B.C.L.R. (2d) 127 (C.A.), and the comments of O'Sullivan J.A. in *Dorion*, above note 27 at 554–55.

122  See *Leask*, above note 118 at 330.

123  *Ibid.* at 326.

124  *Ibid.* at 327. There is authority to the same effect in Manitoba (see *Gillespie*, above note 23) and Quebec (see *Steele*, above note 72 at 160).

the Crown case by virtue of the delay, inconvenience to witnesses, and the public cost of lost court time. Moreover, "the judge should in any event permit counsel to withdraw if the counsel assures the judge that some event has occurred that would make it impossible for the counsel in good conscience to proceed."[125]

This last point, concerning the proper exercise of the court's power to grant or refuse leave to withdraw, is worth accentuating. Placing restrictions on the court's ability to refuse leave demonstrates that the gulf between the reasoning in *C.(D.D.)* and *Leask v. Cronin* is not as gaping as one might suppose at first glance. The Court in *C.(D.D.)* went so far as to emphasize that on some occasions the judge has a *duty* to grant counsel's request for withdrawal.[126] The example given is the case where the client-lawyer relationship has substantially broken down. By the same token, a crucial point made in *Leask v. Cronin* is that an unjustified withdrawal may legitimately attract contempt proceedings in some instances. The British Columbia Supreme Court gave the example of a lawyer withdrawing in an attempt to delay the trial proceeding or otherwise hinder the trial process. This affirmation of the contempt power surely equates with a modest power in the court to require leave to withdraw. After all, how would the refusal to grant leave as envisioned in *C.(D.D.)* be enforced, other than by contempt proceedings?[127]

To sum up, *Leask v. Cronin* and *C.(D.D.)* adopt distinct approaches to the question of the court's supervisory power over defence counsel's withdrawal from a criminal case. The former decision does not require that counsel seek leave in the ordinary course. The latter case always requires that counsel do so. But lawyers in British Columbia will typically seek leave as a matter of courtesy, and they may feel obligated to do so where there is some concern that withdrawal may be viewed as improper by the court. By the same token, lawyers in Alberta may be able to rely upon an automatic right to withdraw where the request for leave relates to an irrevocable and substantial breakdown in the client-lawyer relationship. The difference between the two approaches may thus be fairly modest in practice.

It is worth emphasizing that, even in provinces where leave to withdraw is undoubtedly required, counsel is not ethically obliged to seek leave in every case. We have seen, for instance, that in Ontario the

---

125 *Leask*, above note 118 at 330.
126 *C.(D.D.)*, above note 8 at 328 & 330.
127 The court in *C.(D.D.)* actually refers to the contempt power in this respect: *ibid.* at 326.

rules of professional conduct mandate leave of the court only where there is not sufficient time to allow the client to retain and instruct new counsel.[128] By contrast, rules of the court and case law in some provinces tend to impose a more demanding leave requirement, essentially mandating a leave application whenever counsel has gone on the record in an unqualified manner.[129] It may thus be necessary to bring a formal application to withdraw if counsel has acted for the client in an unqualified manner on a court appearance and new counsel has not officially gone on the record.

**Advice:** A lawyer may not be prepared to commit to appearing as counsel at trial, and may wish to avoid later having to bring an application to withdraw (or to minimize the danger of leave to withdraw being denied). In such circumstances, the prudent step is to expressly articulate to the court the limited nature of the retainer at the time of counsel's first appearance, and to continue to do so on each subsequent appearance unless and until the status of the retainer changes.[130]

No matter what province one is dealing with, if the court refuses to allow a lawyer to terminate the relationship, counsel should think long and hard before taking the drastic step of actually withdrawing. A contempt citation is possible even in jurisdictions that follow the reasoning in *Leask* v. *Cronin*, and in Ontario the rules of professional conduct make withdrawal in the face of an order to the contrary an ethical impropriety. If counsel decides to stay on the case in compliance with the court's order, he or she must not eschew the duty to defend the client competently, resolutely, and loyally. Doing so may call for extraordinary patience and understanding by counsel, but the client should not be made to suffer simply because counsel is unhappy with the court's decision.[131] On the other hand, counsel who is forced to continue with a case does not thereby acquire a license to conduct the defence in a manner that violates the rules of professional conduct.

---

128 See Ont. r. 2.09(5). Otherwise, counsel who has gone on the record need only provide the court with written notice: see Ont. r. 2.09(4).

129 See, for example, Ontario *Criminal Proceedings Rules*, r. 25.01; *C.(D.D.)*, above note 8 at 324, 327, & 329.

130 *C.(D.D.)*, above note 8 at 329–30.

131 ABA Model Rule 1.16(c) expressly states that a lawyer must continue with a representation where ordered to do so by the court, despite having good and valid reason to withdraw. See also ABA Model Code DR 2-110(A)(1); and Third Restatement §31(1) & §32(5). The Third Restatement suggests that counsel who is erroneously denied leave to withdraw can do no more than seek to overturn the impugned decision on appeal: see Third Restatement §31, comm. "c", & §32, comm. "d."

**Advice:** Counsel should anticipate and react to ethical problems that raise the spectre of withdrawal well in advance of the trial, if reasonably possible. Careful and prompt reaction to such problems lessens the chance that leave of the court to withdraw will be required, or where required will be denied.

# M. CONFIDENTIALITY

There are duties owed by a lawyer to the client that survive the end of the client-lawyer relationship, and most certainly persist during the withdrawal process, such as the duty not to put a former client's interest in an impermissible conflict or the duty to preserve client property that remains in the lawyer's possession. Prime among such duties is the lawyer's obligation concerning confidentiality. Maintaining confidences despite the retainer's termination encourages the client to be candid with counsel during the life of the relationship, secure in the knowledge that the confidences will never be revealed. Both ethical rules and case law indicate that counsel must keep a client's confidences not only during the course of the retainer but also after counsel's employment has terminated.[132]

**Example:** Counsel acts on a guilty plea, following which the matter is put over for sentencing. Prior to the sentencing, the client accuses the lawyer of misrepresenting the possible repercussions of the plea. The relationship suffers a breakdown, and counsel seeks the leave of the court to withdraw. In the application materials, counsel states that the client had admitted guilt and had also admitted that he would have been convicted of a more serious crime had the matter gone to trial. These revelations are irrelevant to the withdrawal application, represent nothing more than an attempt to harm the client, and thus constitute an improper breach of the duty of confidentiality.[133]

It is thus axiomatic that counsel must not reveal confidential information out of spite or revenge where the relationship has dissolved into acrimony. However, on occasion, counsel's duty to maintain confi-

---

132 See section H(7), "Duty Survives End of Retainer," in chapter 4. In the particular context of withdrawal, see also Alta. ch. 14, comm. 3; and B.C. ch. 10, r. 9, as well as *Leask*, above note 118 at 325–26; *C.(D.D.)*, above note 8 at 330; and *Dorion*, above note 27 at 554–55 (per O'Sullivan J.A.).

133 This example is loosely based on the facts in *Lawyer Disciplinary Bd.* v. *Farber*, 488 S.E.2d 460 (W. Va. 1997).

dences while in the course of withdrawing presents a real challenge and is not so quickly amenable to a straightforward solution.

## 1) Providing Reasons for Withdrawal

Keeping the client's confidences can be especially difficult where counsel is seeking leave of the court to withdraw from a case. The challenge is to remain loyal to the client, respecting the secrets with which counsel has been entrusted, but at the same time to convince the court that withdrawal is warranted. In particular, some grounds for withdrawal are not valid or could be the subject of disagreement among reasonable people. Other grounds clearly warrant or mandate termination of the retainer. How is counsel to satisfy the court that the basis of the request is legitimate, without revealing confidential information?

The British Columbia rules grant counsel no leeway with the inquisitive court, expressly addressing the matter of reasons for withdrawal as follows: "If the reason for severance or withdrawal results from confidential communications between the lawyer and the client the lawyer shall not, unless the client consents, disclose the reason for severance or withdrawal."[134] Thus, absent the client's consent, counsel in British Columbia shall not disclose the reason for withdrawal. In Ontario, the special rules dealing with withdrawal in criminal cases state that the lawyer who has withdrawn because of "conflict with the client" should not make any reference to the cause of the conflict, nor to any matter that would violate lawyer and client privilege. Any notice of withdrawal "should merely state that the lawyer is no longer acting and has withdrawn."[135] In Alberta, the practice is said to be that withdrawing counsel merely informs the court that "unhappy differences" have arisen.[136] Some judges may be unimpressed with absolute silence, or these intentionally vague phrases, and wonder whether counsel's request is entirely legitimate and well considered. Nevertheless, the duty of confidentiality requires secrecy, regardless of strong pressure from the court.[137]

---

134 B.C. ch. 10, r. 9.

135 Ont. r. 2.09(4) (commentary). Presumably, the same prohibition applies to a notice of application for leave to withdraw.

136 See C.(D.D.), above note 8 at 330.

137 See *R. v. Woo*, [1991] B.C.J. No. 3087 (C.A.) (QL) ("it is appropriate for counsel merely to announce that he does not propose to carry on"). Consider the interesting approach taken by defence counsel in *R. v. Pornbacher*, [1994] B.C.J. No. 63 (S.C.) (QL), who informed the court that the Law Society had directed that counsel withdraw.

**Example:** A lawyer applies to withdraw during the trial. The court asks for an explanation and is obviously not satisfied with counsel's rote comment that confidentiality mandates silence. The judge accordingly turns her attention to the accused and strongly pressures him to waive the confidence. At this point, the client and counsel are in a difficult bind. The client essentially lacks representation, even though leave to withdraw has not yet been granted, and is probably unfamiliar with the law. Counsel seeking to withdraw does not necessarily have the same interests as the client, and may in fact prefer that confidentiality be waived to provide a stronger basis for the application for leave to withdraw. For these reasons, counsel should attempt to intervene where the court persists in questioning the client, and, if appropriate, suggest that the client receive independent legal advice.[138]

**Cross-reference:** One of the most difficult challenges to counsel's duty to maintain confidentiality occurs where the client persists in a plan to act illegally in conducting the defence. The applicable considerations are discussed in detail in chapter 1, section H, and chapter 7, sections F(4)(a) & G(3)(a).

As a final point, defence lawyers should not jump to the conclusion that the reasons for withdrawal are confidential in every case. In some instances, the reasons do not involve confidential information (for example, a Crown witness was formerly represented by counsel in a related matter, or the client physically attacks counsel and makes allegations of incompetence in open court). It may also be that the confidences will not, if disclosed, cause any material harm to the client, and the client is happy to consent to their revelation. Very occasionally, disclosure against the client's wishes will be permitted, for instance, where counsel is withdrawing because the client refuses to correct a perjurious statement.[139]

## 2) Withdrawal As Implied Disclosure of Confidential Information

Sometimes counsel is able to withdraw without arousing any suspicion as to the reason for terminating the retainer. Take the example where the lawyer discovers early on in the matter that the client has fraudu-

---

138 See *Leask*, above note 118 at 326, where the court observed that the client's waiver of confidentiality occurred owing to improper questioning by the trial judge.
139 See section G(3)(b), "Disclosure," in chapter 7.

lently obtained legal aid and refuses to remedy the situation. The lawyer can probably terminate the relationship without even impliedly revealing confidential information.[140] However, the mere act of withdrawal can sometimes amount to the implied disclosure of confidences, no matter how little counsel says in applying for leave to terminate the retainer. Such is often the case where the client-lawyer relationship abruptly ruptures in the middle of a trial, and the context of the request to withdraw suggests that the client has acted improperly or plans to do so.[141] Sometimes there is no way to avoid this implicit disclosure of confidential information. Nonetheless, the resulting potential for harm to the client is a legitimate factor to take into account where counsel has a discretion in deciding whether or not to seek leave to withdraw.[142]

A different approach is for counsel intentionally to utilize a "noisy" withdrawal in order to disavow any connection to fraudulent acts unknowingly committed on behalf of the client during the course of legal representation. In the United States, the ABA has condoned lawyers withdrawing in a manner that alerts an opponent to the possibility that the client has used counsel's services to commit an ongoing or future fraud.[143] An obvious example of a noisy withdrawal would be counsel notifying a third party that a letter or document previously prepared by counsel should not be relied upon. As we have noted, the line between full disclosure of confidences to avert a future crime and the implied warning of a noisy withdrawal is not always transparent and may boil down to a matter of degree of disclosure.[144] The Ontario rules of professional responsibility expressly identify withdrawal as an appropriate response where the client insists on pursuing an illegal

---

140 In England and Wales, a barrister must withdraw where "legal aid has been wrongly obtained by false or inaccurate information and action to remedy the situation is not immediately taken by his client": see *Bar Code of Conduct*, above note 19 at para. 504(c). This dictate is surely applicable in Canada, for continuing to work on the case and to collect from the legal aid plan would constitute participation in the fraud. All Canadian rules demand that a lawyer withdraw rather than take part in an illegality.

141 See section F(4)(a), "Withdrawal," in chapter 7, as well as section J(4), "The Possible Inapplicability of Any Exception," in chapter 5.

142 For the various factors affecting the exercise of the lawyer's discretion, see section G, "Discretionary Withdrawal by the Lawyer," in this chapter.

143 See ABA Comm. on Ethics and Professional Responsibility, Formal Op. 366 (1992); and Formal Op. 375 (1993).

144 See section J(4), "The Possible Inapplicability of Any Exception," in chapter 5.

end.[145] While the subtleties of implicitly leaking confidences by virtue of withdrawal are not addressed, the tenor of the Ontario rules appears to forbid a so-called noisy withdrawal, at least where a more "quiet" approach is possible.[146]

## 3) Successor Lawyers

A separate matter concerns confidentiality *vis-à-vis* the successor lawyer. It has been suggested that counsel cannot provide the new lawyer with confidential information except as instructed to do so by the former client.[147] On the other hand, it often makes sense for the lawyer to assume that the client consents to passing on such information regarding matters pertinent to the case. What do the applicable ethical rules say? A number of Canadian governing bodies have followed the lead of the CBA Code and adopted a rule stating that "confidential information not clearly related to the matter should not be divulged without the express consent of the client."[148] Although this rule is silent on the point, it would therefore appear that, where expressly instructed, former counsel cannot reveal relevant confidential information or portions of the file to the successor lawyer. In special circumstances, however, the client's wishes may be ignored, for instance, where a future-harm exception applies or former counsel has overriding duties concerning completed client perjury.[149]

**Comparison:** Governing bodies influenced by the CBA Code permit the disclosure of confidential information to a successor lawyer in the ordinary course, at least where relevant to the case and absent instructions to the contrary.[150] However, in Nova Scotia the default position is not to reveal confidential information to the successor lawyer absent *express* instructions.[151] Alberta's rule lies somewhere between these positions, forbidding disclosure of confidential information to the suc-

---

145 Ont. r. 2.03(3) (commentary) (withdrawal suggested as an acceptable response if other remedial measures fail).

146 *Ibid.* The commentary states that, as a general rule, "the lawyer shall hold the client's information in strict confidence."

147 Support for this view is found in M. Orkin, *Legal Ethics: A Study of Professional Conduct* (Toronto: Cartwright, 1957) at 94 [*Legal Ethics*].

148 CBA Code ch. XII, comm. 9. To the same effect, see Sask. ch. XII, comm. 9; and Man. ch. XII, comm. 9.

149 See sections G, "Future Harm or Public Safety," and K, "Duty Not to Mislead the Court," in chapter 5; and section F(4)(a), "Withdrawal," in chapter 7.

150 See the rules cited at note 148, above.

151 See N.S. ch. 11, comm. 11.11.

cessor counsel "unless *expressly or impliedly* authorized by the client."[152] In Ontario, the rules regarding withdrawal make no mention of confidentiality *vis-à-vis* the successor lawyer.[153] British Columbia refers to confidentiality but only pertaining to a reason for termination that "results from confidential information." The rule in British Columbia appears to prohibit disclosure of such reason to anyone, including a successor lawyer, unless the client consents.[154]

An especially dicey problem concerning confidentiality and successor lawyers occurs in instances where counsel withdraws because of conflict of interest.[155] Conflict of interest frequently, though not always, arises owing to confidential information in the possession of counsel that cannot be shared with or used for a client. A classic example is where the lawyer for an accused formerly represented a Crown witness with respect to the same subject matter. Counsel is not permitted to divulge confidential information received during the relationship with the former client to the current client. What is more, the conflict will often require that counsel withdraw from the current client's case. Under these circumstances, the duty of confidentiality owed to the former client who is now a witness continues, and prevents the withdrawn lawyer from making disclosure to the successor counsel. More complicated concerns arise where confidential information is received from one client during the course of multiple representation. The possibility that counsel's duty of confidentiality works to prevent disclosure to the other client(s) is discussed elsewhere.[156] Suffice it to say that, if counsel comes to this conclusion, consistency demands that the information also be withheld from the successor lawyer(s) for the other client(s).

---

152  Alta. ch. 14, comm. 3 (emphasis added). See also Alta. ch. 7, comm. 5, which states that "a lawyer should not convey confidential information to a successor lawyer on a change of solicitors unless satisfied that the client has authorized such disclosure."

153  The Ontario rule mentions privilege, but apparently only in regard to third parties who do not owe the client a professional duty of confidence: see Ont. r. 2.09(4) (commentary).

154  See B.C. ch. 10, r. 9. The disclosure of other confidential information to the successor lawyer is not addressed by the British Columbia rule.

155  This issue may lie behind the rather obscure commentary on multiple representation found in the CBA Code's rule on withdrawal (c. XII, comm. 10), adopted by a number of provincial governing bodies. See also the discussion accompanying notes 164–65, below.

156  See section O, "Other Clients," in chapter 4.

# N. OTHER DUTIES UPON TERMINATION

While confidentiality and notice are especially important duties connected with termination of the client-lawyer relationship, there are other obligations that fall upon the lawyer who has been discharged or withdrawn. Many rules of professional conduct impose upon withdrawing or former counsel a general duty "to minimize expense and avoid prejudice to the client, doing everything reasonably possible to facilitate the expeditious and orderly transfer of the matter to the successor lawyer."[157] More specifically, the lawyer should:

1. deliver to the client or new counsel, in an orderly and expeditious manner, all papers and property to which the client is entitled;[158]
2. give the client all information that may be required about the case;[159]
3. account for all funds of the client on hand or previously dealt with, and refund any amounts not earned during employment;[160]
4. promptly render a final account;[161]

---

157   CBA Code ch. XII, comm. 3. To similar effect, see Sask. ch. XII, comm. 3; Man. ch. XII, comm. 3; N.S. ch. 11, Guiding Principle 2; Ont. r. 2.09(8); Alta. ch. 14, r. 3; and B.C. ch. 10, r. 8 (more a recitation of specific duties than a general statement of principle). Similar are the main American codes, such as ABA Model Rule 1.16(d); ABA Model Code DR 2-110(A)(2); and Third Restatement §33 (all of which state that counsel must take steps "to the extent reasonably practicable to protect the client's interests").

158   See CBA Code ch. XII, comm. 8(a); Sask. ch. XII, comm. 8(a); Man. ch. XII, comm. 8(a); N.S. ch. 11, comm. 11.9(a); Ont. r. 2.09(9)(a); Alta. ch. 14, comm. 4; and B.C. ch. 10, r. 8(e) ("take all reasonable steps to assist in the transfer of the client's file"). This duty is subject to the lawyer's right to a lien, which we believe should generally not be exercised unless the client's matter is over: see section R, "Reporting Requirements, Confidentiality, and Privilege," in chapter 10. Also, where there is a dispute regarding entitlement to papers or other property, the lawyer "should make every effort to have the claimants settle the dispute" (CBA Code ch. XII, comm. 8.

159   See CBA Code ch. XII, comm. 8(b); Sask. ch. XII, comm. 8(b); Man. ch. XII, comm. 8(b); N.S. ch. 11, comm. 11.9(b); and Ont. r. 2.09(9(b). Compare Alta. ch. 14, comm. 4: "It may also be appropriate to provide a final report as to the status of the client's matter."

160   See CBA Code ch. XII, comm. 8(c); Sask. ch. XII, comm. 8(c); Man. ch. XII, comm. 8(c); N.S. ch. 11, comm. 11.9(c); Ont. r. 2.09(9(c); Alta. ch. 14, r. 4; and B.C. ch. 10, r. 8(d).

161   See CBA Code ch. XII, comm. 8(d); Sask. ch. XII, comm. 8(d); Man. ch. XII, comm. 8(d); N.S. ch. 11, comm. 11.9(d); Ont. r. 2.09(9(d); Alta. ch. 14, r. 4; and B.C. ch. 10, r. 8(d). Given that switching counsel usually results in unavoidable duplication of effort by the new lawyer, note 9 to the CBA Code's

5.  cooperate with the successor lawyer for the purpose of facilitating the expeditious and orderly transfer of the matter, minimizing expense and prejudice to the client.[162]

As part of the general duty to cooperate with the successor lawyer, some governing bodies specifically state that the withdrawing lawyer will normally provide any memoranda of fact and law that have been prepared in connection with the matter.[163] These same governing bodies often add that, where the lawyer formerly acted for two or more clients, and ceases to act for any of the clients, cooperation with the successor lawyer(s) is required "to the extent permitted" by the rules and withdrawing counsel "should seek to avoid unseemly rivalry, whether real or apparent."[164] These pieces of advice are at best unnecessary and may even be confusing. The reference to memoranda of fact and law adds little to the general duty to cooperate, and it is better dealt with as part of the obligation to deliver up all documents to which the former client is entitled. Moreover, the commentary dealing with such memoranda seems directed primarily at the issue of confidentiality, a subject that could do with a more direct discussion under the rubric of withdrawal.[165] As for the reference to withdrawing counsel who initially acted for two or more clients, a similar point can be made, but in stronger terms. The commentary devoted to this matter is poorly drafted and somewhat unclear. To the extent that special mention of multiple representation cases is necessary, the central concern should be confidentiality, and this concern should be made express.[166]

Though not explicitly required by Canadian rules, we believe that counsel has an obligation to pass on to the client (or successor lawyer)

---

commentary 8 suggests that former counsel "be generous" in accounting for any monies received but not yet earned, on this point quoting from Panel Discussion, above note 72 at 296.

162  See CBA Code ch. XII, comm. 8(e); Sask. ch. XII, comm. 8(e); Man. ch. XII, comm. 8(e); N.S. ch. 11, comm. 11.9(e); Ont. r. 2.09(9(e)); Alta. ch. 14, r. 3; and B.C. ch. 10, r. 8(e).

163  See CBA Code ch. XII, comm. 9; Sask. ch. XII, comm. 9; Man. ch. XII, comm. 9; and N.S. ch. 11, comm. 11.11. This matter is not discussed in the Alberta, British Columbia, or Ontario rules.

164  See CBA Code ch. XII, comm. 10; Sask. ch. XII, comm. 10; Man. ch. XII, comm. 10; N.S. ch. 11, comm. 11.12; and Ont. r. 2.09(9) (commentary). This matter is not discussed in the Alberta or British Columbia rules.

165  In fairness, most Canadian rules stress that confidentiality survives termination of the client-lawyer relationship in the rule that deals with client confidences: see, for example, the rules cited at note 132, above.

166  Confidentiality concerns relating to multiple-representation and successor counsel are discussed in section M, "Successor Lawyers," in this chapter.

all material communications received following termination, where related to the case and reasonable to do so. Otherwise, the discharge or withdrawal may operate to the client's prejudice. For instance, disclosure materials mistakenly sent to counsel after withdrawal has been accomplished, or a resolution offer received from the Crown, must be passed on to the former client. The Third Restatement is one of the few codes of professional responsibility that specifically imposes this requirement.[167] Yet the general obligation to mitigate prejudice, imposed by most Canadian rules, surely embraces a duty to pass on material communications related to the matter in question.[168]

Where termination occurs because of conflict of interest or concerns regarding competence, and the client appears to require help in finding new representation, counsel has a duty to provide reasonable assistance.[169] Where termination occurs for other reasons, especially where counsel has been discharged without valid cause or withdrawn owing to a serious deception by the client, we do not believe that such a duty applies.[170] Nevertheless, and in spite of inappropriate or treacherous behaviour by the client, counsel must avoid acting out of revenge and should at least provide the client with the names of competent replacement counsel if requested. After all, the faster that new counsel is retained, the sooner withdrawing counsel can end the association with the problematic client.

# O. DUTIES OF A POTENTIAL SUCCESSOR LAWYER AND A SUCCESSOR LAWYER

The lawyer who takes over a case from a colleague whose retainer has terminated, or who is asked to consider doing so by a prospective client, should be guided by a number of considerations and duties. A distinction in this regard can be made between the lawyer who is approached while another lawyer is or may be currently acting (the potential-successor-lawyer situation), and the lawyer who is formally

---

167  See Third Restatement §33(2)(c).

168  The rules referred to at note 159, above, may also dictate this result.

169  See Alta. ch. 14, comm. 3. See also the related discussion in section J, "Duties Arising Once a Retainer is Refunded," in chapter 2.

170  See Alta. ch. 14, comm. 3.

retained following the termination of a retainer with a previous lawyer (the successor-lawyer situation).

# 1) Potential Successor Lawyer

Let us begin with a fairly common scenario. A lawyer is approached by an individual who is, or may be, currently represented by another counsel. This individual is not happy with the existing representation, and wishes to switch to new counsel. Under these circumstances, the rules of professional conduct require that the potential successor counsel satisfy himself or herself that the current lawyer approves of the change or has already withdrawn or been discharged.[171] We do not disagree but prefer the following, more sophisticated, approach:

1. Counsel must first attempt to determine the exact status of the client's legal representation. Some clients may be mistaken, confused, or unclear regarding this point, yet the matter can be clarified with a few simple questions. If uncertainty in this regard cannot be resolved, the interview should go no further absent communication with the other counsel (see point 3, below).
2. If there is any question as to whether the individual is currently represented by another lawyer, counsel should not discuss the case in any detail whatsoever. For one thing, it would be improper to interfere with an existing client-lawyer relationship, and a discussion of the merits of the case may have this effect.[172] But also, delv-

---

171 See CBA Code ch. XII, comm. 12; Sask. ch. XII, comm. 12; Man. ch. XII, comm. 12; N.S. ch. 11, comm. 11.14; Ont. r. 2.09(10); Alta. ch. 14, r. 5; and B.C. ch. 10, note 2.

172 Canadian rules of professional conduct generally prohibit communications with an individual who is represented by counsel regarding the subject matter, though some are clearer than others in this regard and important exceptions exist in some jurisdictions: see, for example, CBA Code ch. IX, comm. 6 & ch. XVI, comm. 8; Sask. ch. IX, comm. 6 & ch. XVI, comm. 8; Man. ch. IX, comm. 6 & ch. XVI, comm. 8; N.S. ch. 13, comm. 13.10 but *not* ch. 14, comm. 14.10 (regarding witnesses); Ont. r. 4.03(2) & 6.03(7); Alta ch. 4, r. 6 & 7, & Interpretation r. 4(o); B.C. ch. 4, r. 1.1 but *not* ch. 8, r. 12.1 (regarding witnesses); N.B. Part D, r. 3; and Yukon Part 2, r. 4. Providing a second opinion is condoned by most rules: see, for example, CBA Code ch. III, comm. 5; Alta. ch. 4, r. 7 & ch. 9, r. 17; B.C. ch. 4, r. 1.1 & ch. 8, r. 12; but see Ont. r. 6.03(7).

ing into the merits may lead to subsequent allegations that privilege has been waived. The better course is to avoid future litigation on the privilege point, and attendant harm to the client, by spurning all substantive discussion of the case.

3.  Counsel should promptly inform the other lawyer that he or she has been approached. This action is often necessary to confirm the exact status of the individual's legal representation. Where the other lawyer has not been discharged or withdrawn, there may be an opportunity to repair the frayed relationship. There are often advantages to the client in not having to change counsel, and it may be that a simple and remediable misunderstanding has led to the problem. Conversely, if the other lawyer is no longer handling the case, information may be obtained that substantially affects counsel's decision whether to accept the matter.[173]

4.  Only if counsel is thoroughly satisfied that the other lawyer has already been discharged, or withdrawn, is it proper to discuss the matter with the prospective client and seriously consider taking on the case.

5.  Where the prospective client has discharged the other lawyer, or is considering doing so, there is no *duty* to advise him or her to attempt to re-establish or maintain the professional relationship. Indeed, it may be improper to pressure the individual unduly in this regard, given the freedom of choice that all accused must have in deciding who to retain as counsel.[174]

6.  The fact that the prospective client has failed to pay an outstanding account from former counsel may justify refusing to take on the case, provided that the individual is not unduly prejudiced as a result.[175]

These guidelines strive to avoid rash meddling in a pre-existing professional relationship, and reflect the importance of basic courtesy

---

173 Counsel must not, however, encourage the other lawyer to breach a current or former client's confidences: see section M(3), "Successor Lawyers," in this chapter.

174 See *McCallen*, above note 9 at 530–32.

175 See section O(2), "Successor Lawyer," in this chapter. The Alberta rules are clearest in stating that an outstanding account to former counsel may be a valid reason to refuse to act for the individual (Alta. ch. 14, comm. 5.

among lawyers, but also recognize that a client must be permitted to discharge a lawyer and hire new counsel if that is his or her wish.[176]

## 2) Successor Lawyer

Once the successor lawyer is properly retained, he or she should represent the client in the normal course like any other. A special issue that frequently arises, however, concerns an outstanding account from the former lawyer. In this regard, Canadian rules of professional conduct are concerned primarily with protecting the former lawyer's interest in receiving payment for outstanding accounts. The rules state that successor counsel may properly urge the client to satisfy any outstanding account with the former lawyer, especially if the latter withdrew for good cause or was capriciously discharged.[177] However, where the trial is imminent or in progress, the successor lawyer should not allow an outstanding debt to former counsel to interfere with the current representation.[178]

A lawyer should exercise caution in taking on a case for a client who has discharged former counsel, or whose counsel has withdrawn, owing to allegations of client impropriety or for any reason that is not immediately apparent. The circumstances that led to the termination of the previous client-lawyer relationship may identify the client as difficult and foretell a similar end to any subsequent relationship. The successor lawyer should consider adopting protective measures where necessary and possible, including a written agreement and advance payment in full. By the same token, counsel should take special care to monitor the relationship and communicate fully with the client on an ongoing basis, the better to avoid repetition of a previous breakdown.

---

176  See Orkin, above note 147 at 93–94. Orkin's work remains one of the best regarding the ethical duties of the prospective successor lawyer.

177  See CBA Code ch. XII, comm. 12; Sask. ch. XII, comm. 12; Man. ch. XII, comm. 12; N.S. ch. 11, comm. 11.14; Ont. r. 2.09(10) (commentary); Alta. ch. 14, comm. 5; and B.C. ch. 10, note 2. In *Legal Ethics*, above note 147 at 94, Orkin takes a more extreme view, opining that counsel should refuse to take on the new case unless the client fully pays any outstanding account with former counsel.

178  CBA Code ch. XII, comm. 12; Sask. ch. XII, comm. 12; Man. ch. XII, comm. 12; N.S. ch. 11, comm. 11.15; Ont. r. 2.09(10) (commentary); Alta. ch. 14, comm. 5; and B.C. ch. 10, note 2. See also J. Morden, "A Succeeding Solicitor's Duty to Protect the Account of the Former Solicitor" (1971) 5 L. Soc. Gaz. 257 at 259.

## P.  RIGHT TO EFFECTIVE ASSISTANCE OF COUNSEL CLAIMS ON APPEAL

Regardless of whether trial counsel withdraws or is discharged or the case ends in the normal course and thereby terminates the professional relationship, the client may decide to argue that counsel conducted the defence so as to violate the right to the effective assistance of counsel. The lawyer facing an ineffective-counsel claim may quite properly decide to fight the allegations. Nevertheless, the reasonable desire to emerge unscathed from a stressful appeal process should not degenerate into petty intransigence and vengeful retaliation. In particular, trial counsel is not permitted to withhold the file from the former client, not even if fees or disbursements remain unpaid.[179] The best response is to deliver up the entire file to appeal counsel upon a proper request being made.[180] Trial counsel can make copies at his or her own expense, if desired or necessary.[181] If trial counsel has trepidation regarding transfer of the file, the proper course of action is to bring an application for directions, and not simply to refuse to hand over the file.[182]

## Q.  DISSOLUTION OF A LAW FIRM OR LAWYER LEAVING A FIRM

Where a law firm dissolves, the contracts between clients and the firm are thwarted. Individual lawyers handling the cases do not automatically continue with the case. Granted, in most instances clients will prefer to retain the services of the lawyer whom they regard as being in charge of their matter.[183] But the final decision rests with the client, whose choice in the matter must be respected. Lawyers whose retainers end by reason of dissolution of a firm are required to adhere to the

---

179  See section R, "Reporting Requirements, Confidentiality, and Privilege," in chapter 10.

180  See Ontario Court of Appeal, "Procedural Protocol Re Allegations of Incompetence of Trial Counsel in Criminal Cases" (effective 1 May 2000) at para. 5.

181  *Ibid.* at paras. 5 & 6. The Court of Appeal's directions provide that, upon taking possession of the file, appeal counsel must make the entire file available for inspection by trial counsel on request, in a timely manner, and permit trial counsel to make copies.

182  *Ibid.* at para 5.

183  See CBA Code ch. XII, comm. 13; Sask. ch. XII, comm. 13; Man. ch. XII, comm. 13; N.S. ch. 11, comm. 11.16; and Ont. r. 2.09(7) (commentary).

ethical rules applicable in all cases of withdrawal.[184] The same guidelines should apply where a lawyer leaves a firm.[185]

# R. TERMINATION FOR OTHER CAUSES

Sometimes events will transpire to end the relationship absent any
intentional impetus from client or lawyer. A client or lawyer may die.
The lawyer may be disbarred or suspended or ordered off the case by
the court owing to conflict of interest alleged by a third party. Most
commonly, the representation may run its natural course, leaving no
further need for professional services. In each of these examples, the
lawyer's authority to continue acting for the client is terminated, and
the duties normally attendant upon termination apply, to the extent
possible in the circumstances, as they would in any other case.

# S.  SUMMARY AND RECOMMENDATIONS

The general rule regarding termination of a retainer is quite simple: a
lawyer can withdraw from a case only based upon good cause and with
notice appropriate in the circumstances. But implementing this standard can sometimes be difficult in practice. We recommend the following guidelines for counsel who is discharged or considering
withdrawal:

1.  The client has an absolute power to discharge counsel. Once dis-
    charged, counsel cannot continue to act on the case (section D).
2.  In contrast to the client, who can terminate a retainer for any rea-
    son whatsoever, a lawyer cannot withdraw from a case absent good
    cause and appropriate notice (section E).
3.  There are a number of occasions where the rules of professional
    conduct require that a lawyer withdraw. The circumstances man-
    dating withdrawal vary from jurisdiction to jurisdiction, but the
    general rule is that a lawyer must withdraw where continued rep-

---

184  See CBA Code ch. XII, comm. 13; Sask. ch. XII, comm. 13; Man. ch. XII, comm.
     13; N.S. ch. 11, comm. 11.16; and Ont. r. 2.09(7) (commentary). In Alberta and
     British Columbia, termination by reason of a law firm's dissolution is not
     expressly addressed in the withdrawal rule. However, this situation would come
     under some combination of the lawyer's residual or discretionary right to with-
     draw and the client's ability to discharge counsel.
185  See Third Restatement §31, comm. "f."

resentation will necessarily compromise service to the client or involve the lawyer in violating legal or ethical duties (section F).

4. In many other circumstances, the lawyer is afforded discretion in deciding whether to withdraw. The rules of professional conduct list various examples of discretionary withdrawal, the unifying theme being a serious breakdown in the components of trust and confidence that are so essential to an effective client-lawyer relationship. Useful factors to consider in exercising this discretion include the extent to which the client-lawyer relationship has been damaged, whether the rift in the relationship can be repaired, and the prejudicial impact of withdrawal upon the client (section G).

5. British Columbia is alone among Canadian governing bodies in providing lawyers with a residual right to withdraw. This residual right applies only where the client will not suffer any unfairness and where withdrawal is not undertaken for an improper purpose. Given the general duty not to abandon a client absent good cause, lawyers in other jurisdictions probably do not enjoy the leeway to withdraw afforded counsel in British Columbia (section H).

6. Counsel in a criminal case should be permitted to withdraw because of substantial non-payment of fees, provided that the client does not suffer undue prejudice as a result. In essence, this means that the unpaid lawyer should not wait until the last minute to withdraw. Counsel should also provide the client with reasonable notice prior to making an application to withdraw for non-payment of fees, providing an opportunity to correct the delinquency (section I).

7. Contrary to the position taken by one of the leading ethical codes in the United States, we do not endorse an option to withdraw simply because continued representation will result in an unreasonable financial burden on the lawyer (section I).

8. A lawyer has a duty to inform the client of his or her intention to withdraw, in advance of the act of withdrawal if possible. Most ethical rules provide that notice must be "appropriate in the circumstances." Appropriate notice will typically include providing the reasons for withdrawal and suggesting that replacement counsel be promptly retained (section J).

9. A lawyer should provide notice of withdrawal to the court and the Crown in most instances. Notice is especially important where the court and the Crown have previously been informed that counsel acts for the accused, as a means of avoiding delay and confusion (section K).

10. Once counsel has gone on the record, leave to withdraw may be required by the rules of professional conduct (for example, Ontario), the rules of the court (for example, Ontario, Quebec), or case law (for example, Alberta). Counsel must therefore ascertain the law in the particular province of practice. Where leave is sought and refused, counsel should continue on with the case, ensuring that the defence is not conducted in contravention of any legal or ethical rules (section L).

11. Counsel owes current and former clients a duty of confidentiality. It is therefore important that client confidences be protected, absent the application of a recognized exception to the duty, both during the withdrawal process and after the client-relationship has terminated. In particular, lawyers should avoid disclosing the reasons for withdrawal when notifying the Crown or the court or when seeking leave to withdraw (section M).

12. The various Canadian rules of professional conduct take different positions regarding the provision of confidential information to a successor lawyer. Some governing bodies forbid disclosure to the successor lawyer absent express consent of the client (for example, Nova Scotia). Others permit disclosure of information relevant to the case (for example, CBA Code). A middle position is to allow for disclosure where expressly or impliedly authorized by the client (for example, Alberta). Counsel should consult the rules applicable in his or her jurisdiction to determine the scope of permitted disclosure (section M(3)).

13. In addition to the duties regarding confidentiality and notice, counsel who is discharged or withdraws has a number of other obligations. These obligations can include delivering the file and property to the client or successor counsel, giving the client all information concerning the case, accounting for funds, promptly rendering a final account, and cooperating with the successor lawyer. We also believe that counsel who is discharged or withdraws has a duty to pass on to the former client all communications received following termination, where related to the case and reasonable to do so. Finally, depending on the circumstances there may be a duty to assist a former client in finding a new lawyer (section N).

14. A lawyer who is approached by a potential client to take over an ongoing case must exercise care not to interfere with any existing client-lawyer relationship. At the same time, however, the lawyer should not prevent an individual from exercising the right to dis-

charge current counsel. A successor lawyer, once retained, should represent the client in the normal course like any other (section O).

15. Where former counsel is the subject of a claim that the right to effective assistance of counsel has been denied, the file must not be withheld from appeal counsel in a misguided effort at self-protection. Rather, former counsel must produce the file, taking copies of documents if desired or arranging to view the file later at appeal counsel's office (section P).

16. Where a law firm dissolves, or a lawyer leaves a law firm, there may be uncertainty regarding the future of a client's representation. The final decision rests with the client, who should be consulted promptly regarding the development (section Q).

17. Sometimes events unrelated to client or lawyer dissatisfaction operate to terminate the client-lawyer relationship. For instance, the death of either participant will end the representation, or the lawyer may be suspended or disbarred. Another possibility is that the court will remove counsel from the record for a conflict of interest. Most common is the natural termination of the retainer once a case has concluded. In all of these cases, counsel is bound by the duties normally attendant upon termination (section R).

## FURTHER READINGS

BOON, A., & J. LEVIN, *The Ethics and Conduct of Lawyers in England and Wales* (Oxford: Hart, 1999)

BURKOFF, J., *Criminal Defense Ethics: Law and Liability*, rev. ed. (St. Paul: West, 2000)

DAL PONT, G., *Lawyers' Professional Responsibility in Australia and New Zealand* *North Ryde: LBC Information Services, 1996)

FORTUNE, W., R. UNDERWOOD, & E. IMWINKELRIED, *Modern Litigation and Professional Responsibility Handbook: The Limits of Zealous Advocacy* (New York: Little, Brown & Co., 1996)

HALL, J., *Professional Responsibility of the Criminal Lawyer*, 2d ed. (New York: Clark Boardman Callaghan, 1996)

HAZARD, G., & W. HODES, *The Law of Lawyering: A Handbook on the Model Rules of Professional Conduct*, 2d ed. (Englewood, N.J.: Prentice Hall, 1993)

HUTCHINSON, A., *Legal Ethics and Professional Responsibility* (Toronto: Irwin Law, 1999)

MacKenzie, G., *Lawyers and Ethics: Professional Responsibility and Discipline* (Toronto: Carswell, 1993)

Martin, G., "The Role and Responsibility of the Defence Advocate" (1969) 12 Crim. L.Q. 376

Morden, J., "A Succeeding Solicitor's Duty to protect the Account of the Former Solicitor" (1971) 5 L. Soc. Gaz. 257

Ontario Court of Appeal, "Procedural Protocol Re Allegations of Incompetence of Trial Counsel in Criminal Cases" (effective 1 May 2000) online: http://www.ontariocourts.on.ca/court_of_appeal/notices/procedural_protocol/index.htm

Orkin, M., *Legal Ethics* (Toronto: Cartwright, 1957)

"Panel Discussion: Problems in Ethics and Advocacy" [1969] in Law Society of Upper Canada, *Defending a Criminal Case* (Toronto: R. De Boo, 1960) 279

Pasano, M., "Permanent Appearance Rules: A Concern for Continuity Imperils Criminal Defense Work" (1993) 7 Crim. Just. 8

Perillo, J., "The Law of Lawyer's Contracts is Different" (1998) 67 Fordham L. Rev 443

Rauf, M., "Must the Court Consent to Defence Counsel Withdrawing for Non-Payment of Fees?" (1996) 3 C.R. (5th) 46

Ross, S., *Ethics in Law: Lawyers' Responsibility and Accountability in Australia*, 2d ed. (Sydney: Butterworths, 1998)

Skurka, S., & J. Stribopoulos, "Professional Responsibility in Criminal Practice" in Law Society of Upper Canada, *42nd Bar Admission Course, 2000, Criminal Procedure Reference Materials* (Toronto: Law Society of Upper Canada, 2000) c. 1

Smith, B., *Professional Conduct for Lawyers and Judges* (Fredericton, N.B.: Maritime Law Book, 1998) c. 8

Wolfram, C.W., *Modern Legal Ethics* (St. Paul: West, 1986)

Zitrin, R., & C. Langford, *Legal Ethics in the Practice of Law* (Charlottesville: Michie, 1995)

# CHAPTER 12

# THE PROSECUTOR

## A. INTRODUCTION

An analysis of the prosecutor's specific ethical obligations must begin with a delineation of the role and the general duty of the Crown. The Crown's unique role in the administration of the criminal justice system shapes the ethical responsibilities of prosecutors. Though in many ways the standards of conduct for prosecutors are similar to those for defence lawyers, prosecutors cannot be guided by the exact same principles applicable to the lawyer appearing for the accused. As we will see, there are particular constraints imposed on prosecutors on account of their "dual role" in the system, constraints that simply would not apply to defence counsel. Granted, defence lawyers to some extent also occupy a "dual role," in the sense that as "officers of the court" they cannot be purely adversarial and exclusively committed to their clients at the risk, for instance, of misleading the court. But defence counsel's obligations to the court are not nearly as extensive as the prosecutor's broad duties to the public interest.

Setting high ethical standards is consistent with the tradition of Crown counsel in this country, who generally carry out their role in an exemplary way.[1] Yet special concerns have been expressed in Canada in the recent past with respect to prosecutorial ethical standards. In

---

1   R. v. *Stinchcombe*, [1991] 3 S.C.R. 326 [*Stinchcombe*]; and R. v. *Bain*, [1992] 1 S.C.R. 91.

1998 Fred Ferguson, a regional Crown counsel in New Brunswick, wrote that "never in the history of our criminal law has there been so much judicial attention focused on the role of prosecutors in the assessment and conduct of criminal prosecutions as in the last decade."[2] Ferguson added that "the reconsideration of the *Marshall*,[3] *Milgaard*,[4] and *Morin*[5] cases have caused reflection, reorientation, and refocusing by all who appear and represent the attorney general in criminal matters." More recently, the Ontario Court of Appeal has released several decisions that are highly critical of trial strategy and tactics employed by particular Crown prosecutors.[6] Far from being unique to Canada, these apposite concerns have surfaced in other jurisdictions, including Australia, England, and the United States.[7]

# B.  THE PROSECUTOR'S DUAL ROLE: MINISTER OF JUSTICE AND ADVOCATE

The Canadian tradition, consistent with other Anglo-American countries, sees the prosecutor occupying a dual role of minister of justice and advocate. There is an uneasy tension between these two roles, and the minister of justice function is at first view difficult to accommodate within an adversarial framework. However, our constitution has long granted prosecutors a special status, distinct from that of a mere opponent at trial. The office of the attorney general, which has its beginnings in thirteenth century England, exercises powers derived from the royal prerogative, defined by Dicey as the residue of discretionary or arbitrary authority residing in the hands of the Crown at any given

---

2    F. Ferguson, "Prosecutorial Assessment of the Case" (1998) National Criminal Law Program, Federation of Law Societies of Canada.

3    See Nova Scotia, *Report of the Royal Commission on the Donald Marshall, Jr., Prosecution*, vol. 1 (Halifax: The Cmmission, 1989) (Chair: T.A. Hickman).

4    See *Reference Re Milgaard*, [1992] 1 S.C.R. 866.

5    Ontario, *Report of the Commission on Proceedings Involving Guy Paul Morin* (Toronto: Queen's Printer, 1998) (Chair: F. Kaufman).

6    See *R. v. Ahluwalia* (2000), 149 C.C.C. (3d) 193 (Ont. C.A.) [*Aluwalia*]; *R. v. Rose* (2001), 153 C.C.C. (3d) 225 (Ont. C.A.) [*Rose (Ont. C.A.)*]; and *R. v. Robinson* (2001), 153 C.C.C. (3d) 398 (Ont. C.A.) [*Robinson*].

7    See K. Crispin, "Prosecutorial Ethics" in S. Parker & C. Sampford, eds., *Legal Ethics and Legal Practice: Contemporary Issues* (Oxford: Clarendon Press, 1995) 189.

time.[8] As chief law officer of the Crown, the provincial attorneys general head a ministry of the government and are members of the executive that assumes primary responsibility for the administration of the criminal law, in accordance with the separation of powers. At the federal level, the minister of justice is *ex officio* Her Majesty's attorney general.[9] At the same time, the attorney general acts as prosecutor in individual cases, through Crown counsel who are appointed as agents to prosecute on his or her behalf. These Crown counsel are accountable to the provincial attorneys general or federal minister of justice (as the case may be), who in turn are responsible finally to the legislature.[10]

## 1) Role as Minister of Justice

Because the attorney general is ultimately responsible to the public, and plays a special constitutional role, the lawyers who carry out the day-to-day function of prosecuting cases owe an overarching duty to achieve justice by exercising their powers fairly. The common law has hence long recognized the prosecutor's special duty, in the conduct of a criminal trial, "to be assistant to the Court in the furtherance of justice, and not to act as counsel for any particular party or person."[11] A leading exposition of this sentiment remains the classic *dictum* of Mr. Justice Rand in *R. v. Boucher*:

> It cannot be over-emphasized that the purpose of a criminal prosecution is not to obtain a conviction, it is to lay before a jury what the Crown considers to be credible evidence relevant to what is alleged to be a crime. Counsel have a duty to see that all available legal proof of the facts is presented: it should be done firmly and pressed to its legitimate strength but it must also be done fairly. The role of the prosecutor excludes any notion of winning or losing; his function is a matter of public duty than which in civil life there can be none charged with greater personal responsibility. It is to be efficiently per-

---

8   See *R. v. Power,* [1994] 1 S.C.R. 601 [*Power*], referring to D. Morgan, "Controlling Prosecutorial Powers — Judicial Review, Abuse of Process and Section 7 of the *Charter*" (1986-87) 29 Crim. L.Q. 15 at 20–21.

9   See *Department of Justice Act,* R.S.C. 1985, c. J-2, s. 2(2).

10  The situation is somewhat different in Nova Scotia, where a quasi-independent Public Prosecution Service was established following recommendations made by the Marshall Inquiry: see Nova Scotia *Public Prosecutions Act,* S.N.S. 1990, c. 21. See the discussion in P. Stenning, "Independence and the Director of Public Prosecutions: The Marshall Inquiry and Beyond" (2000) 23 Dal. L.J. 385.

11  *R. v. Thursfield* (1838), 173 E.R. 490.

formed with an ingrained sense of the dignity, the seriousness and the justness of judicial proceedings.[12]

In short, the prosecutor does not act in the largely partisan sense usually required of defence counsel by the adversarial system, but as a promoter of the public interest in achieving justice.

This notion that prosecutors must temper partisanship has been expressed by stating that counsel appearing for the prosecution should regard themselves as "ministers of justice."[13] By "minister of justice," we are referring to the role of a public officer engaged in the administration of justice (*not* to the federal cabinet minister who is elected to Parliament and heads the Department of Justice). Our Supreme Court has taken up this language, stating that "the tradition of Crown counsel in this country in carrying out their role as 'ministers of justice' and not as adversaries has generally been high."[14] Similarly, it has been said that prosecutors are "quasi-judicial officers."[15] Others, seeking to emphasize the role and responsibility of the prosecutor as a decision maker on a broad policy level, whose actions shape the character, quality, and efficiency of the criminal justice system, have also termed the prosecutor an "administrator."[16] Still another formulation sees the prosecutor playing a role as a "symbol of authority and spokesperson for the community in criminal matters."[17] Such monikers incorporate several aspects of the prosecutor's role, yet all are accurate insofar as they accord great importance to the linchpin obligation to advance the public interest by seeking a fair and just result in the prosecution of criminal matters.[18]

The public interest in achieving justice demands unwavering fidelity to the truth-seeking function of the criminal justice system. It also necessitates respect for the constitutional rights of the accused, as promoted by our due-process model of justice, allegiance to the con-

---

12   R. v. *Boucher* (1954), [1955] S.C.R. 16 at 23–24 [*Boucher*]. These sentiments have been repeatedly affirmed in subsequent Supreme Court of Canada cases: see, for example, *Power*, above note 8 at 616; and R. v. *Cook*, [1997] 1 S.C.R. 1113 at 1124 [*Cook*].

13   R. v. *Puddick* (1865), 176 E.R. 662.

14   See, for example, *Nelles* v. *Ontario*, [1989] 2 S.C.R. 170 at 191; and *Stinchcombe*, above note 1 at 341.

15   See R. v. *Logiacco* (1984), 11 C.C.C. (3d) 374 at 379 (Ont. C.A.) [*Logiacco*]; and R. v. *Gayle* (2001), 154 C.C.C. (3d) 221 at 250 (Ont. C.A.) [*Gayle*].

16   ABA Prosecution Standard, 3-1.2 (b).

17   *Logiacco*, above note 15 at 379.

18   See R. v. *Hillier* (1994), 115 Nfld. & P.E.I.R. 27 (Nfld. C.A.). See also *Royal Commission on the Donald Marshall, Jr., Prosecution*, above note 3 at 238.

cept of equality of application, and a keen sense of proportion and substantive justice in pursuing a course of action that can have a significant impact on the liberty and reputation of the accused.[19] The idea that the rights of the accused should somehow bear upon the duties of the Crown is worth stressing. In 1955 the English lawyer Christmas Humphreys stated that the duty of prosecuting counsel is "to assist the defence in every way."[20] In our post-*Stinchcombe* era, where extensive disclosure obligations are well accepted, this opinion is not particularly startling.[21] Nonetheless, Humphrey's comment "offers a useful exhortation for prosecutors to remember that those they prosecute may conceivably be innocent and they should be given every chance to answer the case against them."[22] This approach has relevance at the investigative stage, as well as during the trial itself, for the mere laying of charges can severely effect a person's well being, even if he or she is eventually acquitted.

Another aspect of the prosecutor's role as "minister of justice" that deserves special emphasis is the need for independence.[23] Though accountable to Parliament and the courts, the attorney general and his or her agents are permitted liberal discretion in making decisions affecting the prosecution of criminal cases, and they must be secure from political or social pressures. A guarantee of independence encourages courageous decisions where needed and thus works to safeguard the public interest. Indeed, the principle of independence in the exercise of the prosecution function is an important constitutional convention that infuses the office of attorney general.[24]

Certainly, the prosecutor must consider public needs and community concerns in reaching a decision as to the best course of action to take in any given circumstance. But, in some matters, the prosecutor's duty clearly lies in the defiance of community pressures, though

---

19   See S. Fisher, "In Search of the Virtuous Prosecutor: A Conceptual Framework" (1988) Am. J. Crim. L. 197 at 236–37.

20   C. Humphreys, "The Duties and Responsibilities of Prosecuting Counsel" (1955) Crim. L.R. 739 at 741.

21   Prior to *Stinchcombe*, above note 1, the exhortation to "assist the accused" as an ethical mandate was especially apposite: see *R. v. Lemay* (1951), [1952] 1 S.C.R. 232 at 241 [*Lemay*]; as well as the observations of Mr. Justice Binnie in *R. v. Jolivet*, [2000] 1 S.C.R. 751 at 762 [*Jolivet*].

22   Crispin, above note 7 at 189.

23   See *R. v. Smythe* (1971), 3 C.C.C. (2d) 97 at 110 (Ont. C.A.), aff'd (1971), 3 C.C.C. (2d) 366 at 370; *R. v. Saikaly* (1979), 48 C.C.C. (2d) 192 at 196 (Ont. C.A.); and *R. v. Mitchell* (1975), 33 C.C.C. (3d) 98 at 105 (Ont. C.A.).

24   See M. Rosenberg, "The Ethical Prosecutor in the Canadian Context" (1991) Federal Prosecutors' Conference.

always within the confines of the law. As one commentator has noted, the only mind the prosecutor must make up is his or her own.[25] In *R. v. Curragh Inc.*, McLachlin and Major JJ., in their dissenting opinion, remind us that since the Crown is charged with the broad duty to ensure that every accused person is treated fairly, it is "especially in high profile cases, where the justice system will be on display, that counsel must do their utmost to ensure that any resultant convictions are based on facts and not on emotions. When the Crown allows its actions to be influenced by public pressure the essential fairness and legitimacy of our system is lost."[26] More provocatively, it has been observed by a prosecutor that "the change in societal attitudes, principally the abandonment of deference to authority, coupled with the proliferation of vocal, intense interest groups, the advent of political correctness, the directives of zero tolerance and the monster of sensational journalism all conspire to put dangerous pressures on prosecutors, in more and more cases, at many more stages during the process."[27]

Canadian rules of professional conduct affirm that prosecutors play a special, justice-seeking role in the adversarial justice system. The CBA Code states that the prosecutor's prime duty "is not to seek to convict, but to present before the trial court all available credible evidence relevant to the alleged crime in order that justice may be done through a fair trial upon the merits . . . [The prosecutor] must act fairly and dispassionately . . . ."[28] Most provincial codes of professional conduct have adopted the CBA position, in identical or similar terms.[29] The Federal Prosecution Service Deskbook issued by the Department of Justice Canada (hereafter referred to as the "FPS Deskbook") contains language similar to that used in the codes of professional conduct.[30] The FPS Deskbook also mentions the need for prosecutors to undertake their functions with "objectivity" and "impartiality," wording that further underlines the minister of justice role. In the United States, England and Australia, the applicable rules of professional con-

---

25 S. Gillers, *Regulation of Lawyers: Problems of Law and Ethics*, 3d ed. (Boston: Little, Brown, 1992) at 393.

26 *R. v. Curraugh Inc.*, [1997] 1 S.C.R. 537 at 588.

27 J. Walsh, "Ethics and the Investigator" (1999) National Criminal Law Program, Federation of Law Societies of Canada.

28 CBA Code ch. IX, comm. 7.

29 See, for example, B.C. ch. 8, r. 18; Ont. r. 4.01(3); N.S. ch. 17; N.B. Part C, r. 12; Alta. ch. 10, r. 28.

30 Department of Justice Canada, *The Federal Prosecution Service Deskbook* (Ottawa: Department of Justice, 2000) [*FPS Deskbook*].

duct apply the same general ethical standards to the prosecutor's function.[31]

We can easily understand that Crown Counsel is not an ordinary advocate, and undertakes special duties as part of his or her role as minister of justice, by looking at the case of *R. v. J.(G.P.)*.[32] There, counsel appeared for the complainant on a third-party production hearing brought pursuant to s. 278.1 of the *Criminal Code*. The accused was acquitted, and the Crown appealed the trial judge's ultimate production ruling. On the appeal, counsel who had acted for the complainant at trial appeared for the Crown. The Manitoba Court of Appeal noted that Crown counsel plays a quasi-judicial role directed towards achieving a just result in the public interest. A complainant's lawyer has no such broad duty, and in the context of a s. 278.1 application may well take a different position from the Crown regarding production. In the view of Mr. Justice Philp, a single counsel could not fulfill both roles, and there was "an appearance of impropriety in counsel's role as Crown counsel on the appeal."[33]

In summary, the prosecutor's linchpin duty is to seek justice in the public interest, which encapsulates several related principles:

1. A prosecutor can seek a conviction but must all the while strive to ensure that the defendant has a fair trial.
2. The prosecutor's goal is not to obtain a conviction at any cost but to assist the court in eliciting truth without infringing upon the legitimate rights of the accused.
3. At each stage of the criminal justice process, the discretion vested in the prosecutor should be exercised with objectivity and impartiality, and not in a purely partisan way.
4. Self-restraint for the sake of fairness requires that the prosecutor resist the unbridled desire to obtain punishment of the accused.[34]

---

31    See, for example, ABA Model Rule 3.8; ABA Prosecution Standards, s. 3-1.2; General Council, *Code of Conduct for the Bar of England and Wales* (London: The Council, 1990) [*Bar Code of Conduct*] (General Standards and Standards Applicable to Criminal Cases, Responsibilities of Prosecuting Counsel) §11; and The Barristers' Rules (New South Wales & Queensland) (ModelRules, r. 17.47–59; and New South Wales, Professional Conduct and Practice Rules, r. 23, A. 62–71.

32    (2001), 151 C.C.C. (3d) 382 (Man. C.A.).

33    *Ibid.* at 400.

34    See Fisher, above note 19 at 204.

## 2)  Role as Advocate

The flip side of the prosecutor's role as a minister of justice is the necessary tempering of the partisan function undertaken by most other
lawyers. As the CBA Code states, in adversary proceedings the ordinary
lawyer's function as advocate is "openly and necessarily partisan."[35]
Accordingly, the lawyer is not normally obliged to assist his or her
adversary. But we have seen that the prosecutor, as a "minister of justice," cannot wholeheartedly embrace partisanship.[36] Does this mean,
however, that the prosecutor cannot work hard in seeking to secure a
conviction? Just how vigorous and zealous can the prosecutor be in
presenting a case?

Ultimately, the prosecutor is not only a minister of justice, but also
an advocate. As an advocate, he or she is expected to discharge all
duties with competence, earnestness and vigour.[37] In *R. v. Cook*, the
Supreme Court of Canada affirmed that in the adversarial process the
Crown can act as a "strong advocate" and that it is permissible and
desirable that prosecutors vigorously pursue a legitimate result to the
best of their ability.[38] The Court went so far as to add that the prosecutor as strong advocate is a critical element of this country's criminal
law mechanism.[39] As respected English barrister David Pannick says,
"the obligation to act fairly does not mean that the prosecuting counsel is compelled to avoid advocacy."[40] The prosecutor's distinct mission
thus requires that he or she advance the case as advocate, while at the
same time taking measures to protect the opponent's case as well.

Of course, there can be a great difficulty in reconciling the adversarial nature of the prosecutor's role with the non-adversarial duty of a
"minister of justice." It has been said that "our adversary system makes
it extremely difficult to be a fair prosecutor,"[41] and that "the potential

---

35   CBA Code ch. IX, comm. 15.
36   See *Cook*, above note 12 at 1124.
37   See *Berger* v. *United States*, 295 U.S. 78 at 88 (1985); *R.* v. *Chambers* (1990), 59
     C.C.C. (3d) 321 [*Chambers*]; and *R.* v. *Daly* (1992), 57 O.A.C. 70 at 76 (C.A.)
     [*Daly*].
38   *Cook*, above note 12 at 1124.
39   *Ibid.*
40   D. Pannick, *Advocates* (Oxford: Oxford University Press, 1993) at 115.
41   M. Manning, "Abuse of power by Crown Attorneys" in Law Society of Upper
     Canada, *The Abuse of Power and the Role of Independent Judicial System in Its
     Regulation and Control* (Toronto: Law Society of Upper Canada, 1979) 571 at
     580.

is there for terrible conflict."[42] Consider, for example, the heavy pressures placed upon Crown counsel to win cases as a means of securing career advancement. "The most idealistic prosecutor would have few illusions about his future prospects if every person he prosecuted were to be acquitted. This is, perhaps, rarely taken into account at a conscious level but it adds to the overall ethos of rivalry and hence the need to win."[43] A special strength of character is thus required if Crown counsel is to resist getting too caught up in a "culture of winning" or a "conviction psychology" and is not to lose sight of the need to make sure that the accused is treated fairly. As we have seen, the comments by Mr. Justice Rand in *Boucher* come close to endorsing the view that the prosecutor must remain entirely oblivious to the prospect of victory or defeat. Certainly, in some cases a prosecutor has to concede either that the Crown's case has not been proven or that an injustice would occur in the case of a conviction. To the extent that we can speak of winning, the victory lies in doing justice, not in gaining a conviction.[44]

Some observers of the criminal justice system fear that vigorous advocacy by the Crown, such as arguing for conviction on the facts of a case, tarnishes the ideal of the prosecutor.[45] On the other hand, some argue that prosecutors must engage in "vigorous partisan advocacy."[46] Neither position is acceptable absent careful qualification. Submissions that call for a conviction are not inconsistent with a prosecutor's duty to the public interest. Assuming that the accused has been given the unfettered opportunity to make full answer and defence, and the prosecutor has no reason to doubt the accuracy of the evidence placed before the trier of fact, the call for a guilty verdict is entirely proper. On the other hand, the prosecutor who acts in an overly vigorous and partisan manner risks subverting the primary duties of fairness, impartiality, and candour in seeking justice.

Another way of posing the same question is to ask whether the prosecutor as minister of justice can act in a zealous manner. The eth-

---

42   G. MacKenzie, *Lawyers and Ethics, Professional Responsibility and Discipline*, looseleaf (Scarborough, Ont.: Carswell, 1993) at 6-16–6-17.

43   J. Hunter & K. Cronin, *Evidence, Advocacy and Ethical Practice: A Criminal Trial Commentary* (Sydney: Butterworths, 1995) at 187.

44   R. Jackson, "The Federal Prosecutor" (1940) 31 J. Crim. L. & Criminology 2 at 4.

45   L. Sossin, "Crown Prosecutors and Constitutional Facts: The Promise and Politics of *Charter* Damages" (1994) 19 Queen's L.J. 372.

46   D. Butt, "Malicious Prosecution: Rejoinder" (1996) 75 Can. Bar Rev. 335 at 338–39.

ical norm of zealous advocacy properly applies to a prosecutor, to the extent that as an advocate he or she can work hard to persuade the trier of fact. Once again, however, we stress that this zeal must be exercised within proper limits, consistent with the primary duty to the public interest. One should perhaps therefore speak of a "controlled zeal," a modified version of the traditional zealous advocate.

It might nonetheless be argued that prosecutors are sometimes justified in pushing the outer limits of zealousness in response to perceived truth-defeating tactics employed by defence counsel. Prosecutors may feel that they are sent into battle with a blunted sword, while their opponents' forensic weapons are sharpened to a razor's edge, and that self-defence can require aggressive measures.[47] There are two responses to this proposition. First, by relying upon the principle against self-incrimination, defence counsel is not defeating the truth but rather promoting his or her client's legitimate constitutional rights. To the extent that defence counsel obtains an advantage by reason of basic constitutional guarantees, the criminal justice system is simply operating as intended. Second, where defence counsel acts improperly, the idea that unethical retaliation by the prosecutor is justified should be rejected. For instance, how should a prosecutor respond to a personal attack by defence counsel in the summation to the jury? The tendency in Canada and in England is to discourage the "eye for an eye" response, because the result may be to create an impediment to a fair trial.[48] While the prosecutor can certainly respond to improper defence actions, the public interest does not allow a departure from normal ethical standards in doing so.

In a perfect world, the boundary between acceptably zealous advocacy by the Crown and impermissible prosecutorial abuse would always be clear and not open to disagreement. But drawing fine lines in black and white is not realistic. The controversy over the acceptable degree of advocacy practised by Crown counsel will probably never cease, given the dynamics of the adversary system and the inherent tension between a prosecutor's dual roles as minister of justice and forceful advocate.

---

47  B. Civiletti, "Prosecutor as Advocate" (1979) 25 N.Y.L. Sch. L. Rev. 1 at 17–19.
48  See, for example, *R. v. Peruta* (1992), 78 C.C.C. (3d) 350 (Que. C.A.) [*Peruta*]; Pannick, *supra*, at 114–19. In contrast, it seems that in the United States the doctrine of "invited response" has been applied to justify vigorous reaction to aggressive defence behaviour.

## 3) Ethical Guidelines

The rules of professional conduct in Canada devote minimal attention to the role of the prosecutor. While most provincial jurisdictions have policy manuals for Crown counsel, one of the best sources of ethical guidance comes not from the governing bodies but rather from the FPS Deskbook.[49] This source is thus worth reviewing in more detail in two respects. First, the FPS Deskbook articulates the general principles that we have already discussed: public-interest considerations require Crown counsel to exercise judgement and discretion as ministers of justice that limit the ordinary function of advocates; fairness, moderation, and dignity should characterize the conduct of Crown counsel during criminal litigation; and the trial process should not become a personal contest of skill or professional pre-eminence, although prosecutors are not prevented from conducting trials with vigour and thoroughness.[50]

A second aspect of the FPS Deskbook that warrants specific mention is the detailed standards set out for prosecutors, standards that in our view are helpful in developing ethical guidelines for prosecutors. In particular, the manual sets out important guiding principles and elaborates as to how these principles can be promoted:

1) The duty to ensure that the responsibilities of the office of the attorney general are carried out with integrity and dignity. Counsel can fulfil this duty:

- by complying with the rules of ethics;
- by exercising careful judgment in deciding the case to be presented for the Crown, what witnesses to call, and what evidence to tender;
- by acting with moderation, fairness, and impartiality;
- by adequately preparing for each case;
- by not becoming simply an extension of a client department or investigative agency;
- by conducting plea and sentence negotiations in a manner consistent with the policy set out in this manual.

2) The duty to preserve judicial independence. Counsel can fulfil this duty:

- by not discussing matters relating to a case with the presiding judge without the participation of defence counsel;

---

49   Above note 30 at §9 (The Duties and Responsibilities of Crown Counsel).
50   *Ibid.* at §9.3.

- by not dealing with matters in chambers that should properly be dealt with in open court;
- by avoiding personal or private discussions with a judge in chambers while presenting a case before that judge; and
- by refraining from appearing before a judge on a contentious matter when a personal friendship exists between Crown counsel and the judge.

3) The duty to be fair and to appear to be fair. Counsel can fulfil this duty:

- by making disclosure in accordance with the policy set out in this manual;
- by bringing all relevant cases and authorities known to counsel to the attention of the court, even if they may be contrary to the Crown's position;
- by not expressing personal opinions on the evidence, including the credibility of witnesses, in court or in public;
- by not expressing personal opinions on the guilt or innocence of the accused in court or in public;
- by asking relevant and proper questions during the examination of a witness and by not asking questions designed solely to embarrass, insult, abuse, belittle, or demean the witness. Cross examination can be skilful and probing, yet still show respect for the witness;
- by respecting the court and the proceedings while vigorously asserting the Crown's position; and
- by never permitting personal interests or partisan political considerations to interfere with the proper exercise of prosecutorial discretion.

These guidelines constitute an important component in the evolution of standards of professional conduct for Canadian prosecutors.

In the United States, the ABA Prosecution Standards, although not intended to serve as disciplinary rules, offer an even more detailed guide to professional conduct.[51] These standards cover the general organization of the prosecution function, the investigative function of the prosecutor, plea discussions, the trial, and sentencing. In England, the bar's Code of Conduct contains specific provisions as to the responsibilities of prosecuting counsel, while the Code for Crown Prosecutors is the equivalent of the FPS Deskbook.

---

51   ABA Prosecution Standards.

# C. THE PRINCIPLE OF PROSECUTORIAL DISCRETION

"The *sine qua non* of a prosecutor's duty is discretion. This is recognized as essential to the effective working of our system. Yet, it is this feature that makes the prosecutor so vulnerable to pressure. Discretion is our Achilles' Heel. It is actually easier not to exercise it. The grief often comes when we do."[52]

Many decisions concerning the operation of the criminal justice system involve the exercise of a discretion by the prosecutor. Prosecutors exercise discretion in the decisions to prosecute; to proceed by way of indictment or summary conviction; to oppose or consent to bail; to prefer an indictment; to withdraw a charge; to enter a stay; to consent to elections and re-elections; to appeal; to consent to an adjournment; to intervene in private prosecutions; and to provide pre-trial disclosure. Prosecutorial discretion is also exercised in the selection of witnesses and in the sentence process. As Mr. Justice La Forest stated in *R. v. Beare*, "a system that attempted to eliminate discretion would be unworkably complex and rigid."[53] In short, the prosecutor's discretion is an essential feature of the criminal justice system.

Not surprisingly, the Supreme Court of Canada has clearly affirmed that the existence of prosecutorial discretion does not offend the principles of fundamental justice.[54] As to judicial control of this discretion, the courts have articulated several principles. First, the exercise of a discretionary power is not absolute and can sometimes be reviewed by the courts.[55] Second, the prosecutor's broad discretion is not well suited for judicial review and should be afforded deference.[56] Third, on a case-by-case basis, the exercise of discretion can be reviewed under the doctrine of abuse of process, which gives the courts a residual ability to remedy an abuse of the court's process in the clear-

---

52    Walsh, above note 27.
53    *R. v. Beare*, [1988] 2 S.C.R. 387 [*Beare*]. For a review of various aspects of the prosecutor's discretion, see B. Archibald, "The Politics of Prosecutorial Discretion: Institutional Structures and the Tensions between Punitive and Restorative Paradigms of Justice" (1998) 3 Can. Crim. L. Rev. 69 at 80–81; as well as W. Gorman, "Prosecutorial Discretion in a *Charter*-Dominated Trial Process" (2000) 44 Crim. L.Q. 15.
54    See *Cook*, above note 12; *Beare*, above note 53; and *Jones v. R.*, [1986] 2 S.C.R. 284.
55    See *R. v. T.(V.)*, [1992] 1 S.C.R. 749 [*T.(V.)*].
56    *Ibid.* at 762.

est of cases.[57] Fourth, a judicial stay is not an automatic remedy for past Crown misconduct, since a stay is appropriate only where necessary to prevent further damage to the integrity of the judicial process (that is, Crown misconduct does not necessarily vitiate the criminal justice process and justify termination of the proceedings).

## 1) Policy and Guidelines

In most of the areas of prosecutorial discretion identified above, the *Criminal Code* provides no guidelines for the exercise of this power. However, in Canada and elsewhere in the Commonwealth, as well as in the United States, attorneys general have typically issued policy statements or directives that provide prosecutors with guidance. At the federal level in Canada, these policies and directives are set out in the FPS Deskbook and are intended "to assist prosecutors in the principled discharge of their prosecutorial duties while informing the public of the basis upon which prosecutorial discretion is exercised."[58] This is not to say, however, that the courts are bound by such guidelines. For instance, in *R. v. K.(M.)*,[59] the Department of Justice had adopted a policy of "zero-tolerance" in cases of domestic violence, and the accused was charged with assaulting his son. The Manitoba Court of Appeal held that this policy position regarding charging was subject to judicial review and was objectionable because it nullified prosecutorial discretion. In *R. v. Catagas*,[60] the same appeal court similarly accepted that the Crown has the ability, in the exercise of prosecutorial discretion, to stay proceedings in an individual case but has no right to dispense with the application of a statute in favour of a particular group or race. The Crown policy was subject to judicial intervention because a dispensing power was automatically applied in favour of a particular group.

Though our courts have not intervened to lay down detailed rules governing the exercise of a prosecutor's discretionary power,[61] excep-

---

57   See *Power*, above note 8; *R. v. O'Connor*, [1995] 4 S.C.R. 411; and *Canada (Minister of Citizenship and Immigration) v. Tobiass*, [1997] 3 S.C.R. 391 at 427 [*Tobiass*].

58   *Supra*, Part I, chap. 9.

59   (1992), 74 C.C.C. (3d) 108 (Man. C.A.).

60   (1977), 38 C.C.C. (2d) 296 (Man. C.A.).

61   In *Power*, above note 7, reference was made to *United States v. Redondo-Lemos*, 955 F.2d 1296 at 1299 (9th Cir. 1992), in which Kozinski J. observed that "even were it able to collect, understand and balance all of these factors, a court would find it nearly impossible to lay down guidelines to be followed by prosecutors in future cases."

tionally they have done so with respect to disclosure, beginning with the landmark decision in R. v. *Stinchcombe*.[62] Prior to *Stinchcombe*, prosecutors in some Canadian jurisdictions enjoyed close to an absolute discretion concerning whether information under their control should be disclosed to the defence. In *Stinchcombe*, the Supreme Court of Canada set out guidelines for Crown disclosure. What had been primarily an ethical obligation thus assumed legal and constitutional elements. The components of the disclosure obligation are analysed further below in section D.

The need for policies and guidelines to help prosecutors discharge their responsibilities is undisputed. However, these aids may only incidentally serve as ethical standards, and are not necessarily commensurate with rules of professional conduct. For instance, in the chapter on the "Decision to Prosecute," the FPS Deskbook sets out the main criteria that Crown counsel must consider when deciding whether to proceed with charges. After setting out the factors that must be taken into consideration by the prosecutor in exercising the discretion to prosecute, the Deskbook points out that this decision cannot be influenced by personal feelings, possible political advantage, disadvantage to the government, or the possible effect on the career of the prosecutor. It must also not be based on race, national or ethnic origin, colour, religion, sex, or other grounds of discrimination. These criteria are based on high standards that, on the one hand, are consistent with the Crown's primary duty as minister of justice and, on the other, leave to the particular decision maker an amount of latitude to exercise discretion. Within these boundaries, the prosecutor exercises an unfettered discretion. Yet the ethical propriety of the prosecutor's decision to prosecute is not necessarily in issue just because an administrative guideline has not been respected. It is also possible that compliance with an administrative guideline does not, without more, guarantee ethical behaviour.

# D. PROSECUTORIAL DISCLOSURE

In 1969 Brian A. Grosman, in his book *The Prosecutor: An Inquiry Into the Exercise of Discretion*,[63] denounced the lack of transparency, consistency, and coherence on the part of the Crown in making (or not

---

62    Above note 1.
63    B. Grosman, *The Prosecutor: An Inquiry Into the Exercise of Discretion* (Toronto: University of Toronto Press, 1969).

making, depending on the case) pre-trial disclosure. At that time, no legislative provisions in Canada required complete disclosure by the prosecution before trial, and there was no duty placed upon the police or prosecution to open their files to an accused. Grosman's study concluded that prosecutors frequently viewed pre-trial disclosure as a favour exchanged with certain defence lawyers. By 1977, the situation had not changed appreciably, leading Stanley Cohen to wonder whether the Crown's attitude towards disclosure had not become "truly anathema to the rule of law."[64]

In the intervening years, however, a new CBA Code was adopted, in 1974 to be exact. This Code provided that a prosecutor "should make timely disclosure to the accused or his counsel of all relevant facts and witnesses known to him, whether tending towards guilt or innocence."[65] It was on the basis of this ethical rule that in *Bledsoe* v. *Law Society of British Columbia*,[66] the Court of Appeal upheld a verdict of guilty rendered by the professional discipline committee against a lawyer who, as a prosecutor in a 1977 murder case, had deliberately not advised defence counsel in a timely manner of the existence of witnesses favourable to the defence. The ethical rule as articulated in *Bledsoe* was clearly a forerunner to the constitutional obligation later recognized in *Stinchcombe*.

This is not to deny that in the 1980s many prosecutors co-operated with defence counsel in making disclosure available on a voluntary basis.[67] But such practice varied from one province to another and also depended on the nature of the case and the individual prosecutor involved. Then came the 1991 judgment of the Supreme Court of Canada in *R.* v. *Stinchcombe*. As already mentioned, *Stinchcombe* added a legal and constitutional dimension to the ethical component of the duty to disclose. In the sections immediately following, we will begin by providing an overview of the current law on disclosure, focusing on the basic constitutional principles that lay the foundation for the

---

64   S. Cohen, *Due Process of Law: The Canadian System of Criminal Justice* (Toronto: Carswell, 1977) at 139.

65   CBA Code ch. VIII, comm. 7. In contrast, the current edition of the FPS Deskbook provides no specific ethical guidelines pertaining to disclosure obligations, perhaps because the area is now so well-developed by the courts.

66   (1984), 13 C.C.C. (3d) 560 (B.C.C.A.) [*Bledsoe*].

67   This rather haphazard approach was acknowledged in Law Reform Commission, *Disclosure by the Prosecution* (Report No. 22) (Ottawa: Minister of Supplies and Services Canada, 1984).

resulting ethical duties, before moving on to look at the ethical duties themselves.[68]

## 1) The Crown Disclosure Obligation after *Stinchcombe*

It is now well settled, not only that the Crown has an obligation to disclose, as provided by *Stinchcombe* in reference to the right to make full answer and defence enshrined in section 7 of the *Canadian Charter of Rights and Freedoms*, but also that the accused enjoys a discrete constitutional right to disclosure.[69] The Crown's failure to disclose can therefore constitute an independent breach of the accused's constitutional rights. As to the scope of this duty, the Crown must disclose to the defence all relevant information under its control, whether inculpatory or exculpatory, regardless of whether the information pertains to evidence that the Crown intends to adduce at trial. A discretion is left to the Crown on certain issues.[70] For instance, the timing and manner of disclosure remain a matter of discretion, subject to review by the courts. Also, the Crown has some leeway in excluding what is clearly irrelevant, withholding the identity of a person to afford protection from harassment or injury, and enforcing a legal privilege.

Because the Crown's obligation to disclose is a continuing one,[71] new information may have to be provided to defence counsel during the trial, and sometimes even after conviction. Thus, the expression "pre-trial disclosure," often used before *Stinchcombe*, is a less than totally accurate reflection of the real scope of the disclosure. Moreover, though the obligation prevails for any material in the possession of the Crown, the courts have also held that the Crown has a duty to obtain from the police all relevant information.[72] These aspects of the disclosure obligation flow naturally from the overarching principle that lies at the obligation's core, namely, that "the fruits of the investigation

---

68   For useful syntheses on the law on disclosure, see F. Iacobucci, "Crown Disclosure Since *Stinchcombe*" (1998) National Criminal Law Program, Federation of Law Societies of Canada; and S. Chapman, "Prosecutorial Disclosure" (1997) National Criminal Law Program, Federation of Law Societies of Canada. Note that Crown counsel may also be required to make disclosure or provide notice under the particular terms of a statute: see, for example, *R. v. Dumont* (2000), 149 C.C.C. (3d) 568 (Ont. C.A.).

69   *R. v. La*, [1997] 2 S.C.R. 680 at 692 [*La*].

70   See *Stinchcombe*, above note 1; and *R. v. Egger*, [1993] 2 S.C.R. 451 at 466–67 [*Egger*].

71   See *R. v. Chaplin*, [1995] 1 S.C.R. 727 [*Chaplin*].

72   See *R. v. O'Grady* (1995), 64 B.C.A.C. 111 (C.A.); *R. v. S.(S.E.)* (1992), 100 Sask. R. 110 (C.A.); and *R. v. Gagné* (1998), 131 C.C.C. (3d) 444 (Que. C.A.).

which are in the possession of counsel for the Crown are not the property of the Crown for use in securing a conviction but the property of the public to be used to ensure that justice is done."[73] This central principle is closely aligned with the Crown's ethical duty, in the role of minister of justice, to seek justice in the public interest.

## 2) The Ethical Components of Crown Disclosure

The nature of the legal and constitutional disclosure obligations incumbent on the Crown perfectly reflects the duality of the prosecutor's role. The parameters set by the courts require the prosecutor to be, more than just an advocate, a minister of justice who has a responsibility to see that the accused is treated fairly with respect to the ability to make full answer and defence. In *R. v. Chaplin*,[74] the Supreme Court of Canada held that the Crown obligation to disclose all relevant and non-privileged evidence, whether favourable or unfavourable to the accused, requires that the Crown exercise the utmost good faith in determining which information must be disclosed and in providing ongoing disclosure.[75] The Court added that departures from these obligations "are treated as serious breaches of professional ethics."[76] In this particular context, it would be prudent for Crown counsel to adopt the advice that "if in doubt, give it out."[77]

Inherent in the obligation to disclose is the duty to preserve the fruits of the investigation.[78] In cases where evidence is lost, the Crown will have to show that the loss or destruction is not owing to unacceptable negligence. Whether reasonable steps have been taken will, in many cases, require the Crown to show good faith. Needless to say, a knowing participation in the destruction of evidence, or even failure by a prosecutor to inform the court of his or her knowledge that the police have destroyed relevant materials, could constitute a serious breach of ethics.[79]

---

73   *Stinchcombe*, above note 1.
74   Above note 71.
75   *Ibid.* at 739.
76   *Ibid.*
77   J. McMahon, "Crown Disclosure Obligations — If in Doubt, Give it Out" (2000), National Criminal Law Program, Federation of Law Societies of Canada,, referring to the principle stated in *Stinchcombe* that the Crown should err on the side of inclusion.
78   See *Egger*, above note 70 at 472; and *La*, above note 66 at 689.
79   *R. v. Innocente* (2000), 183 N.S.R. (2d) 1 (S.C.).

The ethical duties underlying Crown disclosure were reiterated in the 1999 Report of the Criminal Justice Review Committee of Ontario. The Committee framed these duties as follows: it is a serious disciplinary offence for the Crown to fail to disclose to the defence as required; it is inappropriate for Crown counsel to limit or refuse disclosure in a case, contingent upon defence counsel agreeing to limit a preliminary inquiry in order to ensure efficient use of court time (this does not preclude counsel from agreeing to shorten or waive a preliminary inquiry); and it is inappropriate for the attorney general to withhold disclosure, contingent upon defence counsel providing an undertaking not to share the information with the client.[80]

The ABA Prosecution Standards state that it is unprofessional conduct to "intentionally fail to make timely disclosure to the defence" and to "fail to make a reasonably diligent effort to comply with a legally proper discovery request."[81] Additionally, the Standards suggest that "a prosecutor should not intentionally avoid pursuit of evidence because he or she believes it will damage the prosecution's case or aid the accused."[82] This latter ethical duty is especially interesting. It means that, just as it is unprofessional for defence counsel to adopt the tactic of remaining intentionally ignorant of relevant facts known to the accused in order to avoid ethical restrictions in conducting the client's defence,[83] so it is improper for the prosecutor to engage in a comparable tactic regarding disclosure. The duty of the prosecutor in the United States is thus to acquire all the relevant evidence regardless of potential impact on the success of the prosecution.[84] American prosecutors are not, however, obliged as a matter of course to conduct investigations specifically designed to collect exculpatory evidence.[85]

Granted, the American prosecutor takes more initiatives at the investigatory stage than do Crown counsel in Canada, a situation perhaps warranting especially strong ethical rules to ensure good faith in

---

80    See Ontario, Criminal Justice Review Committee, *Report of the Criminal Justice Review Committee* (Toronto: Queen's Printer, 1999) (Co-Chairs: H. Locke, J.D. Evans, & M. Segal) Recommendations 30–32.

81    ABA Prosecution Standard §3-3.11.

82    *Ibid.* Standard 3-3.11 is virtually identical to that imposed by ABA Model Rule 3.8(d) and ABA Model Code DR 7-103(B).

83    See section F(4), "Advoidance Techniques Restricting Client-Lawyer Communications, Wilful Blindness, Woodshedding, and Viewing Guilt as Completely Irrelevant," in chapter 1, and section F(1), "Acquiring Knowledge that the Client Intends to Commit Perjury," in chapter 7.

84    See ABA Prosecution Standard §4-3.2(b).

85    J. Hall, Jr., *Professional Responsibility of the Criminal Lawyer*, 2d ed. (New York: Clark Boardman Callaghan, 1996) at 420.

the performance of the prosecutor's dual role. But in our system, a prosecutor may decide to request a supplementary investigation from the police when certain elements of the evidence need clarification. If the investigation uncovers evidence that may weaken the prosecution's case, such evidence must be disclosed. Moreover, if the Crown obtains information that points to the existence of exculpatory material, wilful blindness is not an option. Crown counsel must conduct further investigation, and at the least he or she should promptly inform the defence of the development. Of course, disclosure to the defence may be delayed if revelation would jeopardize an ongoing investigation.[86] While such delay is likely not necessary in the case of exculpatory evidence, each case must be approached on its particular facts.

It is worth underlining that not every breach of the legal and constitutional duty to disclose constitutes a violation of an ethical duty. Non-disclosure can result, for instance, from mere inadvertence, a misunderstanding of the nature of the evidence, or even a questionable strategy adopted in good faith.[87] These lapses may represent a denial of the accused's constitutional rights, but an ethical violation often requires more. A finding of professional misconduct must be based upon an act or omission revealing an intentional departure from the fundamental duty to act in fairness.[88] Thus, a judicial determination that disclosure has wrongfully been withheld will not necessarily reveal a breach of ethics. Conversely, an egregious breach of ethics may in some cases have no appreciable effect on the fairness of the trial, when appropriate remedies can cure any harm suffered by the accused.[89] From an ethical point of view, the issue bears as much upon the conduct and knowledge of the Crown lawyer as on the resulting impact upon the trial process. A prosecutor's ethical delict becomes more serious where he or she knowingly causes significant harm to the accused. Yet a prosecutor cannot be excused for unacceptable misconduct with respect to disclosure simply because the failure did not have a serious impact on the trial. On the other hand, ethical misconduct is not always dependent upon a finding that the Crown violated the accused's right to disclosure.

This potential distinction between the ethical duty and the legal/constitutional duty finds support in the wording employed by the rules of professional conduct and associated commentary in Alberta.

---

86  See *Stinchcombe*, above note 1 at 336.
87  See *R. v. Ford* (1993), 78 C.C.C. (3d) 481 (B.C.C.A.) [*Ford*].
88  See *Bledsoe*, above note 66.
89  See *Tobiass*, above note 57 at 428.

Rule 28(d) of the Law Society of Alberta's Code of Professional Conduct provides that prosecutors "must make timely disclosure to the accused or defence counsel (or to the court if the accused is not represented) of all known relevant facts and witnesses, whether tending towards guilt or innocence." The Commentary to this rule makes clear that the ethical dictate is not intended to establish general government policy or to interfere with the proper exercise of prosecutorial discretion. "Rather, the Law Society's scrutiny of conduct involving an exercise of discretion will be limited to circumstances in which the discretion was exercised dishonestly or in bad faith."[90]

However, drawing too sharp a distinction between the general government policy and a governing body's ethical guidelines can lead to difficult cases, and dubious results. In *Krieger* v. *Law Society of Alberta*, the judge of first instance held that the Law Society of Alberta had jurisdiction to initiate disciplinary proceedings against a Crown prosecutor insofar as the proceedings related to issues of dishonesty or bad faith.[91] But on appeal, the Alberta Court of Appeal held that Law Society cannot proceed with a complaint, regardless of a *prima facie* case of bad faith, where to do so necessarily requires undertaking a review of the attorney general's decision on the matter. On the facts in *Krieger*, the attorney general had determined that the conduct of the prosecutor did not involve any dishonesty or bad faith, and therefore the Law Society was barred from addressing the same issue in disciplinary proceedings.[92]

The court in *Krieger* succinctly stated the rationale for its approach, derived from the principle of prosecutorial independence: "The Law Society has no authority to conduct a review of a decision of the attorney general," said the court, "because it has no jurisdiction over the Crown as an entity or over the office of attorney general."[93] The Court of Appeal conceded that the Law Society has jurisdiction to examine the conduct of prosecutors *qua* lawyers, thus making a prosecutor accountable if he or she exercised a discretion dishonestly or in bad faith, but only where the attorney general had not already exoner-

---

90   Alta. ch. 10, comm. 28.
91   *Krieger* v. *Law Society of Alberta* (1997), 149 D.L.R. (4th) 92 (Alta. Q.B.) [*Krieger* (Q.B.)].
92   *Krieger* v. *Law Society of Alberta* (2000), 191 D.L.R. (4th) 600 at 614 (Alta. C.A.).
93   *Krieger* (Q.B.), above note 91 at 114.

ated the prosecutor.[94] To put the matter another way, the Law Society in Alberta was bound by the finding of the attorney general's office that the prosecutor did not act dishonestly or in bad faith.

This degree of deference to the attorney general risks becoming a total prohibition against governing bodies regulating the conduct of prosecutors. After all, what is to stop the attorney general from issuing a summary determination of good faith in all cases where the actions of a prosecutor are challenged, simply to defeat the governing body's jurisdiction? Conversely, does it make sense that the Law Society would have kept jurisdiction if, contrary to the facts in *Krieger*, the attorney general came to no conclusion on the matter? One also has to wonder whether, in light of *Krieger*, the Attorney General in Alberta could formulate detailed ethical standards and then argue that these standards represent an exercise of discretion and independence that totally supplants the Law Society's ethical rules.[95]

## 3) Disclosure and Plea Discussions

It is worth examining the particular application of the prosecutor's ethical obligations regarding disclosure in the context of plea discussions. The obligation to make disclosure is most often described in terms of the duty to disclose all evidence that may assist the accused at trial. But what of information that is relevant primarily in relation to plea discussions?

Let us assume, for example, that the Crown has made full disclosure in the normal fashion and that plea discussions are now under way. In conducting plea discussions, the prosecutor is obviously bound by the prohibition against acting in bad faith or misleading defence counsel.[96] As the ABA Prosecution Standards observe, "truth is required in the presentation of facts, whether or not they are mitigating facts."[97] But more than this, the Crown's ethical duty to act fairly, and to assist the defence where necessary to ensure that justice is done, bears heavily upon disclosure obligations. The CBA Code implicitly refers to the need for full disclosure of matters affecting plea discus-

---

94   See also *Hoem* v. *Law Society of British Columbia* (1985), 20 C.C.C. (3d) 239 (B.C.C.A.) (holding that the professional governing body has no power to review Crown counsel's decision whether to lay or proceed with a charge).

95   These issues may soon be addressed by the Supreme Court of Canada, as the Court has granted leave to appeal in *Kreiger*: see *Kreiger* v. *Law Society of Alberta*, [2000] S.C.C.A. No. 598 (S.C.C.).

96   See section R, "Duty to Act Fairly Respecting the Crown," in chapter 8.

97   See ABA Prosecution Standard §3-4.1 (commentary).

sions, stating that a Crown lawyer must ". . . make timely disclosure to the accused or defence counsel (or to the court if the accused is not represented) of all relevant facts and known witnesses, whether tending to show guilt or innocence, or *that would affect the punishment of the accused.*"[98] Contrast this language with the more direct, yet narrower, position taken by the ABA Prosecution Standards. The Standards prohibit prosecutors from making false representations in the course of plea discussions, but do not require disclosure of exculpatory evidence at this stage. The Commentary to Standard 3–4.1 opines that "although the prosecutor is under no obligation to reveal any evidence to the defence counsel in the course of plea discussions," if facts are presented, they must be truthful.[99] This statement of principle does not meet Canadian constitutional requirements, and given the wording of the CBA Code, probably falls short of our governing bodies' ethical standards as well.

Let us consider the issue in more detail through the examination of a hypothetical problem. In the course of the plea discussions, the prosecutor learns that the star Crown witness has just testified in another proceeding, in a different country, and has contradicted testimony previously given at the preliminary hearing in Canada. The prosecutor is almost certain that counsel for the accused is not aware of this development. Is disclosure required during the plea discussions? One could conceivably argue that the CBA Code does not mandate disclosure, for the information would not "affect the punishment of the accused." Even if one accepts this interpretation, which is rather narrow and unsatisfactory, disclosure surely remains an ongoing obligation up until the point where the matter has definitively concluded. Certainly, if a plea of guilty has not yet been registered, it seems to us that disclosure must be made in our hypothetical scenario, because a substantial inconsistency provided under oath is relevant to the witness's credibility. Disclosure may weaken the prosecutor's case and convince the accused to withdraw from the plea discussions or insist upon a more favourable resolution, but such a result is commensurate with the Crown's overriding duty to seek justice.

Let us take another example. Suppose that the prosecutor, during plea discussions, fails to reveal to defence counsel the death of the victim who is the main witness. The witness did not testify at a preliminary inquiry or provide a sworn video statement. If the accused eventually pleads guilty, can he or she later complain that the prose-

---

98   CBA Code ch. IX, comm. 9 (emphasis added).
99   ABA Prosecution Standard §3-4.1 (commentary).

cutor misled defence counsel by not making disclosure of this information, and seek to vitiate the plea? Developing our hypothetical example more specifically, assume that the two lawyers have reached an agreement on the sentence, but a few days before the date set for entering the plea, Crown counsel learns that the witness has died. Must the Crown make disclosure? Again, if we apply a narrow interpretation of the CBA Code, it could arguably be said that this piece of information does not "affect the punishment of the accused." Yet we prefer to view this information as falling within the ambit of the ethical duty to disclose. The information *does* effect the accused's potential punishment, and his or her adherence to the plea bargain, because knowledge of the death will likely lead the accused to withdraw consent to the bargain.

The contrary approach is taken in *People v. Jones*, a 1978 decision of the New York Court of Appeals.[100] The court found no denial of due process where the prosecutor failed to disclose that the complaining witness in a robbery prosecution had died four days before a plea was entered. The court held that this circumstance would not have "constituted exculpatory evidence, i.e., evidence favourable to an accused where the evidence is material either to guilt or to punishment."[101] Furthermore, the court noted that there is no duty to disclose "non evidentiary information pertinent to the tactical aspects of a defendant's determination not to proceed to trial."[102] No prosecutor is obliged to "share his appraisal of the weaknesses of his own case (as opposed to specific exculpatory evidence) with defence counsel."[103] This was not an instance of a positive misstatement or misrepresentation, and the court observed that "silence should give rise to legal consequences only if it may be concluded that the one who was silent was under an affirmative duty to speak."[104] This statement is consistent with ABA Prosecution Standard 3-4.1, noted above, which does not require disclosure of exculpatory evidence at the plea discussion stage.

We believe that the approach taken in *People v. Jones* is not consistent with the Canadian tradition of prosecutorial ethics. Even before *Stinchcombe*, in a panel discussion held in Toronto in 1990, participants expressed views that left no doubt as to the proper conclusion: if the Crown knows that an essential witness is dead, and the case can no

---

100  *People v. Jones*, 44 N.Y.2d. 76 (1978) [*Jones*], cert. denied 439 U.S. 846 (1978).
101  *Jones, ibid.* at 87.
102  *Ibid.* at 88.
103  *Ibid.* at 88.
104  *Ibid.* at 88.

longer be proved, the Crown has a duty not only to make disclosure but to go further and to stay the case.[105] This approach is solidified by the subsequent decision in *Stinchcombe*. Since disclosure remains an ongoing obligation, and plea discussions are undertaken by defence counsel on the assumption that the Crown can prove its case, any substantial impediment in the Crown's case must be disclosed to the defence.[106]

## 4) Disclosure at Sentencing

It follows from the above discussion, and in particular the wording of the CBA Code, that consistent with the *Stinchcombe* rationale and the general duty to act fairly, a prosecutor is bound to inform the accused of all relevant evidence that could mitigate the punishment. This uncontentious position is elaborated upon in the ABA Prosecution Standards, which endorse the following guidelines:

> (a) The prosecutor should assist the court in basing its sentence on complete and accurate information for use in the presentence report. The prosecutor should disclose to the court any information in the prosecutor's files relevant to the sentence. If incompleteness or inaccurateness in the presentence report comes to the prosecutor's attention, the prosecutor should take steps to present the complete and correct information to the court and to defense counsel.
>
> (b) The prosecutor should disclose to the defense and to the court at or prior to the sentencing proceeding all unprivileged mitigating information known to the prosecutor, except when the prosecutor is relieved of this responsibility by a protective order of the tribunal.[107]

---

105 See especially the comments by Richard Peck, at the Criminal Lawyers' Association Annual Convention and Education Programme, Toronto, 20 October 1990 [*CLA Annual Convention*]. The other panellists were Frank Marrocco, Mr. Justice G.A. Martin, Mr. Justice Morris Fish, Saul Froomkin, and Robert Car Counselter.

106 "Crown counsel's obligation to disclose is a continuing one and disclosure of additional relevant information must be made when it is received": Ontario, Attorney General's Advisory Committee, *Report of the Attorney General's Advisory Committee on Charge Screening, Disclosure, and Resolution Discussion* (Toronto: Queen's Printer, 1993) (Chair: G. Arthur Martin), Purpose and General Principles of Disclosure #5 [*Martin Committee Report*].

107 ABA Prosecution Standard §3–6.2.

# E.  ETHICAL RESTRAINTS ON ADVOCACY

As stated above, the distinctive feature of the prosecutor's role as advocate is a tempered zealousness, characterized by the restraining general duty to seek justice, not convictions. Such restraint need not necessarily impede the prosecutor's efficiency in conducting the Crown case or in practising the art of persuasion. A prosecutor "can be powerful and determined without being unethical or unfair,"[108] and the obligation to act fairly does not mean that the prosecutor is "compelled to avoid advocacy."[109] As Mr. Justice Binnie stated in *R. v. Rose*, "while Crown counsels are expected to be ethical, they are also expected to be adversarial."[110] It becomes imperative to explore the difficulties that a prosecutor can face in the exercise of the adversarial function.

## 1)  Guidelines Provided by Rules of Professional Conduct and The FPS Deskbook

The FPS Deskbook contains a number of guidelines that bear upon the prosecutor's role as advocate. Culling these from the review conducted above in section B(3), we can focus in particular upon the following dictates:

The duty to act with integrity and dignity:

1.  By exercising careful judgment in determining the case to be presented for the Crown, what witnesses to call, and what evidence to tender.
2.  By acting with moderation, fairness, and impartiality

The duty to be fair and to appear to be fair:

1.  By not expressing personal opinions on the evidence, including the credibility of witnesses, in court or in public.
2.  By not expressing personal opinions on the guilt or innocence of the accused in court or in public.
3.  By asking relevant and proper questions during the examination of a witness and by not asking questions designed solely

---

108 J. Dangerfield, "Ethical Problems for Crown Attorneys" (1992) National Criminal Law Program, Federation of Law Societies of Canada.
109 Pannick, above note 40 at 115.
110 *R. v. Rose* (1990), 129 C.C.C. (3d) 449 at 463 (S.C.C.) [*Rose (S.C.C.)*]. See also *Jolivet*, above note 21 at 765, where Binnie J. similarly states that Crown counsel "is entitled to have a trial strategy and to modify it as the trial unfolds, provided that the modification does not result in unfairness to the accused."

to embarrass, insult, abuse, belittle, or demean the witness. Cross-examination can be skilful and probing, yet still show respect for the witness.

4.  By respecting the court and the proceedings while vigorously asserting the Crown's position.[111]

The CBA Code of Professional Conduct speaks of the role of the advocate in general terms, applicable to all counsel, as follows: "When acting as an advocate, the lawyer must treat the tribunal with courtesy and respect and must represent the client resolutely, honourably and within the limits of the law."[112] Presumably, the general guidelines set out respecting all counsel define the advocate's duty for lawyers who act for the Crown. That is to say, in acting as advocate, the prosecutor is not to seek to convict but rather must see that justice is done through a fair trial upon the merits, and must act fairly and dispassionately.[113]

The ABA Prosecution Standards are especially detailed regarding the prosecutor's ethical approach to advocacy, and state:

### Standard 3–5.7 Examination of Witnesses

(a) The interrogation of all witnesses should be conducted fairly, objectively, and with due regard for the dignity and legitimate privacy of the witnesses, and without seeking to intimidate or humiliate the witness unnecessarily.

(b) The prosecutor's belief that the witness is telling the truth does not preclude cross-examination, but may affect the method and scope of cross-examination to discredit or undermine a witness if the prosecutor knows the witness is testifying truthfully.

(c) A prosecutor should not call a witness in the presence of the jury who the prosecutor knows will claim a valid privilege not to testify.

(d) A prosecutor should not ask a question which implies the existence of a factual predicate for which a good faith belief is lacking.

### Standard 3–5.8 Argument to the Jury

(a) In closing argument to the jury, the prosecutor may argue all reasonable inferences from evidence in the record. The prosecutor should not intentionally misstate the evidence or mislead the jury as to the inferences it may draw.

---

111  *FPS Deskbook*, above note 30, §9.3.1, §9.3.3.
112  CBA Code ch. IX.
113  See CBA Code ch. IX, comm. 7.

(b) The prosecutor should not express his or her personal belief or opinion as to the truth or falsity of any testimony or evidence or the guilt of the defendant.

(c) The prosecutor should not make arguments calculated to appeal to the prejudices of the jury.

(d) The prosecutor should refrain from argument which would divert the jury from its duty to decide the case on the evidence.

## 2) Bail Hearings

In *R. v. Brooks*,[114] Mr. Justice Hill offered the following observations regarding Crown counsel's obligations concerning bail hearings:

> Crown counsel are expected to exercise discretion to consent to bail in appropriate cases and to oppose release where justified. That discretion must be informed, fairly exercised, and respectful of prevailing jurisprudential authorities. Opposing bail in every case, or without exception where a particular crime is charged, or because of a victim's wishes without regard to individual liberty concerns of the arrestee, derogates from the prosecutor's role as a minister of justice and as a guardian of the civil rights of all persons.

> Because the police and the prosecution have significant discretion to exercise respecting the release of accused persons, the administration of criminal justice logically expects that these parties will not simply dump all bail decisions into contested hearings before the courts. Not only does this serve to choke the operation of the bail courts but, as said, the statutory and constitutional regime demands otherwise.

> In those instances where a show cause hearing is reasonably justified, and an adjournment is not requested, all parties should be prepared to proceed with witnesses available and properly admissible evidence. In turn, the court is expected to conduct a judicious hearing applying the statutory and judge-made standards necessary to ensure a fair hearing.[115]

These sentiments reflect the basic duties of Crown counsel in exercising prosecutorial discretion. Quite obviously, the bail context does not permit for a relaxed standard of Crown conduct. Thus, a prosecutor cannot be overly adversarial at bail proceedings, at least not where the result would be to derogate from the overall interests of justice.

---

114 (2001), 153 C.C.C. (3d) 533 (Ont. S.C.J.).
115 *Ibid.* at 543.

## 3) Jury Selection

The Crown prosecutor cannot dispense with the public interest and violate fundamental principles of justice in the jury selection process. Seeking to exclude individuals from the jury on the basis of race or ethnicity is especially pernicious. This point is made in R. v. *Gayle*,[116] where Mr. Justice Sharpe reviewed the law on point and concluded:

> In my view, it follows from the *quasi*-judicial nature of the Crown's discretionary powers and from the overriding values of the *Charter* that there are circumstances where a court will review and constrain the exercise of the Crown's right of peremptory challenge. It seems to me that if the exercise of the power is at odds with the *quasi*-judicial nature of the Crown's duty, or at odds with the basic rights and freedoms guaranteed by the *Charter*, a court can and should intervene as has been done in relation to other discretionary Crown powers: see R. v. *Pizzacalla* (1991), 69 C.C.C. (3d) 115 (Ont. C.A.). In particular, it is my view that public confidence in the administration of justice would be seriously undermined if Crown counsel were permitted to exercise the power of peremptory challenge on racial or ethnic grounds. The rationale for peremptory challenges is to foster confidence in the fairness and impartiality of jury trials. The Crown should not be permitted to subvert that rationale by using peremptory challenges to achieve precisely the opposite result.[117]

On the facts of *Gayle*, the Court held that the appellant failed to make out a case that the trial Crown had improperly utilized the peremptory challenge power.[118]

## 4)  Opening Statement and Closing Address to the Jury

In Canada, contrary to the United States, an improper opening statement rarely occurs. Prosecutors seem more inclined to respect the narrow purpose and scope of the opening statement, which is used to state the evidence expected during the trial and to acquaint jury members with the matters upon which they are to pass judgment.

Any doubt as to the impact that an opening statement can have on the trial process has been dispelled by the recent judgment of the Supreme Court of Canada in R. v. *Jolivet*.[119] In the opening address,

---

116 Above note 14.
117 *Ibid.* at 252.
118 *Ibid.* at 252–53.
119 Above note 21.

Crown counsel mentioned that he would call witness "B" to corroborate the main prosecution witness, who was an informer. Subsequently, however, he advised that witness "B" would no longer be called. The Supreme Court held that any unfairness created by the Crown's change of position, and the trial judge's refusal to allow defence counsel to attack the change in closing submissions, did not warrant a new trial. Nevertheless, *Jolivet* should serve to remind prosecutors of the significance that may attach to an apparently inoffensive opening statement, owing to later unforeseen events.

More serious problems are likely to arise out of a prosecutor's closing address to the jury. Since *R. v. Boucher*,[120] decided almost fifty years ago, courts have expressed in the strongest terms their disapproval of inflammatory or irregular summations given by prosecutors, mainly because of the serious consequences for the fairness of the trial and the criminal justice system as a whole. Often, a new trial has been held to be the only remedy to correct the injustice. As long ago as 1963, in *R. v. Tremblay*, Owen J.A. wrote that "enough has been written to demonstrate that there must be a new trial by reason of the actions [here an inflammatory speech] of the Crown prosecutor. By the time the presiding judge addressed the jury the damage had been done."[121] The Ontario Court of Appeal intervened in several recent cases because of improprieties exhibited in Crown counsel's closing address, reiterating that "unless and until Crown counsel stop this kind of improper and prejudicial conduct, this Court will regrettably have to remit difficult and sensitive cases of this nature back for a new trial at great expense to the emotional well-being of the parties, not to mention the added burden to the administration of justice."[122]

### a)    Inflammatory Language and Tone

Inflammatory speeches must be avoided. Addresses that are calculated to appeal to the emotions of the jury instead of reason and common sense are unethical.[123] Thus, prosecutors must not launch diatribes

---

120  Above note 12.
121  *R. v. Tremblay* (1963), 40 C.R. 303 at 309 (Que. Q.B.).
122  *R. v. F.(A.)* (1996), 30 O.R. (3d) 470 at 472 (Ont. C.A.). See also *R. v. S.(F.)* (2000), 144 C.C.C. (3d) 466 (Ont. C.A.) [*S.(F.)*]; *Robinson*, above note 6; and *Rose* (Ont. C.A.), above note 6.
123  *See R. v. Romeo* (1991), 62 C.C.C. (3d) 1 (S.C.C.) [*Romeo*]; *R. v. Kaufman* (2000), 151 C.C.C. (3d) 566 (Que. C.A.) [*Kaufman*]; *R. v. Moubarak*, [1982] C.A. 454 (Que. C.A.) [*Moubarak*]; *R. v. Charest* (1990), 57 C.C.C. (3d) 312 (Que. C.A.) [*Charest*]; *R. v. B.(R.B.)* (2001), 152 C.C.C. (3d) 437 (B.C.C.A.); *R.*

against the accused, be disrespectful and sarcastic,[124] employ invective,[125] or make wholly inappropriate and irrelevant remarks (such as comparing the defendant's group home to a Nazi death camp).[126]

## b)    Expressing a Personal Opinion

Neither Crown[127] nor defence counsel[128] is entitled to express a personal opinion about a witness, an issue or the case in general. First, counsel's personal opinion is not relevant. Second, such an opinion may contaminate the jury's reasoning, leading to a decision based on an assumed verification of facts that is extraneous to the evidence. Third, allowing an advocate to assert a personal belief puts the opponent who properly refrains from doing so at a disadvantage.[129] On the other hand, if both counsel express their personal opinion, one in response to the other, there is a risk that the one who is more renowned or more talented possesses an advantage.

This last point leads us to a related issue. Does it matter, from Crown counsel's perspective, that an inflammatory reply is preceded by defence counsel's own excesses? In Canada, if not necessarily in the United States, the answer must be in the negative.[130] Ethical duties do not recede in proportion to the improprieties of opposing counsel. On this point, David Pannick criticizes the American doctrine of "justified response," which uses a rather simplistic "tit for tat" reasoning to discount the ethical duties ordinarily demanded of counsel:

> That defence counsel is also at fault is no excuse whatsoever for misbehaviour by the prosecution to the detriment of the unfortunate defendant: the impediment to a fair trial caused by the prosecutor introducing his personal opinions is the same whether or not he was

---

v. *Ballony-Reeder* (2001), 153 C.C.C. (3d) 511 (B.C.C.A.); and *R.* v. *C.(R.)* (1999), 137 C.C.C. (3d) 87 (B.C.C.A.).

124   See *R.* v. *Dupuis* (1967), 3 C.R.N.S. 75 at 83 (Que. C.A.).

125   *Ibid.*; *S.(F.)*, above note 122 at 477.

126   See *R.* v. *Therrien*, [1990] A.Q. No. 921 (Que. C.A.) (QL).

127   See *Chambers*, above note 37 at 335: "There can be no doubt that it was improper for Crown counsel to express a personal opinion as to the veracity of the witnesses." See also *Robinson*, above note 6 at 417; and *Kaufman*, above note 123 at 573–74.

128   See *R.* v. *Finta* (1992), 73 C.C.C. (3d) 65 (Ont. C.A.); and *Peruta,* above note 48.

129   See M. Orkin, *Legal Ethics: A Study of Professional Conduct* (Toronto: Cartwright, 1957) at 105; and E. Levy, "The Closing Address by Defence Counsel" (1992) National Criminal Law Program, Federation of Law Societies of Canada.

130   See *Peruta*, above note 48 at 375ff; and *R.* v. *Henderson* (1999), 134 C.C.C. (3d) 131 at 144 (Ont. C.A.) [*Henderson*].

provoked. If defence counsel impermissibly asserts the personal views of the advocates, the prosecuting counsel should explain to the jury that such opinions are irrelevant to the issue and that he will therefore keep his opinions to himself and will concentrate on presenting to the jury the case for the prosecution. It is essential for courts to control and punish the introduction by prosecuting counsel of their personal opinions of the guilt or innocence of defendants in criminal trials. There is an unacceptable risk that the jury will decide the case by reference to the opinion of the authoritative prosecuting counsel rather than on the evidence presented in court; defence counsel will be tempted, by way of rebuttal, to express their own view of their client's innocence; and any lawyer who, showing greater sensitivity and a finer appreciation of the true role of the advocate, does not wish to express a view may wrongly be thought by the jury to be a prosecutor who does not believe the defendant to be guilty or a defence attorney acting for a client whose innocence he doubts.[131]

To sum up, personal opinion tends to make the prosecutor's credibility and judgment an issue at trial. Naturally, such matters are irrelevant, and crossing the line represents unprofessional conduct. In this vein, in *R. v. Moubarak*, the Quebec Court of Appeal reproached Crown counsel for having stated in his closing address to the jury: that the police do not arrest the innocent but only the guilty; that he was personally convinced of the guilt of the accused; that a defence counsel's task is to make sure his client is acquitted, while Crown counsel has no case to win or lose; and that he could attest to the integrity of the police investigators.[132] Similarly, in *R. v. Boyko*, it was held to be irregular to express a personal opinion on the credibility of witnesses.[133] In *R. v. S.(F.)*, Crown trial counsel was reprimanded for telling the jury that he was an honest and just person, and adding that if the jury was not convinced of the appellant's guilt it was because he

---

131 Pannick, above note 40 at 118–19. This point is also made in *R. v. D.(C.)* (2000), 145 C.C.C. (3d) 290 at 318–19 (Ont. C.A.) [*D.(C.)*], where the court criticized Crown counsel for responding to a perceived impropriety by defence counsel with an inflammatory comment made to the jury. The proper course would have been to make an objection to the trial judge, and to seek a correcting direction from the court.

132 See *Moubarak*, above note 123.

133 *R. v. Boyko* (1975), 28 C.C.C. (2d) 193. See also *R. v. McDonald* (1958), 120 C.C.C. 209 at 222 (Ont. C.A.).

had failed to do his job successfully.[134] The Court of Appeal for Ontario overturned the conviction and ordered a new trial.

### c)   Alluding to Facts that are not Properly in Evidence

The ethical rule regarding facts not properly in evidence was recently stated in *R. v. Rose*, where the majority observed:

> [Crown] counsel should not advert to any unproven facts and cannot put before the jury as facts to be considered for conviction assertions in relation to which there is no evidence or which come from counsel's personal observations or experiences . . . . Crown counsel is duty bound during its jury address to remain true to the evidence, and must limit his or her means of persuasion to facts found in the evidence presented to the jury.[135]

Many other cases hold to the same effect. In *R. v. Clarke*, the prosecutor alluded to the possibility of reprisals by fellow inmates against a Crown witness, in an attempt to explain the witness's testimony, though no evidence had been led in this regard.[136] In *R. v. St-Laurent*, the Crown boldly suggested in the closing address that the evidence led to firm conclusions regarding the blood types of the accused and the victim, thus tending to prove the prosecution theory.[137] This supposition was mere speculation, and the Crown's brazen theory was ultimately discredited before the Court of Appeal by fresh evidence that directly addressed the factual issue. *R. v. Robinson* is a case where the Crown improperly urged the jury to use evidence of prior misconduct to infer that the accused was the type of person to commit the offence, even though character had not been put in issue.[138] Finally, in *R. v. Hay*, Crown counsel improperly and unfairly suggested that the accused and the registered owner of a car found to contain a large quantity of marijuana were one and the same person. In fact, the prosecutor was aware of evidence, not before the court, suggesting that the accused and registered owner were *not* the same person.[139] In all of

---

134  *S.(F.)*, above note 122 at 473.

135  *Rose (S.C.C.)*, above note 110 at 494. See also *Pisani* v. *R.* (1971), 1 C.C.C. (2d) 477 (S.C.C.) [*Pisani*]; *R. v. Munroe* (1995), 96 C.C.C. (3d) 431 (Ont. C.A.), aff'd [1995] 4 S.C.R. 53. For a case where the Crown's jury address was not held to be improper in this regard, see *R. v. Phillips* (2001), 154 C.C.C. (3d) 345 (Ont. C.A.).

136  *R. v. Clarke* (1981), 63 C.C.C. (2d) 224 (Alta. C.A.).

137  *R. v. St-Laurent* (1990), 57 C.C.C. (3d) 564 at 567 (Que. C.A.).

138  *Robinson*, above note 6.

139  *R. v. Hay* (1982), 70 C.C.C. (2d) 286 (Sask. C.A.) [*Hay*].

these cases, the courts disapproved of Crown counsel playing fast and loose with the rules of evidence by referring to information not properly before the trier of fact.

## d)   Discrediting the Legal System

In *R. v. Swietlinski*,[140] it was held to be unacceptable for a prosecutor conducting a parole eligibility hearing with a jury (under what is now section 745.6 of the *Criminal Code*) to urge the jurors not to make a decision in accordance with the law if they feel that the law is bad. The effect of Crown counsel's remarks to the jury was to imply that the procedure set out in the *Criminal Code* was unduly favourable to the applicant, and to urge the subversion of Parliament's intent regarding early parole. Addresses that support this sort of nullification of the law are at odds with the ethical duty to respect the rights of the accused and to strive to achieve justice in the public interest.

## e)   Conclusion: The Duty to Be Accurate and Dispassionate

In *R. v. Charest*,[141] Mr. Justice Fish wrote that "the Crown should press fully and firmly every legitimate argument tending to establish guilt, but must be 'accurate, fair and dispassionate in conducting the prosecution and in addressing the jury'."[142] This point was reiterated in *R. v. Rose*.[143] As Lori-Renée Weitzman, a Crown prosecutor in Montreal, has written:

> The duty of the Crown is to present its case in furtherance of the goal of seeking justice and not vengeance, and certainly not for the personal satisfaction of winning a case. An overzealous prosecutor, influenced by a desire to win a case, 'get' the accused or beat the defence is not performing her duty as an impartial officer of justice.[144]

Tempered advocacy, not unbridled partisanship, must guide the prosecutor's actions and words.

---

140  *R. v. Swietlinski*, [1994] 3 S.C.R. 481 at 497.
141  Above note 123.
142  *Ibid.* at 330 (quoting from *Pisani*, above note 135 at 478).
143  *Rose (S.C.C.)*, above note 110 at 494.
144  L.-R. Weitzman, "The Closing Address of the Prosecutor" (1998) National Criminal Law Program, Federation of Law Societies of Canada.

## 5) Examination of Witnesses

We can review the prosecutor's ethical obligations towards witnesses by studying, in turn, the examination-in-chief (or direct examination), cross-examination, and re-examination. The focus will be upon the ethical issues relating to the prosecutor's courtroom behaviour towards witnesses. In this respect, a distinction has to be made between rules that apply specifically to the prosecutor and those that concern all lawyers in the conduct of a trial. In the latter case, no consensus seems to prevail as to, for instance, which guidelines should be followed respecting communication with witnesses who are still giving evidence.[145] In Ontario, special rules have been adopted,[146] but some commentators have suggested that these rules are too stringent.[147] Moreover, neither the CBA Code nor any other provincial governing body has followed Ontario's path. In any event, rather than address the general rules pertaining to contact with witnesses during testimony, we intend to review those ethical principles applicable to the issue of examination of witnesses by prosecutors.

### a)   Direct Examination

A prosecutor must never forget the ethical limitations imposed on the examination of witnesses, which are more demanding than the basic restrictions imposed by the rules of evidence. He or she cannot subject witnesses to "degrading, demeaning or otherwise invasive or insulting questioning"[148] or, as the FPS Deskbook states, should not ask questions "designed solely to embarrass, insult, abuse, belittle, or demean the witness."[149] Nor should Crown counsel ignore the rules of evidence in conducting direct examination, for instance, by persistently asking leading questions on matters that are contentious.[150]

ABA Prosecution Standard 3-5.7(c) covers a slightly unusual issue, providing that "[a] prosecutor should not call a witness in the presence of the jury who the prosecutor knows will claim a valid privilege not to testify." The rationale behind this prohibition derives from the neg-

---

145   See, for example, *R. v. Montgomery* (1998), 126 C.C.C. (3d) 251 (B.C.S.C.).

146   See Ont. r. 4.04.

147   J. Sopinka, *The Trial of an Action* (Toronto: Butterworths, 1981) at 106ff; A. Mewett, *Witnesses* (Scarborough, Ont.: Carswell, 1991) at 6-5 & 6-6.

148   ABA Prosecution Standard §3–5.7 (commentary). This Standard also provides that the examination should be conducted "with due regard for the dignity and legitimate privacy of the witness."

149   *FPS Deskbook*, above note 30 at §9.3.3.

150   See *Rose* (S.C.C.), above note 110 at 233–34 & 234–38.

ative inference that can be drawn by the jury where a witness invokes a privilege. The prosecutor is therefore advised to canvass the matter first in a *voir dire*, outside the presence of the jury. Though these situations are more likely to occur in the United States, because of the privilege granted to many witnesses under the Fifth Amendment, relevant precedent exists in Canada. In R. v. *Fortin*, the Crown lawyer surprised defence counsel by calling the accused's former lawyer as a rebuttal witness.[151] The element of surprise apparently extended to the former lawyer himself, who, on initially being questioned in chief by the Crown, enquired in the presence of the jury whether the accused agreed to waive legal-professional privilege. The situation worsened when the trial judge, despite an objection from defence counsel, asked the accused outright if he waived the privilege. This judicial pressure left the accused with little choice but to waive privilege in the presence of the jury. On appeal, the Court of Appeal ruled that Crown counsel's behaviour in calling the witness undermined trial fairness, and a new trial was ordered.

## b)    Re-examination

In approaching re-examination, a prosecutor may be tempted to discuss the case privately with the witness. Cross-examination may have led to troubling responses. The witness, initially called by Crown counsel, will generally be cooperative in response to a friendly request for a chat. As we have mentioned, there is no firm consensus as to the proper ethical approach where a lawyer wishes to speak to his or her witness before re-examination. Nevertheless, the basic principles of fairness and impartiality that bind the prosecutor help to dictate the proper course of conduct. The case of R. v. *Peruta* serves as a useful illustration of how *not* to handle the problem.[152]

Peruta was charged with first-degree murder, and a pathologist testified for the Crown as to the sequence of various injuries suffered by the deceased. It became clear, by the end of defence counsel's cross-examination, that the pathologist's opinion was favourable to the accused. Crown counsel obtained an adjournment before the re-examination, despite defence counsel's objection. When the trial resumed, the pathologist was re-examined, and he performed a volte-face in changing his opinion to one that now favoured the Crown's theory. In re-cross-examination, the pathologist admitted that Crown counsel

---

151  R. v. *Fortin*, [1997] A.Q. No. 2887 (C.A.) (QL).
152  *Peruta*, above note 48.

and the police had expressed disappointment in his responses in cross-examination, and had spent time reviewing his testimony.

On appeal, the Quebec Court of Appeal determined that the prosecutor's conduct was highly improper. Though the trial judge had not warned the witness that he was forbidden to discuss his testimony with anyone, the court held that Crown counsel should have known better and at the least was required to ask the leave of the court before communicating with the witness during his testimony. The court also observed that the special relationship that frequently develops between Crown counsel, the police, and forensic experts must not be improperly exploited. Crown counsel should have cautioned himself against the temptation of taking advantage of these ties in order to influence the witness. It follows from *Peruta* that, even in the absence of any global agreement as to the ideal guidelines for handling communication with a witness just prior to re-examination, the pervasive duty for a prosecutor is to act fairly and impartially. Unfortunately, the trial Crown lawyer in *Peruta* acted unprofessionally in not resisting the temptation to use his favourable working relationship with the pathologist in order to engineer a change in testimony.

### c)   Cross-examination

"In the midst of a cross-examination of the accused, the dual roles of Crown counsel as both an advocate and a minister of justice may not appear easily reconciled."[153] Nonetheless, a review of recent decisions leads to the conclusion that Crown counsel is subject to the same duties in the cross-examination of witnesses, and especially the accused, as apply in delivering a closing speech to the jury. One might expect that the acceptable scope of vigorous cross-examination is well known to all Crown counsel, based upon decades of precedent following *R. v. Boucher*.[154] However, improper cross-examination by some Crown counsel unfortunately continues. In 1999 the Ontario Court of Appeal referred to an "unfortunately ever-growing line of authority relating to improper cross-examination by Crown counsel,"[155] and the court has subsequently added to the line in cases such as *R. v. Robinson* and *R. v. Rose*.[156] A prosecutor can always launch a skilful, probing, and

---

153 *Henderson*, above note 130 at 145.

154 Above note 12.

155 *R. v. White* (1999), 42 O.R. (3d) 760 at 764 (C.A.) [*White*]. See also *R. v. Walker* (1994), 90 C.C.C. (3d) 144 (Ont. C.A.); *R. v. Bricker* (1994), 90 C.C.C. (3d) 268 (Ont. C.A.); *Daly*, above note 37; *R. v. Stewart* (1991), 62 C.C.C. (3d) 289 (Ont. C.A.); *Henderson*, above note 130 at 144.

156 *Robinson*, above note 6; and *Rose* (*Ont. C.A.*), above note 6.

devastating cross-examination.[157] But once cross-examination becomes unfair, an ethical duty has been breached and the accused's legal and constitutional rights improperly infringed.

Whether improper cross-examination causes a miscarriage of justice giving rise to intervention by an appellate court goes beyond the scope of our analysis. It is enough to note that improper conduct in a cross-examination may be saved by the proviso in section 686(1)b)(iii) of the *Criminal Code*, while still constituting unethical conduct.[158]

We will now examine several different examples of impropriety by the Crown in conducting cross-examination.

### (i) Abusive and Unfair

There are a myriad of ways in which Crown counsel can engage in abusive and unfair cross-examination. It is unprofessional to be "frequently irrelevant, often distracting and repeatedly abusive and insulting [and to] have belittled and demeaned the appellant in the eyes of the jury,"[159] or to adopt a sarcastic tone and repeatedly insert editorial commentary calculated to humiliate the accused,[160] or to be "inappropriately sarcastic, flippant and disrespectful"[161] toward the accused. In *R. v. Robinson*, Mr. Justice Rosenberg offered the following strong criticism of Crown counsel's cross-examination of the accused:

> In my view, Crown counsel's cross-examination of the appellant was highly improper. From start to finish, it was designed to demean and denigrate the appellant and portray him as a fraudsman, a freeloader and a demented sexual pervert. Many of the questions posed were laced with sarcasm and framed in a manner that made it apparent that crown counsel personally held the appellant in utter contempt. In many respects, this was not a cross-examination but an attempt at character assassination.[162]

Such cross-examination tactics constitute a breach of Crown counsel's ethical duty and will frequently lead to a new trial.

---

157 See *Logiacco*, above note 15.
158 See *R. v. Brown*, [1995] 2 S.C.R. 273.
159 *Logiacco*, above note 15 at 379.
160 See *R. v. R.(A.J.)* (1994), 94 C.C.C. (3d) 168 (Ont. C.A.).
161 *S.(F.)*, above note 122 at 474.
162 *Robinson*, above note 6 at 416. To similar effect, see *Rose (Ont. C.A.)*, above note 6 at 241.

### (ii)  Undermining a Truthful Witness

We have earlier examined the limits that defence counsel faces in cross-examining the truthful witness.[163] Prosecutors must abide by these limits, and then some. This is not to say that a Crown lawyer cannot put aside personal opinion or knowledge regarding the credibility of a witness, and invoke the usual cross-examination techniques to test opportunity and capacity to observe, recollect, or describe. However, as ABA Prosecution Standard 3–5.7(b) suggests, we believe that the prosecutor's role forbids use of cross-examination to "discredit or undermine a witness if the prosecutor knows the witness is testifying truthfully."[164] To allow the prosecutor to act otherwise would conflict with his or her overall duty as a minister of justice. An analogy can be drawn to the prohibition against submitting to the jury an hypothesis that may look reasonable on its face but that Crown counsel knows in fact to be wrong.[165]

### (iii)  Reference to Disclosure Materials

A number of recent cases have underlined the serious risks run by Crown counsel in suggesting, in the cross-examination of an accused, that the latter's testimony is suspect because he or she has received full disclosure of the Crown's case.[166] Absent evidence that substantiates such a suggestion, indicating, for example, that the accused has tailored his evidence precisely to conform to the disclosure, courts have declared this tactic to be unacceptable. As Mr. Justice Doherty has stated in R. v. White, "that inference, no matter how logical, cannot be drawn without turning fundamental constitutional rights into a trap for accused persons. Where any such suggestion seeps into the cross-examination of an accused, it must be eradicated by the trial judge."[167]

### (iv)  Unfounded Questions

Crown counsel must not suggest facts to witnesses that cannot be proven, especially considering the impact on the fairness of the trial

---

163  See section K(1), "Cross-Examining the Truthful Witness," in chapter 1.

164  ABA Prosecution Standard §3-5.7(b).

165  See *Hay*, above note 139.

166  See *R. v. Cavan* (1999), 139 C.C.C. (3d) 449 (Ont. C.A.); *R. v. Khan* (1998), 126 C.C.C. (3d) 523 (B.C.C.A.); *R. v. Peavoy* (1997), 117 C.C.C. (3d) 226 (Ont. C.A.); and *White*, above note 155. In an analogous vein, it is improper for Crown counsel to cross-examine the accused so as to suggest that he or she should have made a statement to police upon arrest: see, for example, *R. v. Poirier* (2000), 146 C.C.C. (3d) 436 (Ont. C.A.); *R. v. Paris* (2000), 150 C.C.C. (3d) 162 (Ont. C.A.); and *R. v. Schell* (2000), 148 C.C.C. (3d) 219 (Ont. C.A.).

167  *White*, above note 155 at 382.

where this occurs during cross-examination of the accused.[168] As Mr. Justice Lamer, as he then was, stated in *R. v. Howard*, "it is not open to the examiner on cross-examination to put as a fact, or even a hypothetical fact, that which is not and will not become part of the case as admissible evidence."[169] The Crown must be certain that there is a solid foundation for the questions, as opposed to mere speculation, innuendo or an unreliable source.[170]

*(v)  Demanding a Comment on the Credibility of Other Witnesses*
It is improper for Crown counsel, when cross-examining an accused, to demand an assessment of the credibility of other witnesses. The danger with such questioning lies in the strong (and improper) inference that the accused person bears an onus to provide a motive for adverse testimony. Such an inference impermissibly undermines the presumption of innocence. Not surprisingly, the result may be the overturning of a conviction and an order for a retrial.[171]

## 6)  Trial Strategy and Calling Witnesses

The duty of the Crown to act fairly does not preclude the use of a trial strategy aimed at securing a conviction, so long as the strategy does not result in unfairness to the accused.[172] As Binnie J. stated in *R. v. Jolivet*, "it is not the duty of the Crown to bend its efforts to provide the defence with the opportunity to develop and exploit potential conflicts in the prosecution's testimony. This is the stuff of everyday trial tactics and hardly rises to the level of an 'oblique motive'."[173] Similarly, in *R.*

---

168  See *R. v. Wilson* (1983), 5 C.C.C. (3d) 61 at 85 (B.C.C.A.); *R. v. Nealy* (1986), 30 C.C.C. (3d) 460 (Ont. C.A.); and *R. v. Gaultois* (1989), 73 Nfld. & P.E.I.R. 337 (Nfld. C.A.). In *R. v. Hofung* (2001), 154 C.C.C. (3d) 257 (Ont. C.A.), the prosecutor was criticized for using cross-examination to elicit impermissible hearsay from the testifying accused.

169  *R. v. Howard*, [1989] 1 S.C.R. 1337 at 1347. See the discussion in *D.(C.)*, above note 131 at 318–18, expressing some doubt regarding the seemingly contrary opinion provided by *R. v. Bencardino* (1973), 15 C.C.C. (2d) 342 (Ont. C.A.).

170  See E. Levy, *Examination of Witnesses in Criminal Cases*, 4th ed. (Scarborough, Ont.: Carswell, 1998) at 412–15. ABA Prosecution Standard §3-5.7, in its commentary, states that it is an improper tactic to attempt to communicate impressions by innuendo, where the prosecutor has no evidence to back up a suggestion.

171  See, for example, *R. v. Masse* (2000), 134 O.A.C. 79 (C.A.); *Rose (Ont. C.A.)*, above note 6 at 241.

172  See *Jolivet*, above note 21 at 765.

173  *Ibid.*

v. *Ford*, Southin J.A. dismissed emphatically the argument that the "Crown must do everything it can to prevent an accused from, so to speak, digging his own grave in front of the jury."[174]

Moreover, it has long been established that the Crown has no obligation to call a witness considered unnecessary to the prosecution case.[175] As stated by the Supreme Court of Canada in *R. v. Cook*, the Crown possesses a fair deal of discretion in regard to calling witnesses, and only improper or oblique motives will justify judicial intervention to check the exercise of this discretion.[176]

Australian courts have endorsed an especially aggressive version of prosecutorial adversarial tactics, arguably going so far as to undercut the usual obligation to make full disclosure.[177] In *R. v. Jamieson*,[178] for instance, defence counsel called a witness, expecting that privilege would be invoked and no testimony would be given. In fact, all indications suggested that the witness would provide evidence harmful to the defence if he decided to testify. But defence counsel expected the privilege claim and hoped that the trier of fact would use the claim to draw an inference favourable to the accused. The Crown anticipated this strategy and took the counter-measure of granting the witness immunity from prosecution. However, the Crown did not tell the defence lawyer of this development. The witness was called by the defence, and because of the immunity agreement did not claim privilege, instead providing testimony damning to the accused.

It is obvious that the defence case in *Jamieson* was undermined because of the prosecution strategy, but the tactic drew no ire from the judiciary. Rather, the Supreme Court of New South Wales (Court of Criminal Appeal) observed: "[I]f from one point of view it is possible to say that the Crown laid a trap for the defence [by keeping silent], . . . it could be more appropriate to say that the Crown permitted defence counsel to trap himself."[179] In Canada, this type of strategy would probably run afoul of the legal and ethical principles relating to Crown disclosure. Admittedly, the tactics of defence counsel were of highly dubious ethical validity, because a lawyer should not seek to manipulate the system to suggest facts that are not true. Nevertheless,

---

174 *Ford*, above note 87 at 499.
175 See *Lemay*, above note 21; *R. v. Yebes*, [1987] 2 S.C.R. 168; *Cook*, above note 12; and *Jolivet*, above note 21.
176 See *Cook*, above note 12 at 1128.
177 See, for example, *R. v. Van Beelen* (1972), 6 S.A.S.R. 534; *Lawless v. R.* (1979), 142 C.L.R. 659.
178 (1992), 60 A. Crim. R. 68 (C.C.A.).
179 See also Hunter & Cronin, above note 43 at 207.

the Crown is not entitled to dispense with disclosure obligations, and be guided by a "tit for tat" principle of advocacy, simply because defence counsel plans to use an improper trial strategy.[180]

# F.  DUTY OF CANDOUR

The duty of candour encompasses the need to act honestly and truthfully in the lawyer's dealings with the administration of justice. Not only the courts, but also all other parties to the criminal justice system, depend on Crown counsel's honesty at every stage of the process. Candour requires that Crown counsel avoid misleading the court on the facts and the law and take curative steps to investigate, and if necessary remedy, possible falsehoods perpetrated against the court.

Examples of conduct prohibited by reason of the duty of candour are contained in commentary 2 of the CBA Code's Chapter IX, and apply to all lawyers, including prosecutors. For instance, an advocate may not:

> (e) knowingly attempt to deceive or participate in the deception of a tribunal or influence the course of justice by offering false evidence, misstating facts or law, presenting or relying upon a false or deceptive affidavit, suppressing what ought to be disclosed or otherwise assisting in any fraud, crime or illegal conduct;
> (f) knowingly misstate the contents of a document, the testimony of a witness, the substance of an argument or the provisions of a statute or like authority;
> (g) knowingly assert something for which there is no reasonable basis in evidence, or the admissibility of which must first be established;
> (h) deliberately refrain from informing the tribunal of any pertinent adverse authority that the lawyer considers to be directly in point and that has not been mentioned by an opponent;
> [. . .]
>
> (j) knowingly permit a witness to be presented in a false or misleading way or to impersonate another.[181]

---

180  See the related discussions in sections B(2), "Role as Advocate," and E(2)(b), "Expressing a Personal Opinion," in this chapter.

181  ABA Prosecution Standard §3-5.6 is to the same effect. See also the *Bar Code of Conduct*, above note 31 at §11.7, which states that "[i]t is the duty of prosecuting counsel to assist the Court at the conclusion of the summing-up by drawing attention to any apparent errors or omissions of fact or law."

What is more, and this is a crucial point that does not apply to defence counsel, prosecutors have a general duty to take action to prevent the court from being misled, regardless of the source of the threat or the fact that no Crown lawyer, actor or witness is implicated. Defence counsel can rely upon the principle against self-incrimination and an especially strong partisan role to remain silent in the face of falsehood, as long as he or she is not complicit (for instance, by calling a witness who is known or later determined to be lying).[182] Crown counsel is not resolutely partisan in this way, has a general duty to seek justice and preserve the truth-finding function of the process, and thus is bound by a different set of ethical standards. Let us consider now some concrete situations that illustrate the prosecutor's special duty of candour.

## 1) The Prosecutor Learns That a Crown Witness has Testified Falsely

At the well-known 1969 Panel Discussion on criminal law ethics, the participants were confronted with the following example.[183] At a trial for armed robbery, an accomplice who has been convicted and sentenced, after completing his evidence-in-chief and cross-examination, steps down from the witness box as the court adjourns for the day. Passing the counsel table, the witness says to the Crown lawyer words to the effect that he "lied a little bit." On instructions from the prosecutor, a police officer interviews the accomplice that night at the jail. The following morning, before the conclusion of the Crown's case, the police officer informs the prosecutor that there is nothing to worry about, because the accomplice was lying solely in regard to a collateral matter.

Responding to this scenario, the panellists agreed that Crown counsel should disclose the developments to defence counsel. They also took the position that the perjurious witness has to be recalled to the stand and asked whether the conversation with the Crown took place. If he admits to making the statement in question, then defence counsel can be left to cross-examine him as to the nature of the lie.[184]

---

182 See chapters 1, 5, & 7.

183 "Panel Discussion: Problems in Advocacy and Ethics" in Law Society of Upper Canada, *Defending a Criminal Case* (Toronto: R. De Boo, 1969) 279 at 335.

184 Denial of the statement may lead to other problems, especially if the Crown lawyer is the only individual who heard the comment and thus becomes a potential witness.

We thus see that the duty of candour requires full disclosure to the defence. Concomitantly, the prosecutor is prohibited from attempting to hide the perjury, and certainly cannot attempt to aid the witness's lie by posing related questions in re-examination. Nor can the Crown lawyer rely on the false testimony in making submissions to the trier of fact in closing. It does not matter whether the falsehood occurs in examination-in-chief, in cross-examination or in re-direct, or even that the witness is called by the defence. Mere inconsistency by a witness does not equate with misleading testimony and hence does not on its own require remedial action by the Crown. Yet, whenever the Crown comes by information that suggests a reasonable possibility that the court has been or will be misled, action must be taken.

The full extent of the Crown's duty of candour, and the degree to which this duty surpasses what might normally be expected of defence counsel, is seen in the case of *R. v. Ahluwalia*.[185] There, the appellant had pleaded guilty to drug-related offences and then sought to stay the proceedings based on entrapment. A key Crown witness on the entrapment application was an American police agent, handled by FBI officers, who repeatedly testified to having a single criminal conviction. The entrapment argument was rejected, but, following sentencing, defence counsel learned that the agent had several convictions. He asked the Crown for an explanation. The Crown lawyer confirmed the more extensive criminal record, and hence the agent's perjury, and added that neither the Crown law office nor the Canadian police were aware of this information prior to defence counsel's post-trial request. Ultimately, however, the Crown refused to make inquiries, principally of the FBI, as to why the agent's criminal record and the trial perjury had not been disclosed.

The Ontario Court of Appeal was disturbed by the nature of the perjury, observing that the Crown disclosure provided to trial counsel perfectly matched the lie told by the agent at trial. It thus appeared, though no finding could be made on the point, that the state may have been complicit in misleading the court and denying the accused his rights. Indeed, it seemed that the agent's FBI handler, who was aware of the true state of affairs, was in court when the perjury occurred yet said nothing. Mr. Justice Doherty was thus unimpressed with the Crown's failure to investigate further. He held:

> The Crown has obligations to the administration of justice that do
> not burden other litigants. Faced with its own witness's perjury and

---

185 Above note 6.

the fact that the perjured evidence coincided with the incomplete disclosure that the Crown says it innocently passed to the defence, the Crown was obliged to take all reasonable steps to find out what had happened and to share the results of those inquiries with the defence. In my view, the Crown did not fulfill its obligations to the administration of justice by acknowledging the incomplete disclosure discovered by the defence, and after making limited inquiries, professing neither a responsibility for the incomplete disclosure nor an ability to provide any explanation for it. The Crown owed both the appellant and the court a fuller explanation than it chose to provide.[186]

There can thus be a positive obligation to undertake an investigation, not only as a means of exposing a falsehood, but also to uncover the reason for the court having been misled. What is more, this obligation is not extinguished with the conclusion of trial, at least where the circumstances are such that the standard for the admission of fresh evidence can be met.

Perhaps closer to the line is complicity in misleading the court where the aim is to achieve justice. This strange possibility is presented by the facts in the intriguing case of *In Re Friedman*,[187] which involved a disciplinary action against a prosecutor. In order to obtain proof of bribery by two defence lawyers, the prosecutor authorized police officers to accept bribes from the lawyers and give false testimony as requested. The prosecutor also arranged for the witnesses to be absent from court proceedings, in accordance with the defence lawyers' illegal plan. The charges were dismissed, following which the lawyers were arrested.

The court that heard the initial case learned of the deception, and a disciplinary board recommended that the prosecutor be censored. But the Supreme Court of Illinois, in a majority decision, discharged the prosecutor. The two dissenting judges convincingly argued that lawyers cannot be excused for conduct that deceives the court, regardless of a valid ulterior motive or the limited impact of the deception. Two of the majority judges took a different view, arguing that the prosecutor's conduct was unethical but concluding that no sanction should be imposed because the prosecutor acted without the guidance of precedent and there was considerable consensus among experts that he acted properly in conducting the investigation. The remaining two majority judges relied upon Monroe Freedman's statement that

---

186 *Ibid.* at 213.
187 392 N.E.2d 1333 (Ill. 1979).

"motive is a primary consideration in making judgments regarding the ethical quality of conduct," and held that the prosecutor's temporary deception of the court, for a laudable purpose, violated no ethical prescriptions.

Given the Supreme Court of Canada's discomfort regarding state-sanctioned illegalities, even when directed at achieving valid ends,[188] we would not expect exoneration of the *Friedman* prosecutor in the context of Canadian ethical standards. The proper approach would be for the prosecutor to conclude the investigation prior to the presentation of fabricated evidence, if possible, or to attempt to obtain immunity in advance from the courts via an *ex parte* application. We take solace in the fact that four of the six judges in *Friedman* held that the prosecutor's conduct was improper. In essence, disciplinary censure was avoided because the circumstances were unique and novel and the lawyer was therefore seen to deserve some leeway.

## 2) The Prosecutor Realizes That Evidence May Have Been Obtained Unfairly

It may be that the prosecutor learns of a *Charter* violation that has the potential for impact on the admissibility of relevant evidence, and yet the facts surrounding the violation are not known to the defence. Such information falls within the legal, constitutional, and ethical duties to disclose and should be revealed to the defence. The need to be candid and open extends beyond facts pertaining to the elements of the offence charged, to encompass matters that bear upon the legitimate exercise of the accused's constitutional rights or the admissibility of the evidence.[189] Information pertaining to a possible *Charter* violation should therefore be disclosed to defence counsel.

## 3) The Court or Defence Counsel Has Made an Error Favouring the Prosecution

Crown counsel may become aware of an error or misapprehension by the judge or defence counsel that inures to the prosecution's advan-

---

188 See *R. v. Campbell*, [1999] 1 S.C.R. 565 [*Campbell*].

189 See M. Blake & A. Ashworth, "Some Ethical Issues in Prosecuting and Defending Criminal Cases" (1998) Crim. L.R. 16 at 27; and ABA Prosecution Standard §3-5.6(b)(c). See also *Egger*, above note 70; *R. v. Hutter* (1993), 86 C.C.C. (3d) 81 (Ont. C.A.); and *R. v. Pearson* (1994), 89 C.C.C. (3d) 535 at 558 (Que. C.A.). See also *R. v. Creswell* (2000), 149 C.C.C. (3d) 286 at 300–02 (B.C.C.A.).

tage. In England and Wales, the bar's Code of Conduct imposes a positive obligation on prosecuting counsel to assist the court at the conclusion of the summing-up by drawing attention to any apparent errors or omissions of fact or law. Presumably, an error by the court or defence counsel would fall within the ambit of this rule, triggering disclosure by the Crown. The FPS Deskbook has no companion provision, only stating that prosecutors must reveal "all relevant cases and authorities known to counsel," something that applies to any lawyer.[190] In our view, the obligation should be more extensive and general, working to require Crown lawyers to inform the court and/or defence counsel whenever a misapprehension has likely occurred regarding a material matter.

## 4)  Witness Preparation

There are numerous subtle ways in which prosecutors can intentionally or inadvertently encourage a witness to mislead the court. The following guidelines will protect against such improper conduct.

1.  Crown lawyers must avoid pushing a witness to conform his or her version of events to better accommodate a legal theory.
2.  Leading questions in interviews also run a danger of causing some witnesses to alter testimony to comply with whatever is perceived as most desirable for the Crown. Naturally, this danger does not exist with respect to every Crown witness, and counsel must use common sense in determining when leading questions are appropriate.
3.  The witness must not be advised to use particular language in an effort to alter the meaning of the testimony to something more favourable to the prosecution. However, suggesting particular wording to encourage clarity of description is not problematic.
4.  A witness cannot be presented with favours, not even subtle ones, to encourage cooperation, without carefully considering the propriety of such action. Obviously, our courts have permitted some witnesses to be paid for their testimony. But there are cases where the provision of benefits may go too far, such as taking steps that directly permit a witness to engage in illegal drug use. Any actions that might reasonably be construed as bestowing a benefit on the witness should be disclosed to the defence.

---

190 *FPS Deskbook*, above note 30 at §9.3.3.

5. Recommending that the witness actively take steps to present well in court is unobjectionable, but suggesting that demeanour be shaped artificially to bolster reliability of the witness' testimony is improper. For instance, the witness cannot be told to express confidence and certainty in identifying the alleged perpetrator of the crime, if in fact the identification is equivocal.

6. Sometimes a witness is a former accomplice or co-accused who has decided to cooperate. In interviewing such a witness, Crown counsel must avoid digging for information that reveals defence strategies or confidential information shared under a joint-defence arrangement. Such questioning might constitute an improper infringement of the accused's joint defence privilege. Arguably, the witness should thus be initially briefed not to reveal confidential information concerning the conduct of the accused's defence.

7. Telling a witness that he or she cannot broach a particular subject in direct examination is entirely proper, and perhaps even required. For instance, the Crown might want to caution the witness against discussing a prior incident revealing the accused's bad character. Conversely, a prosecutor must refrain from coaching the witness to reveal inadmissible evidence during cross-examination, in order to surprise and disrupt the defence.

At the end of the day, prosecutors should follow the general rule of encouraging the witness to tell the truth, whether or not the truth is helpful to the Crown case, and avoid taking any measures that risk distorting the witness's testimony.

## 5)  Failure to Disclose Material Information on an *Ex Parte* Application

Canadian rules of professional conduct invariably include a requirement that counsel be candid and make full disclosure to the court in bringing an *ex parte* application. The CBA Code states, for example, that "[w]hen opposing interests are not represented, for example, in *ex parte* or uncontested matters, or in other situations where the full proof and argument inherent in the adversary system cannot be obtained, the lawyer must take particular care to be accurate, candid and comprehensive in presenting the client's case so as to ensure that the court is not misled."[191] The rationale is explained in this commentary and flows

---

191 CBA Code ch. IX, comm. 15.

from the fact that the adversarial process usually relied upon to sort out the truth in litigation is much reduced on an *ex parte* application.

The need to be candid with the court in making an *ex parte* application is especially important for Crown lawyers, who often seek orders in the absence of any opposing party. Examples are orders to intercept private communications or to restrain or seize suspected proceeds of crime. The danger in failing to make full disclosure is illustrated in the case of *R. v. Derksen*.[192] There, the Crown applied with notice to continue the detention of goods seized under proceeds-of-crime legislation pursuant to an *ex parte* order.[193] The respondents applied to set aside the original *ex parte* order, on the grounds that the Crown had failed to disclose to the court the existence of a pertinent agreement between the parties. Under this agreement, the goods had previously been returned to the respondents after a police seizure, subject to certain conditions being fulfilled.

The court in *Derksen* accepted the respondents' arguments and refused to extend the order on the grounds of the lack of disclosure of material information to the court. Observing that Crown counsel had failed to adhere to the applicable rules of professional conduct regarding *ex parte* applications and full disclosure, the court opined that counsel had engaged in a "serious breach of professional ethics."[194] The appeal on this issue was dismissed, on the ground that the Crown had no right of appeal. However, the Saskatchewan Court of Appeal noted that the trial judge's comments criticizing the Crown for failure to make full disclosure were "superfluous" to the judgment at first instance.[195] Moreover, the Law Society of Saskatchewan subsequently considered the conduct of the prosecutors and determined that there was no basis to commence a further investigation into the matter. Finally, on our review of the case, the conclusion that Crown counsel breached an agreement with the defence, hid information from the issuing judge, or otherwise acted improperly seems quite a stretch. Full disclosure is essential in bringing any *ex parte* application, but Crown counsel in *Derksen* does not appear to have violated this duty.

---

192 (1998), 126 C.C.C. (3d) 554 (Sask. Q.B.) [*Derksen*].
193 See s. 462.35 of the *Criminal Code*, R.S.C. 1985, c. C-46.
194 *Derksen*, above note 192.
195 *R. v. Derksen* (1999), 140 C.C.C. (3d) 184 at 193 (Sask. C.A.).

## 6) Raising a Theory Inconsistent with Facts Not in Evidence

Sometimes Crown counsel has access to information which, for a valid reason, cannot be disclosed to the accused. For instance, the Crown might have possession of private counselling records that a complainant successfully argues should not be produced to the defence.[196] Or perhaps information pertaining to a confidential informant is kept secret because the innocence-at-stake exception does not apply. While information can on occasion properly be withheld from the defence, the prosecutor cannot present an argument or invoke a theory that to his or her knowledge is inconsistent with such information. Such conduct would be unfair to the accused and amount to misleading the court.[197]

## 7) Improper Contact with Potential Jurors

In the unusual case of *R. v. Kirkham*,[198] a Crown lawyer was charged with two counts of obstructing justice contrary to section 139(2) of the *Criminal Code*, in connection with the original Robert Latimer murder trial. The first count alleged that the prosecutor authorized police officers to collect personal information about potential jurors in an attempt to obtain an unfair advantage over the defence. The second count alleged that, despite knowing that potential jurors had been directly contacted by police, he failed to promptly advise defence counsel and the court of such contacts. Though the prosecutor was acquitted on both counts, the court reserved some harsh language for his actions. In particular, the court was unimpressed with the failure to inform the court promptly upon learning that the police had contacted three prospective jurors. Counsel avoided conviction largely because, in the view of the court, there was no policy in place to provide professional guidance regarding contact with prospective jurors. Moreover, it was not obvious to counsel that his failure to contact the court or defence counsel would result in an obstruction of justice, since he believed that he would be able to keep the "tainted" jurors off

---

196 See ss. 278.2 to 278.91 of the *Criminal Code*, above note 193; as well as *R. v. Mills*, [1999] 3 S.C.R. 668.

197 See *Hay*, above note 139.

198 *Kirkham* (1998), 126 C.C.C. (3d) 397 (Sask. Q.B.).

the actual jury. On a principled basis, however, the trial judge held that counsel should have promptly informed the court once he learned of the direct contact with the prospective jurors.[199]

# G. DUTIES RELATED TO CHARGING AND STAYING DECISIONS

In this section, we will address two main topics of discussion that pertain to a prosecutor's decision to proceed with a case. First, to what extent can or should the prosecutor become involved in the initial decision to lay a charge? Second, what factors can properly be taken into account in deciding whether to lay a charge or to stay proceedings? As we have seen again and again, the prosecutor's actions must be guided by the duties of fairness and impartiality.

## 1) Involvement of Crown Counsel in Laying a Charge

There are two contrasting approaches to the role of Crown counsel in the decision whether or not to lay a charge.[200] Some jurisdictions, like Quebec, British Columbia, and New Brunswick, require approval by Crown counsel before a charge can be laid by a police officer. For instance, section 4 of Quebec's *An Act Respecting Attorney General's Prosecutors* provides that the prosecutor's duty is to "authorize prosecutions against the offenders."[201] This duty should be viewed as a screening process, or a safeguard against ill-founded charges, given that the police can ignore a prosecutor's advice and proceed to lay the charge before a justice of the peace. In contrast, the role of prosecutors

---

199 *Ibid.* at 407–08 & 410.

200 See generally, J. Pearson, "The Prosecutor's Role at the Investigative Stage from an Ontario Perspective" Federal Prosecutor Service XXth Annual Conference (2000); and J. Brooks, "Ethical Obligations of the Crown Attorney — Some Guiding Principles and Thoughts" (2001) 50 U.N.B.L.J. 229 at 233–34.

201 R.S.Q., ch. S-35, s. 4. The *Manuel de Directives*, No ACC-3, revised 95-02-23, which offers more detailed guidelines for prosecutors, provides that if the police officer in charge of an investigation disagrees with the prosecutor's decision, the matter is referred to that prosecutor's superior: see s. 9.

in provinces such as Ontario is more restricted. In Ontario, the police have absolute control over the laying of charges and need not obtain prior approval or input from a Crown lawyer.[202] The situation in Nova Scotia is similar, as recently described by Mr. Justice Cromwell, writing for the majority in R. v. *Regan*:

> There is no dispute on this appeal that the responsibility and authority to make the decision to charge criminal offences in this Province rests with the police. There is also no dispute that the Crown may, on request, properly give legal advice to the police in the course of an investigation, including advice about the strength of the case. Moreover, there is no dispute that the Crown has the authority to stay charges that have been laid by the police. Accordingly, there may be disagreement between the police and the Crown about whether charges should proceed.[203]

The differing approaches to the prosecutor's role in the pre-charge stages of a matter, and the ultimate decision whether to lay a charge, reflect contrasting views as to the need for, and degree of, police independence. Some commentators see the independence of the police as a constitutional convention, mandating that Crown lawyers play no part in making the final decision whether or not to lay charges.[204] In this vein, the Supreme Court of Canada has recently stated in R. v. *Campbell*, a case that involved the RCMP, that "a police officer investigating a crime is not acting as a government functionary or as an agent of anybody. He or she occupies a public office initially defined by the *common law* and subsequently set out in various statutes."[205] The Court added that "the police are independent of the control of the executive government."[206] At the same time, however, the complexity of many criminal investigations, involving for instance, proceeds of crime, often demands that police and Crown lawyers work together at the pre-

---

202 See *Martin Committee Report*, above note 106 at 37, accurately noted that "[a]s a matter of law, police officers exercise their discretion in conducting investigations and laying charges entirely independently of Crown counsel."

203 R. v. *Regan* (1999), 137 C.C.C. (3d) 449 at 511 (N.S.C.A.), currently on appeal before the Supreme Court of Canada, [1999] S.C.C.A. No. 514 (QL) [*Regan*].

204 See Rosenberg, above note 24.

205 *Campbell*, above note 188 at 588.

206 *Ibid.* at 589.

charge stage. As long as the independence of the police is not unduly hampered, we see no problem with this type of cooperation.[207]

Where Crown counsel have some involvement in the pre-charging process, a question may arise as to the propriety of certain actions. Pre-charge conduct by prosecutors was directly addressed in R. v. *Regan*, where the pre-charge interviewing of witnesses by Crown counsel was attacked by the defence as improper. The judge at first instance expressed the view that pre-charge witness interviewing inevitably prevents the Crown from properly exercising the discretion to stay charges later if required in the public interest. This problem was perceived to occur because "[i]t is impossible to retain the requisite level of objectivity by conducting lengthy (and no doubt emotional) pre-charge interviews." However, this fairly stringent prohibition on pre-charge interviews was rejected by a majority on appeal. Mr. Justice Cromwell refused to accept that pre-charge interviewing causes any inevitable tainting of a prosecution, and preferred to retain flexibility on the question of Crown pre-charge interviews, relying on numerous policy reasons. In particular, Cromwell J.A. stated:

> (i) Several factors require close co-operation between investigators and prosecutors. The complexity of many modern prosecutions, particularly in drug and commercial crime cases, the requirements that the police comply with the Charter, and the requirement for pre-authorization of investigative techniques, especially wire-tap, are examples.
>
> (ii) The trial judge's insistence on a strict separation of roles of the police and the Crown would make it difficult or impossible to maintain integrated offices comprised of lawyers and investigators in areas such as war crimes, proceeds of crime and competition offences.
>
> (iii) There are several provisions in the Criminal Code and other federal statutes that require the consent of the attorney general of Canada to institute proceedings. I do not understand why it would be in the public interest to preclude the attorney general, personally or through counsel, from interviewing witnesses in deciding whether to grant such consent.
>
> (iv) The trial judge's decision, while expressly not dealing with pre-charge screening, seems to me to inevitably have an adverse effect on such screening. In my view, there is no good reason why such screening should depend solely on the police assessment of credibility, par-

---

207 For a discussion of a prosecutor's duties in advising the police prior to a charge being laid, see M. Code, "Crown Counsel's Responsibilities When Advising the Police at the Pre-Charge Stage" (1998) 40 Crim. L.Q. 326.

ticularly in the case of witnesses such as "jail house" informers and those seeking immunity or other benefits. Any banning of pre-charge interviewing would not serve the administration of justice in such cases.

(v) There are sound policy arguments favouring a role for the Crown in charging decisions rather than confining the Crown's role to staying charges after they have been laid. As Edward L. Greenspan and George Jonas said in their book, Greenspan, The Case For the Defence (1987) at page 16: "Leaving the decision to lay charges up to the Crown may reduce the chances of frivolous or inhumane (and costly) prosecutions. It may also reduce the needless overcrowding of the courts." I do not make this point to cast doubt in any way on the clear position in this Province that the duty and responsibility for the form and content of charges laid belongs with the police. I simply note that, contrary to what the trial judge implies in his reasons, there is nothing inherently suspect about Crown involvement in the charging decision.

(vi) The prosecution policies of both New Brunswick and Ontario permit pre-charge witness interviewing. While the judge made no clear finding on this point, there was abundant evidence on the point which he apparently did not reject. It would be strange if an aspect of criminal practice which is acceptable in one Province should be found to offend the Charter in another.[208]

Ultimately, the more extensive the participation of Crown counsel at the pre-charge stage, the greater the risks of at least appearing to act unfairly and with a lack of objectivity.[209] Counsel must therefore exercise caution in playing a role prior to charges being laid, and at all times strive to act impartially and in the best interests of justice.

In short, in some provinces the police act with more independence, and with less Crown supervision, than in others. However, in all Canadian jurisdictions the prosecutor acquires total control of a criminal matter once charges have been laid. At this stage, the question may arise as to whether an existing charge should be withdrawn or stayed. The prosecutor has total control over such a decision and exercises a broad discretion in deciding upon the proper course of action to

---

208 *Regan*, above note 203 at 513–14.

209 In jurisdictions where the Crown typically becomes involved prior to a charge being laid, such as Quebec, prosecutors are also more vulnerable to being sued for malicious prosecution: see, for example, *Quebec (P.G.) v. Proulx*, [1999] R.J.Q. 398 (Que. C.A.), currently on appeal before the Supreme Court of Canada; and *Quebec (P.G.) v. Chouinard*, [1999] R.J.Q. 2245 (Que. C.A.).

take.[210] We now turn to the factors that should inform the prosecutor's decision whether to lay or stay a criminal charge.

## 2) Applying the Discretion: Sufficiency of Evidence and Public Interest

Our common law tradition does not require the automatic laying or prosecuting of a charge every time an allegation of criminal conduct is made.[211] Rather, the decision whether or not to launch and continue a prosecution requires the exercise of a discretion. The decision whether to prosecute thus becomes, to borrow the words of the Martin Committee, a pivotal event that "prevents the process of the criminal law from being used oppressively."[212] Given the substantial consequences that a charge can have for the liberty and security of an accused, the fact and appearance of fairness is crucial. As Monroe Freedman has pointed out, it may be that the Crown never wins or loses a case, but even the accused who is exonerated after being charged may "carry for life the severe scars of that encounter with justice."[213] Exercising the discretion to lay or stay a charge is thus vital to the integrity of the system and the rights of individuals who may have been or may be accused of a criminal offence.

We have already seen that the existence of prosecutorial discretion does not offend the principles of fundamental justice,[214] and in keeping with this position, courts have afforded considerable deference to the exercise of the discretion to prosecute.[215] "A judge does not have the authority to tell prosecutors which crimes to prosecute or when to prosecute them."[216] The courts have refused to interfere with Crown discretion in this regard except in cases of flagrant impropriety, in essence applying the demanding standard of abuse of process.

---

210 See Rosenberg, above note 24 at 6; *R. v. Dowson*, [1983] 2 S.C.R. 144; *Kostuch (Informant)* v. *Alberta (A.G.)* (1995), 101 C.C.C. (3d) 321 (Alta. C.A.); *R v. Osiowy* (1989), 50 C.C.C. (3d) 189 (Sask. C.A.); and *Quebec (A.G.)* v. *Chartrand* (1987), 40 C.C.C. (3d) 270 (Que. C.A.).

211 See Rosenberg, above note 24 at 16; and Archibald, above note 53 at 81–83.

212 *Martin Committee Report*, above note 106 at 51.

213 M. Freedman, *Lawyers' Ethics in the Adversary System* (Indianapolis: Bobbs-Merill, 1975) at 29.

214 See section C, "The Principle of Prosecutorial Discretion," in this chapter.

215 See *Power*, above note 8.

216 *T.(V.)*, above note 53, quoting Powell J. in *Wayte* v. *United States*, 470 U.S. 598 (1985).

What then are the factors to consider in exercising the discretion? The *Criminal Code* provides no guidance on this point, nor do Canadian rules of professional conduct have anything specific to say. The Supreme Court of Canada has noted a number of considerations that can properly bear upon the decision to prosecute, including the strength of the case, the general deterrence value of proceeding with the charge, and the government's enforcement priorities.[217] Most attorneys general in Canada have adopted policies or standards that help delineate the proper exercise of the prosecutorial discretion. The leading current example is the FPS Deskbook, which sets out the criteria regarding the decision to prosecute. The manual reflects what is accepted wisdom in setting out two main prongs that determine whether a prosecution will be launched or continued: first, the evidence must be sufficient to warrant proceeding, meaning that there exists a reasonable prospect of conviction; and second, the public interest must otherwise justify prosecuting the charge.[218]

The FPS Deskbook goes further, however, providing more detail by setting out a number of irrelevant criteria, which must *not* be taken into account in deciding to proceed with a prosecution. According to the manual:

> A decision whether to prosecute must clearly *not* be influenced by any of the following:
>
> (a) The race, national or ethnic origin, colour, religion, sex, sexual orientation, political associations, activities or beliefs of the accused or any other person involved in the investigation;
> (b) Crown counsel's personal feelings about the accused or the victim;
> (c) Possible political advantage or disadvantage to the government or any political group or party; or
> (d) The possible effect of the decision on the personal or professional circumstances of those responsible for the prosecution decision.[219]

Relying on any of these enumerated factors constitutes a serious breach of the prosecutor's fundamental duty to act with fairness and impartiality. Even where a prosecution is clearly justified, reliance on an

---

217 See *T. (V.)*, above note 53 at 761. In describing these factors, however, the court was making the point that such considerations are not easily amenable to judicial review, resulting in the limited degree of judicial supervision already mentioned.

218 See also Brooks, above note 200 at 233–34.

219 *FPS Deskbook*, above note 30 at §15.4.

irrelevant or improper factor in launching or continuing with a case seriously detracts from the appearance of justice.[220]

### 3) Staying a Charge

As to the stay of a charge, it is well settled that, though an individual has the right to initiate a private prosecution, the attorney general has the right to intervene and take control of the matter. Included in the right to intervene and take control is the power to direct a stay pursuant to section 579 of the *Criminal Code*. Except in cases of flagrant impropriety, the exercise of this discretion to stay will not be interfered with by the courts.

## H. PLEA DISCUSSIONS

The chapter devoted to plea discussions focuses on the ethical duties of defence counsel and has much to say that applies equally to prosecutors. In this section, we will briefly examine some of the corollary ethical duties that apply in particular to Crown counsel.

### 1) A Principled Approach

The FPS Deskbook sets out the following helpful principles that should guide any prosecutor's approach to plea and sentence negotiations: fairness; openness in soliciting and weighing the views of those involved in the Crown's case; accuracy for the development of a consistent and informed practice; and the interest of the public in the effective and consistent enforcement of the criminal law.[221]

### 2) Duty Not to Delay Resolution Discussions

Crown counsel should act expeditiously in responding to a plea-resolution initiative proposed by defence counsel. Indeed, it is often advisable for prosecutors to take the initiative themselves by contacting defence counsel regarding the possibility of a plea resolution. Overall, Crown counsel should ensure that resolution discussions are undertaken after disclosure has been completed, provided that a plea resolution is in the public interest.

---

220 See Rosenberg, above note 24 at 16.
221 *FPS Deskbook*, above note 30 at §§20.2, 20.3.7, & 20.3.8.

## 3)  Overcharging

It is improper for Crown counsel to proceed with more charges than are justified on the evidence, merely as a means of providing extra bargaining power during plea discussions. It is especially improper for Crown counsel to offer expressly to drop a charge in exchange for a concession by the accused, where the charge is not justified in the first place. Similarly, a more serious charge than is warranted on the evidence should not be laid in order to pressure the accused to plead guilty to a less serious offence arising out of the same transaction.[222] However, it is not *per se* improper to lay overlapping charges where all are justified by the evidence, for instance, a charge of "over 80" and impaired driving or theft and possession of proceeds.

## 4)  Misleading the Court

Crown counsel can negotiate with defence counsel regarding the facts to be relied on for the purposes of sentencing. It is not acceptable, however, to reach an agreement respecting facts that amounts to misleading the court. In this respect, the FPS Deskbook offers guidance (and seems to place further restrictions on Crown counsel) by prohibiting the following agreements:

> (a) An agreement not to advise the court of any part of the accused's provable criminal record which is relevant or could assist the court;
>
> (b) An agreement not to advise the court of the extent of the injury or damages suffered by a victim;
>
> (c) An agreement to withhold from the court facts that are provable, relevant, and that aggravate the offence; or
>
> (d) An agreement to outline facts to the court which, when measured against the essential elements of the offence to which the accused has pleaded guilty, would cause the presiding judge to reject the plea in favour of a plea of not guilty.[223]

---

222  See U.K., Crown Prosecution Service, *Code for Crown Prosecutors*, 4th, ed. (London: Crown Prosecution Service, 2000), s. 7.2, and the *FPS Deskbook*, above note 30 at §20.3.1 both state that it is unacceptable to instruct or proceed with unnecessary additional charges to secure a negotiated plea. See also *United States of America* v. *Cobb* (2001), 152 C.C.C. (3d) 270 (S.C.C.), where an American prosecutor threatened sexual violence against fugitives who persisted in opposing extradition from Canada.

223  *FPS Deskbook*, above note 30 at §20.3.4.

## 5)  Non-disclosure to the Accused

We have already discussed the disclosure requirements applicable to prosecutors, including disclosure of matters relevant to plea discussions.[224] To reiterate, disclosure obligations persist despite the fact that plea discussions are ongoing or a plea agreement has been reached. Where Crown counsel becomes aware of facts that could reasonably modify the defence position in negotiating a guilty plea or adhering to a plea agreement, the proper approach is to disclose such information.

## 6)  Misrepresentations Made to the Accused

Crown counsel must avoid the use of deception in dealing with defence counsel during plea discussions. Extensive disclosure obligations drastically reduce the possibility that defence counsel can be misled in this regard. Nevertheless, prosecutors must take care to conduct discussions in good faith and without knowingly misleading the defence lawyer.[225]

## 7)  The Charge Cannot be Reasonably Supported on the Facts

The Nova Scotia rules of professional conduct state that "a prosecutor has a duty not to negotiate and recommend a plea agreement if the defence, by such agreement, is obliged to plead guilty to an offence or charge not reasonably supported by the facts."[226] Similarly, the FPS Deskbook states that a prosecutor must not "agree to a plea of guilty to an offence not disclosed by the evidence."[227] Consequently, where Crown counsel realizes that the charge cannot be supported by the facts, the charge must be stayed or withdrawn. Pressuring the accused to plead guilty based on groundless allegations is unfair and opens the way for the unpalatable possibility that an innocent accused will plead guilty.[228]

---

224  See section D(3), "Disclosure and Plea Discussions," in this chapter.
225  ABA Prosecution Standard §3-4.1 (commentary).
226  N.S. ch. 17, comm. 17.2.
227  *FPS Deskbook*, above note 30 at §20.3.1.
228  See *CLA Annual Convention*, above note 105 at 31 (G. Arthur Martin).

## 8) Duty to Honour Plea Agreement

As the Commentary to ABA Prosecution Standard 3-4.2 states, "a prosecutor's refusal to honour a plea agreement concerning a recommendation to the Court after a guilty plea is made undermines the voluntariness of the plea and results in fundamental unfairness to the defendant."[229] Unless the public interest would be compromised by continued adherence to a plea agreement, it is thus unacceptable for a prosecutor to refuse to honour a completed plea agreement.[230] Moreover, the public interest can operate to release the Crown from an agreement only in rare circumstances, most particularly where the agreement was obtained by fraud or misrepresentation.[231]

# I.  SUMMARY AND RECOMMENDATIONS

Our summary and recommendations concerning ethics and the prosecutorial function in the criminal justice process are as follows:

1.  The prosecutor has a dual role in the justice process. On the one hand, Crown counsel must seek to act fairly and achieve a just result in the furtherance of the public interest. On the other, the prosecutor can legitimately act as an advocate in striving to obtain a just conviction. Probably the greatest challenge for a prosecutor is reconciling the frequent tension involving these duties (section B).
2.  The rules of professional conduct adopted by many Canadian governing bodies devote minimal attention to the role of the prosecutor, although the general duties of the advocate are often applicable to Crown counsel. Many prosecution services in Canada have adopted policy manuals that bear upon counsel's ethical duties, one of the most comprehensive being the federal Department of Justice's Federal Prosecution Service Deskbook (section B(3)).
3.  A key aspect of the prosecutorial function is the exercise of discretion. While courts are slow to interfere with this discretion, and

---

229 ABA Prosecution Standard §3-4.2. See also *FPS Deskbook*, above note 30 at §20.3.8.2.
230 See CBA Code ch. IX, comm. 12. See also *R. v. Pawliuk* (2001), 157 C.C.C. (3d) 155 at 175 (B.C.C.A.).
231 In *R. v. Obadia*, [1998] R.J.Q. 2581 (C.A.), the Crown convinced the Court of Appeal to increase the sentence agreed to at first instance, because of the accused's subsequent failure to fulfil the terms of the agreement.

Crown counsel must enjoy a substantial amount of freedom in performing their jobs, there are limits as to how the discretion can be exercised. For instance, the discretion cannot be utilized based upon a prohibited ground of discrimination or nullified by adopting an unbending rule of application (section C).

4.  Crown lawyers have legal and constitutional duties to provide full disclosure to the defence. Analogous ethical obligations also guide a prosecutor's actions. These obligations apply in a variety of contexts, including plea discussions and sentencing matters (section D).

5.  A distinctive feature of the prosecutor's role is to temper advocacy with the duty to act in the public interest. Consequently, a Crown lawyer must act fairly in making opening and closing statements to the trier of fact, and cannot use inflammatory language or tone, express a personal opinion, allude to facts not properly in evidence, or ask a jury to disregard the law (sections E & E(2)).

6.  In examining witnesses, Crown counsel must not use degrading or insulting methods. Equally improper is to call a witness to the stand knowing that a privilege will be claimed or a valid objection made by the defence, merely for the purpose of having the trier of fact improperly draw a factual inference from such events. A prosecutor must also desist from priming a Crown witness to modify or alter testimony for the purpose of eliciting favourable evidence during re-examination. Finally, the prosecutor must avoid cross-examination that is abusive and unfair, undermines a truthful witness, or impermissibly erodes the principle against self-incrimination (section E(3)).

7.  The Crown has a broad discretion to decide which trial witnesses should be called as part of the prosecution case (section E(4)).

8.  Lawyers for the Crown owe the court a duty of candour. For instance:
    a.  A prosecutor who learns that a witness has testified falsely must inform the defence lawyer and the court. There may also be a further duty to undertake an investigation to determine the truth, or even the reason behind a deception, where counsel has a reasonable suspicion that a falsehood has been perpetrated on the court (section F(1)).
    b.  Where a prosecutor realizes that evidence has been obtained in a manner that violates the Charter, and also knows that the defence is not aware of the violation, disclosure of the problem should be made to the defence (section F(2)).
    c.  An error by the court or defence counsel, operating to the advantage of the Crown, should not be relied upon to obtain a conviction (section F(3)).

d. In preparing for the trial a prosecutor must take care not to encourage or permit a witness to stretch or bend the truth (section F(4)).

e. Full disclosure must be made to the court in bringing an *ex parte* application (section F(5)).

f. A Crown lawyer should not raise or rely upon a theory that is inconsistent with known facts (section F(6)).

g. It is improper to have contact with potential jurors in an effort to influence the course of the case (section F(6)).

9. In Canada, different jurisdictions approach the charging function in different ways. Some provinces largely leave the charging role to the police. Others have Crown counsel provide a screening mechanism prior to charges being laid (section G(1)).

10. In providing advice regarding the laying of a charge, or deciding whether to proceed with a charge, Crown counsel enjoys a broad discretion. Nonetheless, a charge should not be pursued absent a reasonable prospect of conviction. As well, a decision to proceed should not be influenced by considerations personal to the prosecutor, irrelevant political considerations, or prohibited grounds of discrimination (section G(2)).

11. The prosecutor must carry out plea discussions in an ethical manner. Fairness, openness, accuracy, and promotion of the public interest are among the proper considerations to take into account. The prosecutor should not overcharge, or rely upon overcharging, in an effort to leverage a better plea result. Additionally, the plea agreement should not serve to mislead the court in any way. Finally, a Crown lawyer is bound by the usual duty to make full disclosure even during the plea-discussion process (section H).

## FURTHER READINGS

ALSCHULER, A., "The Prosecutor's Role in Plea Bargaining" (1968) 36 U. Chi. L. Rev. 50

ARCHIBALD, B., "The Politics of Prosecutorial Discretion: Institutional Structures and the Tensions between Punitive and Restorative Paradigms of Justice" (1998) 3 Can. Crim. L. Rev. 69

BLAKE, M., & A. ASHWORTH, "Some Ethical Issues in Prosecuting and Defending Criminal Cases" (1998) Crim. L.R. 16

BROOKS, J., "Ethical Obligations of the Crown Attorney — Some Guiding Principles and Thoughts" (2001) U.N.B.L.J. 229

BUTT, D., "Malicious Prosecution: Rejoinder" (1996) 75 Can. Bar Rev. 335

CALARCO, P., "S.(F.): When Crowns Go Bad (Again!)" (2000) 31 C.R. (5th) 173

CHAPMAN, S., "Prosecutorial Disclosure" (1997) National Criminal Law Program, Federation of Law Societies of Canada

CIVILETTI, B., "Prosecutor as Advocate" (1979) 25 N.Y.L. Sch. L. Rev. 1

CODE, M., "Crown Counsel's Responsibilities When Advising the Police at the Pre-Charge Stage" (1998) 40 Crim. L.Q. 326

COHEN, S., *Due Process of Law: The Canadian System of Criminal Justice* (Toronto: Carswell, 1977)

COOPER, H., "Representation of the Unpopular: What Can the Profession Do about this Eternal Problem?" (1974) 22 Chitty's L.J. 333

CRISPIN, K., "Prosecutorial Ethics" in S. Parker & C. Sampford, eds., *Legal Ethics and Legal Practice: Contemporary Issues* (Oxford: Clarendon Press, 1995)

DANGERFIELD, J., "Ethical problems for Crown Attorneys" (1992) National Criminal Law Program, Federation of Law Societies of Canada

FERGUSON, F., "Prosecutorial Assessment of the Case" (1998) National Criminal Law Program, Federation of Law Societies of Canada

FISHER S., "In Search of the Virtuous Prosecutor: A Conceptual Framework" (1988) Am. J. Crim L. 197

FLOWERS, R., "A Code of Their Own: Updating the Ethics Codes to Include the Non-Adversarial Roles of Federal Prosecutors" (1996) 37 B.C. L. Rev. 923

FREEDMAN, M., *Lawyers' Ethics in the Adversary System* (Indianapolis: Bobbs-Merill, 1975)

GILLERS, S., *Regulation of Lawyers: Problems of Law and Ethics*, 3d ed. (Boston: Little, Brown, 1992) 393

GLENN, H., "Professional Structures and Professional Ethics" (1990) 35 McGill L.J. 424

GORMAN, W., "Prosecutorial Discretion in a *Charter*-Dominated Trial Process" (2000) 44 Crim. L.Q. 15

GREEN, B., "Why Should Prosecutors Seek Justice" in Symposium: "The Changing Role of the Federal Prosecutor" (1999) 26 Fordham Urb. L.J. 607

GROSMAN, B., *The Prosecutor: An Inquiry Into the Exercise of Discretion* (Toronto: University of Toronto Press, 1969)

HALL, JR. J., *Professional Responsibility of the Criminal Lawyer*, 2d ed. (New York: Clark Boardman Callaghan, 1996)

HUMPHREYS, C., "The Duties and Responsibilities of Prosecuting Counsel" (1955) Crim. L.R. 739

HUNTER, J. & K. CRONIN, *Evidence, Advocacy and Ethical Practice: A Criminal Trial Commentary* (Sydney: Butterworths, 1995)

IACOBUCCI, F., "Crown Disclosure Since *Stinchcombe*" (1998) National Criminal Law Program, Federation of Law Societies of Canada

JACKSON, R., "The Federal Prosecutor" (1940) 31 J. Crim. L. & Criminology 2

LAW REFORM COMMISSION OF CANADA, *Disclosure By the Prosecution* (Report No. 22) (Ottawa, Minister of Supplies and Services Canada, 1984)

LAW SOCIETY OF UPPER CANADA, *Defending a Criminal Case* (Toronto: R. De Boo, 1969)

LEVY, E., *Examination of Witnesses in Criminal Cases*, 4th ed. (Scarborough, Ont.: Carswell, 1998)

LEVY, E., "The Closing Address by Defence Counsel" (1992) National Criminal Law Program, Federation of Law Societies of Canada

MACKENZIE, G., *Lawyers and Ethics, Professional Responsibility and Discipline*, looseleaf (Scarborough, Ont.: Carswell, 1993)

MANNING, M., "Abuse of Power by Crown Attorneys" in *The Abuse of Power and the Role of an Independent Judicial System in its Regulation and Control* (Toronto: Law Society of Upper Canada, 1979) 571

MATHESON, JR. S., "The Prosecutor, the Press, and Free Speech" (1990) 58 Fordham L. Rev. 865

MCMAHON, J., "Crown Disclosure Obligations — If in Doubt, Give it Out" (2000) National Criminal Law Program, Federation of Law Societies of Canada

MEWETT, A., *Witnesses* (Scarborough, Ont.: Carswell, 1991)

MORGAN, D., "Controlling Prosecutorial Powers — Judicial Review, Abuse of Process and Section 7 of the *Charter*" (1986-87) 29 Crim. L.Q. 15

Nova Scotia, *Report of the Royal Commission on the Donald Marshall, Jr., Prosecution* (Halifax, The Commission, 1989) (Chair: T.A. Hickman)

ONTARIO, ATTORNEY GENERAL'S ADVISORY COMMITTEE, *Report of the Attorney General's Advisory Committee on Charge Screening, Disclosure, and Resolution Discussions* (Toronto: Queen's Printer, 1993) (Chair: G. Arthur Martin)

ONTARIO, *Report of the Commission on Proceedings Involving Guy Paul Morin* (Toronto: Queen's Printer, 1998) (Chair: F. Kaufman)

ORKIN, M., *Legal Ethics: A Study of Professional Conduct* (Toronto: Cartwright, 1957)

PANNICK, D., *Advocates* (Oxford: Oxford University Press, 1993)

PEARSON, J., "The Prosecutor's Role at the Investigative Stage from an Ontario Perspective" (2000) XXth Annual Federal Prosecutor Service Conference

ROACH, K., "The Attorney General and the *Charter* Revisited" (2000) 50 U.T.L.J. 1

ROSENBERG, M., "The Ethical Prosecutor in the Canadian Context" (1991) Federal Prosecutors' Conference

ROSS, S., *Ethics in Law: Lawyers' Responsibility and Accountability in Australia*, 2d ed. (Sydney: Butterworths, 1998)

SCOTT, J., "The Role of the Attorney General and the *Charter of Rights*" (1986-87) 24 Crim. L.Q. 187

SOPINKA, J., *The Trial of an Action* (Toronto: Butterworths, 1981)

SOSSIN, L., "Crown Prosecutors and Constitutional Facts: The Promise and Politics of *Charter* Damages" (1994) 19 Queen's L.J. 372

STENNING, P., "Independence and the Director of Public Prosecutions: The Marshall Inquiry and Beyond" (2000) 23 Dal. L.J. 385

SUTHERLAND, J., "Role of the Prosecutor: A Brief History" (1998) 19:2 Criminal Lawyers' Association Newsletter 17

UTZ, P., "Two Models of Prosecutorial Professionalism" in W.F. McDonald, ed., *The Prosecutor* (Beverley Hills: Sage, 1979)

UVILLER, H., "The Virtuous Prosecutor in Quest of an Ethical Standard: Guidance from the ABA" (1978) 71 Mich. L. Rev. 1145

WALSH, J., "Ethics and the Investigator" (1999) National Criminal Law Program, Federation of Law Societies of Canada

WEITZMAN, L., "The Closing Address of the Prosecutor" (1998) National Criminal Law Program, Federation of Law Societies of Canada

ZACHARIAS, F., "Structuring the Ethics of Prosecutorial Trial Practice: Can Prosecutors Do Justice?" (1991) 44 Vand. L. Rev. 45

# TABLE OF CASES

# INDEX

# ABOUT THE AUTHORS

**Honourable Mr. Justice Michel Proulx**

Hon. Mr. Justice Michel Proulx has been a member of the Court of Appeal of Quebec since 1989. Prior to his appointment, he had a distinguished litigation practice, mainly in criminal law, from 1963 to 1989. He also served as Adjunct Professor of Law at McGill University from 1967 to 1989.

**David Layton**

David Layton was gold medallist at Dalhousie Law School in 1987, and obtained a graduate degree in law from Oxford University in 1989. He subsequently clerked for the late Chief Justice Brian Dickson at the Supreme Court of Canada. He has written extensively on legal matters in a wide variety of publications, and currently practises criminal and civil litigation in Vancouver.